RACE AND SLAVERY
IN THE WESTERN HEMISPHERE:
QUANTITATIVE STUDIES

Race and Slavery in the Western Hemisphere:

Quantitative Studies

EDITED BY

Stanley L. Engerman and
Eugene D. Genovese

CONTRIBUTORS

Alan H. Adamson - Roger Anstey - Frederick P. Bowser

Michael Craton - Philip D. Curtin - K. G. Davies

Jack Ericson Eblen - Stanley L. Engerman

Eugene D. Genovese - Claudia Dale Goldin

Theodore Hershberg - Mary Karasch - E. Phillip LeVeen

Sidney W. Mintz - Colin A. Palmer - Johannes Postma

George Shepperson - Richard B. Sheridan - Richard Sutch

Peter H. Wood - Harold D. Woodman

PRINCETON UNIVERSITY PRESS

Library of Congress Cataloging in Publication data will
be found on the last printed page of this book

Printed in the United States of America
by Princeton University Press, Princeton, New Jersey

Reproduction, translation, publication, use,
and disposal by and for the United States Government
and its officers, agents, and employees acting
within the scope of their official duties,
for Government use only, is permitted.

TO THE MEMORY OF
Alfred H. Conrad

Preface

Race and Slavery in the Western Hemisphere: Quantitative Studies points up the difficulty in predicting the course of scholarship. During the late 1960s there were raging debates as to whether black studies and black history had a legitimate place in the university curriculum. Many feared, not entirely without reason, that they would be artificial creations or, at best, "soft" subjects that undermined scholarly standards. And now we have this volume which shows that black history has become the leading arena in the effort to apply quantitative methods to historical research.

Race and Slavery is the fourth volume in the series, *Quantitative Studies in History*, sponsored by the History Advisory Committee of the Mathematical Social Science Board (MSSB) in order to encourage the application of mathematical methods to historical analysis. MSSB was established in 1964 under the aegis of the Center for Advanced Study in the Behavioral Sciences "to foster advanced research and training in the application of mathematical methods in the social sciences." The following fields are each represented on MSSB by one member: anthropology, economics, history, geography, linguistics, political science, psychology, and sociology. The three methodological disciplines of mathematics, statistics, and computer science are also represented. Members of MSSB are appointed, subject to the approval of the Board of Trustees of the Center, for a term of four years. At the present time the members of MSSB are:

Preston S. Cutler, Center for Advanced Study in the Behavioral Sciences

Michael F. Dacey, Department of Geography, Northwestern University

Roy G. D'Andrade, Department of Anthropology, University of California—San Diego

William K. Estes, Department of Psychology, Rockefeller University

Leo A. Goodman, Departments of Sociology and Statistics, University of Chicago

Kenneth C. Land, Russell Sage Foundation and Department of Sociology, Columbia University

R. Duncan Luce, School of Social Sciences, University of California —Irvine (Chairman)

Allen Newell, Department of Computer Science, Carnegie-Mellon University

Stanley Peters, Department of Linguistics, University of Texas

Roy Radner, Departments of Economics and Statistics, University of California—Berkeley

William H. Riker, Department of Political Science, University of Rochester

Herbert A. Simon, Department of Industrial Relations, Carnegie-Mellon University

Charles Tilly, Departments of History and Sociology, University of Michigan

MSSB has established advisory committees to plan its activities in the various substantive fields with which it is concerned. The current members of the History Advisory Committee are listed on page ii above.

Supported by grants from the National Science Foundation,[1] MSSB has organized five major classes of activities.

(1) *Training Programs*, which last from two to eight weeks during the summer, are designed to provide young pre- and post-Ph.D.'s with intensive training in some of the mathematics pertinent to their substantive field and with examples of applications to specific problems.

(2) *Research and Training Seminars*, which last from four to six weeks, are composed of both senior scientists and younger people who have already received some training in mathematical applications. The focus is on recent research, on the intensive exploration of new ideas, and on the generation of new research. The training is less formal than in (1); it has the apprentice nature of advanced graduate work.

(3) *Advanced Research Workshops* last from four to six weeks, but they are almost exclusively restricted to senior scientists and are devoted to fostering advanced research. They afford the possibility of extensive and penetrating contact over a prolonged period, which would otherwise probably not be possible, of men deeply steeped in research.

(4) *Preparation of Teaching Materials*. In some areas, the absence of effective teaching materials—even of suitable research papers—is a very limiting factor in the development of research and teaching activities within the university framework. The Board has, therefore, felt that it could accelerate the development of such materials, in part, by financial support and, in part, by help in organizing their preparation.

[1] This volume was prepared with the support of National Science Foundation Grant number GS-3256. Any opinions, findings, conclusions, or recommendations expressed below are those of the authors and do not necessarily reflect the views of NSF or MSSB.

(5) *Special Conferences.* Short conferences, lasting a few days, are organized to explore the possibilities of the successful development of mathematical theory and training in some particular area that has not previously been represented in the programs, or to review the progress of research in particular areas when such a review seems warranted.

Robert William Fogel, for the
History Advisory Committee, MSSB

Chicago, Illinois
August 1974

Contents

CONTENTS

Introduction

THIS VOLUME contains papers presented at a conference, "An International Comparison of Systems of Slavery," held at the University of Rochester on March 9-11, 1972, and sponsored by the Historical Advisory Committee of the Mathematical Social Science Board. In arranging the conference and selecting the contributors we were more interested in the approach to problems and the methods employed than in the filling out of a preselected geographical or chronological pattern, although we did find it necessary to impose some restrictions —all papers were confined to slavery in the Western Hemisphere, or to its African origins, from the fifteenth to the nineteenth centuries. We also selected those papers which seemed to ask the most interesting questions and to open up new areas of inquiry rather than those which, while applying more sophisticated quantitative analysis, dealt with more traditional topics. Despite, or maybe because, of these criteria, the papers seem to us to contain certain unifying threads, which certainly became apparent during the three days of stimulating discussions at the conference. We found much that was new and interesting on the ostensibly well worked subject of slavery.

In preparing the volume for publication we found it useful to rearrange the essays from the order and the groupings in which they were presented at the conference but have not been able to include all of the remarks of the formal commentators or any of the comments made by participants during the general discussion.* A few of the formal commentaries, which by general consent were indispensable, have been included; in several cases these were rewritten after the conference to fit in with the revised format. Authors of papers had several months to modify the version presented and therefore the commentaries also had to be revised somewhat.

We both feel somewhat constrained in our introductory remarks, since we have reserved the final summary remarks on the papers for ourselves, and some basic issues of substance and method will be discussed in greater detail then. Here we shall make only a few methodological remarks. The conference participants included historians, economists, sociologists, and anthropologists. As expected, there were differences among the disciplines in sophistication in the use of analytical and quantitative techniques. Economists, in particular, insisted on the basic specification of a model to be applied

* A list of all participants is given in the Appendix at the end of the volume.

to the historical issues, the application of more formal quantitative techniques to estimate the various parts of the model, and a greater emphasis on detailing the exact results of each particular study. The Goldin and LeVeen essays, for example, start from the economists' basic supply and demand model and proceed to estimate the importance of the various components subsumed under that dichotomy by the application of various techniques of empirical estimation. Although the particular specifications of the model may be criticized, there was no disagreement with the importance of the question under consideration or with the usefulness of the attempt to answer the historical question. The importance of the issues has been clearly established in the historical literature, as well as in the writings of contemporaries. They were not selected for analysis because of their amenability to analytical techniques. But, although the techniques have been useful in the study of certain questions, there are other questions for which these contributions have proven to be of more limited value. In these cases, which we think well illustrated by some of the methodologically more traditional papers, we need to seek alternative ways to study the problem rather than to condemn quantitative techniques out of hand for not being able to answer all questions.

The nature of quantitative techniques varies from the very formal statistical regression analysis, as in Goldin's paper, to basic counting of cases, as illustrated in several papers that provide new breakdowns of archival and manuscript data and provide a firmer base from which to pursue certain issues. Imprecise or incomplete as some of these counts may seem they do provide a more manageable and understandable order of magnitude than the usual "some," "more," "less," and other quantitative terms whose rough order of magnitude are considerably less well defined. On this level the papers of Bowser, Karasch, and Postma provide important additions to our knowledge; at more complex levels the various interpolations by Anstey and the cross-tabulations and quantitative comparisons of Hershberg do the same for their topics. In a less expected way the use of quantitative techniques provides an extremely useful basis to examine the primary material in archival and manuscript form which are the basis of much of the historians' work. These methods provide a framework for extracting much information that might otherwise be lost or else made available in such a way as to obscure the general significance of each unique document. In this sense quantitative methods are not new or "revolutionary," but are often used by historians. The more explicitly and self-consciously that they are used, however, the more fruitful will be the examination and the greater the possibility of devising effective sampling designs to organize the data. At an early stage of historical work simple counting can provide the best quantitative tool for analysis. Wood and Craton, for example, use this device to throw forward a number of valuable hypotheses and interpretations.

Quantitative and analytical techniques, like all tools, are only as good as their user. In good hands the product is good; in poor hands the product can be worthless. We believe that this volume contains articles based upon tools well-used, that the findings have interest and importance, and that, in numerous places, the mode of attack and analysis demonstrates the value of these methods for the study of long standing problems in history and the social sciences.

In the process of arranging the conference we were aided by funds and facilities provided by the University of Rochester.

In editing the volume we were greatly assisted by the other two members of the editorial committee, Philip Curtin and Sidney Mintz. Editorial details were undertaken by Laura Levine Frader and, at Princeton University Press, by Polly Hanford. The index was prepared by Donald K. Moore.

Stanley L. Engerman
Eugene D. Genovese

PART ONE:
THE SLAVE TRADE

I

The Volume and Profitability of the
British Slave Trade, 1761-1807

ROGER ANSTEY

WHAT WAS the extent of the British slave trade in the last half century before abolition?[1] From what portions of the African coastline did the slaves come and what was the relative importance of the different coastal regions in the supply of slaves? To these questions answers have been attempted, usually in monographs on the various national branches of the slave trade: more recently, however, Philip D. Curtin has published *The Atlantic Slave Trade: A Census,*[2] on the volume and flows of the Atlantic slave trade during the four centuries for which it endured. What I attempt here is not only to look closely at a fifty-year period, but, as far as possible, to go beyond the published sources to which Curtin necessarily confined himself.

On any reckoning, the British slave trade was the largest single national branch in the second half of the eighteenth century[3] and, given the limited period, it is possible to use the varying kinds of evidence according to availability and quality on almost a year by year basis. Broadly speaking, the evidence falls into the two categories of export and import shipping data. Strongest of all is the evidence of actual imports into the Americas, for, even though it never comprehends all the importing entrepôts, this evidence permits one to establish ratios of landed slaves per ton.[4] Such evidence

---

[1] Apart from particular acknowledgments which are to follow, I gratefully recognize the assistance given me by colleagues in the University of Kent—Mr. J. M. Bevan, Professors Peter Bird and Walter Hagenbuch and Dr. David Ormrod. Externally Mr. Frank Sanderson helped me greatly with his knowledge of Liverpool MS collections on the slave trade and Professor Ralph Davis and Dr. P. D. Richardson gave me valuable guidance. I also learned much from discussion of an earlier version of this paper at the conference.

[2] Madison, Wis., 1969.

[3] See Averil MacKenzie-Grieve, *The Last Years of the English Slave Trade, Liverpool, 1750-1807*, London, 1941, for a rather general approach to the subject.

[4] Unless otherwise indicated, "tons" in this paper are, or must be assumed to be, measured tons. In about 1700 the two were equivalent but "by 1775 most ships carried more than they measured," i.e., a ship of 100 tons measured was 100 + x tons burden/deadweight. The ratio was not constant and so no formula can readily be applied to convert one into the other. There is the yet graver obstacle

3

can then be combined with the more abundant clearance lists wherein, in varying combination, one has the names of ships, masters or owners, tonnage, number of slaves "gone for" or, after 1788, "licensed to carry." Finally, there is some evidence of the relative importance to the British slave trade of the different regions of the Atlantic coastline of Africa, while mortality figures can also be worked out.

For the decade 1761-1770, clearance lists, though in various forms, are our evidence. For Bristol there are two overlapping lists [5] but the Customs authorities had not originally sought to discover the number of slaves "gone for." However, "upon enquiring we find that upon an average computation the number of slaves taken in by each ship in the above account amounted to nearly 250." [6] This will be taken as 248,[7] while the number of clearances is 249.[8] The Liverpool return for the decade yields the more precise information of the number of slaves "gone for" and there is no alternative but to rely on the one sample which relates slaves "gone for" to slaves actually loaded that I have so far discovered, a sample which suggests that a slaver took on board about 95 percent of the intended cargo.[9] The evidence for London is less satisfactory since the one decennial clearance list [10] does not clearly distinguish between slave ships and ships engaged in the trade in gum, ivory, timber, and gold. Edward Long, however, cites a precise one-year estimate which

---

that the records do not usually specify which type of ton they are using. But from 1773 the use of the measured ton was encouraged in official records and from 1786 this became compulsory. All the official records here used are post-1773, though in certain cases collated after 1773, and we can only assume that measured tons are meant. A sample comparison of the tonnages in Norris' list of Liverpool slave ships in 1790 at least shows in most cases an exact correspondence with the measured ton figure as reproduced from the Liverpool Port Registry books. When there is a difference it is not usually significant (Ralph Davis, *The Rise of the English Shipping Industry in the Seventeenth and Eighteenth Centuries*, London, 1962, pp. 7n, 372, 374; Great Britain. *Parliamentary Papers, Accounts and Papers*, 1792, xciii, hereafter cited as *A&P*; Robert Craig and Rupert Jarvis, *Liverpool Registry of Merchant Ships*, Manchester, 1967).

[5] Great Britain, Public Record Office, *Board of Trade Papers* (hereafter cited at *BT*), 6/3 fols. 91-98, 150-189.

[6] *Ibid.*, fol. 98.

[7] Coincidentally the average cargo for all British slavers in 1771 has been given as 248 (F. W. Pitman, *The Development of the British West Indies, 1700-1763*, reissue, London, 1967, p. 67).

[8] As so often, there are minor discrepancies between the two sets of returns and one must simply take the more credible alternative.

[9] The sample consists of 9 ships belonging to Tarleton and Backhouse of Liverpool, a leading slave-trading firm, in voyages of 1787 and early 1788 (*A&P*, xxiv [633]).

[10] *BT 6/3*, fols. 150-189.

4

says London employed 58 ships for 8,136 slaves in 1771.[11] This is puzzling because of the small—by Liverpool and Bristol standards—cargoes thus denoted, but significant because the (good) clearance lists already referred to are, at 56 virtually the same as Long at 58. The best resolution of the problem which we can offer is to apply this ratio of 58:8,136 to the undifferentiated list of London clearances,[12] yielding a total for the decade of 49,097 slaves loaded. Added to the Liverpool and Bristol figures this gives a total of 306,022 slaves loaded in the decade 1761-1770. To these data the mortality rate for the period 1769-1787, which has been established (see Appendix 1) at 8.5 percent, must be applied.[13] On these bases we

[11] *Treatise upon the trade from Great Britain to Africa* (1772), cited in E. Long, *History of Jamaica*, London, 1774, I, 492n.

[12] This mode of calculation, while it tends sharply to lower the volume of the London slave trade, necessarily has the effect of raising the number of ships and increasing the tonnage, which must be attributed to it. It is possible that Long is to be taken as meaning that 56 London ships in the African trade took off 8,136 slaves but that not all of these ships actually loaded slaves. Alternatively, London-Africa ships may have bought relatively large amounts of African produce, and relatively small numbers of slaves. A related puzzle is the relatively large number of ships recorded as constituting the import trade from Africa—290 in 1761-1770, 445 in 1771-1780, and 193 in 1781-1787. It seems most likely, however, that this list is not of ships which returned directly from Africa but of ships which included African produce in their homeward cargoes. If so, this would help to explain the low slave-loading rate of London ships. It also surmounts the very great difficulty in postulating that in those three decades, 20%, 40%, and 25% of all clearances for Africa were in the out and back trade. For the Africa inward and outward clearances on which these percentages are based see *A&P*, 1789, xxvi, [646a], pt. iv, and n. 44 below.

[13] No allowance is made, either in this or subsequent decades, for the effect of ship loss, as distinct from mortality on ships which reached the Americas. There was no systematic recording of ship loss, but the evidence suggests that this did not happen frequently. When pressed on the question by the Commons Select Committee, Captain Fraser said that in his twenty years' experience of the trade he had seen none, and heard of only "very few" losses on the African coast (*A&P*, 1790, xxix [698], 50). Such losses as did occur seem to have been suffered more in Caribbean waters, especially in wartime at the hands of enemies. But it must be remembered that the slaves on board were likely still to have reached the Americas though they would rightfully have to feature under a different national total. The work of Craig and Jarvis on registration lists of Liverpool ships, by making it possible to work from analogy of the "ceased registrations," i.e., losses, in the port's trade as a whole would suggest that, in the 1790s, for instance, an average of 12.5% of the tonnage standing on the register at a given date in one year had ceased to be registered twelve months later (R. Craig and R. Jarvis, *Liverpool Registry of Merchant Ships*, Manchester, 1967, pp. 143, 149; I am grateful to Professor David Bartholomew for assistance in the use of these statistics). But such analogical reasoning cannot tell us what proportion of the 12½% were lost either after they had landed their slaves, or were simply scrapped at the end of their voyage, which latter must have been very common. It seems best to make no allowance for ship loss and perhaps to counterbalance this item by the con-

can establish a decennial figure of 306,022 slaves exported by English slave traders and 280,010 landed, in 1,341 vessels of 150,628 tons.

The volume of the English slave trade in the first six years of the next decade can be measured from the same kind of evidence and with the same assumptions. The resulting figure is 205,968 slaves loaded and 188,461 landed in 901 ships of 97,628 tons. In the remainder of the decade, however, there are no individual port clearance lists, but only an aggregated annual figure of all tonnage clearing for Africa.[14] It is clear from this that there was a very sharp decline in the slave trade—a result, no doubt, of the activities of American privateers during the earlier years of the Revolutionary War and it would seem wise to apply to the slave trade the same proportionate reduction as affected all clearances for Africa. As regards the Middle Passage, the same figure for mortality obtains as for the earlier part of the decade. The decennial total, on these assumptions, becomes 253,521 loaded and 231,972 landed, in 1,074 ships of 120,168 tons.

Both the aggregated national clearance list and a list of total Liverpool clearances for Africa [15] reveal 1779 as the low point of the English slave trade during the war. These same lists also combine to attest that a significant degree of recovery preceded the Peace of Paris in 1783 and that recovery to prewar levels was completed in that year. For the Liverpool slave trade in the years 1781 and 1782 we can take the total tonnage cleared from the port, less the 5 percent which Gomer Williams attested was the percentage of its African trade in commodities other than slaves.[16] For the next six years we can obtain a figure for slave ship tonnage cleared from Liverpool by taking the number of slave ships recorded as clearing according to a 1797 account by an "eye-witness-Liverpool" [17] and projecting a tonnage

---

siderable evidence that, at a guess, 5% of ships participating in the slave trade went unrecorded. For example, well over this percentage of Liverpool ships employed in the slave trade in 1790, as listed by Norris, are not included in the port clearance lists for the year, or for 1789, or 1791, and this when not only the value of the ships but of the cargo is carefully itemized (A&P, 1790, xxix [500-509]).

[14] A&P, 1789, xxvi (646a), pt. iv, no. 1.

[15] Genuine "Dicky Sam," Liverpool and Slavery: An Historical Account of the Liverpool-African Slave Trade, reissue, Newcastle-upon-Tyne, 1969, p. 137; also published in Donnan, Documents Illustrative of the History of the Slave Trade to America, Washington, 1930-1935, iv, 48-49.

[16] Gomer Williams, History of the Liverpool Privateers and Letters of Marque with an Account of the Liverpool Slave Trade, reissue, London, 1967, Appendix xiv. Also printed in part in Donnan, ii, 625.

[17] Liverpool and Slavery, p. 107. This source also gives a figure for slaves landed, 1783-1793, but this last information has not been used since it postulates much larger cargoes than do other sources. The apparently convincing sterling

for them from the tonnages of all ships listed as clearing for Africa from the port.[18] To arrive at the tonnage engaged in the British slave trade as a whole, of which there is no direct evidence, we can use published returns which give Liverpool a 70 percent share in 1789-1790 and assume a more or less regular—as from the revival of the slave trade in 1781—increase in that percentage from the known 67 percent of 1771-1776.[19] Slaves landed can now be projected from total tonnage with the aid of a very large sample of landings in the British West Indies from 1783 to 1788 inclusive—130,873 slaves landed in 65,660 tons of shipping.[20] For the last two years of the decade we have a Register-General of Shipping list of numbers and tonnage of slave vessels clearing from the three British ports,[21] but need to project the number of slaves landed on a different basis, since Dolben's Act brought about a marked reduction in carryings per ton from this time onward. The ratio of landings per ton for the year 1791 has therefore been taken—41,496 slaves in 29,018 tons.[22] Mortality continues at 8.5 percent until 1788 when it increases to 9.6 percent.

The evidence for slave carryings in the years 1791-1800, though often varying in kind from that available for the preceding decades, is better than ever. From 1795 onward we have near-comprehensive port clearance lists, including tonnage and/or "slaves allowed" figures, and from 1796 we have substantially complete information on slave landings in the British West Indies. For the early and mid-nineties, as we have already seen, we have especially good mortality samples, while for the years 1791-1797 we possess an extremely full and detailed analysis of the voyages of some 350 slavers together with sparser, but still valuable, information about 550 more.[23] In both

---

value of the slaves which also is given in the table is revealed as nothing more than the anonymous author's assumption of £50 per head. The list itself is printed in Donnan, II, 625.

[18] *Liverpool and Slavery*, p. 137.

[19] But note that the 70% is of tonnage and 67% of slaves loaded. The best evidence in each case demands that we admit this minor inconsistency.

[20] *A&P*, 1789, xxvi (646a) and *A&P*, 1790, xxxi, (705).

[21] *A&P*, 1792, xxxv (768), 1-9.

[22] See Table 1.

[23] This provides detailed and often complete itineraries of the voyages up to the time of clearance from the West Indies for home. The information really is remarkably full—it occupied three clerks' whole time for a year: the vessel's name and tonnage together with port and date of clearance; the date and place of arrival on the African coast; the number of slaves taken on board from the time of arrival and the number that died while the vessels were still on the coast, or who were relanded or transshipped, all divided into the categories of Men, Women, Boys, and Girls; the date and place of clearance from the African coast with the

Table 1. The British Slave Trade 1781-1790

Period	Estimated Liverpool Tonnage in Slave Trade	Liverpool Ships	% of Liverpool Slave Trade to British Slave Trade	Projected Total Tons	Projected Total Ships	Projected Slaves Imported	Mortality	Total Loaded
1781	5,434	41	68	7,991	60		8.5	
1782	5,899	45	68	8,675	66		8.5	
1783	12,294	85	68	18,079	125		8.5	
1784	8,426	59	68	12,391	87	235,041	8.5	257,269
1785	10,148	73	69	14,707	106		8.5	
1786	13,212	87	69	19,148	126		8.5	
1787	12,455	72	69	18,051	104		8.5	
1788	13,027	71	69	18,880	103		9.6	
1789	11,081	61	71	15,510	85	59,824	9.6	66,177
1790	18,266	94	69	26,325	136		9.6	
Total				159,757	998	294,865		323,446

av. = 8.64

Sources: see text.

halves of the decade, the fact that first the Lords List A and subsequently Customs Office lists give us large samples of slaves imported into the West Indies enables us to make major use of import data. For 1791-1795 the Lords List A makes it abundantly possible to estimate a figure for the average size of landed cargoes, while for the second five years (although the Lords List continues to 1797 it is significantly less full in its last two years), figures of virtually all tonnage and slaves arriving in the British West Indies enable us to arrive at a ratio of slaves per ton landed.[24] It only remains to relate this import data to the number of clearances for the slave trade from English ports, or, in respect of 1796-1800, the slightly finer category of tonnage cleared. In the former case the Lords Lists are a most comprehensive guide, while the proper collation of port clearance lists, which begin from 1795, gives us almost an embarrassment of overlapping estimates.[25] Our conclusions are tabulated in Table 2.

---

total of slaves on board, and who died on the middle passage, again divided by age and sex; the place of arrival in the West Indies, and the dates of arrival and clearance. Added to this list, which for subsequent convenience we shall term Lords List A, is a list of some 560 vessels described as "such ships as appear by any entries in the Customs House Books to have been engaged in the Slave Trade." For one reason or another their log books and surgeon's journals had not been deposited with the Customs authorities and the information given is restricted to the ship's name and tonnage, and the place and date of clearance from Britain. We shall call this table Lords List B. The direct value of these two lists is evidently for the decade 1791-1800 but they possess some analogical value for the decade before and for the period 1801-1807. This return of slave shipments is in the House of Lords Record Office under Order Date 10 July 1799.

[24] Since rather more than half of the slavers clearing in a given year landed their cargoes the next year, the slaves per ton ratio shown in the list below represents the mean of the tonnage and slaves landed figures for adjoining years (A&P, 1806, XIII [783-797]).

Year	Tonnage	Slaves	Slaves per Ton
1796	8,963	14,976	
1797	13,053	19,499	1.37
1798	23,939	32,776	1.41
1799	22,761	35,914	1.47
1800	31,379	36,159	1.33
1801 (½ year)	12,713	17,519	1.21

The Lords List B gives the names of a number of ships lost or sold, and these have been subtracted from the annual totals. It is highly likely that the number of slaves per ton landed in foreign possessions (the direct foreign trade was about 25% of the whole) was higher, since the Acts regulating numbers could not be enforced in this case. No weighting has, however, been given for this.

[25] For instance, in the overlap year, 1795, the list of clearance in A&P, 1806, XIII (783 & 795) enables us to add eleven ships not recorded in the Lords lists, and to subtract two which are shown to be not engaged in the slave trade. From 1795, there are two lists summarizing port clearances, as well as the port lists detailing

TABLE 2. THE BRITISH SLAVE TRADE 1791-1800

Period	Ships Clearing for Slave Trade	Tonnage Clearing for Slave Trade	Average Cargo Loaded	Average Slaves Per Ton	Total Landed	Mortality %	Total Loaded
1791	156	29,018	266		41,496	9.5	45,852
1792	186	35,293	263		48,918	8.4	53,404
1793	75	15,885	320		24,000	5.5	25,397
1794	141	27,341	308		43,428	3.2	44,864
1795	92	17,098	306		28,152	2.7	28,933
1796	111	20,755		1.57	32,585	3.4	33,732
1797	112	23,479		1.41	33,105	4.2	34,556
1798	163	36,756		1.47	54,031	4.0	56,282
1799	163	37,212		1.33	49,492	4.0	51,554
1800	142	35,700		1.21	43,197	4.0	44,997
TOTAL	1,341	278,537			398,404		419,571

SOURCES: see text.

In the years 1801-1807, the last period of the British slave trade, the same method can be used as in the second half of the previous decade. By direct evidence of very substantial samples we have figures of slaves per ton landed, for the years up to 1805 inclusive, and can assume that for the remaining two years of the trade this rate remained

the names, tonnages and/or slaves allowed figures of individual ships. The first of the summary lists (A&P, 1806, XIII [797]) covers the years 1795-1804 and is well known since Gomer Williams reproduced it, with slight errors, in his *History of the Liverpool Privateers*, p. 680, whence it was copied by Donnan, II, 632, Table 291. The second list (A&P, 1806 VII [199]) was produced by the Registrar-General of Shipping, as opposed to the Inspector-General of the Customs, and gives the national total of ships clearing "for Africa and the West Indies," together with their tonnage, from 1796 to 1805. The number of vessels clearing for Africa *and* the West Indies, which is undoubtedly synonymous with vessels engaging in the slave trade, was arrived at by subtracting from the total of all clearances to Africa those vessels which subsequently returned directly from Africa. In every year to 1800 the number of ships in the second list is higher—by about 9% of the aggregate. To take the first list as an exclusive guide would be to ignore the additional ships seemingly detected by the Registrar-General; to rely only on the second list risks such inflation of the number of vessels engaged in the slave trade as would result from under-recording of the return of ships engaged in the out and back Africa trade. It therefore seems right to draw the mean. To do this the "slaves allowed" figures in the first list are converted into tonnage cleared on the basis of 1.6 slaves per ton up to 1799 inclusive, and 1.03 per ton for the remaining year. The change stems from the more stringent regulations which came into force on 1 August 1799 (though because the great proportion of slavers in that year took pains to clear before the new law came into effect, it had no perceptible effect that year) and the figure of 1.03 is the average of slaves allowed per ton on all Liverpool clearances in the first two full years of the new regulations. The second list is less well-known and is as follows:

the same.[26] In arriving at tonnage cleared from British ports we face the continuing problem of variation in the different clearance lists, compounded by the absence of figures other than for Liverpool after the end of April 1806. Only in 1801, however, need we resort to taking the mean, since in the remaining three years for which we have two sets of figures, the Customs House list, which is the higher, in each year, is to be preferred since it is based on named individual ships.[27] For 1805 we must use the one summary list—the Registrar-General's —which we have, and for the remaining years use the Liverpool clearances [28] and the assumption that in that period the London and Bristol trade continued at the 15 percent of the whole which it had been in the twelve months ending 30 April 1806.[29] On mortality, we shall simply assume the same figure of 4 percent which was taken for the later nineties: there appear to be no estimates of mortality specifically for the last years of the British trade.

We can now, therefore, tabulate in Table 4 the estimated number of slaves loaded and landed in the British slave trade between 1761 and 1807. Curtin's "preferred series" of slaves loaded in the British trade

Year	Ships	Tons
1796	118	21,252
1797	120	25,092
1798	165	37,822
1799	170	39,655
1800	150	37,621
1801	158	38,259
1802	150	36,916
1803	100	23,151
1804	138	31,823
1805	132	32,490

Note: See Table 2 for the yearly totals, 1791-1800.

[26] The same approach to tonnage and slaves arriving in the British West Indies as was detailed in n. 24, with projections for years where the figures are wholly or partly lacking, gives the following figures per year of clearance for slaves per ton landed (A&P, 1806, xiii [777-781, 798-801]).

$$1801 : 1.05$$
$$1802 : 0.96$$
$$1803-1807 : 0.99$$

[27] "Slaves allowed" on the list can be transposed into tonnage cleared at the 1801 ratio of .97 tons per slave allowed.

[28] Donnan, ii, 48-49 (Table 33) where I have assumed that the tonnage figures include the assumed 5% of vessels engaged in the out and back African trade, and made the necessary deduction. It is claimed in *Liverpool and Slavery*, p. 137, however, that the total tonnage at this time was devoted to the slave trade. The preferred figures for tonnage clearing in each year are given in column 3 of Table 3.

[29] A&P, 1806, xiii (802-804).

ROGER ANSTEY

TABLE 3. THE BRITISH SLAVE TRADE 1801-1807

Period	Ships Clearing for Slave Trade	Tonnage Clearing for Slave Trade	Slaves per Ton Landed	Slaves Landed	Mortality %	Slaves Loaded
1801	153	37,485	1.05	39,359		40,999
1802	157	39,853	0.96	38,259		39,853
1803	99	24,177	0.99	23,935		24,932
1804	147	35,782	0.99	35,424	4.0	36,900
1805	132	32,490	0.99	32,165		33,505
1806	131	29,002	0.99	28,712		29,908
1807	87	19,901	0.99	19,702		20,523
TOTAL	906	218,690		217,556		226,620

SOURCES: see text.

in this period is 1,386,300: [30] our estimate, 10.3 percent higher, is based on material not known to Curtin's authorities and therefore supersedes his results.

Given these decennial totals we can now proceed to an estimate, tabulated in Table 5, of the coastal distribution of slave exports. For the decade 1761-1770 we can apply to the overall British slave trade the declared destinations of all Liverpool slavers and adopt essentially the same procedure for the following decade but assuming that the same pattern existed for 1777-1780, in respect of which we have no information, as for 1771-1776.[31] For the decade 1781-1790 direct evidence is lacking and we must consequently take the mean of the percentage distributions of the preceding and the

TABLE 4. ESTIMATED NUMBER OF SLAVES, LOADED AND LANDED, BRITISH SLAVE TRADE 1761-1807

Period	Loaded	Landed
1761-70	306,022	280,010
1771-80	253,521	231,972
1781-90	323,446	294,865
1791-1800	419,571	398,404
1801-1807	226,620	217,556
TOTAL	1,529,180	1,422,807

SOURCES: see text.

[30] Curtin, p. 142.
[31] BT 6/3, fols. 99-129.

12

TABLE 5. COASTAL DISTRIBUTION OF THE BRITISH SLAVE TRADE 1761-1807

Region	1761-70	1771-80	1781-90	1791-1800	1801-1810	Total
Senegambia	11,812	8,062	6,243	2,811	1,518	30,446
%	3.86	3.18	1.93	0.67	0.67	1.99
Sierra Leone	26,777	28,268	25,649	19,720	10,651	111,065
%	8.75	11.15	7.93	4.70	4.70	7.26
Windward Coast	74,578	47,561	42,501	31,510	17,019	213,169
%	24.37	18.76	13.14	7.51	7.51	13.94
Gold Coast	26,838	20,484	35,417	57,985	31,319	172,049
%	8.77	8.08	10.95	13.82	13.82	11.25
Bight of Benin	26,683	24,820	18,630	7,259	3,921	81,315
%	8.72	9.79	5.76	1.73	1.73	5.32
Bight of Biafra	112,249	117,355	140,764	170,975	92,348	633,691
%	36.68	46.29	43.52	40.75	40.75	41.44
Congo, Angola	27,083	6,997	54,177	129,354	69,867	287,478
%	8.85	2.76	16.75	30.83	30.83	18.80
TOTALS	306,022	253,521	323,446	419,571	226,620	1,529,180

NOTE: In the crucial years 1791-1800 about ¼ to ⅓ of the total voyages do not specify the part of the African coast cleared from. To record such a proportion as "unknown" would involve heavy distortion, and so, throughout the table, the percentages are of known clearance regions; cf. Curtin, p. 150.

following decade. For the latter we can invoke the strong evidence of very large samples for each year of the decade.[32] The final seven years have left almost no evidence about distribution and so the pattern of 1791-1800 will be assumed. Perhaps the most striking trend is the declining importance of the whole coast down to the eastern edge of the Bight of Benin, with the exception of the Gold Coast, the re- markably constant share of the Bight of Biafra, and the rise in im- portance of Congo and Angola.

How profitable was the British slave trade in this last half century of its existence? "Eye-witness" of Liverpool, writing in 1797, estimated that a decade earlier the profit on the Liverpool slave trade was "upwards of thirty per cent"[33] and a figure of this order has not infrequently been cited with general approval by later historians;[34] in any event it is a truism to say that the slave trade has generally been regarded as highly lucrative. Nor has this considerable profit- ability merely the significance of a somber commentary on human nature, for the triangular trade, of which the slave trade was an integral part, has for half a century, at least, been regarded as an

[32] Based on Lords List A up to 1795 and on British West Indies arrival lists from 1796-1800 (A&P, 1801-1802, IV [451ff]).

[33] Liverpool and Slavery, p. 111.

[34] See, e.g., Eric Williams, Capitalism and Slavery, New York, 1961, pp. 36-37.

important source of the capital which made possible the Industrial Revolution. "The triangular trade," writes Eric Williams, "made an enormous contribution to Britain's industrial development. The profits from this trade fertilized the entire productive system of the country." [35] Serious though the difficulties in constructing an estimate of profitability are, the interest and significance of the question warrant an attempt.

The assessment of the volume of the British slave trade, just completed, provides a starting point, for we can immediately link volume to what is, on the whole, good evidence of the slave trader's main return—the price paid for his slaves in the Caribbean. For the first three decades under our view we have good evidence—20 indications, usually of "prices round" (expressed in £ sterling, or readily convertible thereto) for the decade 1761-1770, 33 for the following decade, and 29 for the period 1781-1790. There is therefore a firm basis for attributing to those decades average prices for newly landed slaves of £29, £34, and £37 respectively. For the nineties, when there are seven indications only, we must postulate £50, and for the years 1801-1807, when there are some half-dozen indications, we must suggest £60.[36]

---

[35] *Ibid.*, p. 105. See also p. 63: "It was only the capital accumulation of Liverpool which called the population of Lancashire into existence and stimulated the manufactures of Manchester. That capital accumulation came from the slave trade whose importance was appreciated more by later historians." In this section, it should be noted, Williams is stressing the regional role of profits from the slave trade. Elsewhere he is careful to observe that profits from the triangular trade were not the only source of capital for the Industrial Revolution (see pp. 52, 98).

[36] Note the compatibility of the estimates for the first three decades with the opinion of Norris, a Liverpool slave trader, who informed the Privy Council Committee in 1789 that the average price commanded by new slaves in the West Indies between 1763 and 1788 was £28-£35, and with the evidence of Evan Baillie, a West Indian slave factor, that the average value of cargoes before the American war was from £25 to £33, that this had increased from £30 to £40 thereafter and in 1789-1790 to between £42 and £50. Dr. Phillip LeVeen's calculations, based primarily on the Rogers Papers (Great Britain, Public Record Office, Chancery 107/1-15) and the Davies-Davenport MSS (Great Britain, University of Keele, Raymond Richards Collection of miscellaneous Historical Materials; see below), have led to somewhat lower average selling prices. Extrapolating them from his graph, and assuming a conversion rate of $5 to £1 sterling, they appear to be £32, £38, £39, £40, and £40 for the five decades, an average of £37.8 (E. Phillip LeVeen, "British Slave Trade Suppression Policies 1821-1865: Impact and Implications," Ph.D. dissertation, University of Chicago, 1971, pp. 9-10 and Appendix A). I am most grateful to Dr. LeVeen for making available to me a copy of his valuable work. My own sources are: A&P, 1789, xxvi (646a), pt. iii, Answers of Witnesses from the various islands to Q 29; *ibid.*, pt. iv, nos. 17 and 18; A&P, 1790, xxix (698), 94, 194, 199, 230, 305, and 637-

We have thus arrived at the basic element of one of the major components of an overall voyage account: but that gross sale price was subject to significant deductions. The first category of deductions comprised those made in the West Indies: the captain's, mates', and surgeon's commissions, the commission payable to the slave factor and on the remitting home of the bills of exchange given in payment for the slaves, and various disbursements made by the ship's captain, including part of the crew's wages, which it was evidently the custom to offset against the price paid for the slaves. These deductions were rated by Gomer Williams at 19 percent, while study of an admittedly small number of voyage accounts shows a range of between 14 percent and 20 percent.[37] We shall take 18 percent as the norm.

The next deduction results from the financial structure of the British slave trade at this period. Although slavers sometimes brought home part cargoes of West Indian produce,[38] the need to avoid a long waiting period in the Caribbean had combined with the ever more common practice of freighting the tropical staples home in specially built West Indiamen, partly to exclude slave ships from a share in this trade in our period. The remittance home of the net proceeds on slave sales was thenceforward made in bills of exchange which, says Richard Sheridan, "probably accounted for the bulk of the returns

---

638; L. J. Ragatz, *The Fall of the Planter Class in the British Caribbean, 1763-1833*, reissue, New York, 1963, p. 191; Francis E. Hyde, Bradbury B. Parkinson, and Sheila Marriner, "The Nature and Profitability of the Liverpool Slave Trade," *Economic History Review*, 2d ser., 5 (1952-1953), 370, 375-376; Bradbury B. Parkinson, "A Slaver's Accounts," *Accounting Research*, ii (1951), 148-149; Michael Craton and James Walvin, *A Jamaican Plantation: The History of Worthy Park, 1670-1970*, London, 1970, p. 131; Stanley Dumbell, "The Profits of the Guinea Trade," *Economic Journal*, ii (1931), 256; J. M. Hodson, "The Letter Book of Robert Bostock, a Merchant in the Liverpool Slave Trade, 1789-1792," *Liverpool Bulletin*, iii (1953), 41, 45, 47, 57; *The Commerce of Rhode Island*, Boston: Massachusetts Historical Collections 7th ser., ix, 1914, i, 338-339, 346, 398, 425, 461 and *ibid.*, Boston, 1915, ii, 14; Davies-Davenport MSS (Great Britain, University of Keele, to whom I am grateful for permission to use this source), Voyage Accounts, RR57/1, 3, 4, 5, 8, 9, 10 (provisional classification). Evidence from voyage account of *Mars* (1804), *Kitty's Amelia* (1805), and *Enterprise* (1806), kindly supplied by Mr. Frank Sanderson; *A&P*, 1847-1848, xxii, (536), Slave Trade Select Committee, 3d Rep., pars. 5653-5654, 5690-5694, Evidence of Thomas Tobin.

[37] *Liverpool and Slavery*, p. 111; Accounts of two voyages of the *Hawke* (Hyde et al., 375-376); of the *Plumper* (Parkinson, "A Slaver's Accounts," 148-149); of the *Emilia* (*A&P*, 1790, xxix [698, 637-639]), and several accounts from the various Liverpool collections kindly supplied by Mr. Frank Sanderson.

[38] The accounts of the *Hawke's* second voyage (above) show this, as does Professor Walter Minchinton's, "The Slave Trade and the West India Trade," an unpublished article kindly communicated to me.

15

after 1750." [39] Now the bill of exchange was not payable immediately upon receipt, but at so many months' "sight." We must therefore include an item for discounting as a deduction from the net remittance home. Thomas Clarkson, who investigated the working of the slave trade for himself, assessed the average "sight" of the bills at twenty four months, and other good evidence supports this.[40] The discount rate for two years has been taken as 10 percent in the years of peace, and 12 percent in the wartime years [41]—5 percent and 6 percent per annum respectively.

The final item on the credit side of the account is the written-down, or residual, value of the slave ship and its equipment on its return to the home port. Only sometimes do series of voyage accounts reveal the value of a ship and its outfit on its return, but some thirteen voyage accounts, estimates, or the equivalents—which appear to contain a balancing spread of both new and old ships—indicate written-down value of ship and equipment at the termination of a voyage. These values can then be adjusted for price changes and averaged over the total tonnage. The resulting residual value per ton figure

---

[39] R. B. Sheridan, "The Commercial and Financial Organization of the British Slave Trade, 1750-1807," *E.H.R.*, 2d ser., 11 (1958), 252-253. See also *A&P*, 1789, XXVI (646c), pt. IV, no. 1, where evidence of the Assemblies and Agents of the West Indian Colonies is summarized: "The ships bringing negroes from Africa are not generally employed in transporting the produce of the West India islands, and . . . the number of such vessels, which are employed in transporting produce, bears little or no proportion to the whole."

[40] Thomas Clarkson, *Essay on the Impolicy of the Slave Trade*, London, 1788, p. 28. Clarkson goes on to show that the average point in time at which the slave trader had to meet the bills by which he had financed the voyage was thirteen months after the voyage had begun. If this is adjusted to take account of the quite considerable cash outgoings which all voyage accounts show were made before the voyage began, the point becomes zero + nine months. Coincidentally, it was at approximately this point that the bills of exchange for slave sales were tendered in the West Indies. For the further evidence on the period of bills see Davies-Davenport MSS, RR 57/1, Voyage Accounts of *Hawke* (1780), RR 57/3, of *May* (1772 and 1773), and RR 57/4, of *Badger* (1777); *Liverpool and Slavery*, p. 115; see also Sheridan, 253-263 *passim*. Thomas Tobin, who as a young man had captained a slave ship between about 1798 and 1807, told the Commons Select Committee on the Slave Trade in 1848 that ". . . the payments were made in one, two, and three years' bills, and unless they were rich houses they could not do anything with those bills." (*A&P*, 1847-1848 [536], par. 5690, Evidence of Thomas Tobin). But for our purposes inability to obtain a discount does not matter: to have the prior use of his money the slave merchant would have had to borrow at the going rate for an average period of two years.

[41] S. Homer, *A History of Interest Rates*, New Brunswick, 1963, pp. 163-164, 181-186. Average discount over the decades is therefore 5.2%, 11.0%, 10.4%, 11.6%, and 11.4%. (In the 1760s the discount period was one year only.)

16

can then, in turn, be adjusted for each decade so that for the five decades we have, respectively, £5.4, £6.0, £6.4, £7.6, and £9.5 per ton.[42]

On the debit side the principal items were the ship and its equipment, the cargo, wages, provisions, customs, insurance, and miscellaneous expenses. The evidence presented on this relates particularly to 1787 and 1790 respectively, and must be adjusted in accordance with the movement in prices and insurance rates and the two-stage introduction of restriction on the numbers of slaves that could be carried. The conclusion of the extensive calculations made in Appendix 2 is the following outset cost per ton for the successive decades— £45.8, £51.7, £52.2, £55.0, and £53.4.

It may be objected that accounting on this basis ignores two important items. The first is the profit on West India produce brought home on the third leg of the triangular voyage, and the second the profit of such African produce as ivory, camwood, and gum which slavers sometimes bought if opportunity offered. But as regards the first objection, we have already seen that by the beginning of our period, slavers normally came home part loaded from the Caribbean, bringing the proceeds of the sale of slaves in bills of exchange. Exceptions there undoubtedly were, but, more fundamentally, since our concern is with the slave *trade* and its profits, we can ignore what was a possible and marginal profit in the operation of a slave-based economy. The other practice, the inclusion of African produce in a slaver's homeward cargo doubtless was as common as Hyde, Parkinson, and Marriner assert it to have been.[43] We are not, as such, concerned with the profitability of this trade for it was, though an integral part of the trade of slave ships, distinguishable from the trade in slaves. In balance sheet terms, however, a proportion of the voyage capital must be attributed to this African commerce and the outset of the slaving enterprise correspondingly reduced. The evidence regarding the relative importance of this commerce in ivory, redwood,

---

[42] Davies-Davenport MSS, RR 57/1, *Hawke* (1780 and 1781), RR 57/3, *May* (1772 and 1774), RR 57/4, *Badger* (1774), and RR 57/6, *Swift* (1770); four voyage estimates in BT 6/7; Parkinson, 148-149 (*Plumper*, 1768), Hodson, 56-57 (*Little Ben*, 1792). We also include evidence from one voyage of a Dutch slaver, because so meticulously accounted (W. S. Unger, "Bijdragen Tot de Geschiedenis van der Nederlandse Slavenhandel: 2. De Slavenhandel der Mittelburgsche Commercie Compagnie, 1732-1808," *Economich—Historisch Jaarbock* (1958), p. 108. Where tonnages were not given, these were worked out by the application of the average of slaves per ton landed during the decade.

[43] Hyde *et al.*, p. 372.

etc., is not entirely satisfactory, but it suggests that it should be rated at 5 percent.[44]

Whatever the inadequacies of this mode of calculation, and at least its assumptions and methods have been indicated in enough detail for modification to be offered, we can now project such figures as the amount of capital investment in the slave trade, the yield on that capital, both in money and as a percentage on the amount invested in the voyage. The primary purpose of these calculations has been to arrive at the return to the slave trader, but only a slight

---

[44] *A&P*, 1789, xxvi (646a), pt. iv, no. 2 gives the alleged number of ships bringing imports directly from Africa, together with their tonnage and the value of their cargoes, in the period 1761-1787, as follows:

Period	Ships	Tons	Value of Cargo in £
1761-1770	290	29,004	451,150
1771-1780	445	45,448	682,099
1781-1787	193	30,417	555,912

A difficulty about this list is that it gives a figure for the number of ships in the direct trade far higher than all the other evidence about the out and back trade warrants—an average of 45 a year between 1771 and 1780, for instance, with 69, 66, and 71 in three of those years. Yet the captain of a ship in this direct trade told the 1789 committee that he reckoned the number of ships employed in it as from 12 to 14 in each of the two previous years (*ibid.*, pt. iv, Appendix to no. 2), while Gomer Williams attests that less than 5% of Liverpool African ships, namely from 5 to 8, were employed in the direct trade (*Liverpool Slave Trade*, Appendix xiv). If one builds on the evidence of a Bristol merchant in the direct trade, also given to the 1789 committee (*A&P*, 1789, xxvi [646a], pt. iv, Appendix no. 2) that about half of the ivory (the second most valuable commodity after redwood) brought from Africa was carried in slave ships, and applies this proportion to all African produce, and if we assume that the return mentioned above really did refer to imports directly from Africa, we must conclude that, in the decade 1771-1780, for example, slave ships carried another £ 682,099 worth of African produce, demanding another 45,448 tons of shipping. But this is not credible, for total tonnage of slave ships in the decade was 120,168 and all other evidence is against the necessary implication that African produce amounted, tonnage wise, to 38% of the capacity of slave ships.

The alternative procedure would be to assume that the figures given for direct importation from Africa really relate to imports direct *and* in slave ships, and to assume that half of these by value came in slave ships as part cargo and half in out and back ships. In other words, the value of produce brought in slave ships in the sample decade 1771-1780 is either £ 682,099, or one half of this sum £ 341,050. As percentages of the sum of the value of the produce and the gross sale value of the slaves, these figures are 8.2% and 4.3% respectively. If the second assumption is applied to the exiguous evidence about imports in the period after 1787 (*A&P*, 1808, xi [220]) the percentage results are, for the decades before and after 1771-1780, 2.6, 3.5, 2.8, and 3.8. This assumption is to be preferred since the alternative involves accepting an implausibly high number of ships as engaged in the direct trade, but the percentage figure will be rounded up to 5, and applied to each decade.

18

refinement can indicate the contribution of the slave trade to national resource growth. The main component of this is simply the slave trader's profit, but to this must be added the discounting percentage since this is a transaction within the metropolitan economy.

The profit level of about 9.5 percent which has been put forward is, in the event the same as Phillip LeVeen's estimate, carried out by different methods, of a decennial profitability of 9.5 percent circa 1800.[45] The estimates are also compatible with much contemporary evidence save that the good profitability of the 1760s is rather a far cry from Clarkson's observation that between 1763 and 1772 the Liverpool slave trade was running at a loss, and the return in the seventies and eighties perhaps subserves Tarleton's observation that the trade expected profits to run out at rather over 10 percent.[46] It is surely unlikely that better evidence will ever show the slave trade to have been, in this period, a bonanza, or even that it could be made to show a return "upwards of thirty per cent profitability." The circumstantial evidence for discrediting the notion of a bonanza is in any event powerful. In a trade with open access, reports of rich killings must inevitably have led to a rush of investment. The supply of slaves would be unequal to the new demand and prices would rise. Various market forces, such as a decline in sugar prices would, probably sooner rather than later, mean difficulty in disposing of the slaves at a good, or any, profit and the probability of a loss. If high profits look improbable on circumstantial as well as on statistical grounds, there is strong analogical evidence for the proposition that the British slave trade could have sustained a much lower overall rate of return.

Such a low rate was precisely the experience of the Dutch Middleburg Company for which the most meticulous accounts imaginable have been preserved, and which have been worked upon and to some extent processed by the Dutch scholar, Dr. Unger. From the near-complete series of voyage accounts of 66 slaving voyages of the Middleburg Company between 1761 and 1800 (there are equally complete accounts of a further 35 voyages between 1732 and 1760) Unger has, on the fullest information,[47] tabulated (in Flemish Pounds) the

[45] LeVeen, p. 28, Table 3.

[46] Clarkson, p. 29. But he went on to say, more puzzlingly, that in the seventies Liverpool merchants failed for the sum of £710,000 and that in the late eighties it is considered as a fact, at the ports where it is carried on, that it is a losing trade at the present day; Great Britain. British Museum. Add. MSS 38, 416 fol. 103, Tarleton to Hawkesbury.

[47] "We get from the account-current a detailed picture of the financial results. First the debit side: foremost we see an account of the costs of the building of the

TABLE 6. VOLUME AND PROFITABILITY OF THE BRITISH SLAVE TRADE 1761-1807

	1 Voyages	2 Tons	3 Slaves Landed	4 Slaves Landed per Ton	5 Average Gross £ Sale Price	6 Gross Receipts on Slaves £	7 Net Receipts (82%) £
1761-70	1,341	150,628	280,010	1.86	29	8,120,290	6,658,638
1771-80	1,074	120,168	231,972	1.93	34	7,887,048	6,467,379
1781-90	998	159,757	294,865	1.85	37	10,910,005	8,946,204
1791-1800	1,341	278,537	398,404	1.43	50	19,920,200	16,334,564
1801-1807	906	218,690	217,556	0.99	60	13,053,360	10,703,755
AGGREGATES	5,660	927,780	1,422,807	1.53	42.1	59,890,903	49,110,540

	8 Net Receipts after Discounting £	9 Residual Value Less 5% for Produce £	10 Total Credit £ (Cols. 8+9)	11 Outset Less 5% for Produce £	12 Profit/£	13 % Profit	14 Resource Increment £ (Cols. 7+9 − Col. 11)
1761-70	6,312,389	772,721	7,085,110	6,553,824	531,286	8.1	877,535
1771-80	5,755,967	684,958	6,440,925	5,902,051	538,874	9.1	1,250,286
1781-90	8,015,799	971,323	8,987,122	7,922,350	1,064,772	13.4	1,995,177
1791-1800	14,439,755	2,011,037	16,450,792	14,553,558	1,897,234	13.0	3,792,043
1801-1807	9,483,527	1,973,677	11,457,204	11,094,144	363,060	3.3	1,583,288
AGGREGATES	44,007,437	6,413,716	50,421,153	46,025,927	4,395,226	9.5	9,498,329

[£202,092 p.a.]

TABLE 7. PROFIT AND LOSS IN THE TRIANGULAR TRADE OF THE
MIDDLEBURG COMPANY 1741-1800 [a]

Period	Outlay (in Flemish £)	Profit or Loss (£)	Net % Return or Loss	Average Voyage Length	% Annual Return or Loss	No. of Voyages
1741-50	110,934	−479	−0.43	16	−0.32	10
1751-60	282,603	+32,393	+11.46	17	+8.09	22
1761-70	511,543	+36,376	+7.11	17	+5.07	33
1771-80	425,036	−615	−0.14	18	−0.09	24
1781-90	132,932	−4,934	−3.73	24	−1.87	6
1791-1800	76,134	−6,530	−8.58	32	−3.21	3
1741-1800	1,538,642	+56,211	+3.65	17[b]	+2.58	98
1761-1800	1,145,105	+24,657	+2.15	18[b]	+1.43	66

[a] Distilled from Unger, pp. 87-91.
[b] This ignores the much extended voyage times in the two decades when voyages were few, 1781-1800.

original capital investment and voyage expenses, on the one hand, and the returns on the other. In the case of the Middleburg Company a cargo of produce was always brought home, having been purchased with the proceeds of the sale of the slaves, which in their turn had been bought by the trade goods initially sent out, thus completing the cycle. We are therefore here concerned not with the slave trade, but rather with the triangular trade. From the tabulation so thoroughly worked out by Unger it is readily possible to work out profit and loss over the four decades for which, though with decreasing momentum, the Dutch slave trade lasted.

There are, of course, the voyages that looked highly profitable, such as that of the *Het Vergenoegen* which returned 37.38 percent on an investment of £23,507, or £13,432 (sterling),[48] in 1786-1787,

ship, sometimes stating the measurements and the contents of the cargo. At the end of the voyage, the value hereof is written on the credit side, which will be put under Debit with the next voyage. Then follow the accounts and 'Home coming expenses,' next the purchase of the cargo and the expenses on the return cargo. In *Credit*: the yield of the imported and sold return goods . . . (as specified in the accompanying Captain's statement which lists the successive transactions on the voyage) . . . and the above-mentioned book value of the ship." Unger, pp. 106-107.

[48] Assuming an exchange rate of 35 Flemish shillings to the pound sterling. This was the approximate rate in 1811 (see Patrick Kelly, *Universal Cambist and Commercial Instructor being a General Treatise on Exchange including the Monies, Coins, Weights and Measures of all Trading Nations and Colonies*, London, 1811, I, 35, 276 and II, 9. The average of first monthly quotations 1752-1761 was 35s 5¾d. (J. Castaing, *Course of the Exchange*). I am indebted to Dr. Ormrod for the latter figures.

but against such seemingly lucrative ventures must be set the fact that, since voyages always took over twelve months, this figure is much lower when expressed as an annual rate of return. On the other hand, there could be losses at the level of the 59.41 percent sustained by the *De Geertruida en Christina* in 1783-1785. To remark the chance of high reward and the possibility of serious loss is to pinpoint an attitude to risk which had to exist if the slave trade, with all its hazards, was to be carried on at all. But at another level the significant thing is the overall return on capital. This is shown in decennial divisions for each of the four decades in our period that the trade lasted. The samples for the eighties and nineties, however, are too small to be very meaningful, and compensatory depth will be lent to the demonstration by adding the figures for the two immediately preceding decades. Both voyage profit and loss and annual profit and loss are included, the latter being arrived at proportionately by averaging total voyage duration in each decade.

All in all we perhaps have to realize that profits in eighteenth century overseas trade generally were probably much lower than we have tended to suppose. And if persistence in a trade giving an annual return of 1.43 percent over 40 years, or 2.58 percent over 60 years, was worth while for a Dutch Company, then a 9.5 percent return for the British trade over 47 years was very respectable indeed.

But what was "respectable" in terms of contributions to the capital requirements of the Industrial Revolution? Stanley Engerman has recently indicated the lines on which this can be measured. What follows here are crude calculations on lines suggested to me by a reading of Engerman but which in some respects do not follow his work. The extent of slave trade "profits" (in the sense of Resource Increment), according to our estimate, was about 9 million in almost a half-century and the annual average will be taken as £200,000. Now by 1800 the national ratio of investment to national income, according to Deane and Cole was about 7 percent,[49] and in our crude calculation we will take this figure as constant for the half-century. National income, again following Deane and Cole, rose from £130 million circa 1700 to £232 million in 1801;[50] we shall assume

[49] Phyllis Deane and W. A. Cole, *British Economic Growth 1688-1959*, Cambridge, 1964, pp. 259-264. I am most grateful to Dr. Engerman for sending me a preliminary copy of his paper "The Slave Trade and British Capital Formation in the Eighteenth Century: A Comment on the Williams Thesis," *Business History Review*, 46 (Winter 1972), 430-443. The form of the approach to Deane and Cole was suggested by me by this paper.

[50] Deane and Cole, pp. 156, 282.

an average of £180 million for the whole period. Total national investment was, therefore, at 7 percent, £12,600,000 per annum. If we assume that the proportion of slave trading profits invested followed the national 7 percent ratio, then £14,000 per annum was invested—which is exactly 0.11 percent of total national investment.

An alternative assumption is theoretically credible, namely that all the profits of the slave trade were invested. In this event the contribution of the slave trade to total national investment rises sharply, but still to the not very dizzy height of 1.59 percent. A further theoretical assumption is that all invested slave trade profits (7 percent of the whole) went into the formation of industrial capital. In our period this sector amounted to about 20 percent of the total, i.e., £2,520,000 per annum, and so invested slave trade profits would amount to 0.56 percent of this. Of course this percentage would rise dramatically if we assumed that all slave trade profits were put into industrial capital formation, namely, to 7.9 percent. There were varying implausibilities about all of the last three of these four possibilities, especially when we recall the lure of the land and of the funds, the concern to diversify into other trades and the need of the slave trader to eat. There is one sense in which these negative judgments can be qualified. Liverpool, the principal slaving port, was, of course, the port of Lancashire and the cotton industry. It is not unreasonable to suggest that geographical propinquity would result in a relatively large proportion of this capital formation in Lancashire cotton coming from the profits of a major activity of Liverpool. If slave trading profits of nearly all three British ports (i.e., with no deduction in respect of London and Bristol) were applied to cotton, and with the knowledge that the capital stock in the industry increased by about £400,000 per annum from 1780 onward,[51] we can assess the contribution made by slave trading profits on our first and our second assumptions. The results are 3.3 percent and 50.0 percent respectively. Credible though the notion of significant flow of slave trading profits into cotton is, this latter figure can only stem from a number of extreme assumptions and can be dismissed.

The prima facie case, urged by Williams and others, for some special contribution of slave trading profits to capital formation in cotton remains, but to be really significant such a contribution would

---

[51] *Ibid.*, p. 262. Cf. the relatively recent brief discussion of the role of slave trade and plantation profits in capital formation in the Industrial Revolution. See T. S. Ashton, *An Economic History of England: The Eighteenth Century*, London, 1955, p. 125, and M. W. Flinn, *Origins of the Industrial Revolution*, London, 1969, p. 46.

need to be shown—apart from being regionally and industrially concentrated—to be related to the proposition that outside capital in-
fusion was relatively low (most industrial investment being financed,
it has been argued, from profits) so that the importance of slave trade
capital in relation to all outside capital would have manifestly been
greater. It might also be necessary to "play the multiplier effect" and
assume that slave trade capital went into rapidly expanding and
highly profitable industries. Meanwhile, the most credible contribution of slave trade profits to capital formation is—at 0.11 percent—
derisory enough for the myth of the vital importance of the slave
trade in financing the Industrial Revolution to be demolished.

The West India plantation economy and its role in capital formation in Britain is a different case, and one which it is not immediately
relevant to consider here. Suffice it to say that here, too, recent
scholarship would seem to show that this contribution cannot have
been considerable. Indeed, on certain premises, the plantations
economy brought actual loss to the nation.[52]

[52] See R. B. Sheridan, "The Wealth of Jamaica in the Eighteenth Century,"
E.H.R., 2d ser., 18 (August 1965), 292-311, and "A Rejoinder," *ibid.*, 21 (April
1968), 46-61; R. P. Thomas, "The Sugar Colonies of the Old Empire: Profit or Loss
for Great Britain," *ibid.*, 30-45; K. G. Davies, "Essays in Bibliography and
Criticism XLIV: Empire and Capital," *ibid.*, 13 (1960-1961), 105-110; Richard
Pares, "Economic Factors in the History of the Empire," *E.H.R.*, 1st Series, 7
(1936-1937), 119-144.

APPENDIX 1

Mortality

THERE are three principal sources. Captains and others in the slave trade were closely questioned on mortality by the Privy Council Committee of Enquiry into the slave trade and, although they sometimes spoke from memory, and on occasion in round numbers, their evidence constitutes a large random sample, spanning the years 1769-1787 (A&P, 1789, LXXXIV [646a], pt. II). For 1789 mortality on large samples of cargoes arriving in the British West Indies was

APPENDIX TABLE 1. SLAVE MORTALITY RATES 1761-1807

Period	Loaded	Died	% Mortality, or Mean % Mortality
1761-70 ⎫	12,792	1,085 (1769-87)	8.5
1771-80 ⎬			
1781-87 ⎭			
1788-90	11,014	1,053 (1789)	9.6

	BWI Imports Sample			Sample Based on Logs and Journals			
Period	Loaded	Died	% Mortality	Loaded	Died	% Mortality	
1791	15,108	1,397	9.2	19,978	1,945	9.7 (1791)	9.5
1792	26,971	2,468	9.2	26,705	2,040	7.6 (1792)	8.4
1793	11,720	859	7.3	10,043	376	3.7 (1793)	5.5
1794	14,611	394	2.7	11,864	434	3.7 (1794)	3.2
1795	7,157	224	3.1	7,605	164	2.2 (1795)	2.7
1796				8,317	283	3.4 (1796)	3.4
1797				11,433	480	4.2 (1797)	4.2
1798-1800 ⎫							4.0
1801-1807 ⎭							

NOTES: 1. There is a marked discrepancy in the two overlapping lists in one year only, 1793.
2. There is no allowance made for mortality accruing from ship loss.
3. There was great variation in mortality according to the coastal region of loading. The breakdown in the BWI imports sample is R. Senegal to R. Volta, 4.1%; R. Volta to Gaboon, 13.1%; Loango to Angola, 2.8%. The coastal divisions are not identical, but this mortality distribution is reflected in insurance rates payable on slave consignments to Jamaica in 1788.

From Calabar	15%	From Windward Coast	7%
From Bonny	10%	From Gold Coast	5%

(Stephen Fuller MS, "Letter Book I," Fuller (Agent for Jamaica) to Jamaica Committee of Correspondence, 20 February 1788.)

recorded (*A&P*, 1795-1796, xlii [849]). At 9.6 percent this is higher—puzzlingly—than the 8.5 percent of the earlier period when there was unrestricted packing. Although this earlier figure, *faute de mieux*, will be retained, an estimate of, say 10 percent would be no less valid. For 1791 to 1795 there is a resumption of the 1789 B.W.I. arrivals sampling, while for 1791-1797 I have worked out figures from the collated logs of masters and surgeons (Lords A List). For the period in which these last two sources overlap, the mean has been drawn. Figures for blank years are based on ad hoc derivation from adjacent years. There seem to be no mortality figures for 1798 onward.

APPENDIX 2

THE OUTSET

THE largest sample of ship, outfit, and cargo costs is Norris' detailed tabulation of all the ships engaged in the Liverpool slave trade in 1790 (A&P, 1792, xciii) and which is invested with the authority of his considerable local knowledge, and familiarity with the trade. When the components of the list are adjusted to exclude tenders on the African coast and other items which evidently distort, we are left with a valuation—ship, outfit, cargo, and 6 percent insurance—of £45.5 per ton. Now this estimate was in the period after Dolben's Act of 1788, which regulated the size of slave cargoes and when the outset cost *per ton* must necessarily have been lower than before regulation. (This results from the fact that while the ship and outfit component of cost per ton remains constant, the cargo cost per ton must decline because that ton is not permitted to carry as many slaves, and so does not require to carry out as much cargo). We can quite easily project a cost per ton figure for the pre-Dolben period by applying to the cargo component of the figure of £45.5 per ton (at 65 percent, justified below, this is £29.6) the ratio of average number of slaves per ton landed in the period before and after Dolben, i.e., 1.85:1.43 (see p. 20 above). The result is that the cargo component must be increased to £38.3 and the revised overall outset figure becomes £54.2 per ton. But we do not only depend on projection for we have summary estimates of outset costs in 1787, before regulation. Figures provided by Tarleton, a leading Liverpool slave trader, give the average value of 80 Liverpool slave ships, totaling 14,028 tons, with their cargoes, as £47.1 per ton, while another account accords to 30 British African ships of 4,195 tons a value of £57.2 per ton (A&P, 1789, xxvi [646a] pt. iv, no. 3). We also possess three voyage calculations or accounts for this period which give outset per ton figures of £52.5, £53.6 and £58.5 respectively. (B.M. Add. MS 38416, Liverpool Papers, fol. 23, James Jones to Hawkesbury, 14 February 1788; BT6/7, General Calculations respecting the effect of Sir William Dolben's Bill and Tarleton and Backhouse's estimate of profits of voyage of *Eliza*.) Since these last three figures include insurance at 6 percent, as does the projection, we should assume that the summary Bristol figure of £57.2 also includes insurance, but that the summary Liverpool figure of £47.1 per ton does not. This evidence is not good enough to justify strict averaging, but we are perhaps erring on the conservative side if we postulate an outset figure, including 6 percent insurance, of £52 per ton for 1787. We are not, however, justified in taking the peacetime insurance rate for every year up to—or for that matter after—1788, since 1761-1762, 1776-1780, and 1781-1782 must be regarded as wartime years in which insurance can be taken as increased to 12 percent. These wartime years must therefore be debited with an outset cost of £55 per ton.

Dolben's Act came into force during 1789 and so the years 1761-1788 will be costed on a "pre-Dolben" basis. The ensuing period 1789-1799 inclusive forms a unity. We have already observed that cost per ton, at a 6 percent insurance rate, runs out at £45.5 per ton in a given year (1790) in this period. However, the years 1793-1799 inclusive were wartime years and a 12 percent insurance rate raises the cost per ton to £48.1. The last year of this decade, also a year of war, is subject to yet another complication stemming from a further measure of restriction in 1799, which will be taken as effective from 1800 onward. This additional restriction on slaves licensed per ton necessarily reduced still further the cost per ton since still less cargo per ton would be required for the yet smaller number of slaves allowed. From the exhaustive Norris sample we discover that the cargo constituted 65 percent of the total valuation in the early post-Dolben years, and we already know that whereas slaves per ton allowed from 1789 were 1.60, there were only 1.03 from 1800. The cargo percentage (65) must therefore be reduced by .57/1.60 as compared with the cost per ton figure for a year in the 1790s. This same further limitation of course lasted for the remainder of the life of the British slave trade. Of the final part decade, 1801-1802 will be taken as years of peace, and 1803-1807 as years of war. The final complication that we must take account of is the price changes over the years, since our projections so far have been on a constant price level basis. In contrast to the long middle years of the eighteenth century, prices in the Revolutionary and Napoleonic war period rose sharply, and it will be necessary to adjust the rates per ton which we have established by reference to the Schumpeter-Gilboy index of consumer prices (B. R. Mitchell, *Abstract of British Historical Statistics,* Cambridge, 1962, p. 469). After careful consideration we have used the Consumer Goods index rather than the index of Consumer Goods other than Cereals. This second index trails behind the first and the effect of using it would be to lower outset costs and hence improve profitability. The only period in which there is a really striking difference is 1801-1807—profits of nearly 9 percent as compared with 3.3 percent—but the aggregate profit, 1761-1807 merely rises from 9.5 percent by about 2 percent (see Table 6). It is, of course, necessary to remember that when the Norris valuation was taken the price index stood at 124, while the 1787 estimates were made when the index stood at 117. The outcome of these various calculations is shown in Appendix Table 2.

A disturbing discrepancy of the years after 1791, however, is that the outset in the few, raw, voyage accounts we have, even when adjusted to include insurance at 12 percent and a valuation for ship cost, usually omitted in the originals, does not add up to more than £45-£47 and £44-£46, respectively, in the two decades. This is a conclusion based on 9 voyages and 7 ships and we must prefer Norris's much more exhaustive sample, speculating that in the 9 voyage sample cargo might, as Hyde, Parkinson and Marriner have pointed out was sometimes the case, have in some instances been valued at wholesale cost (see Dumbell, "Profits of the Guinea Trade," passim, and information from the Dumbell MSS kindly communicated by Mr. Sanderson). The validity of a per ton figure in the £45-£55 range for the British trade up to 1788 is borne out by the fact that a per ton figure for 98 voyages of the Middleburg Company 1741-1800 is £58.3 (Sterling) per ton. When this is adjusted to reflect the apparently different composition of that Company's balance sheet, compared with what we assume to have been included in the British estimates, and with insurance at 6 percent added, the result is at the very least £50.0 (Sterling) per ton. This is a crude measure only since detailed comparison of how the two national calculations were made is not possible. Also the Dutch "Last" is taken as 2 tons, but whether they were measured tons, as with the British, or, as is perhaps more likely, tons burden, it is not possible to say. If the Dutch "Last"/Tonnage ratio is to tons burden, the Dutch outset cost in tons of tons measurement must be higher (see Table 7 and Unger, *Bijdragen*, pp. 87-89, 107-110).

No attempt has been made to adjust cargo values for the years before and after 1787-1790 to take into account the fact that slave prices on the African coast were rising through our period. It appears that they may have increased by about 25 percent during our period (P. Curtin, "The Atlantic Slave Trade, 1600-1800," in *The History of West Africa*, ed. J. F. Ajayi and Michael Crowder, Longmans, 1971, I, 255 and information kindly supplied by Richard Bean). However, our evidence about cargo values comes from years not long after the midway point of our period.

The reason why the insurance rate of 6 percent must be increased to 12 percent for the war years is simply that in wartime insurance was necessarily higher. At points in the Revolutionary and Napoleonic Wars insurance for slave ships rose as high as 20 percent (*A&P*, 1847-1848 [536], par. 5680, Evidence of Thomas Tobin), but a conservative figure of 12 percent for the years of warfare will be adopted. This figure is also analogically compatible with insurance rates for vessels engaged in the out and back West India trade contained in Richard Pares, *A West India Fortune*, London, 1950, p. 223. It does not concern us whether or not slave traders actually insured. If one includes insurance, no deduction for ship losses had to be made. In fact wartime losses could be quite high—15 Liverpool slavers out of 97 in 1800 for example (information kindly supplied by Mr. Frank Sanderson).

APPENDIX TABLE 2. CALCULATIONS OF COSTS

Period	Outset Cost per Ton p.a. at Constant Prices	Price Change Factor	Outset Cost per Ton p.a. Adjusted for Price Changes	Decennial Average
1761-62 (War)	£55	$\frac{94}{117}$	£44.2	
1763-70 (Peace)	£52	$\frac{104}{117}$	£46.2	
1761-1770				£45.8
1771-75 (Peace)	£52	$\frac{114}{117}$	£50.7	
1776-80 (War)	£55	$\frac{112}{117}$	£52.6	
1771-1780				£51.7
1781-82 (War)	£55	$\frac{116}{117}$	£54.5	
1783-88 (Peace)	£52	$\frac{122}{117}$	£54.2	
1789-90 (Peace)	£45.5 First post-Dolben period begins.	$\frac{119}{124}$	£43.7	
1781-1790				£52.2

APPENDIX TABLE 2. CALCULATIONS OF COSTS *(continued)*

Period	Outset Cost per Ton p.a. at Constant Prices	Price Change Factor	Outset Cost per Ton p.a. Adjusted for Price Changes	Decennial Average
1791-92 (Peace)	£45.5	$\frac{122}{124}$	£44.8	
1793-99 (War)	£48.1	$\frac{146}{124}$	£56.6	
1800 (War)	£36.9 Second post-Dolben period begins.	$\frac{212}{124}$	£63.1	
1791-1800				£55.0
1801-1802 (Peace)	£35.0	$\frac{201}{124}$	£56.7	
1803-1807 (War)	£36.9	$\frac{175}{124}$	£52.1	
1801-1807				£53.4

II

The Origin of African Slaves:
The Dutch Activities on the
Guinea Coast, 1675-1795

JOHANNES POSTMA

THE QUESTION of origin of African slaves is one of the most perplexing problems of the Atlantic slave trade and will undoubtedly never be solved to satisfaction.[1] By identifying the relative significance of certain coastal areas and specific ports from which slave ships departed this study, it is hoped, will make at least a small contribution toward unraveling this problem.

Two limitations in the scope of this study should be recognized at the outset. First of all, the data and resulting conclusions presented here apply only to the Dutch share of the Atlantic slave trade, which represented approximately 10 percent of the total traffic,[2] and should therefore not be construed as necessarily representative of the overall pattern. Secondly, the mystery of the ultimate origin of slaves in the African interior is a subject far too complex to be treated within the scope of this paper; ethnographic and oral sources of Africa and the Black communities in the Western Hemisphere will need to be consulted for that problem.

Unpublished Dutch documents constitute the principal source for this study. Although rarely consulted for slave trade history, Dutch archives have collected a wealth of relevant papers as a result of a significant entrenchment on the West African coast and a lengthy participation in the African slave trade by that nation. During the greater part of the seventeenth and eighteenth centuries the Dutch operated generally more than a dozen trading stations on the Guinea

---

[1] See, for example, Philip D. Curtin and Jan Vansina, "Sources of the Nineteenth Century Atlantic Slave Trade," *Journal of African History* 5 (1964); also the relevant portions in Philip D. Curtin, *The Atlantic Slave Trade: A Census,* Madison, Wis., 1969.

[2] For an assessment of the volume of the Dutch trade see Johannes Postma, "The Dimension of the Dutch Slave Trade from Western Africa," *Journal of African History* 13 (1972). For a tabulated summary of this article see Table 7 below.

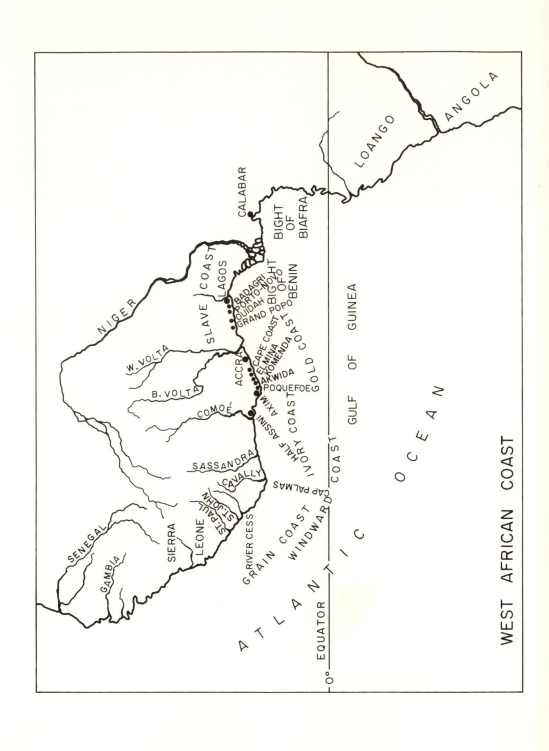

NIGER

LOANGO

ANGOLA

CALABAR

BIGHT OF BIAFRA

SLAVE COAST

LAGOS

BADAGRI
PORTO-NOVO
OUIDAH
GRAND POPO

BIGHT OF BENIN

OFO

BENIN

GULF OF GUINEA

W. VOLTA

B. VOLTA

ACCRA

CAPE COAST
ELMINA
KOMENDA
AKWIDA
POQUEFOE
AXIM
ASSINI

GOLD COAST

COMOÉ

HALF ASSINI

IVORY COAST

SASSANDRA

CAVALLY

WINDWARD COAST

CAP PALMAS

SENEGAL

GAMBIA

SIERRA

LEONE

ST. JOHN

ST. PAUL

G. RIVER CESS

GRAIN COAST

ATLANTIC OCEAN

0° EQUATOR

WEST AFRICAN COAST

Coast (roughly the coastline between contemporary Senegal and Gabon), and they took an active part in the slave trade from approximately 1630 until 1795.[3]

The Dutch WIC (West India Company), chartered in 1621 and dissolved in 1791,[4] played a prominent role in the slave trade. For about one century, from 1629 until the early 1730s, the Dutch participation in the Atlantic slave trade was almost exclusively executed by the WIC. Protected by a governmental charter, the company started with a commercial monopoly on both the African and American shores of the Atlantic. While this monopoly was gradually cut back the WIC retained complete control over the Dutch slave trade until 1730, and in the Gold Coast (modern Ghana) area as late as 1734. (Here the Dutch had their heaviest concentration of trading stations, with the Castle at Elmina as administrative center.) Even after the loss of its trade monopoly the company continued to exercise considerable control over the acquisition of slaves, as it continued to man and operate the coastal trading stations. After 1730, however, the bulk of the Dutch slave trade was carried by Dutch free traders, who either obtained their slaves from the company stations or from African merchants along the coast.[5]

Numerous factors helped determine where Europeans acquired their slaves. In addition to existing institutions and political and economic conditions in a given area in Africa which influenced the supply of slaves, slaves from certain regions were in greater demand than those from other areas. Literature based on English sources, for example, has emphasized the desirability of Gold Coast slaves, particularly those from Kormantin.[6] Undoubtedly these were Akan slaves, who came to be known for their cooperative character and their

---

[3] The most complete history of the Dutch slave trade to date is the unpublished Ph.D. dissertation by this author: Johannes Postma, "The Dutch Participation in the African Slave Trade: Slaving on the Guinea Coast, 1675-1795," Michigan State University, 1970. See also Pieter C. Emmer, "The History of the Dutch Slave Trade; A Bibliographical Survey," *Journal of Economic History* 32 (September 1972), 728-747.

[4] The WIC went bankrupt in 1674 but was reorganized during the following year under the same name. The old company is generally styled the "old" or "first" WIC, and its successor the "second" WIC.

[5] A detailed discussion of the organization and operation of the WIC on the African Coast, and also the techniques involved in the acquisition of slaves by both the company and the free traders can be located in Postma, "The Dutch Participation," Chaps. II and III.

[6] Daniel P. Mannix and Malcolm Cowley, *Black Cargoes: A History of the Atlantic Slave Trade, 1518-1865*, New York, 1962, p. 17.

willingness to work. Eighteenth century Dutch sources confirm these notions about Gold Coast slaves.[7]

Slaves from the Bight of Biafra, on the other hand, were considered very undesirable. A Dutch document dating from the 1660s singles out slaves from Calabar, the Cameroons, and Rio Del Rey (most likely Ibos) as completely undesirable because of their "malicious" and "stubborn" nature and their tendency to commit suicide.[8] This caution against Biafran slaves was repeated in subsequent WIC directives, primarily because the Spanish *Asientos* (contracts with the Spanish crown regulating the importation of African slaves to its American colonies) refused to accept slaves from this region.[9] As a result very few WIC slavers obtained their cargoes here.[10] An eighteenth century pamphlet serving as a guide for free traders broadened the area for undesirable slaves and mentions Benin, Gabon, and the Cameroons as areas from which slaves should not be obtained because they were regarded as "lazy" and "cowardly." [11] These warnings against Biafran slaves must have made a lasting impression on Dutch slavers, for they seldom purchased slaves in these regions.

Contrary to the English preference for Gold Coast slaves, a WIC directive of the early eighteenth century indicated that Slave Coast slaves were much more desirable in the West.[12] This was at a time when the WIC was just beginning to purchase slaves in large quantities on the Gold Coast. With the passing of time they overcame this bias, for Dutch free traders were encouraged to get slaves on either the Gold or Slave Coasts since they were much preferred over slaves from the Grain Coast (Liberia). Angola slaves were said to be cheaper, and by implication therefore less desirable than Guinea Coast slaves.[13] Some West India planters, however, preferred the slaves from Angola. Since the middle passage from Angola was also shorter, this may explain why the Dutch continued to send a substantial number of slaving vessels to the Loango-Angola Coast.[14]

---

[7] Verspreidde West Indische Stukken (hereafter referred to as VWIS), Rijksarchief, The Hague, Folder 13, Documents 11/24/1789 and 3/11/1791.
[8] Gemeente Archief Rotterdam, Rotterdam, vol. 802.
[9] West Indische Compagnie (hereafter referred to as WIC), Rijksarchief, The Hague, vol. 783, Document 13, Art. 4.
[10] WIC, vol. 832, p. 420; vol. 833, p. 377.
[11] D. H. Gallandat, *Noodige Onderrichtingen voor Slaafhandelaren*, Middelburg, Netherlands, 1769, pp. 438-439.
[12] WIC, vol. 56, p. 43.
[13] Gallandat, pp. 438-439.
[14] The Dutch concentrated their efforts primarily on the Loango Coast, north of the Zaire or Congo river, but they always referred to the area as Angola. For an analysis of the trade in this region see P. M. Martin, *The External Trade of*

For the purpose of making a quantitative assessment of slave origin in regard to the Dutch slaving activities four separate coastal regions can be identified: the Slave Coast, the Gold Coast, the Ivory-Windward Coast, and the Loango-Angola coastal region. Owing to the relative independence of the WIC Angola trade, comparatively little data has been preserved for this area. All evidence indicates, however, that the Dutch traded there without interruption during the WIC monopoly as well as during the free trade period. According to Unger's study of MCC (Middleburgsche Commercie Compagnie) slaving activities, 26.8 percent of that company's slavers obtained their cargoes in Angola.[15] The only useful statistics of this region on the WIC trade are the assignments (*tourbeurten*) of slaving voyages made by the WIC directors in Holland. Approximately half of the estimated total number of assignments can be documented.[16] Covering the period of 1675-1747, of a total of 140 assignments 42 were destined for the Angola region. The remainder were divided as follows: 74 to the Slave Coast, 7 to Elmina (Gold Coast), 4 to either Elmina or the Slave Coast, 3 to Calabar, and the remaining 10 had mixed or optional destinations. This suggests that the Loango-Angola trade constituted nearly one-third (42 of 130 specific destinations) of the total WIC slaving effort. Considering that the Dutch slave trade was much smaller during the WIC monopoly than during the free trade, and that the MCC may have sent a larger proportion of its ships to Angola than other Dutch free traders, 25-30 percent of the overall Dutch trade would seem to be a reasonable estimate for the Loango-Angola trade.[17]

As is confirmed by the data listed in Table 1, before 1720 the WIC acquired the bulk of its slaves on the Slave Coast and only a small portion on the Gold Coast. During the last quarter of the seventeenth century only one slaver was recorded departing from the Gold Coast for its Atlantic crossing, and only two other slavers had Elmina indicated as their destination,[18] which makes the contrasts for those two regions even more obvious for the earlier period. When warfare deprived the Dutch of their Slave Coast markets during the first decade of that century, the WIC began to buy large numbers of

---

the Loango Coast, 1576-1870: The Effects of Changing Commercial Relations on the Vili Kingdom of Loango, Oxford, 1972.

[15] W. S. Unger, "Bijdragen tot de geschiedenis van de Nederlandse slaven-handel," *Economisch-Historisch Jaarboek*, xxviii (1958-1960), 38.

[16] These assignments are tabulated in Appendix C of Postma, "The Dutch Participation," pp. 258-263.

[17] See Table 4 and the accompanying explanation.

[18] See Table 2, and also Appendixes A and C in Postma, "The Dutch Participation."

Gold Coast slaves. After a brief period of normalization, this practice was repeated during the middle of the second decade. Then during the 1720s the rise of the Dahomey state and its attendant political upheavals forced the WIC to rely increasingly more on the Gold Coast for its slaves. This trend is clearly demonstrated in Tables 1 and 2. In 1726, the WIC Director-General, chief WIC official in Africa, reported that the "Gold Coast has become a slave coast." [19] Throughout the eighteenth century, the Dutch search for slaves gradually shifted westward. If during the 1720s the Gold Coast became the principal source, twenty years later the Windward Coast had even superseded the former.

A shortage of slaves during the second decade of the eighteenth century forced the WIC to attempt buying on the Upper Coast or Windward Coast. An experiment in this region with a company slaver in 1716 met with unsatisfactory success,[20] and the WIC itself never depended on the Windward Coast as an important source of supply for slaves. At best, small company vessels would trade along the coast and buy a few slaves along with other products; these slaves were then taken to Elmina and there boarded on a WIC slaver or placed in stock at the Castle.[21]

The situation changed considerably with the freeing of the slave trade. In 1744, the Director-General reported that most of the free traders purchased their slaves on the Windward and Ivory Coasts, going to Elmina only to complete a deficient cargo.[22] A sample of the trading activities of 56 free trade vessels confirms that an average of 69 percent of the slaves had been obtained before the Gold Coast was reached. This pattern of free trade slaving is clearly illustrated in Table 3. Since the sample in this table consists almost exclusively of MCC ships, this percentage may be slightly exaggerated. Some free traders, such as the ships of the Rotterdam company of Coopstad and Rochusen, frequently contracted their whole slave cargo from the Director-General at Elmina.[23] Other free traders may have done this also, which would have slightly raised the tabulated Gold Coast share of 31 percent. In light of the foregoing and the approximate figures under consideration, it seems reasonable to round off the Gold Coast–Windward-Ivory Coast ratio to a 35-65 percentage.

[19] WIC, vol. 487, p. 63.
[20] WIC, vol. 485, p. 564.
[21] Archief van de Nederlandse Bezittingen ter Kuste van Guinea, Rijksarchief, The Hague, vol. 85, Instructions 6/3/1718.
[22] WIC, vol. 113, p. 187.
[23] J. Hudig, *De Scheepvaart op West Afrika en West-Indie in de achtiende eeuw*, Amsterdam, 1926, p. 30.

The practice of contracting slaves at Elmina may also have a similar bearing on the volume calculated for the Loango-Angola trade, since Unger's percentage of 26.8, mentioned earlier, was also based on MCC records. This would justify lowering the overall average for this region slightly. Table 4 presents a regional comparison regarding the origin of slaves purchased by Dutch free traders.

Turning to a detailed assessment of each of the four slaving regions in particular, the Loango-Angola trade can be dismissed rather quickly on grounds that insufficient data is available to determine the relative importance of specific ports or regions. The Slave Coast ports were all in such close proximity that a differentiation would not throw much light on the problem of ultimate slave origin. It is safe to assume the slaves acquired at Offra, Ouidah, Appa, Jakin, and the Popos were probably drawn from the same or similar sources. Only the lodge at Badagri was removed a considerable distance and perhaps drew on different interior sources, but this lodge was established in 1737 when the importance of the Slave Coast as a source of supply began to decrease drastically. Table 5 indicates the WIC lodges on the Slave Coast and the years during which they were in use. Unfortunately the complete record of the slaves procured at these lodges has been lost. During the WIC monopoly period there was generally one lodge at a time which supplied all or most of the slaves for the WIC ships. On a few occasions the WIC had more than one lodge.

The Windward Coast was one of the longest stretches of coastline where the Dutch slaved. Free traders acquired their slaves from a large variety of small coastal trading centers along the coast. Commercial data of fifty-six free traders, indicating places where slaves were purchased, has been tabulated in Table 3. As a space-saving device several minor trading points have been grouped together in areas, except for Cape Lahou and Grand Bassam. Cape Lahou clearly emerges as the most prolific supplier of slaves on the Windward Coast. According to the available sample more than 50 percent of the slaves bought in this region came from Cape Lahou. The neighborhood of River Cess also supplied a large percentage of slaves to the Dutch free traders.

The Dutch never established trading stations on the Windward Coast, with the result that slaving captains traded directly with African middlemen. An additional consequence of this limited cross-cultural contact between Europeans and Africans was that Dutch documents contain very little information about the inhabitants of the Windward Coast and the political developments in this region.

In this respect the Gold Coast is quite a contrast to the Windward

Coast, because on this short coastline the Dutch had erected nearly all their African trading stations and fortifications. As a result of this concentration of WIC administration on the Gold Coast, it is possible to give a more detailed account of the Dutch slaving activities here, both in regard to the global figures and the relative significance of the various centers of trade on the Gold Coast. Unfortunately no complete set of commercial statistics, such as the payment of head money,[24] for example, has survived; however, portions of this record have survived and are listed in Table 6. This record, used in conjunction with the information from free trade slavers listed in Table 3, allows one to draw a number of tentative conclusions. Both sets of data clearly establish the commercial preeminence of Elmina during the free trade period. According to both tables the WIC headquarters contributed about 40 percent of all the slaves purchased by Dutch free traders on the Gold Coast and Slave Coast combined. Other trading stations supplying considerable numbers included Axim, Shama, Kormantin, and Accra. Trade at the various lodges and forts fluctuated with the political conditions in their vicinity. Without a comprehensive set of statistics on the commercial activity at each lodge, it is impossible to determine these fluctuations in the trade. In a sense, the lodges between Annamabu and Accra could be treated as one, since the supply of slaves at these places was generally dominated by Fante traders.

Based on an earlier assessment of the total volume of the Dutch slave trade, summarized in Table 7, estimates of the nearly half a million slaves involved are tabulated in Table 8. For the Loango-Angola trade the formula of one-third for the WIC and one-fourth for the free trade has been employed, except for the WIC consignments after 1731 which obtained slaves on the Gold Coast exclusively. The Category of "rented ships," apparently a predecessor to the free trade practice,[25] has been treated like the WIC trade. In determining the relative significance of the Guinea Coast regions the samples produced in Tables 1-3 have been utilized as models.

In summary, the trade in the Loango-Angola region remained relatively stable, although its percentage of the total Dutch trade declined slightly. This relative decline was largely due to the significant increase of the Dutch trade on the Ivory Coast. During the eighteenth century a definite shift of the Dutch slaving activities westward along the Guinea Coast is discernible. Whereas in the beginning of

[24] This was a fee paid by company officials to the WIC for the privilege of selling a slave to free traders.
[25] For a broader explanation see Postma, "The Dutch Participation," pp. 108-109.

the century the Slave Coast was clearly the principal source for slaves, after the 1730s this area had become virtually negligible and the Ivory Coast had outdistanced all other regions as a source of slaves. The Gold Coast, while insignificant in the traffic during the seventeenth century, became a significant source of supply for the Dutch for the duration of the eighteenth century.

TABLE 1. SLAVE ORIGINS BASED ON WIC DEPARTURES

Period	Gold Coast		Slave Coast		Angola		Mixed & Misc.	
	No. of Slaves	No. of Ships	No. of Slaves	No. of Ships	No. of Slaves	No. of Ships	No. of Slaves	No. of Ships
1700	100	(1)*	1,553	(3)	—		1,050	(2)
1701	—		1,575	(3)	525	(1)	124	(1)*
1702	—		—		—		—	
1703	—		513	(1)	525	(1)	439	(1)
1704	279	(1)*	906	(2)	525	(1)	525	(1)
1705	896	(2)	925	(2)	—		—	
1706	1,277	(3)*	1,093	(2)	525	(1)	—	
1707	424	(1)	2,285	(4)	525	(1)	525	(1)
1708	—		873	(2)	—		612	(1)
1709	—		2,105	(4)	—		—	
1710	—		1,685	(4)*	—		—	
1711	—		1,102	(2)	—		525	(1)
1712	—		1,154	(2)	—		—	
1713	—		585	(1)	—		525	(1)
1714	166	(1)*	1,755	(3)	525	(1)	—	
1715	410	(2)*	1,153	(2)	525	(1)	—	
1716	146	(1)*	1,088	(2)	—		—	
1717	175	(1)*	1,962	(3)	—		—	
1718	719	(1)	881	(2)	—		1,002	(2)
1719	—		525	(1)	1,050	(2)	525	(1)
1720	—		596	(1)	525	(1)	—	
1721	1,483	(3)	1,128	(2)	1,050	(2)	—	
1722	562	(1)	—		—		525	(1)
1723	865	(2)	—		525	(1)	1,575	(3)
1724	423	(1)	525	(1)	—		1,130	(2)
1725	2,028	(4)*	587	(1)	525	(1)	—	
1726	991	(2)	—		—		1,012	(2)
1727	1,224	(2)	525	(1)	—		1,377	(2)
1728	1,028	(2)*	525	(1)	—		1,273	(2)
1729	525	(1)	2,072	(3)	—		—	
1730	323	(1)	409	(1)	—		—	
1731	1,558	(3)	1,597	(3)	—		—	
1732	1,140	(2)	525	(1)	—		1,412	(2)
1733	1,514	(2)	1,789	(3)	—		—	
1734	1,549	(4)**	1,191	(2)	—		—	
1735	1,194	(3)*	2,160	(3)	—		370	(1)
TOTAL	20,891	(47)	37,260	(68)	4,752	(14)	13,801	(27)

SOURCES: see Table 2.

NOTE: Asterisks signify irregular and unusually small slaving vessels. It should be kept in mind that the Angola figures are spotty and far from complete. The bulk of the slaves listed in column "Mixed and Miscellaneous" belong either with the Gold or the Slave Coast figures, but the sources did not specify the ports of departure clearly.

TABLE 2. COMPARATIVE GOLD AND SLAVE COAST EXPORTS

	Gold Coast		Slave Coast	
Year	No. of Slaves	Annual Average	No. of Slaves	Annual Average
1675-99	136	(5)	23,355	(934)
1700-1709	2,868	(287)	11,828	(1,183)
1710-19	1,616	(162)	11,890	(1,189)
1720-29	9,129	(913)	5,969	(597)
1730-35	7,278	(1,213)	7,585	(1,264)
1736-	5,618	—	—	—

SOURCES: Tables 1 and 2: The information is gleaned from numerous letters, reports, and accounts of the WIC. A compilation of more expanded data of 233 WIC slaving voyages is located in Postma, "The Dutch Participation in the African Slave Trade," Appendix A.

NOTE: These figures should not be construed as the total of Dutch slave exports from these regions. They are intended to compare the relative significance of the slave trade for the two areas.

TABLE 3. SAMPLE ORIGIN OF SLAVES

Year Cargo Purchased

Places of Origin	1741	1746	1753	1753	1754	1755	1755	1756	1756	1757	1758	1761	1762
Sierra Leone Coast	2	2	18	2		8	15	2	2	27	56		5
St. Paul and St. John Rivers	143	154	9		47		13		2	12	1		
River Cess to Cape Palmas		10	9	31		58	69	3	4	75	78	10	6
Rivers Cavalla to Saassandra			34	1	6	16	8	10	12	11	4		2
Cape Lahou		106	34	43	77	94	60	30	98	97	162	121	179
Grand Bassam	2	2	1	21	7	8		13	9	6			14
Assine to Axim	13	13	8			1	2		1	6	4		4
Not identified			15		4	92	30	9	24	12	17		2
Windward and Ivory Coast combined	145	287	128	98	141	277	197	67	152	246	322	131	212
Axim	3	4		2		12	1		4	2	2		11
Poquefoe													
Akwida							2		3	4	4		
Butri													
Takoradi										1			
Secondi			1				9		7				
Shama	2												
Komenda	32	20	3		13								
Elmina			10	84			52	1		55	9	97	80
Cape Coast													
Mori													
Annamabu	61	3		9	37			90	62			73	
Kormantin				124				44	54				
Apam													
Berku			52										
Accra			12										
Keta			1										
Eppee													
Popo			34										
Not identified	4	62	28		40			32					
Gold and Slave Coasts combined	102	89	141	219	90	12	64	167	130	62	15	170	91
TOTAL	247	376	269	317	231	289	261	234	282	308	337	301	303

SOURCE: MCC, vols. 224-1414; Hudig Archief Rotterdam, vols. 41-42.
NOTE: This sample of 50 slaving voyages represents slightly more than 5% of the total free-trade traffic.

TABLE 3. SAMPLE ORIGIN OF SLAVES (Continued)

Places of Origin	Year Cargo Purchased												
	1763	1763	1764	1765	1765	1765	1767	1767	1768	1769	1769	1769	1770
Sierra Leone Coast		10				1	2	1			1	4	5
St. Paul and St. John Rivers					2		7					3	
River Cess to Cape Palmas	11	59	3		28	31	20	9			13	18	18
Rivers Cavalla to Saassandra		10	8		13	3	35	6	175		28	7	16
Cape Lahou	297	154	191	167	165	174	43	149			105	140	98
Grand Bassam		2	4			2	5	24	2		27	8	32
Assine to Axim			5		4		4	7	4				
Not identified	4	7	3		24	6	119	18			6	7	18
Windward and Ivory Coast combined	312	242	214	167	239	217	235	214	181		180	187	187
Axim			3			6	18	35			7		5
Poquefoe													
Akwida			2										5
Butri			6			2					6		14
Takoradi											7		6
Secondi					1	1		10			7		3
Shama													
Komenda													17
Elmina		24	48		16	16	32		61		55		23
Cape Coast		5											
Mori		6							7				
Amamabu							40						
Kormantin		15				25							
Apam						4			1				
Berku						5							
Accra				71		8							
Keta										4			
Eppee													
Popo													
Not identified						13				63			
Gold and Slave Coasts combined		63	59	71	17	80	90	45	69	67	82		73
TOTAL	312	305	273	238	256	297	325	259	250	67	262	187	260

TABLE 3. SAMPLE ORIGIN OF SLAVES (Continued)

Places of Origin	Year Cargo Purchased												
	1771	1771	1771	1772	1772	1773	1773	1774	1774	1775	1775	1775	1776
Sierra Leone Coast	1					2					2		11
St. Paul and St. John Rivers	14	7		4		10	14		11	4	30	37	71
River Cess to Cape Palmas	32	16		6		7	11	5	11	11	6	14	9
Rivers Cavalla to Saassandra	11	47	131							6	113	134	139
Cape Lahou	91			74		108	120	59	87	84	4	4	6
Grand Bassam	6		14	3		8	7	6	6	2			3
Assine to Axim	7	10	13		1	7				9			
Not identified	12	32	2	45			8			8	13	15	
Windward and Ivory Coast combined	174	112	160	132	1	142	160	72	115	124	168	204	239
Axim	3	9	34			2				114			6
Poquefoe													10
Akwida		3											8
Butri	7	4	18										
Takoradi	12			29									
Secondi												5	
Shama												2	
Komenda	28			118							10		
Elmina								1	169			51	6
Cape Coast													
Mori						12	27	4			80		
Annamabu								40					
Kormantin								54					
Apam		64		10				47					
Berku						12	27						
Accra													
Keta								4					
Eppee								5					
Popo								118					
Not identified					106								
Gold and Slave Coasts combined	50	80	52	157	106	26	54	273	169	114	90	58	30
TOTAL	224	192	212	289	107	168	214	345	284	238	258	262	269

TABLE 4. ORIGIN OF SLAVES DURING THE FREE TRADE

Region	%
Loango-Angola Coast	25
Windward Coast	50
Gold Coast [a]	25
TOTAL	100

SOURCE: Tables 1 and 3.
[a] The relatively small contribution of the Slave Coast is included in the Gold Coast figures.

TABLE 5. WIC LODGES ON THE SLAVE COAST

Region	Period
Offra	1660s-1691
Ouidah	1670s-1724
Jakin	1726-1734
Appa	1732-1736; 1742-1749; 1754-1755
Badagri	1737-1744; 1748
Popo	1738-1740; 1744; 1752-1760

SOURCE: Personnel Rosters in WIC, vols. 101-115, 487-491.

TABLE 6. SAMPLE OF SLAVE ORIGIN ON THE GOLD COAST

Locations	1725 8 mo.	1727 8 mo.	1735 9 mo.	1738-1740 17 mo.	1742-1743 18 mo.	1752-1754 24 mo.	Totals 84 mo.
Axim	77	64	42	25	692	39	939
Poquefoe	—	1	45	3	174	16	239
Akwida	—	—	25	28	93	5	151
Butri	26	34	33	30	20	21	164
Takoradi	—	89	65	54	65	6	279
Secondi	55	231	115	81	234	22	738
Shama	112	134	218	114	560	19	1,157
Komenda	26	15	376	67	149	4	637
Elmina	1,095	826	768	178	435	159	3,461
Mori	47	49	72	8	8	19	203
Kormantin	265	174	263	62	298	3	1,065
Apam	24	37	97	—	54	660	872
Berku	8	40	37	19	8	99	211
Accra	103	97	58	32	307	311	908
TOTAL	1,838	1,791	2,242	701	3,097	1,383	9,214

SOURCE: WIC, vol. 102, pp. 160, 167, and 284; vol. 108, pp. 32, 41, 46, and 53; vol. 112, p. 336; vol. 113, p. 294; vol. 290, p. 609; vol. 484, pp. 418-419.

TABLE 3. SAMPLE ORIGIN OF SLAVES (*Continued*)

Places of Origin	Year Cargo Purchased											Total
	1777	1777	1778	1778	1778	1779	1779	1780	1787	1788	1792	
Sierra Leone Coast		44	155		1	94	94	138	2		3	699
St. Paul and St. John Rivers		3		13	3	9	103	47				259
River Cess to Cape Palmas	54	64		72	15	55	9	47	20	42	6	1,508
Rivers Cavalla to Saassandra	1	6			16				65	11	13	454
Cape Lahou	66	105	71	105	75	33	77	32	33	149	69	4,961
Grand Bassam	25	12		25	29	25	23		16	17		419
Assine to Axim		3			17	5	2	7	1			187
Not identified	15			15	42	2	11					606
Windward and Ivory Coast combined	161	237	226	230	198	223	319	271	137	219	91	9,093
Axim	11		16							4		314
Poquefoe												10
Akwida		8										35
Butri		2			3		14					74
Takoradi						12						72
Secondi												40
Shama												30
Komenda											6	34
Elmina	112	42	154		11	63		103		47	78	1,682
Cape Coast												5
Mori					17							149
Annamabu												402
Kormantin					17							97
Apam												397
Berku												91
Accra												101
Keta												9
Eppee												5
Popo									47			152
Not identified												395
Gold and Slave Coasts combined	123	52	154	16	48	75	14	103	47	51	84	4,094
TOTAL	284	289	380	246	246	298	333	374	184	270	175	13,187

TABLE 7. GLOBAL ESTIMATES FOR THE DUTCH SLAVE TRADE

Period	WIC Trade	Rented Ships	Free Trade	Totals	Annual Average
1630-74	70,000			70,000	1,500
1675-80	18,302			18,302	3,050
1681-90	15,437			15,437	1,544
1691-1700	23,155			23,155	2,316
1701-10	23,822			23,822	2,382
1711-20	23,624			23,624	2,362
1721-30	25,424	3,000	4,215	32,639	3,264
1731-40	17,374 [a]		30,420 [a]	47,794	4,779
1741-50	2,250		52,984	55,243	5,524
1751-60	356		50,994	51,350	5,135
1761-70			62,921	62,921	6,292
1771-80			40,300	40,300	4,030
1781-90			9,695	9,695	970
1791-94			3,500	3,500	880
TOTAL 1675-1794	149,753	3,000	255,029	407,782	3,398
Overall	219,753	3,000	255,029	477,782	

SOURCES: Tables 2, 3, 7, 8, 9, 10, and 11 in my dissertation.
[a] The estimated figures for the years 1731-1735 were for the WIC 13,167 and for the free traders 18,378.

TABLE 8. REGIONAL ORIGINS OF THE DUTCH SLAVE TRADE, 1675-1795

Period	Loango-Angola	Slave Coast	Gold Coast	Ivory Coast	Windward Coast	Totals
1675-1700	19,000 (731)[a] 34%[b]	35,900 (1,381) 64%	2,000 (77) 2%	—	—	56,000
1710-35	35,300 (1,009) 31%	36,000 (1,029) 32%	25,600 (731) 23%	10,500 (300) 9%	4,200 (120) 4%	111,600
1736-95	58,100 (968) 24%	1,900 (32) 1%	16,500 (1,025) 26%	84,600 (1,410) 35%	33,200 (553) 14%	239,300
TOTAL	112,400	73,800	89,100	95,100	37,400	407,800

SOURCES: Tables 1-4.
[a] This line indicates the annual averages for the period.
[b] Regional percentages for the period are listed in this line.

49

III

A Quantitative Analysis of the Impact of British Suppression Policies on the Volume of the Nineteenth Century Atlantic Slave Trade

E. PHILLIP LEVEEN

IN 1808 BRITAIN declared participation by its citizens in the slave trade illegal, and during the following decade virtually all other nations similarly abolished the slave trade. At first, without effective methods of enforcement, these laws had little impact, and so with the conclusion of the Napoleonic Wars the volume of slaves exported annually across the Atlantic rose to about 70,000—a level very close to late eighteenth century peak averages. To stem this tide, Britain sent its navy to patrol the African coast where it remained in growing degrees of strength until after 1865, capturing slavers and taking other actions designed to hinder traders.

On the diplomatic front, Britain pursued an aggressive foreign policy designed to influence other nations (namely, Spain, Portugal, Brazil, France, and the United States) to enforce antislave trade provisions against their citizens, either by sending their own navies to the African coast, and/or by granting the Royal Navy the right to search and condemn slavers sailing under their colors. These diplomatic efforts, as well as the tactics and conduct of the navy along the African coast, have received considerable attention.[1] However, in

---

[1] Of the large number of works on abolition and other aspects of antislave trade policies, the following are of importance: Leslie Bethell, *The Abolition of the Brazilian Slave Trade*, Cambridge, England, 1970; Thomas Buxton, *The African Slave Trade: Its Remedy*, 2 vols., Philadelphia, 1839; W.E.B. DuBois, *The Suppression of the African Slave Trade*, New York, 1896; Reginald Coupland, *The British Anti-Slavery Movement*, London, 1933; Basil Davidson, *Black Mother: The African Slave Trade*, Boston, 1961; K. O. Dike, *Trade and Politics on the Niger Delta*, Oxford, 1956; Warren Howard, *American Slavers and the Federal Law, 1837-1860*, Berkeley, 1963; W. L. Mathieson, *Great Britain and the Slave Trade, 1839-1865*, London, 1929; D. P. Mannix and M. Cowley, *Black Cargoes: A History of the Atlantic Slave Trade, 1518-1865*, New York, 1962; Christopher Lloyd, *The Navy and the Slave Trade: The Suppression of the African Slave Trade in the Nineteenth Century*, London, 1949; W.E.F. Ward, *The Royal Navy and the Slavers: The Suppression of the Atlantic Slave Trade*, London, 1970; Eric E. Williams, *Capitalism and Slavery*, Chapel Hill, 1942.

spite of the lively debates in Parliament over what we might today term the "cost effectiveness" of the suppression policies, there has never been a systematic attempt to estimate the probable impact of such policies on the volume of the slave trade. This is not to imply that no estimates exist. Many proponents of the policies have pointed to the 160,000 slaves rescued by the navy and the 1,500 ships it captured and brought to court during the 45 years it patrolled the coast as evidence of its effectiveness. Others have charged that the navy's major impacts were to increase the hardships of the middle passage for the slaves, leading to greater slave mortality and, at the same time, to enhance slaver profits without significantly reducing the volume of the trade.

This essay argues in favor of a considerably higher estimate of the effect of British suppression policies on the volume of the trade than has been made previously. Our analysis presents evidence which

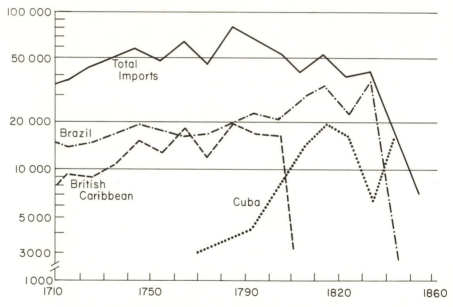

Average Annual Quantities of Slaves Imported to the Americas, 1710 – 1870.

FIG. 1. Source: Philip D. Curtin, *The Atlantic Slave Trade: A Census*, Madison, Wis., 1969, pp. 34, 211, 216, 234.

TABLE 1. ESTIMATED SLAVE IMPORTS OF THE AMERICAS, 1701-1810 AND 1811-1870 (000 OMITTED)

Region	1701-21	1721-40	1741-60	1761-80	1781-1810	Total	Percent
United States	19.8	50.4	100.4	85.8	91.6	384.0	5.8
Spanish Territories	90.4	90.4	90.4	121.9	185.5	578.6	9.6
British Caribbean	160.1	198.7	267.4	335.3	439.5	1,401.3	23.2
French Caribbean	166.1	191.1	297.8	335.8	357.6	1,348.4	22.3
Brazil	292.7	312.4	354.5	325.9	605.9	1,891.4	31.3
Other	126.0	83.3	86.7	100.5	83.0	484.0	8.0
Total	855.1	926.3	1,197.2	1,309.7	1,763.1	6,051.7	100.0
Annual Average	42.8	46.3	59.9	65.5	58.8	55.0	

Region	1811-20	1821-30	1831-40	1841-50	1851-60	1861-70	Total	Percent
Caribbean (Cuba, Puerto Rico)	117.7	170.6	143.6	58.2	145.5	66.2	702.0	37.0
United States	10.0	10.0	10.0	10.0	10.0	1.0	51.0	2.7
Brazil	266.8	325.0	212.0	338.3	3.3	—	1,145.4	60.3
Total	394.5	505.6	365.8	406.5	158.8	67.2	1,898.4	100.0
Annual Average	39.5	50.6	36.6	40.7	15.9	6.7	31.6	

SOURCE: Philip D. Curtin, *The Atlantic Slave Trade: A Census*, Madison, Wis., 1969, pp. 216, 234.

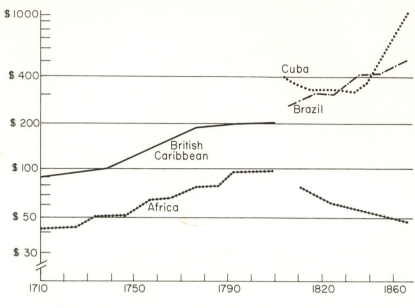

Decennial Averages of Prices in : Africa, British Caribbean,
Cuba, Brazil.

FIG. 2. *Source:* E. Phillip LeVeen, "British Slave Trade Suppression Policies,"
Ph.D. diss., University of Chicago, 1971, pp. 139-155.

demonstrates that the navy's influence forced the prices of newly
imported slaves to Brazil and Cuba to rise as much as twice what
they would have been without such interference.[2] Thus, while considerable numbers of slaves continued to be imported illegally into
the Americas during the nineteenth century (Figure 1 and Table 1),
the higher slave prices (Figure 2) implied a smaller importation,
assuming that the demand for slaves was not completely inelastic.
That is, not only did the navy prevent some slave cargoes from reaching their destination, but also, through the combined effects of higher
operating costs and greater risk of loss, the navy deterred some po-

[2] Cuba and Brazil were, for our purposes, the only major slave markets during
the nineteenth century which accepted new imports. Puerto Rico and the United
States and some other Caribbean Islands also continued to import some slaves,
but numerically these imports were insignificant in comparison with those of
Cuba and Brazil.

54

tential traders from entering the trade and caused some buyers to seek substitutes for slave labor, or to produce less sugar and coffee.

In order to derive an estimate of the navy's impact upon the trade, we require estimates of the percentage shift of the slave supply curve, its elasticity, and the elasticity of the demand for slaves. However, because of the limitations on the length of this essay, we shall omit considerations concerning these elasticities and give only the parameter values used in making the impact estimate. The supporting evidence for these values may be found elsewhere.[3] In this paper we shall concentrate upon the shift in the supply curve as a result of suppression policies. The approach is to disaggregate the slave supply process and suggest the nature and extent of the influence of the navy upon each of its components.

The Slave Supply Curve

We begin by isolating four components of the supply process: (1) the African suppliers who provided for the collection and transportation of slaves to the coast;[4] (2) the coastal factors who maintained slave stocks, prepared slaves for the middle passage, and served as a bridge between the European traders and the African suppliers; (3) the Atlantic traders responsible for the middle passage; and (4) the distributors of new slaves to potential owners in Cuba and Brazil. These four components are listed in Table 2 together with estimates of the share of the total cost going to each. In two cases, the amount of profits—net income received per slave—are also given (see figures in parentheses). The bottom half of Table 2 indicates the hypothesized costs and profits which would have obtained had there been no suppression. In the following pages, we shall suggest reasons why these recorded differences between the hypothesized and the observed costs were a consequence of suppression policies.

THE AFRICAN SUPPLY COSTS

There is no evidence that the navy directly influenced the mechanisms for collecting and delivering slaves to the coast. Indirectly, however, by blockading only West Africa for the first two decades of the illegal trade, the navy forced some distributional changes in the pattern of

[3] E. Phillip LeVeen, "British Slave Trade Suppression Policies, 1821-1865: Impact and Implications," Ph.D. dissertation, University of Chicago, 1971.
[4] For more on the African supply mechanism, see Philip Curtin, "The Slave Trade and the Atlantic Basin: Intercontinental Perspectives," in *Key Issues in the Afro-American Experience*, ed. N. Huggins, M. Kilson, and D. Fox, New York, 1971.

TABLE 2. SUMMARY OF SUPPLY COST DATA (PER SLAVE)

Period	Place	African Cost (1)	Factor Cost (2)	Shipping Cost (3)	Distribution Cost (4)	Market Price (5)
			Suppressed Trade			
1800	Caribbean	75	20	68.5 (13.2)	26.5 (7.5)	190
1821-40	Cuba	29	29	179.5 (84.0)	62.7 (40.0)	300
1841-50	Cuba	35	30	185.0 (123.0)	100.0 (76.0)	350
1851-65	Cuba	20	32	336.0 (275.0)	190.0 (100.0)	575
1821-40	Brazil (A)[a]	30	30	127.5 (63.5)	62.5 (n.a.)	250
1821-40	Brazil (B)[b]	30	30	127.5 (58.5)	62.5 (n.a.)	250
1841-50	Brazil	35	30	185.0 (132.0)	85.0 (n.a.)	325
			Nonsuppressed Trade			
1821-40	Cuba	35	15	48.1 (9.5)[c]	30.0 (21.6)	128
1841-50	Cuba	35	15	46.0 (8.5)	64.0 (52.8)	160
1851-65	Cuba	30	10	36.7 (7.5)	159.3 (100.0)	236
1821-40	Brazil	35	15	43.0 (9.0)	32.0 (n.a.)	125
1841-50	Brazil	35	15	43.0 (10.0)	31.0 (n.a.)	124

[a] Refers to the 15 percent Brazilian trade remaining north of the Equator.
[b] Refers to the remaining 85 percent Brazilian trade below the Equator.
[c] Figures in parentheses are profits; their calculation is discussed in the text.

trader demand; more slaves were purchased in the South-Central and Southeast African markets than during the eighteenth century. In general, slaves from these more distant markets were cheaper than those purchased from West Africa, but the longer voyages to the American markets increased mortality and freight costs which more than offset the initial cost advantage. Therefore, even those traders who escaped the direct influence of the navy incurred higher combined slave and freight costs on the average than they would have with no suppression force. The slave prices paid African suppliers are listed in Table 2, column 1; variations in these prices in different importing markets, or for the same market over time, reflect different or changing compositions of exporting markets.[5] After 1840, the blockade was extended to most of the coast, causing some shift back to West Africa as the risk was more evenly spread out to include the formerly safe market regions; therefore, the distributional effects on slave prices indicated above were less important.

[5] For greater detail, see LeVeen, p. 154.

56

FACTOR COSTS

Very little quantitative data are available on the costs of factoring. One estimate for the late eighteenth century suggests that west coast factors charged about 25 percent of the African price for their services.[6] The large trading houses in Liverpool and Bristol kept representatives on the coast to help facilitate the collection and bulking of potential slave cargoes for which they received 5 percent of the final selling price in the Caribbean, though it is unlikely that this was the total factoring charge.[7] During the nineteenth century, factoring became increasingly important to successful slaving and undoubtedly became more costly. Slave ships were most vulnerable when loading slaves and so, to minimize time onshore, transactions which formerly may have taken place at a leisurely pace on shipboard were removed to onshore factories which served as a collection point for slaves and as a storage facility for the barter goods used in the trade. Factors supplied more services during the nineteenth century. Skilled European carpenters were retained to construct the necessary outfit on the ships so that slavers could avoid detection and prosecution under the equipment clauses (whereby a ship could be condemned for having the articles of the slave trade on board, even if it was not carrying slaves).[8] Factors also helped to change ship registries or facilitate ownership transfers which could help some slavers escape prosecution, even if caught by the navy, depending upon the laws obtaining at any given time. Factors also served to convert gold and other European currencies carried by slavers into goods and currencies which could be traded for slaves in the interior, thus eliminating for slavers the tedious bargaining process and time-consuming

---

[6] See Marion Johnson, "The Ounce in Eighteenth-Century West African Trade," *Journal of African History* 7 (1966), 213.

[7] Two unpublished sets of papers and accounts of the slaving activities of two slaving houses in eighteenth century Britain have been used to find information on this type. The official citation for the Rogers Papers is: Great Britain, Public Record Office (hereafter P.R.O.), Chancery 107, 1-15. These papers cover the mid-1780s to 1793 and are also available on microfilm from Duke University. The other set, the Davenport Papers, is available from Love Library, University of Nebraska, Cat. No. L74730. The original set is in the archives of Keele University, United Kingdom. This set of papers refers to the period 1760 to 1785. Several of the shipping accounts from these papers have been published in other articles; see F. E. Hyde *et al.* "The Nature and Profitability of the Liverpool Slave Trade," *Economic History Review,* 2d ser., 5 (1952-1953), 368-377, and B. B. Parkinson, "A Slaver's Accounts," *Accounting Research* II (1951), 144-150.

[8] Stationing Europeans on the African coast must have been expensive, given the high mortality rates to which they were subjected. British personnel sent to Sierra Leone, for example, received large increments over their regular salaries for such service.

unloading of cargoes which were common during the eighteenth century.[9] Risks in factoring also increased as the navy began to harass factories with its guns or with raiding parties; and for this reason, as well as from possible monopoly power, the profits of the factor probably increased.[10]

It is unlikely that the factoring institutions would have been as highly developed or as costly to operate had traders been free to trade without fear of the navy. We, therefore, assume that without the navy the factor's operating costs would have been reduced, and profits would have remained at their eighteenth century levels (though no division of costs and profits is suggested for lack of sufficient data). Table 2, column 2, lists the factoring costs, and the relative change between the actual and hypothetical costs is given in Table 6, column 2.

SHIPPING COSTS

Of all the components, the Atlantic slave trader's costs were the most influenced by the navy. There are two parts to the effect of the suppression on the shippers. First, the navy forced slavers to take precautions to avoid detection, and these resulted in increased operating costs. Second, by increasing the probability of loss, the navy influenced the rate of return, thus forcing profits higher. Both effects are now considered.

---

[9] For a description of the nineteenth century factory on the Nigerian coast, see D. Turnbull, *Travels in the West: Cuba*, London, 1840, pp. 403-406. The description is based upon captured slaver papers. The company which owned the factory also owned the slave ships. The Europeans in charge of running were noncapital contributing, profit-sharing members of the company. Also, see David Ross, "The Career of Domingo Martinez in the Bight of Benin, 1833-64," *J.A.H.* 6 (1965), 79-90.

[10] Evidence is cited that Martinez had an annual business of $200,000 on which he cleared $80,000 in one year, which would mean that at least 40% of the slave price paid by the shipper was payments to the factor; see Ross, *op. cit.* We do not otherwise have much information on the costs and profits of factoring during the nineteenth century. From the Parliamentary hearings on the slave trade, however, it is possible to get some idea of the factor's value-added component of slave price paid by the trader. Several observers reported that slave prices in the interior of West Africa ranged from $25 to $45. Naval commanders, however, reported that slavers paid up to $100 per slave on the coast, with the most likely price of about $60 per slave. This suggests that factoring plus transportation to the coast may have added as much as $40 per slave, which is double the late eighteenth century charge reported by Marion Johnson. In Southeast Africa, slave prices in the interior were reported to be lower—about $5—while prices on-board ship were $20-25; see Great Britain, Parliament, House of Commons & Command, *Parliamentary Papers*, 1847-1848, xxii, Report 1, 66-70, and *Parliamentary Papers*, 1852-1853, xxxix, 37, 55 (and elsewhere).

CHANGES IN OPERATING COSTS

The device employed to measure the effects of the navy on freight costs is a series of shipping accounts designed to represent different periods of the nineteenth century for Cuba and Brazil.[11] Each account contains an estimate of the conditions existing under the influence of the navy and an estimate of the conditions which we assume would have existed without the navy. These accounts and a discussion of their construction may be found elsewhere.[12] The relevant information from the accounts is summarized in different tables and figures of this paper.

A comparison of the eighteenth century slave trade [13] with the rest of eighteenth century shipping [14] reveals few important differences between the trades. However, during the nineteenth century the costs and the structure of the slave trade diverged considerably from those of the rest of overseas shipping. From slaver capture records and from consular reports,[15] which contain time series data on ship size, slave loading rates, slave mortality rates, and length of voyages, the structure of the nineteenth century slave trade emerges.[16] During the nineteenth century the slave trade differed from the rest of the shipping industry most strongly in ship size, manpower requirements,

[11] Brazil and Cuba are treated separately for two reasons: (1) Brazil is closer to the source of supply and, therefore, cost conditions were different and (2) until 1830, the Brazilian market was legally open to ships of some countries as long as they traded south of the Equator. The Brazilian market is further divided into two parts—one for the trade above the Equator, the other for the trade below the Equator. Brazilians continued to trade on the West African coast in spite of increasing risks from the navy partly because costs were so much lower and partly because of historic trading ties, which conferred upon Brazilian tobacco a unique advantage in bartering for slaves; see Pierre Berger, *Flux et reflux de la traite des nègres entre le golfe de Benin et Bahia de Todos os Santos du 17ᵉ et 19ᵉ siècles,* The Hague, 1968; also, Johnson, p. 210.

[12] See LeVeen, Appendixes.

[13] The major sources of these accounts are listed in n. 7; see also Elizabeth Donnan, *Documents Illustrative of the History of the Slave Trade to America,* Washington, D.C., 1930, II, 570-580; Brantz Mayer, *Captain Canot: An African Slaver,* New York, 1968, p. 101; Howard, pp. 607-608. *Parliamentary Papers,* 1847-1848, XXII (623), "Report from the Select Committee on the Slave Trade," 395.

[14] Ralph Davis, *The Rise of the English Shipping Industry,* London, 1962. Gary Walton, "A Measure of Productivity Change in American Colonial Shipping," *E.H.R.,* 2d ser., 21 (1968), 268-283.

[15] The most important single Parliamentary source of data is: *Parliamentary Papers,* 1845, XLIX, 590-633.

[16] For nineteenth century data, see Ward, *op. cit.;* Lloyd, *op. cit.;* Howard, *op. cit.;* and George Dow, *Slave Ships and Slaving,* Salem, Mass., 1927.

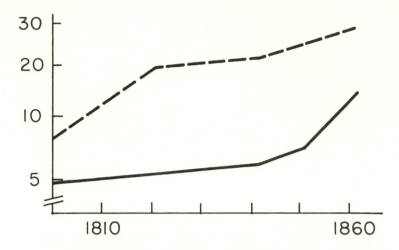

Tons per man in the slave trade
(solid line), and in the general shipping
industry (dotted line).

FIG. 3. *Source:* LeVeen, p. 23.

wages, and insurance [17] (Figures 3, 4, and 5; Table 3). The productivity gains of 3 percent per year which prevailed in ocean shipping during the first half of the nineteenth century (made possible by the use of larger ships with smaller crews) did not occur in the slave trade. There were no technical reasons why large ships could not be used in the trade; in fact, considerably larger ships were used in the late eighteenth century than were used during the peak periods of the 1840s. The preference for small ships was probably related to a desire to escape detection and perhaps to the risk-averting nature of the traders who would prefer to minimize the loss (at the expense of

[17] Douglass North, "Sources of Productivity Change in Ocean Shipping, 1600-1860," *Journal of Political Economy* 76 (1968), 953-970.

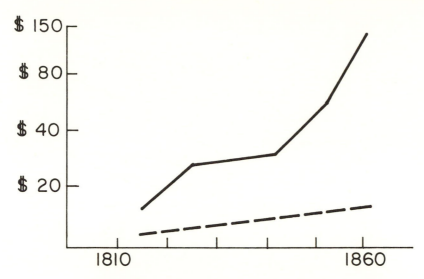

Monthly wages in the slave trade
(solid line), and in the general shipping
industry (dotted line).

FIG. 4. *Source:* LeVeen, p. 24.

some profits if successful) if the ship were captured.[18] If ships had been larger, it is likely that economies of scale in the use of men would have been possible in the slave trade as in other shipping, though perhaps to a lesser extent, owing to the problems of controlling a hostile cargo.[19] The higher insurance and wages reported in the slave trade were certainly related to the increasing probability of loss and of penalty imposed by the naval blockade. Therefore, in the hypothetical accounts of the unsuppressed slave trade, larger ship

[18] From the capture records and consular reports, it appears that the smallest ships were used where the naval blockade was most effective along the West African coast, and the largest ships were used where there was little effective suppression—in Southeast Africa. Between 1834 and 1843, ships from Southeast Africa to Brazil averaged 214 tons, while those from West Africa averaged 98 tons.

[19] Large slave ships were used at the end of the trade and had tons per man ratios close to those in the rest of shipping (Table 3).

61

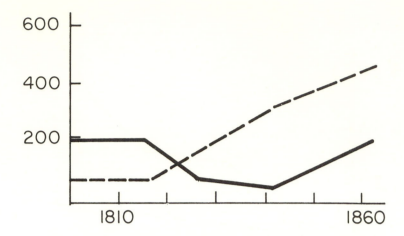

Ship size (tons) in the slave trade
(solid line), and in the general shipping
industry (dotted line).

FIG. 5. *Source:* LeVeen, p. 24.

size, lower wage rates, lower insurance rates,[20] somewhat lower mortality rates,[21] and higher tons per man ratios have been used to bring the slave trade closer to the rest of the industry. The operating costs which actually existed in the trade are listed in the upper half of Table 2, column 3 (it is necessary to subtract the profits estimate to obtain the operating cost component of total shipping costs). The costs which would have existed are listed in the lower half of the same column. The difference in operating costs brought about by the influence of the navy can be seen in column 3, Table 6 (see figures in parentheses).

[20] There is limited information about insurance. Some report that only the hulls of the ships were insured, but few purchased insurance; see R. R. Madden, *The Island of Cuba*, London, 1849, p. 33, and Turnbull, p. 367.
[21] The data on mortality rates are remarkably good for the eighteenth century. Rates of between 9 and 15% were common. We also have information about the nineteenth century which suggests that mortality rates did not change dramatically as was often alleged. This problem is considered later in the paper; see n. 43.

TABLE 3. SUMMARY OF DATA RELATING TO SHIP SIZE, CREW SIZE, AND CARRYING CAPACITY

Period	Average Tons, per Ship	Standard Error	No. Obs.	Slaves per Ton, Loaded	S.E.	No. Obs.	Tons per Crewman	S.E.	No. Obs.
1824-27[a]	134.0	60.4	58	2.2	1.2	34	5.1	1.9	53
1825-32[b]	162.0	76.2	64	1.9	1.4	39	n.a.		
1834-43[b]	154.2	75.6	226	2.8	.9	53	10.1	2.0	112
1838-45[c]	113.1	63.0	387	4.5	1.8	90	n.a.		
1845-48[c]	143.0	90.0	160	4.3	1.9	33	8.0	4.5	130
1849-52[d]	168.0	101.0	95	2.7	1.1	22	n.a.		
1855-64[e]	203.0	157.0	107	2.5	1.0	21	13.6	7.9	51
1857-60[f]	262.5	107.0	101	1.9	.5	33	n.a.		

[a] Returns of Mixed Commission courts, Great Britain, *Parliamentary Papers*, 1828, XXVI, 89. This data refers largely to the Cuban trade and the W. African component of the Brazilian trade.

[b] Report of the British consuls compiled by the Foreign Office. *Parliamentary Papers*, 1845, XLIX, 593-633. This data refers largely to the Brazilian trade. The slave loading rate is lower in part because the observation was made upon the returned cargo, some of which died en route (as compared with other returns which were recorded on the African coast). Crews suffered mortality too, and therefore this rate may be higher than those recorded near the coast because of a mortality differential.

[c] Returns of the Vice Admiralty and Mixed Commission courts. *Parliamentary Papers*, 1840, XLIV, 1ff; 1842, XLIV, 500ff; 1850, IX, 349ff.

[d] Returns of the Vice Admiralty and Mixed Commission courts. *Parliamentary Papers*, 1852-53, XXIX, 289ff.

[e] Returns of Vice Admiralty courts, *Parliamentary Papers*, 1861, LXIX, 360; 1865, LVI, 520.

[f] See Warren Howard, *American Slavers and the Federal Law*, Berkeley, 1963, Appendixes H, I, and J. These data refer specifically to ships of American origin in the trade.

The impact of the navy on operating costs appears to be much lower in the final periods than during earlier ones. This is the result of the assumption that after 1840 slavers insured themselves instead of outright purchasing an insurance policy. If there was no insurance, some of the expenses of buying the policy were eliminated, but the returns from selling a slave would have to be higher in order to induce the slaver to undertake the increased risk. Indeed, Table 6, column 4, indicates that the impact on profits was greater during those same times when insurance was not available. Had insurance continued to be available at high premiums, the removal of the navy would have reduced operating costs by reducing insurance premiums. Thus, some of the cost changes which are recorded in the profits effect probably belong in the operating cost effect for these latter periods. This distinction, however, has no effect on the overall impact estimate.

CHANGES IN THE PROFITABILITY OF SLAVING

We turn now to the consideration of changing profits associated with the shipping cost component of the slave supply curve. Table 4, column 1, indicates the changing profits per slave successfully delivered. The figures in the lower half of the same column indicate what the profits would have been, assuming a 10 percent expected rate of return on capital invested in shipping. Contemporary critics of the suppression squadron were fond of exclaiming over the slave trade's huge profits, which they believed would insure the continuation of slaving no matter what tactics the navy might adopt. Indeed, according to the evidence in columns 1 and 3, gross profits per slave were very much above eighteenth century levels.

Why the large increase in profits? Part of the reason is related to the impact of suppression policies upon the likelihood that a given slave trade investment would fail. Almost all observers of the trade agreed that the navy imposed losses upon traders.[22] To quote a Royal Navy commander of the suppression squadron, "The profitable result is pretty well calculated by the merchant . . . he fits out four vessels, and expects to lose three; if he should lose only two, he would consider himself lucky." However, few people saw the causal connection between probability of loss and high profits or the relationship between suppression and slave price rises. Investors in the slave trade were primarily concerned that average profits—that is, the gains from successful voyages minus the losses from unsuccessful ventures—were high enough to bring at least a competitive rate of return on their investment. Therefore, as the navy increased the probability that a given venture would fail, and thereby reduced average profits, it discouraged investment in the slave trade. Smaller investment implied fewer slaves transported to the Americas which, in turn, caused slave prices to rise in Brazil and Cuba and fall in Africa. This divergent price movement caused profits on successful voyages to rise, as can be seen in Table 4, column 1. Expected profits —which are the profits of a successful voyage, weighted by the probability of success, minus the losses of an unsuccessful voyage, weighted by the probability of failure—were substantially lower than profits on a successful voyage, as can be seen in Table 4, column 6.[23]

[22] Table 5 contains a derivation of the possible impact of the navy upon the probability of loss.

[23] The calculation of the expected profit is as follows: The simplifying assumption made is that a given venture has two possible outcomes, each with a known probability (given in col. 5). If the venture fails, the investor loses the amount listed in col. 4. Thus, col. 6 is the mathematical expectation of the two outcomes.

TABLE 4. SUMMARY OF RATE OF RETURN DATA (PER SLAVE) [a]

Period	Place	Profit (1)	Capital Outlay[c] (2)	(1)÷(2) (3)	Capital Risked[d] (4)	Probability of Loss[e] (5)	Expected Profit (6)	(6)÷(2) (7)
				Suppressed Trade				
1800	Caribbean	$ 13.2	$138.5	9.5%	$ 6.8	5.0%	$12.0	8.8%
1821-40	Cuba	79.0	130.0	62.0	37.0	40.0	32.7	25.0
1841-50	Cuba	123.0	96.0	128.0	96.0	50.0	13.5	14.0
1851-65	Cuba	275.0	120.0	223.0	120.0	60.0	38.0	31.8
1821-40	Brazil (A)[b]	63.5	111.0	57.0	29.0	35.0	31.2	28.0
1821-40	Brazil (B)	58.5	120.0	48.0	20.0	20.0	42.0	35.0
1841-50	Brazil	132.0	94.0	140.0	94.0	50.0	19.0	20.4
				Nonsuppressed Trade				
1821-40	Cuba	9.2	85.5	10.8	4.2	5.0	8.5	10.0
1841-50	Cuba	9.5	89.0	10.5	2.6	3.0	8.9	10.0
1851-65	Cuba	7.2	70.0	10.2	1.6	2.0	7.0	10.0
1821-40	Brazil	8.9	82.0	10.5	3.9	5.0	8.2	10.0
1841-50	Brazil	9.3	90.0	10.2	1.6	3.0	9.0	10.0

[a] Calculated from accounts, see text.
[b] See note "b," Table 2.
[c] Source: Accounts, see text. Composed of the cost of ship, outfit, cargo, stores, and insurance.
[d] If insurance was available, then it was sole component of this category, if no insurance then risked capital is the same as capital outlay, col. 2.
[e] See Table 5.

To summarize, by increasing the probability of loss, the navy caused the profit component of slave costs to rise and forced an upward shift in the slave supply curve.

Another interesting aspect of the navy's impact on profits can be seen by comparing eighteenth and nineteenth century expected rates of return on investment (that is, expected profits divided by the capital investment per slave) which were three to five times higher during the nineteenth century.[24] (See Table 4, column 7.) So even if account is taken of the above-discussed effect of the navy upon the probability of loss and on profits of successful voyages, there is still some unexplained differential in profit levels. The most likely reason for the observed increase in expected rate of return in slaving during the nineteenth century relates to the increased riskiness and uncertainty of investing in the trade. If risk is defined as the variance of outcomes from the mathematically expected outcome of an investment, then as the impact of the navy became more significant, the slave traders faced greater divergences in the returns from individual ventures. Assuming that investors were risk averters (that is, if two investments had the same mathematical expectation, they would prefer the one which was more likely to succeed), then, in order to induce investment into an increasingly risky trade, higher expected returns would be necessary.

In addition to its effect upon risk, the navy may have indirectly helped create monopoly power in the slave trade, which might also help explain the higher profits. The chances of capture were probably greater for the new or the small independent trader who either did not know how or was unable to avoid detection by the navy. Information about the trade probably became more difficult to find, and the facilities of quick slave delivery in Africa were less accessible to the trader who did not have contacts or the funds to set up a network of slave factories.

Another explanation for the observed higher expected returns is our possible failure to include in the calculations all the costs of trading. Traders may have employed costly practices to escape detection. The practice of sending decoys is often mentioned as a method by which slavers kept the navy busy investigating ships, while the real

---

In economic terms the mathematical expectation is what an investor would be most likely to earn were he to send several ships on slaving expeditions.

[24] The expected rates of profit listed in Table 4, col. 6, are gross profits. No allowance has been made for interest costs on the initial capital outlay. To obtain the net return, some interest rate must be subtracted from the rates listed. If a 4% rate is used, the eighteenth century rate is about 5% which is very similar to rates found by Davis, pp. 378-379.

slavers carried out their missions. Goods for slave barter and slave equipment were sometimes sent as part of a legitimate cargo and then transferred at the factory. Another frequently used device was the purchase of several registration papers of different countries to take advantage of the latest legal loopholes which might grant a ship of a given nationality immunity from the Royal Navy. It is usually assumed that this method was costless, but other evidence suggests that registration papers were not cheap.[25] Nor was this tactic infallible since laws were subject to change and to different interpretation by commanders on the coast. There was considerable uncertainty as to which flag was safe at any given time.[26] At any rate, none of these devices was costless, and if they were important, profits may have been lower than those recorded.

Finally, it is possible that the profits estimated are artificially high because the probability of loss used to estimate the expected rates of return may be systematically too low—more captures may have occurred than have been recorded (Table 5).[27] None of these considerations substantially alters the conclusions about the navy's impact, for all can be related to the influence of the navy. Therefore, the only change, as far as this analysis is concerned, would be a

[25] Turnbull, p. 380, states that the cost of obtaining fictitious papers from the Portuguese was 15% of the value of the ship and cargo.

[26] A criticism usually leveled at the U.S. policy of summarily granting registration to anyone was that it permitted everyone to travel under the U.S. flag which, in principle, was supposed to be immune from British forces. Thus, it is supposed that there existed a giant loophole through which most of the trade after 1840 was permitted to be carried on without fear of capture. In reality, it has not been shown that the number of ships traveling under U.S. registry was a very large percentage of the total. In fact, Curtin has shown that from records kept by the British Consul in Rio very few of the ships sailed under U.S. colors. Perhaps registration papers were more difficult to obtain than critics believed. Perhaps registration papers were not infallible means of escaping the navy. British officers frequently arrested ships they suspected of sailing under false registry in spite of protests of the U.S. government. Howard (pp. 241-250) suggests that the British captured many American ships: 14 between 1837 and 1840; 51 between 1840 and 1860. Howard believed that about 60% of all ships were caught during the 1850s. United States citizens apparently became more involved in the trade after 1850, and the character of style of trade changed; larger ships, different African factoring procedures, and higher profits (see Ross, *op.cit.*).

[27] The number of ship captures officially recorded may be an understatement because ships which were sunk or driven ashore and never brought to court are not included in the records. After 1845, the British Vice Admiralty courts handled most of the slave cases, and with this shift, more ships were sunk on the spot and not brought to court; see Bethell, "The Mixed Commissions for the Suppression of the Transatlantic Slave Trade in the Nineteenth Century," *J.A.H.* 7 (1966), 79-93. During the 1850s, the Spanish and Portuguese navies made several captures off the coast of Cuba. These are not included in the statistics.

TABLE 5. ESTIMATES OF THE TOTAL SHIPS[a] IN THE SLAVE TRADE AND PERCENT DETAINED
(ANNUAL AVERAGES)

Period	Place	Slaves Imported (000)	Slaves per Ton[b]	Average Ship Size[b] (tons)	Complete Voyages[c]	Total Complete Voyages	Total Ships Captured[a]	Total Ships in Trade	Percent Ships Detained
1821-30	Cuba	18.1	2.2	135	61.0	156.5	14.4	170.9	15.3[e]
	Brazil	32.5	2.0	170	95.0				
1831-40	Cuba	15.4	4.5	110	29.6	78.1	34.0	112.1	46.5[e]
	Brazil	21.2	2.8	155	48.5				
1841-50	Cuba	6.8	4.3	140	11.6	86.7	70.5	157.2	45.0
	Brazil	33.8	3.0	150	75.1				
1851-60	Cuba	15.6	2.7	200	28.8	34.9	19.3[f]	54.2	35.6
	Brazil	.3	2.7	200	6.1				
1861-70	Cuba	6.7	2.5	300	8.9	8.9	6.1[f]	15.0	40.5
	Brazil								

[a] Ships and voyages are the same.
[b] See Table 3 for data source.
[c] Divide the number of slaves imported by the product of slaves per ton and average ship size.
[d] See LeVeen, "British Slave Trade Suppression Policies," p. 100, for sources.
[e] Only 20 percent of the Brazilian trade is assumed under the influence of the navy, and the percent detained refers to this part of the Brazilian trade, and to the total Cuban trade.
[f] These are the official British statistics; however, see n. 26 for reasons why these data are probably understated.

TABLE 6. THE SOURCES OF MARKET PRICE REDUCTION UNDER "NO-SUPPRESSION" ASSUMPTION

Period	Place	African Cost (1)	Factor Cost (2)	Operating Cost (3)	Profits (4)	Distribution Cost (5)	Total Reduction (6)
1821-40	Cuba	+2.0%	-4.6%	-19.1%	-24.8%	-11.0%	-57.5%
		(+20.0)^a	(-48.0)	(-60.0)	(-88.0)	(-49.0)	
1841-50	Cuba	0.0	-4.2	-6.5	-33.0	-10.3	-54.0
		(0.0)	(-50.0)	(-40.0)	(-93.0)	(-28.0)	
1851-65	Cuba	+1.8	-3.5	-5.4	-47.8	-5.1	-60.0
		(+50.0)	(-67.0)	(-51.0)	(-96.0)	(-19.0)	
1821-40	Brazil (A)	+1.9	-6.0	-12.1	-21.7	-12.1	-50.0
		(+17.0)	(-50.0)	(-47.0)	(-86.0)	(-50.0)	
	Brazil (B)	+1.9	-6.0	-14.4	-19.4	-12.1	-50.0
		(+17.0)	(-50.0)	(-56.5)	(-85.0)	(-50.0)	
1841-50	Brazil	0.0	-4.7	-5.4	-38.0	-14.2	-62.0
		(0.0)	(-50.0)	(-30.0)	(-93.0)	(-59.0)	

SOURCE: Table 2.
^a Figures in parentheses are the percentage reduction in each component.

shift in the relative shares of the components of the total impact if actual costs were higher than recorded costs (Table 6).

Looking now at the bottom half of Table 4, we examine the derivation of the profits for the hypothetically unsuppressed trade. The calculations of columns 1 and 6 depend upon the assumed probabilities and rates of return which would have prevailed during the nineteenth century. Probabilities of loss are based upon nonslave trade maritime insurance rates, though these estimates are larger than the maritime rates to account for the possibility of continued piracy at a higher level than elsewhere and the possibility of loss from slave mutinies. The 10 percent expected profit rate assumed is arbitrary—risk-free rates on British consuls varied between 3 and 4 percent during this time. Ten percent is higher than the estimated eighteenth century rate, and it should, therefore, have the effect of biasing the navy's impact downward. Given the 10 percent profit rate, the expected profits per slave are calculated; then working backward, given the probabilities of loss, the per slave profits (Table 4, columns 1 and 3) for a successful voyage are derived. Finally, the influence of the navy on profits and thus on slave prices is summarized in Table 6, column 4.

DISTRIBUTION AND SELLING COSTS

The final component of the supply mechanism—the cost of selling and distributing slaves in the importing markets—was least influenced by the navy [28] (Table 2, column 4). We have almost no information about these markets in the nineteenth century; but during the previous century, a considerable portion of the final slave price went to selling commissions (about 5 percent), to brokerage and credit fees (5 percent), and to other credit charges.[29] Credit problems no doubt persisted into the nineteenth century. Brazilian traders became large landholders as a result of the debts owed them by the planters.[30] There were increasing problems associated with distributing illegally

[28] It is assumed that British diplomatic efforts had no effect on internal conditions in Cuba and Brazil, which is unlikely. However, it is probable that without these efforts the process of distributing slaves in Cuba and Brazil would have been less costly.

[29] Payment for slaves was usually in the form of bills of exchange which carried with them the risk of default and were usually not payable at face value for between one and three years, making the effective price received lower by a discount and a risk factor.

[30] One of the forces in favor of abolition which developed in Brazil was that of planters who were in debt to the slave traders and who had lost much of their land as they defaulted on payments with the depression of the late 1840s in the coffee industry; see Bethell, *Abolition*, pp. 313-315.

imported slaves—the trade was officially illegal in Cuba after 1820 and in Brazil after 1830. In addition to finding buyers, the importer had to contend with government officials, which meant increasingly liberal bribes. In Cuba a slave could be brought in for $10 in bribes in 1830; but by the mid-1850s, total expenditures for bribes and identification cards came to over $140 per slave.[31]

In Brazil slave prices in the interior, at the mines, and at sugar and coffee plantations cost 20 percent more than at the coast. This increase may be ascribed to transportation and mortality expenses as well as credit costs.[32]

It is assumed that these higher costs which prevailed during the nineteenth century would not have been lower even if there had been no British suppression (except that slave mortality after arrival might have been higher, which would have represented a cost to distributors).

The profit estimates in parentheses (Table 2, column 4) are highly speculative. They include bribes, if known, and 35 percent brokerage and selling fees in Cuba; this is the rate which may have been typical for the eighteenth century factoring profits in the Caribbean.[33] The effects of the naval influence are summarized in Table 6, column 5.

Finally, Table 6, column 6, gives the combined effects of all forms of the navy's impact. In general, it is found that prices of the *quantity of slaves actually imported* would have been between 50 and 62 percent lower, depending on the place and decade, had the suppression force been withdrawn.

The Derivation of the Impact Estimate

The preceding analysis shows that, for a given quantity of slave imports, if the navy had been withdrawn slave prices in the Caribbean and Brazil would have been considerably lower than they actually were, which in turn implies that more slaves would have been demanded. The extent of this increase depends upon both the elasticity of demand and the elasticity of supply curves. If either elasticity is low, then the shift of the supply curve would have had little impact on the quantity of imports. As indicated earlier, we cannot devote space in this essay to a consideration of these values. Table 7 lists the parameter values used in estimating the derived demand elasticity, and Table 8, column 2, lists the values used for the

[31] Mayer, p. 101; Howard, pp. 607-608.
[32] *Parliamentary Papers*, 1847-1848, xxii, 51; also, see Bethell, p. 77.
[33] Robert P. Thomas, "The Sugar Colonies of the Old Empire: Profit or Loss for Great Britain?," *E.H.R.*, 2d ser., 21 (1968), 30-46.

71

TABLE 7. ESTIMATES OF DERIVED SLAVE DEMAND ELASTICITY

Period	Place	η_w[a] (1)	q[b] (2)	e[c] (3)	η_h[d] (4)	α[e] (5)	σ[f] (6)	ξ[g] (7)	η_d[h] (8)
1821-40	Cuba	−1.5	.10	1.0	−24.0	.35	1.0	1.0	−1.95
1841-50	Cuba	−1.5	.18	1.0	−13.0	.35	1.0	1.0	−1.90
1851-65	Cuba	−1.5	.25	1.0	−9.0	.30	1.0	1.0	−1.60
1821-40	Brazil	−1.5	.15	1.0	−15.0	.35	1.0	1.0	−1.94
1841-50	Brazil	−1.5	.40	1.0	−7.5	.35	1.0	1.0	−1.70

SOURCES: see text.

[a] η_w is the world price elasticity of demand for sugar in all cases except for the final decade in Brazil where it is the same elasticity, but of coffee.

[b] q is the share of the world market allocated to Brazil and Cuba.

[c] e is the elasticity of supply of other sugar and coffee producers.

[d] η_h is the home price elasticity for sugar and coffee. It is derived from the following:

$$\eta_h = 1/q \cdot \eta_w - (1-q)/q \cdot e$$

[e] α is share of slave costs in total sugar (coffee) production costs.

[f] σ is the elasticity of substitution.

[g] ξ is the elasticity of supply of other factors.

[h] η_d is the derived demand elasticity for slaves. It is calculated as follows:

$$\eta_d = \frac{\eta_h\sigma - [(1-\alpha)\sigma - \alpha\eta_h]\xi}{\alpha\sigma - (1-\alpha)\eta_h + \xi}$$

Source for formula: R. Muth, "The Derived Demand Curve for a Productive Factor and the Industry Supply Curve," *Oxford Economic Papers* 16 (July 1964), 226.

supply elasticity.[34] The results of combining the elasticity values with the supply curve shift are given in the last two columns of Table 8, while the formula used to compute the estimates is given in footnote "d" of the table. The remainder of the paper is devoted to further consideration of the final estimates of the numbers imported into the Americas and of those exported from Africa.

INTERPRETATION OF THE IMPACT ESTIMATES

IMPORT ESTIMATES AND POSSIBLE CRITICISMS

CURTIN estimates that nearly 1.5 million slaves were actually imported to Cuba and Brazil between 1821 and 1865, and our analysis suggests that this number would have been about 50 percent larger without

---

[34] The most important aspect of the supply elasticity analysis is that related to the supply response of the African slave suppliers: Did the price of slaves affect the quantity of slaves "produced"? I have argued elsewhere that this supply was price responsive and that the value of the elasticity for this component of the supply process was probably close to one; see LeVeen, pp. 156-168.

TABLE 8. ESTIMATE OF THE IMPACT OF SUPPRESSION POLICIES

Period	Place	(1) [a] η_d	(2) [b] θ	(3) [c] $\dfrac{\overset{*}{S}}{S}$	(4) [d] $\dfrac{\overset{*}{Q}}{Q}$	(5) [e] ΔQ^M (000)	(6) [f] ΔQ^x (000)
1821-40	Cuba	−1.95	1.8	−57.5%	+54.5%	181.0	197.0
1841-50	Cuba	−1.90	2.4	−54.0	+59.0	39.5	41.5
1851-65	Cuba	−1.60	3.0	−60.0	+62.5	139.0	140.0
1821-40	Brazil	−1.94	1.5	−50.0	+42.9	230.0	240.0
1841-50	Brazil	−1.70	1.4	−62.0	+47.7	185.0	201.0
TOTAL						774.5	819.0

[a] See col. 8, Table 7.

[b] θ is the elasticity of the supply curve; see text.

[c] $\dfrac{\overset{*}{S}}{S}$ is the percent downward shift of the supply curve; carried over from col. 6, Table 6.

[d] $\dfrac{\overset{*}{Q}}{Q}$ is the percentage increase in the number of imported slaves estimated in the following way:

$$\frac{\overset{*}{Q}}{Q} = \frac{\eta_d \cdot \theta}{\eta_d + \theta} \cdot \frac{\overset{*}{S}}{S}$$

[e] ΔQ^M is the number of slaves which would have been imported without suppression. It is calculated by taking the product of col. (4) and the appropriate import estimate from Table 1.

[f] ΔQ^x is the estimated change in slaves exported from Africa. Its calculation is discussed in the text.

suppression. We now turn to arguments which suggest that the suppression impact estimates are either too low or too high.

In addition to the deliberate attempt to understate the suppression policy impact by selecting conservative values of various parameters used in estimating demand and supply elasticities and the supply curve shift, there are two other factors which might be cited to support the thesis that our impact estimates are unduly low. First, some of the estimates of actual slave imports collected by Curtin and employed in this study are probably too low, thus making the impact estimates also too low. Klein has investigated slave imports to Rio during the nineteenth century and has found substantially higher imports than were reported by British consuls, upon whose reports Curtin's work is

TABLE 9. ESTIMATED POPULATIONS OF BRAZIL AND CUBA, 1800-1872

Period	Slave	Free Afro-Cuban	White	Total
		Cuba		
1804	180,000 (35) [a]	90,000	234,000	504,000
1817	199,145 (36)	114,058	239,830	553,045
1827	286,942 (41)	106,494	311,051	704,482
1841	421,649 (43)	147,787	408,966	978,402
1855	366,421 (35)	179,012	498,752	1,044,185
1861	399,872 (29)	213,167	748,534	1,361,573
		Brazil		
1800	1,000,000 (33)	2,000,000		3,000,000
1819	1,107,389 (33)	2,488,743		3,396,123
1823	1,147,515 (29)	2,813,351		3,960,856
1850	2,500,000 (32)	5,520,000		8,020,000
1872	1,510,806 (15)	8,419,672		9,930,478

SOURCES: Cuba: Herbert Klein, *Slavery in the Americas*, Chicago, 1967, p. 202. Brazil: Stanley Stein, *Vassouras*, Cambridge, 1957, p. 294.

[a] Numbers in parentheses indicate percentage of the total population represented by the slave population.

largely based.[35] It is possible that other work will show similar results for Cuba.

The second argument, based upon a possible relationship between profits of slave ownership, slave mortality rates, and slave replacement costs, suggests that if planters were able to reduce slave mortality rates by sacrificing some present output per slave (e.g., by working slaves less hard or by spending more on their nutritional and health requirements) then as replacement costs rose, they would profit by adopting measures to increase slave life spans. A similar argument can be made for increasing slave import prices causing an increase in the number of slaves bred domestically. If such options were open to planters, and underlying cost conditions permitted, it is possible that planters could substitute domestically bred for imported slaves as import prices increased because of naval activities. Such options imply that the derived demand elasticity estimates we used may be too low, which further implies greater impact estimates of the quantity of slaves imported than the above estimates. Whether our neglect of these alternatives is a serious omission depends upon grower reaction to the

[35] Klein's import estimates are not yet published; they were communicated to me in private correspondence.

higher prices. Did planters take measures to decrease mortality rates, increase fertility rates, or increase the proportion of females in the imports from Africa? Some contemporaries observed that plantation conditions did improve as slaves became more valuable, and others thought that producers were increasingly willing to raise slaves domestically.[36] A survey of sixty slave cargoes captured by the navy between 1830 and 1840 indicates that the ratio of males to females on board slave ships declined from over 4.4:1 during the first five years to 2.3:1 during the latter five years.[37] However, while this difference is statistically significant, and while such an increase in the proportion of females could have had an important impact on birth rates, we cannot necessarily relate the shift in the ratio to changing planter preferences for increased domestic breeding since the ratio is also affected by supply conditions on the African coast and women may have been more available during the latter period. Another piece of relevant evidence comes from Eblen's work on the Cuban population during the nineteenth century which is contained in this volume. His conclusion is that fertility rates, especially among slaves, may have actually declined between 1820 and 1860 in Cuba; if true, this finding would tend to discredit arguments in favor of better treatment of slaves, since declining fertility rates may have been an indicator of the harshness of slave existence.[38] However, it remains possible that increasing the proportion of females may have outweighed the effect of declining fertility rates, so that the number of domestically born slaves may have increased during the period. The resolution to this problem requires a more detailed analysis of the demography of slave populations of both Cuba and Brazil. Eblen's efforts are directed at the entire black population, which includes a substantial minority of free blacks, and although he operates under the assumption that the two groups did not differ greatly in mortality or fertility, it is possible that important differences between slaves and free blacks did exist. One final note on the costs of breeding versus importing slaves: the calculation presented in the following footnote implies that there was little incentive to raise slaves domestically before 1850, for as long as

[36] For a detailed account of these observations as well as a rigorous mathematical development of an economic model which contains the relationship between profitability, slave mortality and fertility rates, interest rates, and prices of slaves and crops see Dave Denslow, Jr., "Economic Considerations in the Treatment of Slaves in Brazil and Cuba," unpublished mimeo., Department of Economics, University of Florida.

[37] *Parliamentary Papers*, 1842, XLIV, 500-599.

[38] For some additional corroborative evidence, see Franklin Knight, *Slave Society in Cuba During the Nineteenth Century*, Madison, Wis., 1970, pp. 73-75.

expected slave prices remained below $600, they were cheaper to import than breed.[39] Although slave prices did not rise above $600 in Cuba until after 1850, it is possible that planters anticipated the price rise before that date and began to import more women for the purpose of increasing the domestically born slave stock.

We turn now to arguments which might be advanced to suggest that the impact estimates are too generous. First, some might argue that the white populations of Cuba and Brazil would not have permitted the increased imports because of fear that larger slave populations would have increased the risks of costly rebellion, such as occurred in Haiti in 1790. However, because of the high mortality during the process of seasoning (the period during which the slave became accustomed to the environment of the plantation), and because of generally high mortality and low fertility of seasoned slaves, the increased numbers of slaves, which we hypothesize would have been imported without the navy's interference, would not have drastically altered the slave/population ratios in either Cuba or Brazil; a numerical example is given in the following footnote for the case of Cuba.[40] In neither Cuba nor Brazil would the additional slave imports

[39] In deciding whether to raise his own slaves or to continue to import them, the producer must look at the costs of rearing a slave until he or she reaches a productive age (about 14 years old), and the costs of a newly imported slave in 14 years. The rearing costs are as follows: Annual costs, including food, health, and clothing for an adult slave were about $50; we assume that similar expenses for a child would be lower, say, $20 per year. The annual costs, including interest, for 14 years comes to $500. The child might die, and the lost investment from such mortality must be added on to the cost of the successfully reared child. Assume that the chance of mortality per child for 14 years is 10%; we then must add $50 to the cost above. Children required a mother's care, especially for the first half-year of life, which meant that her services were lost to the plantation. Taking $80 as the value of the mother's yearly productivity (the annual cost of a slave) and assuming one-half year's productivity lost to the plantation, and compounding the $40 at 5% for 14 years, this cost comes to about $80, making the total cost at least $630. This does not include the probable effect of reduced average productivity of the slave stock from having a larger proportion of women necessary to increase the birth rate—women could not do the hard labor that a man could do. Slave prices in Cuba and Brazil did not exceed $600 for newly imported slaves until after 1850. Whether producers anticipated these higher import costs in the late 1830s is difficult to say, but probably they did not, thus explaining the continued preference for imported slaves.

[40] The slave population of Cuba was 36% of the total population in 1820 and 43% in 1841. We estimated earlier that, in the absence of suppression, 180,000 additional slaves would have been imported during this period. Of these, about 25% would have died during seasoning, and about 26% of the remaining slaves would have died during the twenty years (assuming that the mortality rate for seasoned slaves was 3%). These additional slaves would have increased the slave population through their offspring. If we assume that the sex composition of these additional slaves would have been two males to each female, about 45,000 females

have brought slave/population ratios even close to the levels of those islands which had uncontrollable rebellions, most of which had ten slaves to each European. In Cuba, even with the additional slaves, the ratio would have been close to one slave per each European, and the ratio would have been considerably lower in Brazil. Moreover, both Spain and Brazil encouraged relatively lenient manumission policies which gave rise to large free black populations. The possibility, either through escape or by legal methods, of becoming a member of this population may have helped provide a safety valve for the most discontented slaves.[41] It is doubtful that policy makers would have balked at permitting these additional imports of slaves then. There is even some evidence that Spain, in an attempt to keep Cuba dependent upon its authority, wanted a large slave population as a threat to possible independence-minded colonialists.[42]

A second argument in favor of a too generous estimate of the impact has been raised by Philip Curtin. He suggests that, if the volume of slaves imported were to have increased, the mortality rate of the slave population would also then have increased since a larger percentage of the population would have been composed of new arrivals from Africa—the group which had the least immunity to disease. Mortality rates of newly arrived slaves, though lower than comparable rates for newly arrived whites or Chinese, were still much higher than for seasoned and second-generation slaves.[43] The relevance of these higher mortality rates associated with the larger number of unseasoned slaves to our impact analysis is as follows: If the navy had been withdrawn and greater numbers of new slaves had been imported, higher average mortality rates would have increased slave costs to planters, which, in turn, would have implied higher total production costs of coffee and sugar. If such cost increases were

---

would have survived seasoning, of which perhaps 36,000 could have reproduced (assuming all females to be between 15 and 45 years old, and 20% childless). We do not have estimates of slave fertility rates, but using the high rate of 200 births per 1,000 females per year, and taking into account the mortality of slaves, these assumptions imply about 53,000 children during the twenty years. Of these, perhaps 35,000 would have survived until 1841. The net result is: of the additional 180,000 slaves imported, about 134,000 including offspring would have survived until 1841, and therefore the slave population in Cuba in 1841 would have been 557,000 or about 50% of the entire population of Cuba, instead of the actual 43%.

[41] This is Herbert Klein's thesis in his *Slavery in the Americas: A Comparative Study of Virginia and Cuba*, Chicago, 1967. For a contrary point of view, see Knight, *op. cit.*

[42] Hubert S. Aimes, *A History of Slavery in Cuba: 1511-1868*, New York, 1907, pp. 143ff, suggests that the population mix was a political issue in Cuba.

[43] See Philip Curtin, "Epidemiology and the Slave Trade," *Political Science Quarterly* 83 (1968), 190-216.

important, they could have partially offset the production cost decreases permitted by the hypothesized lower slave import prices.[44] Thus, the impact estimates, which do not include this possible mortality effect, might be overstated. However, it is unlikely that increased slave imports would have dramatically affected average mortality rates and hence production costs would have increased only slightly—see following footnote for a numerical example.[45] Consequently, this argument, while technically correct, is of little importance.

EXPORT ESTIMATES

Exports from Africa would have been 820,000 more without suppression policies. This is more than the imports because of the mortality factor. More slaves had to be exported from Africa than the number imported because between 10 and 15 percent died en route to the markets. There is some evidence that the navy increased the mortality rates by forcing slavers to take precautions to avoid detection which resulted in even less sufferable conditions for slaves during the passage. However, several systematic investigations of middle passage mortality rates have shown that this effect, if it existed at all, was of minor importance.[46] Insofar as the navy did indeed increase slave mortality, its impact on the African exports was diminished from what

[44] In pointing out this mortality rate effect, Curtin did not draw out this implication for slave costs. His argument is that increasing slave imports in any given time would increase demand for slaves at future times even more; see Curtin, "The Slave Trade and the Atlantic Basin," p. 89.

[45] To illustrate the effect of increasing the number of unseasoned slaves on mortality rates, let us suppose that in 1830 the rural slave population of Cuba was about 260,000 and that about 30,000 of these had been imported within the past three years (which was approximately the seasoning period). Assuming that mortality of the unseasoned group was 10% per year, and 3% for the seasoned slaves, then average mortality for the entire rural population was about 3.85%. (The accounts of Worthy Park, a Jamaican plantation, provide interesting evidence of the impact of importing large numbers of slaves on slave mortality rates. See Michael Craton and James Walvin, *A Jamaican Plantation: The History of Worthy Park, 1670-1770*, Toronto, 1970, pp. 128ff) We now assume that the additional imports of slaves permitted by withdrawing the navy would have doubled the rate of importation into Cuba. This implies that in 1830 about 18% of the rural slave population would have been unseasoned, which further implies an average mortality rate for the entire population of 4.26%. Slave replacement costs therefore would have increased by 11%. But since slave replacement costs were only about 16% of total costs of producing sugar (see LeVeen, Appendix B), the total increase in sugar costs stemming from the mortality effect would have been only 1.5%.

[46] For an excellent survey of several sources, see Curtin, "Postscript on Mortality," in *The Atlantic Slave Trade*, Madison, Wis., 1969, pp. 275-281; also, Klein, "The Trade in African Slaves to Rio de Janeiro, 1795-1811: Estimates of Mortality and Patterns of Voyages," *J.A.H.* 10 (1969), 533-540, and Howard, p. 238.

it would have been had it not caused higher mortality rates. This analysis assumes that the navy increased average mortality rates by 2 percentage points which is about a 20 percent increase in the rate. It is impossible to determine from the existing evidence whether this is a high or a low estimate. If it is high, then the estimated impact on Africa of the suppression policies was greater than that recorded; if low, then the impact estimate is overstated.

The estimate of the suppression policy impact may overstate the true effect on Africa for another reason. The navy "rescued" almost 160,000 slaves while pursuing the slave trade, a number frequently taken as the measure of its effectiveness. If one assumes that the navy simply restored the 160,000 individuals to their homelands, then the export figures are a true estimate of the impact. However, slaves rescued by the navy were not usually restored to their homelands but rather went to Sierra Leone or Cuba, depending upon where they were captured. Thus, the actual numbers exported during the nineteenth century were larger than imports by the mortality factor plus the number of slaves captured by the navy and not returned home. The total exports from Africa *during the suppressed trade period* thus appears to have been the 1.5 million imports plus the number of slaves captured by the navy, 160,000, plus the mortality en route of 183,000, making a total actual disruption of 1,843,000. This compares with a disruption of 2.5 million exports which would have occurred without the intervention of the navy. Therefore, the policy impact on Africa was about 657,000 exports.

The numbers of slaves exported from Africa is only a partial indicator of the suffering and hardship imposed by the slave trade on African society. Insofar as the procurement of slaves involved death and dislocation for many Africans who were never exported in the slave trade, any reduction in export demand, which brought about a reduction in the level of damaging slaving activities, should be counted as a gain for Africa.[47] One estimate of the repercussions of slave exports on African society is that for every slave exported, one African

[47] One of the arguments sometimes made in favor of the slave trade was that the Africans exported were already living in some form of domestic slavery and so were simply exchanging masters (with the implicit understanding that white masters were more benevolent). This argument has been forcefully destroyed by those who know the institution of domestic slavery in Africa which did not resemble slavery in the Americas; see, for example, A. Norman Klein, "West African Unfree Labor Before and After the Rise of the Atlantic Slave Trade," in *Slavery in the New World,* ed. L. Foner and E. Genovese, Englewood Cliffs, N.J., 1969, and Allan Fisher and Humphrey Fisher, *Slavery and Muslim Society in Africa,* New York, 1971.

died either in the process of raiding or of being raided or in transit to the coast and waiting for a ship. Even if this is a high guess (we have no way of knowing), the 660,000 fewer exports must have led to fewer deaths in Africa.[48]

OTHER BRITISH POLICY IMPACTS

WE have been examining only one of several British policies which affected the volume of the slave trade. For example, British diplomatic efforts to bring about the enforcement of stricter antislave trade laws in Cuba and Brazil may have affected the costs of carrying on the trade within those countries. Corrupt governors and other officials in Cuba were brought to the attention of Spanish authorities by British observers, and the names and numbers of slave traders were recorded by the consul there. Such efforts may have increased the costs of making transactions, but they have not been estimated in this analysis. The importance of such activities would be difficult to determine; but British diplomatic pressure on Brazil during the 1840s to end the trade is credited with influencing the decision to abolish the trade, which was done abruptly in 1850, although the institution of slavery continued until 1888. It is possible that the trade would have continued to import thousands of Africans until abolition sentiment, which eventually forced the end of the institution of slavery and also forced the end to the trade many years after 1850.[49]

Abolition of the slave trade from British territories apparently curtailed any further significant illegal import of slaves into those territories. Had these territories been permitted to continue trading, it is not likely they would have maintained their eighteenth century averages of 15,000 per year because of their reaching maturity and because of a declining competitive position (which was not the result of labor costs) as their soils continued to wear out. However, assuming the slave populations continued to require replacement at a rate of 1 percent a year, an annual import to the British Caribbean Islands could have amounted to 7,000 slaves per year; there were 700,000 slaves in the region in 1831 at the time of emancipation. Thus, had

---

[48] In passing it should be noted that undoubtedly the navy had other impacts on Africa. African political systems and economies were disrupted by the cessation of the slave trade. These are topics which cannot be covered in an essay of this scope, however.

[49] See Bethell. One explanation which Bethell does not discuss is the fact that Brazil's slave labor force was close to 2.5 million slaves in 1850, and the economy had recently undergone a recession which had hurt coffee planters. It is possible that the demographic factors, and not political pressures, were decisive in bringing about the early end to the trade.

there been no abolition and had the British not declared the institution illegal, an additional 300,000 slave imports into the Caribbean (and, perhaps, more to the United States) could have resulted.

Finally, not all British policies helped reduce the slave trade's volume. The abolition of the prohibitive sugar duties on slave-grown sugar after 1848 had the effect of encouraging the demand for slaves in Cuba. Using parameter values already estimated for the earlier impact analysis, it is possible to derive a measure of the impact of the adoption of these policies. As shown in detail elsewhere, these policies probably accounted for an additional 50,000 slaves exported from Africa to Cuba after 1848, of which perhaps as many as 5,000 died en route.[50]

[50] See LeVeen, pp. 78-80.

IV

The Living and the Dead:
White Mortality in
West Africa, 1684-1732

K. G. DAVIES

Toward the end of *The Atlantic Slave Trade* Philip D. Curtin briefly discusses mortality among white crews of slave ships, the subject which first drew Clarkson to the Bristol docks. On 598 French slaving voyages between 1748 and 1792 one crew member in six died: "The death rate per voyage among the crew was uniformly higher than the death rate among slaves in transit at the same period." [1] Clarkson's own estimates for Bristol and Liverpool slavers were even higher, in excess of 200 per 1,000 per voyage, five times greater than the mortality of crews in the East Indian trade and twenty times greater than in the Newfoundland trade. [2] These data led Curtin in the last paragraph of his book to ponder the social cost of the slave trade to Europeans. Taking his estimate of 2½ million slaves exported from Africa by British slave traders between 1690 and 1807, and applying ratios of one slave to two-thirds of a ton of shipping and one seaman to every five tons, it appears that about ⅓ million British seamen were employed in the trade in these 117 years. [3] If something like the French death rate of one in six were found to prevail among the British, it would follow that about 50,000 seamen died in the slave trade. This kind of arithmetic is unsatisfactory; but, for the want of evidence as comprehensive as the French, it is difficult to improve on.

Curtin points out that in computing the social cost to Europe of the slave trade the fate of shore-based white personnel in Africa must also be taken into account. [4] In this more restricted aspect of the subject British sources are better, at least for the late seventeenth and early eighteenth centuries. The purpose of this essay is to explore those

[1] Philip D. Curtin, *The Atlantic Slave Trade: A Census*, Madison, Wis., 1969, pp. 282-283.   [2] *Ibid.*, p. 285.
[3] K. G. Davies, *The Royal African Company*, New York, 1970, pp. 193-194, for discussion of these ratios.
[4] *Atlantic Slave Trade*, p. 286, and see the same author's *The Image of Africa*, London, 1965, esp. pp. 483-487.

sources and to examine living conditions and mortality rates among Europeans on the West African slave stations.

SOURCES

THE records used in this investigation are those of the Royal African Company (1672-1750), and principally the "Lists of the Living and the Dead." [5] These lists were compiled in Africa and sent to London where they were entered in books kept for that purpose: the originals are not known to have survived. They were meant to be made up at regular intervals, but in practice, either through the laziness of the Company's officials or through lack of opportunity to send, the intervals were irregular. Occasionally as many as four lists were sent from the Gold Coast in one year; sometimes three; more often two; at times only one. Fewer lists were sent from the other stations (Gambia, Sierra Leone, etc.) than from the Gold Coast, and at even less regular intervals. For the purpose of collecting mortality data this irregularity does not matter much: each list was intended to report on the period back to the date of the last list. Unfortunately there are gaps, small ones resulting from inefficient record keeping in Africa or London, and some larger ones resulting from the disappearance of entire books. These make it impossible to compile figures for the whole period of the Company's history. Luckily enough evidence remains for parts to be studied in a reasonably coherent and continuous way.

The lists record the names and ranks (or trades) of the living on the given day, the names of the dead with date of death, the names of discharged persons, and, with less consistency, other casualties such as desertions, postings, and promotions. One reason for keeping them was to enable the Company in London to keep track of the payment of wages. Some men received all their pay in Africa, the sums being credited to the account of the station. Others were paid partly in Africa and partly by allotments to dependents in England. Pay began on landing in Africa, though an advance of wages before sailing was customary, and ended at death or discharge. Hence the need for accurate and up-to-date reports. The question of "dead pay"—failing to report a death in Africa so that someone could go on drawing the wages—naturally arises. All that can be said is that, among the many reproaches in letters from London to Africa, this particular charge does not occur often enough to raise serious doubts about the lists. If "dead pay" was being claimed silently and successfully, the effect would of course be to diminish the number of deaths notified to Lon-

[5] Great Britain, Public Record Office (hereafter, P.R.O.), T. 70/1441-1448.

don: nobody had an interest in reporting a death that had not taken place.

At the same time it must be admitted that the record-keeping was crude and that the statistics derived therefrom must also be regarded as crude. Men, and not merely those in transit or just arrived, simply vanish from the lists. There is an appearance of greater consistency and perhaps of greater accuracy in the eighteenth century than in the seventeenth: the Company's failure to compete with the separate traders in the slave trade may have given their writers more leisure to keep establishment records.

Besides the "Lists of the Living and the Dead," some books of passenger lists have been preserved for the period under examination.[6] They appear not to be a reliable record of the total number of men sent to Africa (see below) but they are useful in the reconstruction of the service of an individual: they make it possible to establish the date of his landing in Africa, and hence, the number of days, weeks, months or years he lived there. Some passenger lists record ages and nationalities of men going to Africa.

MEN

SOME men were recruited in Africa. There were a few deserters from Dutch or Danish service; some Portuguese or mulattoes with names like Gomes or Lopez; the occasional volunteer of any nationality from a passing ship; and a handful of free Africans ("Black Tom, cooper") or half-breeds ("Edward Barter, linguister"). The Company could not afford to be particular. In April 1722, when 52 pirates were hanged at Cape Coast, 19 others, according to Captain Johnson's *General History of the Pirates*, were sentenced to the marginally less severe punishment of serving the African Company for seven years: [7] 12 appear in the "Lists of the Living and the Dead," of whom 7 died within two months of being sentenced.

These occasional recruitments in Africa amounted to only a small fraction of the total number of men in service: the great majority came out from England and were English. Thus, of 563 persons enrolled as passengers on the Company's ships between 1701 and 1720 and whose nationalities are recorded, 510 were "English" or (from 1707) "British"; 20 were "Scottish" or (from 1707) "North British"; Welsh were not distinguished from English. Of the rest, 7 were Dutch, 4 German, 4

---

[6] *Ibid.*, T. 70/1435-1439.

[7] Charles Johnson, *A General History of the Pirates*, ed. Philip Gosse, London, 1927, II, 84-87.

K. G. DAVIES

TABLE 1. ENROLLMENTS FOR AFRICA 1694-1732

5-Year Period	Gold Coast	Whydah	Gambia	Sherbro	S. Leone	Cabinda	Total
1694-98	251	—	99	43	—	—	393
1699-1703	213	—	165	53	43	—	474
1704-08	163	—	79	—	15	—	257
1709-13	267	—	36	19	18	—	340
1714-18	141	—	26	61	—	—	228
1719-23	256	130	260	—	69	50	765
1724-28	64	13	47	—	39	—	163
1729-32 (4 years)	134	—	106	—	—	—	240
TOTAL	1,489	143	818	176	184	50	2,860

NOTE: These figures refer to a continuously unprofitable period in the Company's history. Greater numbers probably went out between 1672 and 1688.

Irish (many more Irish went out in 1721), 3 French, 3 "Guinea," 3 "black," 2 "Jamaican," and 1 each Swede, Dane, Swiss, Muscovite, Indian, and "Foreign."

Most recruits can be placed in one of three principal classes: officers, tradesmen, and soldiers. Although soldiers were sometimes regarded as tradesmen, it was very rare for anyone to be made an officer who had gone out in a lower rank. Illiteracy was probably the bar. The Company's northern stations (Gambia, Sierra Leone, Sherbro) were headed by an agent or governor, the Gold Coast establishment either by an agent-general or governor-general or by a committee of three chief merchants. Next came chief factors and factors who commanded smaller stations like Accra, and below them writers who were generally young men of 17 or 18 years and upwards. Other officers appearing in the lists were: a lieutenant in charge of the soldiers, a surveyor, a minister, a surgeon, and a register. Salaries were to some extent negotiable. Sir Dalby Thomas, who commanded on the Gold Coast from 1703 to 1711, earned £1000 a year plus allowances plus a commission, but this was quite exceptional.[8] In 1702 the standard rate of pay for chief merchants was £300 a year plus £100 for diet, for chief factors £100 plus £50, for factors £40 plus £50, and for writers £10 plus £40. By 1720 writers were getting £30 a year salary.

Tradesmen included armorers, carpenters, coopers, masons, bricklayers, blacksmiths, and occasionally miners. Their standard rate of pay in 1702 was £30 a year with £15 for diet, but bigger money had often to be paid to attract competent men. Judging by the complaints

[8] Davies, p. 253.

86

of the Company's officers in Africa, the skills of these tradesmen were inadequately tested before recruitment. Of about equal rank with the tradesmen were the sergeants, gunners, surgeon's mates and bomboys, some of whom were promoted from among the soldiers, some appointed in England. A few sailors were recruited for manning coasting vessels.

By far the largest category of recruits consisted of soldiers, presumably quite untrained. Of 894 persons enrolled for the Gold Coast between 1694 and 1713, 170 were officers, 158 tradesmen, 480 soldiers. Soldiers were paid £12 a year, with £13 for diet.

The ages of men going to Africa are stated in certain passenger lists, though their reliability cannot be vouched for. The average is higher than expected: 25.6 years for 695 men of all ranks enrolled between 1701 and 1720. The oldest recruit observed was 64, the youngest (children apart) 12. The average age of officers was slightly less than that of tradesmen and soldiers, owing to the recruitment of youthful writers. One might guess that a good many men entering the African service had already failed at some other job.

The list of enrollments, as already mentioned, are of doubtful accuracy. In most cases where a check is possible fewer persons arrived in Africa than were enrolled in England, owing to discharges and desertions before the ship sailed as well as to deaths *en voyage*. On the other hand, more men can sometimes be found on a station than can be accounted for by the enrollment lists. Table 1 is offered, with these reservations, as a rough guide to the number of men going to Africa and to the relative importance of the different stations. There is a further qualification that men for Whydah were commonly sent on ships bound for the Gold Coast: many more than 143 were posted there in this period.

WOMEN AND CHILDREN

AT times the Company was mildly encouraging toward wives wishing to accompany their husbands to Africa. Although the number who did so was small, it is greater than expected: out of 3,114 enrollments from 1694 to 1744, 106 (3.4 percent) were women, mostly wives with a few maidservants. One man, William Browne, in the Cape Coast garrison in 1694, turned out to be a woman, Mary Wilson.

In some cases, perhaps all, wives of tradesmen and soldiers were taken on the strength and given an allowance for food of £12 a year on the understanding that they would nurse the sick when required.[9]

---

[9] Great Britain, P.R.O., T. 70/55, pp. 2-3.

Now and again, but rarely, a complete family can be found traveling together. Such were the Levenses, father (a surgeon), mother, two children, and maid, who sailed for Whydah in 1721. They landed on 27 May: all five were dead within six weeks.

Of the 106 recorded enrollments of women 44 took place in 1720-1721 when the Duke of Chandos was trying to put new life into the moribund Company. Not as many as 44 sailed: the fate of 22 who did was as follows. One was drowned at Madeira, eleven died within two months of landing in Africa and four more in the third to eighth months after arrival, four came home after a very short stay, one cut her throat after three months, and one deserted with her husband and child and may have become a pirate.

MORTALITY ON THE GOLD COAST: 1684-1732

THE Company's principal fort on the Gold Coast was Cape Coast Castle. There were smaller forts or factories at Accra, Anashan, Anomabu, Dixcove, Egya, Fort Royal (the old Danish fort Frederixborg), Kommenda, Sekondi, Tantamkweri, and Winnebah, though not all were continuously occupied. Cape Coast generally contained between 50 and 100 men in the early eighteenth century, the larger out-stations between 10 and 20, the smaller between 1 and 5. Depending on the incidence of mortality and the flow of recruits from England, the total strength of the Gold Coast establishment fluctuated between 100 and 200 men: the average in the thirty-nine years to be examined was 141.

"Lists of the Living and the Dead" are unsatisfactory before 1684, and have not survived for 1698-1702 or 1713-1716. As already mentioned the number of lists compiled varied from year to year. In Table 2 the number of men alive and in service has been obtained from the *first* list surviving for each year. This was likelier to have been compiled in the earlier than in the later months of the year, and was commonly dated in March or April: the high season for arrival of recruits (see below) and well before the deadliest months of the year, June and July (see below). Had the *last* list in each year been selected, the figures obtained would probably have been different. It is important to make this clear because the average number of men in service furnishes the dividend for calculating a kind of death rate. In addition to men reported dead and discharged, a number deserted on the coast, were kidnapped by pirates, or were posted away on the Company's service. These are difficult to compute but seem not to have averaged more than 3 or 4 a year over the whole period, possibly fewer.

The average death toll of 38 per annum is 27 percent of the average

TABLE 2. GOLD COAST 1684-1732

Period	Average No. of Living	Average No. of Dead p.a.	Average No. of Discharged p.a.
1684-88	153	40	13
1689-93	152	35	25
1694-97	142	49	8
(4 years)			
1703-07	157	34	14
1708-12	141	36	10
1717-21	125	38	14
1722-26	130	40	8
1728-32	127	35	14
Average over 39 years	141	38	12

number of living, which is probably as near to a death rate as it is possible to get in a population of this kind. It is of course extremely crude, owing to fluctuations in the size of the establishment at different times of the year; and it conceals a good deal of variation both from quinquennial period to period and from year to year. The average death rate for 1694-1697 was 34.5 percent; for 1703-1707, only 21.6 percent. The highest in a single year appears to be 57 percent in 1694; the lowest, 13 in 1691.

The average discharge rate over thirty-nine years was 8.5 percent, rising as high as 16.4 percent in 1689-1693 and falling as low as 5.6 percent in 1694-1697. All signs point to unusually healthy conditions prevailing on the Gold Coast from about 1687 to about 1691 (death rate in these years 17.2 percent, discharge rate 11.8 percent) followed by an unusually sickly time from about 1692 to about 1695 (death rate, 39.5 percent, discharge rate, 11 percent).

MORTALITY AMONG NEW ARRIVALS

ONE reason for caution in accepting this death rate is that it does no kind of justice to the heavy incidence of mortality among men newly arrived from Europe. The purpose of this section is to examine that incidence: the method is to use examples drawn from different parts of the coast. These examples were chosen for convenience, where coherent lists of enrollments and mortality coincide.

(I) GOLD COAST 1695-1696

Four ships, *Averilla, John Bonadventure, Falconberg,* and *Kendal,* arrived at Cape Coast between 9 January 1695 and 13 August 1696.

A total of 84 passengers were enrolled in England: 12 officers, 19 tradesmen, 5 sailors (for coasting sloops), 47 soldiers, and 1 woman. Five of the tradesmen (all carpenters) deserted before embarkation; 6 men died *en voyage;* 73 landed. Of those who landed, 7 (9.6 percent) died in the first four months, 34 (42 percent) in the first year. Owing to defects in the records the fate of the 39 who survived the first year is not in every instance ascertainable: only 3 are known to have been discharged from the Company's service but 9 were still alive after six years, 2 after eleven years and 1 after seventeen years. Despite arriving at Cape Coast toward the end of a singularly unhealthy time (1692-1695), this party by comparison with others was a fairly lucky one.

(II) GOLD COAST 1719-1720

Seven ships, *Victory, Mary, Anne, Generous Jenny, King Solomon, Hannibal,* and *Sarah,* arrived at Cape Coast between 4 February 1719 and 18 January 1720. The number of passengers enrolled in England was 79: 23 officers, 11 tradesmen, 38 soldiers, 3 women, 1 child, 2 blacks. Ten, including two of the women, the child, and the blacks, were not recorded on arrival: either they did not sail or they died *en voyage* or they were not taken onto the Gold Coast establishment. Of the 69 who are known to have landed, 29 (42 percent) died in the first four months, 43 (64 percent) in the first twelve months. In this example the subsequent careers of the 26 who survived the first year are reasonably well-documented: 7 died in the second year, 2 in the third, 2 in the fourth, 1 in the fifth, and 3 in the seventh; 6 are known to have been discharged after periods of service of from one to seven years. The fate of the remaining 5 is not known: 1 disappears from the record after a year's service, the other 4 lived at least five years but are not reported as discharged. Despite the death of two-thirds of this party in the first year, at least 10 (14.5 percent) were alive and in service four years after landing.

(III) WHYDAH (OUIDAH) 1721

The *Carlton* for Whydah had a passenger list of 61. Seven deserted or were discharged before sailing, but one more must have been recruited: 55 appear to have embarked, 2 died *en voyage,* and 53 landed on 27 May 1721. Thirty-seven (69.6 percent) of those who landed died in the first four months, nearly all of them in the first two months. Only four more died in the rest of the first year, making 41 (77.3 percent). Of the 12 who did not die in the first year, 6 had been discharged soon after landing and 1 more was discharged after twelve months. It follows that of the 53 who landed, there remained in the Company's service one year later just 5: 2 of them survived to be discharged and 1 lived to 1729 and was then "seiz'd by the Dahomys and supposed to be dead."

The swiftness with which death overtook more than two-thirds of this party appears on the evidence examined to be exceptional. It is unlikely to have been caused by sickness on shipboard. The same ship landed 14 men and 2 women at Cape Coast, only 3 of whom died in 1721 and 4 of whom were still alive in 1730.

(iv) GAMBIA 1721

In 1720 the Company planned to extend its activities in the Gambia. After sending no men there for four years, three transports, *Otter*, *Gambia Castle*, and *Martha*, were prepared. Part, perhaps the greatest part, of the recruiting was undertaken by Colonel David Dunbar (presumably the same who was later lieutenant-governor of New Hampshire) who was expected to go out himself as governor. At the last moment he did not go, occasioning a number of desertions among those he had recruited. One ship, the *Otter*, recruited her complement in Ireland, the only transport in Company service known to have done so. More women than usual were attached to this party.[10]

The total enrollment on the three ships was 200 but not that many embarked. Some deserted; some fell sick, the *Martha's* captain being instructed to put "incurables" ashore; 9 were formally discharged before sailing, including a "soldier" aged 10 and a man found to have been "convicted of felony at the Old Bailey on account of My Ld. Cobham's Jewells." Probably about 170 sailed. At least one man deserted at Madeira, and the chaplain also left the party following "barbarous treatment" from the captain of the *Otter*. There landed in the Gambia 160 persons, the largest number sent there in any year in the Company's history. *Otter* arrived on 4 February 1721, *Martha* on 2 April, and *Gambia Castle* on 9 May. There were 17 women and 5 children.

On 12 June 1721, 48 men, 1 woman and 1 child deserted the fort, joined the crew of the *Gambia Castle* in seizing that vessel, sailed to the West Indies and turned pirates.[11] One of the deserters, Lieutenant John Massey, surrendered himself in England and was hanged in 1723; at least one other was hanged at St. Kitts. These 50 deserters have been removed from the following calculations of mortality.

[10] Details in this and next paragraph come from *ibid.*, T. 70/46, pp. 51ff; *ibid.*, T. 70/55, pp. 1ff.

[11] J. M. Gray, *A History of the Gambia*, Cambridge, England, 1940, pp. 167ff.

91

Of the 110 who did not desert, 5 were discharged at once or soon after landing, 49 (44.5 percent) died in the first four months, and 79 (71.8 percent) in the first twelve months. One year after landing, there remained, out of the 160 who went ashore 26 still in the Company's service: 5 of these 26 died in the second year of service and 2 in the third year; 2 were killed in 1725 when James Fort blew up; 2 served at least seven years; 9 are known to have been discharged after serving four years or more. Special mention must be made of Anthony Rogers (Roggers, Rodgers) who went out as factor in the *Martha* in 1721: he rose to be governor of James Fort in 1725, was discharged to England, reenlisted and returned to the Gambia for a second tour, again survived, and was finally discharged in 1733.

(v) GAMBIA 1705

This example is based on a list compiled on 3 March 1705 which furnishes data on 81 men who had entered the Company's service in 1703-1705. The immediately preceding "Lists of the Living and the Dead" have not survived, and it is possible that the deaths of some of the new arrivals in those years had already been posted to London before this record was compiled. This example may therefore be not perfectly comparable with those already given.

Working from the information provided, 7 (8.6 percent) of these 81 men died in the first four months of service and 38 (47 percent) in the first twelve months. Of the remaining 43 there is no further report on 13; at least 15 were still alive after three years service; and 3 are known to have been discharged.

(VI) SIERRA LEONE 1722

Like no. v above, this example is taken from a contemporary report (i.e., has not been constructed on cards) and is subject to the same qualification. The report is dated 4 April 1722 and supplies data on 78 men in Sierra Leone: 4 of them, at the time of the report, had neither died nor completed one year's service and have been removed from the following computation. Of the remaining 74, 2 had been discharged and 16 had completed their first year; 30 (40.5 percent) had died within four months of entering the service and 54 (73 percent) within twelve months. Five of the survivors had served for at least four years.

(VII) SUMMARY

Assembling the above data, the results are given in Table 3. These six examples exhibit much variation, as one would expect. Three (nos. iii, iv, and vi above) show heavy mortality in the first two months; one (no. ii) shows moderate to heavy mortality; the other two

TABLE 3. 460 NEW ARRIVALS IN AFRICA 1695-1722

Month of Death	(i)	(ii)	(iii)	(iv)	(v)	(vi)	Total	Percentage of Persons Landed	Cumulative Percentage
1st	–	9	11	3	–	9	32	7.0	7.0
2nd	1	5	24	29	3	14	76	16.5	23.5
3rd	2	9	–	7	3	7	28	6.1	29.6
4th	4	6	2	10	1	–	23	5.0	34.6
5th	12	3	2	8	3	2	30	6.5	41.1
6th	5	1	–	11	6	2	25	5.4	46.5
7th	4	5	1	5	8	4	27	6.0	52.5
8th	3	1	1	2	7	12	26	5.7	58.2
9th	–	2	–	3	3	–	8	1.7	59.9
10th	3	–	–	–	1	–	4	0.8	60.7
11th	–	1	–	–	2	3	6	1.3	62.0
12th	–	1	–	1	1	1	4	0.8	62.8
Dead in 1st Year	34	43	41	79	38	54	289		
Discharged in 1st Year	–	–	7	5	–	1	13		
Survivors after 1st Year	39	26	5	26 [a]	43	19 [b]	158		

[a] Omitting 50 deserters.

[b] Plus 4 who at date of report had neither died nor completed a year's service.

show hardly any. Taking the two Gold Coast examples (nos. i and ii), 25.2 percent died in the first four months and 54 percent in the first year; the comparable figures for the other stations (nos. iii-vi) are 38.6 percent and 66.7 percent. These variations make it necessary to treat with caution any general statement based on Table 3.

With this qualification, it appears:

1) One man in three died in the first four months in Africa, more than three men in five in the first year.
2) In three examples, the second month was the deadliest. This apart, other months down to and including the eighth were about equally deadly. Thereafter the number of deaths fell sharply.
3) The Gold Coast was healthier than other stations.[12] It is to be

[12] This is not the view of Alexander Bryson, *Report on the Climate and Principal Diseases of the African Station*, London, 1847, p. 15. But in the period considered here, living conditions were better at Cape Coast than anywhere else. There were more men, hence better facilities. Whereas the Gambia, Sierra Leone, and Sherbo stations were deserted and reoccupied more than once, Cape Coast was always occupied and there were always some old hands there to advise and encourage newcomers. It is quite feasible that Cape Coast was more hospitable to Europeans about 1700 for reasons which have nothing to do with "climate."

remembered that more men went there than to all the other stations added together.

The problem of how many of the men who survived the first year lived to be discharged has not been tackled statistically because the number involved was at almost all times so small that occasional defects in the records could produce major distortions. A personal impression is that the myth of men who survived the first year living for a long times does not gain much support from these records. Three years was the standard term of engagement. Certainly there were some who survived three years, chose to stay in Africa and soldiered on for a dozen years or more: there were even one or two who went home and came back for a second tour. Such cases were exceptional. Certainly, the number of deaths of second- and third-year men, were it firmly established, would be much smaller than for first-year men; but this is because there were far fewer of them left to die. Taking the data in Tables 2 and 3 and adding scraps of other evidence accumulated in the course of this investigation, it is tentatively proposed that out of 10 men going to Africa at this time, 6 died in the first year, 2 more in the second to seventh years, and 1 was discharged: the fate of the tenth is best left in doubt.

SEASONAL MORTALITY

PREVAILING explanations of the incidence of sickness and death in the tropics attached much importance to a damp climate. However inaccurately the medical connection may have been made, the statistical correlation between mortality and the "rainy season" seems to have been a close one. Tables 4 and 5 present an analysis by months of 1,517 deaths on the Gold Coast and 458 deaths in the Gambia.

TABLE 4. MONTHLY MORTALITY ON THE GOLD COAST 1683-1734

Month	1683-89	1690-99	1702-14	1716-22	1725-34	Total	Percentage
January	29	17	31	20	22	119	7.9
February	21	14	26	18	21	100	6.6
March	22	23	19	30	22	116	7.8
April	11	30	33	45	23	142	9.4
May	17	31	28	38	23	137	9.0
June	16	59	48	46	34	203	13.4
July	36	48	43	42	40	209	13.8
August	23	21	44	29	18	135	8.9
September	8	17	19	16	10	70	4.6
October	16	15	21	21	16	89	5.9
November	32	20	18	24	11	105	6.2
December	12	8	32	27	13	92	6.0

TABLE 5. MONTHLY MORTALITY IN THE GAMBIA 1684-1726

Month	1684-89	1690-99	1702-14	1716-26	Total	Percentage
January	3	11	8	5	27	6.0
February	8	10	5	4	27	6.0
March	7	4	4	12	27	6.0
April	4	4	2	6	16	3.5
May	5	4	4	15	28	6.1
June	10	10	7	14	41	8.9
July	21	12	20	25	78	17.0
August	15	18	13	32	78	17.0
September	8	7	17	11	43	9.4
October	4	5	14	11	34	7.4
November	4	7	4	8	23	5.0
December	8	10	12	6	36	7.8

Some variation between the two regions will be noticed. On the Gold Coast, June and July were the deadliest months of the year; August was better, and September and October were the healthiest months of the year. In the Gambia, July and August were worst, accounting for a third of all deaths; June to September for more than half. April in Gambia, with only one-fifth the number of deaths recorded in July, appears singular.

There is some evidence that this seasonal rhythm was appreciated in London and taken into account in timing the arrival of ships carrying passengers to the Gold Coast. Of 51 ships carrying ten or more men to Cape Coast, 14 arrived in the healthy months of September-December, 31 in the relatively healthy months of January-April, and only 6 in the deadly months of May-August. For the Gambia, a very small sample of 17 ships shows a roughly even distribution of arrivals through the year: 5 in January-April, 7 in May-August, and 5 in September-December. The British Army seems not to have given much thought to the timing of the arrival of fresh troops on foreign stations until 1767.[13]

OTHER EVIDENCE

THE nonstatistical material in the Company's archives (letters, minutes, etc.) has not been thoroughly searched in connection with this inquiry, and might yield some information. Little is to be expected in the way of identification of diseases: the period under consideration is well before the publication of Lind's *Essay on Diseases*

[13] File on this subject in Great Britain, P.R.O., C.O. 5/167, fols. 33-35d, 66-69d.

Incidental to Europeans in Hot Climates (1768). "Fevers" and "fluxes" are the usual diagnoses.

The singular experience of the Gambia party in 1721 produced a certain amount of comment, much of it connected with the mass desertion of 50 persons in the Company's service and the seizing of the *Gambia Castle* but some concerning the fate of those who did not desert. A letter written by the Company in London on 23 January 1722 contains the following passage:

> We are sorry to find the Mortallity & sickness has been so great amongst you, wch we presume might be occasioned by the rains coming so soon after your arrival [February-May 1721], but as we hope those who have survived are by this time pretty well seasoned, we hope they as well as those since sent over will enjoy their healths better & be more capable of rendring the Compa. the service they were appointed for.[14]

A reply to this letter from the Company's agent in Gambia, dated 17 September following, suggests that 1722 was as bad as 1721:

> The latter part of this rainy season has been very fatal to our people, the old standards as well as the new, as your honours will perceive by our list of the living & dead, which with the death of all our surgeons strikes such a damp upon all our people that they give themselves up for dead as soon as they are taken ill, which no doubt contributes much towards it, for it has been often observed that few people Escape in this Country who believe they shall dye in it.[15]

Several interesting points are made in these letters, but none more deserving of attention than the Company's hope that in future more men would live "& be more capable of rendering the Compa. the service they were appointed for." This pragmatic reaction to the news from Gambia appears to be typical of the Company's attitude toward the death of so many of its employees.

Assets at Death

Surviving the first year did not mean making one's fortune: the proof, if any be needed, is furnished by inventories of the assets of 123 persons dying on the Gold Coast between 1718 and 1722.[16] Customarily, the possessions of the deceased were inventoried on the

[14] *Ibid.*, T. 70/55, p. 22.
[15] *Ibid.*, T. 70/27, Gambia, 17 September 1722.
[16] *Ibid.*, T. 70/1499-1500.

day of death or the day following; his personal effects sold; and the wages due to him computed. The result was a gross sum, expressed in marks, ounces, etc., of gold, from which deductions were then made for personal debts, debts owing to the Company, and funeral expenses. The balance, if any, was remitted to the next-of-kin in England.

Of 47 soldiers whose inventories have survived none was worth, gross, as much as £10; 17 were worth between £5 and £10; and 30 less than £5.[17] Much the biggest item was wages due; personal effects were often no more than a shirt and trousers. Subtracting debts and funeral expenses, only one soldier left more than £5 to be remitted to England; 30 of the 47 left nothing at all.

The officers did a little better. Inventories of 38 agents, factors, etc., dying between 1718 and 1722, show that after deductions 5 left more than £100 to be remitted to England and 5 others between £50 and £100. On the other hand, 14 officers left less than £25 net, 9 left nothing, and 1 left a debit balance. From the entire sample of 123 men of all ranks only two can be said to have done well. One was William Johnson, Agent-General at Cape Coast, who died on 14 June 1718 after about fifteen months service in Africa: he left £2,689 2s. 8½d. net, part of which may represent effects brought out from England. The other was Thomas Bennett, Chief at Accra, who died on 25 April 1718 after about two years on the Gold Coast: £423 2s. 3½d. was remitted to England on his account and he had credit in the Company's books for a further £431 12s. 3½d.

CONCLUSION

"THE African disease environment," Dr. Curtin states, "claimed the life of half the European merchants, factors, officials and soldiers sent out to man the slave trading posts."[18] In the period comprehended within this investigation the statistics are grimmer, with well over one-half dead in the first year and no certainty that more than one-tenth got back to England. Whether the experience of the Dutch and French in Africa was as bad remains to be seen. Bosman thought not: ". . . if the State of Health in *Guinea* be computed by the number of the *English* which dye here, certainly this Country must have a much more unhealthful Name in *England* than with us." Elsewhere he admitted that "few come hither who are not at first seized by a Sickness which carries off a great many."[19]

[17] Valuing one ounce of gold at £4.
[18] Curtin, *Atlantic Slave Trade*, p. 286.
[19] William Bosman, *A New and Accurate Description of the Coast of Guinea*, London, 1967, pp. 50, 106.

Why did white men expose themselves to these conditions? A complete answer to this question would tell more about English society in the eighteenth century than about Englishmen in Africa. Low as wages were in the African Company's service they were marginally better than at home. The common soldier earned £12 a year in Africa with £13 added for food, say 10s. a week. In London about 1700 an unskilled laborer received 1s. 8d. a day, rising to 2s. a day by 1750; less in other parts of the country; and in some places less than half as much.[20] And in Africa a man could be sure of continuous employment as long as he wanted it. Unemployment at home, or underemployment, probably explained the majority of enrollments. As for the risks of the African station, the three chances in five of being dead within a year, it is unlikely that they were known beforehand to recruits, and it is a moral certainty that the Company's recruiters kept quiet about them. No doubt the officers had a better idea of what they were letting themselves in for. They gambled with their lives in a version of Russian roulette in which more chambers were loaded than empty. A few did well, though none except Sir Dalby Thomas with his £1,000 a year and his commission did magnificently. The majority died early and died poor. It is possible to see them as victims of their own greed and inhumanity, but the same can hardly be said of the rank and file. In them it is difficult to remember anything but more victims of the slave trade.

[20] Charles Wilson, *England's Apprenticeship*, London, 1965, p. 344, based on Gilboy.

V

Comment

GEORGE SHEPPERSON

ALTHOUGH THIS Conference is entitled "Comparative Systems of Slavery," it is limited in its range to the Western Hemisphere and, with a few glances at eastern Africa, largely to West Africa. It is, in fact, about a system of slavery rather than about systems: about the trans-Atlantic system stemming from Western Europe and West Africa in the fifteenth and sixteenth centuries down to the last years of the nineteenth century. What the essays in this Conference volume are comparing is a collection of variants within a single system. This, of course, is a highly valuable exercise and may well throw new light on many aspects of the trans-Atlantic system. But it is not a comparison of systems of slavery in the way that it would have been if, for example, the four centuries of the trans-Atlantic system of slavery had been compared with, at its greatest extent, the trans-Saharan slave trade to the North African coast during the seventeen centuries in which it is known to have existed or, at a lesser level, during the twelve centuries following the Arab conquest of North Africa. Nor, for that matter, have comparisons been attempted between the trans-Atlantic system of slavery and that other notable trans-oceanic system, the Indian Ocean slave trade which, in one form or another, was "probably a constant factor"[1] on the southern and eastern African coasts from the second century A.D. to the end of the nineteenth century. It may be argued that, in numbers and economic consequences, the trans-Saharan and the Indian Ocean slave trades, although they lasted over much longer periods than the trans-Atlantic slave system, were of much less importance. Professor J. D. Fage, to be sure, has called sharply into question the estimate of 34 to 24 million slaves from West to North Africa provided by Raymond Mauny; and has claimed that "it is safer to conclude that, extending over a very much longer period, the trans-Saharan trade removed fewer Negroes than the Atlantic trade, and that its effect on the West African population

---

[1] Joseph E. Harris, *The African Presence in Asia: Consequences of the East African Slave Trade*, Evanston, 1971, p. 5, quoting G. Mathew, "The East African Coast until the Coming of the Portuguese," in R. Oliver and G. Mathews, eds., *History of East Africa*, London, 1963, pp. 101, 121.

99

during the time the Atlantic trade was operating was relatively minor." [2] In a similar fashion, Professor Joseph E. Harris in his recently published, pioneering work on the African presence in Asia, has implied that the Indian Ocean trade was less than nineteenth century abolitionists like David Livingstone believed, on the grounds that "the trade from East Africa did not become the kind of big business that developed in West Africa." [3] Both of these generalizations are open to question. But, even if one accepts them and gives to the trans-Atlantic system of slavery pride of place in all matters of scale, I think that it is true to say that only a limited light can be thrown on it by an examination of variants within it. Comparisons must be developed outside the system as well as within it. The two obvious external comparisons are the trans-Saharan and the Indian Ocean slave trades. But there are many others—as Bruno Lasker's often-neglected but valuable first chapter, "Memories and Remnants of Slavery," should remind us.[4]

My approach, indeed, to the four admirable papers on aspects of the trans-Atlantic slave trade which we have before us will be on the macrocosmic rather than on the microcosmic level. Many points of detail, I am sure, I can leave in others' hands, particularly those questions which Professors Anstey and LaVeen have raised about Professor Curtin's very important work.

The first general question that I want to raise is one of chronology. The essays in this conference volume, of course, are necessarily somewhat arbitrarily selected, following, as they must, the current research interests of their authors. Nevertheless, bearing this in mind, I cannot help regretting that we have only an essay on the volume and profitability of the Atlantic slave trade after 1761 and not one as well on the period before this. Of course, as Professor K. G. Davies tells us, from a British point of view, the period from 1694 to 1732 in the fortunes of the Royal African Company was one of continuous unprofitability. But this was not necessarily the case with other European states. Professor Postma's useful study of the Dutch West India Company takes us back to 1621, although his attention is not focused primarily on numbers of slaves and profitability. His Table 1 on Slave Origins, 1700-1735, however, gives interesting detail. It would have been useful if he had elaborated on the "Mixed and Miscellaneous" category in this. While not so large as the Gold Coast, Slave Coast, and

---

[2] J. D. Fage, "Slavery and the Slave Trade in the Context of West African History," *Journal of African History* 10 (1969), 399.

[3] Harris, *The African Presence*, p. xiii.

[4] Lasker, *Human Bondage in Southeast Asia*, Chapel Hill, 1950.

Angolan groups of slaves, they are, comparatively speaking, not a small group, and many of us would be interested to learn more of the territorial composition of this group. Concentration on the post-1761 period often operates in a teleological atmosphere because it is difficult to avoid the question of the relationship between capital accumulation and the emergence of the Industrial Revolution. It is not, I think, accidental that Professor Anstey's paper finishes with a reference to this problem.

Furthermore, by concentrating on the period from the 1760s onward, one's attention is shifted from the full sweep of the Atlantic slave trade since the late fifteenth century. Not only does this mean that one misses many interesting case studies—for example, the correspondence and papers in the Sheffield Central Library of Benjamin Spencer, London Merchant, and his slaving voyages in 1755 and 1756 —but I think it also has the tendency to divert one's attention from the multilateral rather than bilateral nature of trade in the Atlantic economy from about the opening of the sixteenth to the end of the eighteenth century. Could the supply of colonial primary products have developed as fast as it did without the supply of African slaves? When Professor Anstey writes, ". . . since our concern is with the slave *trade* and its profits we can ignore what was a possible profit in the operation of a slave-based economy," this tendency seems to be at work. I think we must ask ourselves if it is altogether a realistic exercise to attempt to abstract the slave trade from the total Atlantic economy in the period from, roughly, 1500 to 1800—or, indeed, later.

An example of this sort of problem is, I feel, provided in Professor Anstey's attempt to "establish a reasonable percentage figure for the deductions made from gross sale figures." Speaking of some of the items in such an estimate, he declares that "payment was usually made in the form of bills of exchange at up to twenty-four months or even more. To get his money earlier, the slave merchant had, of course, to accept a discount." He then goes on to quote Thomas Clarkson on the ramifications of all this: "In six months . . . [the slave trader's bill] for spirits is brought him. . . . In fourteen, he must account for his East India assortments, and in eighteen for those of Manchester and Birmingham." And Professor Anstey goes on to say that it could be argued that the commission for discounting a bill should be reckoned as one of the slave trader's costs but that he has not done this "nor made any allowance for loss or protracted delay by disputed bills, which appears to have been not infrequent." In view of the ramifications of the slave trade and slavery in the wider economy of Europe's relations with the New World and the manner in which

101

these complemented and supplemented each other, interlocked with Europe's economic relations with the Middle and Far East, the problem of disentangling such amounts might well have been formidable, if not impossible.

Professor Anstey, it seems to me, gets close to this problem when he notes that "attempts to gauge the profitability of the slave trade by such means as the simple comparison of the price paid for slaves on the West African coast, and the price reserved for them in the Americas, are largely meaningless, given the commercial and financial complexities of the triangular trade." And, with special reference to the Middleburg Company, he states that, "We are therefore here concerned not with the slave trade, but rather with the triangular trade." I am, however, wondering just how useful this triangular trade concept is. This geometrical metaphor has, I think, been overworked by historians for far too long. The slave trade was, if we must employ geometrical images, often part of a quadrilateral trade across the Atlantic; and, in its full ramifications into the Middle and Far East, it was often part of an octagonal trade.

In all this, I am arguing not merely for a wider consideration of the Atlantic slave trade in time but also in space. To estimate volumes, profitability, and mortality rates within such a broad chronological framework, of course, poses formidable difficulties—not the least of which is the use of sources in non-European languages such as Arabic, Gujerati, etc. But if we wish to attempt such calculations, then I think that we must extend our efforts into more than one hemisphere.

Similarly, if we want to make estimates of the full significance of British naval suppression policies against the slave trade, we must not stop in 1865. Until the end of the century, if not longer, the British navy continued its antislavery actions against the Indian Ocean-based slave trade, as works such as Captain Sulivan's *Dhow Chasing in Zanzibar Waters* [5] and the British East African Slave Trade Committee's Report of 1871 remind us. In this respect, the contrast between the chronological limits of Professor LeVeen's valuable dissertation (1821 to 1865) and of his paper which speaks in general terms of "the nineteenth century slave trade" exposes him to criticism, for an estimate of the numbers of slaves taken by the British navy throughout the nineteenth century must include those captured from Arab as well as from European vessels. His useful study places emphasis largely on the Western Hemisphere, although, at times, Pro-

[5] G. L. Sulivan, *Dhow Chasing in Zanzibar Waters on the Eastern Coast of Africa*, London, 1873.

102

fessor LaVeen is obliged to reach out into the Indian Ocean, as when, for example, he tells us, in passing, that "the navy forced some distributional changes in the pattern of trader demand: more slaves were purchased in the South-Central and the Southeast African markets than during the eighteenth century"; and that, if prices were lower, the increased mortality and freight costs on longer voyages "more than offset the initial cost advantage."

With the exception of Professor Postma's, the emphasis in these essays is quantitative. Qualitative changes, however, brought about by the slave trade in the age of the expansion of Europe, ought not to be neglected. The social factor, it can be argued, is as important as the numerical, although, obviously, the two interact. We have interesting examples of the social factor in this volume: for example, Professor Davies' assertion that "a good many [English] men entering the African service has already failed at some other job"; and his distinction between the officers of the Royal African Company who had the opportunity, if luck ran for them, of a considerable increase in their incomes, and the rank-and-file Britishers who were, as he puts it, also "victims of the slave trade." What he has to say about the gambler's attitude of the officers seems to reinforce Professor Anstey's interesting comments on the risk psychology—perhaps "risk psychosis" would be a better expression—of the slave traders.

Examples of other social consequences of the Atlantic slave trade are to be observed in Professor LeVeen's essay when, employing Leslie Bethell's work with reference to British naval suppression policies and possible increases in slave prices, he indicates that "Brazilian [slave] Traders became large landholders as a result of the debts owed them by the planters."

Of greater social consequence, however, was possibly another effect of British naval suppression policies before the end of the American Civil War: the dispersal of groups of politically conscious (potentially and actually) "Liberated Africans" in West Africa, especially Sierra Leone, where they became ultimately important elements in the rise of African nationalism.

Professor LeVeen's paper may also be made the occasion to remind ourselves once again of the widespread ramifications of the African slave trade that are revealed in and symbolized by the enormous and complicated correspondence in connection with the suppression of the slave trade from 1816 to 1892 that is filed in the Public Record Office, London, under the general heading of "F.O. (Foreign Office) 84. Slave Trade," in 2,276 volumes.

If these British Foreign Office papers have been extensively—al-

103

though not exhaustively—worked over, Professor Postma does us a valuable service by indicating to us a group of records which have been "rarely consulted for slave trade history": the Dutch archives, with their wealth of material.

In passing, I should like to take this opportunity of pointing out that, beyond the Public Record Office, London, and a number of better-known and more accessible private collections of papers, there are also several British repositories to which scholars interested in the slave trade could pay greater attention. There is, to begin with, the India Office Library, a small example of whose riches is a record of slave prices in Madagascar between 1735 and 1753. And there are local British sources: for example, the Lancashire Record Office at Preston with, among other slaving items, a letter of 1752 describing a voyage with 130 slaves to Virginia via the Gambia from the Isle of Man.

If the Isle of Man can, in some obscure manner, find its way into the Atlantic slave trade, I am sure that Glasgow, Scotland, with its intimate links with the American tobacco trade, cannot be denied a place. Yet it always gets left out of considerations of the Atlantic slave trade—although, quite obviously, it is difficult to imagine that any future research could ever make it a rival of London, Liverpool, and Bristol, that triumvirate of British slave-trading cities.

But, in similar fashion, Birmingham, England, often gets overlooked, although the ramifications of its gun trade with the slave trade are clear, as the letter-books of the firm of Farmer and Galton, between 1751 and 1757, in the Birmingham Public Library, illustrate. All of these and other local British sources indicate the ramifications and complexities of the slave trade.

But, to return to Professor Postma's work. His paper, in space and time, supplements the work of Dr. Walter Rodney on the Upper Guinea area; and, like him, in my opinion, Professor Postma redresses the balance a little which appears to be swinging in a direction very much against the normal when one considers that, in reaction against abolitionist exaggerations, the tendency of some recent work has been almost to make the slave trade and slavery bear more heavily on the whites than on the Africans. Professor Postma, although reacting against the overexaggeration of the horrors of the Middle Passage, stresses that the process of acquiring slaves on the African coast was longer and "often more traumatic and costly in terms of death rates for slaves and slavers alike."

I wonder, however, if his claim that the Dutch treated their slaves better than other Europeans, albeit for commercial reasons, is quite justified. How does this square with the revelations of Dutch brutality in the narrative of Captain J. G. Stedman, a British naval officer in the Scottish brigade in the service of Holland; [6] or with the opening words of the chapter on slavery under the Dutch in Sir Harry Johnston's study of the blacks in the New World, "The Dutch were hard taskmasters: as slaveholders disliked perhaps more than the British or the British Americans"? [7] Perhaps we must distinguish between slaveholders and slave traders: always, I feel, a tenuous distinction to maintain.

Professor Postma, drawing upon an early nineteenth century Dutch source, declares that many slaves, in spite of the horrors associated with their capture, "feared an even worse lot was awaiting them on the other side of the Atlantic, to be eaten by these [and he quotes] 'white savages.' " This "white men are cannibals" rumor was widespread during the four centuries of the European slave trade and it continues into the period of the European Partition of Africa and well into the colonial period. It was a widely held folk belief which, in my opinion, deserves serious and detailed investigation throughout Africa and the areas of the African diaspora.

Discussion of Professor Postma's interesting essay may be made the occasion to point out an aspect of the European slave trade and an interesting variant of the European slave system which is not mentioned, I believe, by any of the contributors to this Conference. I refer to the establishment of slavery by the Dutch East India Company at the Cape of Good Hope and its extension into the South African hinterland during the period from 1658 to 1834. Numbers were not large. But they were not insignificant, rising from 891 slaves as against 1,334 Europeans at the Cape in 1701 to 25,754 slaves as against 21,746 whites in 1797.[8] The Dutch East India Company slave trade to and in South Africa—and the internal trade seems to have been as important as the external—drew on both the Western and the Eastern Hemispheres for its supply, although most slaves came from the East African trade (through Zanzibar and Madagascar) and from India and South East Asia. The Cape slave community has been rightly called "almost cosmopolitan," [9] with a color-line of its own developing between lighter skinned domestic and artisan slaves

---

[6] *Narrative of an Expedition to Surinam*, London, 1796.

[7] Sir Harry Johnston, *The Negro in the New World*, London, 1910.

[8] Victor De Kock, *Those in Bondage. An Account of the Life of the Slave at the Cape in the Days of the Dutch East India Company*, Cape Town and London, 1950, p. 237.

[9] Isobel Eirly Edwards, *Towards Emancipation: A Study in South African Slavery*, Cardiff, 1942, p. 15.

GEORGE SHEPPERSON

of Indian and South East Asian origin in the more urbanized regions of the Cape and those of African origins working on the farms in the western Cape and frontier districts. I hope we shall not forget in our discussions the South African experience of slavery, standing midway between the trans-Atlantic and the Indian Ocean slaving spheres.

Finally, it is clear that the approach in most of these essays has been quantitative; and, although the various measurements provided can be scaled up or down, according to the availability of new evidence and the refinement of scholarly techniques, I am sure we would agree that their authors have done us all an important service. But I hope that we shall not forget that there are elements associated with the Atlantic slave trade—and, indeed, with its ramifications into other trades and industry in eastward and other directions—which cannot at the moment—and probably never will—be measured. I refer to its effects on white culture. Because we cannot measure such an impact, should we be inclined, at a time of long-overdue scholarly reaction against abolitionist exaggerations, to minimize this? Should we dismiss out of hand such assertions as that by Professor W.E.B. Du Bois when he wrote that "the result of the African slave trade and slavery on the European mind and culture was to degrade the position of labour and the respect for humanity as such"; [10] or Mr. C.L.R. James's claim that the "rationalizations for the Atlantic slave trade . . . raise a compelling challenge to the whole matter of what indeed constitutes a civilization"?" [11] I hope that, in our preoccupation with the more measurable, we shall not overlook the less measurable and immeasurable matters that the slave trade has left with us.

[10] W. E. Burghardt Du Bois, *The World and Africa: An Inquiry into the Part which Africa Has Played in World History*, New York, 1965, p. 18.
[11] "The Atlantic Slave Trade and Slavery: Some Interpretations of Their Significance in the Development of the United States and the Western World," *Amistad* 1 (1970), 163-164.

VI

Measuring the Atlantic Slave Trade

PHILIP D. CURTIN

THE CONTRIBUTIONS by Messrs. Anstey, Davies, LeVeen, and Postma are a major advance in the general and continuing task of better measuring and better understanding the Atlantic slave trade. Anstey and Postma revise our knowledge of the numbers of slaves shipped by the principal European carriers, and their new information about the sources of the trade in West Africa is still more important. LeVeen and Anstey move on to the more difficult problem of measuring the relationship between the slave trade and other aspects of the Atlantic economy of the eighteenth and nineteenth centuries, while Davies advances into the barely investigated field of historical demography and historical epidemiology. These three areas of investigation fall into an order of precedence from what we know best (though still very incompletely), to what we know least—from numbers carried to the Atlantic economy to demography and epidemiology. And the order may be one of ultimate significance as well, since the numbers carried are only data for solving more important questions of why and how.

Since Postma and Anstey explicitly revise and correct some of the data I published in my *Atlantic Slave Trade,* the first task is to see what their work contributes to the whole picture as it is now known. Both studies depend on shipping data. As such, they tell little that is new about the total size of the Atlantic slave trade, simply because shipping data are too incomplete to be used for the construction of a general total. Overall totals have come so far mainly from import data, estimates or enumerations of slaves entering the importing regions, the estimates often based on population figures.[1]

Shipping data, however, are more precise, and they are the most reliable source for the origins of slaves in Africa. Once enough shipping data are on hand, they can be used to fill out the estimates to arrive at a total slave export from Africa, at least for certain periods.

---

[1] Philip D. Curtin, *The Atlantic Slave Trade: A Census,* Madison, Wis., 1969, pp. 15-93 (cited hereafter as *AST*).

The major unknowns when I first wrote were the numbers carried by the Dutch, Danes, and North Americans. The best global figures available for these carriers were five contemporaneous estimates. These took the form of capacity estimates; in effect, the trade that *could be* carried when everything went well. They are therefore unreliable as a guide to the actual annual average trade, but they can be treated as a guide to the distribution of the trade among major carriers, when the set of available estimates was averaged and treated as a consensus of "expert" opinion. With the assumption that the expert witnesses of the time knew what they were talking about, and that all carriers fell below capacity by about the same amount, the annual average trade of the known carriers (France, England, and Portugal) could be used to estimate the annual average trade of the Dutch, Danes, and North Americans.[2]

The total I arrived at by this method is now seriously modified. Postma's work shows that I was quite wrong about the Dutch trade, but the nature of the error is itself indicative. My calculations showed the Dutch carrying an annual average of about 3,500 slaves, while Postma shows them carrying 3,424 each year over the period 1761-1794. So far so good. The closeness of the two figures seems to confirm the method and the assumptions, at least in regard to the Dutch trade. The mistake was all my own; I assumed that the Dutch would have continued to carry about the same number of slaves on through to 1810, instead of stopping short in 1794, as they did. As a result I came up with a total trade of 174,000, against Postma's measured total of 116,000 for 1761-1810. If any lesson can be drawn it is, first of all, that statistics work, and, second, that no amount of sophisticated method can overcome wrong assumptions about nonquantitative history. Any historian on his toes should have known in this case that the Dutch could hardly have sustained the annual average of the 1780s through the turmoil of the Wars of the French Revolution and Napoleon. Quantitative history, in short, is no substitute for nonquantitative history, it simply goes on where the other leaves off.

The same exercise can now be done over with the benefit of Anstey's new data for the British slave trade and Postma's for Dutch exports of 1761-1810. The result appears in Table 1.[3] Since the corrected British total is higher and the corrected Dutch total is lower than the first effort, the corrected grand total of slaves exported from Africa in 1761-1810 is not very great—an increase from 3,338,300

[2] *AST*, pp. 217-220 and Table 64, p. 212.
[3] The new table here is thus a revision of Table 64, p. 212 in *AST*.

TABLE 1. SLAVE EXPORTS BY CARRIERS, CALCULATED FROM CONTEMPORANEOUS ESTIMATES, 1761-1800

Carrier	Percentage Distribution by Carrier Indicated by Five Contemporaneous Opinions:					Mean of cols. 1-5 (6)	Total Slaves Exported, by Carrier, Based on Other Data (7)	Total Exports Projected from col. 6 (8)	Percentage of Total Slave Exports, following cols. 7 and 8 (9)
	(1) 1768	(2) 1780	(3) 1788	(4) 1788	(5) 1798				
England	51.0	46.9	51.3	48.5	57.9	51.1	1,529.2	1,529.2	44.6
France	22.6	21.4	27.0	24.2	—	19.0	546.4	546.4	15.9
Portugal	8.4	25.7	13.5	16.2	26.3	18.0	1,010.4	1,010.4	29.4
Dutch	10.9	4.3	5.4	5.4	—	5.2	116.4	116.4	3.4
Danes	1.2	1.7	2.7	2.7	—	1.7	—	58.4	1.7
U.S.	6.1	—	—	3.0	15.8	5.0	—	171.6	5.0
TOTALS	100.0	100.0	100.0	100.0	100.0	100.0	—	3,432.4	100.0

SOURCES: col. 1 quoted from Ad. Mss. 18960, f. 37 by Frank W. Pitman, *The Development of the British West Indies, 1700-1763*, New Haven, 1917, p. 70; col. 2 quoted from "Mémoire sur la côte d'Afrique," Archives nationales, K 907, 38 and 38 bis, by J. Machat, *Documents sur les établissements français de l'Afrique occidentale au xviiie siècle*, Paris, 1906, pp. 132-133 [dated to 1779-1783 evidence]; col. 3 estimate of Robert Norris quoted in Pitman, *West Indies*, p. 71; col. 4, W. Young, *West India Common-Place Book*, London, 1807, p. 5; col. 5, J. Badinel, *Some Account of the Trade in Slaves from Africa*, London, 1842, p. 105; col. 8 from AST Table 63, p. 211 and from Postma's Table 7 (above).

to 3,432,400, or a change of about 2.8 percent. Even this much change, however, has some interesting implications. For one thing, it can be checked against the import data to see whether the two forms of calculations from independent sources give consonant results. In *The Atlantic Slave Trade* I did this, though I was forced to set aside the Portuguese-Brazilian portion of the trade as a self-contained system, since the Brazilian import estimates for this period came from shipping data. For the rest of the trade, the task was to compare the number of slaves potentially available for import into the Americas against the estimates of those actually imported, and the available number indicated by shipping data fell short of the number imported by 8 percent.[4] That is not a bad result, considering the quality of the data, but the same calculation can be made again but with the improved shipping data supplied by Postma and Anstey, the gap narrows to only 1 percent.

The Postma and Anstey data are still more important in their implications for the geographical origin of slaves exported from West Africa. Anstey's work with the records of Liverpool shipping provides very large samples of the declared destinations in the 1760s, 1770s, and 1790s. This leaves the decade 1801-1810, where both of us were forced to assume that the pattern of the 1790s continued, for lack of other evidence.[5]

The 1780s poses a neat problem in historical reconstruction on slim evidence. Anstey's solution was to interpolate by using the mean of the 1770s and 1790s. My solution, lacking his evidence for the 1770s and 1790s, was to use instead an estimate made for a Privy Council committee by Robert Norris, a prominent slave trader. The neighboring decades, the interpolations, and Norris' estimates are compared in Table 2. It is clear that Norris was in line with the Liverpool data for almost every part of the coast, in the sense that his estimate lies between the percentages indicated for the earlier and later decades, and this is true of the two Bights as well if they are taken as a single area. The question then becomes one of probability. Is it more probable that the pattern of the trade shifted evenly throughout the decade of the 1780s, or that it rose or fell more suddenly near the beginning or end of that decade? Mathematically, the probability is no greater for one year than for another. Arithmetic interpolation simply expresses the expectation that late shifts and early shifts will cancel one another. In this case, Norris' general accuracy is confirmed by the

---

[4] *AST*, p. 217.
[5] *AST*, p. 150, Table 43, cols. 8-9.

TABLE 2. A COMPARISON OF ESTIMATES OF BRITISH SLAVE EXPORTS
FROM AFRICA, 1781-1790

Conventional Coastal Regions	Percentage of Total British Slave Exports from Africa		
	1771-80	1781-90	1791-1800
Senegambia			
Liverpool shipping data	3.2	1.9	0.7
Robert Norris		0.9	
Sierra Leone			
Liverpool shipping data	11.2	7.9	4.7
Robert Norris		4.7	
Windward Coast			
Liverpool shipping data	18.8	12.2	7.5
Robert Norris		5.4	
Gold Coast			
Liverpool shipping data	8.1	11.0	13.8
Robert Norris		13.5	
Bight of Benin			
Liverpool shipping data	9.8	5.8	1.7
Robert Norris		16.8	
Bight of Biafra			
Liverpool shipping data	46.3	43.5	40.1
Robert Norris		29.0	
Angola			
Liverpool shipping data	2.8	16.8	30.8
Robert Norris		29.7	
	100.0	100.0	100.0
Alternate Calculation Aggregating the two Bights			
Liverpool shipping data	56.1	49.3	41.8
Robert Norris		45.8	

fact that his figures are within the bounds of the earlier and later
decades in so many instances. The question then is whether Norris'
knowledge of the date of shift in the pattern of the trade was likely
to be better than random. Given the fact that his knowledge of the
general levels of the trade from each area was far better than random,
it is a safe assumption that his knowledge would extend to other
aspects of the trade. Norris' estimates for the 1780s are therefore
to be preferred to interpolation.

Postma's data can be rearranged in decennial totals according to
the importance of each coastal region in West Africa.[6] These decennial

[6] Total quantities exported by the Dutch each decade are taken from Postma's
Table 7, and then distributed according to the coastal region of origin. These
distributions for 1711-1740 are taken from the indications of his Table 1, with
the category "mixed and miscellaneous" reassigned to the Gold Coast and Wind-

TABLE 3. ESTIMATED REGIONAL SLAVE EXPORTS FROM WEST AFRICA BY FRENCH, BRITISH, PORTUGUESE, AND DUTCH SHIPPING (IN 000's)

Region	1711-20	1721-30	1731-40	1741-50	1751-60	1761-70	1771-80	1781-90	1791-1800	1801-10	Totals	Percent
Senegambia	30.9	22.5	26.2	25.0	22.5	14.1	12.1	20.3	6.2	2.0	181.8	5.4
Sierra Leone	5.9	15.0	14.9	18.4	11.8	28.4	32.1	17.7	20.3	10.7	175.2	5.2
Windward Coast	30.6	47.6	55.2	97.4	53.7	112.8	68.0	30.8	33.9	17.0	547.0	16.2
Gold Coast	46.6	72.7	85.6	76.3	54.0	46.7	36.9	60.8	61.7	31.3	572.6	17.0
Bight of Benin	166.1	131.7	132.4	80.9	77.8	101.9	87.9	142.4	64.6	53.8	1039.5	30.8
Bight of Biafra	—	4.5	45.1	71.3	100.7	125.2	126.5	114.8	173.5	92.3	853.9	25.3
TOTALS	280.1	294.0	359.4	369.3	320.5	429.1	363.5	386.8	360.2	207.1	3370.0	100.0

SOURCES: Anstey, Table 5 (above); Postma, Tables 1, 3, 4, and 7 (above); Curtin, *The Atlantic Slave Trade*, Table 62 (p. 207), Table 60 (p. 200), and Table 43 (p. 150). Note that the Portuguese-carried exports from Sierra Leone coast are not included. See text, p. 113.

totals can then be added to the French and Portuguese estimates I have already published, and to the English figures following Anstey's revision (though keeping Norris' distribution for the 1780s). The result appears in Table 3—and in Tables 4-9 and Figures 1-3 and 5-7 for the individual coastal regions. Though this kind of calculation cannot be very accurate, it is considerably better than the tables and graphs I printed before Anstey's and Postma's studies were available.[7] The Danish and North American slave trades are still omitted. The Danish omission is not so important, since they traded mainly on the Gold Coast and somewhat on the Bight of Benin, and their trade faded out in the latter part of the period, just as the Dutch did. Even in their better days of the 1780s, contemporaries assigned them only 2.4 percent of the whole slave trade.[8] The North Americans are a more serious omission, especially for the last two decades of this survey. Rated by contemporaries as carrying only 3 percent of the whole slave trade in 1788, their share rose to an estimated 15.8 percent in 1798. Since they were more active in some regions than in others, a total of 10,000 to 15,000 slaves a year in the 1790s could make a really important difference in the export pattern of certain regions.[9] Americans were especially active, for example, in Senegambia and the conventional Sierra Leone (which covers the whole region from the Casamance River to Cape Mount). A small but unmeasured trickle of Portuguese-carried exports from "Sierra Leone" (especially from the Portuguese post at Bissau) is also omitted, though this was comparatively small. It was recorded at an annual average of only 700 a year in 1788-1794,[10] and it probably never exceeded 1,000 a year for any significant length of time.

---

ward Coast in due proportion. The information for 1731-1735 is taken as valid for the whole decade 1731-1740. From 1741 to 1800, the distribution to coastal regions is based on the sample data in Table 3. In order to detect the pattern commensurate with the projections in my *Atlantic Slave Trade*, I have made Sierra Leone a separate category from the Windward Coast. The marginal region Assini to Axim is also usually considered part of the Gold Coast, but it *is* marginal and the quantities traded are not enough to be significant. It is therefore left as Windward Coast. Following Postma's indications, it is assumed that 12.5% of the total Dutch slave trade came from Angola and the ports north of the Congo in 1731-1740, and 25% thereafter.

[7] That is, Table 3 here supersedes Table 66, p. 221 of *AST*, and Figures 1-3 and 5-7 supersede Figure 16, pp. 224-225 of *AST*.

[8] *AST*, Table 64, p. 212 and p. 223n.

[9] In short, the totals in cols. 9 and 10 will be about 15% lower than actuality, *if* the American trade was distributed in the same proportions as the whole slave trade. They could vary more widely, to the extent that the North American trade deviated from the general pattern.

[10] George E. Brooks, Jr., *Yankee Traders, Old Coasters, and African Middlemen*, Boston, 1970, pp. 24-72; Jorge Faro, "O movimento comercial do porto de Bissau de 1788 a 1794," *Boletim cultural da Guiné Portuguesa* 14 (1959), 231-258.

TABLE 4. SENEGAMBIA SLAVE TRADE (EXPORTS 000's) 1711-1720 TO
1801-1810

| | Exported by | | |
Period	British	French	Total
1711-20	20.6	10.3	30.9
1721-30	9.1	13.4	22.5
1731-40	13.9	12.3	26.2
1741-50	17.3	7.7	25.0
1751-60	16.2	6.3	22.5
1761-70	11.8	2.3	14.1
1771-80	8.1	4.0	12.1
1781-90	2.9	17.4	20.3
1791-1800	2.8	3.4	6.2
1801-10	1.5	0.5*	2.0
TOTAL			181.8

* Shipments recorded during the Peace of Amiens.

Even where the new data alter points of detail, they confirm the broadest pattern of supply to the Atlantic slave trade. The most striking feature is highly erratic supply from particular regions, in contrast to a reasonably even rise of total supply to a peak in the 1780s, followed by a decline. As LeVeen points out, the total supply from Africa was not only regular but followed a pattern of apparent response to rising prices and a high price-elasticity of supply. But this pattern would only be true of Africa in general, an aggregate of many different regions, any one of which furnished slaves idiosyncratically with little apparent reference to the prices offered. In short, where "Africa" appears to supply slaves in response to economic demand, the individual coastal regions appear to supply slaves in response to their own patterns of political affairs, anarchy, civil and international warfare.

Turning to these export profiles on a region-by-region basis, the Senegambian pattern is little changed from the earlier projections now corrected by Anstey's data. The decade most clearly out of line with other evidence is 1711-1720, which may be twice the actual figure.[11] Otherwise, the projections seem to be in line with other evi-

[11] France and England were at war until 1713, and James Island was unfortified from 1709 to 1717. Even after both nations returned to Senegambia trade, contemporaneous estimates, which should be interpreted as the capacity of the Senegambia trade in a good year, not a statistical annual average, indicate a trade of about 2,700 per year. Total exports at that level for seven years would come to 18,900 for the decade, in place of the indicated 30,900. See AST, pp. 223-228, and my forthcoming work on the economic history of Senegambia, c. 1650-1850.

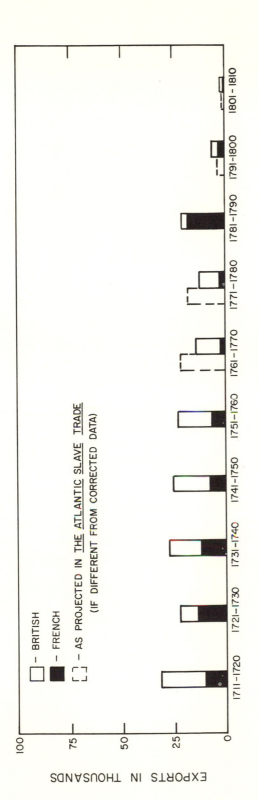

SENEGAMBIA SLAVE TRADE
1711-1720 to 1801-1810

Figure 1

PHILIP D. CURTIN

TABLE 5. SIERRA LEONE SLAVE TRADE (EXPORTS 000's) 1711-1720 TO 1801-1810

| Period | Exported by | | | Total |
	British	French	Dutch	
1711-20	5.9	—	—	5.9
1721-30	15.0	—	—	15.0
1731-40	14.9	—	—	14.9
1741-50	15.5	2.9	—	18.4
1751-60	9.0	0.9	1.9	11.8
1761-70	26.8	1.2	0.4	28.4
1771-80	28.3	0.8	3.0	32.1
1781-90	15.3	2.4	—	17.7
1791-1800	19.8	0.5	—	20.3
1801-10	10.7	—	—	10.7
TOTAL				175.2

dence, and the alternation between the French and English carriers follows the known pattern of international affairs. That is, the French share dropped in the late 1750s as the English came to dominate the sea lanes, and it stayed low through the 1760s and 1770s because the English held Saint Louis at the mouth of the Senegal from 1758 to 1779, leaving the French with Gorée as their only fortified trading post. In the 1780s, the situation was reversed when the French recaptured Saint Louis and destroyed the English James Fort at the mouth of the Gambia (1779), leaving the English without a fortified post during the next decade. Since the Gambia and Senegal were alternate routes to the interior, the level of the trade remained relatively constant, simply shifting from one river to the other.

Sierra Leone's export profile is modified much more sharply by the new data, and the change removes some of the problems of interpreting my older projection. It showed a peak in the 1780s, which could not be explained by any local events, and low figures for the 1760s and 1770s, which should have been a period of high exports. In the hinterland, the rise of the Almamate of Futa Jallon from the mid-1720s, with a continuing *jihad* or holy war against neighboring peoples into the 1740s, accounts for the comparative rise in slave exports over that period, and the decline in the 1750s corresponds to a period of peace and stability during the late reign of Karomoho Alfa. The second and more military phase of the Almamate came with the reign of

116

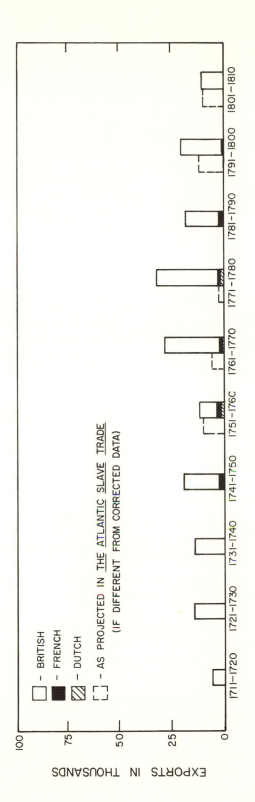

SIERRA LEONE SLAVE TRADE
1711-1720 to 1801-1810

Figure 2

TABLE 6. WINDWARD COAST SLAVE TRADE (EXPORTS 000's) 1711-1720
TO 1801-1810

| Period | Exported by | | | Total |
	British	French	Dutch	
1711-20	14.7	15.9	—	30.6
1721-30	7.5	40.1	—	47.6
1731-40	18.4	36.8	—	55.2
1741-50	25.5	39.8	32.1	97.4
1751-60	28.6	1.2	23.9	53.7
1761-70	74.6	2.5	35.7	112.8
1771-80	47.6	2.9	17.5	68.0
1781-90	17.6	6.8	6.4	30.8
1791-1800	31.5	1.0	1.4	33.9
1801-10	17.0	—	—	17.0
TOTAL				547.0

Ibrahima Sori, in the 1760s through the 1780s. The high export figures for those decades are accounted for by his further wars.[12]

The Windward Coast from Cape Mount in present-day western Liberia to Assini in eastern Ivory Coast is the part of West Africa least known from European records. The Europeans found this coast with few good anchorages, steep beaches and high surf, broken only occasionally by a river mouth, usually even then with an offshore bar that prevented passage from open sea into the river by any but surf boats. Few, if any, stayed on shore long enough to learn about local politics or the patterns of trade from the hinterland. Figure 3 shows a two-peaked profile, with one very high peak in the 1740s and a second in the 1760s, but the division by carriers makes it clear that the general profile is in fact a combination of three separate tendencies by the three principal carriers. The French became important from the 1720s through the 1740s, then dropped out. Both English and Dutch trade reached a peak in the 1760s, and then declined. By the early nineteenth century, when other coastal regions still supplied the illegal trade, the Windward Coast had virtually dropped out as a source of slaves.

Postma's data are crucial to an explanation of this pattern, since they break the trade into sub-regions within the Windward Coast as a whole. The percentages by sub-regions can be taken from his Table

[12] The best recent summary history of this region is by Yves Person in H. Deschamps, ed., *Histoire générale de L'Afrique noire de Madagascar et des archipels*, Paris, 1970-1971, I, 283-303.

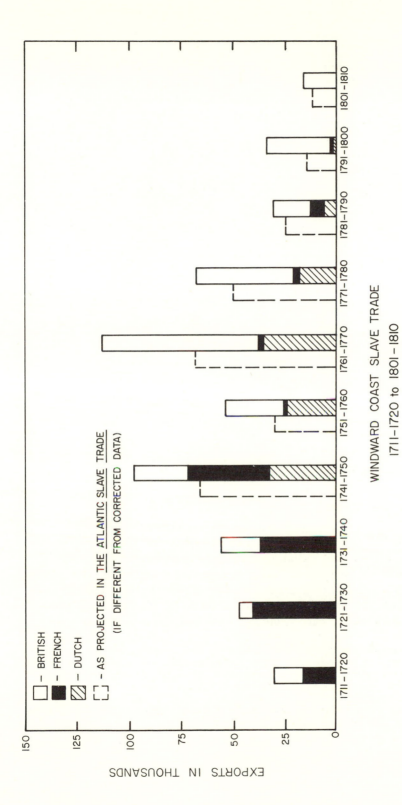

WINDWARD COAST SLAVE TRADE

1711-1720 to 1801-1810

Figure 3

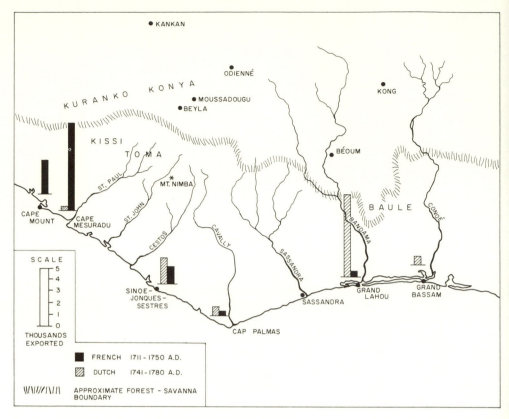

KANKAN

ODIENNÉ

KONG

KURANKO   KONYA

MOUSSADOUGU
BEYLA

KISSI

TOMA

BÉOUM

MT. NIMBA

ST. PAUL

ST. JOHN

CESTOS

CAVALLY

SASSANDRA

BANDAMA

BAULE

CONOÉ

CAPE
MOUNT

CAPE
MESURADU

SCALE

5
4
3
2
1
0

THOUSANDS
EXPORTED

SINOE-
JONQUES-
SESTRES

SASSANDRA

GRAND
LAHOU

GRAND
BASSAM

CAP PALMAS

FRENCH   1711 - 1750 A.D.

DUTCH   1741 - 1780 A.D.

APPROXIMATE FOREST - SAVANNA
BOUNDARY

THE "WINDWARD COAST"

Figure 4

3.[13] When these are combined with the projected French exports for 1711-1750 (from Table 3), the results appear on Figure 4. It is instantly clear that "the Windward Coast" is a deceptive aggregate, that Dutch trade was actually concentrated in a small part of the whole 600-mile stretch of coastline. The sub-regional origin of the French Windward Coast trade of the early eighteenth century shows a similar reality.[14]

[13] The trade was heavier in some decades than in others, but the number of observations in Postma's table appears to be roughly proportional to the extent of the Dutch trade in any particular decade. The overall average should therefore be accurate enough to indicate the general sources of the trade over the whole period 1741-1780.
[14] Gaston Martin, *Nantes au xviii⁰ siècle: L'ère des négriers (1714-1774)*, Paris, 1931, pp. 188, 207, 212, 218.

120

The "Windward Coast" that provided the peak of the 1740s was far away from the "Windward Coast" that furnished the Dutch exports of the later period.

With these more precise indications of coastal origin, it is possible to suggest hypothetical events in the interior that account for the two peaks from the two principal regions of supply. The heavy French exports from the Cape Mount-Cape Mesuardo region seem to be accountable to the eastward expansion of the Kuranko out of what is now Sierra Leone into present-day upper Guinea-Conakry, pushing toward Konyan and driving the Kissi south in the process. The beginning of the Kuranko movement is generally put at the end of the seventeenth century, and it coincided with the development of a new trade route through the forest to the coast. Malinke *juula* (or traders) belonging to Kamara lineages moved south from Konyan into the forest, where they set up a number of small states in Toma country (now northern Liberia and southeastern Guinea-Conakry). From this base, they kept their old commercial contacts with the north and also pushed a regular trade route through Vai country to the region of Cape Mount and Cape Mesurado (present-day Monrovia). It is possible that the Kamara wars among the Toma may also have furnished slaves among the French exports of the early eighteenth century.[15]

The second major route through the forests, the Bandama River leading down to Grand Lahou, is explicable on environmental grounds; this is the narrowest point in the forest belt anywhere between Sierra Leone and the eastern Gold Coast. Sometime in the seventeenth century, Malinke-speaking *juula* or merchants moved south to establish a commercial base at Boron. From there they developed trade routes through to the coast near Grand Lahou.[16] This through route from the interior was cut, however, by the westward movement of Akan refugees from Asante in the middle of the eighteenth century. These were the Baule who settled between the lower Bandama and Komoe Rivers displacing the many Senufo and Guro already there.[17] The Baule wars with their neighbors seem to be the most probable source of the high rate of export from Grand Lahou in the second half of the eighteenth century, though it is possible that some slaves also came through from the Juula kingdom of Kong further north.

Postma's detailed information on ports of shipment from the Gold Coast has less obvious meaning. Many different paths led down to the

[15] Person, I, 284.
[16] *Ibid.*, 285.
[17] P. Mercier, in Deschamps, ed., *Histoire générale de l'Afrique noire*, I, 326.

121

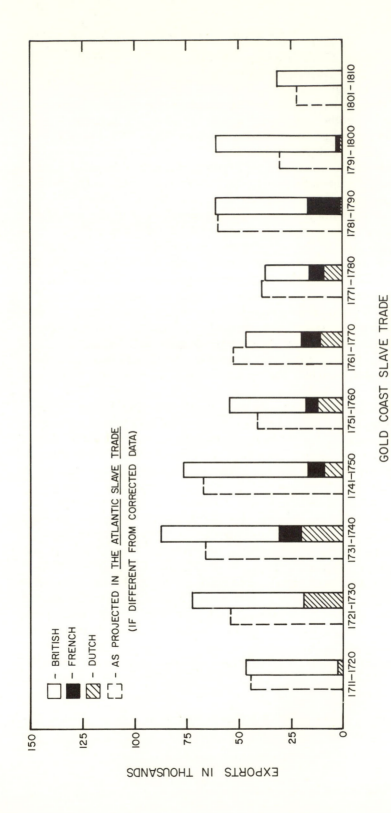

EXPORTS IN THOUSANDS

□ — BRITISH
■ — FRENCH
▨ — DUTCH
⊏⊐ — AS PROJECTED IN THE ATLANTIC SLAVE TRADE
       (IF DIFFERENT FROM CORRECTED DATA)

GOLD COAST SLAVE TRADE
1711-1720 to 1801-1810

Figure 5

TABLE 7. GOLD COAST SLAVE TRADE (EXPORTS 000's) 1711-1720 TO
1801-1810

	Exported by			
Period	British	French	Dutch	Total
1711-20	44.0	—	2.6	46.6
1721-30	54.2	—	18.5	72.7
1730-40	56.1	9.1	20.4	85.6
1741-50	59.4	7.6	9.3	76.3
1751-60	36.5	5.3	12.2	54.0
1761-70	26.8	8.8	11.1	46.7
1771-80	20.5	7.3	9.1	36.9
1781-90	43.9	16.0	0.9	60.8
1791-1800	58.0	2.4	1.3	61.7
1801-10	31.3	—	—	31.3
TOTAL				572.6

coast from Asante and other inland states, so that nearly any point
could serve as a possible alternative for the shipment of slaves
originating in Asante or beyond, much as the Gambia and Senegal
were alternate outlets for the slave trade from the Manding culture
area. Nor does Postma's data change the general profile of slave exports from the Gold Coast. It merely raises the curve above the level
projected from French and English data alone. The large difference
between the original and these revised projections for the 1790s
comes from the fact that Anstey discovered greater British slave ship-

TABLE 8. BIGHT OF BENIN SLAVE TRADE (EXPORTS 000's) 1711-1720 TO
1801-1810

	Exported by				
Period	British	French	Dutch	Portuguese	Total
1711-20	55.8	16.7	17.5	76.1	166.1
1721-30	30.2	18.2	11.3	72.0	131.7
1731-40	27.3	32.1	21.4	51.6	132.4
1741-50	26.8	4.1	—	50.0	80.9
1751-60	12.0	23.6	.5	41.7	77.8
1761-70	26.7	40.0	—	35.2	101.9
1771-80	24.8	35.3	.7	27.1	87.9
1781-90	54.7	65.7	—	22.0	142.4
1791-1800	7.3	8.6	—	48.7	64.6
1801-10	3.9	—	—	49.9	53.8
TOTAL					1039.5

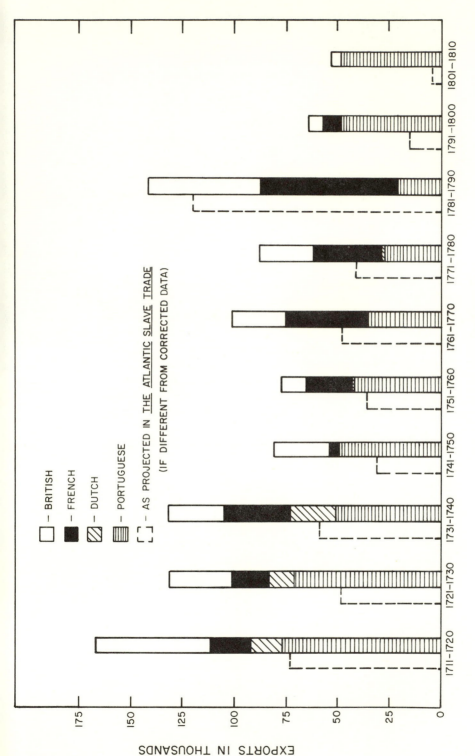

BIGHT OF BENIN SLAVE TRADE
1711-1720 to 1801-1810

Figure 6

Legend:
☐ – BRITISH
■ – FRENCH
▨ – DUTCH
▥ – PORTUGUESE
┌┄┐ – AS PROJECTED IN THE ATLANTIC SLAVE TRADE
      (IF DIFFERENT FROM CORRECTED DATA)

EXPORTS IN THOUSANDS
175   150   125   100   75   50   25   0

1711-1720   1721-1730   1731-1740   1741-1750   1751-1760   1761-1770   1771-1780   1781-1790   1791-1800   1801-1810

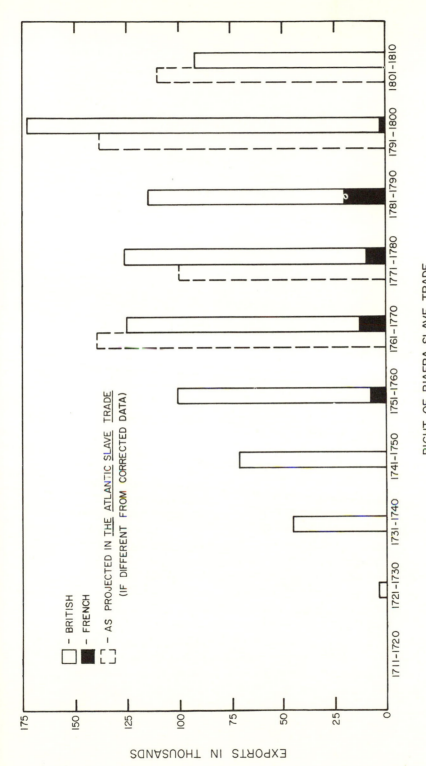

BIGHT OF BIAFRA SLAVE TRADE
1711-1720 to 1801-1810

Figure 7

□ — BRITISH
■ — FRENCH
⊏⊐ — AS PROJECTED IN THE ATLANTIC SLAVE TRADE
      (IF DIFFERENT FROM CORRECTED DATA)

EXPORTS IN THOUSANDS

PHILIP D. CURTIN

TABLE 9. BIGHT OF BIAFRA SLAVE TRADE (EXPORTS 000's) 1711-1720 TO
1801-1810

	Exported by		
Period	British	French	Total
1721-30	4.5	—	4.5
1731-40	45.1	—	45.1
1741-50	71.3	—	71.3
1751-60	93.2	7.5	100.7
1761-70	112.2	13.0	125.2
1771-80	117.4	9.1	126.5
1781-90	94.4	20.4	114.8
1791-1800	171.0	2.5	173.5
1801-10	92.3	—	92.3
TOTAL			853.9

ments at this time than were indicated by the published record at the time I first made this calculation. The new totals are in fact somewhat higher for all shipping areas in the 1790s.

The new projections for the Bight of Benin are much higher than those based on French and British data alone because of Portuguese trade from here to Brazil, but here (and for the Bight of Biafra) the new data tend to smooth the curve of total exports without changing its basic shape.

A somewhat changed pattern of regional origins emerges for the whole century 1711-1810. Earlier projections showed the Bight of Biafra as the largest supplier, while the new projections shift the dubious honor to the Bight of Benin, "the slave coast" in eighteenth century usage. To the west, the Gold Coast and Windward Coast appear at about the same level, with a sharp drop to lower levels for the Senegambia and Sierra Leone. The total exports from these two western regions would have been somewhat higher because of the North American trade, but even if the total American exports projected on Table 1 were divided equally between these two regions, their totals would only rise to about half of those indicated for the Gold or Windward Coast.

The question of slave-trade profitability has drifted decade after decade through the historical literature without a serious challenge. In spite of the known failure of most of the large chartered companies, and in spite of some studies of small samples of the trade, the general assumption was that it must have been immensely profitable. Part of the belief came from antislave-trade propagandists of the early

126

nineteenth century. Part came from the evangelical faith that so immoral a trade had to be fanastically profitable, or else men would not have entered it.

In the light of any hard evidence now available, however, it is even a little surprising that Anstey's calculations show as high a rate of profitability as they do. Dr. Unger has shown that the Dutch trade, at least as represented by the Middleburg Company, was not especially profitable between 1761 and 1800. The French trade seems to have been even less so. At least, the French slave traders convinced the government on that score. After 1758, French slavers received a direct subsidy of 100 *livres tournois* (equivalent to £3.98) for each slave delivered to the French colonies, and it was raised to 160 livres in 1787 (£6.37 at the exchange then current). In effect, the government paid one-third to one-quarter of the African cost of slaves, which easily accounts for the French success in the 1780s against Dutch competition.

The social cost of slavery and the whole South Atlantic System to the Europeans is another problem, well beyond that of mere account-book profit or loss. K. G. Davies' study of the "Lists of the Living and the Dead" brings in some startling evidence, and it also points up some continuing problems. One is the statistical problem faced by historians who cannot ask questions of the past. One of the most valuable sources for the epidemiology of Europeans in West Africa is a study like Davies', where he can trace whole drafts of men over a number of years. Otherwise, the deaths per thousand present are deceptive at best. As Davies shows, a crude death rate of 270 per thousand is possible in a situation where new recruits were actually dying at more than twice that rate in their first year. We know in theory that one of the crucial factors making for differential death rates among newcomers is the childhood disease environment. In theory again, such rates might well be lower among people who had grown up where malaria was endemic, even if the *plasmodia* were different from the *P. falciparum* of West Africa. But most of the studies now available deal with Englishmen, not with Portuguese or Brazilians or even men from the south of France. T. W. Shick's study of black Americans emigrating to Liberia in the early nineteenth century shows that those from the southern states survived better than those from the north—and that the fact of African descent a few generations back was little protection.[18] No estimate of the over-all

[18] Tom W. Shick, "A Quantitative Analysis of Liberian Colonization from 1820 to 1843, with Special Reference to Mortality," *Journal of African History* 12 (1971), 45-60.

cost of the slave trade to the carriers as well as the slaves will be possible until comparative data are published for other carriers. But the theoretical importance of further epidemiological studies is greater still, since it enters a very important and barely explored problem of the historical relations between man and disease before modern medical practice began to distort the evidence.

PART TWO:
SOCIAL AND DEMOGRAPHIC ASPECTS
OF SLAVE POPULATIONS

VII

"More Like a Negro Country": Demographic Patterns in Colonial South Carolina, 1700-1740

PETER H. WOOD

DURING THE first twenty-five years after the founding of South Carolina in 1670, roughly one out of every four settlers was a black. These first black Carolinians, scarcely more than a thousand in number, came from the West Indies, and most were retained as slaves by a small number of aspiring white immigrants from Barbados. During the quarter century after 1695 this racial balance shifted markedly, so that by the time the colony's Proprietors gave way to a royal government in 1720, Africans had outnumbered Europeans for more than a decade. But the coastal area's population, if free Indians are excluded, still totaled fewer than 19,000 people.

In 1722 the settlement's central town, with its low houses and unpaved streets, remained small enough so that a suggestion to change the name from Charlestown to Charles City was easily ignored.[1] However, 25,000 barrels of rice and nearly as many barrels of tar and pitch were already crossing local wharves annually.[2] By this time, moreover, the direct importation of slaves from Africa had been well under way for several years. As rice production expanded these shipments would increase. Only in 1741, as a result of the Stono Uprising and other disturbances, was a prohibitive duty imposed upon new slaves in an effort to curtail further growth of the black majority. But before 1740 the racial demography of the colony had already been firmly established.

"Carolina," commented a Swiss newcomer named Samuel Dyssli in

[1] South Carolina Department of Archives and History (SCDAH), Columbia, *South Carolina Upper House Journal (SCUHJ)*, mfm. BMP/D487, 15 June 1722. Charlestown did not officially become Charleston until 1783. A slightly shorter version of this essay appears in Peter H. Wood, *Black Majority: Negroes in Colonial South Carolina from 1670 through the Stono Rebellion*, New York, 1974. Figure 1 and Map 1 are reproduced here by courtesy of Alfred A. Knopf.

[2] M. Eugene Sirmans, *Colonial South Carolina: A Political History, 1663-1763*, Chapel Hill, 1966, p. 132.

131

1737, "looks more like a negro country than like a country settled by white people." [3] The pages which follow suggest the demographic context for Mr. Dyssli's striking observation, which could not have been made about any other mainland colony. If early demographic patterns were determined by the nature of the settlement, they also helped to shape that settlement, and it is difficult to consider the general history of colonial South Carolina without first having some factual knowledge of who lived there and where they came from. This essay explores, with as detailed statistical data as could be mustered, various demographic aspects of the Afro-American majority as it materialized within the colony's total population between 1700 and 1740. The exploration depends primarily upon three kinds of resources: gross population data, annual slave import statistics, and a unique census of the households in one central parish.

II

POPULATION statistics for the first generation are scarce and a bit confused. It is clear, however, that prior to the end of the seventeenth century the percentage of blacks in the tiny settlement had begun to increase. An undated manuscript from shortly before 1700 states: "South Carolina hath nott above 2000 whites & those not ye wealthyest of men in Americah; yett . . . they have procured as many or more Negroes whose labours are Equall to yᵉ English." [4] The exact moment at which black inhabitants exceeded white may not have come until 1708, for data collected in that year showed the two groups almost even, with just over 4,000 in each. This census report, although rough, provides a valuable profile of the colony, for the Governor and Council broke the survey into distinct categories and indicated the change in each group over the five years since 1703. Their report is summarized in Table 1. [5]

---

[3] Samuel Dyssli, Charlestown, 3 December 1737, *South Carolina Historical and Genealogical Magazine* (*SCHGM*), 23 (July 1922), 90.

[4] "Some weighty considerations relating to America . . . ." This anonymous and undated manuscript appears as item 64 in the Archdale Papers, on mfm. at the SCDAH.

[5] W. Noel Sainsbury Transcripts of Records in the British Public Record Office Relating to South Carolina 1663-1782, 36 vols. (SCDAH), v, 203-204. The first five volumes of this series were published in facsimile edition (Columbia, S.C., 1928-1947) and will be referred to as BPRO *Trans.*: the unpublished volumes will be abbreviated as BPRO Trans. Sirmans (p. 60) has added these figures wrongly. More significant, however, may be the fact that Verner W. Crane seems to have obtained slightly different totals from the actual BPRO manuscripts, Colonial Office papers, 5:1264, p. 82. *The Southern Frontier, 1670-1732*, Ann Arbor, 1929, p. 113.

DEMOGRAPHIC PATTERNS IN SOUTH CAROLINA

TABLE 1. SOUTH CAROLINA POPULATION AS REPORTED BY THE GOVERNOR AND COUNCIL, SEPTEMBER 17, 1708

	Projected Figures for 1703	Reported Changes Since 1703	Reported Figures for 1708
Free men	1,460	−100	1,360
Free women	940	−40	900
Free children	1,200	+500	1,700
White servant men	110	−50	60
White servant women	90	−30	60
TOTAL WHITES	3,800	+280	4,080
Negro men slaves	1,500	+300	1,800
Negro women slaves	900	+200	1,100
Negro children slaves	600	+600	1,200
TOTAL NEGRO SLAVES	3,000	+1,100	4,100
Indian men slaves	100	+400	500
Indian women slaves	150	+450	600
Indian children slaves	100	+200	300
TOTAL INDIAN SLAVES	350	+1,050	1,400
TOTAL POPULATION	7,150	+2,430	9,580

Due to commerce in war captives, Indian slaves can be seen as the fastest growing segment of the population between 1703 and 1708.[6] This was a short-term trend that contributed directly to the frontier wars of the ensuing decade, after which the Indian presence would diminish rapidly.[7] Among whites, despite the arrival of newcomers, the number of adults declined by nearly 6 percent during the five-year

[6] English colonists had overpowered the Savannah Indians during these years. It is noteworthy that among Indian slaves the percentage of women reported was high, the percentage of children low. Free Indians still constituted by far the largest population group in the colony at this time, but they do not appear in this report or in others cited later. For an estimate of their numbers, see William J. Rivers, A Sketch of the History of South Carolina, Charleston, 1856, p. 239.

[7] Frank J. Klingberg, ed., The Carolina Chronicle of Dr. Francis Le Jau, Berkeley, 1956, p. 109. At the time of the Tuscarora War Le Jau wrote (20 February 1712):

our Traders have promoted Bloody Warrs this last Year to get slaves and one of them brought lately 100 of those poor Souls. . . . I don't know where the fault lyes but I see 30 Negroes at Church for an Indian slave, and as for our free Indians—they goe their own way and bring [up] their Children like themselves with little Conversation among us, I generally Pceive something Cloudy in their looks, an Argumt. I fear, of discontent. I am allso Informed yt. our Indian Allyes [the Yamasees] are grown haughty of late.

133

Population Trends in
Colonial South Carolina, 1700-1740

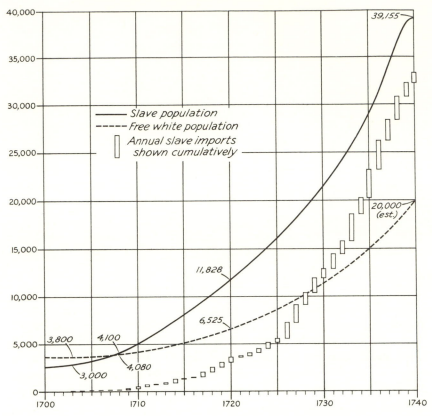

FIG. 1.

span. By contrast, the number of black adults rose more than 20 percent in the same period, owing to natural increase as well as importation. The high proportion of children among the whites (42 percent) suggests a populace with a high rate of mortality. Among black slaves the proportion of children is lower (29 percent), but their total number of children doubled in the course of five years, arguing a high rate of natural population growth among Africans. These different rates of growth continued through the ensuing decade.

The contrast between black and white growth rates in the proprietary colony is suggested by Figure 1. Epidemics, Indian wars, and emigration meant that the white population rose by scarcely 2,500

134

between 1708 and 1721 inclusive, while the Negro population added over 4,000 by natural increase and above 3,600 more through imports during the same period (cf. Tables 1 and 2). Using data drawn from Tables 1 through 3, it is possible to demonstrate that the annual rate of the black population increase in excess of the number of immigrants was a surprising 5.6 percent during the thirteen years before 1721.[8] Support for these numerical calculations can be found in a 1714 statute which raised the duty on black slaves in hopes of reducing their importation. The legislators observed that "the number of negroes do extremely increase in this Province, and through the afflicting providence of God, the white persons do not proportionably multiply."[9] By the time the Crown assumed control in 1720 it was apparent to all contemporaries that South Carolina, unlike the other mainland English colonies, was dominated demographically by migrants from West Africa.[10] They predominated in terms of total numbers, pace of immigration, and rate of natural increase.

III

IN 1720 the rough population figures accepted in London for the new royal colony were 9,000 whites and 12,000 Negroes, and as is often the case with colonial statistics the figure for Africans was

---

[8] The annual rate of population increase in excess of the number of immigrants was computed by: (1) subtracting the total imports during the interval from the net change in population over the period; (2) adding the net increase in excess of the imports to the initial year population; and (3) computing the compounded annual rate of increase between the initial year's population and the final year's estimated population as calculated in (2). To interpret this calculation as referring to the natural increase of the initial year's slave population requires the assumption that births to the imported slaves are equal to the deaths among the imports.

[9] Thomas Cooper and David McCord, eds., *The Statutes at Large of South Carolina,* Columbia, 1836-1841 (hereafter cited as *Statutes*), VII, 367. It is necessary to keep in mind that some part of the increase in slaves during these years was due to masters importing individual Negroes from the West Indies for their own personal use rather than for sale. No duty was paid on these slaves (*Statutes,* III, 56-68), hence they may not appear in a tabulation of imports such as Table 3 below. See Converse D. Clowse, *Economic Beginnings in Colonial South Carolina, 1670-1730,* Columbia, 1971, p. 204.

[10] At about this time the colony's agent, Joseph Boone, was asked, "Are the Inhabitants increased or decreased of late and for what Reasons," and he gave the following reply:

Within these last 5 years the White Inhabitants have annually Decreased by Massacres of Indians and flying off of Great Numbers to places of greater safety. . . . Yett the Number of Blacks in that Time have very much increased for the Pitch and Tarr Trade Prodigiously increasing here made the Inhabitants [word faded] in to buying of Blacks to the great endangering [of] the Province.

"Querys for Mr Boon," The Wake Letters, mfm., SCDAH. Cf. nn. 16, 19 below.

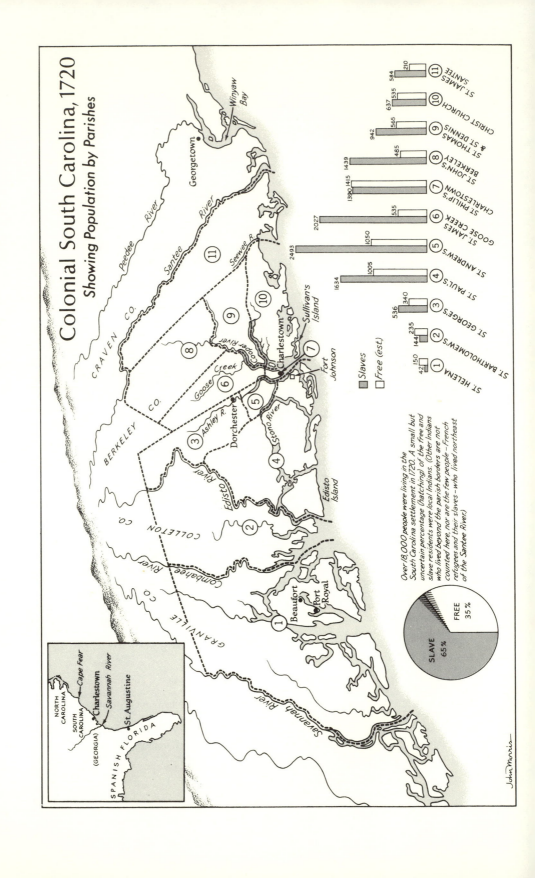

Colonial South Carolina, 1720
Showing Population by Parishes

Slaves

Free (est.)

① ST. HELENA — 42 / 150
② ST. BARTHOLOMEW'S — 144 / 235
③ ST. GEORGE'S — 340 / 536
④ ST. PAUL'S — 1005 / 1634
⑤ ST. ANDREW'S — 1050 / 2493
⑥ ST. JAMES GOOSE CREEK — 535 / 2027
⑦ ST. PHILIP'S CHARLESTOWN — 1390 / 1415
⑧ ST. JOHN'S BERKELEY — 485 / 1439
⑨ ST. THOMAS & ST. DENNIS — 565 / 942
⑩ CHRIST CHURCH — 535 / 637
⑪ ST. JAMES SANTEE — 210 / 584

Over 18,000 people were living in the South Carolina settlement in 1720. A small but uncertain percentage (hatching) of the free and slave residents were local Indians. (Other Indians who lived beyond the parish borders are not counted here, nor are the few people – French refugees and their slaves – who lived northeast of the Santee River.)

SLAVE 65%

FREE 35%

Georgetown

Winyaw Bay

Santee River

Peedee River

CRAVEN CO.

Seewee R.

Charlestown

Sullivan's Island

Fort Johnson

BERKELEY CO.

Cooper River

Goose Creek

Dorchester

Ashley R.

Stono River

Edisto River

Edisto Island

COLLETON CO.

Combahee River

GRANVILLE CO.

Beaufort
Port Royal

Savannah River

NORTH CAROLINA

SOUTH CAROLINA

Cape Fear

Charlestown

(GEORGIA)

Savannah River

St. Augustine

SPANISH FLORIDA

John Morris

TABLE 2. POPULATION FIGURES FOR SOUTH CAROLINA BY PARISH, 1720

| | Figures Submitted by Governor Moore | | | Additional Calculations | | | |
Parishes (listed from northeast to southwest)	A. Taxable Acres	B. Taxpayers	C. Slaves	D. Estimated Free Pop. (B×5)	E. Estimated Total Pop. (C+D)	F. Estimated % Slaves (E/C)	G. Taxable Acres per Person (A/E)
St. James Santee	117,274	42	584	210	794	74	148
Christ Church	57,580	107	637	535	1,172	54	49
St. Thomas & St. Dennis	74,580	113	942	565	1,507	63	50
St. John's (Berkeley)	181,375	97	1,439	485	1,924	75	94
St. Philip's (Charlestown)	64,265	283	1,390	1,415	2,805	50	23
St. James Goose Creek	153,267½	107	2,027	535	2,562	79	60
St. Andrew's	197,168¾	210	2,493	1,050	3,543	70	56
St. George's	47,457	68	536	340	876	61	54
St. Paul's	187,976	201	1,634	1,005	2,639	62	71
St. Bartholomew's	30,559	47	144	235	379	38	80
St. Helena	51,817	30	42	150	192	22	270
TOTAL	1,163,319¼[a]	1,305	11,828	6,525	18,393	65	63

[a] Moore actually gives 1,163,239¼ acres as the total for this col, which reflects an error in either the transcription or the addition. For comment on this mistake and for further breakdown of acreage figures, see Clowse, *Economic Beginnings*, pp. 253-255.

notably more precise than that for Europeans.[11] But it was not until the following March, when census data from each parish was delivered under oath to the tax commissioners in Charlestown, that a detailed picture was available. (See Map, p. 136.) The interim Governor, James Moore, Jr., promptly forwarded to England, "An Exact account of the Number of Inhabitants who pay Tax in the Settlement of South Carolina for the yeare 1720 with the Number of Acres and Number of Slaves in each parish." [12] Moore's account, which provides the basis for Table 2, places the slave population at 11,828, or within 2 percent of the estimated figure of 12,000.[13]

Moore's totals for taxable land (over 1,100,000 acres) and for South Carolina taxpayers (1,305) as given in columns A and B can be confirmed from other sources.[14] Moreover, since the number of taxpaying heads of households in each parish is known, it is possible to estimate the full number of white inhabitants through the accepted formula of multiplying by five.[15] The resulting total of 6,525 whites (column D) checks remarkably well with the total of 6,400 obtained a year earlier by Colonel Johnson, using the other traditional formula of multiplying militia rolls by four.[16] The estimate of 6,525 white colonists in 1720

[11] This is not to say that slave totals were never misrepresented. For example, in 1720 colonial agents put South Carolina's Negro population at "14 or 15,000" when they were trying to dramatize the threat of insurrection. (BPRO Trans., VIII, 253-254). But it is safe to say that officials usually possessed better demographic information on blacks than on whites. "The White Inhabitants," wrote Governor Glen in 1749, "may be in number Twenty five Thousand, and the Negroes at least Thirty nine Thousand, of these I can be more positive, as Taxes are paid for them." BPRO Trans., XXIII, 369-370.

[12] BPRO Trans., IX, 22-23; also in BPRO, *Calendar of State Papers, Colonial*, XVIII, 39.

[13] This total is higher but apparently more accurate and inclusive than several which followed. After an act of 1721 imposed a tax "upon Negro, Indian, Mustee and Molato Slaves from the age of Seven years to the Age of Sixty inclusive," a revenue estimate for 1724 put 9,100 persons in this category. (BPRO Trans., XI, 51.) Limitations by age, incomplete returns, or even the incursions of an epidemic could all help explain the similarly smaller figure of 9,570 slaves submitted to the S.P.G. in 1722. Society for the Propagation of the Gospel, "Facsimiles," p. 61, Library of Congress.

[14] A revenue estimate of 1724 lists 1,116,000 acres of taxable land, and an earlier representation to the King puts the number of taxable inhabitants near 1,300. BPRO Trans., XI, 51; *ibid.*, 19.

[15] James H. Cassedy, *Demography in Early America: Beginnings of the Statistical Mind, 1600-1800*, Cambridge, 1969, p. 73.

[16] *Ibid.* Johnson, then governor, had informed the Lords of Trade, 12 January 1720 (BPRO Trans., VII, 233-234):

Tis computed by the Muster Roles & other observations that at present we may have about 1600 Fighting Men, from 16 to 60 Years of Age every body in the Province within that Age being inlisted, and obliged to bear Arms and by the Comon Computacon of 4 Persons in each Family, the whole of the Whits are

represents a more informed if less optimistic calculation than the guess of 9,000 accepted in London.[17] Using this figure of 6,525 Europeans, a sum can be reached for the total population of each parish (column E) and for the percentage of residents who were slaves (column F).

A final column (G), based on the ratio of occupied acreage to total population, indicates how sparsely settled the coastal colony remained in 1720.[18] Since the parishes are ordered geographically in Table 2, it is clear that the southernmost precincts of St. Bartholomew's and St. Helena, lying beyond the Edisto River in the region which had recently been devastated by the Yamasee War, contained few whites and by far the lowest proportion of blacks.[19] Slaves were far more numerous among the small French settlements in the parish of St. James Santee on the northern boundary, and for the colony as a whole slaves already outnumbered free whites by roughly two to one. In the wealthy rice-growing parish of Goose Creek near Charlestown there

---

6400, tis bleived that since the Indian Warr which broke out in Aprill 1715 We are Increased about 100 Inhabitants, wee haveing lost about 400 in the Warr and have had the Accession of about 500 from England, Ireland and other places.

[17] Sirmans, p. 132, arrived at a total of 7,800 whites from Moore's figures. Sirmans' total was accepted by Frank Robert Hawkins, who recently reviewed general population data in his unpublished M.A. thesis at the University of Wisconsin, "Legislation Governing the Institution of Slavery in Colonial South Carolina," Madison, 1968, chap. II. Various estimates for the colonial period appear in Evarts B. Greene and Virginia D. Harrington, *American Population Before the Federal Census of 1790*, New York, 1932, pp. 172-179.

[18] Slightly earlier Thomas Nairne had observed, "This Province is capable of containing about 60 times the Number of its present Inhabitants." *A Letter from South Carolina*, London, 1710, p. 8.

[19] Francis Yonge, "A Narrative of the Proceedings of the People of South-Carolina in the Year 1719," in Peter Force, ed., *Tracts and Other Papers Relating Principally to the Origin, Settlement, and Progress of the Colonies in North America, from the Discovery of the Country to the Year 1776*, Washington, 1836-1846, II, 7:

In this War near 400 of the Inhabitants were destroy'd with many Houses and Slaves, and great numbers of Cattle, especially to the Southward near Port-Royal, from whence the Inhabitants were entirely drove, and forced into Settlements near Charles Town.

Cf. BPRO Trans., XVII, 88-144; BPRO Trans., XIX, 131. Several years later in "A View of the Trade of South Carolina" (BPRO Trans., X, 2), Yonge, who was one of the colony's agents, told the Lords of Trade and Plantations:

The trade for Beef and pork which was to Barbado's and the several Leeward Caribbee Islands ye Bahamas Jamaica &c has been very much interupted by the late Indian Warr which not only destroyed the Stocks of Cattle but drove most of the Inhabitants to the southward where the great stocks of Cattle were, from their plantations who yet dare not return for fear of the Yamazee Indians who frequently disturb the settlements near Port Royall murder the planters and carry the slaves to S[t] Augustine.

were more than three slaves for every white, and only in Charlestown itself (where calculations based on household size are least reliable) does it appear that the numbers of free and unfree may still have been approximately even.

During the 1720s the white population may have risen by as much as 50 percent to roughly 10,000 people, since one estimate at the end of the decade put the number fit to bear arms at "2500 Men or there-abouts," [20] and another reckoned the taxable inhabitants "to be two thousand Whitemen." [21] But the numbers of the unfree climbed fully twice as fast, approximately doubling within the decade. By 1729 there were "above Twenty Thousand Tythable Negroes," [22] presumably between the ages of 7 and 60. The export of both pitch and tar nearly doubled during the first half of the decade, and confident producers bought slaves on credit before the bottom fell from under the naval stores market in 1727.[23] The drop accelerated the transition to rice already underway, and this shift intensified the demand for labor. Where the colony had imported 1,500 slaves in the first four years of the decade, it imported four times as many during the last four years.

The white population, benefiting from the clearing of the land and the gradual improvement of food, clothing, and housing, probably owed more of its increase to natural growth than in previous decades. But the same economic expansion which improved the lot of free settlers worsened the condition of the unfree. Among slaves the rate of natural increase appears to have declined as the rate of importation swept upward. All told nearly 9,000 newcomers arrived from Africa during the 1720s,[24] an immigration which was almost equal to the net increase in the slave population. A slight rise in the death rate and decline in the birth rate of the black population would not be surprising. In many European colonies of the South Atlantic the drive to secure profits or remove debts by increasing the production of a plantation economy expanded the demand for slaves and created a

[20] James Sutherland came to South Carolina in November 1722 and served as the commander of Johnson's Fort on Charlestown Harbor. Sometime between 1729 and 1732 he submitted a letter to the Lords of Trade, an undated copy of which is in the Coe Papers of the South Carolina Historical Society (SCHS), Charleston:

Charleston, my Lord, . . . hath ab^t 300 brick Houses in it, the rest Timber, & is inhabited by about 600 white Men from 16 to 60 years of Age. . . .

I believe there are 2500 Men or thereabouts, fit to carry Arms, from 16 to 60: But as to the number of Whites & Negroes in this Colony, I cannot be certain.
[21] George Burrington to the Lords of Trade, 23 July 1730, BPRO Trans., XIII, 373-374.
[22] Ibid., p. 373.
[23] For a discussion of major economic and demographic trends in this decade, see Clowse, chaps. VII and VIII.
[24] See Table 3.

willingness to buy Negroes on credit. As slave imports rose to meet demand, the cost of individual slaves was reduced somewhat. Ironically, this would have increased white callousness toward the conditions of resident slaves and heightened white impatience with the costly and time-consuming process of sustaining black children as eventual members of the labor force. All these tendencies worsened the prospects for natural population growth among slaves and heightened the demand for slave imports. A vicious circle was thereby established in which it appeared advantageous to stress the importation of "salt water" slaves rather than the survival of those at hand. On some Caribbean sugar islands the natural rate of increase fell below zero for generations with the advent of intensive staple agriculture.[25]

Somewhat the same phenomenon seems to have occurred in South Carolina during the decades after 1720, as rice rose from the status of a competing export product to become the colony's central preoccupation. White colonists who responded to the opportunity for profit by investing in labor and expanding the production of staples soon faced declining export prices which in turn intensified the urge to broaden production further.[26] Pressures to expand cultivation, increase crop yield, raise efficiency, and reduce overhead all worked directly to depress the lot of the slave.[27] Intensification of the plantation system could have impaired the family stability usually associated with a high birth rate,[28] reduced life expectancy, and increased the incidence of disappearances or departures.

[25] Philip D. Curtin, *The Atlantic Slave Trade: A Census,* Madison, Wis., 1969, p. 32n, and chap. III.

[26] Governor Nicholson had written to the Lords of Trade, 21 April 1723 (BPRO Trans., x, 77):

> We have already had more ships and vessels in respect of Tonnage than was ever known in the Country and it is supposed there is loading enough for them and for those that are expected but the people are afraid that their Comodity of Rice pitch and Tarr their being so much of it will come to a Low market.

[27] The squeeze produced by this downward spiral was suggested in Governor Johnson's report of 1731. The governor pointed out that during the previous decade South Carolina had "more than doubled the produce in Rice, which imploys more than double the Negroes." But he went on to lament that the price of this commodity had declined so rapidly that 50,000 barrels of rice exported in 1731 returned hardly £4,000 more than had been brought by fewer than half that many barrels in 1721, "altho it is the Labour of Double the Number of Negroes, near three times the quantity of Land Planted, and the same proportion of Labour to make it marketable." "Governor Johnson's Answers to Queries," 16 December 1731, Parish Transcripts, box marked "Md. and other colonies," folder for S.C., 1720-1752, p. 18, New-York Historical Society (NYHS).

[28] Cf. Orlando Patterson, *The Sociology of Slavery: An Analysis of the Origins, Development and Structure of Negro Slave Society in Jamaica,* London, 1967, pp. 108-110.

141

Departures, in fact, deserve a separate comment. Runaways were a constant feature of colonial life, and careful analysis of black slaves in this category has only just begun.[29] From the earliest years of the Carolina colony, many absentees obtained refuge among the Tuscarora Indians to the north or among the Spaniards to the south. Even before 1700 both Virginia and South Carolina claimed that the sparsely settled North Carolina region was harboring runaways of all sorts,[30] but the total numbers both there and at St. Augustine were probably in the hundreds, not in the thousands.

Authorized departures, that is slave exports, were a slightly different matter. Most of the slaves exported from South Carolina before 1720 were Indians, not Negroes. Large-scale reexport of Africans by ship from Charlestown harbor, primarily to Georgia, did not develop until after that colony legalized slavery in 1751.[31] In the intervening decades, however, it is possible that the overland exportation of slaves into North Carolina was considerable, even though little documentation remains.[32] Maurice Moore, who accompanied his brother

[29] Gerald W. Mullin, *Flight and Rebellion: Slave Resistance in Eighteenth-Century Virginia*, New York, 1972, theorizes about runaways in that colony. Russell Blake at the University of Michigan has engaged in a quantitative study of runaways in colonial South Carolina.

[30] North Carolina was charged with sheltering deserting wives, stolen horses, and runaway servants and slaves, passing both north-to-south and south-to-north. Governor Henderson Walker offered the following defense in a letter of 10 October 1699. William L. Saunders, ed., *The Colonial Records of North Carolina*, Raleigh, 1886-1890, I, 513-514.

> We have (besides statutes against Vagrants) a particular law y^t injoyns all persons on a penalty to apprehend runaway Negros and prohibits ye harboring of them on ye penalty of ten shillings every night over & above all damage y^t can be proved & I purpose to recommend it to ye next Assembly if any thing may be done more effectually to prevent such a mischief Not long ago information was made to me & ye Council that one Grand at ye Sand-banks had entertained some persons suspected to be runaways. . . . I myself at my own charge sent as far as Pamplico after those runaways and since here [hear] advice y^t some of y^m died by famine in ye uninhabited part of this Government And I believe many other y^t fly this way are lost after ye same or such like manner endeavoring to escape to S. Carolina.

[31] Exportations of slaves from Charlestown between 1735 and 1775 are summarized in W. Robert Higgins, "The South Carolina Negro Duty Law," unpublished M. A. thesis at the University of South Carolina, Columbia, 1967, pp. 245-259, 263-265. Higgins points out (p. 19) that the duty law of 1716 (*Statutes*, II, 649-661), which allowed for the first time a 75% remission of duty on Negroes reexported within six months of arrival, may have been intended to help Charlestown slave traders expand the size and range of their commerce.

[32] Kenneth W. Stetson, "A Quantitative Approach to Britain's American Slave Trade, 1700-1773," unpublished M.S. thesis at the University of Wisconsin, Madison, 1967, pp. 48, 53. Stetson assumes that one-third of North Carolina's slave imports came from Virginia and two-thirds from South Carolina. This puts as many as 9,000 slaves moving from South Carolina to North Carolina between 1720 and

Col. James Moore on the Tuscarora expedition of 1712, remained in North Carolina and exerted a dominant influence for more than a quarter-century. Much of the family's power may have derived from the fact that they supposedly brought about 1,200 slaves into the colony.[33]

Census materials for South Carolina are spotty, but attrition through death, desertion, and exportation seems to have been high enough so that the Negro population scarcely sustained itself for several decades. Guesses made in 1734 as to the number of slaves range from 22,000 to 30,000,[34] with the proper total probably falling almost half way in between.[35] Assuming the correct figure to be around 26,000, it is notable that even though roughly 15,000 new slaves were imported from Africa over the next six years, the colony's black population was tabulated at only 39,155 in 1740.[36] If the question of departures is ignored for the moment, it is possible to calculate the annual rate of black population increase in excess of the number of immigrants for the two decades by using the precise counts of the black population made in 1720 and 1740, along with the import data from section four below. A population which had been increasing at a rate of 5.6 percent per annum before 1720, appears to have been decreasing at a rate of 1.1 percent per annum over the next twenty years.[37] If substantial exportations to North Carolina are taken into account the shift becomes less drastic, but it does not disappear.

Nevertheless, expanded importation more than offset any increase in slave mortality or export figures, causing the total black population to rise more rapidly than ever, as Figure 1, based upon Table 3

1740. Such movement undoubtedly occurred, but Stetson's calculation remains no more than a very rough estimate. (Stetson puts South Carolina's rate of natural increase among Negroes at zero for the total period 1700-1773.)

[33] SCHGM, 37 (January, 1936), 14-15.

[34] Document of 9 April 1734, BPRO Trans., xvi, 398-399; "Extract of the Reverend Mr. Bolzius's Journal" in Force, Tracts, iv, part 5, 18.

[35] An estimate of "twenty four Thousand Negroes" was probably a bit low. Document of 8 March 1734, Parish Transcripts, p. 15a of folder cited in n. 27, NYHS.

[36] A committee report to the colonial legislature, 2 March 1742, listed 2,447 town slaves and 36,708 slaves in the outlying counties. This census was based on assessments made the previous spring for the year 1740, and it appears in the South Carolina Commons House Journal for 1741-1742 (p. 460). These published journals (referred to hereafter as SCCHJ) include Alexander S. Salley, ed., Journal of the Commons House of Assembly, 21 vols., Columbia, 1907-1946; and J. H. Easterby and Ruth S. Green, eds., The Colonial Records of South Carolina, ser. i: The Journal of the Commons House of Assembly 1736-1750, 9 vols., Columbia, 1951-1962.

[37] See n. 8 above for the basis of the calculation.

TABLE 3. RECORD OF ANNUAL SLAVE IMPORTS, 1706-1739, AS IT APPEARS
IN *Gentleman's Magazine* OF 1755 (xxv, 344)

Years	Negroes	Vessels	Years	Negroes	Vessels
1706	24	68		4,504	1,919
1707[a]	22	66	1724	604	122
1708	53	81	1725	439	134
1709[b]	107	70	1726	1,728	146
1710	131	92	1727	1,794	126
1711	170	81	1728	1,201	141
1712	76	82	1729	1,499	157
1713	159	99	1730	941	165
1714	419	121	1731	1,514	184
1715[c]	81	133	1732	1,199	182
1716[c]	67	162	1733	2,792	222
1717[d]	573	127	1734	1,651	209
1718	529	114	1735	2,907	248
1719	541	137	1736	3,097	229
1720	601	129	1737	2,246	239
1721	165	121	1738	2,415	195
1722	323	120	1739	1,702	225
1723	463*	116			
	4,504	1,919		32,233	4,843

[a] The trade of this province to 1708 was only in exporting provisions to the sugar islands, from whence they had their supply of *European* goods, &c. and there were not above 200 Negroes in the province, although now there is above 50,000
  About this time they began to make tar, pitch, and turpentine.
[b] At this time they began to make and export rice.
[c] Time of the great *Indian* War, when many inhabitants left the prov.
[d] Before this time the trade was chiefly carried on in small coasting vessels, who made three or four voyages *per ann.* but after this in large ships to *Europe,* and smaller vessels to *America.*
[e] About this time two new ports of entry, &c. for shipping was allowed, *viz.* *Port Royal,* to the southward, and *George Town,* to the northward, each about 60 miles from *Charles Town,* and the number of negroes or vessels in those parts are not in this account.

* Donnan (*Documents,* IV, 255) reprints the annual totals, 1706-24, which were given in the *Report of the Committee of the Commons House of Assembly of the Province of South Carolina on the State of the Paper Currency of the said Province* (London, 1737) and were repeated in Edward McCrady, *History of South Carolina under the Proprietary Government* (New York, 1897), p. 723. They are identical to those in Table 3, except for the difference—apparently an ancient copying error— for 1723, where 436 is given. There is no way to know which figure is correct.

suggests. Aware of this steep rise and frightened by the Stono Rebellion of 1739, the white minority passed a law curtailing slave imports into South Carolina for three years, beginning in 1741.[38] This

[38] *Statutes,* III, 556-568.

prohibitive duty of the early 1740s, plus the later disruptions of war and depression, limited slave imports for the entire decade so drastically that the total black population may even have declined. It was estimated at roughly 40,000 in 1742 and 1745,[39] and although Governor Glen put the Negro total "above Forty thousand" in 1747,[40] he reduced his figure to "at least Thirty nine Thousand" two years later on the basis of tax records.[41]

Governor Glen could still add concerning the slaves in 1747, "I do not find that their number diminishes, but . . . the contrary." [42] The evidence, however, was hardly decisive, and the validity of his assertion would again rest upon the extent of exports, both recorded and unrecorded. It does appear that the rate of natural increase had been down for a full generation, and that imports continued to be the dominant factor in the growth of slave numbers until well after the Revolution. Still, Glen seems to have spoken with authority in 1754 when he stated of arriving slaves:

> these Importations are not to supply the place of Negroes worn out with hard work or lost by Mortality which is the case in our Islands where were it not for an annual accretion they could not keep up their stock, but our number increases even without such yearly supply.[43]

By the mid-1700s, therefore, the South Carolina slave population may have regained the positive rate of natural increase which would characterize it over the course of the next century.

IV

A SURPRISING amount of data is available concerning the arrival of new slaves. Increasing productivity after 1720 made it possible for the colony's economy to absorb whole shiploads of laborers, and a differential duty encouraged direct importation of Africans. A customs fee of £10 was imposed for each adult slave brought from Africa, while five times as much was charged for the entry of any Negro man or woman who had spent more than six months in the Western Hemi-

[39] BPRO Trans., xxi, 20-21: "Md. and other colonies," Parish Transcripts, S.C., 1720-1749, p. 38, NYHS.
[40] BPRO Trans., xxii, 275-276. Glen was emphasizing the colony's importance as a consumer of coarse English woolens and may have exaggerated Negro numbers slightly for that purpose.
[41] BPRO Trans., xxiii, 369-370 (cf. n. 11 above).
[42] Ibid.
[43] Elizabeth Donnan, ed., Documents Illustrative of the Slave Trade to America, Washington, 1930-1935, iv, 313.

sphere.[44] Direct transatlantic traffic in turn meant the use of larger ships, and a gradual increase in the average size of slave cargoes, even though the ratio (common to the entire slave trade) of roughly two slaves per ton aboard a fully loaded vessel probably altered little during the century.[45]

Increased shipping opened the possibility for other commercial centers on the coast, and in the mid-1720s Georgetown on Winyaw Bay to the north and Beaufort near Port Royal to the south were made legal ports of entry.[46] Captains were drawn to these spots for a variety of reasons. A few sensed the prospect of conspiring with local officials to avoid the colony's Negro duty.[47] Other ships' masters touched at the

---

[44] *Statutes*, III, 159-170. The wealthier Caribbean colonies often forwarded to the mainland slaves who were too weak and sickly ("refuse") on the one hand or too clever and dangerous on the other. As early as 1693 the Carolina Assembly prohibited the entrance of any slaves from Barbados who had been convicted for conspiracy or insurrection (*SCCHJ*, 1693, p. 15). The idea of a differential duty was first mentioned in an act of 1703 (see *SCCHJ*, 1703, pp. 33, 34, 63; *Statutes*, II, 200-206), and it is conceivable that it was urged by Proprietors with financial interest in the African trade. But the primary intention was undoubtedly to preclude weak or dangerous slaves from the West Indies. Compare the fact that during deliberations over a duty bill in Virginia in 1710, the Council addressed the following communication to the House of Burgesses (Donnan, IV, 91-92):

And foreasmuch as most of the Negroes imported from her Majesty's Plantations are either such as are transported for crimes or infected with diseases, the Council submit to the consideration of your house whether it may not be proper that a higher duty be laid on them then on Negroes imported directly from Africa.

[45] For the estimate of two slaves per ton in the trade generally, see Curtin, p. 134. On a single day in 1726 the 50-ton brigantine *America* brought 116 Negroes into port followed by the ship *Greyhound*, a galley listed at 100 tons and carrying 187 slaves. BPRO Trans., XI, 147, 243.

[46] See Table 3, note e. The towns themselves had first been established in 1705 and 1711 respectively. Joseph I. Waring, *A History of Medicine in South Carolina, 1670-1825*, Columbia, 1964, pp. 26-27. In 1743 it was noted that the County Comptrollers at Port Royal and Winyaw, like the Public Treasurer in Charlestown, charged a fee of £4 for every entry of a cargo of Negroes. 17 January 1743, *SCCHJ*, 1742-1744, p. 155.

[47] On 22 February 1733, the Lower House alerted the Upper that John Caruthers, a slaving captain familiar with Carolina, had brought 162 Africans to the colony in December aboard the galley *Molly*, landing 100 at Charlestown and taking the rest to Winyaw. "Caruthers made a manifest to the Comptroller of the One Hundred Negroes Imported in the ship into the Port of Charlestown only, without making any Manifest of the Sixty two Negroes landed at the Port of Wyneaw or taking any proper measures for the payment of the Duties arising on the Importation of said Sixty two Negroes." On 3 March the Upper House reported back after looking into the matter "that we find John Brown the Comptroler, has not been only very remiss in his Duty, but indeed guilty of Notorious Falsity (we might almost say Forgery)." They urged the appointment of "some other more fit person for that Employment which we think is a trust almost equal to that of the Treasurer & shou'd therefore be put into the hands of a person of Credit and

146

outports in search of a homeward cargo when supplies in Charlestown lagged.[48] And still others may have brought slaves who were in such poor condition that they could not compete in the Charlestown slave market but could be sold off slowly, with liberal credit, to white residents of the outlying districts.[49] (More than two dozen of the slaves brought into Port Royal from Angola aboard the *Susannah* in 1736 had still not been sold in 1739 according to a notice in the *Gazette*.) [50] However, the slaves who entered the colony through these ports (and therefore went unnoted in the Charlestown records) came intermittently aboard small vessels, and their total numbers were insignificant before mid-century.

The arrival of more slaves in larger shipments, for which higher prices were charged and greater debts incurred, led inevitably to broader advertising and more careful accounting of imports.[51] Statistics for the South Carolina slave traffic increase in availability with the importance of the trade, and at certain points overlapping records can be combined for remarkable completeness. The longest single series of import figures appeared in *Gentleman's Magazine* in 1755 and is repro-

---

Ability," but on 7 March the Lower House requested Brown only be reprimanded "Considering that he has been an old Servant to this House." Three years later (26 March 1736), the Governor and Council reported that they had "advice that a Negro Ship is shortly expected to arrive at Port Royal in this Govt. & as there is not a Treasurer or Comptroller appointed for that Port," they took the occasion to name authorities "to receive such Dutys as may become due to the Public in that port & likewise in that of Winyaw." These incidents from the legislative journals are copied in Parish Transcripts, S.C., Box I, folder 4, pp. 30-31 and folder labeled "Minutes of Council and Burgesses, 1734-1740," p. 7, NYHS. There is special irony in the fact that the Treasurer in Charlestown at this time was himself engaged in embezzling funds from the Negro duties. SCCHJ, 1734-1735, pp. 128, 129, 405, 406, 524.

[48] The S.C. *Gazette*, 23 November 1834, carried an "Account of all the Vessels that are cleared outwards at the Port of George Town Winyaw in South-Carolina, from the first of November 1733. to the first of November 1734 with the Lading of each Vessel." Pitch and other naval stores were going directly to England and the northern maritime colonies, but the small amount of rice passing through the port at this time went south to Charlestown.

[49] A petition to the Council in 1727 from white inhabitants of Santee and Winyaw concerning inequities in the Negro tax may have reflected the condition of slaves reaching Georgetown at this time. "Your Honors know how unjust the Tax is," complained the citizens; "the Aged, sucklings [and the] Decrepit pay the same Tax as the best Negroes in the province." BPRO Trans., XII, 213.

[50] S.C. *Gazette*, 17 March 1739. The *Susanna* had left 30 Negroes in Barbados. Since she was almost the only vessel for South Carolina in the mid-1730s which did this, it may be an indication of failing health among her slaves. Donnan, II, 431. Cf. item 43 in the appendix.

[51] On the increasing size of debts and the changing methods of payment during the 1730s, see the letter to the S.C. *Gazette*, 9 March 1738, reprinted in Donnan, IV, 291-294.

duced as Table 3 above. It derives from records kept by the customs officer in Charlestown, who recorded imports and exports and published the totals in annual tables, according to a calendar year which ended 1 November. Most of these tables have disappeared, but those that survive provide contemporary checks on the slave import figures from the English magazine. The customs house data reprinted in the South Carolina *Gazette* for the year ending 1 November 1735, for example, show 248 entering vessels (only a fraction of which carried Negroes) and 2,907 arriving slaves,[52] just as in Table 3. Comparable data for the year ending 1 November 1739 agree with the *Gentleman's Magazine* listing of 1,702 Negroes imported into Charlestown.[53] The accuracy of the figures can be further verified by the records of the Treasury Office, which was responsible for collecting duty on Negroes brought into Charlestown.[54]

V

THE Treasury Records constitute an invaluable source of immigration data in their own right, for the General Duty Books contain a continuous account of money collected for the importation of slaves into Charlestown between 1735 and 1775.[55] Except when prohibitive duties were in effect for brief spans (1741-1744 and 1766-1768) the standard basic tax on each new slave from Africa for the half-century before the Revolution was £10 for persons over 10 and £5 for those under that age, though after 1740 a third rate was established for smaller children.[56]

[52] S.C. *Gazette*, 8 November 1735. The fact that these figures were accepted by contemporaries is borne out by a letter in the S.C. *Gazette*, 2 April 1737. The author, "Mercator," clearly used these numbers to compute the fact that 10,447 Negroes were imported in the previous four years while only 5,153 had arrived in the four years prior to that.

[53] "Record of Imports and Exports for the Port of Charlestown, 1 Nov. 1738-1 Nov. 1739," John Carter Brown Library, Providence, Rhode Island.

[54] The Treasury Records appear to have been separate from customs house data, for the tax books were kept according to the old style calendar until 1752, beginning the year on 25 March and dividing it at 29 September. The earliest series of import figures based on this source shows that between 29 September 1721, and 29 September 1726, 3,528 slaves were imported, while the customs total for the same five years, counting from 1 November, is 3,557. Donnan, IV, 267.

[55] The most extended treatment of these colonial duties is Higgins, "The South Carolina Negro Duty Law." Focusing on Charlestown slave merchants, Higgins was the first person to use the Treasury Records to explore Negro imports systematically. The Treasury Records themselves are in the SCDAH and are available on microfilm.

[56] What became of the ten-year-olds, and who determined the Africans' ages in the first place are unanswered questions. The ambiguous division was clarified somewhat by the 1740 act which set the arbitrary height of 4 feet 2 inches as the

Between the years 1735 and 1740, while only two rates were still in effect, the Treasurer recorded not only the total duty paid by each importer but also the number of slaves in every shipment. It is therefore possible to calculate the exact number of minors aboard each ship, since only one combination of full and half rates could yield the precise duty paid. For example, £ 100 paid for twelve slaves indicates the arrival of eight adults and four children. As a result these records, complimented by material from the *Gazette* and other sources, offer the opportunity for a detailed recreation of Negro arrivals from Africa. This five-year reconstruction is given in the appendix at the end of the chapter, and aside from minor exceptions noted there the picture it gives is a thorough one. This compilation for import data between March 1735 and March 1740 is summarized in Table 4.

Within Table 4 the importation statistics have been broken down by year according to the regions of origin listed in the South Carolina sources. The number of shipments may not be totally exact, since different merchants occasionally paid duties on separate groups of slaves arriving in the same vessel. More importantly, the division according to place of origin is by no means entirely precise. Sixteen of the eighty shipments were simply listed as coming from "Africa," while for seven other shipments the origin was given as "Africa" in one record and as some more specific point in another source.[57] It was commonplace for slaving ships to work their way along the coast picking up slaves at a variety of ports in one or more regions. Thus, since an explicit locality is named for four-fifths of the shipments in this sample, the question becomes whether any inferences can be drawn from that listing about the regional origins of the slaves being transported? This question is made more intriguing by the fact that Table 4 would seem to suggest that roughly seven out of every ten Africans imported into Charlestown during this period came from the area then called Angola near the Congo River.

Might captains have stated their final African point of departure without reference to the places where they had obtained most of their slaves? This seems unlikely, since Carolinians—official and unofficial— were more interested in the origin of the cargo than in the course of the ship. Moreover, if a point of departure was being recorded, more ships would have given a specific port and fewer would have listed

---

dividing line between young and old and added a third tariff of 2 pounds 10 shillings for children under 3 feet 2 inches, leaving only infants to enter duty free. *Statutes*, iii, 556-558.

[57] In the appendix I have chosen to list the specific origin for these seven vessels and to mark each with an asterisk.

TABLE 4. AFRICANS ARRIVING IN CHARLESTOWN, S.C. (MARCH 1735-MARCH 1740) BY YEAR AND BY ORIGIN OF SHIPMENT

Treasury Yr. March-March	From Angola				From Gambia				From Elsewhere in Africa				From West Indies, etc.				Total			
	Shipments	Over Age 10	Under 10	Total	Shipments	Over Age 10	Under 10	Total	Shipments	Over Age 10	Under 10	Total	Shipments	Over Age 10	Under 10	Total	Est. No. of Shipments	Slaves Over Age 10	Slaves Under Age 10	Total No. of Slaves
1735-36	6	1,858	171	2,029	—	—	—	—	4	569	43	612	3	4	6	10	13	2,431	220	2,651
1736-37	12	2,474	417	2,891	2	163	25	188	1	196	28	224	3	22	1	23	18	2,855	471	3,326
1737-38	5	789	38	827	—	—	—	—	1	194	34	228	4	7	0	7	10	990	72	1,062
1738-39	6	1,276	330	1,606	3	291	23	314	3	453	122	575	1	12	0	12	13	2,032	475	2,507
1739-40	2	590	102	692	2	178	25	203	5	894	186	1,080	3	33	8	41	12	1,695	321	2,016
5 Yr. Total	31	6,987	1,058	8,045	7	632	73	705	14	2,306	413	2,719	14	78	15	93	66	10,003	1,559	11,562
% of total slaves	69.6%				6.1%				23.5%				0.8%				100%			
Average size of shipment	260				101				194				7				175			
% Over 10	86.9%				89.7%				84.8%				83.9%				86.5%			
% Under 10	13.1%				10.3%				15.2%				16.1%				13.5%			

"Africa." [58] It is true that many slave ships, even those bound for the most northerly American ports, dropped down toward the equator to find favorable winds and currents for the voyage west, but since time was a crucial factor few vessels would have ended their African stay by sailing southeast to the Angolan ports unless absolutely necessary. It seems more likely that while numerous English slavers worked the coast further northward, certain larger vessels suited to the longer voyage sailed more directly to the Angolan region for their cargo. [59] No doubt many of these ships took on Africans elsewhere. An advertisement in 1733, for example, announced the arrival of "a choice Cargo of SLAVES, imported from the GOLD COAST and ANGOLA." [60] But it seems safe to assume that a majority of the passengers aboard ships reported to be from "Angola" were drawn from the slave sources of that region.

However, this does not explain why such a high proportion of these shipments came to South Carolina. Less than 15 percent of the total English slave trade during the 1730s derived from the Congo-Angola region according to the most recent estimate, and it is unclear why more than half the Negroes leaving Loanga, Malimba, and other Angolan ports in English ships appear to have ended up in Charlestown. [61] It could be that the "separate traders" who dominated the Carolina market found easier access at Angola, since both the source and the destination remained on the perimeter of the English slaving world. But we must know a good deal more about Angolan slave trading before we can be certain about general export figures or the motivations of particular captains.

To fully explain this marked departure from the established patterns of the English slave trade, it will also be necessary to know a great deal more about specialized demand among American slave purchasers. Did preferences expressed in Charlestown reflect precise knowledge and specific needs on the part of the purchasers? (For example, what explains their repeated interest in obtaining "tall" slaves?) [62] Or did they merely represent an acceptance of those

[58] Nor did "Africa" designate ships passing through the West Indies, since stopovers in Caribbean ports seem to have been specifically recorded.

[59] Perhaps the volume of trade there was great enough upon occasion to offer the inducement of obtaining a large shipment in a brief time.

[60] S.C. *Gazette*, 14 April 1733.

[61] Curtin, p. 150 (Table 43), estimates total English slave exports from Angola and Mozambique combined at less than 30,000 for the 1730s, or less than 15,000 for the latter half of the decade.

[62] Elizabeth Donnan, "The Slave Trade into South Carolina Before the Revolution," *American Historical Review* 33 (1927-1928), 816-817.

151

nationalities still available after the West Indian planters had exerted their choice?[63] It is evident that Carolina slave merchants and their customers were fully capable of distinguishing between Africans from different regions, though opinions about the relative merit of certain groups may have been based more upon hearsay and coincidence than deep-rooted facts.[64] The stated preference of Carolina masters was for slaves from Gambia (which helps explain why the few shipments from that region were carefully designated) or the Windward and Gold Coasts.[65] On the other hand, Angolans were valued more highly than slaves from the Bight of Biafra, so it seems doubtful that their presence in the slave pens of Charlestown was simply the result of some prejudice in the larger Caribbean ports against Angolans.[66]

[63] Not only were regional preferences at work in the West Indies, but distinctions were regularly being made between different Africans from the same region. A Jamaican factor, who traded the best of incoming slaves to the Spanish for gold, remarked in 1737 that "The ships from Angola and Calabar bring in three assortments of negroes. The first for us, the second for the Planters, And the third for the illicit traders." John Merewether to Peter Burwell, 30 September 1737, Donnan, *Documents,* II, 461.

[64] Distinctions made by purchasers of African slaves in the eighteenth century bear a striking resemblance to attitudes characteristic of the employers of cheap European labor in the nineteenth and early twentieth centuries. The stereotypes applied to Gambians, Ibos, Coromantees, and Angolans were not different in kind from those later applied to Irish, Swedes, Jews, Slavs, and Italians. Racial, ethnic, and religious distinctions were mixed; shrewd analysis and sensible lore became intermingled with shifting social and personal prejudices. Word of a shipboard rebellion in Benin or of several Ibo suicides in Carolina could do a great deal to shape labor demands. The influential slave merchant, Henry Laurens, once wrote to his agent to send "fine, healthy, young Negro lads & Men, if such [are available] of any Country except Ebo." *SCHGM,* 27 (October 1926), 211.

[65] Curtin, p. 157. Laurens, for example, stated his desire for slaves from "Gambia & Windward coast . . . or the Angola Men such as are large." Philip Hamer and George C. Rogers, eds., *The Papers of Henry Laurens,* Columbia, 1968—, I, 258.

[66] Whatever the cause of this apparent Angolan concentration, it altered rapidly, so that a rough estimate of slaves entering South Carolina through the rest of the century is probably correct to put those from Angola at less than 40% (still more than double their proportion in the British slave trade as a whole and nearly twice the percentage of Angolans estimated among all Africans entering North America). Portuguese exportation from Angola doubled during the middle third of the century, and diminishing British contact with that region could be one explanation for the shift in the origins of Carolina's slaves. During the two decades immediately preceding the Revolution, when the colony's slave imports were greatest, English activity in Angolan ports was negligible. Curtin, pp. 150 (Table 43), 157 (Table 45), 207 (Table 62).

Conceivably, the predominance of new Angolans during the late 1730s became linked in some real or imagined way with the unrest at the end of that decade, prejudicing masters against slaves from that region. A contemporary account of the 1739 Stono Uprising, in which more than sixty people were killed, makes special reference to the fact that "Amongst the Negroe Slaves there are a people brought from the Kingdom of Angola in Africa." It was argued that as a result of missionaries in Angola, a number of these slaves professed Catholicism or spoke Portuguese, which was said to be close enough to Spanish so that the Spaniards

Not only were Angolans predominant among new Negroes between 1735 and 1740, but they arrived in distinctively large shipments. Vessels coming from that most distant of the major slaving regions averaged 260 persons per cargo.[67] By contrast, cargoes from the middle reaches of the African coast averaged less than 200 and those from the northern region of the River Gambia averaged scarcely 100.[68] All told, the capacities of slaving vessels entering Charlestown probably remained somewhat below the average for the English trade as a whole, which reached nearly 250 slaves per ship by the third quarter of the century.[69]

While the size of individual shipments varied widely, the ratio of adults to children remained remarkably constant. Overall, 86.5 percent of the slaves in the sample were judged to be above 10 years old, and the figures from each region conform closely.[70] Shipments from Gambia had the lowest percentage of children, perhaps because adults from that region were highly valued. In general, buyer preferences as to age and sex, like preferences in nationality, must have been taken into consideration by slave merchants and weighed constantly against the other complexities of a precarious trade. Before the three-year embargo on Negroes expired in the summer of 1744, a Charlestown merchant wrote to the owner of a schooner in Barbados that ideal slave cargoes for Carolina would include "especially Boys & Girls of abo.ᵗ 15 or 16 y.ʳˢ of Age . . . ⅔ Boys & ⅓ Girls."[71]

---

in St. Augustine were particularly successful in encouraging them to rebel or escape. "An Account of the Negroe Insurrection in South Carolina," in Allen D. Candler and Lucien L. Knight, eds., *The Colonial Records of the State of Georgia*, Atlanta, 1904-1916, xxii, pt. 2, p. 233. For a full account see Wood, *Black Majority*, chap xii.

[67] Since less than half the trading ships entering Charlestown accounted for 70% of the incoming slaves, any calculation of slave origins based upon numbers of shipments would underestimate the Angolan contingent.

[68] New Negroes shipped from the West Indies entered in consignments so small that some may have escaped the Treasurer's records. They did continue to arrive, however, for a correspondent to the *Gazette* (9 March 1738) observed, "I have known many Slaves bought in *Barbadoes, &c* and sent here for Sale which have been sold with good Profit."

[69] Curtin, pp. 133-134, 147.

[70] It is notable that in the only earlier sample of incoming Negroes divided by age—734 Africans arriving aboard five ships in the summer of 1726—the full duty was paid for 86.1% of the slaves. BPRO Trans., xi, 243-244; also in Donnan, *Documents*, iv, 267-268.

[71] Robert Pringle to Edward Pare, owner of the *Charming Sarah*, 5 May, 1744, Letterbook of Robert Pringle, 1737-1745, SCHS. This is not dissimilar to the advice which Henry Laurens conveyed to his slave trading agents, Smith & Clifton, in the following decade: "Purchase that number of very likely healthy People, Two thi[r]ds at least Men from 18 to 25 Years old, the other young Women from 14 to 18." Hamer and Rogers, eds., *The Papers of Henry Laurens*, i, 295.

A look at South Carolina's copious but unstudied inventories from this period underscores the effects which such importation patterns had on the black demography of the region. One inventory, drawn up for the estate of John Cawood in 1726, is specially valuable since it lists age as well as monetary value for each of thirty-nine slaves.[72] Youth predominates, for almost half (19 of 39) are 18 or under, while only six are over 40. For the younger slaves exact ages are given, and most were probably born on Cawood's estate. But among the sixteen who were born before 1700 ages are rounded off, and it is interesting to speculate about their origins. Most, like Angola Phillis whose age was estimated at 30, were undoubtedly born in Africa and imported after the turn of the century, although Indian Jane (also 30) was clearly an American by birth. The two most elderly slaves, Old Cate born in 1662 and Old Betty born in 1666, probably began life in the West Indies, since their exact ages were known to the appraisers.

If the slave trade helped shape age distribution, it also played a part in determining the sex ratio among slaves. Rising imports reflected a consistent preference for men over women which perpetuated the imbalance of earlier years and limited the prospects for a high birth rate which could restore a more even ratio between the sexes. An analysis of the twenty-three inventories covering estates with more than ten slaves filed in the eighteen months after 1 January 1730 yields a sample of 714 slave names.[73] Of the 663 persons who can be identified by sex, 64.2 percent (426) are men and only 35.8 percent (237) are women. In the future, even broader statistical samples taken from import and inventory records over a longer time span may yield a more precise and continuous demographic picture.

VI

It is valuable in the meantime to explore one further source of data. The letters written by the missionaries of the Society for the Propagation of the Gospel contain very different and even more detailed

[72] "Inventory of John Cawood, Esq.," 4 January 1726, Miscellaneous Records (1726-1727), B, 542-552, typed vol., SCDAH. Cawood was a well-to-do citizen whose diverse enterprises illustrate the state of the young economy. In Charlestown, where Cawood's older and more valuable slaves were located, he maintained a town house, a "skin store," and a smith shop, but he also owned a plantation at Ashepoe employing twenty-eight slaves. His brother-in-law, William Gibbon, was a Charlestown merchant (*SCHGM*, 19 (April 1918), 69). But Cawood himself appears to have been—like many others of his generation—part merchant, part Indian trader, part artisan, and part planter.

[73] I have drawn these documents from: Wills, Inventories, and Miscellaneous Records, vol. 62-B (1729-1731), SCDAH.

figures on the increasing Negro population. These plentiful records, still almost completely unpublished, have never been combed adequately for demographic material, but certain pieces of census data which the churchmen sent back to London have appeared in print. These published figures provide varied insights, depending upon the location of the minister's parish and his own specific interests.

The reports of Thomas Hasell, for example, from the northern parish of St. Thomas east of the Cooper River provide clear evidence of the relative and absolute decline in the number of Indian slaves during the 1720s.[74] In that year Hasell noted the nonwhites in his parish as more than 800 Negroes and 90 Indian slaves. Four years later he recorded 950 blacks but only 62 enslaved Indians,[75] and in 1728 he estimated, "There are in this parish about 1,000 negro and 50 Indian slaves."[76] In the survey of 1730 inventories mentioned above, only 18 of 714 slaves were identified as Indians or mustees. This represents only 2.5 percent of the slave population. Eight of them resided on the two largest plantations, and the majority were women and children.

Letters from St. Bartholomew's, between the Edisto and Combahee Rivers, suggest the evolution of a frontier parish into a predominantly Negro rice district within a generation. In 1715 the Rev. Nathaniel Osborne estimated there were "near an Hundred and Twenty Familys" in this region, but most were forced out by the Indian war and five years later there were less than half as many whites and only a minority of blacks.[77] No missionary settled there again until the 1730s, but by 1736 Thomas Thompson reported to the S.P.G. Secretary that, "In the parish of St. Bartholomew there are one hundred and twenty families of white people, and twelve hundred negroes."[78] In the next seven years, with the expansion of rice production, the free population

[74] This significant shift had begun well before the Yamasee War and was accompanied by a decline in the cash value of Indian slaves. In 1722 (when Negro slaves were worth several hundred pounds in Carolina currency) the government offered Col. Theophilus Hastings £50 for each remaining Yamasee he could take, dead or alive. It was added that "in Case he Engages the Creeks or any other Indians utterly to destroy the Said nation of Yamasees the Said Hastings for such Extraordinary Service Shall be paid out of the Publick Treasury of the Province the Sum of One Thousand pounds." SCUHJ, mfm. BMP/D487, 14 June 1722, SCDAH. (Hastings returned with five scalps and three captive Indians, two of whom were set aside by Governor Nicholson as gifts for the Prince and Princess of Wales. SCCHJ, 1724, pp. 15, 50.)

[75] Frank J. Klingberg, *An Appraisal of the Negro in Colonial South Carolina*, Washington, 1941, p. 32.

[76] Klingberg, *Appraisal*, p. 34.

[77] SCHGM, 50 (October 1949), 175. Cf. Table 2 above.

[78] *Ibid.*, p. 178.

rose from roughly 600 to more than 900 [79] while the number of slaves fully tripled to "between three and four thousand." [80] When William Langhorne submitted "An Account of the Spiritual State of St. Bartholomew's Parish" in 1752, he numbered the Europeans at 1,280 and the "Heathens and Infidels" at 5,200.[81] Dramatic population shifts such as this in the rice-growing parishes south of Charlestown must have proved significant factors in the unrest which filled the colony in the late 1730s and early 1740s.

The most precise population data acquired by the S.P.G. derive from St. George's Parish, offering a localized perspective for some of the patterns already mentioned. This thin strip of prosperous lowland stretched toward the northwest from just below Dorchester, touching the Ashley River on one side and the Edisto on the other. It had been split off from the older parish of St. Andrews during the expansion which followed the Yamasee War, and by 1720 it already had nearly 70 taxpayers and more than 500 slaves.[82] Rapid growth over the next few years meant that there were more than 100 households with a total of 1,300 slaves in St. George's when the Rev. Francis Varnod filed his unique census of the parish in January 1726. This minister's account, long published, has been subjected to almost no analysis, yet it provides an invaluable close-up of one segment of the colony at the end of the first quarter of the eighteenth century.[83]

Varnod listed by name 108 heads of households, probably in some geographical order, and placed a "D" after those fifty-two who were religious dissenters. After each name he recorded six figures: the numbers of white people ("Men," "Women," and "Children") and the numbers of slaves ("Men," "Women," and "Children") within that household. Two of the land holdings—totally dissimilar in nature—clearly belonged to absentees. "Sam Wraggs Plant[ation]" was the property of the leading Charlestown slave merchant and contained

[79] This estimate is based upon Thompson's statement, 23 April 1743, that "There are not above 240 White men in this parish." *Ibid.*, p. 180.

[80] *Ibid.*, pp. 182-183, Thompson wrote of his white parishioners (16 August 1743):

They pretend that their parish is poor and cannot well defray the charges of a Church and parsonage; but tis well known that for some years past there is no parish in the Province That has produced a greater, and few (if any) so great a quantity of rice; that there are between three and four thousand slaves in it, and several considerable Stores, which besides the land, make it richer than some parishes in England itself.

[81] *Ibid.*, p. 200.

[82] Table 2 above.

[83] Varnod's census is printed in Klingberg, *Appraisal*, pp. 58-60. Sirmans, p. 145, makes brief use of it, but the number of slaves has been added incorrectly.

fifty-seven slaves and a white overseer; "Nath Wickams Pl": was worked by four slave men, one woman and a child entirely on their own. Eleven of the households are listed in the names of women, in some cases even when white men were present.

Below the list of householders Varnod recorded the presence of twenty-four people under the separate category of "Free negroes and Indians." Guy (a Negro), Nero (an Indian), and a woman named Sarah each lived alone. An Indian named Sam Pickins and a Negro named Robin Johnson both lived separately with a wife and four children, and Johnson's household also included nine slaves: three men, three women, and three children. The presence of these two dozen people is significant, for it illustrates the fact that free nonwhites could still find ways to subsist, at least marginally, within the confines of this frontier society. As slavery based on race became increasingly central to the colony's social and economic system, the incongruous status of such people grew more and more untenable. As early as 1726 the most striking fact about this group was its small size. Whatever the social importance of these anomalous residents, statistically they represent less than 2 percent of the parish's non-Europeans. It is therefore logical to leave them aside while examining the bulk of both the free and slave population more closely, and they have been excluded from the calculations which follow.

The parish's white minority totaled 537. Just over 50 percent (271) were regarded as adults, and 56 percent of these were men. There were eight households with no white men and seven others with more women than men, but almost half the holdings contained one man and one woman listed as white. Assuming most of these couples to be conjugal units, the sizes of the families they were raising can be summarized as follows:

TABLE 5. CHILDREN IN 53 WHITE HOUSEHOLDS WITH ONE MAN AND ONE WOMAN

Children per household	0	1	2	3	4	5	6	7	Total
Number of households	3	13	14	7	10	3	2	1	53
Number of children	0	13	28	21	40	15	12	7	136

Nearly 40 percent of these homes (21) contain two or three children: 16 have one child or none, and 16 others have 4 offspring or more. The child/parent ratio in these 53 households averages to 2.57 children for every mother. This ratio is somewhat higher (2.82/1) when calculated from the 73 households with one white woman present (but

157

not necessarily one white man), and it is slightly lower (2.24/1) when the total number of white children is divided by the total number of white women in the parish.

The numbers of white men varied little from household to household. Apart from the large farm of Benjamin Perriman with 8 men (plus 2 women, 9 children, and a slave man and child) and that of Roger Sumner with 5 men (plus 2 women, 3 children, and 3 adult slaves), all the other households in the parish contained fewer than 4 free men. On 70 of the holdings there was only one white man, and there were merely two or three on 28 of the other estates. (This is not a surprising distribution in a recently settled parish where fresh land was readily available for new arrivals and for children as they came of age. Numerous family connections can be seen among the names of property owners on Varnod's list.) The size of white households as a whole is worth noting. If one discounts the two plantations with absentee owners, the 1726 census shows 106 households with 536 white members, or 5.06 per household. This figure varies little in accordance with the size of the plantation, and it lends specific confirmation to the process of multiplying the number of taxpayers by five to estimate the white population, as in Table 2 above.

The slaves in St. George's Parish by 1726 were almost entirely Negroes, and there were scarcely half a dozen Negroes present who were not slaves, so it is possible to view the black population and the unfree population as roughly coequal. Varnod's list enumerates exactly 1,300 slaves, more than 70 percent of the parish's total inhabitants. By this time, therefore, slaves numbered 12 per household (as opposed to 8 in 1720), and since 21 residences in the parish included no slaves at all, there were an average of 15 Negroes on each of the remaining 87 tracts. However, they were by no means evenly distributed, as Tables 6 and 7 show, and a slave born in St. George's Parish or brought there to work was far more likely to dwell on a large plantation than on a small one. There were 40 tracts with from 1 to 5 slaves and a total of 90 holdings which contained fewer than 20 slaves, but only one-third of the unfree population worked on these lands. Two-thirds of the slaves resided on only 18 plantations in groups which ranged from 25 to 94, and more than 20 percent were located on the largest three of these.

The contrasting distribution of Africans and Europeans is seen more clearly in Table 7, which sorts out households according to their combined total of free and unfree persons. There were fewer than ten people in half the units (column A) and here whites outnumbered slaves by 5 to 2. But in the other half (columns B through F), which

TABLE 6. DISTRIBUTION OF SLAVES PER HOUSEHOLD, ST. GEORGE'S PARISH, S.C., 1726

No. of slaves per household	0	1	2	3	4	5	6	7	8	9	10	11	12	13	14	15	16	17	18	19	20	21	22	23	24
No. of households	21	13	4	12	8	3	4	1	3	2	3	2	2	2	6	0	1	0	1	2	0	0	0	0	0
No. of slaves	0	13	8	36	32	15	24	7	24	18	30	22	24	26	84	0	16	0	18	38	0	0	0	0	0
% of Total slave pop.	8.0%						7.9%					12%					5.5%								

No. of slaves per household	0-24	25-49	50-74	75-99	Totals
No. of households	90	11	4	3	108
No. of slaves	435	371	232	262	1,300
% of total slave pop.	33.4%	28.5%	17.9%	20.2%	100%

TABLE 7. DISTRIBUTION OF SLAVES AND WHITES IN RELATION TO TOTAL HOUSEHOLD SIZE, ST. GEORGE'S PARISH, S.C., 1726

Number of slaves and whites in household	A. 1-9	B. 10-19	C. 20-29	D. 30-39	E. 40-49	F. 50-99	G. Totals
Number of households	54	31	6	5	5	7	108
% of total households	50%	29%	6%	4.5%	4.5%	6%	100%
Number of people	305	449	146	185	220	532	1,837
% of total population	16.6%	24.4%	8.0%	10%	12%	29%	100%
Number of slaves	86	277	100	147	196	494	1,300
% of all slaves	6.6%	21.3%	7.7%	11.3%	15.1%	38%	100%
Number of whites	219	172	46	38	24	38	537
% of all whites	40.7%	32%	8.6%	7.1%	4.5%	7.1%	100%
Ratio of slaves per one white	0.4	1.6	2.2	4	8.2	13.4	2.4
Ratio of slaves per five whites (average size of white household)	2	8	11	20	41	67	12

DETAILS OF THE SEVEN LARGEST HOUSEHOLDS (COL. F ABOVE) AS LISTED IN VARNOD'S CENSUS

	Whites			Slaves		
	Men	Women	Children	Men	Women	Children
Walter Izard	2	1	4	29	23	39
John Williams	1	1	1	48	24	22
Alex Skeene, Esq.	3	2	1	27	18	32
Sus: Baker D[issenter]	3	3	5	26	17	18
Eliz. Diston D[issenter]	2	1	2	19	18	24
Sam Wragg Plant[ation]	1	—	—	35	12	10
Jos: Blake	1	1	3	16	17	20
	13	9	16	200	129	165

TABLE 8. DISTRIBUTION OF SLAVES AND WHITES BY SEX AND AGE, ST. GEORGE'S PARISH, S.C., 1726

	Men	Women	Children	Total	% of Total Pop.	Children per Woman	Men per 100 Women	% of Adults
Slaves	484	376	440	1,300	70.8%	1.17	129	66.2%
Whites	152	119	266	537	29.2%	2.24	128	50.5%
Combined	636	495	706	1,837	100%	1.43	128	61.6%

contained five-sixths of the total population, slaves outnumbered whites by nearly 4 to 1. On the seven plantations listed by Varnod with more than 50 residents (two of which were run by women), there were more than 13 slaves for every white person.

As Table 8 indicates, the ratio between the sexes among the adult slaves (129 men to 100 women) was almost exactly the same as the ratio among their white owners (128 to 100). But this similarity is deceptive in considering family patterns, for slave distribution was extremely arbitrary and was dictated by white economic considerations. Although in half of the white homes adults were balanced by sex, less than one-sixth of the adjacent slave quarters had an equal number of men and women. Fifteen slave men and 6 women belonged to Lilia Hague; 18 men and 8 women lived on the Warring plantation; 6 men and 13 women were bound to John Baker's estate. Negro women outnumbered men on 31 percent of the slaveholding estates (while females predominated in only 13 percent of the white households), but more often Negro men were in a majority. Not surprisingly, this was especially true on the largest plantations. Two hundred men labored on the seven biggest tracts, where the ratio was 155 men to 100 women. As has been noted, masters increasingly sought and obtained shipments of slaves which were nearly two-thirds men as plantation agriculture intensified. As a result, while the sex ratio for Europeans grew more balanced, that for Africans was becoming more disproportionate. A sample of slaves taken from inventories in 1730 and 1731 shows that by that time the ratio of slave men to women on sizable plantations throughout the colony was 180 to 100.[84]

Although the slave population was undoubtedly young as a whole, the St. George's census shows a low percentage of Negro children. While only half of the white inhabitants were listed as fully grown,

[84] See n. 73 above.

nearly two-thirds of all slaves (66.2 percent) were numbered as adults. Few explanations seem sufficient.[85] Undoubtedly slave imports which concentrated upon young adults raised the percentage of grown-ups somewhat, but by the same token they introduced numerous women of child-bearing age. It would therefore seem that the birth rate itself among potential Negro mothers was lower in 1726 than it had been earlier, for there was an average of only 1.17 children for each slave woman in the parish, scarcely half the average (2.24) of the free population.

No single argument explains the high proportion of adults and the associated low birth rate. They are best understood in terms of the general worsening of black living conditions associated with the intensification of staple agriculture. This process would never result in quite the degree of malnutrition, overwork, abortion, and infant mortality which prevented slave populations in the Caribbean from sustaining themselves. But by the 1720s and 30s the arbitrary grouping of slaves to create and maintain plantations in the wilderness already had adverse effects upon Negro family life. Men and women were thrown together in increasingly random proportions on increasingly large holdings as the period progressed. And far from giving license to any innate promiscuity imagined by white masters, such conditions apparently served more to frustrate desires for enduring intimacy and reduce the likelihood of procreation.

This reduced rate of natural growth is easily overlooked in view of the considerable net increases in the black population. The slaves listed by Varnod generated enough profits for their owners so that hundreds of new blacks were brought into the parish every year. When Varnod's successor, the Rev. Stephen Roe, filed a parochial report in 1741, the number of slaves owned in St. George's had risen to

[85] The difference might in some measure arise from (1) the economic double standard whereby full duty was paid on any African over ten, with young slaves assuming adult work loads before their white contemporaries, but it seems doubtful that Negro children were classed as adults much earlier than their white counterparts. (2) Since high rates of mortality and large numbers of children often fit together in demographic data, another source of the discrepancy between slave and white age distribution could be a continuation of the higher death rate among Europeans which had characterized the colony in the previous generation. (3) Conceivably the sale of slave children could have decreased their percentage somewhat, but since labor was clearly in demand in the parish it is unlikely that Negro children would have been sent elsewhere. (4) A few mulatto children born to slave mothers might have passed into the household of a white father (a dissenter named Bacon had no white women and one slave woman, no slave children and five free children, on his plantation), but miscegenation would have increased the numbers born into servitude.

162

roughly 3,300, an increase of more than 250 percent in fifteen years.[86] According to Roe's report there were by this time "Few or no wandering Indians," and what was more striking, the white population had actually diminished to 468 persons in 139 households. Errors on the minister's part or sickness among his parishioners could account for this decline in slight measure, but emigration was undoubtedly the primary factor.[87] As a result of these shifts in the population of St. George's Parish, the average number of slaves per household in 1741 was three times higher (24) than it had been twenty years before. Moreover, in the two decades after 1720 this parish near the geographic center of the colony had altered from a situation where scarcely 60 percent of its inhabitants were unfree to a point where nearly 90 percent were enslaved.

These demographic changes were being repeated to varying degrees in each of the other lowland parishes. Everywhere during the period between the beginning of royal government in 1720 and the imposition of the slave embargo in 1741 plantation agriculture expanded and intensified. For the blacks, directly involved in the grueling process of rice production, the birth rate declined and the mortality rate (and runaway rate) may have increased. As natural growth slackened the importation of new slaves intensified greatly, with the net result that the number of Africans rose more rapidly than the number of Europeans.

"If a great number of negroes could have made South Carolina secure," wrote Benjamin Martyn in 1741, the English colony would have had little to fear, "for she is computed to have at least forty thousand blacks." But the presence of so many African slaves offered little in the way of security to Europeans whose adult males numbered "not above five thousand; and these . . . at too great a distance from one another for the public safety." On the contrary, said Martyn, repeating a generalization which was common among whites at this time,

> The greater number of blacks, which a frontier has, and the greater the disproportion is between them and her white people, the

---

[86] Klingberg, *Appraisal*, p. 87. Roe stated that the 468 white inhabitants owned 3,347 slaves, but he listed the number of heathens and infidels as 3,287. Two things contribute to this discrepancy. One is the fact that certain Negroes were counted as Christians (roughly 85 professed to be of the Church of England and 15 were communicants); the other is the fact that some slaves were "settled at Remote Plant[ati]ons out of y[e] Parish."

[87] As lowland holdings were enlarged during the 1740s there is evidence that the number of households in St. George's decreased, and after 1750 a further number of white residents would take their slaves and move to Georgia.

more danger she is liable to; for those are all secret enemies, and ready to join with her open ones on the first occasion. So far from putting any confidence in them, her first step must be to secure herself against them.[88]

No single demographic fact did more to shape the subsequent history of South Carolina than the emergence of this clear-cut black majority soon after 1700. For two centuries the children of these black Carolinians would continue to be viewed in large measure as "secret enemies" by the white minority which lived among them. The actual size and contribution of this early concentration of black colonists, whose descendants are now spread from coast to coast, is only beginning to be explored within the present generation.

[88] [Benjamin Martyn], *An Impartial Inquiry into the State and Utility of the Colony of Georgia*, London, 1741, reprinted in Georgia Historical Society, *Collections*, I, 1840, 167.

APPENDIX

Appendix Table 1 which follows has been compiled from the Treasury Records in the South Carolina Department of Archives and History and from evidence in the South Carolina *Gazette*.[1] It covers slave imports into Charlestown between March 1735 and March 1740. Arrivals for each of the five years (from March to March) are listed in separate sections, and a summary of the data is presented in Table 4 above. For a few entries the dates of arrival and sale are unknown and the names of the captain, the importer, and the vessel itself have not been determined and remain blank. Where I have found general and specific listings for the origin of a shipment (implying the vessel stopped at more than one port), I have given the specific name, accompanied by an asterisk which indicates that another source lists the shipment as originating in "Africa." The point of origin for two shipments and the numerical data for several others have been arrived at indirectly; these have been enclosed in parentheses.

Certain slaves are missing from this tabulation. First of all, Negroes who had spent more than six months in other colonies were subject to a £50 duty designed to prevent the transportation of miscreants from the Caribbean to Carolina.[2] Although the *Gazette* of 8 November 1735 listed the arrival of 236 slaves from the West Indies in the previous year, the Treasury records for the year ending the following March show only 72 slaves incurring the higher rate, and all but two were reexported with a remission of duty. Almost no slaves were taxed at the £50 rate and almost none were reexported during the remainder of the decade. These two small categories of slaves imported from or shipped to other colonies tended to cancel each other out in these years and can therefore be ignored.

Several of the most valuable Negroes aboard each ship were designated "privilege slaves," since it was the captain's privilege to sell them for his own profit. No doubt the importer often paid the duty and handled the sale of these slaves, but there were instances when the captain paid the duty himself.[3] Some commanders may have

---

[1] Useful but much less complete compilations are available in Donnan, *Documents*, IV, 279-280 (Table 152), 296ff (Table 158).

[2] *Statutes*, III, 160-161.

[3] It appears from the Treasury Records that this applies to items 20, 31, 36, 51, 56, and 62 in Appendix Table 1 and perhaps to items 9, 34, 45, 58, 60, 63, 78, and 79 as well.

avoided paying the duty altogether, and the same could apply to the occasional "ventures" allowed other ships' officers. At any rate, the number of privilege slaves is small enough to be ignored statistically, even in calculating the average size of shipments. Besides these slaves, the Treasury Records omit a few babes-in-arms who entered untaxed and also those Africans (perhaps several hundred) who arrived at Georgetown and Port Royal. No slaves smuggled into the colony duty-free would appear, but there is little evidence of such activity in the 1730s.

Gazette Notice	Date of Sale	Vessel	Captain	Source of Shipment	Duty in £	Slaves	Adults	Children	Importer
1735									
1. Apr. 19	Apr. 29	Morning Star	W. Hamley	Angola	2,965	324	269	55	B. Savage & Co.
2. May 10	May 14	Rainbow	R. Morgan	Africa	1,450	153	137	16	J. Wragg & Co.
3. May 17	May 28	London, Frigate	J. Sutherland	Angola	3,510	378	324	54	Cleland & Wallace
4. June 28	July 2	Dove	R. Fothergill	Angola	2,060	208	204	4	J. Wragg & Co.
5. July 12	July 16	Amoretta	D. Jones	Africa	(2,280)	(233)	(223)	(10)	B. Savage & Co.
6. July 26	July 31	Diana	J. Malone	Windward & Gold Coast	(670)	(68)	(66)	(2)	
7. Aug. 2	Aug. 6	Faulcon	S. Sanders	Angola*	3,610	363	359	4	Jenys & Baker
8. Aug. 30	Sept. 10	Molly	J. Carruthers	Angola	3,820	398	366	32	B. Godin
9.				Africa	400	40	40	0	R. Hill
10. Sept. 13	Sept. 24	Happy Couple	-. Hill	Coast of Guinea*	1,105	118	103	15	J. Wragg & Co.
1736									
11. Jan. 17	Jan. 21	Berkley	P. Stockdale	Angola*	3,470	358	336	22	Jenys & Baker
12.				Barbados	20	4	0	4	James Crokatt
13.				Providence	40	5	3	2	J. Wragg & Co.
14.				Jamaica	10	1	1	0	J. Frasier

Appendix Table 1 (*continued*)

Gazette Notice	Date of Sale	Vessel	Captain	Source of Shipment	Duty in £	Slaves	Adults	Children	Importer
15. June 26	June 30	Amoretta	D. Jones	Africa	2,100	224	196	28	B. Savage & Co.
16. June 26	June 30	Scipio, Galley	R. Smith	Angola*	2,330	262	204	58	Jenys & Baker
17. Aug. 7	Aug. 11	Bonetta, Pink	P. Comyn	Angola	3,610	382	340	42	J. Wragg & Co.
18. Aug. 21	Aug. 25	Garlington	H. Watts	Gold Coast & Angola	2,740	289	259	30	Jenys & Baker
19. Aug. 21	Aug. 25	Princess Caroline	J. Coe	Gambia	1,390	148	130	18	Hill & Guerard
20.				Gambia*	50	5	5	0	J. Coe
21. Sept. 18	Sept. 22	London	J. Sutherland	Angola	2,960	319	273	46	Cleland & Wallace
22. Sept. 18	Sept. 25	Dorothy	W. Douglas	Antigua	30	3	3	0	"To be sold at Publick Vendue at the usual place"
23.				Barbados	190	19	19	0	S. Haven
24.				Angola	420	44	40	4	B. Savage & Co.
25.				Gambia	315	35	28	7	J. Wragg & Co.
26.				N. Carolina	5	1	0	1	A. Scharmahorn
27. Oct. 16	Oct. 27	Speaker	H. Flower	(Angola)	(3,225)	(356)	(289)	(67)	J. Wragg & Co.
28. Oct. 30	Nov. 2	Shepard	M. Power	Angola	(3,205)	(350)	(291)	(59)	"
29. Nov. 6	Nov. 10	Phoenix	D. Arthur	Angola	(2,745)	(300)	(249)	(51)	
1737									
30. Jan. 8	Jan. 19	Loango	T. Dolman	Angola	3,170	337	297	40	B. Savage & Co.
31.				Angola	190	19	19	0	T. Dolman
32. Feb. 5	Feb. 9	Mary	R. Pollixsen	(Angola)	(960)	(101)	(91)	(10)	J. Wragg & Co.
33.				Angola	1,230	128	118	10	P. Jenys
34.				Angola	40	4	4	0	H. Powell

Gazette Notice	Date of Sale	Vessel	Captain	Source of Shipment	Duty in £	Slaves	Adults	Children	Importer
35.	May 28	Amoretta	D. Jones	Africa	2,040	221	187	34	B. Savage & Co.
36.				Africa	70	7	7	0	D. Jones
37.	July 23	Pine-Apple	D. Hallowe	Angola	1,470	157	137	20	J. Wragg & Co.
38.	July 30	Pearl, Galley	E. Hardwick	Angola	2,415	247	236	11	Hill & Guerard
39.				Montserrat	10	1	1	0	R. Austin
40.				London	10	1	1	0	A. Sutton
41.				Mobile	40	4	4	0	R. Lampton
1738									
42.				Angola	815	83	80	3	Montaigut & Curry
43.		Susannah, Snow		Angola	770	79	75	4	Cattell & Austin
44.				Angola	2,600	260	260	0	Hill & Guerard
45.				Angola	10	1	1	0	B. Cross
46.				London	10	1	1	0	T. Shubrick

APPENDIX TABLE 1 (continued)

Gazette Notice	Date of Sale	Vessel	Captain	Source of Shipment	Duty in £	Slaves	Adults	Children	Importer
47. Mar. 2	Mar. 15	Shepherd	M. Power	Angola*	2,665	354	179	175	J. Wragg & Co.
48. Apr. 6	Apr. 12	London Merchant	J. Thomas	Angola	2,680	292	244	48	
49. Apr. 15	Apr. 19	London, Frigate	J. Pickett	Angola	2,265	254	199	55	Cleland & Wallace
50. Apr. 27	May 3	Amoretta	J. Crode	Africa	1,720	208	136	72	B. Savage & Co.
51.				Africa	60	7	5	2	J. Crode
52. May 18	May 24	Bettsey	A. Duncomb	Angola	2,145	223	206	17	Cleland & Wallace
53. June 29	July 6	Speaker	H. Flower	Angola/St. Christophers	2,880	306	290	16	J. Wragg & Co.
54. July 27	Aug. 2	Mary	J. Coe	Gambia	995	101	98	3	"
55. July 27	Aug. 9	Princess Caroline	W. Johnson	Gambia	1,595	169	150	19	Hill & Guerard
56. Aug. 17	Aug. 23	Seaflower	J. Ebsworthy	Gambia	155	16	15	1	W. Johnson
57.				Africa/St. Christophers	1,450	149	141	8	J. Wragg & Co.
58.				Angola	10	1	1	0	W. Mathews
59.				Gambia	230	23	23	0	Yoemans & Escott
60.				Gambia	40	4	4	0	John Thomson
61. Oct. 12	Oct. 25	Maremaid	W. Wilson	Angola	1,605	170	151	19	Hill & Guerard
62.				Angola	60	6	6	0	W. Wilson
63.				Gambia	10	1	1	0	J. Dalrymple
64. Nov. 16	Nov. 22	Squirrel	J. Dyke	Africa	1,910	211	171	40	B. Savage & Co.
65.				Antigua	120	12	12	0	Hill & Guerard

(March, 1740)

* See Appendix text, above.

VIII

The Breeding of Slaves for Sale and the Westward Expansion of Slavery, 1850-1860

RICHARD SUTCH

ONE OF THE tenets which distinguishes the "revisionist" approach to the study of American slavery is the assertion that the American slaveowner was able to regard his slaves solely as capital assets, no different in kind from acres of land, from farming implements, or from work animals.[1] According to this view, the Southern planter made his decisions to buy or sell slaves, and to employ them at one task or another based only upon economic criteria without thought of the humanity or inhumanity involved. Because the slaveowner retained slaves for the purpose of employing their labor in a profit-maximizing agricultural enterprise and because the market for his output was quite competitive, only the planter who employed his slaves in the most efficient manner could earn sufficient return to justify their price. The pressure of the competitive system made human gestures which were incompatible with maximum economic efficiency a luxury only a few could afford.

This competitive mechanism is used to explain a seeming paradox

[1] The author would like to express his thanks to Harriet Fishlow for advice on several demographic problems, to William Parker and Robert Gallman for the use of data which they collected from the manuscripts of the 1860 Census of Population and Agriculture, and to James Foust and Gavin Wright for providing the information necessary to make use of that data. Robert Fogel and Stanley Engerman kindly made available data on the relative price of slaves which they collected from estate appraisal records. The net migration estimates reported in the appendix were made in collaboration with John Lyons and were part of a larger study conducted by the author, John Lyons, and Richard Roehl. Research assistance was ably provided by Lynnae Wolin and Bruce Vermeulen. The advice and criticism from many of the participants of the Conference has encouraged me to revise and, I trust, improve on the original draft. I am particularly indebted to Stanley Engerman, Herbert Klein, Eugene Genovese, Robert Fogel, and C. Vann Woodward for suggestions. Financial support was provided by the Computer Center and the Institute of International Studies, both at the University of California, Berkeley. A Ford Foundation Faculty Fellowship enabled the author to devote more time than he might otherwise to this study.

which arises when comparing the American slave system with those of other places and other times. The blacks in the American South seem to have been better cared for in terms of food, living conditions, and medical attention than slaves in other systems. Yet the American slave, unlike his counterparts in most other countries was stripped of his humanity. He was thought of as subhuman and therefore not deserving of common human dignities. In this respect the American slave seems to have been the most cruelly treated of all. This duality of treatment arose because of the competitiveness of the antebellum American economy. It was the market system which adjusted the price of the slave to equal the present discounted value of his future expected labor, and it was this system which guaranteed good physical treatment. The slaveowner was repaid for his care by the high resale value of his property.

For this market to work, however, slaveowners had to be prepared to buy and sell slaves whenever their price fell out of line with their expected value. This meant, among other things, that considerations of the slave's wishes in the matter were out of the question. Husband and wife were separated, and even children were sold separately from their mothers when economics dictated the profitability of such action. If this market in human capital was to work efficiently and smoothly, the goods traded had to be divorced from their humanity.[2] Only when the black man became regarded as subhuman could the white man treat him as a simple physical asset without troubling his conscience.

A natural implication of this view of the American slave system is that some slaveholders would find it profitable to practice "slave breeding," for the same economic reasons that led some nineteenth century Southern farmers to practice mule breeding. Since the market value of a young adult field hand undoubtedly exceeded the costs of raising him from childhood, there would be those slaveholders who would see the opportunity to specialize in raising slaves for sale, and many others who would supplement their income from agriculture by the sale of slaves not needed for their labor on the farm.[3] According to

[2] It should be pointed out that these statements need apply only to the marginal transactors. There can be (and there was in the antebellum South) a sizable number of slaveowners who refuse to participate in the market for slaves and who respect some measure of their slaves' dignity. However, it is in the nature of the economics of such a situation that these individuals will not be able to make the adjustments necessary to conduct their plantations at maximum economic efficiency. Such slaveowners will pay a price for their principles—a lower rate of return on their capital than they could otherwise earn.

[3] That slave breeding is an implication of an economic model in which slaves are treated by their owners as capital assets was clear to contemporary economists. The most famous discussion is that of John Elliott Cairnes, *The Slave Power:*

this approach to American slavery, these slaveowners could disregard the questions of the morality and the humanity of such a callous treatment of sexual relations and of marriage and family ties precisely because they were able to view the slave as simply another form of property, no different in kind than the horses and asses owned by the mule breeder.

Many observers of the American South have commented on this aspect of the economics of slavery, and have presented supporting evidence for the existence of slave breeding from plantation records, diaries, the autobiographies of slaves and ex-slaves, records of slave auctions, and the observation of contemporary travelers.[4] This direct evidence, however, is rather limited, perhaps because of the natural reticence that contemporaries would have had in recording details of such practices.[5] As a result, there is still room for debate about the extent and nature of slave breeding. It appears that those writers who accept the relevance of the theoretical model which treats slaves as capital assets have found the evidence sufficient to conclude that the slaveowner systematically interfered with the sexual life of his slaves.[6] Other writers, who have not accepted the slave-asset model or who have applied it cautiously, have denied that breeding was extensively practiced. They suggest that while some owners were forced by economic necessity to sell those slaves who were not needed for plantation work when they reached maturity, nevertheless the slave-

---

Its Character, Career, and Probable Designs: Being an Attempt to Explain the Real Issues Involved in the American Contest, London, 1862. This point was also important to the economic analysis of American slavery by Alfred H. Conrad and John R. Meyer, "The Economics of Slavery in the Antebellum South," *Journal of Political Economy* 66 (April 1958), reprinted in Alfred H. Conrad and John R. Meyer, *The Economics of Slavery and Other Studies in Econometric History,* Chicago, 1964. The page references in this essay are to the book. Among other points, they concluded that "breeding returns were necessary . . . to make the plantation operations on the poorer lands as profitable as alternative contemporary economic activities in the United States" (p. 82).

[4] Several of the more important commentaries on slave breeding, but by no means an exhaustive list, include Frederic Bancroft, "The Importance of Slave-Rearing," chap. IV of *Slave-Trading in the Old South,* Baltimore, 1931; Lewis C. Gray, *History of Agriculture in the Southern United States to 1860,* Washington, 1933, II, 661-663; and Kenneth M. Stampp, *The Peculiar Institution: Slavery in the Ante-Bellum South,* New York, 1956, pp. 245-251.

[5] Kenneth Stampp, for example, has noted that "evidence of systematic slave breeding is scarce indeed, not only because it is unlikely that many engaged in it but also because written records of such activities would seldom be kept" (*The Peculiar Institution,* p. 245). Slaveowners frequently denied the charge made by the antislavery movement that breeding was common.

[6] See, for example, Conrad and Meyer.

owners accepted whatever natural increase their slaves presented to them.[7]

One of the implications of the approach which argues that slaves were treated as capital assets and that plantation decisions were made on solely economic grounds, is that arrangements to increase fertility would have been most frequently practiced on the poor lands of the border states and along the Atlantic coast. In these areas the economic returns to agriculture, given the price of slaves and the land-labor ratios observed, were below those obtainable elsewhere in the South.[8] If the slaveowners in these regions were to obtain more typical rates of return on their investment, they would have had to resort to slave breeding to augment their income. The slaveowners in the west where the soils were more fertile could, given the price of slaves and the observed land-labor ratios, on the other hand, earn normal rates of return without resorting to breeding. Presumably, the typical planter in a southwestern state would have preferred to see his female slaves working in the field than to have them indisposed with pregnancy or occupied with children. This suggests that the border states and eastern coastal states would be exporting slaves while the western states would be importing them.

There is conclusive evidence of this regional pattern of slave migration in the Census returns which report much higher rates of population increase in the western slave states than in the eastern or border states. In Table 1 I present the percentage change in population between 1850 and 1860 in each slave state. There is no question that the states with poorer soil were providing slaves for the rapidly growing western regions.

It is possible to infer the magnitude of the migration flows as well as the age and sex distribution of the slaves who were exported across state boundaries, from the Census returns. The appendix to this article details the methodology I have employed to make such estimates.

---

[7] This debate over the existence of slavebreeding is only a portion of a much wider dispute over the applicability of the competitive market model to the slave economy. For a collection of the more important papers in this debate, including Stanley Engerman's review of it, see Hugh G. J. Aitken, ed., *Did Slavery Pay? Readings in the Economics of Black Slavery in the United States*, Boston, 1971.

[8] This is precisely the argument of Conrad and Meyer. In an article on the profitability of slavery, I computed the rate of return implied by the observed agricultural yields, land-labor ratios, and the price of slaves. I found that if only average female fertility is forthcoming, the older areas with poor soils would yield rates of return in the neighborhood of 3.6 to 4.0% in 1859, while the highly fertile alluvial soils yielded returns on the average of between 7.1 and 8.7%. Richard Sutch, "The Profitability of Ante-Bellum Slavery—Revisited," *Southern Economic Journal* 31 (April 1965), Table VIII, p. 376, reprinted in Aitken, p. 240.

176

TABLE 1. DECENNIAL GROWTH RATES OF THE SLAVE AND FREE
POPULATIONS AND THE NUMBER OF SLAVEOWNERS, BY STATE,
1850-1860

	Decennial Rate of Growth of:		
	Slave Population (%)	Free Population (%)	Slaveowners (%)
Texas	213.9	172.8	182.4
Arkansas	135.9	99.2	91.4
Florida	57.1	63.5	46.4
Mississippi	40.9	19.6	33.9
Louisiana	35.5	37.8	6.6
Missouri	31.5	79.5	26.8
Alabama	26.9	23.4	15.1
All slaves states	23.4	29.2	13.7
Georgia	21.1	13.5	6.8
Tennessee	15.1	9.3	8.8
North Carolina	14.7	13.8	22.5
Kentucky	6.9	20.6	0.7
South Carolina	4.5	6.2	4.3
Virginia	3.9	16.5	−5.3
Maryland	−3.5	21.8	−14.1
District of Columbia	−13.6	26.7	−16.8
Delaware	−21.5	23.7	−27.5

SOURCES: Computed from data in the following:
U.S. Census Office, *The Seventh Census of the United States: 1850,* Washington, 1853, pp. xlii-xliv.
U.S. Census Office, *Population of the United States in 1860 . . . The Eighth Census,* Washington, 1864, pp. 592-597.
U.S. Census Office, *Agriculture of the United States in 1860 . . . The Eighth Census,* Washington, 1864, pp. 224, 247-248.

Table 2 presents my estimate of net slave exportation and importation as a percentage of the potential population for each slave state based on these calculations. The estimates suggest that the major exporting states were the border states: Delaware, District of Columbia, Maryland, and Kentucky. South Carolina, Virginia, Tennessee, and North Carolina were also exporting substantial portions of their potential slave populations. The major receiving states were Texas, Arkansas, and Florida. Louisiana and Mississippi were also expanding their slave stocks significantly through importation.

Whether this migration was produced by the exportation of slaves by professional slavetraders or by the movement of entire plantations is another issue which has been considerably debated. The fact that only three of the states and the District of Columbia show a decline in

177

TABLE 2. THE ESTIMATED RATE OF SLAVE EXPORTATIONS AND
IMPORTATIONS, BY STATE, 1850-1860

Exporting States	Exportation Rate[a] (%)	Importing States	Importation Rate[a] (%)
Delaware	32.6	Texas	130.7
District of Columbia	20.1	Arkansas	79.3
Maryland	19.7	Florida	27.4
Kentucky	15.8	Louisiana	17.4
South Carolina	13.4	Mississippi	12.7
Virginia	12.0	Alabama	3.8
Tennessee	10.3	Missouri	0.1
North Carolina	7.3		
Georgia	2.4		
Average	10.8	Average	19.6

SOURCES: Computed from data presented in the Appendix.
[a] Defined as the estimated number of exports or imports as a percentage of the estimated number of slaves who would have resided in the state in 1860 had no migration taken place.

the number of slaveholders according to Table 1, and that even in these states the rate of slave exportation exceeded the decline in slaveholdings, suggests that a substantial number of slaves transported across state boundaries left their home plantations, their former masters, and perhaps their families behind them.

The estimates of the export flows by age and sex for the selling states are given in Table 3. The estimates of the net imports into the buying states (excluding Missouri) are presented in Table 4.[9] The tables indicate that over one-quarter of a million slaves were exported from the eight selling states to the six buying states during the last decade of slavery, nearly one slave out of every fifteen. These slaves represented over 12 percent of the value of the potential slave population had no migration been allowed. A conservative estimate of their sale prices values these slaves at $200 million, or approximately $20 million per year.[10]

[9] Henceforth, I use the terms exporting states and selling states interchangeably. Likewise, the term buying state will be used to refer to the importing states. The division made in Table 2 is used to define the two groups. However, Missouri is frequently excluded from consideration since on balance it showed very little net importation.

[10] These figures are based on the relative prices of slaves by age and sex compiled by Robert Fogel and Stanley Engerman and an assumed value of $1,000 for an average male between 20 and 29 years old. Since Fogel and Engerman estimate that the average price in Louisiana of a male of this age in 1850 was $1,079.63 and the average price of a prime male field hand over the decade 1851-1860 has been estimated by Conrad and Meyer to be $1,424.00 (p. 76), I feel the estimate given is a lower bound.

TABLE 3. NET EXPORTS OF SLAVES FROM SELLING STATES, BY AGE AND SEX, 1850-1860

Age in 1860	Delaware, Maryland, District of Columbia, and Virginia		North and South Carolina		Kentucky and Tennessee		Georgia		Total Selling States	
	Male	Female	Male	Female	Male	Female	Male	Female	Male	Female
Under 10	6,582	8,444	5,342	4,131	11,955	11,009	866	-186	24,745	23,398
10-14	4,076	4,403	5,607	5,807	2,991	2,809	1,119	322	13,793	13,341
15-19	6,257	7,068	6,584	7,871	3,954	4,625	758	649	17,553	20,213
20-29	15,974	15,962	14,044	11,768	11,057	11,102	2,941	2,128	44,016	40,960
30-39	6,212	4,889	4,916	4,553	6,103	4,021	1,395	883	18,626	14,346
40-49	2,642	1,856	2,738	2,724	2,068	1,520	123	30	7,571	6,130
50-59	1,969	1,359	-704	-595	-318	161	681	584	1,628	1,509
60 and over	2,071	1,141	2,135	2,208	1,028	994	-559	-325	4,675	4,018
Age unknown	238	186	6,216	5,933	32	25	92	43	6,578	6,187
TOTAL	46,021	45,308	46,878	44,400	38,870	36,266	7,416	4,128	139,185	130,102
	91,329		91,278		75,136		11,544		269,287	

SOURCES: Based on data presented in the Appendix.

TABLE 4. NET IMPORTS OF SLAVES INTO BUYING STATES, BY AGE AND SEX, 1850-1860

Age in 1860	Texas and Arkansas		Mississippi and Louisiana		Florida		Alabama		Total Buying States	
	Male	Female	Male	Female	Male	Female	Male	Female	Male	Female
Under 10	13,130	12,983	7,930	5,476	1,571	1,359	2,518	3,466	25,149	23,284
10-14	10,489	10,390	2,030	1,093	832	903	-93	156	13,258	12,542
15-19	10,494	11,179	5,135	6,600	815	779	568	1,333	17,012	19,891
20-29	18,939	18,009	20,879	19,224	1,788	1,602	2,868	2,874	44,474	41,709
30-39	9,736	9,220	7,841	3,868	837	696	1,247	806	19,661	14,590
40-49	5,016	5,171	1,891	-222	555	497	-9	344	7,453	5,790
50-59	2,349	2,147	-352	-580	299	278	-659	-298	1,637	1,547
60 and over	2,027	1,971	1,938	1,391	142	170	490	348	4,597	3,880
Age unknown	212	225	6,546	5,921	-122	79	-3	3	6,633	6,228
TOTAL	72,392	71,295	53,838	42,771	6,717	6,363	6,927	9,032	139,874	129,461
	143,687		96,609		13,080		15,959		269,335	

SOURCES: Based on data presented in the Appendix.

In Table 5 the interstate flows are presented as a percentage of their respective cohorts. The pattern of exports across the age categories reveals that slaves between 15 and 39 in 1860 were exported out of the selling states at a much higher rate than slave children or the elderly. This implies that the slaves were not primarily exported in family units complete with their children and their parents. Rather it appears that a substantial exportation of young adults without children or parents took place.

The sexual distribution of exported slaves is also suggestive. We would expect the slave breeder who did not respect the custom of monogamous sexual relations for his slaves to sell more men than women. Consistent, then, with the suggestion that the exporting states had a greater tendency to breed slaves than the buying states is the fact that 7 percent more males than females were exported. Males were in excess among exports by 14.3 percent in the age class 20 to 49. Among those slaves who were 20 to 29 in 1850 and 30 to 39 ten years later, 29.8 percent more males than females were exported.

The evidence on slave migration is ample to conclude that a substantial interstate trade in human beings took place and that eastern and border state planters sold slaves to this trade. However, from this evidence alone, we can deduce nothing about the nature of the slave breeding operation. Was it merely the practice of selling off the surplus slaves, or did the slaveowner interfere in the conjugal and sexual life of his slaves in order to increase the number of children born?

It is in this latter sense that the term "slave breeding" is properly

TABLE 5. EXPORTATION AND IMPORTATION RATES, BY AGE AND SEX COHORTS, 1850-1860

Age in 1860	Exports of Selling States as a Percentage of Their 1850 Population Surviving to 1860		Imports of Buying States as a Percentage of Their 1850 Population Surviving to 1860	
	Male	Female	Male	Female
Under 10	6.4	6.0	12.3	11.1
10-14	7.6	7.7	14.3	14.9
15-19	12.1	13.4	24.8	28.0
20-29	18.7	18.0	40.7	39.4
30-39	13.8	10.5	25.6	18.9
40-49	9.0	7.2	14.0	11.4
50-59	3.3	3.2	5.8	6.1
60 and over	9.9	8.4	23.0	21.2

SOURCES: Based on data presented in the Appendix.

181

applied.[11] Some historians object to the use of this term. They suggest that it is dehumanizing and carries with it the implication that "barnyard" techniques were employed. That the term is dehumanizing is granted. However, that is precisely the point. It would have been dehumanizing to encourage increased fertility by any technique, whether it consisted solely of rewards offered for childbearing or was carried to the extreme of forced matings. If the slaveholder did interfere in the sexual life of his slaves, it was because he was willing to dehumanize them for the sake of his own profit.

The techniques employed in this essay to examine the extent and nature of slave breeding are indirect. They are based on the limited demographic data contained in the Federal Census Returns of 1850 and 1860. They can tell us very little about the devices employed to encourage fertility. The issue of whether the "barnyard" implications are warranted cannot be determined from the census data I have chosen to examine. In any case, it is not my intention that the term should carry such implications. I use it to cover all practices which were intended to increase the number of children born over and above the numbers otherwise obtainable.

Despite the richness of the information available in the Censuses of 1850 and 1860 on the free population, only limited data were collected on the slave population. The slave schedules list only the owner's name and county of residence and the sex, age, and color (black or mulatto) of each slave owned. The slaves were not grouped into families nor were their names given. Yet the age-sex distributions alone allow us to compute a crude index of fertility by taking the ratio of slave children under one year of age to the number of women of childbearing age. In Table 6 we present these ratios for both census years for each of the slave states.[12] The states are ordered in the table by the percentage of their slave population which was exported during the decade as reported in Table 2.

An examination of the table will reveal that there is a tendency for the selling states to have a higher "fertility" ratio than the buying states. In 1850 the only buying state with a fertility ratio higher than South Carolina, the least fertile of the selling states, was Arkansas.

---

[11] I believe this is the sense in which Conrad and Meyer have used the term. In any case, the assumptions they employed to compute the rate of return to breeding imply such enormously high birth rates that positive mechanisms to promote fertility would seem to have been required to achieve them. N. G. Butlin, *Ante-Bellum Slavery: A Critique of a Debate*, Canberra, 1971, pp. 32, 40.

[12] For most purposes I have combined the two states of Maryland and Delaware with the District of Columbia because of their small size and the urban nature of the District.

TABLE 6. THE INFANT-WOMEN RATIO FOR THE SLAVE POPULATION, 1850-1860

State	Number of Children Under 1 per Thousand Women of Childbearing Age [a]		
	1850	1860	Average
Maryland, Delaware and the District of Columbia	162	160	161
Kentucky	182	200	191
South Carolina	137	163	150
Virginia	152	178	165
Tennessee	175	189	182
North Carolina	178	178	178
Georgia	145	174	159
Average: Selling states	157	177	167
Missouri	180	188	184
Alabama	134	162	148
Mississippi	129	151	140
Louisiana	102	132	117
Florida	130	160	145
Arkansas	134	163	148
Texas	132	170	151
Average: Buying states [b]	124	153	139

SOURCES: Computed from data in the following sources:

U.S. Census Office, *The Seventh Census of the United States: 1850*, Washington, 1853, pp. xlii-xliv.

U.S. Census Office, *Population of the United States in 1860 . . . The Eighth Census*, Washington, 1864, pp. 594-595.

[a] The definition of the period of childbearing is somewhat arbitrary. I have adopted the practice of counting all women between the ages of 20 and 39 and one-half of the women between 15 and 19.

[b] Excluding Missouri.

After ten years this pattern apparently had not changed. The states with the lowest ratios of infants to women (Louisiana, Mississippi, and Florida) were among the buying states. At the same time the selling states such as Virginia, Kentucky, North Carolina, and Tennessee have fertility ratios which rank relatively high.[13]

It would be a mistake, however, to place too much reliance on comparisons of the ratio of infants to women. This ratio does not measure fertility accurately because of two important defects. The numerator of the ratio includes only those infants alive at the date of the census,

---

[13] Spearman's coefficient of rank correlation between the ranking of the average fertility presented in Table 6 and the ranking of each state by its rate of slave exportation is .633.

183

thus differential rates of infant mortality will distort the measure. Moreover, there is considerable evidence that the census has consistently underenumerated the number of infants relative to other age groups.[14] To the extent that the degree of such underenumeration was not uniform across the states, the "fertility" ratios in Table 6 cannot be compared with each other.

In an attempt to partially correct for these biases the ratio of infants to women was also computed for the *white* population.[15] Since differences between the states in infant mortality and census underreporting can be reasonably supposed to affect the white population in the same manner as they affect the black population, the ratios for the whites can be used to standardize the slave data. Accordingly, the average white fertility ratio was divided into the slave ratio for each state to produce an index of relative fertility. Table 7 presents the results. Judged by the magnitude of this index, North Carolina stands first. This should be interpreted as follows: of all the slave states North Carolina exhibits the highest fertility of its slave population relative to the fertility of its white population. Slave fertility in North Carolina was, in fact, 8.5 percent higher than white fertility. The relative fertility of slaves in the selling states according to Table 7 was .960, substantially above the figure for the importing states located in the west (.747). The states are ordered in Table 7 by their respective rates of net exportation reported in Table 2. Note the strong relationship between that ordering and the index of relative slave fertility.[16]

---

[14] The introduction to the Census volume of 1850 stated: "In many counties the assistant marshals have adopted one year as the lowest designation of age; and, therefore, the [children *under* 1 year of age] as published in those counties; show proportionately small. This was often the case with slaves" (U.S. Census Office, *The Seventh Census of the United States: 1850*, Washington, 1853, p. xxxix, footnote). This tendency of the enumerators would, of course, also exaggerate the number of children reported as between 1 and 4 years of age. But there is other evidence that the total number of slave children under 5 was also consistently underestimated. The number of male slaves aged 10 to 14 reported in the Census of 1860 was 276,928 while this same cohort was measured in 1850 when they were under 5 as containing only 267,088. The difference cannot be explained by immigration since importation of slaves was illegal at this time and the illegal importation of slaves or the enslavement of free persons was comparatively negligible. The data are from *The Seventh Census*, p. xliv, and U.S. Census Office, *Population of the United States in 1860 . . . The Eighth Census*, Washington, 1864, pp. 594-595.

[15] Including "civilized Indians" but excluding the free colored.

[16] The Spearman coefficient of rank correlation between the ordering of the fertility index in Table 7 and the rank of each state by its rate of slave exportation is .899. It might be objected that this index of relative fertility will still be biased if the infant mortality among slaves relative to whites was higher in the buying states than in the selling states. However, careful examination of the

TABLE 7. AN INDEX OF RELATIVE SLAVE FERTILITY, 1850-1860

State	The Average of the 1850 and 1860 Infant-Women Ratios		Index of Relative Slave Fertility
	Slave	White	
Maryland, Delaware and the District of Columbia	161	156	1.032
Kentucky	191	194	.985
South Carolina	150	150	1.000
Virginia	165	166	.994
Tennessee	182	185	.984
North Carolina	178	164	1.085
Georgia	159	186	.855
Selling states	167	174	.960
Missouri	184	203	.906
Alabama	148	185	.800
Mississippi	140	185	.757
Louisiana	117	149	.785
Florida	145	190	.763
Arkansas	148	213	.695
Texas	151	212	.712
Buying states [a]	139	186	.747

[a] Excluding Missouri.

On the basis of the published data it seems safe to conclude that the selling states exhibited a significantly higher rate of slave births than did the states with the more fertile soil in the southwest. This conclusion is supported by an examination of individual cotton plantations. The manuscript returns of the Assistant Marshals who enumerated the population for the Census of 1860 have been retained by the National Archives.[17] The manuscript returns of the 1860 Census of Agriculture for most states have also been preserved in state archives or university libraries. These agricultural returns for the southern

mortality data reported by race in the 1850 Census revealed that infant slave mortality was actually *higher* in the selling states than the buying states. Alabama and Texas were the only two importing states with high infant slave mortality relative to the healthiest of the selling states, South Carolina. This result was also confirmed by standardizing the slave infant mortality ratios by the infant mortality ratios for the free population. If the fertility ratios reported in Table 7 were to be corrected for infant mortality, the distinction between the buying states and the selling states would be exaggerated not diminished.

[17] Katherine H. Davidson and Charlotte M. Ashby, United States General Services Administration, The National Archives, *Records of the Bureau of the Census*, Washington, 1964.

RICHARD SUTCH

states have been collected by the University of North Carolina Library.[18]

The enumeration schedules list each free inhabitant, each farm, and each slaveholding separately. For each slaveholding the manuscripts provide a complete age and sex distribution of the slaves owned. While it is not possible to match the slave children with their parents from these schedules, they can nevertheless be employed to estimate fertility ratios for individual plantations. These estimates will have several important advantages over those based on the aggregate data. With the more detailed age data (compared to the broad age classes of the published tabulations) one can more precisely estimate the population at risk of pregnancy. Moreover, by restricting the analysis to the slaveholdings owned by farmers or planters the results will be based only upon the agricultural slave population. This will have an important impact on the fertility measures since many of the non-agricultural slaves were held as domestic servants by owners who had only one slave.

For the purposes of an unrelated series of studies, William Parker and Robert Gallman have drawn a sample of 5,230 farms from the manuscript agricultural returns of the 413 counties which produced at least 1,000 bales of cotton in 1859. The sample consists of approximately 1.67 percent of the farms in those counties.[19] Of the 5,230 farms, 2,588 were operated by slaveowners, who together reported owning 40,576 slaves. The distribution of these farms by state is given in Table 8.

The Parker-Gallman sample does not include or underrepresents the border states because it is restricted to the cotton-growing region of the South. While these border states may have sheltered substantial slave breeding operations, this sample is nevertheless suited to test the Conrad and Meyer assertion that slave breeding was prevalent among *cotton planters* of the Old South. Moreover, to the extent that the non-cotton areas of the South were the chief breeding areas, the use of the Parker-Gallman sample builds a degree of conservatism into the data.

[18] Samuel M. Boone, "Agricultural and Manufacturing Census Records of Fifteen Southern States for the Years 1850, 1860, 1870 and 1880," Chapel Hill, 1966.
[19] See William N. Parker, ed., *The Structure of the Cotton Economy of the Antebellum South,* Berkeley, 1970, particularly the articles by Robert Gallman, James Foust and D. E. Swan, and Gavin Wright for more detail on this sample. Also see James Donald Foust, "The Yeoman Farmer and Westward Expansion of U.S. Cotton Production," unpublished Ph.D. dissertation, University of North Carolina at Chapel Hill, 1967, for an extensive discussion of the sampling procedure employed.

186

TABLE 8. THE DISTRIBUTION OF SLAVEHOLDINGS AND SLAVES BY STATE, PARKER-GALLMAN SAMPLE OF COTTON FARMS, 1860

State	Slaveholdings		Slaves	
Virginia	26		540	
North Carolina	202		2,091	
South Carolina	328		5,942	
Georgia	492		7,460	
Tennessee	207		2,380	
Subtotal: Selling states		1,255		18,413
Florida	32		451	
Alabama	424		6,477	
Mississippi	377		6,509	
Arkansas	127		1,395	
Louisiana	136		4,293	
Texas	237		3,038	
Subtotal: Buying states		1,333		22,163
TOTAL	2,588		40,576	

NOTE: The four cotton counties in Missouri were excluded from the original Parker-Gallman sample because of the unavailability of the Agricultural Census manuscripts for that State.

In the Parker-Gallman study the age and sex distribution of the slaveholdings associated with each plantation was collected from the slave schedules and condensed into 36 age-sex classes. Children under 5 were divided into infants under six months old and all others. The age brackets thereafter are in five-year increments up to age 79 (that is 5-9, 10-14, 15-19, . . ., 75-79). There is also an open class of those 80 and over.

Rather than use the number of infants as our measure of fertility, I have chosen to use the total number of children 14 years and under. This assumes that children under 15 were rarely sold separately. While there is considerable evidence that children were separated from their parents for sale,[20] it is probable that this practice was not frequent.[21] The reasons for this were both moral and economic. The optimal time to sell a slave was apparently between the ages of 16 and 21.[22]

[20] Bancroft, pp. 208-214.
[21] Ulrich Bonnell Phillips, American Negro Slavery: A Survey of the Supply, Employment and Control of Negro Labor as Determined by the Plantation Regime, New York and London, 1918, p. 369; and Bancroft, p. 214. According to Stampp, a Louisiana State law prohibited the sale or importation of children under 10 without their mothers, p. 252.
[22] If each slaveholder had access to other factors of production (land, capital, work animals, etc.) at prices equal to their marginal product in perfectly divisible

187

RICHARD SUTCH

The advantage of using the broad definition of children is that this measure is less likely to be distorted by underreporting than is the number of infants and it allows us to look at fifteen years of fertility experience rather than the first six months of 1860. A disadvantage of this measure, on the other hand, is that it may blur the distinction between the regions. Since women with children were frequently sold and transported from one region to another, a woman who was under the influence of a high-fertility slave region may have been moved with her children to a low-fertility region and this transfer would push the observed fertility ratios together.

The number of children on each plantation is compared with the number of women times the number of years each woman was in the child-bearing age span of 15 through 44 during the previous fifteen years. In addition each year of fertility experience was converted to a prime-fertility-year equivalent by multiplying it by the relative chance of conception associated with that age, compared with the years of peak fertility (ages 20-24).

The reproductive potential at each age was estimated using the pre-1942 fertility experience of the women of the Cocos-Keeling Islands born between 1873 and 1927. These women experienced the highest gross reproduction rate ever recorded for any population (4.17). It is widely believed that their age-specific fertility patterns approach a biological maximum. The Cocos Islands society was characterized by especially early marriage (16 was the most popular age for women at their first marriage) and frequent premarital conceptions. Health standards were high, venereal disease absent, nursing periods were short, and birth control unknown. There was apparently no economic pressure to restrain population growth.[23]

In Table 9 the Cocos Islands fertility data are used to produce an

amounts, it would make no difference to the present value of a newborn slave at what age he would be sold. The present value of his future expected net product on the home plantation could be made to equal his present sale price through appropriate additions of land and capital. However, since this availability of complementary factors was not present (particularly in the case of land) a plantation with excess slaves would have found it optimal to sell a slave when he reached physical maturity.

[23] T. E. Smith, "The Cocos-Keeling Islands: A Demographic Laboratory," *Population Studies* 14 (November 1960). I have chosen to use the Cocos Islands fertility pattern rather than that of the Hutterite women, a group also characterized by high fertility, because the Hutterites rarely married before the age of 20 and premarital conception was very infrequent. Thus the marital fertility rates before the age of 20 are extremely high (marriage usually followed a premarital conception in order to legitimize the birth) while the rates defined to include all women below that age are extremely low.

TABLE 9. WEIGHTING FACTORS FOR EACH COHORT OF WOMEN
(COCOS ISLANDS)

Age Cohort	Average Number of Live Births per 1,000 Women	Index of Potential Fertility (age 20-24=1)	Average Number of Years of Fertility per Woman during Preceding 15 Years	Average Number of Prime Fertility Equivalent Years per Woman during Preceding 15 Years [a]
10-14	1.64	.000	0	0.00
15-19	139.12	.509	3	1.53
20-24	371.46	1.000	8	5.55
25-29	360.02	.970	13	10.45
30-34	311.72	.839	15	13.38
35-39	282.54	.761	15	13.32
40-44	139.26	.375	15	11.06
45-49	15.6	.000	12	7.36
50-54	0.0	.000	7	3.40
55-59	0.0	.000	2	.75

SOURCE: T. E. Smith, Table 8, p. 109.

[a] The value of this weighting factor is computed for the jth cohort by the formula $3F_j + 5(F_{j-1} + F_{j-2}) + 2F_{j-3}$ where F_j is the potential fertility index for the jth cohort.

index of potential fertility. This index was the one used to weight each year of fertility experience during the preceding fifteen years for the women in each cohort. The result is a measure of the average number of years of prime-fertility equivalents experienced by women in each cohort.

In Table 10 I present the ratio of children to women-years of prime-fertility experience on the Parker-Gallman slave farms. Each of the selling states had higher fertility ratios than did the buying states. Moreover, the fertility rates observed are extremely high. The prime fertility rate observed in the Cocos Islands was 371.46 children per thousand women. The ratios in Table 10 are diminished by the mortality of the children.[24] Therefore, the South Carolina ratio of 355 children per thousand years of prime-fertility experience must be close to the maximum that could be obtained. In the selling states almost 20 percent of the farms with five or more slave women had fertility ratios exceeding 333 per thousand. By contrast the buying states had only 13 percent of their farms in that high fertility category.

[24] But increased by the mortality of women. However, the probability of a slave dying before age 15 was greater than the probability that his mother would die before he reached that age. Therefore, the net effect of mortality would reduce the "fertility" rates presented.

189

TABLE 10. THE RATIO OF CHILDREN TO WOMEN ON SLAVE FARMS, PARKER-GALLMAN SAMPLE, 1860

State	Number of Children, 0-14, per Thousand Women-Years of Prime Fertility Experience	
South Carolina	354.6	
Tennessee	320.2	
Georgia	314.3	
North Carolina	309.8	
Selling states (includes Virginia)		323.0
Mississippi	283.6	
Alabama	267.6	
Texas	263.9	
Arkansas	260.5	
Louisiana	244.6	
Buying states (includes Florida)		268.8
All states		294.7

The statistical evidence seems strong: the slave women of those states with poor or exhausted soils conceived children more frequently than the women of the southwestern slave states where agricultural productivity was much higher. But is this alone evidence that the slaveowner of the eastern and border slave states interfered with the sexual lives of his slaves? Perhaps the differences in fertility arose simply as the result of selective exportation. If a young woman who was either pregnant or with small children under her care was less likely to be moved south because of the hazards of the journey or because of her diminished potential as a field-hand than her barren counterpart, then this mechanism alone could have produced the relatively higher ratios of children to women in the east.

That this suggestion is implausible can be demonstrated by computing the number of barren women who would have had to be exported from the selling states and imported into the buying states to fully explain the differences in the 1860 fertility ratios presented in Table 6. This calculation suggests that fully one-third of the women of childbearing age who were exported across state lines would have had to have been barren if the other two-thirds were of average fertility.[25] This is an implausibly high figure. Even if one were willing

[25] There were 43,005 infants under 1 in the six importing states (excluding Missouri) in 1860. The national average was 167.68 infants per one thousand women of childbearing age. To account for these infants these states would have required 256,471 women of average fertility. There were actually 280,180 women

to accept it, it suggests a degree of selectivity in the interstate slave trade that is incompatible with the notion that slaves were not being bred for sale. If breeding was not typically a part of the eastern slaveowner's business, why should he sell off barren women and retain those capable or willing to bear children? I suggest that the evidence is more consistent with the hypothesis that the higher apparent fertility ratio in the older states was the result of a systematic and widespread interference with the sexual life of the slaves.

How the higher fertility ratios were induced cannot be determined from the census data. However, the suggestion that eastern slaveowners encouraged or forced their slaves into polygamous or promiscuous relationships can be investigated by examining the ratio of women to men in the different regions. A slave breeder, with no scruples regarding the virtues of serial monogamy for slaves, would not need to have one man for each woman. He could have each man impregnate many women.

The aggregate data indicate that, if there were breeders operating farms with unusually high women per man ratios, they did not affect the overall sex ratios in their states. Table 11 presents the ratio of women to men in 1850 and 1860 for each slave state. The states are ranked by their estimated rate of slave exportation between 1850 and 1860 with the selling states first. There is no obvious relationship between the sex ratios and the ranking of the states.[26] Moreover, all of the ratios are quite close to one. At the extreme was South Carolina, which shows a surplus of 7.5 women per one hundred men.

The aggregate data obscure some important differences, however. It was likely that slaves held for non-agricultural and non-domestic purposes would be male.[27] Since the slave states differed sharply in the percentage of slaves engaged in non-agricultural occupations, a restriction of the analysis to farms should yield a different pattern. It also was apparently true that on farms with only one slave, males dominated as the preferred sex. This is illustrated by the Parker-Gallman sample. The total number of slave women, 15 to 44 years of age, included in the sample was almost exactly equal to the total number of men. The women-per-man ratio was 1.010 (1.042 for the selling states

---

of childbearing age. Thus 23,709 women (over 8%) would have had to have been barren women imported into the region. According to our estimate 66,245 slave women were brought into this region.

[26] Spearman's coefficient of rank correlation between the rank of the states by the women per man ratio presented in Table 11 and their rate of slave exportation is .046.

[27] Robert S. Starobin, *Industrial Slavery in the Old South*, New York, 1970, p. 11.

TABLE 11. The Ratio of Slave Women to Men, 15 to 39, 1850 and 1860

State	1850	1860	Average
Maryland, Delaware and the District of Columbia	.986	.984	.985
Kentucky	.976	.977	.977
South Carolina	1.075	1.074	1.075
Virginia	.944	.953	.949
Tennessee	1.012	1.029	1.021
North Carolina	.998	.986	.992
Georgia	1.042	1.034	1.038
Average: Selling states	1.007	1.008	1.007
Missouri	.987	.978	.983
Alabama	1.004	1.005	1.005
Mississippi	1.015	1.003	1.009
Louisiana	.943	.938	.941
Florida	.994	.970	.982
Arkansas	.986	.971	.979
Texas	1.057	1.010	1.034
Average: Buying states[a]	.993	.986	.990

[a] Excluding Missouri.

and 0.986 for the buying states). However, when we exclude the farms without any women, the average ratio becomes 1.232. Significantly, this tendency of farms to have a surplus of women was most pronounced in the selling states where the excess of women over men reached 300 per thousand. In the buying states the surplus was 200 per thousand, still a surprising figure.

These abnormally high ratios of women to men seem to be related to slave breeding. Table 12 presents the ratio of children to adults cross classified by the ratio of women to men. Since children represent the "output" of a slavebreeding operation and the number of adults represents the "inputs" it can be seen that over a wide range of sex ratios the "productivity" could be increased by increasing the number of women to men.

There was a limitation to the extent the sex ratio could be distorted to increase productivity, however. As the ratio of women to men increased, the fertility of the women decreased, as is indicated in Table 12. This was probably the result of an increased risk of venereal disease coupled with a type of passive resistance on the part of the slaves to the disruption or absence of a stable family life implied by the shortage of men.

The unequal sex distributions on the slave plantations suggest that

TABLE 12. PRODUCTIVITY AND FERTILITY RATES ON FARMS WITH FIVE OR MORE
WOMEN, PARKER-GALLMAN SAMPLE, 1860

Sex Ratio Women per Man	Ratio of Children, 0-14, to Adults, 15-44		Number of Children per Thousand Years of Prime Fertility Experience		Number of Farms with Five or More Women	
	Selling States	Buying States	Selling States	Buying States	Selling States	Buying States
R > 3.0[a]	1.37	0.85	233.6	122.4	19	11
2.0 < R ≤ 3.0	1.36	1.09	245.1	222.2	22	18
1.5 < R ≤ 2.0	1.27	1.07	275.1	229.2	42	42
1.1 < R ≤ 1.5	1.14	0.97	248.1	233.3	66	86
1.0 ≤ R ≤ 1.1	1.01	0.88	232.6	209.6	36	44
R < 1.0	0.99	0.81	276.0	239.8	63	132

[a] Includes farms with no men.

a substantial portion of the slaveowners were overtly practicing slave breeding. Consider the implications of assuming that the sex distributions *do not* imply the practices of polygamy or promiscuity.

In Table 13 we have recomputed the fertility rates presented in Table 10 under the new assumption that only married slave women had children and that the maximum number of married couples existed on each plantation. The maximum number of couples is equal to the number of women or the number of men, whichever is less.

TABLE 13. THE RATIO OF CHILDREN TO COUPLES ON SLAVE FARMS,
PARKER-GALLMAN SAMPLE, 1860

State	Number of Children, 0-14, per Thousand "Married" Women-Years of Prime Fertility Experience	
South Carolina	491.7	
Tennessee	439.0	
North Carolina	431.6	
Georgia	415.3	
Selling states (includes Virginia)		440.9
Arkansas	383.8	
Mississippi	357.0	
Alabama	343.0	
Texas	340.5	
Louisiana	284.2	
Buying states (includes Florida)		339.7
All states		381.2

193

Since we do not know which of the women on those plantations with surplus women would have been married, in such cases we assume that each married woman had the average number of prime-fertility years of experience of all the women in the holding. Any farm without men was omitted from the computation.

The fertility ratios in the eastern selling states computed in this manner seem unbelievably high. For the selling-state farms as a group, average "marital" fertility would have to have been 441 per thousand at ages 20 through 24, which exceeds the measured fertility of the 20 to 24 year old Cocos Islands women by 70 per thousand and approaches even the extremes of individual experience. A woman would have to have nearly ten surviving children by the time she was 44 to equal 441 live children per thousand married prime-fertility equivalent years of experience observed as average on the selling-state farms in the Parker-Gallman sample. The average for South Carolina is 492 per thousand, 120 per thousand above the Cocos Islands standard. It seems safe to conclude that a substantial portion of slave women in these states conceived children by men to whom they were not married.

As a final test of the hypothesis that breeding farms existed in the antebellum South a search was made of the Parker-Gallman sample for examples of farms with a disproportionate number of women and large numbers of children. Lest we unjustly charge one of the Parker-Gallman slave owners, we have adopted a restrictive definition of a breeding farm. The first criterion employed was that the farm must have a ratio of women to men in the 15 to 44 age group so large as to occur less than 10 percent of the time by chance *if* the men and women were distributed randomly.[28] This is an extremely conservative criterion since it assumes that there was no tendency for slaves to be bought and

---

[28] The Parker-Gallman sample records 9,185 women between 15 and 44 and 9,098 men. If these males and females were distributed randomly to each of the plantations, the expected sex distribution on a plantation of any given size would be given by a hypergeometric distribution. However, since the number of slaves is large the binomial distribution provides an extremely close approximation. The binomial theorem tells us that the probability that exactly x of the slaves on a plantation with n slaves between the ages of 15 and 44 will be female is:

$$P \left(\begin{array}{c} x \\ n \end{array} \right) = \frac{n!}{x! \, (n\text{-}x)!} \, (.5024)^x \, (.4976)^{n-x}$$

where .5024 is the fraction of slaves mentioned in the Parker-Gallman sample who are women, and .4976 is the fraction who are men. The expected number of women on a plantation with n adults is .5024 n with a standard deviation of approximately $[n/4]^{\frac{1}{2}}$. Note that the criteria I have adopted automatically exclude any farm with less than four men and women.

owned in family units. If slaves are frequently coupled, nearly equal sex distributions ought to be observed much more frequently than would be the case with a random distribution. Actually only 87 farms (3.4 percent) of the 2,588 slaveholdings sampled had such extreme sex distributions. From this list of 87 farms we deleted those on which the number of children was low enough to be explained solely by the maximum number of couples; that is, the number of men. To give men over 44 the benefit of the doubt we included *all* men 15 years old and over. The procedure established was to compute the number of children under 15 per 1,000 years of prime fertility experience represented by the women on the plantation and then to multiply this fertility measure times the ratio of women, aged 15 to 44, to men 15 and over. This gives us a "marital fertility rate," assuming every man over 15 was married. If this "marital" fertility rate was less than 375 per thousand, the farm was deleted.[29] Forty farms were excluded on this ground, leaving 47. Table 14 lists each of the 47 suspect breeding farms.

These 47 farms had a total of 439 women, nearly 5 percent of all the women included in the Parker-Gallman sample. Fourteen of the 47 were located in South Carolina, 29 altogether in the selling states, and 18 in the buying states (six in Alabama). The women on the 29 selling-state breeding farms accounted for 7.3 percent of the total number of women in the selling states who were included in the Parker-Gallman sample.

In addition to the 47 farms listed in Table 14 there were 527 farms (20.4 percent of the slaveholders in the sample) which had three or fewer men and a ratio of women to men larger than two. The majority of these farms (436, or 16.8 percent of the sample) had no men at all. All of these farms are distributed in Table 15 by the number of women and children. Seventy-six percent of them had children present. While it is certain that some of these farms represent cases of slave widows with their children, it is not likely that a large fraction of them can be explained in this way.

None of the evidence presented in this essay is direct, all of it is circumstantial. However, the case provided by this circumstantial evidence is strong enough to conclude that many slaveowners in the American South systematically bred slaves for sale. These slave breeders were concentrated in the border states and in the states along the Atlantic coast. They held disproportionately large numbers of

---

[29] The peak fertility experience of the Cocos Islands women was 371.46 per thousand for the 20 to 24 year old cohort.

TABLE 14. SUSPECTED BREEDING FARMS FOUND IN THE PARKER-GALLMAN
SAMPLE, 1860

State and County	Women 15-44	Men 15-44	Children 0-14
North Carolina			
Johnson	5	1	10
Pitt	11	4	23
Wake	38	28	120
South Carolina			
Abbeville	6	1	13
Abbeville	11	5	30
Abbeville	5	1	9
Colleton	18	6	28
Darlington	14	6	39
Darlington	5	1	12
Edgefield	14	7	26
Edgefield	5	1	17
Fairfield	9	4	11
Greenville	5	1	5
Marion	16	1	20
Union	11	5	31
Union	10	5	46
Williamsburgh	14	4	39
Georgia			
Clark	4	0	10
Crawford	18	6	22
Harris	6	0	8
Jones	5	1	13
Lowndes	9	2	16
Macon	4	0	6
Muscogee	5	1	5
Oglethorpe	9	3	18
Tennessee			
Carroll	7	2	15
Fayette	12	5	22
Fayette	6	1	11
Giles	7	2	12
Florida			
Hamilton	16	7	32
Alabama			
Barbour	14	8	44
Dekalb	4	0	11
Jackson	5	1	5
Limestone	8	3	11
Marengo	5	0	4
Wilcox	6	1	10
Mississippi			
Holmes	4	0	7
Holmes	11	6	23
Marshall	13	5	29
Rankin	8	3	16

TABLE 14 *(Continued)*

State and County	Women 15-44	Men 15-44	Children 0-14
Arkansas			
Ashley	4	0	2
Drew	22	2	27
Phillips	7	2	7
Sevier	4	0	8
Louisiana			
Claiborne	5	1	5
Texas			
Grimes	10	5	19
Harrison	4	0	5
Selling states	289	104	637
Buying states	150	44	265
TOTAL	439	148	902

TABLE 15. THE NUMBER OF SLAVE CHILDREN RESIDING ON FARMS WITH SELECTED SEX RATIOS, PARKER-GALLMAN SAMPLE, 1860

	Number of Farms with							
	No Men and			One Man and		Two Men and		Three Men and
Number of Children	One Woman	Two Women	Three Women	Three Women	Four Women	Five Women	Six Women	Seven Women
0	112	9	—	2	1	—	—	—
1	83	12	2	4	—	—	—	—
2	44	17	1	3	—	—	—	—
3	55	11	2	5	1	—	1	—
4	23	6	4	9	2	1	—	—
5	14	4	2	10	1	—	—	—
6	6	9	1	4	3	2	—	1
7	4	2	3	5	2	—	—	—
8	2	3	—	2	6	2	—	—
9	1	1	1	4	2	1	1	—
10	—	1	—	3	—	—	—	—
11	—	—	1	2	—	—	—	1
12	—	—	—	—	—	2	—	—
13	—	—	—	—	—	2	—	1
14	—	—	—	—	—	—	—	—
15	—	—	—	—	1	1	—	1
16	—	—	—	—	—	—	—	—
17	—	—	—	—	—	1	—	—
TOTAL	344	75	17	53	19	13	2	4

women in the child-bearing age group. They fostered polygamy and promiscuity among their slaves. The products of this breeding operation were sold or transported to the southwestern slave states, predominately as young adults. There is little possibility that this practice was innocent; it appears to have been the logical outcome of a system which treated slaves as assets, a system that stripped men of their humanity so that the market for their labor could operate efficiently and so that the profits of their exploiters could be maximized.

APPENDIX

Estimates of the Net Importation and Exportation of Slaves By Age, Sex, and State Between 1850 and 1860

THE data on the importation and exportation of slaves reported in the text were computed from the age and sex tabulations of the slave population reported in the 1850 and 1860 Census reports.[1] These estimates rely on techniques for computing net migration from such data which have been worked out by Hamilton (1934), Hamilton and Henderson (1944), and Siegel and Hamilton (1952).[2] These techniques produce an estimate of the population which would be expected in each region at the end of the decade had there been no migration by the application of survival rates to each age-sex-race cohort enumerated at the beginning of the decade. The difference between the expected population and the enumerated population of each cohort at the end of the decade is an estimate of the net out-migration from the region between the two censuses.

The survival rate technique begins with the simple identity:

$$(1) \qquad P_o + B - D + M = P_1$$

which says that the aggregate population of a region at the beginning of the period (P_o) plus the number of births within the time period

[1] U.S. Census Office, *The Seventh Census of the United States: 1850*, Washington, 1853; and U.S. Census Office, *Population of the United States in 1860 . . . The Eighth Census*, Washington, 1864.

[2] C. Horace Hamilton, "Rural-Urban Migration in the Tennessee Valley Between 1920 and 1930," *Social Forces* 13 (October 1934); C. Horace Hamilton and F. M. Henderson, "Use of the Survival Rate Method in Measuring Net Migration," *Journal of the American Statistical Association* 44 (June 1944); Jacob S. Siegel and C. Horace Hamilton, "Some Considerations in the Use of the Residual Method of Estimating Net Migration," *Journal of the American Statistical Association* 47 (September 1952). The computational techniques used to prepare the estimates reported here are described at greater length in Richard Sutch, Richard Roehl, John Lyons, and Michael Boskin, "Urban Migration in the Process of Industrialization: Britain and the United States in the Nineteenth Century," *Working Papers in Economic Theory and Econometrics*, no. 162, Berkeley, Center for Research in Management Science and Institute of Business and Economic Research, August 1970. Also see the discussion of Everett S. Lee, "Migration Estimates," in Simon Kuznets and Dorothy Swaine Thomas, eds., *Population Redistribution and Economic Growth, United States 1870-1950*, vol. I, "Methodological Considerations and Reference Tables," Philadelphia, 1957.

(B) less the number of deaths (D) plus the *net* in-migration (M) must equal the aggregate population at the end of the period (P_1). For every age-sex-race cohort there is a similar identity. For example, for slave females ten to twenty years old at the beginning of the period the formula becomes:

$$P_o - D + M = P_1,$$

where the variables are defined as before except that they now refer to the 10- to 20-year-old female cohort. A different relationship exists for the cohort of children born during the decade; for that group the population identity is written:

(3) $$B - D + M = P_1.$$

The age-sex tabulations for the slave population provide the information on P_o and P_1. If data on births and deaths of slaves were available, these identities could be used to compute an age and sex breakdown of the net migration. Unfortunately, neither of the censuses provide sufficiently reliable statistics on the number of births and deaths.[3] However, sufficient information on mortality and fertility rates of slaves is available to allow an estimation of these numbers.

First, it is helpful to rewrite equation (2) as follows:

(4) $$P_o - D_n + M_p - D_{mb} - D_{ma} = P_1.$$

Here, P_o and P_1 are defined as before; D_n refers to the number of those nonmigrants in the region who die during the period; M_p denotes the total number of *potential* migrants into the region at the beginning of the period (the number of people who would have migrated had no one died during the period); D_{mb} is the number of the potential migrants who died *before* they migrated into the region in question; and D_{ma} is the number of potential migrants who died during the period but *after* arriving in the region. The net migration is the number of potential migrants less those who died before migrating ($M = M_p - D_{mb}$). I assume that the number of deaths in any given cohort

---

[3] "The Tables of the Census which undertake to give the total number of Births, Marriages, and Deaths in the year preceding the first of June, 1850, can be said to have very little value. Nothing short of a registration system in the States will give these data with even approximate truth; and, where such a system has been established, difficulties have continually occurred, requiring a very long period of time to be removed. Against all reasonings, the facts have proved that people will not, or cannot, remember and report to the Census taker the number of such events, and the particulars of them, which have happened in the period of a whole year to eighteen months prior to the time of his calling." U.S. Census Office, *The Seventh Census of the United States: 1850*, p. xxxiv.

between the two census dates can be obtained by applying the appropriate mortality rate to the original cohort population. Symbolically this can be written as:

(5) $$D_n = dP_o.$$

where d is the rate of mortality of individuals belonging to the age, sex, and race cohort in question. Substitution of equation (5) into equation (4) produces:

(6) $$(1-d)P_o + M - D_{ma} = P_1.$$

In this formulation the term $(1-d)$ is a survival ratio—the fraction of the given cohort which survives the period from the first census to the second. The equation is more conveniently written in terms of the survival ratio, s, as follows:

(7) $$sP_o + M - D_{ma} = P_1.$$

To compute M one must estimate D_{ma}. Applying the same survival rate to the potential migrants as was applied to the non-migrants one can estimate the sum of D_{mb} and D_{ma}: [4]

(8) $$(1-s) M_p = D_{mb} + D_{ma}.$$

It is next assumed that D_{mb} equals D_{ma}. If the total number of potential migrants within a period were distributed uniformly throughout the census decade, one would expect more to have died after moving than before since the probability of dying generally rises with age. On the other hand, the morbidity preceding death may deter migration in a sizable number of cases. This will have an opposite effect: death will overtake more of the potential migrants before they move than after. I assume these two effects roughly cancel leaving an equal chance of dying before as after moving for a member of the potential migrant group. With this assumption equation (8) can be solved for D_{ma} in terms of M:

(9) $$D_{ma} = \frac{(1-s)}{(1+s)} M.$$

Substituting this last expression into equation (7) and solving for M yields [5]

---

[4] There are at least two objections to this assumption. (1) Migrants are likely to be hardier people than nonmigrants (even in the same age-sex cohort). (2) Migration is a dangerous and health-destroying process, thus migrants are exposed to greater risks of death. It will be observed that these two effects work in opposite directions. The assumption made can be thought of as requiring that these two factors exactly cancel.

[5] This equation is identical to one suggested by Siegel and Hamilton (p. 491), although their derivation was based on a different argument.

(10)
$$M = \frac{(1+s)}{2s}(P_1 - sP_o).$$

Equation (10) was used to estimate the net slave migration into each state by age and sex.[6] With the exception of the survival ratios, all the information required is available in the age classification tables of the published censuses.

The real difficulty in estimating net migration lies in obtaining accurate estimates of the survival ratios by age, sex, and region. Accurate estimates are particularly important because of the sensitivity of the results to small changes in the survival ratio. Appendix Table 1 illustrates this fact by presenting the estimated net exports between 1850 and 1860 from Virginia of female slaves who were between 30 and 39 years of age in 1860 for several assumed survival ratios. As can be seen, a substantial change in the rate of out-migration can be produced by small changes in the survival rate.

C. H. Hamilton has demonstrated that the appropriate survival rate for use in migration calculations is the "census survival rate" computed directly from the census tabulations. Estimates based on life tables will compound and transmit any errors in the reporting of ages to the

APPENDIX TABLE 1. AN ILLUSTRATION OF THE SENSITIVITY OF NET MIGRATION ESTIMATES TO THE SURVIVAL RATIO [a]

Survival Rate	Net Out-Migration	Rate of Out-Migration[b]
.75	1,914	6.9
.76	2,328	8.3
.77	2,735	9.6
.78	3,148	10.9
.79	3,534	12.1
.80	3,925	13.3
.81	4,312	14.4

[a] This illustration is based on female slaves 20 to 29 years old in 1850 and 30 to 39 years old in 1860 in the State of Virginia. The number enumerated in this cohort in 1850 was 36,974 and in 1860, 26,090. The survival rate employed for this cohort in the calculations below was .780. U.S. Census Office, *The Seventh Census of the United States: 1850,* Washington, 1853, p. xliv; and U.S. Census Office, *Population of the United States in 1860 . . . The Eighth Census,* Washington, 1864, pp. 594-595.

[b] Defined as a percentage of the expected population in 1860 on the assumption of no migration.

[6] The equation does not apply to the cohorts born during the intercensal period. Estimating these flows requires estimates of fertility by region. A technique for including these cohorts in the calculations is discussed below.

migration estimates.[7] The census survival rate is simply a measure of the decline (or increase) of each age-sex cohort between successive censuses for a closed population. In the case of a population which was not affected by immigration or emigration the national survival ratio for each cohort can be computed directly from the age tabulations of the total population. While the United States experienced considerable immigration during the decade of the 1850s, over 2½ million between the two Censuses, almost all of the arrivals were white. Of the few blacks who did immigrate, it can be safely concluded that they joined the "free colored" population rather than the slave population.[8] Blacks, nevertheless, could pass out of the slave population into either the free colored population or foreign countries through manumission or successful escape. The available evidence, however, indicates that such departures were rare,[9] and to the extent that they did take place it is entirely appropriate for our purposes to consider them as equivalent to a slave death. They would be so treated by the slaveowner. No adjustments were made to the slave population for the purpose of estimating the survival rates.

Appendix Table 2 presents the census survival ratios for the slave population based on the Census data. The distortions in the age dis-

---

[7] C. Horace Hamilton, "Rural-Urban Migration in the Tennessee Valley"; id., "Practical and Mathematical Considerations in the Formulation and Selection of Migration Rates," *Demography* 1 (1965); and id., "Effect of Census Errors on the Measurement of Net Migration," *Demography* 2 (1966). It can be established that censuses generally underenumerate the number of children under 5 years of age relative to other age groups. Thus it is frequently found that a census will report more persons 10 to 15 years of age at one census than it reported as under 5 years of age ten years previously. A life table would yield an estimate of the survival ratio for this cohort of less than one and thereby attribute the improved enumeration of this age cohort in every region to net migration—greatly exaggerating the true migration flows.

[8] The raw immigration data was published yearly by the United States Department of State. The data were not classified by race. However, if we judge race by national origin we find that during the decade only 134 immigrating passengers arrived from African countries and only 10,437 from the West Indies (see Sutch, Roehl, Lyons, and Boskin, Table C-2, p. 78). The birthplaces of the slave population were not collected in the Federal Censuses of either 1850 or 1860. However, the nativity of the entire population was collected in 1870 and tabulated separately by race. In that year only 9,645 blacks—less than two per thousand— were born in foreign countries (U.S. Census Office, *The Statistics of the Population of the United States . . . Ninth Census*, Washington, 1872, Table VI, p. 336). The illegal importation of slaves into the United States was undoubtedly negligible during this period. See Philip D. Curtin, *The Atlantic Slave Trade: A Census*, Madison, Wis., 1969, pp. 73-75.

[9] In the year preceding the 1850 Census 1,467 slaves were freed by their owners and 1,011 escaped and were fugitive at the time of Census. U.S. Census Office, *Statistical View of the United States*, Washington, 1854, p. 64.

203

APPENDIX TABLE 2. DECENNIAL CENSUS SURVIVAL RATIOS OF THE SLAVE POPULA-
TION, BY AGE AND SEX COHORTS, 1850-1860

Age of Cohort 1850	1860	Number of Males in Cohort 1850	1860	Male Survival Rate	Number of Females in Cohort 1850	1860	Female Survival Rate
Under 5	10-14	267,088	276,928	1.037	273,406	264,320	.967
5-9	15-19	239,163	220,365	.921	239,925	228,481	.952
10-19	20-29	397,649	355,018	.893	395,825	343,023	.867
20-29	30-39	289,595	218,346	.754	282,615	220,520	.780
30-39	40-49	175,300	140,791	.803	178,355	139,002	.779
40-49	50-59	109,152	79,776	.731	110,780	75,926	.685
50-59	60-69	65,254	46,219	.708	61,762	44,124	.714
60-69	70-79	38,102	15,433	.405	36,569	15,724	.430
70+	80+	19,361	6,615	.342	20,720	7,948	.384

SOURCES: Computed from data in:
U.S. Census Office, *The Seventh Census of the United States: 1850*, Washington,1853, p. xliv.
U.S. Census Office, *Population of the United States in 1860 . . . The Eighth Census*, Washington, 1864, pp. 594-595.

tributions caused by misreporting or underenumeration are apparent in the survival ratios shown. No true survival ratio could exceed one, and the higher survival ratios for the males in the 40 to 49 year old 1860 cohort than for the 30 to 39 1860 cohort is very unlikely to reflect a true mortality reversal. Rather, these peculiarities reflect a systematic underenumeration of young children and of age heaping in the 20 to 29 year old cohort. However, to the extent that the degree of under-enumeration and age heaping at each age is uniform across the states under study, use of the census survival ratios will automatically correct for this bias while the use of life table survival ratios would introduce serious errors.[10]

Equation (10) was used to estimate the migration for each cohort born before the 1850 Census. A complete estimate of migration must also include the migration of those slaves born within the decade. This cohort required a different technique, one based on equation (3). Solving that equation for the net migration of children one obtains:

(11) $$M = P_1 - (B - D).$$

Here M is the migration of children under ten of a given sex, P_1 is the number of children in that cohort enumerated in the region at the end of the decade, B is the number of births in the region during the

---

[10] Daniel O. Price, "Examination of Two Sources of Error in the Estimation of Net Internal Migration," *Journal of the American Statistical Association* 50 (September 1955), 691-693.

intercensal period, and D is the number of deaths occurring to members of this age-sex cohort.

The absence of reliable data on the number of births prevents the use of the survival rate technique to estimate the quantity $(B-D)$, the number of children born in the region and surviving until the end of the decade. Instead, I computed this number by estimating slave fertility ratios for each state which were then used to distribute all slave children under ten years of age at the end of the census decade to a state of birth. This procedure does not permit an estimate of the number of children who migrated and then died before the end of the decade. There is therefore a tendency to understate the migration flows in this cohort relative to the other cohorts.

The state fertility ratios were estimated by taking the weighted average of the ratio of infants under one year of age to women of childbearing age at both the initial and terminal censuses.[11] These fertility ratios were then converted to an index by dividing each state's ratio by the appropriate national ratio computed in the same manner.

In order to distribute the slave children to their region of birth a census-decade fertility ratio for the nation as a whole was computed as the ratio of all slave children under 10 years of age to the average of women who were 15 to 39 at the first census and women who were 20 to 39 a decade later. This definition has the property that it includes all of the women who were 15 to 29 at the first census (and hence 25 to 39 at the second census) and in addition it counts with a weight of one-half those women who were 30 to 39 at the first census (40 to 49 at the second) and those women who were 10 to 14 at the first census (20 to 24 at the second).

This ratio of children to women (1.0110 for male children and 1.0279 for females) was multiplied by the state fertility index previously mentioned to obtain a state fertility ratio. This ratio was then multiplied by the average number of women of childbearing age in the state during the decade, computed in the same manner as that cohort was for the nation. Appendix Table 3 presents the distribution of slave children under 10 in 1860 to their state of birth.

Appendix Table 4 presents the net importation of slaves into each of the slave states by age and sex. The ages given in the table are the ages of each cohort in 1860. Appendix Table 5 presents the importations as a percentage of the number of individuals in the given cohort who would have resided in the region at the end of the decade had no migration taken place; that is, the population of the cohort at the first census times the appropriate survival ratio.

[11] Women of childbearing age were defined as one-half the women 15 to 19 years old plus all women 20 to 39 years old.

APPENDIX TABLE 3. DISTRIBUTION OF SLAVE CHILDREN UNDER AGE TEN IN 1860 TO THEIR STATE OF BIRTH

State	Average Number of Women of Childbearing Age	Weighted Average State Fertility Ratio		Distribution of Children to State of Birth	
		Male	Female	Male	Female
Delaware	379	.727	1.016	275	385
Maryland	14,633	1.101	1.063	16,116	15,547
District of Columbia	773	.550	.614	425	475
Virginia	74,893	1.047	1.080	78,442	80,921
North Carolina	48,247	1.168	1.157	56,347	55,827
South Carolina	67,995	.943	.985	64,144	66,945
Georgia	72,752	1.030	1.031	74,986	74,982
Florida	8,488	.950	.949	8,069	8,052
Alabama	67,415	.959	.963	64,668	64,919
Mississippi	65,271	.895	.929	58,377	60,647
Louisiana	53,465	.740	.785	39,544	41,990
Texas	19,933	1.035	1.027	20,642	20,472
Arkansas	13,671	.966	1.017	13,201	13,896
Tennessee	43,122	1.176	1.187	50,723	51,203
Kentucky	35,160	1.230	1.246	43,258	43,800
Missouri	16,602	1.218	1.179	20,229	19,580

APPENDIX TABLE 4. NET IMPORTATION (+) OR EXPORTATION (−) OF SLAVES, BY AGE, SEX, AND STATE, 1850-1860

Age in 1860	Delaware Male	Delaware Female	Maryland Male	Maryland Female	District of Columbia Male	District of Columbia Female	Virginia Male	Virginia Female
Under 10	−2	−119	−2,739	−2,342	−72	−114	−3,769	−5,869
10 to 14	−30	−28	−1,014	−1,016	8	100	−3,040	−3,459
15 to 19	−49	−21	−704	−1,058	44	28	−5,460	−6,017
20 to 29	−228	−125	−3,378	−3,135	−213	−248	−12,155	−12,454
30 to 39	−132	−103	−2,168	−1,508	−81	−130	−3,831	−3,148
40 to 49	−28	−19	−702	−648	−22	−14	−1,890	−1,175
50 to 59	−6	−4	−327	−368	−13	15	−1,623	−1,002
60 to 69	−2	−4	−202	−149	−10	−14	−711	−226
70 to 79	−2	5	−95	−80	0	0	−169	131
80 and over	1	−3	−138	−101	2	−7	−745	−693
Age unknown	0	0	−4	−9	0	0	−234	−177
TOTAL	−478	−421	−11,471	−10,414	−445	−384	−33,627	−34,089
AGGREGATE	−899		−21,885		−829		−67,716	

Age in 1860	North Carolina Male	North Carolina Female	South Carolina Male	South Carolina Female	Georgia Male	Georgia Female	Florida Male	Florida Female
Under 10	−1,977	−570	−3,365	−3,561	−866	186	1,571	1,359
10 to 14	−1,342	−1,505	−4,265	−4,302	−1,119	−322	832	903
15 to 19	−3,259	−4,198	−3,325	−3,673	−758	−649	815	779
20 to 29	−5,228	−4,748	−8,816	−7,020	−2,941	−2,128	1,788	1,602
30 to 39	−1,930	−1,856	−2,986	−2,697	−1,395	−883	837	696
40 to 49	−1,016	−969	−1,722	−1,755	−123	−30	555	497
50 to 59	1,485	1,610	−781	−1,015	−681	−584	299	278
60 to 69	−731	−496	−1,058	−1,126	402	458	−15	14
70 to 79	317	195	−282	−428	−109	−325	52	93
80 and over	−72	−70	−309	−283	266	192	105	63
Age unknown	−20	−32	−6,196	−5,901	−92	−43	−122	79
TOTAL	−13,773	−12,639	−33,105	−31,761	−7,416	−4,128	6,717	6,363
AGGREGATE	−26,412		−64,866		−11,544		13,080	

APPENDIX TABLE 4 (Continued)

Age in 1860	Alabama		Mississippi		Louisiana		Texas	
	Male	Female	Male	Female	Male	Female	Male	Female
Under 10	2,518	3,466	4,673	4,093	3,257	1,383	8,915	9,443
10 to 14	−93	156	1,232	873	798	220	7,252	7,301
15 to 19	568	1,333	2,578	3,483	2,557	3,117	7,071	7,469
20 to 29	2,868	2,874	8,363	8,919	12,516	10,305	11,911	11,584
30 to 39	1,247	806	2,304	872	5,537	2,996	6,618	6,358
40 to 49	−9	344	117	−592	1,774	370	3,364	3,504
50 to 59	−659	−298	−493	−601	141	21	1,702	1,525
60 to 69	630	354	1,311	933	173	91	766	676
70 to 79	−230	−230	−212	−144	216	186	310	371
80 and over	90	224	215	179	235	146	223	205
Age unknown	−3	3	4,967	4,740	1,579	1,181	211	225
TOTAL	6,927	9,032	25,055	22,755	28,783	20,016	48,343	48,661
AGGREGATE	15,959		47,810		48,799		97,004	

Age in 1860	Arkansas		Tennessee		Kentucky		Missouri	
	Male	Female	Male	Female	Male	Female	Male	Female
Under 10	4,215	3,540	−5,527	−4,541	−6,428	−6,468	−407	122
10 to 14	3,237	3,089	−1,220	−901	−1,771	−1,908	531	800
15 to 19	3,423	3,710	−1,932	−2,129	−2,022	−2,496	542	324
20 to 29	7,028	6,425	−4,915	−4,139	−6,142	−6,963	−451	−745
30 to 39	3,118	2,862	−2,768	−1,868	−3,335	−2,153	−1,024	−244
40 to 49	1,652	1,667	−1,118	−973	−950	−547	119	339
50 to 59	647	622	845	561	−527	−722	−7	−29
60 to 69	568	505	−666	−572	−415	−435	−23	23
70 to 79	93	80	13	5	50	66	62	91
80 and over	67	134	−13	−25	3	−33	84	98
Age unknown	1	0	−11	−5	−21	−20	−51	−35
TOTAL	24,049	22,634	−17,312	−14,587	−21,558	−21,679	−625	744
AGGREGATE	46,683		−31,899		−43,237		119	

APPENDIX TABLE 5. NET IMPORTATION OF SLAVES, AS A PERCENTAGE OF THE 1850 COHORT SURVIVING TO 1860, 1850-1860

Age in 1860	Delaware		Maryland		District of Columbia		Virginia	
	Male	Female	Male	Female	Male	Female	Male	Female
Under 10	-.61	-26.10	-15.22	-13.49	-14.09	-20.00	-4.46	-6.74
10 to 14	-15.90	-16.09	-13.58	-14.73	3.96	45.97	-7.76	-9.29
15 to 19	-23.85	-12.39	-11.07	-16.55	-22.96	10.24	-16.76	-18.11
20 to 29	-60.23	-41.81	-30.01	-30.49	-53.49	-43.36	-22.89	-25.22
30 to 39	-82.58	-54.32	-35.53	-25.97	-44.95	-39.20	-12.71	-10.91
40 to 49	-52.03	-29.02	-20.47	-18.48	-21.57	-7.33	-9.25	-6.22
50 to 59	-26.48	-13.57	-15.15	-18.32	-19.55	12.03	-12.06	-8.35
60 to 69	-14.12	-25.45	-14.81	-11.27	-25.67	-15.19	-8.27	-2.92
70 to 79	-61.72	105.71	-19.76	-15.83	0.00	0.00	-5.48	4.36
80 and over	41.81	-78.21	-50.24	-32.47	34.43	-43.45	-50.29	-36.29
Age unknown	0.00	0.00	-46.23	-55.60	0.00	0.00	-55.20	-53.34
TOTAL	-35.28	-29.91	-20.16	-19.14	-25.96	-15.88	-11.72	-12.19
AGGREGATE	-32.55		-19.66		-20.06		-11.95	

Age in 1860	North Carolina		South Carolina		Georgia		Florida	
	Male	Female	Male	Female	Male	Female	Male	Female
Under 10	-3.39	-.99	-4.85	-4.92	-1.15	.25	21.78	18.88
10 to 14	-4.99	-5.96	-13.07	-13.50	-3.30	-1.01	24.29	27.72
15 to 19	-15.12	-18.73	-13.33	-13.71	-2.84	-2.37	30.62	28.46
20 to 29	-16.08	-15.36	-21.75	-17.35	-6.76	-4.93	44.69	40.82
30 to 39	-10.68	-10.11	-12.48	-10.33	-5.45	-3.27	28.63	24.23
40 to 49	-9.24	-8.93	-10.42	-9.82	-.80	-.19	30.35	27.58
50 to 59	24.06	27.22	-8.13	-10.20	-7.70	-6.55	30.44	30.27
60 to 69	-15.15	-10.97	-17.03	-18.01	8.62	9.77	-2.37	2.46
70 to 79	21.52	12.58	-12.83	-18.09	-5.87	-16.63	27.08	54.48
80 and over	-9.21	-6.96	-31.67	-25.04	37.04	22.86	137.81	79.73
Age unknown	-28.90	-28.24	-55.60	-55.96	-39.38	-31.25	-35.25	0.00
TOTAL	-7.58	-7.07	-13.91	-12.92	-3.13	-1.74	27.66	27.04
AGGREGATE	-7.33		-13.41		-2.43		27.36	

Age in 1860	Alabama		Mississippi		Louisiana		Texas	
	Male	Female	Male	Female	Male	Female	Male	Female
Under 10	3.96	5.43	8.42	7.10	8.66	3.46	72.92	77.89
10 to 14	−.30	.54	4.52	3.32	4.63	1.31	136.85	148.37
15 to 19	2.40	5.45	12.04	15.83	18.66	21.81	176.18	174.14
20 to 29	7.62	7.87	25.13	27.89	56.04	47.17	182.08	177.45
30 to 39	5.22	3.31	10.22	3.72	28.19	16.02	157.16	143.38
40 to 49	−.06	2.26	.78	−4.00	10.91	2.58	133.78	130.36
50 to 59	−7.89	−3.69	−6.75	−8.83	1.52	.29	133.07	118.48
60 to 69	13.97	8.22	38.13	29.75	4.10	2.62	120.43	114.14
70 to 79	−15.05	−15.50	−16.67	−11.80	17.59	18.11	205.19	259.89
80 and over	16.80	40.25	50.54	41.37	49.34	33.95	413.09	358.67
Age unknown	−34.67	0.00	452.04	492.18	2607.16	4864.29	221.70	198.58
TOTAL	3.30	4.35	13.29	12.06	20.26	14.49	130.59	130.89
AGGREGATE	3.82		12.67		17.42		130.74	

Age in 1860	Arkansas		Tennessee		Kentucky		Missouri	
	Male	Female	Male	Female	Male	Female	Male	Female
Under 10	46.21	36.87	−10.50	−8.55	−13.66	−13.57	−2.01	.62
10 to 14	77.76	76.22	−5.58	−4.30	−9.50	−10.64	6.58	10.32
15 to 19	106.75	109.87	−11.24	−11.71	−13.09	−15.58	8.30	4.97
20 to 29	128.33	124.73	−17.26	−14.98	−24.59	−28.80	−4.25	−7.31
30 to 39	83.88	78.31	−16.91	−11.37	−23.24	−15.65	−15.75	−3.91
40 to 49	81.37	81.89	−12.24	−10.42	−11.46	−6.73	3.80	10.12
50 to 59	62.56	63.87	17.65	11.50	−11.06	−14.72	−.42	−1.52
60 to 69	122.81	121.87	−21.27	−17.92	−15.65	−15.28	−2.86	2.49
70 to 79	60.74	54.88	1.57	.54	6.79	7.23	28.61	33.49
80 and over	156.88	284.01	−3.57	−5.15	.97	−6.54	103.74	80.09
Age unknown	0.00	0.00	−42.38	−30.89	−30.34	−30.89	−53.59	−54.06
TOTAL	81.78	76.82	−11.18	−9.40	−15.70	−15.84	−1.08	1.31
AGGREGATE	79.30		−10.29		−15.77		.10	

IX

On the Natural Increase of Slave Populations: The Example of the Cuban Black Population, 1775-1900

JACK ERICSON EBLEN

I. Introduction

IN THE SLAVEHOLDING areas of the eighteenth and nineteenth centuries, births, deaths, and other vital events were seldom recorded systematically and few censuses were taken.[1] Estimates of population sizes, movements, and characteristics made by contemporaries were usually subjective. Microanalytical studies based on the scattered data usually available are of questionable comparative value, when used either with one another or with studies of whole populations, for it is often uncertain that they are in any sense representative. In the continuing debate over slavery in the Western Hemisphere, however, comparative studies have utilized various combinations of aggregated and disaggregated data, along with other sources, to support every position. From all the sources it is generally assumed, but not proved, that Caribbean and Latin American slave populations were not ordinarily self-reproducing. One of the currently popular inferences stemming from this assumption, in tandem with the rapid natural increase of the black population of the United States during the antebellum period, is that slavery was less severe or "bad" in the United States than elsewhere. It would be equally logical to conclude that health and mortality conditions now are substantially "better" in Cuba, for example, than in the United States, since the crude death rate in the United States is currently about 50 percent higher than it is in Cuba.

Raw population data, used indiscriminately, may seem to support such inferences in particular cases. On closer examination, however, they may not. Both aggregated and disaggregated data can be ex-

[1] The author gratefully acknowledges the support for this study granted from the Penrose Fund by the American Philosophical Society, and the aid and advice freely given by Franklin W. Knight and Trudi J. Eblen. Additional documentation is available from the author.

211

tremely difficult to interpret, and their indiscriminate comparison is likely to produce inappropriate, misleading or inaccurate results. The main reasons for this are that disaggregated data may not be representative, on the one hand, and aggregates are always made up of a variety of components in differing combinations. Where the data are scant, the variety and combination in each case may be unknown.

Data for populations subject to large-scale migration—such as those for most Caribbean islands and Brazil in the late eighteenth century and in the nineteenth—are not immediately or directly comparable, either with one another or with data for one like the black population of the United States during the same general time period—where slave importation (that is, migration) was slight and in relative terms probably insignificant. In like manner, raw data for slaves in an area where there was extensive and continuous manumission cannot be directly compared with data for slave populations where there was little or no manumission. Raw data for slaves alone, in other words, include only population remnants—the survivors of persons born or brought into slavery who have not been manumitted. In order to analyze a single slave population or compare several correctly, it is therefore necessary to consider fully the effects of migration and, if possible, manumission. If information is lacking on manumission, a slave population can be analyzed adequately only with reference to the total black population, both free and slave.

We are fortunate to find aggregate data that cover even a few items of interest for most populations. Ordinarily, these data are for scattered dates, they are known to be accurate only within wide margins, and careful scholars understandably treat them lightly. Often we find only crude estimates of the total size of the black population, usually divided into free blacks and slaves, and of the volume of the slave trade. Such data could be very revealing, but the derivation of meaningful vital rates must be accomplished by indirect methods. The most meaningful vital rates are the intrinsic ones. These can be calculated from a minimum of data which includes, in addition to the kinds specified above, a series of population estimates for dates that are reasonably close together and at least one census with a good age breakdown.

Minimal data are available for Cuba from 1775 to 1900. When analyzed they show that, contrary to the commonly assumed natural decline, the intrinsic rate of increase of the slave population was remarkably high until nearly the end of slavery. Insofar as the Cuban experience was representative of Latin American slaveholding areas, one of the most interesting comparisons that can be made is between it and the demographic history of slavery in the United States. This comparison shows, when one takes account of all demographic variables, that the intrinsic rates of the two populations were very similar.

The vital rates of primary interest are the birth rate, death rate, and growth rate or rate of increase. The first is calculated by dividing the number of births in a year by the population at midyear; the second is calculated by dividing the number of deaths in a year by the average population at risk during the year. Both are annual rates, consequently the difference between the two is an annual growth rate. The growth rate can also be measured by the size of a population at two points in time. The formula for calculating what is called the continuous rate of increase is:

$$\frac{P_1}{P_o} = e^{rn}$$

where P_1 is the number of people in the population at the second, or more recent, date;

P_o is the number of people in the population at the first, or earlier, date; and,

e^{rn} is the exponential function of natural logarithms, e^x, wherein the exponent, x, is the product of the annual rate of growth (r) times the length of the interval (n) in years.

Birth and death rates are expressed in terms of numbers of events per thousand people in the population, which is to say, the quotients are multiplied by 1,000. The rate of increase is sometimes expressed as a simple quotient or a percentage, but it is now more commonly expressed in the same terms as the other rates, and this convention shall be used throughout the paper. An annual growth rate of 20 thus means 20 per thousand and is the same thing as a 2.0 percent annual rate of increase.

Rates calculated by using the above methods, or others, are not necessarily equivalent. Those derived from unadjusted population totals, used either in the continuous formula or in the calculation of birth and death rates, for example, are referred to as observed or crude rates. Those based on adjusted data which compensate for the effects of migration, if any, and reflect only the experience of the native-born, or of any other single population in its entirety, are called natural rates of change. (As used in this paper, the natural growth rate of the native-born black population is the rate for a population which includes the native-born progeny of foreign-born women except where specified to the contrary.) The rates for a population that is both closed—or from which the effects of migration have been eliminated

—and has a stable or quasi-stable age structure are intrinsic ones. Similarly, if crude or natural rates are so standardized as to reflect the ones that the same population would exhibit if its age structure were stable or quasi-stable, they become intrinsic rates. In other words, crude rates are ones derived from raw population data, natural rates are those calculated for a closed population, and intrinsic rates are ones reflecting the characteristics of a closed population with a stable age structure. All three rates will be the same only in the case of a closed stable population, but if enough information is available, the crude or natural rates of another population can be translated into intrinsic ones. This is important since only intrinsic rates have much comparative value.

It is obvious that no slave population was completely closed. Slaves entered through importation or enslavement and left by manumission or escape. All can be considered as forms of migration, but in most cases, the only available measure is one of importation. In a few instances, like that of the United States during the nineteenth century, net migrations were numerically small enough to be negligible, and the total black population can be treated as if it had been closed. Moreover, since slaves constituted the overwhelming majority of all blacks, rates derived for the total black population can be taken as slave rates. In Cuba, and perhaps most other Latin American and Caribbean areas, by contrast, free blacks constituted a much larger proportion of the total black population, while immigration occurred on a relatively large scale and was more or less continuous. As a result, the total black population cannot be treated as if it was closed, and its vital rates cannot be estimated without reference to immigration. Furthermore, in the absence of additional information, the vital rates for the slave population cannot be measured precisely on the basis of those for the total black population unless it can be demonstrated that free black and slave rates were approximately the same. In both the Cuban and United States examples, it is clear that vital rates for slaves cannot be estimated until rates for the total black population have been obtained.

One way to deal with the effects of immigration is to calculate an immigration rate, subtract it from the crude, or observed, growth rate, and take the result to be the rate of natural increase. If annual data are available an immigration rate can be calculated in the same manner as birth and death rates. If the data are for a longer period a mid-interval estimate is generally made. To do this it is assumed both that the immigrants arrived in equal numbers each year and that the total population increased by equal increments during each year of the interval. The immigration rate is thus calculated by dividing the average annual number of immigrants by the mid-interval population —which is estimated at halfway between the size of the total population at the beginning and at the end of the time period—and the result is multiplied by 1,000. A crude growth rate can be calculated in the same way, by using the continuous formula, or by some other method, but if the mid-interval formula is used to calculate the immigration rate it should also be used, for consistency, to determine the crude rate of change.

Table 1 gives the data upon which the following study is based and crude growth rates for the total Cuban black population calculated by using both the mid-interval and the continuous rate formulae. As can be seen, the results differ. The amount of difference depends on a combination of the size of the population at each end of the interval and the length of the interval. Table 1 also includes mid-interval rates of immigration and mid-interval rates of natural increase. Philip D. Curtin's rates of natural change for the Cuban slave population are all negative,[2] indicating that it was a naturally declining population, whereas most of the rates in Table 1, which, again, is for the total black population of Cuba, are positive. Neither set of rates, however, is very useful or informative.

Simple rates like those in Table 1 do not readily lend themselves to interpretation or comparison for several reasons. For one thing, the base population for each set of intercensal rates contains a substantial, and different, percentage of immigrants and immigrants' children. Each set of rates is therefore the product of a unique age structure and of a series of singular sex ratios—that is, of peculiar relationships between the numbers of males per hundred females in each age group. The age and sex structure of a population is determined by a combination of the age and sex characteristics of its immigrant element and the fertility and mortality experience of each its native- and foreign-born (that is, immigrant) components. As such, identical crude rates—or natural rates like those in Table 1—for two separate populations may have entirely different meanings, and the rates for a single population may vary a great deal over time even though its underlying characteristics and intrinsic rates are stable. Thus, none of the rates in Table 1 is necessarily comparable with any other, nor can any of them be assumed to be comparable with rates calculated for another population. The latter point is implicit in the age distributions of the

---

[2] *The Atlantic Slave Trade: A Census*, Madison, Wis., 1969, pp. 31-41, but see esp. Table 9B on p. 40.

TABLE 1. THE CUBAN BLACK POPULATION, 1774-1919, NUMBERS OF SLAVES IMPORTED, AND ANNUAL RATES OF POPULATION INCREASE

Census Date	Interval between Censuses (years)	Black Population		Number of Slaves Imported[a]			Annual Rates of Increase (×1,000)			
		Total Number	Percent Slaves		Interval Total	Annual Average	Continuous Rate for Total Pop'n	Mid-Interval Formula		
								Total Pop'n	Imported Slaves	Net Rate[b]
1774-75	17.0	75,180	59.0	(a) (b)	47,730 28,000	2,808 1,647	26.9	26.4	29.0 17.0	-2.6 9.4
1791-92	25.0	118,741	54.0	(a) (b)	129,070 148,800	5,163 5,952	39.0	36.2	23.8 27.4	12.4 8.8
1816-17	10.5	314,983	63.3		103,500	9,857	21.1	21.1	27.8	-6.7
1827	14.5	393,436	72.9		176,500	12,172	27.9	27.5	24.8	2.7
1841-42	19.0	589,333	74.1		170,900	8,995	1.2	1.2	15.1	-13.9
1860-61	16.5	603,046	62.9		61,500	—	-12.3	-12.3	—	-12.3
1877	10.0	489,249	44.3		—	—	7.8			
1887	12.0	528,798	—		—	—	-4.6			
1899	8.0	505,543	—		—	—	23.3			
1907	12.0	608,967	—		—	—	21.2			
1919	12.0	784,811	—		—	—				

SOURCE: Derived from data in *Census of the Republic of Cuba, 1919,* Havana, n.d., pp. 263-284, 307; and in Curtin, *Atlantic Slave Trade,* pp. 34, 35-41. The method of calculation is explained in the text. Orientals are *not* included in the black population data in this table. Data from the 1855-57 "censuses" are not included because their validity is higher suspect; moreover, since they occurred so close in time to the 1860-61 census and contain few age categories, they could not have contributed to the analysis.
[a] The alternative numbers of slaves labeled (a) and (b) are discussed in the last paragraph in Section II.B of the text.
[b] "natural" increase.

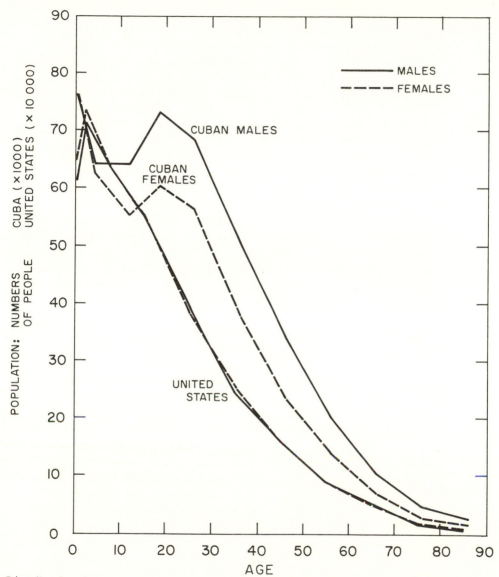

Distribution by age and sex of the black population in the United States and Cuba in 1860 (Plotted by ten-year age groupings).

Figure 1

total black populations of the United States and Cuba as enumerated in the censuses of 1860. These are shown in Figure 1. The differences in the two age structures, stemming from the large-scale importation of slaves into Cuba, are apparent; the others are more subtle.

The curve drawn for any population to show death rates by age (referred to as age-specific death rates) will be U-shaped. Death rates are relatively high at the youngest ages, decrease to their lowest point between 10 and 15, then increase slightly through the early adult years, after which age-specific rates rise sharply with age. The Cuban population of 1860, to be sure, had a high concentration of people in the age groups subject to minimum death rates, but it also had a relatively extraordinary concentration in the older ages. Clearly, no rate that does not compensate for the unusual age structure of that population can seriously be taken as a measure of natural growth. Because of the large numbers of people in the old age groups, the crude death rate could conceivably exceed the crude birth rate, and a crude rate of change might indicate that the population was declining when, in fact, it was reproducing about as rapidly as possible and would exhibit a high growth rate were it not for the unusual age distribution.

II. Manipulations and Analysis

A. General Method and Assumptions

In the analysis that follows, the limited data available for Cuba are used in conjunction with stable population models to obtain intrinsic rates. Since the models presuppose a closed population, the first step is to remove the imported slaves, or immigrants, from the total number of slaves and free blacks enumerated at each census. This amounts to separating the foreign-born from the native-born component of the population, and these terms shall be used in this sense throughout the paper. Once the foreign-born are removed, the remaining population at each census date can be treated as closed and in terms of stable population theory. After making some adjustments for probable errors in the data, intrinsic rates can be obtained for the native-born population at each census date and generalizations can be made for the entire period from 1775 to 1900. Finally, by using these rates and generalizations, together with the census age distributions of 1841 and 1860, it is possible to estimate the probable differences, in any combination, between the rates for native- and foreign-born slaves and native- and foreign-born free blacks.

The following analysis utilizes a number of assumptions. The first is that Curtin's are the best estimates of slave imports to Cuba and that they are substantially correct. As it turns out, they are consistent with the census data and appear to be very good. The second assumption is that the census data for the total black population are reasonably accurate. Again, the results indicate that they are correct within rather narrow limits. The third assumption is that the natural increase of the native-born black population followed a discernible secular trend for which a smooth curve could be drawn. This assumption necessarily glosses over the sometimes violent fluctuations in death rates known to have typified preindustrial societies—the results of wars, epidemics, famines, and natural disasters—as well as normal variations in birth rates. The fourth assumption is that the mean age of the slaves imported annually was 20 years throughout the period from 1775 to 1865. Judging from the age structure of the 1860 census, this is a reasonable assumption. The fifth assumption is that mortality conditions among slaves imported into Cuba during the period from 1775 to 1865 were no better than the average of all Latin American countries for which there are reliable estimates. Another way of stating the same assumption is that the age-specific death rates of blacks in Cuba could not have been lower than those of mixed populations in Latin America around the end of the nineteenth century.

B. CALCULATION OF FOREIGN-BORN SURVIVORS AT EACH CENSUS

Before the foreign-born population could be removed from the enumerated population totals, the numbers of immigrants alive at each census date had to be determined. This was done by reducing the annual average number of imported slaves for each time period in such a way as to account for the probable range of mortality experiences. The reduction of import data was carried out through the use of three mortality schedules selected to comprehend that range. Table 2 summarizes the three mortality schedules. It gives both five-year survival ratios—the probabilities of surviving from each exact age, x, to the one five years older ($_5p_x$)—and the numbers of individuals of both sexes who would survive to any specified exact age (l_x) out of each radix of 100,000 persons alive at exact age 20. Of every 100,000 (or 1,000) slaves imported in a given year, 84,598 (or 846) would be alive ten years later, if the Arriaga mortality schedule were applicable, for example; sixty years later, at exact age 80, there would be 3,576 (or 36) survivors. The single-year survival ratios actually used in the calculations below were obtained by linear interpolation from the figures in Table 2.

The first mortality schedule, reflecting the minimum applicable

219

TABLE 2. THE THREE MORTALITY SCHEDULES, FOR BOTH SEXES

	Arriaga Composite $e_{20}=30.2$		West 3 $e_{20}=30.3$		Maghreb $e_{20}=24.5$	
Exact Age x	Mean $_5p_x$ Values [a]	Number of Survivors at Age x	Mean $_5p_x$ Values [a]	Number of Survivors at Age x	Original Survivors at Age x	Number of Survivors at Age x
20	.92595	100,000	.92304	100,000	43.3	100,000
25	.91364	92,595	.91390	92,304	39.0	90,069
30	.90199	84,598	.90176	84,357	34.0	78,521
35	.88753	76,307	.88904	76,070	29.0	66,974
40	.86940	67,725	.87416	67,629	24.0	55,427
45	.84663	58,880	.86046	59,119	19.5	45,034
50	.81782	49,850	.82473	50,870	15.4	35,565
55	.77964	40,768	.78691	41,954	11.9	27,482
60	.72722	31,784	.71000	33,014	8.8	20,323
65	.65415	23,114	.63010	23,440	5.8	13,394
70	.55486	15,120	.51268	14,770	2.9	6,697
75	.42627	8,389	.37161	7,572	.8	1,847
80	—	3,576	—	2,814	—	—

SOURCES: See nn. 3, 4, 6, and text for derivation of table.

[a] The $_5p_x$ values are the probabilities of surviving from age x to x+5—from 20 to 25, from 25 to 30, and so on.

age-specific death rates, was derived from twelve life tables developed by Eduardo E. Arriaga for a group of Latin American countries. The most recent tables were for the year 1900.[3] The twelve life tables were combined to create a mortality schedule for both sexes (hereafter called the Arriaga composite) in the following manner. First, the mean of Arriaga's five-year survival ratios ($_5p_x$) was calculated for each age interval by sex. In the two cases where his tables did not differentiate between sexes, the survival ratios were included in the calculations for each sex. Then the mean survival ratios for each sex in each interval were averaged.

The second mortality schedule was derived from Ansley J. Coale and Paul Demeny's Model West tables which are based primarily on Western European and twentieth century North American experience.[4] Mortality level 3 in the West family of tables was chosen because it has approximately the same expectation of life at age 20 as

[3] New Life Tables for Latin American Populations in the Nineteenth and Twentieth Centuries, Berkeley, 1968, pp. 21-22, 29-33, 82-87, 135, 170-173, 248-251. Specifically, the life tables used were for Bolivia in 1900; Brazil in 1872, 1890, and 1900; Costa Rica in 1864, 1883, and 1892; Guatemala in 1893; Mexico in 1895 and 1900; and Paraguay in 1886 and 1899.

[4] Regional Model Life Tables and Stable Populations, Princeton, N.J., 1966, esp. pp. 4, 30-31, 78-79, 126-127, 174-175, for West level 3.

the Arriaga composite but reflects a slightly different pattern of age-specific death rates. The West 3 schedule used in this study was calculated in the same manner as the Arriaga composite, except that the derivation began with probabilities of dying $(_5q_x)$ rather than probabilities of surviving $(_5p_x)$.[5]

The third mortality schedule was chosen to represent the effects of what are likely to be about the worst mortality conditions under which a human population can survive. It is called Maghreb-type mortality by the scholars who devised the life table, Gy. Acsádi and J. Nemeskéri,[6] and is based on epipalaeolithic data from North Africa. The Maghreb schedule used here was converted directly from the column for number of survivors (l_x) in the life table, which is for both sexes.

If the intrinsic rates of the Cuban black population between 1775 and 1900 fell within the limits of the three mortality schedules, as assumed, the following generalization would be valid. The birth rate probably could not have exceeded 55 or 56 per thousand, the death rate could not have been less than about 34 nor more than 39, and the maximum growth rate would have been between 16 and 22 per thousand a year. This generalization does not rule out any lower growth rate or a precipitous decline, nor does it identify possible differentials between the rates of components of the population. It simply defines a realm of possibilities.

By circumscribing the realm of intrinsic rate variation as above it is feasible to begin with the hypothesis that both native- and foreign-born slaves were subject to the same age-specific death rates and that the mortality schedule applicable to all slaves was very similar or identical to the one applicable to all free blacks. It cannot be assumed that newly imported slaves were immediately affected by the mortality conditions prevailing in Cuba, for mortality rates were clearly much higher in the slave trade than on the plantation. It must be supposed that a substantially higher than average loss was visited upon newly imported slaves, and for this reason, only the survivors of the trauma of migration and "seasoning" can be assumed to have experienced the same age-specific probabilities of survival as native-born blacks.

---

[5] The two probabilities are simply different expressions of the same thing. Mathematically, $_5p_x = 1 - {_5q_x}$. A standard text that discusses the construction and use of life tables and the calculation of basic demographic rates is George W. Barclay, *Techniques of Population Analysis*, New York, 1958. See esp. chaps. 2, 4.

[6] *History of Human Life Span and Mortality*, Budapest, 1970, pp. 266-267. See also their discussion of the derivation of the table, pp. 138-161.

Since the exact period of trauma and extent of loss are unknown, each of the three mortality schedules was applied to the import data in three ways. Each of the three optional applications produced a distinct set of possible numbers of foreign-born survivors for each census date. The first option was to apply each schedule as though newly imported slaves sustained no abnormal losses. In the cases of the Arriaga composite and West 3, these estimates of foreign-born could be deemed unrealistically high and might be dismissed out of hand. The second option allowed for the loss of 10 percent of each year's imports within the first year. From mean age 21 on, each of the three mortality schedules was applied as if there was no additional abnormal loss. The second option or something between it and the third seems to be the most probable representation of reality. Under the third option, each year's imports were subjected to a 10 percent loss during both the first and the second year. Thereafter, beginning with mean age 22, the remainder was treated as in the first two options.

The effect of the second and third options is to reduce rather substantially the expectation of life at age 20 of newly imported slaves. In the most extreme situation—that of Maghreb Option III— a newly arrived slave of age 20 would have an expectation of living fewer than 20 more years. If he survived to age 23, however, he could expect to live another 22.9 years. In other words, if he adapted, under this option or the second, a newly imported slave's life expectancy actually increased until it equaled that of native-born slaves or free blacks who were his age.

The import data (Table 1) for the period through 1800 are such that it was necessary to add one more facet to the calculations. The data for the period after 1800 are for sufficiently short intervals and they are unambiguous enough that, regardless of known annual fluctuations, a straight annual average could be used in the calculations for each intercensal interval. It is clear from Curtin's data that there was a general increase in the annual level of slave imports during the early nineteenth century, but it is not clear whether average annual imports were about the same throughout the period before 1800 or increased between 1775 and 1800. The uncertainty arising from this, and the small size of the base populations in 1774-1775 and 1791-1792, therefore made it unwise to use only a single annual average for the quarter century. Instead, both an annual average for the whole period was used and a somewhat arbitrarily selected pair of annual averages —one for the period 1775-1791 and the other for the period 1792-1800. The latter reflected a hypothetical increase in the numbers of slaves imported during the last decade of the century. The two distributions of the import data through 1800 are referred to as alternatives (a) and (b) within each option and affect the estimates of foreign-born survivors through 1840.

C. FIRST APPROXIMATIONS: NATIVE-BORN POPULATION AND NATURAL GROWTH CURVE

First approximations of the size of the native-born population at each census date were made by subtracting the total number of foreign-born survivors under each option (and alternative, where applicable) from the total number of blacks enumerated. A series of native-born estimates was derived for each set of differences, and a series of rates of natural increase was calculated for each set using the continuous growth rate formula cited earlier. In this instance, the native-born growth rates are for a population that includes the native-born progeny of both native- and foreign-born blacks. For convenience the calculated numbers of foreign-born survivors for a census year were taken to be the numbers of foreign-born persons present at the exact time the census was taken. The censuses of 1774-1775, 1791-1792, 1816-1817, 1841-1842, and 1860-1861 were used as though they had been taken on 31 December of the first year. The census of 1827 was assumed to have occurred in midyear, and those of 1877, 1887, and 1899 were used as though taken at midyear even though it is known that they were not. The additional refinement of calculating to the month of each census, when it was known, was neither necessary nor warranted by the quality of the data. (The intercensal intervals used are listed in Table 1.)

A more important refinement was the calculation of growth rates for overlapping time periods. In addition to rates for successive census intervals, rates were calculated for all possible periods represented by the intervals between each census and the second and third censuses that followed it. In the case of 1816-1817, for example, rates were calculated for the interval to the succeeding census, in 1827, and also for the periods between 1816-1817 and 1841-1842 and between 1816-1817 and 1860-1861. The overlapping rates could be used to determine the appropriate manner of dealing with intercensal rates for successive censuses which changed abruptly and in such a way as to indicate that there were errors in enumeration at one or more censuses, errors in the import data, or both.

The calculation of more rates also provided sets of rates for more uniform periods of time. Sets were obtained for periods of 10 to 20 years, 22 to 37 years, and 39 to 53 years. Even a cursory examination of these estimates shows that, almost without exception, the Cuban black population was increasing rather than declining and that during much of the period from 1775 to 1900 it was increasing rapidly. The range of variation for almost every set of rates is relatively narrow. It is therefore feasible and appropriate to begin generalizing the data by using the mean values of the rates for each interval. The nature of

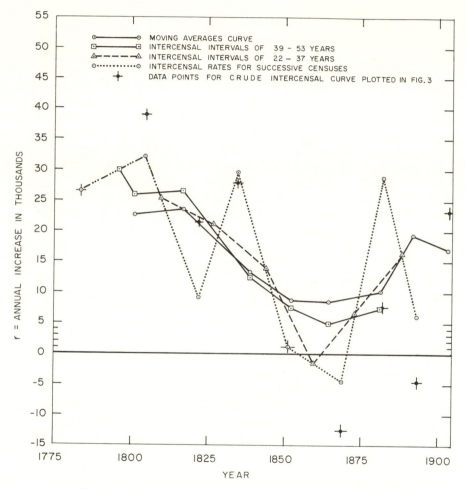

Natural growth rate curves for the native-born black population of Cuba, 1775-1900, based on intercensal rates for intervals of different lengths and moving averages.

Figure 2

the data clustering shows that a secular trend line can be drawn with some ease.

In Figure 2 the mean rates of growth, located at the midpoints of their intervals, are connected to form three curves which illustrate the trends of rates corresponding generally to the three sets of intervals described above. The dotted curve connects the intercensal rates for successive censuses; the broken line includes rates for intervals of 22 to 37 years (and thus also includes some early rates for successive censuses); and the solid line with squares at the data points connects rates for period of between 39 and 53 years. There is, in other words, no overlapping in the first curve, a small amount in the second and a considerable amount in the third, and the three can be taken to represent increasing steps in the generalization of the data. A fourth curve—the solid line between data points in circles—connects the moving averages of intercensal rates for successive censuses.

The highly generalized natural growth curve in Figure 3, which was extracted from the four curves in Figure 2, provides a good approximation of rates of natural increase for use in the next stage of analysis. The curve in Figure 3 largely ignores the one in Figure 2 that is based on the rates between successive censuses, and also the first data points for the other intercensal curves. The first data points in Figure 2 were arbitrarily set on the assumption that the ratio of foreign-born to native-born blacks was the same in 1774-1775 as in 1791-1792. For this reason alone they cannot be taken very seriously. But more importantly, it turns out that the number of foreign-born survivors in 1791-1792, using *any* option, is *in*sufficient to make up for the difference between the derived rate of natural increase for the native-born population and the assumed maximum intrinsic growth rate that could have been achieved by the women in the native-born population alone.

In constructing the generalized growth curve it was assumed that the gross reproduction rate of native-born women was unlikely to have exceeded 3.5.[7] This presupposes an intrinsic birth rate of not more than 52 or 54. If the corresponding death rate is fixed at between

---

[7] The gross reproduction rate is defined as the number of *daughters* a hypothetical cohort of 1,000 women entering the childbearing period would have during their lives, if they were subject to the age-specific birth rates observed or posited, and if none of the cohort were to die before the childbearing period was completed. The rate is the sum of the age-specific *birth* rates alone, and does not take into account mortality conditions. Since the sex ratio at birth favors males, a gross reproduction rate of 3.5 (or 3,500 as defined here) presupposes that the women in question give birth to somewhat more than twice as many children—an average of about 7.1 children per woman.

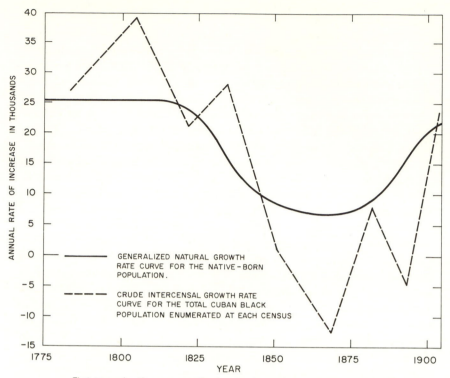

First approximation, or generalized, natural growth rate curve for the native-born
black population of Cuba, and crude growth rate curve for the total black population
of Cuba, 1775 – 1900.

Figure 3

34 and 37, the maximum growth rate attainable by the women in the
native-born population would have been about 20 per thousand. Any
additional natural increase in the native-born population would have
to be attributed to the fecundity of foreign-born women. It was also
assumed that about 20 percent more foreign-born than native-born
women were needed to produce any given rate of increase. This percentage was selected arbitrarily to reflect the probable lower fertility
of foreign-born women arising from the permanent scars of enslavement, both psychological and physiological, and the likelihood that
the mean age of foreign-born women was higher than that of native-
born. Finally, the maximum number of foreign-born women present
at each census date was estimated on the basis of known sex ratios at
between a third and a quarter of the calculated numbers of survivors.

226

Using these criteria the natural growth rate of 29 (from Figure 2) for the native-born black population in 1791-1792, for example, was adjusted downward to 25.3.

The ends of the generalized natural growth curve for the native-born population in Figure 3 were located arbitrarily; at the beginning on the basis of an assumed constant rate of growth until about 1816, and at 1900 on the basis of observed growth rates for Cuban blacks in the twentieth century. The crude growth rate curve for the total black population, as enumerated at each census (which includes foreign-born persons), is also plotted in Figure 3 for contrast. It cannot be too strongly emphasized that the generalized natural growth curve for the native-born population is only an estimate of *possible* growth which lays the foundation for refining the data and generating a more adequate, and final, growth curve.

D. DERIVATION OF THE FINAL NATIVE-BORN POPULATION ESTIMATES AND NATURAL GROWTH CURVE

The first step in deriving final estimates of the native-born population at each census date was to calculate intermediate estimates. These were calculated in such a way as to provide the best fit between the original census data and the growth rates taken from the generalized growth curve in Figure 3 where it intersects the midpoints of intercensal intervals. Once obtained, the intermediate estimates were examined for credibility. The examination began with a consideration of females since reproductive capacity is a primary determinant of population growth. A common definition of the reproductive period, which will be used later when treating the native-born population alone, is age 15 through 44, inclusive. It could not be used at this point, however, because there is no way to estimate the number of foreign-born women of these ages at each census date. Women 15 years of age or older were used instead.

The number of native-born women age 15 or older was estimated at 30 percent of the total native-born population at each census.[8] The

---

[8] This percentage was derived from an examination of the percentage age distributions in both the Coale and Demeny and in the United Nations model life tables. Greatest weight, however, was given to the distributions of the United Nations models at mortality level 20, where the expectation of life at birth is 30 years. These distributions appear to correspond most closely to the experience of the Latin American areas represented in the life tables from which the Arriaga composite mortality schedule was calculated. The percentage of women age 15 or older is nearly constant within any given mortality level in the United Nations models, and the deviating networks allow for considerable variations in mortality patterns. Therefore, in estimating that about 30% of the population was women

ranges of relationships between the numbers of women age 15 or older present in the native-born population and the probable numbers of women the same ages in the foreign-born population were calculated as follows. First, the number of foreign-born women age 15 or older was estimated at a third of the total number of foreign-born survivors present at each census. This gives slightly more women than appear to have been among the foreign-born survivors in 1860. Second, the number of foreign-born women was estimated at a quarter of the total number of foreign-born. This gives slightly fewer than appear to have been among the foreign-born survivors in 1841.

Ratios of foreign-born women age 15 or older per thousand native-born women the same ages were calculated for each census date using each of the extreme estimates of native-born women 15 or older as divisor and each of the estimates of surviving foreign-born women, under each of the three mortality conditions, as dividends. These ratios thereby represent the ranges of possibility within any given set of conditions. The mortality conditions selected represent the worst mortality under each the Maghreb and the West 3 schedule, and the "best" under the Arriaga composite. The three sets of estimates presumably encompass the entire range of conditions and relationships for any census date.

The range of ratios is quite large. In 1816-1817, for example, there could have been anywhere from 389 to 798 foreign-born women

---

age 15 or older, one does not restrict the actual population either to a single or to an unchanging age distribution.

The percentages of women age 15 or older within models at differing rates of growth range from approximately 27.5 to 32.5. If the intermediate estimate of the total native-born population at each census is assumed to have a possible error of 5 percent, then the least number of women age 15 or older present in the population can be calculated by combining minima $[(.95P_x)(.275)$, where P_x is the total native-born population in year $x]$, and the most women can be calculated by combining maxima $[(1.05P_x)(.325)]$. These calculations effectively account for errors both in the total intermediate population estimates and in the possible numbers of women age 15 or older present. They also help to avoid creating a self-fulfilling situation in which results are tied in advance to the Arriaga composite and a life expectation at age 20 of 30 years.

See *Age and Sex Patterns of Mortality. Model Life Tables for Under-Developed Countries*, United Nations, Sales no.: 55.XIII.9; *The Concept of a Stable Population. Application to the Study of Populations of Countries with Incomplete Demographic Statistics*, United Nation, Sales no.: E.65.XIII.3 (English ed., 1968), *passim*, but esp. pp. 78-81, 99-105. Latin American applications of the methods in the latter publication are in J. R. Rele, *Fertility Analysis Through Extension of Stable Population Concepts*, Berkeley, 1967. Two other studies in the Population Monograph Series of the Institute of International Studies which were valuable throughout this study, but particularly at this stage, are O. Andrew Collver, *Birth Rates in Latin America: New Estimates of Historical Trends and Fluctuations*, Berkeley, 1965, and Eduardo E. Arriaga, *Mortality Decline and Its Demographic Effects in Latin America*, Berkeley, 1970.

age 15 or older per thousand native-born women the same ages. Some of the ratios are unacceptable, and the various relationships provide insights that help in selecting the most appropriate mortality schedule for each date. As in the derivation of the generalized growth curve, however, the ratios were used here primarily to discover if foreign-born women were present in sufficient numbers at each census date to account for any natural increase in the native-born population that could not be attributed to native-born women.

As explained previously, the foreign-born estimates for 1774-1775, and consequently the estimated number of native-born, are arbitrary. Nevertheless it was not difficult to obtain final estimates from the relationships between the intermediate estimates for native-born and foreign-born women. The highest ratios (360-471) indicate that if the foreign-born women had been as fertile as the native-born, they could have added between 36 and 47 percent to the natural increase of the native-born population. Only under such conditions, and if an annual increase of 17.5 to 18.6 were attributed to the native-born women, could the natural growth rate have been 25.3 in 1774-1775. In order to allow a margin for error, the estimated size of the native-born population in 1774-1775 was increased, from 65,120 to 73,000, the numbers of foreign-born survivors were decreased correspondingly, and the growth curve was bent down to a lower annual rate.

The manipulation of the other data was slightly more complicated because of their interrelatedness. Any change made in the data for one census required an adjustment in the annual growth rates for both adjacent intercensal periods, creating a wavelike effect on the data for all other censuses, or both. In general, the rules followed in manipulating the data were (1) to adjust both the intermediate native-born population estimates and the growth rates as little as possible; (2) to stay within the 5 percent margin of accuracy assumed for the intermediate estimates; (3) to retain a mean sum of the estimated native-born and foreign-born populations within 5 percent of the enumerated census figures; and (4) to arrive at final estimates for the native-born population, and rates of natural increase for the native-born population, which were such that the estimated numbers of foreign-born survivors derived from the Maghreb mortality schedule would be sufficient to account for any natural increase in the native-born population that could not reasonably be attributed to the native-born women. The minimum number of foreign-born women needed at each census date was calculated in a manner that allowed for their having been slightly less fertile than native-born women. The method and reasoning used here will be considered more fully in the next two sections.

229

In addition to the adjustments made on the bases just outlined, the final population estimates and growth rates were keyed to the observed age distributions of the free black and slave populations in the censuses of 1841 and 1860. These distributions were essential to the determination of the shape of the growth curve during the most critical period—from the beginning of the sugar revolution to the end of slavery. For the earlier dates a satisfactory determination of growth rates could be made on the basis of probable native-born natural increases and numbers of foreign-born women. By 1840 it is evident that the rate of natural increase was declining, but by that date any estimate of the native-born population would in itself be sufficient to account for all of the natural increase.

The final estimate of the native-born population in 1860-1861 was calculated before those for the other census dates beginning in 1841 because the census of 1860 provided the most detailed age breakdown. The 1860 age distributions were first graphed (Figure 4) and the numbers of children under 15 were used to project a smooth curve (the dotted line) representing a quasi-stable age distribution. The averages of the numbers of free black male and female children were used for projecting the smooth curve since these data show no evidence of containing significant numbers of foreign-born. Both the possibilities that children were underenumerated and that there were manumitted children in the free black population were ignored; if the two did not cancel each other out they would introduce inconsequential errors. The slave data for children 8 to 15, inclusive, appear to contain very significant numbers of foreign-born, but the absolute numbers of slave and free black children under 8 were almost exactly the same in 1860. Consequently a native-born slave population between ages 8 and 15 which also equaled that of the free blacks could be hypothesized. Children under 15 then constituted around 40 percent of the total native-born black population.[9] This produces a final estimate of 438,000 for the native-born population in 1860-1861.

---

[9] See n. 8. As earlier, 30 percent of the native-born population was assumed to have been women age 15 or older, but in this instance, a different set of relationships was presupposed, for the population is known to have been increasing at a lower annual rate than before. The growth rate and the percentage of women 15 or older are inversely related within a given mortality level. Similarly, the percentage of women 15 or older and the stable-model death rate are inversely related if the annual rate of increase is held constant. It is reasonable to suppose that part of the declining growth rate around 1860 was associated with a higher intrinsic death rate, hence the same percentage for women 15 or older was as appropriate at this point as it had been earlier. If the sex ratio is assumed to have been 100, 30 percent of the population would also have been males 15 or older, and children under 15 would have constituted 40 percent of the total population.

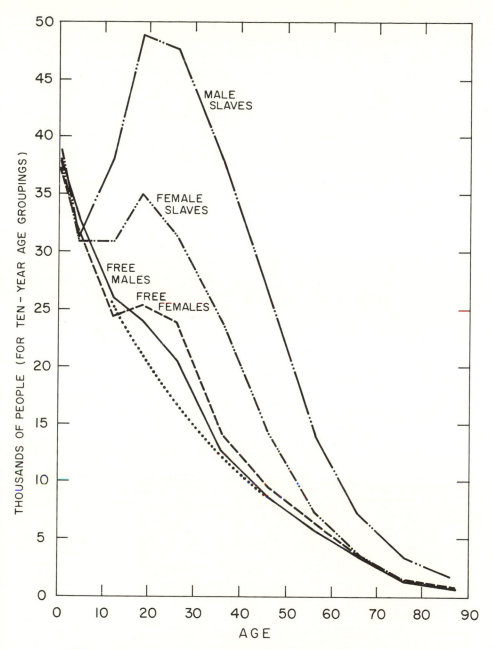

Distribution by age and sex of the free black and slave populations of Cuba, as enumerated in the Census of 1860 and plotted by ten-year age groupings.

Figure 4

The age breakdown in the 1841 census is less adequate than that of the 1860 census so the estimate for 1841 was made to provide the smoothest growth curve that seemed warranted between 1816 and 1860. The 1841 census lumped children under 16 together, and the free black data first had to be reduced to approximate the number of children under 15. Unlike the free black data, the number of slave children was not equally divided between males and females, and an additional complicating factor was that the number of female slave children was about 1.65 times greater than the free counterpart. In order to adjust the 1841 slave data, the proportions of slave to free black females in the various age groups of the 1860 census were used. A single proportion was extracted from the 1860 data and used to estimate the number of slave children in 1841 who could be counted as native-born. From this point the procedure was the same as used for 1860.

The final estimate of 321,000 native-born blacks for 1841 is only about 5 percent more than the intermediate estimate. The one for 1860-1861, however, is substantially above the intermediate estimate. The sum of the 1860-1861 final estimate for the native-born population and even the lowest estimate of foreign-born survivors is also higher than the total black population enumerated in 1860. The sum of the Maghreb III foreign-born survivors and the final estimate of native-born is about 7 percent above the census total. The sum using Arriaga II is almost 18 percent in excess of the number of people enumerated. This discrepancy can be attributed to any or all of four factors: (1) a large underenumeration in the census of 1860, (2) errors in the computation of the native-born population, (3) the inappropriateness of the Arriaga II estimate, or (4) the hurricanes of 1844 and 1846 and the waves of cholera, smallpox, and yellow fever that struck the Island during the 1850s.[10] While, if anything, the census of 1860 probably erred in the direction of underenumeration, there is nothing in the relationships between its figures and those of the adjacent census to suggest that the errors were unusually large. There is a possibility that the number of native-born is underestimated, in which case the discrepancy is minimized, but there is no possibility, with the procedures used here, that the native-born population is overestimated. The possibility that Arriaga II overestimates the number of foreign-born survivors in 1860 is more likely, but the "natural" disasters of the 1840s and 1850s provide the principal explanation for the differences between the sums and the census enumerations.

[10] See Franklin W. Knight, *Slave Society in Cuba During the Nineteenth Century*, Madison, Wis., 1970, pp. 54-55.

The effects of the disasters upon the black population age 15 or older can be measured roughly by the difference between the total black population enumerated in 1860 and the sum of the final native-born estimate and any estimate of foreign-born survivors. The reason is that the census shows what size the population was, whereas the sums indicate what it should have been. Neither the estimates of the numbers of foreign-born survivors nor the final estimate of the native-born population provides for sudden losses resulting from natural disasters. Consequently, those people who died "early" and otherwise would have been alive in 1860 are counted in the estimates as if they were still alive at that date.

The natural disasters of the 1840s and 1850s affect the interpretation of both the 1860 data and the final estimates for the succeeding two censuses. Thus the final estimates of the native-born population in 1877 and 1887 were made by projecting forward the relationships between the estimated sums and the enumerated total in 1860 and by making some minor adjustments to compensate for the effects of the Ten Years' War. The projections are such that the mean of the sums of the final estimate for the native-born population in 1887 and the various estimates of foreign-born survivors is only about 3 percent higher than the total number of blacks enumerated in the census. Through 1887, estimates of both foreign- and native-born populations can thus be made satisfactorily and a smooth growth curve of some merit can be drawn. Owing to the extended conflict during the 1890s and United States occupation, it is not feasible to do more than suggest a growth trend beyond 1887 and guess at what the native-born population might have been in 1899. Since the growth rate after 1900 was about 20, however, one can hypothesize that an S-shaped secular trend curve, wavering around 20 for about a century and a half—from around 1770 to 1920—would have been the most probable one if there had been no natural disasters or wars.

Table 3 gives the final native-born population estimates, and examples of the relationships between the estimated numbers of foreign- and native-born women age 15 or older. The growth rate curve derived from the calculations is shown in Figure 5. The intercensal rates that would result within a range of error of 1 percent at each census date are plotted on either side of the growth curve. The dotted line is discussed below.

E. SOME THEORETICAL CONSIDERATIONS

Before turning to an examination of probable differences between the vital rates of free blacks and slaves or between native- and foreign-

TABLE 3. FINAL ESTIMATES OF THE NATIVE-BORN CUBAN BLACK POPULATION, 1774-1899, AND RATIOS OF FOREIGN-BORN TO NATIVE-BORN WOMEN 15 YEARS OF AGE OR OLDER

Census Date & Rate of Increase (1,000's) [Range]^a	Native-born Population		Foreign-born Populations and Ratios					
	All Ages	Women 15 Years of Age or Older	Mortality Schedule Option Used	Total Number	Women as a Third of All Foreign-born		Women as a Quarter of All Foreign-born	
					Number	Ratio^a	Number	Ratio^a
1774-75 r=19.6	73,000 [73,730-72,270]	21,900 [23,960-19,870]	Arriaga-IIa	24,030	8,010	334-403	6,010	251-302
			West 3-IIIb	12,880	4,290	179-216	3,220	134-162
			Maghreb-IIIb	12,240	4,080	170-205	3,060	128-154
1791-92 r=23.0	105,000 [106,050-103,950]	31,500 [34,470-28,590]	Arriaga-IIa	37,960	12,650	367-443	9,490	275-332
			West 3-IIIb	20,340	6,780	197-237	5,090	148-178
			Maghreb-IIIb	19,330	6,440	187-225	4,830	140-169
1816-17 r=22.6	190,000 [191,900-188,100]	57,000 [62,370-51,730]	Arriaga-IIa	117,830	39,280	630-759	29,460	472-570
			West 3-IIIb	111,180	37,060	594-716	27,800	446-537
			Maghreb-IIIb	100,120	33,370	535-645	25,030	401-484
1827 r=21.2	239,000 [241,390-236,610]	71,700 [78,450-65,070]	Arriaga-IIa	178,050	59,350	757-912	44,510	567-684
			West 3-IIIb	166,360	55,450	707-852	41,590	530-639
			Maghreb-IIIb	147,870	49,290	628-758	36,970	471-568
1841-42 r=19.2	321,000 [324,210-317,790]	96,300 [105,370-87,390]	Arriaga-IIa	259,600	86,530	821-990	64,900	616-743
			West 3-IIIb	240,910	80,300	762-919	60,230	572-689
			Maghreb-IIIb	210,620	70,210	666-803	52,660	500-603
1860-61 r=11.1	438,000 [442,380-433,620]	131,400 [143,770-119,250]	Arriaga-II	271,950	90,650	631-760	67,990	473-570
			West 3-III	248,490	82,830	576-695	62,120	432-521
			Maghreb-III	205,740	68,580	477-575	51,440	358-431
1877 r=3.3	479,000 [483,790-474,210]	143,700 [157,230-130,410]	Arriaga-II	184,350	61,450	391-471	46,090	293-353
			West 3-III	166,440	55,480	353-425	41,610	265-319
			Maghreb-III	123,880	41,290	263-317	30,970	197-237
1887 r=4.1	495,000 [499,950-490,050]	148,500 [162,480-134,760]	Arriaga-II	115,740	38,580	237-286	28,940	178-215
			West 3-III	104,790	34,930	215-259	26,200	161-194
			Maghreb-III	69,690	23,230	143-172	17,420	107-129
1899 r=19.0	531,000 [536,310-525,690]	159,300 [174,300-144,560]	Arriaga-II	54,770	18,260	105-126	13,690	79-95
			West 3-III	50,270	16,760	96-116	12,570	72-87
			Maghreb-III	29,910	9,970	57-69	7,480	43-52

SOURCE: See discussion in text.

NOTE—The intercensal annual growth rates are: 1774-91, 21.4; 1792-1816, 23.7; 1817-27, 21.9; 1827-41, 20.3; 1841-60, 16.4; 1861-77, 5.4; 1877-87, 3.3; 1887-99, 5.8.

^a Bracketed figures under All Ages were calculated by increasing and decreasing the final estimate of the total native-born population by 1%. Bracketed figures under Women 15 Years of Age or Older were calculated as 27.5% of the lower population total in brackets and 32.5% of the higher total. Ratios are for the ranges of foreign-born women per thousand native-born and were calculated using the bracketed figures for native-born women.

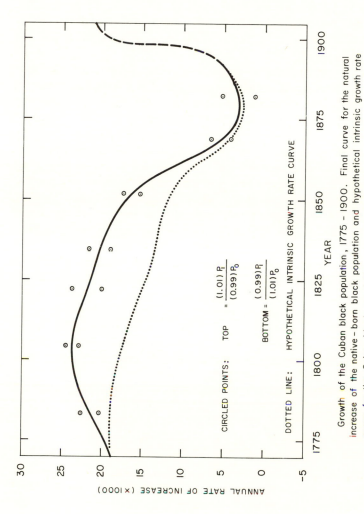

Growth of the Cuban black population, 1775 - 1900. Final curve for the natural increase of the native - born black population and hypothetical intrinsic growth rate curve for the Cuban black population.

Figure 5

born blacks, let us consider some general demographic relationships that pertain to the estimates derived to this point and affect the next stage of analysis. As noted in the introduction, a closed population must have a crude birth rate equal to its crude death rate to remain the same size over time. If two populations have a crude birth rate of 30, but the first has a crude death rate of 40 while the second has one of 30, the first population will decrease at an annual rate of 10 per thousand, or 1.0 percent, whereas the size of the second will not change.

The crude death rate is a summation of the effects of the age-specific death rates on a population, and if the two populations just considered had stable or quasi-stable age structures, it would be unreasonable to expect the first, with a death rate of 40, which in this situation is an intrinsic rate, to increase or even to be able to increase at the same rate as the second. If the two populations were the same size, the first would have fewer women in the childbearing ages of 15 to 44, inclusive. For the two populations to remain the same size, the one subject to the higher death rate would have to produce more children with fewer women. The first population could keep up with the second only if (1) a larger proportion of its women had children with the same frequency as the women in the second, (2) the same proportion of women in each population had children but the women in the first were more fertile, or (3) a larger proportion of the women in the first population both had children and had them more frequently than in the second.

The percentage of women age 15 to 44 who remain childless—that is, who pass through the childbearing years without having children—is influenced by numerous factors and may vary considerably from population to population and over time. The average frequency with which the childbearing women in a population actually have children, called the childbearing interval, may also vary a great deal. Both the degree of childlessness and average spacing of children affect the birth rate. Various combinations of their effects on the birth rate are shown in Table 4.

In a stable or quasi-stable population, the interaction of childlessness, fertility (as measured by the childbirth interval), and mortality not only determines the rate of increase, but when mortality conditions are severe, effectively limits the population's *potential* for growth. To illustrate this point, suppose we have a population subject to each of the four mortality schedules in Table 4, and that in each instance the maximum reproductive capacity is reached when 20 percent of the women age 15 to 44 are childless and the remaining,

TABLE 4. EFFECTS OF VARYING DEGREES OF CHILDLESSNESS AND DIFFERING CHILDBEARING INTERVALS ON THE INTRINSIC BIRTH RATE AT FOUR LEVELS OF MORTALITY

Mortality Level, and Childbearing Interval, in Years	Intrinsic Birth Rates Resulting When the Percentage of Childless Women in the Female Population 15-44 is:										
	0	20	25	30	35	40	45	50	60	70	80
Maghreb-type mortality (intrinsic death rate=*c*. 39)											
2.5	67	54	50	47	44	40	37	34	27	20	13
3.0	56	45	42	39	36	34	31	28	22	17	11
3.5	48	38	36	34	31	29	26	24	19	14	10
4.0	42	34	32	29	27	25	23	21	17	13	8
West 3 mortality (modified intrinsic death rate=*c*. 37)											
2.5	77	62	58	54	50	46	42	39	31	23	15
3.0	64	51	48	45	42	39	35	32	26	19	13
3.5	55	44	41	39	36	33	30	28	22	17	11
4.0	48	39	36	34	31	29	26	24	19	14	10
Arriaga composite (intrinsic death rate=*c*. 34)											
2.5	83	67	62	58	54	50	46	42	33	25	17
3.0	70	56	52	49	45	42	38	35	28	21	14
3.5	60	48	45	42	39	36	33	30	24	18	12
4.0	52	42	39	36	34	31	29	26	21	16	10
West 5 mortality (modified intrinsic death rate=*c*. 31)											
2.5	92	73	69	64	60	55	50	46	37	27	18
3.0	76	61	57	53	50	46	42	38	31	23	15
3.5	65	52	49	46	43	39	36	33	26	20	13
4.0	57	46	43	40	37	34	31	29	23	17	11

SOURCE: Computed from the life tables previously cited by using the mean numbers of women between ages 15 and 44 in the stable populations.

childbearing women have an average of one child every third year. The childbearing interval would then be three years, the average childbearing woman would have a total of ten children, and the average number of children born to all women who lived through the reproductive period would be eight. Suppose, further, that the applicable death rates are 39 for the Maghreb-type population, 37 for the West 3, 34 for the Arriaga composite, and 31 for the West 5. Under the childbearing conditions specified, the birth rates for the four populations, in the same order as the death rates, would be 45, 51, 56, and 61. Given the same (assumed maximum) childbearing conditions, then, the Maghreb-type population would increase at a rate of 6 per thousand a year, the West 3 at a rate of 14, the Arriaga at a rate of 22, and the West 5 at a rate of 30. Expressed in terms of the greatest difference, the West 5 population would have a (potential) growth rate five times greater than the Maghreb-type.

It would take the Maghreb-type population about 140 years to double in numbers under the conditions specified above, whereas the West 5-type would double about every 23 years. A modern population whose females have an expectation of life at birth of 70 years (West 21), by contrast, would have a birth rate of around 125. Its death rate would be less than 4, so the population would increase at an annual rate of over 120 and double about every six years. Although no rates such as these can be found, the comparison illustrates the implications of the hypothetical reproductive behavior for modern, low mortality groups. Conversely, it is equally evident that, if the relatively low, modern fertility levels had prevailed in *any* of the four high mortality populations posited, they all would have died out very quickly.

F. DERIVATION OF VITAL RATES

Up to this point we have obtained final estimates of the total numbers of native- and foreign-born blacks at each census and of native-born growth rates. We have also estimated the numbers of women age 15 or older in each the native-born and the foreign-born population, but these figures cannot be used to determine with any precision if there were fertility differentials, for each population contained a different proportion of women in the reproductive ages 15 to 44, inclusive. The number of native-born women 15 to 44 could be estimated easily for any date: in all models of moderate-to-high mortality, they constitute about 44 percent of the females, or approximately 22 percent of the total native-born population.

The numbers of foreign-born women 15 to 44 could be estimated only within broad limits. These limits were defined by the sex ratios of the survivors of imported slaves within the range of numbers of survivors calculated by using the Maghreb and Arriaga mortality schedules. First, the proportions of *all* foreign-born survivors 15 to 44 at each census date were estimated as being the proportions of the total numbers of survivors who had been imported within the twenty-five years immediately preceding the census. The two proportions obtained for each census date—one for Maghreb-type mortality, the other for the Arriaga composite—were then multiplied by the corresponding numbers of foreign-born women age 15 or older previously estimated (Table 4) for each census date by assuming that a third, then a quarter, of all foreign-born survivors at any time were females.[11]

[11] The method of estimating the numbers of foreign-born women 15 to 44 is justified by the initial assumption that the mean age of all imported slaves was 20 years; any survivors of slaves imported more than 25 years before a census

238

The estimated numbers of foreign- and native-born women in the age group 15 to 44 are given in Table 5. They were used first to calculate the range of percentages of foreign-born in the total female population between the ages of 15 and 44 at each census date. The next step was to determine what share of the natural increase of the total native-born black population at each census date could be attributed to foreign- and to native-born women. This was done by using the rounded mean of the percentages for each date, calculated in the first step, with three hypothetical fertility differentials. These were that (1) foreign- and native-born women were equally fertile; (2) foreign-born women were three-quarters as fertile as native-born; and (3) foreign-born women were only half as fertile as native-born women.[12]

The allocations of rates of natural increase were then used to identify the mortality schedule, or schedules, most appropriate for each census date. This was done by assuming, as earlier, that the maximum acceptable birth rate is 45 under Maghreb mortality conditions, 51 under West 3, and 56 under Arriaga composite. Each maximum acceptable birth rate determines whether or not the growth rate attributed to native-born women at a given date could have been achieved under its allied mortality conditions. The birth rates that native-born women would have to have achieved under each of the mortality schedules used throughout this paper are given in Table 6. The birth rates in column 5 exceed the acceptable maximum before the 1860s and after 1890, and consequently render the Maghreb schedule inapplicable for almost all of the period from 1775 to 1900. The improbable West 3 birth rates can similarly be identified in column 4. If we assume that foreign-born women were always less fertile than native-born, the only acceptable options are in the vicinity of the birth rates italicized in Table 6. This is, of course, only an

---

would have a mean age of 45, and the women would have passed beyond the childbearing years. It is possible that the proportions calculated are slightly high since the survivorship of each group of slaves was not carried all the way to, or beyond, age 80. Since there was minimal survival at the upper ages, however, no significant error can be assumed to have resulted from this procedure.

[12] The equation used for calculating the distributions was:

$$r_{nb} = r_t - fpr_t$$

where r_{nb} is the rate of increase attributed to native-born women 15 to 44,
r_t is the total natural increase at the census year in question (from Table 3),
p is the proportion of women 15 to 44 who were foreign-born, and
f is the proportionate fertility of foreign-born women to native-born—in the first case, 1.00; in the second 0.75; and in the third, 0.50.

TABLE 5. ESTIMATED NUMBERS OF BLACK CUBAN WOMEN OF
CHILDBEARING AGES, 1774-1899, AND PERCENTAGES OF
CHILDBEARING WOMEN WHO WERE FOREIGN-BORN
(IMPORTED AS SLAVES)

Census Date	Percentage of All Foreign-born Age 15-44 [a]	Number of Foreign-born Women 15-44 if Women Were:		Number of Native-born Women 15-44 [c]	Percentage of All Women 15-44 Who Were Foreign-born, Calculated by Using		
		(A) ⅓ of Total [b]	(B) ¼ of Total [b]		(A)	(B)	Rounded Mean, (A&B)
1774-75	—	—	—	16,060	—	—	—
1791-92	100	12,650	9,490	23,100	35.4	29.1	26
	100	6,440	4,830		21.8	17.3	
1816-17	84	33,000	24,750	41,800	44.1	37.2	40
	93	31,030	23,280		42.6	35.8	
1827	87	51,630	38,720	52,580	49.5	42.4	44
	90	44,360	33,270		45.8	38.8	
1841-42	81	70,090	52,570	70,620	49.8	42.7	44
	85	59,680	44,760		45.8	38.8	
1860-61	54	48,950	36,710	96,360	33.7	27.6	29
	61	41,830	31,380		30.3	24.6	
1877	63	38,710	29,040	105,380	26.9	21.6	22
	70	28,900	21,680		21.5	17.1	
1887	30	11,570	8,680	108,900	9.6	7.4	7
	35	8,130	6,100		6.9	5.3	
1899	0	0	0	116,820	0.0	0.0	0

SOURCE: See text and Table 3.

[a] The high percentage in each pair is from the Maghreb schedule, the low is from the Arriaga composite.

[b] The total foreign-born population age 15 to 44 inclusive.

[c] Native-born women 15 to 44 were calculated to be 22% of the total native-born population.

illustration; no argument is advanced that foreign-born women were only 75 percent as fertile as native-born.

Regardless of the assumptions made about differences in the reproductive behavior of native- and foreign-born women, it is clear from the figures in Table 6 that the one mortality schedule applicable throughout the period covered in this paper is the Arriaga composite. Since the only credible birth rates through 1827 are those in the Arriaga column (3), it follows that free blacks and slaves must have lived under similar mortality conditions and that foreign-born women must have been nearly as fertile as native-born. If this was true after 1827 as well as before, West 3 mortality conditions could be attributed to the total black population in 1841, but a convincing argument could

TABLE 6. BIRTH RATES THAT NATIVE-BORN WOMEN OF CHILDBEARING AGES WOULD HAVE TO HAVE ACHIEVED TO PRODUCE THEIR SHARE OF THE NATURAL INCREASE OF THE NATIVE-BORN POPULATION AT DIFFERING MORTALITY LEVELS AND VARYING DEGREES OF FOREIGN-BORN FERTILITY

[1] Census Date and Total Rate of Natural Increase[a] (r)	[2] Relative Fertility: Foreign- to Native-born Women 15-44	[3] Arriaga (34)	[4] Birth Rate Native-born Women Would Have to Have Achieved if the Applicable Intrinsic Death Rate Was West 3 (37)	[5] Maghreb (38)
1774-75	1.00—	[53]	[56]	[58]
r=19.6	.50			
1791-92	1.00	51.0	54.0	56.0
r=23.0	.75	52.5	55.5	57.5
	.50	54.0	57.0	59.0
1816-17	1.00	47.6	50.6	52.6
r=22.6	.75	49.8	52.8	54.8
	.50	52.1	55.1	57.1
1827	1.00	45.9	48.9	50.9
r=21.2	.75	48.2	51.2	53.2
	.50	50.5	53.5	55.5
1841-42	1.00	44.8	47.8	49.8
r=19.2	.75	46.9	49.9	51.9
	.50	49.0	52.0	54.0
1860-61	1.00	41.9	44.9	46.9
r=11.1	.75	42.7	45.7	47.7
	.50	43.5	46.5	48.5
1877	1.00	36.6	39.6	41.6
r=3.3	.75	36.8	39.8	41.8
	.50	36.9	39.9	41.9
1887	1.00	37.8	40.8	42.8
r=4.1	.75	37.9	40.9	42.9
	.50	38.0	41.0	43.0
1899	—	43.0	46.0	48.0
r=19.0				

SOURCE: Derived from Table 5 as explained in text.
[a] The annual rate of natural increase for the total native-born population which includes the native-born progeny of foreign-born women.

not be made for the Maghreb-type having prevailed, either generally or to a large portion of the black population, before 1877. In sum, if allowances are made for fertility differentials, the experience of Cuban blacks seems not to have been atypical, insofar as the norm is defined by the experiences represented in the life tables from which the Arriaga composite was constructed.

By 1860 there is enough leeway between the italicized birth rates in Table 6 and the acceptable maxima for a general decline in fertility to have developed or for significant differences to have emerged between the fertility and mortality levels of both free blacks and slaves and native- and foreign-born blacks. It is thus indeed fortunate that the only census with a satisfactory age breakdown was taken in 1860. From it we can estimate the relative fertility of free blacks and slaves and examine possible differences *within* the *slave* population. The 1860 census age breakdown indicates that slightly over half the children under 8 years of age were slaves. By using the age group 16 to 50 as a substitute for the age group 15 to 44, we find that somewhat more than 59 percent of the women of childbearing ages were slaves. Taken together, the two proportions suggest that on the average 826 free black women produced the same number of children as 1,170 slave women. (In percentages, slave women exhibited about 71 percent of the fertility of free black women, or conversely, free black women were 42 percent more fertile than slave women.) These fertility differentials, of course, presuppose the same mortality conditions among both free blacks and slaves and are for population groups that include both native- and foreign-born individuals. From the preceding paragraph, and Table 6, we know that the death rate could have varied from about 34 to 37.

It can be assumed that almost all of the foreign-born women were in the slave population. If they were less fertile than native-born slave women, foreign-born slave women alone might have accounted for the above differences in the relative fertility of free blacks and slaves. In order to investigate this possibility, the relative fertility of native- and foreign-born slaves in 1860 was estimated using the same techniques as in deriving Table 6. When the estimates of foreign-born women 15 to 44 are examined in conjunction with the age distributions, we find that foreign-born slave women must have constituted between 35 and 37 percent of all slave women in the same age group in 1860. From these percentages we can get a series of allocations of the annual natural increase of the slave population in 1860 by assuming that, since there were equal numbers of slave and free black children under 8 enumerated in the census, the rate of natural increase attributable to each the free black and slave population was the same—which is to say 11.

The allocations of shares of the natural increase of the slave population are given in Table 7, and for the same reasons as in the case of Table 6, the figures in column 5, for Maghreb-type mortality, can be dismissed as untenable. The figures for the Arriaga composite and West 3-type mortality, which are equally credible, thus set ap-

TABLE 7. HYPOTHETICAL ALLOCATIONS OF THE NATURAL INCREASE OF
THE CUBAN SLAVE POPULATION IN 1860 BETWEEN NATIVE- AND FOREIGN-
BORN WOMEN OF CHILDBEARING AGES, AND INTRINSIC BIRTH RATES
NATIVE-BORN WOMEN WOULD HAVE TO HAVE ACHIEVED AT DIFFERING
MORTALITY LEVELS

	[1]	[2]	[3]	[4]	[5]
	Shares of the Natural Increase of the Native-born Slave Population[a]		Birth Rate Native-born Women Would Have to Have Achieved if the Applicable Intrinsic Death Rate Was		
Relative Fertility of Foreign-born Women Age 15-44	Native-born (65-63%)	Foreign-born (35-37%)	Arriaga (34)	West 3 (37)	Maghreb (39)
Foreign-born as fertile as native-born women	7.2-7.0	3.9-4.1	41.1	44.1	46.1
Foreign-born =75% of native-born fertility	8.2-8.0	2.9-3.1	42.1	45.1	47.1
Foreign-born =50% of native-born fertility	9.2-9.0	1.9-2.1	43.1	46.1	48.1

SOURCE: See text.
[a] The native-born slave population which includes the progeny of foreign-born slave women. The natural increase of the slave population was 11.1.

proximate limits for variations in the intrinsic death rate. From the
Arriaga and West 3 figures, it becomes evident that, because the
foreign-born share of the natural increase of the slave population
varies with fertility differentials as it does, both of the following
propositions are valid: (1) If there was a substantial difference between the reproductive behavior of foreign- and native-born slave
women, but the *same* mortality schedule applied to *all* blacks (free
and slave), the reproductive behavior of native-born free blacks and
native-born slaves would have been nearly the same. For example,
if foreign-born slave women exhibited 50 percent of the fertility of
native-born slave women, the intrinsic birth rate of the native-born
slave population would have been 43.1 and the intrinsic birth rate of
the native-born free black population would have been 45.1. (2) If
there was little or no difference between the reproductive behavior
of foreign- and native-born slave women, and if *all* slaves were sub-

ject to higher mortality rates than *all* free blacks, the relative reproductive behavior of the native-born slaves and native-born free blacks would almost certainly have been identical. For example, if *all* free blacks were subject to the Arriaga mortality schedule, *all* slaves were subject to another mortality schedule no more different than one midway between the Arriaga and West 3 schedules, and the reproductive behavior of foreign- and native-born slave women was the same, then the reproductive behavior of *all* free black women and of *all* slave women also would have been the same. To be sure, the intrinsic birth rate of the free black population would have been 45.1, whereas that of the slave population would have been 42.6, but the achievement of these birth rates under the differing mortality conditions would have required the same general reproductive performance. Thus, if the percentage of women childless was the same in each population the childbearing interval would also have been the same.

A similar study of the 1841 data would produce identical results, and from all we now know, it is clear that there were few differences if any between the intrinsic vital rates of the free and slave populations during the relevant period between 1775 and 1900. Consequently, an intrinsic growth rate curve for the total black population is equally valid for each the free and slave components. The dotted line in Figure 5 is an intrinsic growth rate curve (that is, one for the native-born population, free and slave, which includes only children of native-born parents, and has a stable or quasi-stable age structure), premised upon foreign-born women 15 to 44 having exhibited 75 percent of the fertility of native-born women the same ages. This curve represents the most probable central tendency among the various fertility and mortality differentials. The use of different criteria would produce a similar curve, and would do no more than alter the date in the following generalization. As can be seen from a comparison of the two curves in Figure 5, throughout much of the period in question the contributions of foreign-born women to the natural increase of the native-born population effectively masked a secular decline in the intrinsic rate of increase which began around 1790.

III. CONCLUSIONS AND IMPLICATIONS

The results of this study indicate that, prior to the 1870s, mortality rates between those of West 3 and the Arriaga composite almost certainly prevailed. Except for very brief periods, the intrinsic death rate of the Cuban black population fluctuated between 34 and 37, inclusive. From a point between 1860 and 1877 until sometime in the

244

1880s—perhaps until the United States occupation—the intrinsic death rate may have been higher, but this is, of course, at and after the end of slavery. It is unlikely that the intrinsic death rate could have exceeded 35 around 1800, and it appears probable that it increased, perhaps to 37 by the 1870s. As the death rate increased, the intrinsic birth rate apparently declined, more or less regularly, from 52 or 53 in the 1770s and 1780s, to a low of about 40 around 1880. By 1900 it had again increased, to about 44, and the death rate had dropped dramatically. Within the limits imposed by the intrinsic death rate, the Cuban black population increased about as rapidly as could be expected during most (if not all) of the period from 1775 to 1900. More likely than not, the intrinsic changes in fertility and mortality were shared by all elements of the black population. During the relevant period, the intrinsic birth and death rates of the slave population must have equaled or very nearly equaled those of the free black. The configuration of changes in the intrinsic rates is illustrated in Table 8.

The above conclusions can be put in broader perspective by comparing the Cuban vital rates with those of the United States black population in the period from 1820 to 1860.[13] This period was equally

TABLE 8. A PROBABLE CONFIGURATION OF THE CHANGING INTRINSIC RATES OF THE CUBAN BLACK POPULATION, 1775-1900

| Date | Intrinsic Rates (Annual Rates per Thousand) | | |
	Growth Rate	Birth Rate	Death Rate
1774-75	19.0	53.0	34.0
1791-92	18.5	52.5	34.0
1816-17	15.8	50.0	34.2
1827	14.2	49.0	34.8
1841-42	12.9	48.0	35.1
1860-61	8.7	45.0	36.3
1877	2.8	40.0	37.2
1887	3.9	41.0	37.1
1899	19.0	44.0	25.0

SOURCE: This illustration, intended to show central tendencies, is based on the annual growth rates of the intrinsic curve in Figure 5, data in Table 6, and the presumption that the death rate increased during the nineteenth century.

[13] Jack E. Eblen, "Growth of the Black Population in *ante bellum* America, 1820-1860," *Population Studies* 26 (July 1972), 173, 273-289. The figures are revised in a new study, Jack Ericson Eblen, "New Estimates of the Vital Rates of the United States Black Population During the Nineteenth Century," *Demography* 11 (May 1974), 301-319, which confirms the conclusions and implications in the text discussion that follows.

significant in the history of both slave systems—as slavery became more intense in each country just before emancipation—and there are remarkable similarities between the growth curves for the two black populations. The growth curve developed for the United States black population had an annual rate of natural increase of just over 24 between 1825 and 1840. From 1840 to 1860 there was an almost linear decline to a rate of 17.5 in 1860. As in Cuba, the decline continued until the abolition of slavery and began a rapid recovery shortly afterward.

The mean growth rate of the black population of the United States for the period from 1820 to 1860 was 22.5. The high and low rates were those mentioned above—24.0 and 17.5. The survival characteristics of the population were such that the best fit, among the Coale and Demeny models, was obtained around West 5, but it seems certain that mortality rates increased during the period. By 1860 the applicable model life table may have been West 4. The West 4 table has an expectation of life at age 20 of 30.6 for males and 32.6 for females—or an average of 31.6. The West 5 life table has an expectation of 32.9 years of life at age 20 for the two sexes. The death rates associated with these tables vary a great deal with growth rates and cover the range from about 35 to 42.

One of the most serious objections to the West models for these levels is that their infant and early childhood mortality rates appear to be unrealistically high, and those are the ones that both account for the wide variation in the death rate and cause it to be so high. It is for these reasons that others have been used with the West models in this study. The other models reflect more adequately the real, or observed, relationships between age-specific death rates and crude rates. In particular, the correlation between the Arriaga composite and the high mortality United Nations models appears to be quite good.

From the United Nations sources previously cited it appears that intrinsic death rates ought not to vary as much with growth rates as they do in the West models and that, at the higher mortality levels, they ought to be lower. If we accept as correct the expectation of life at age 20 originally estimated in the study of the United States population, but adopt a schedule of vital rates closer to those in the United Nations models—wherein infant and early childhood losses are reduced—we arrive at a new intrinsic death rate of 31 or 32. At the estimated growth rates noted above, these death rates call for a mean birth rate of 54, and for maximum and minimum birth rates of about 55 and 49. These birth rates for the black population of the

United States are based on the assumption that the death rate increased as the growth rate decreased. The significance of the figures can be seen by referring again to Table 4, and as earlier, by assuming that the maximum acceptable birth rate occurs with 20 percent of the women 15 to 44 childless and the remainder average one child every three years. Using these criteria, the black women in the United States (at a modified West 5 or at United Nations level 20) and in Cuba reproduced at about the same level of the capacity allowed within the respective mortality schedules. The similarities between the two populations would be increased if the linkup of the United States population with the models was at West 4 or 4.5, but the nature of the fits with the models and of the intrinsic rates at different times imply that the childbearing intervals of black women in the United States were *longer* or their fertility levels were *lower* than were those of black women in Cuba.

A life table for the British Guiana slave population in the same time period [14] lends further support to the probability that the following generalization is valid: black populations in the Western Hemisphere during the late eighteenth century and in the nineteenth (prior to the end of slavery and during the period of abolition), whether free or slave, lived under very severe and very similar mortality conditions, and reproduced at about the same relative level of capacity. This generalization seems to be valid regardless of wide variations in the white mortality rates, in the lifestyles and attitudes of whites, and in the environmental health risks of different slaveholding areas. Thus the research discussed in this essay shows that the key demographic variables of diverse slave populations were intrinsically akin to one another, not different, and these fundamental similitudes define the framework within which future comparative studies of slave systems must be carried out.

[14] G. W. Roberts, "A Life Table for a West Indian Slave Population," *Population Studies* 5 (March 1952), 238-243. See also Roberts, *The Population of Jamaica,* Cambridge, England, 1957, pp. 34-39. He notes (p. 39) that "it is difficult to obtain any reliable indication of the numbers of free [black] persons in the days of slavery," and treats the slave population separately with only passing reference to the free blacks. Roberts treats the slave population in terms of "natural decrease" but it is clear from his discussion of that population during the period of registration (pp. 39-42), that manumission played a significant role in producing the decrease. It is likely that the birth registration data he presents understate true conditions substantially more than do the death data, and that elderly foreign-born survivors, as in Cuba, affected the Jamaican death rates in such a way as to imply an intrinsic decline when there was in fact a considerable intrinsic increase.

X

Jamaican Slavery

MICHAEL CRATON

IN THE EIGHTEENTH century—for ideological purposes and with dubious accuracy—British slavery was carefully differentiated by British writers from that of other European imperialisms, almost invariably to Britain's advantage. At the same time, Jamaica, being the richest British colony of the type regarded as the most valuable during the mercantilist period, tended to be treated as the British colonial norm, in slavery as in other respects.[1] In this century a similar imperialism of scholarship has tended to generalize from American mainland slavery —particularly that of the cotton plantations in the nineteenth century —for slavery throughout the British Empire as well, if not for all slavery.[2] This tide has recently been reversed, most notably by Eugene Genovese in his *The World the Slaveholders Made*.[3] The model of a preindustrial (or extraindustrial), prebourgeois culture, paternalistically closed, in which profitability was less important than social reciprocation between masters and slaves, was perhaps plausible in the nineteenth century United States context. But it could not be traced equally in the earlier "slave societies" of the British West Indies, with their practical absence of a recognizable master-culture, their absentee owners and exploitative managers both exceedingly interested in profitability and uninterested in the slaves as human beings, and their indubitably alienated blacks.

The result of this revisionism, however, has been to treat the British Caribbean once more too generically. The time has now arrived to show the ways in which Jamaican slavery was peculiarly different

---

[1] This stemmed chiefly from Bryan Edwards' "best-seller" which, though called a general history of the British West Indies was dominated by Jamaica. First published in 1793, it went through three large editions before 1801. Edwards, *The History, Civil and Commercial of the West Indies*, 2 vols., London, 1793.

[2] A trend which originated, paradoxically, from the very first foray by a modern American scholar into the slavery of the British Caribbean; Ulrich B. Phillips, "A Jamaican Slave Plantation," *American Historical Review* 14 (April 1914). Probably the best short bibliography of American slavery is in Eric Foner, ed., *America's Black Past: A Reader in Afro-American History*, New York, 1970, pp. 557-577.

[3] New York, 1969.

from that of other British West Indian colonies, conditioned by differences of geography, topography, historical morphology and demography. It is also necessary to concentrate on the relatively undocumented Jamaican slavery of the eighteenth century, since the period between the ending of the slave trade in 1807 and the emancipation of the slaves in 1838 about which most is known because records and accounts proliferated, or even the period after 1787 when general amelioration laws were first passed, was not typical of Jamaican slavery but significantly atypical.

Situated about 1,000 miles to leeward of those small islands of the Lesser Antilles which the earliest British colonists found most accessible, defensible, and developable as plantations, Jamaica was not acquired until Britain had a firm base in the Caribbean, and could not be exploited properly until the demands of Barbados and the Leewards for capital, labor, and shipping had more or less been satisfied. Consequently, in its first settlement and in the development of sugar plantations Jamaica lagged behind by about thirty years, and even after it became the richest British island always suffered from the anxieties, delays, and higher prices for slaves and other imported commodities which followed from its geographical location.[4]

For other reasons Jamaica's development was not only telescoped but never really completed until the sugar industry passed its apogée around 1775. Jamaica was to remain the largest island developed by the British during the mercantilist period, containing half the population of the British West Indies and responsible for a like share of Britain's Caribbean production and profit, and with some of its 1,000 sugar growing estates situated as far as 25 miles inland. Yet though it contained at least 1½ million cultivable acres, Jamaica was densely forested and riven by mountains and impenetrable tropical *karst* "cockpit" country.[5] These were made all the more difficult to tame by the presence of Maroons and their runaway recruits, who resisted encroachment until 1739 and final reduction until 1796. Ten times as close to Spanish Cuba and French Saint Domingue as to other

[4] See particularly, R. B. Sheridan, *The Development of the Plantations to 1750; An Era of West Indian Prosperity, 1750-1775*, Barbados, 1970.

[5] Edward Brathwaite (*The Development of Creole Society in Jamaica, 1770-1820*, Oxford, 1971) says that Jamaica contains 4 million acres of which 3¾ are cultivable, citing Edwards, *History*, I, 247-248. Yet Jamaica's total area is only 4,400 square miles, or about 2,800,000 acres, of which probably no more than half is actually cultivable in the sense of tillable. In 1752, Governor Trelawny, while estimating that Jamaica's total acreage was 3,840,000, considered 1,706,664 (or 44%) was "mountainous, inaccessible, rocky or barren land," and only 2,133,336 acres (or 56%) was "good plantable land." Trelawny to Board of Trade, 15 August 1752, P.R.O., C.O. 137/25, x, 101.

British colonies, Jamaica was also very vulnerable to outside attack, particularly until two trans-island carriage roads were completed in the later eighteenth century. In all these senses Jamaica remained a dynamic "frontier" society even after Barbados and the Leewards were stabilized and stagnant.

Unlike the islets first colonized, Jamaica was large enough almost to swallow the limited number of whites who were willing to settle there and able to survive. Its original settlement was made by the survivors of the "conquering" army of 1655, who almost immediately established an aristocracy on Harringtonian lines, in which political power, landowning, and rank in the militia were closely matched. Capital and labor poor, these shabby oligarchs were land rich, having been able selfishly to preempt huge acreages long before development was possible. This retarded progress early, but once the "takeoff" occurred around 1730—chiefly through improvements in credit and marketing machinery and the supply of African slaves—the transition to a socioeconomic system dominated by slave sugar plantations was not only rapid but also remarkably uniform. This process was aided by the fact that by that time sugar husbandry and technology, if not slave management as well, had become more or less standardized throughout the Caribbean.[6]

Although, as the largest in size and population, Jamaica after 1750 had more townsmen than any other British West Indian colony, the proportion of its population in rural areas, about 90 percent, was if anything even higher than elsewhere. Jamaica, however, did not develop quite the degree of sugar monoculture suffered by the smaller islands to windward. In 1774, Edward Long estimated that besides 680 sugar plantations there were 600 "polinks and provision places," 500 "breeding pens," 150 coffee, 110 cotton and 30 ginger plantations, 100 pimento "walks," and eight indigo works.[7] Nineteen years later, Bryan Edwards claimed that besides 767 sugar plantations there were 607 coffee estates and no less than 1,047 grazing pens, as well as innumerable smallholdings.[8]

---

[6] For Jamaica's early years, Richard S. Dunn, *Sugar and Slaves: The Rise of the Planter Class in the English West Indies, 1624-1713*, Chapel Hill, 1972, and Michael Craton and James Walvin, *A Jamaican Plantation: The History of Worthy Park, 1670-1970*, London and Toronto, 1970, pp. 12-94. For the remarkable standardization, as well as the almost completely static technology, of sugar production, see Ward Barrett, "Caribbean Sugar Production Standards in the Seventeenth and Eighteenth Centuries," in J. Parker ed., *Merchants and Scholars*, Minneapolis, Minn., 1967, pp. 147-170.

[7] Edward Long, *History of Jamaica*, London, 1774, i, 495-496.

[8] Edwards, *History*, i, ii, 311-315.

MICHAEL CRATON

These figures, however, are somewhat misleading and a clear picture would emerge only if the size of each unit, its ownership and relationship to others were fully analyzed. The majority of provision grounds and a high proportion of the pens listed by Long and Edwards were probably tied directly to the sugar plantations. Moreover, most of the coffee, cotton, ginger, pimento, and indigo plantations were small and, like the unspecified smallholdings, many grew sugar as well. In 1793, Edwards estimated that 80 percent of the Jamaican slaves lived on plantations (the remainder living on smallholdings or in the towns), but only 56 percent on sugar plantations.[9] If the typical Jamaican unit of factory-based sugar plantation with tied grazing and provision land is used, the proportion of the Jamaican slave population involved either directly or indirectly in the production of sugar might be calculated as high as 75 percent, with the average population of integrated units about 240.[10] Corroborating evidence is provided by the facts that in 1770, sugar, rum, and molasses accounted for no less than 89 percent of Jamaica's exports by value, and that this proportion did not fall below 80 percent before the end of slavery.[11]

Slave sugar plantations predominated in Jamaica but it was clearly a monoculture with peculiar characteristics. The topography of Jamaica and the nature of its early colonization determined that the average estate was laid out on more generous lines than in other sugar colonies. This explains the rather high average slave populations of Jamaican estates and consequent low average sugar production, but also the degree to which Jamaican estates were relatively self-sustaining, self-contained and socially closed.

As elsewhere, the amount of cane planted was determined by the capacity of mills and factory, the optimal unit varying between 250 and 400 acres according to soil fertility and rainfall. The average West Indian plantation produced about three tons of sugar per year from every four acres in canes, with a work force equivalent to one slave per acre.[12] Yet in Jamaica, the availability of second- and third-class land decreed that for the acreage in canes there would normally be as much improved pasture-land, and up to four times the area of forest and mountain, in which there would be glades for rough grazing and polinks for the growing of provisions. Because of non-sugar employment there would therefore be a total population on an average

[9] That is, 140,000 out of 250,000 on sugar plantations, 21,000 on coffee plantations, 31,000 on pens, and 58,000 on smallholdings or in towns.

[10] That is, as many as a further 60 in addition to 182, or a total of 184,000 out of 250,000.

[11] Sheridan, p. 47. See Table 1 below.

[12] W. Barrett, p. 153.

252

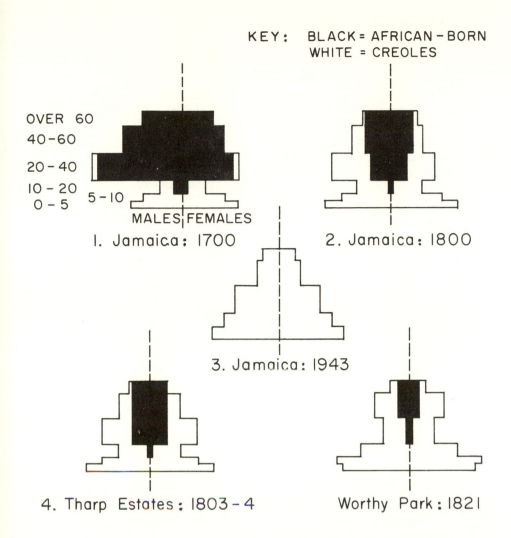

KEY: BLACK = AFRICAN – BORN
       WHITE = CREOLES

OVER 60
40 – 60
20 – 40
10 – 20
0 – 5   5 – 10
       MALES¦FEMALES

1. Jamaica: 1700

2. Jamaica: 1800

3. Jamaica: 1943

4. Tharp Estates: 1803 – 4

Worthy Park: 1821

Jamaican Population Pyramids, 1700 – 1943

Figure I

Jamaican estate equivalent to three slaves for every two acres of canes, with a complement of steers and mules at least two-thirds as numerous.[13]

[13] That is, about 240 slaves for 160 acres of canes and about 160 animals. In 1739 there were said to be 84,000 livestock to 100,000 slaves in Jamaica, and in 1768, 136,000 against 167,000, but proportionately fewer livestock than slaves were located on sugar plantations; Sheridan, p. 41.

253

The ease with which cattle could be grazed and provisions grown aided the cultivation and fertilization of Jamaican estates and made them, and Jamaica as a whole, less dependent upon outside supplies. Cattle pens and provision grounds—useful also for "seasoning" new African slaves—were often separated from the core sugar land of an estate, in the case of inland plantations frequently serving as way stations on journeys to and from the coast.[14] Some Jamaican planters owned several or many estates, but these aggregations (never more profitable than single fortunate estates) did not really represent economic or social consolidation of the type that reached its peak in late nineteenth century Cuba.[15] The factory-based units were rarely contiguous or even adjacent, and their work forces remained almost entirely self-contained and therefore relatively stable. Besides, within each unit there was a much wider range of available jobs than estates on islands like Barbados where sugar monoculture was almost absolute (93 percent in 1770), if not also a relatively larger degree of occupational mobility.[16]

Despite constant attempts to recruit more whites and the fact that Jamaica's white population became the largest in the British West Indies, the Jamaican ratio of blacks to whites became and remained the highest in the British Empire during the slavery period, stabilizing around 1780 at 10:1 overall but being up to six times as high on the largest estates and those farthest inland. These ratios, compared with overall proportions of 4:1 for Barbados, parity for Bermuda, Virginia and Georgia, and a white preponderance of 15:1 for the American Middle Colonies, were among the most important of all social determinants.[17]

Because opportunities outran the available whites, the white indentured laborer almost became an extinct species in Jamaica,[18] and

[14] Craton and Walvin, pp. 59-62.

[15] The Tharp estates in Trelawney, developed after 1765, in which half a dozen contiguous holdings centered around one of the most elaborate factories in Jamaica at Good Hope on the Martha Brae, may have been something of an exception, though its success was either not conspicuous enough or came too late to invite emulation. Aggregations of holdings could, of course, be profitable in other ways, such as speculative sales of superfluous land, the "bleeding" of the least profitable areas for labor, or their diversification into pens or coffee farms.

[16] Sheridan, pp. 29, 47.

[17] Michael Craton, *Sinews of Empire*, London, 1974, chap. II; Edward Brathwaite, "Controlling the Slaves in Jamaica," unpublished paper, Slavery Conference, University of Guyana, 1971, p. 6.

[18] The Pinnock estate in St. Andrew in 1753 cited by F. W. Pitman, "The Settlement and Financing of British West India Plantations in the Eighteenth Century," in *Essays in Colonial History Presented to Charles McLean Andrews*

there were no such pockets of poor rural whites as found in Barbados and other plantation colonies. Jamaica's white population of up to 30,000 included about 3,000 troops, 1,000 merchants, shopkeepers, and urban craftsmen, and 4,000 smallholders.[19] Yet as many as 20,000 were tied to the plantation system, though not as proletarians. Far from ever approaching the Negro slave in status as a laborer and thus identity, the poorest Jamaican whites were found in the very senior and most skilled craftsman posts or on the lower rungs of the managerial ladder. They enjoyed not only an absolute social distinction from all blacks, but also considerable upward mobility and real power from their indispensability as managers, voters, and militiamen for external and internal defense.[20]

Jamaican towns, in which probably 26,000 or about 10 percent of the total population lived by 1775,[21] provided a contrast to rural life but acted more as an irritant or stimulus than a determinant for society as a whole. Spanish Town was crowded with planters during the winter legislative season and at other times, and in all other towns the minority of white merchants and shopkeepers dominated. Yet the Deficiency Laws—taxing estates which did not keep up a certain proportion of whites—and the owners' preference for Britishers determined that the towns would largely be filled by second-class citizens aspiring to middle-class status and the most mobile and ambitious of the slaves. Freed Negroes—who by mutual consent left the plantations as soon as they were manumitted—probably outnumbered the ruling white townsmen by four or five to one, and competed commercially and socially against an almost equal number of Portuguese Jews. Even the urban slaves, numbering perhaps 15,000 by 1775, differed from the plantation majority in enjoying, or suffering from, the aspirations toward locational, occupational, and social mobility which

---

by His Students, New Haven, 1931, pp. 261-270, with its 16 white servants to 280 slaves (on 2,872 acres, of which 242 were in canes) was probably one of the last such examples; Sheridan, p. 45.

[19] Brathwaite, *Development,* pp. 135-136.

[20] ". . . The poorest White person seems to consider himself nearly on a level with the richest, and, emboldened by this idea, approaches his employer with extended hand, and a freedom, which, in the countries of Europe, is seldom displayed by men in the lower orders of life towards their superiors. It is not difficult to trace the origin of this principle. It arises, without doubt, from the pre-eminence and distinction which are necessarily attached even to the complexion of a White Man, in a country where the complexion, generally speaking, distinguishes freedom from slavery. . . ." Edwards, *History,* II, iv, 7-8.

[21] Barry Higman, "Some Demographic Characteristics of Slavery in Jamaica, circa 1832," University of the West Indies Postgraduate Seminar Paper, March 1969, pp. 5, 22; Brathwaite, *Development,* chaps. x, xii.

their smaller groupings and the greater variety of town life seemed to offer.

All these factors sharpened the dichotomy between country and town life and between country and town, merchant and planter factions in colonial politics, which in turn tended to reflect the division between colony and metropolis. Yet, just as fear of social discord concentrated power in the hands of the town whites, who tried to keep the garrison tied to the major towns and tended to play Jews against free blacks and both against the slaves, so it was the plantocracy which throughout the eighteenth century was able to impose its will on the towns. For example, in midcentury the planters were able to promote the building of roads at the island's expense directly to serve their estates and to insist on the building of barracks at strategic inland locations to guard against a Maroon resurgence or organized slave rebellion in the backwoods. Plantocratic power was, only occasionally, partially and temporarily curtailed when an unfriendly Governor was able to concentrate opposing forces, as Charles Knowles did in 1755.[22]

Generally, the importance of the plantation colonies led the imperial government to connive at the process whereby the metropolitan laws were "wonderfully altered" to suit the socioeconomic needs of the colonists.[23] The peculiar needs of each colony's dominant class were therefore catered for. In the case of Jamaica this called for the establishment of security and social control on behalf of the planters. This in turn implied extreme severity at tension points such as towns and isolated estates, or in times of stress such as wars and slave rebellions; but not to the same degree when and where standardization and stability had been achieved. It is easily arguable that by 1790 or thereabouts such a form of stability—amounting to a dynamic equilibrium —had been achieved in Jamaica, based upon the entrenchment of a standard system of estates and the relative stabilization of the population. The best evidence for this lies in the fact that by 1787 it was possible for the slave laws to be moderated considerably and to change their purpose.

As the most valuable colony of all, Jamaica came close to legislative autonomy even though the solidarity of interest between all Jamaican whites meant that there was a greater degree of "democracy" there than almost anywhere within the imperial system. Such plantocrats as

---

[22] Craton and Walvin, pp. 71-78; George Metcalf, *Royal Government and Political Conflict in Jamaica, 1729-1783*, London, 1965, pp. 58-190. The reorganization of 1756 which created Jamaica's three counties, however, may have been something of a defeat for the planters, or at least for parochialism.

[23] Bermudian law of 1730, quoted in Craton, *Sinews of Empire*, chap. IV.

Edward Long were able to discuss the colonial constitution in Lockean terms that were even more ironic and absurd than those employed by Locke's disciples in England or the American colonies since the Jamaican free coloreds as well as the slaves were totally excluded as well as being legislated against.[24]

Indeed, the legislation constricting the right of "free" Negroes, along with the general harshness of the slavery laws, reflected a classic case of social "siege mentality," stemming from racial imbalance coupled with strategic insecurity. In two of the four principles discerned, in the informal slavery code that had evolved in the West Indian colonies by 1789, Jamaica could be judged normal in defining property in slaves and even comparatively enlightened in its laws protecting slaves. Yet in regulations designed to preserve the social order and police the blacks, Jamaica was exceptionally severe.[25]

In Jamaica slaves were regarded absolutely as chattel property at least until 1787, save that provisions were made not to separate slaves from the plantations which depended on their labor. In normal circumstances slaves could not be sold or bequeathed apart from the lands on which they lived, though it was not until 1788 that an Act was passed to forbid the breakup of slave families, where they existed. Despite the development of contrary custom, Jamaican law maintained as long as it could that slaves, being property, could not themselves own property, appear in normal courts on their own behalf, or be manumitted except on the initiative and under the continuing responsibility of their masters or the legislature.

Manumission was made so difficult that free Negroes never amounted to more than 4 percent of the Jamaican population before 1800—or less than half the total of whites.[26] Moreover, clear legal distinctions were made, in a subtly ascending order of practical freedom, between Negroes who had been manumitted by private deeds and public Acts, between those who had themselves been freed and the sons and daughters of freedmen, and between those who were free on the basis of legal form and those who were free by being "recognized as white." The Jamaican custom recognizing mustees' children as white was the most generous to persons of color in the West Indies, but though this was obviously a result of the shortage of whites it was not

[24] Long, *Jamaica*, I, x, Appendix, pp. 156-220.
[25] "A General View of the Principles on Which This System of Laws Appears to Have Been Generally Founded," Great Britain, Commons, *British Sessional Papers*, A/P, 1789, xxvi, 646a, pt. III.
[26] It was said to be 3.7% in 1787, when it was 3.0% for Antigua and 2.6% in Barbados; H. A. Wyndham, *The Atlantic and Slavery*, Oxford, England, 1935, p. 284.

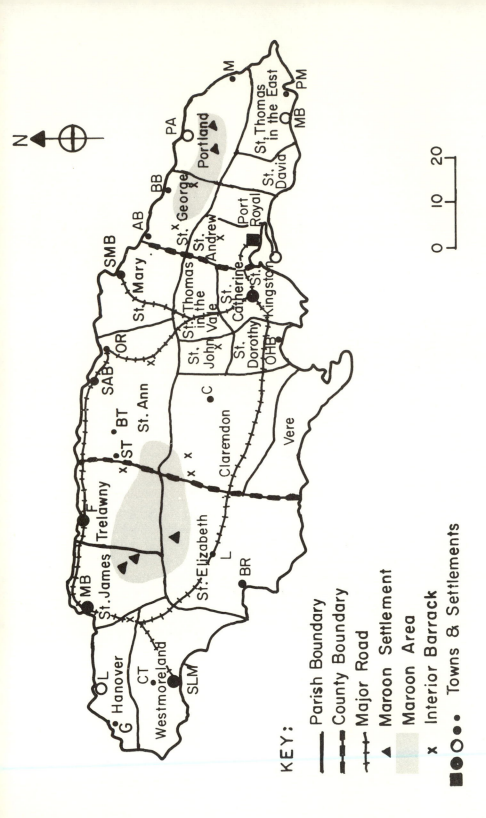

N

KEY:

Parish Boundary
County Boundary
Major Road
Maroon Settlement
Maroon Area
Interior Barrack
Towns & Settlements

JAMAICA, around 1790

0   10   20

M

PM

St. Thomas in the East

Portland

PA

BB

St. George

St. David

AB

St. Mary

SMB

St. Andrew

Port Royal

Kingston

St. Catherine

St. Thomas in the Vale

St. Dorothy

OHB

OR

SAB

St. Ann

BT
ST

Trelawny

F

MB

St. James

Clarendon

Vere

C

St. Elizabeth

L

BR

OL

Hanover

G

CT

Westmoreland

SLM

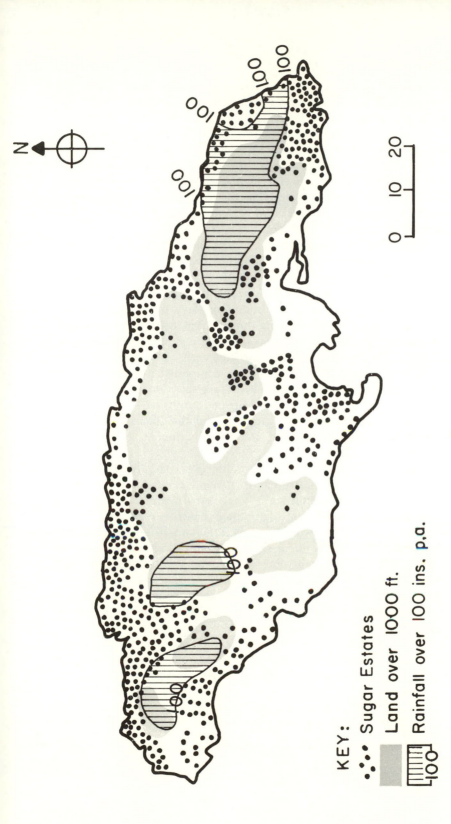

KEY:

∴∴ Sugar Estates

▨ Land over 1000 ft.

▤100 Rainfall over 100 ins. p.a.

JAMAICA, around 1790.

N

0   10   20

really evidence of the slackening of racial and class lines; rather the reverse, since it was based on a redefinition of the quality "white." [27]

The most savage of the Jamaican laws were directed against the slaves who resisted the system. Particularly in the early years described by Hans Sloane and in the aftermath of Tacky's 1760 rebellion described by Long and Edwards, the penalties for rebellion and murder by slaves were medieval in their barbarity. But draconian controls were also applied against the threat of violence, the carrying of weapons, riotous or unsupervised assembly, travel without a pass, running away, drumming and the practice of *obeah*.

Elements of social control were evident in such laws as required regular Vestry returns of slaves, including runaways (and later, details of ages, origins, color, and health), the listing of slaves belonging to absentees, widows, minors, and lunatics, the inventorizing of slaves in wills, the enrollment of deeds involving slave purchases, and the bonding of masters for slaves manumitted. Yet even laws ostensibly aimed at protecting the slaves' interests contained similar elements, as Elsa Goveia has demonstrated for the Leewards. For example, those laws which laid down rules for holidays, compelled masters to maintain their sick and superannuated slaves, regularly to issue food and clothing, and to detail slaves to grow ground provisions were as much designed to standardize practice and prevent the slaves becoming a burden on or an embarrassment to the government as strictly to ameliorate conditions.[28]

The Jamaican slave plantation was, however, largely a law unto itself as long as it posed no threat to general stability and security. Planters and their managerial staffs were hardly controlled at all in the way they established and maintained control over their slaves. The Jamaican legislature was the most reluctant of all to lay down specific scales of punishment for slaves. Moreover, since blacks could not testify save against each other, prosecution would depend upon the whites themselves, who would naturally be reluctant to crack the facade of racial solidarity. Any such legislation was likely to be as much a dead letter as the clause in the 1696 Act enjoining the Christianizing of slaves.[29]

Yet the fact that Jamaica set up a system of slave courts—even with juries, though of freedmen, not peers—in advance of other colonies, and passed legislation uniquely laying down punishments for whites

[27] Brathwaite, *Development*, pp. 167-175.
[28] Elsa Goveia, *The West Indian Slave Laws of the Eighteenth Century*, Barbados, 1970.
[29] *British Sessional Papers*, A/P, 1789, xxvi, 646a.

who violently abused the slaves, did hint that it was recognized that in such a volatile slave colony excessive severity—overstepping the delicate line in slave husbandry between firm management and outright sadism—was as dangerous to social security in general as weakness or lack of uniformity.[30]

The actual quality of life on Jamaican slave plantations (being a subject which naturally has always aroused animus on all sides and has thus been obscured by polemic) is difficult absolutely to ascertain. Yet, given the predicates of uniformity, stability, and self-containment, much can be inferred, both from general data and accounts, and from the particular example of Worthy Park estate, on which detailed analytical work continues.[31]

Jamaican plantation life in the eighteenth century was conditioned by the insecurity and crudity of the backwoods, the disproportion between whites and blacks, and the tendency of the dominant class to limit locational, occupational, and cultural mobility; but also by absenteeism and purely demographic factors such as the proportion of males to females, Africans to Creoles (island-born).

In an island not only separated by an eternity of longing from Africa and by months of sailing from the imperial metropolis, but also with plantations which might be a day's hard ride from the sea or the nearest hamlet and three days from the colonial capital and garrison, the sense of insularity, isolation, and introspection could have been overwhelming. Paradoxically, this may have been in the long run less damaging for the slaves, who were permanently located and had no choice, than for the masters who hankered for the life of the capital or their motherland, or the managerial whites who became almost peripatetic in their restlessness.

Owners, especially if they were resident, might acquire an affection for the land which brought them profit and power and even, in a paternalistic way, for the slaves who provided "the very sinews of West Indian property." The slaves themselves could likewise, in course of time, become attached to the estates as the places of their birth, the burial places of their kin, the only home they knew. Only the salaried whites had no ties with the estate as home or source of

---

[30] Ibid.

[31] U. B. Phillips (1914); Craton and Walvin, A Jamaican Plantation, pp. 125-154; Michael Craton, "Jamaican Slave Mortality: Fresh Light from Worthy Park, Longville and the Tharp Estates," Journal of Caribbean History 3 (November 1971), 1-27. Computer analysis of the entire slave population of Worthy Park between 1783 and 1838, to trace mortality, fertility, health, job mobility, male-female ratios, African-Creole ratios and individual biographies continues, with the aim of producing a book, entitled tentatively, Discovering the Invisible Man.

wealth. On an average they probably spent no more than three years on each estate. They therefore tended to be restless, rootless, callous, being to the blacks they ruled as undifferentiated a force as the mass of blacks appeared to them.[32]

Blacks and whites alike escaped the bonds of the plantations as far as they could, but for the whites this was physically easier. Yet for whites as well as blacks there were ties which bound them to the system and to each other. There was an unacknowledged degree— immediately recognized by some outsiders—to which the whites were occupationally tied, dependent on the blacks and symbiotically related by a subtle admixture of fear, hatred, sex, and grudging respect. This relationship shaped plantation society to the point that foreign visitors saw the owner and upper managerial class as philistinely imitative of metropolitan society and their white hirelings as brutalized barbarians little different in language or habits from the slaves themselves. In the age of the Noble Savage there was also a type of black who was regarded by enlightened men as superior to the "worst sort" of white man, though, like Oroonoko, Friday, or Rasselas, they tended to sound like golliwog dummies of *philosophe* ventriloquists.[33]

When owners were resident (and even more so while they were on extended visits), plantation conditions came closest to that idyllic or quasifeudal model which romantics detect in the pages of M. G. Lewis.[34] Yet by 1790 probably no more than 10 percent of Jamaican owners lived permanently in the Great Houses on their estates. Both success and failure increased absenteeism and its effects. Most West Indian planters sent their children to be educated in England from the beginning and retired there themselves just as soon as they could afford to live in style upon their profits. The very success of Jamaica decreed that from 1730 onward absenteeism became the norm, although many planters reversed the process by sending their eldest sons out to their estates for a period of practical apprenticeship. Even when profits declined few planters returned to Jamaica,

[32] For example, between 1783 and 1796 no fewer than 85 white men lived and worked on Worthy Park estate, yet there were never more than a dozen in residence at any one time. Craton and Walvin, *A Jamaican Plantation*, pp. 144-145.

[33] Sir Charles Prices's famous Coromantine "friend" was one such idealized "Uncle Tom," *British Sessional Papers*, A/P, 1789, xxvi, 646a; Long, *Jamaica*, ii, vii, 77. Such exemplary blacks as Francis Williams could be easily ridiculed in London for the incompleteness of their attempted assimilation. Apparently no one thought to measure them against contemporary colonial whites. Francis Williams, though hardly polished, was probably the best Jamaican Latinist of his day, white or black.

[34] *Journal of a West India Proprietor, Kept During Residence in the Island of Jamaica*, London, 1834.

preferring to increase their debts by continuing to live in the style to which they had accustomed themselves. Accordingly, more and more Jamaican properties sank under the burden of mortgages, falling in due course into the often reluctant hands of the mortgagors, who rarely felt any compulsion to visit the island.[35]

The normal Jamaican estate was therefore run on behalf of an impersonal or quasi-mythical owner, indirectly by a local attorney who often controlled many estates and was paid a percentage of the gross returns, and directly by an overseer and white underlings (called bookkeepers) forced to seek consolation for their poor salaries in the exercise of petty power and in conspicuous consumption.

The very scarcity of whites led to two particular areas of social tension and ambivalence. In Jamaica to a greater degree than elsewhere, senior craftsmen's as well as driver's functions were performed by blacks. This provided not only an area of occupational overlap but a comparatively large slave élite. This unique body of slaves with specialized functions was torn three ways: between the African traditions which provided the means of their leadership, acceptance of the white man's system which provided them with occupational rank, and frustration at the racial lines that remained uncrossable.

Secondly, because plantation whites (often contracted to remain single) were even more deprived of womenfolk of their own color than were the imported blacks, miscegenation was general. This exacerbated the sexual and familial anarchy of Jamaican plantation life, particularly since it was invariably of the artificially one-sided kind of free white men mating with black slave women. The overall effects of miscegenation were limited by the huge preponderance of blacks and the tendency of free coloreds to leave the estates, but the average incidence of coloreds in the population of Jamaican plantations may have been as high as 10 percent by 1834 or 5 percent by 1775.[36] Permanent liaisons were rare and open acknowledgements of love unthinkable, but since white men often freed their colored bastards and sometimes their mistresses too, miscegenation possessed the attractions for the black women of the easiest route to manumission

---

[35] Edwards reckoned that in 1791, 451 or 59% of Jamaican sugar estates were in the hands of their owners but did not estimate how many of these owners were absentees, held several estates, or lived normally in Spanish Town; *History*, I, ii, 311-315.

[36] At Worthy Park, those listed as colored did not rise above 10% before 1800, yet those listed "black" may not all have been serologically pure. For the debate on the number of "coloreds" in the Jamaican population, see Brathwaite, *Development*, pp. 168-171.

or even, over the minimum four generations needed to produce a "Jamaican White," toward full entry into the white man's world.[37]

At the very least, any "lightening of the skin" offered a better chance of occupational mobility since the élite jobs of domestic servant and craftsman generally went first to the colored slaves. Drivers— the third component of the plantations' slave élites—were generally black rather than colored, yet they were rarely African-born save in the earliest years. Such important posts were almost invariably reserved for the apparently most faithful and assimilated of the Creoles. In these ways, the equations not only between laborer and slave, and slave and black were perpetuated, but also the correlation between the degree of assimilation and responsibility, and even between assimilation, responsibility, and degrees of blackness.

Nonetheless, relative to the slaves in other British islands, Jamaican plantation slaves had by 1775 achieved a high degree of locational stability, were likely to be left much to their own devices if quiescent, and had the chance of limited improvement and even responsibility as long as they were Creoles.

Although a few percipient masters recognized the excellent skills many Africans possessed as stockmen or in crafts such as woodworking, the vast majority of new African slaves recruited after Jamaica's early years as a British colony or the very first years of a new estate were shuffled off to join the laboring gangs, there to toil out the remainder of their lives. They were treated as nearly as possible as human draft animals, women as well as men. Given names that were mere labels, they were not educated or Christianized, theoretically not allowed to own even the simplest property, not encouraged to form stable sexual relationships or even set up a permanent house as home. Provided with none but the most rudimentary skills (some not even allowed to work with tools, being simply carriers), and trained only

[37] The following partial table of the identification of 393 manumitted in five Jamaican parishes between 1829 and 1835 is telling:

	Negro	Sambo	Mulatto	Qua-droon	Mustee	African	Creole	Totals
Westmoreland	16	8	29	12	3	1	64	71
Hanover	15	14	16	9	3	2	54	59
St. James	24	7	30	23	2	3	83	86
Trelawney	13	13	22	27	3	5	73	78
St. Elizabeth	50	23	23	3	—	15	83	99
TOTAL	118	65	120	74	11	26	357	393

SOURCE: Higman, "Demographic Characteristics," Table 22, Appendix 4.

where necessary to fill the limited number of more sophisticated plantation tasks, the gangmen and women did not even acquire the language of the master class save to the fractured degree necessary to understand the words of command transmitted by the semi-assimilated and notoriously brutal drivers.

None of these conditions of absolute deprivation and depersonalization could be continued once the slaves were generations removed from Africa. Yet the very degree to which the Jamaican plantation majority was unassimilated, a separate identity was retained. Beyond the ken or care of the master class, in the separate language, music, folklore, and spiritual beliefs of the black laborers, in their cramped cantonments (which sometimes even looked like African villages) or on the often-distant provision grounds which the slaves worked with little supervision on Sundays and even Saturdays out of crop-times with almost African methods of slash and burn and hoeing, a vivid culture or individuality lingered. Until 1807 this was constantly refreshed from Africa, but even before the links were severed it was subtly developed and shaped by the Jamaican environment.[38]

The Jamaican slave culture was in any case syncretic from the beginning. Large tribal groupings such as the Coromantines, Ibos, Congos, Papaws, Chambas, Bandas, Mandingos did retain their separate identities to a degree, but the partly calculated, partly accidental mingling of the Middle Passage determined that black culture was only generically African at most. As time went on, moreover, the generic African life-style was modified by West Indian foods, European clothing, musical instruments and modes, and such status symbols as household possessions, money, the English language, and finally (and probably most important) Christianity. This process of insensible acculturation or "creolization" reached a point before the ending of slavery that the dominant culture of the white Jamaicans was itself substantially influenced by the "African," particularly in language, music, and religion.

The Anglican Church was to prove most obdurate of all elements in white colonial society. The planters throughout the slavery period were a godless lot and the Anglican Church, as far as it operated at all, was strictly a function of the Jamaican Establishment. Only toward the end of slavery days was it persuaded to proselytize the slaves, in the hope of cramming them under the wing of the master church and

---

[38] For Jamaican slave society see U. B. Phillips (1914); F. W. Pitman (1917, 1926); H. O. Patterson, *The Sociology of Slavery*, London, 1967; Craton and Walvin, *A Jamaican Plantation;* Brathwaite, *Development,* and R. B. Sheridan's *Sugar and Slavery,* Barbados, 1973.

thus forestalling the missionary activities of Baptist, Wesleyan, and Moravian sectaries. This hope proved largely vain and most Anglicans unregenerate—for example, using the church as the aegis of the savage oppression of the Baptists and Methodists which occurred after the 1831 rebellion.

For their part, the sectarian chapels, particularly those with separate congregations and black preachers, provided a chance of an alternative society outside the plantation's orbit, complete with its own status patterns and freedom of expression. This began to occur, however, only after about 1785, once the preachings of the Moravians began to take effect and Jamaican blacks were inspired by the words of the black evangelists George Lisle and Moses Baker.

By this time, the Jamaican slaves had already made great gains in the acquisition of status through possessions and money. Many witnesses stated that in practice Jamaican slaves had tenure in their homes and plots, grew provisions and raised stock to sell on their own behalf, and on special occasions dressed in finery which they bought for themselves. In 1789, testimony before the English House of Commons claimed that nine-tenths of the silver coin in Jamaica was in the hands of slaves and that very many of them had the means to purchase their own manumission *if they wished*.[39] If not contentment, this evidence seems to indicate at least a fair degree of acceptance; a preference for slavery as it normally was to those conditions of severe restraint imposed upon free blacks. Even if hopelessly exaggerated, it does imply conditions of stability, or at least equilibrium, in which custom could outweigh the law.

Yet, from beginning to end, uncertainty bedeviled plantation life, for all segments of plantation society. Economic fortune affected the population top to bottom either directly or indirectly. The fact that the determining forces—hurricane, flood, drought, disease, war, rising costs, and fluctuating produce prices—were beyond human control tended to load the owners and attorneys with manic-depression and to contribute to the callousness and fatalism of resident whites and blacks alike.[40] Nothing was more important yet so frustrating as the factors

[39] *British Sessional Papers*, A/P, 1789, xxvi, 646a.

[40] The whites perhaps echoing the brutal fatalism of Captain Phillips (1694): ". . . what the smallpox spar'd the flux swept off to our great regret, after all our pains and care to give their messes in due order and season, keeping their lodgings as clean and sweet as possible, and enduring so much misery and stench so long among a parcel of creatures nastier than swine; and after all our expectations to be defeated by their mortality . . ."; Elizabeth Donnan, *Documents Illustrative of the History of the Slave Trade to America*, 4 vols., Washington, 1930-1935, i, 410.

determining health, mortality, and fertility, since the causal elements —geography, epidemiology,· and demographical factors—were not only immutable but little understood.

Toward the end of the eighteenth century the philanthropists believed that the planters' cruelty and the harshness of the work on plantations contributed most to the lamentable health record of the slaves, and that amelioration, by leading to natural increase, would in due course make the slave trade unnecessary. At the same time, some planters favored a measure of amelioration in the cause of improving slavery's notorious record of inefficiency. In neither respect did amelioration work, T. F. Buxton's horrified disclosure in 1830 of continuing natural decrease convincing the philanthropists that only emancipation would improve conditions, though even the wisest planters were merely converted to a further phase of amelioration while redoubling their efforts to retain slavery itself.[41]

Edward Long, though biased as a planter, was probably more accurate than the philanthropists in attributing the poor health of the slaves chiefly to geographical location and the type of work engaged in rather than overt cruelty and the intrinsic harshness of the work. From personal experience Long reckoned in 1788 that the annual natural decrease (excess of deaths over births) in Jamaica was 2 percent, observing that the least healthy estates were large sugar plantations on the marshy plains (with a natural decrease as high as 6 percent), and the most healthy small coffee plantations in the mountains, many of which maintained their demographic equilibrium.[42]

Edward Long also remarked that fresh Africans could be expected to die off at the rate of 10 percent per year during the first three years of "seasoning," and provided figures which showed that on his own estate in Clarendon a disastrously low birthrate was accompanied by a very low proportion of fertile females, though apparently he had neither the medical knowledge nor the demographic insight to draw the correct etiological conclusions. Philip Curtin, however, has recently pointed out the epidemiological factors which made the Middle Passage a crossroads for the diseases of Europe, Africa, and America, and the inevitability that fresh Africans in the plantations, like all people with low resistance and little immunity, would be bound to

---

[41] Charles Buxton ed., *Memoirs of Sir Thomas Fowell Buxton, Bart . . .*, new ed., London, 1877, pp. 122-126.

[42] Edward Long to William Pitt, 7 March 1788, Great Britain, P.R.O., *Chatham Papers*, 30/8, 153, 40; *British Sessional Papers*, A/P, 1789, xxvi, 646a.

MICHAEL CRATON

suffer disastrously from disease.[43] This would be especially true in crowded conditions, in areas close to the breeding grounds of mosquitoes, or in conditions of extremes of heat, cold, and damp, insufficient or ill-balanced diet, and crushing toil. Modern medical knowledge has also suggested that unstable sexual conditions (resulting partly from the low ratio of women), by encouraging the "promiscuity" for which the slaves were notorious, contributed to the very low fertility rates among slave women as much as poor diet, hard work, and the general ignorance concerning infantile diseases and child care.

Since Africans suffered from higher mortality and lower fertility rates than Creoles, and cargoes of fresh Africans averaged about 60 percent males and contained very few slaves under 20 years of age, the demographic health of Jamaica as a whole and of individual estates at different times can be determined very largely by projections showing ratios of Africans to Creoles and males to females.[44] In Jamaica as a whole around 1670 and on estates in their early years or periods of rapid expansion, when the population would be virtually all African-born, the average age around 25 and the proportion of males as high as 60 percent, it would be likely that the annual birth rate would be no higher than 10 per thousand, and the death rate as high as 100 per thousand, requiring an annual importation of 9 percent simply to keep numbers level.[45]

Once Jamaica as a whole or individual estates had become established, these disastrous rates would have modified, but since the period from 1700 to 1775 was one of general expansion the average annual inflow of fresh Africans merely declined from about 6 percent around 1700 to about 4 percent around 1775. By 1788, however, the rate of general expansion had slowed almost to a stop and the Jamaican need for imported slaves was probably close to Edward Long's figure of 2 percent per year. This implies a deathrate for Jamaica as a whole (and thus for the average estate) of about 40 per

[43] Philip D. Curtin, "Epidemiology and the Slave Trade," *Political Science Quarterly* 83 (June 1968), 190-216.

[44] The average for 121 vessels carrying 41,625 slaves to Jamaica between 1764 to 1786 was 62.2% males. *British Sessional Papers*, A/P, 1789, xxvi, pt. vi.

[45] This projection, however, probably requires some modification for, as Richard Sheridan has recently argued, slave mortality was almost certainly lower in periods of low agricultural intensity, and sugar plantations did not predominate in Jamaica until at least 1700. The same effect can be traced in Barbados' early years. See Sheridan, *Sugar and Slavery*. If Sheridan's arguments are true, the extrapolated natural decrease figures for 1682-1701 in Table 4 below may require some adjustment, though the Jamaican demographic statistics for the earliest period on which Sheridan worked are particularly unreliable—inferior even to those of Barbados.

268

thousand if the overall birthrate was as high as 20 per thousand per year.

African slave importations ceased, perforce, in 1808 with the ending of the slave trade, at a time when Jamaica (thanks partly to the 5 percent longer life expectancy of females) had almost reached a healthy 50:50 ratio of females to males. Natural decrease continued, amounting to about five per thousand as late as 1834, but this was as much due to the "aging and wasting" effect of the cutoff in slave imports as to the continuation of high mortality and low fertility figures. Slave census returns in the 1830s showed that Creole slaves were already increasing naturally, and projections show that Jamaica would have achieved an overall natural increase little later than it actually did (around 1842) had slavery continued. It also seems likely that these demographic effects may have occurred had the amelioration laws never been passed.

A demographically stable and closed society of Creoles—in which the ratio between the sexes was close to parity, which did not demonstrate an unhealthy "bulge" in any age-range, which reproduced itself naturally, and suffered from neither in- or out-migration—was likely to be socially stable as well, as long as political and economic conditions were not severely disrupted by external events. These criteria were as true, in microcosm, for individual estates as for islands as a whole.

Unlike some islands such as Barbados and the Leewards, Jamaica had not quite reached this degree of demographic stability even by the time slavery ended, and in 1775 males still made up about 57 percent of the overall slave population and Africans 64 percent. Yet, though profits declined, sugar production continued to expand until 1805, to the degree that sugar plantation work forces were frequently augmented by gangs of "jobbing slaves" brought in from failing coffee and cotton plantations. As long as the chances of socioeconomic improvement continued to exist for Creole slaves a dynamic social equilibrium was likely. This seems as true for Jamaica as a whole as for the individual estates which continued to flourish most.

Since the social stability of society, however, depends as least as much on the incidence of psychological adjustment as to material wellbeing and demographic health, it is necessary, in conclusion, to consider the question of alienation and resistance to the system by the Jamaican slaves and to speculate on the ways these subtly changed.

Resistance—the slaves' escapism—existed in so many forms short of open rebellion that it is possible to maintain that it was general, and provided as important a social determinant as the constraints which slavery imposed or the assimilation which the system encouraged. At the least obvious and measurable level, the low state of slave health—mental as well as physical—might be largely attributed to resistance. Masters certainly accused slaves of malingering, self-wounding, culpable carelessness in health matters, of procuring abortions, and even committing suicide in order to frustrate them. More calculable, the abysmal level of Jamaican slaves' productivity—probably no higher than 25 percent of that of modern wage-earners performing similar tasks—was almost certainly due more to unwilling-ness to work than to physical incapability.[46] Most masters recognized that overuse of the whip was counter-productive but they were faced with a dilemma. Whatever incentives they tried did not greatly or permanently raise productivity. Freedom from work was the only "incentive" which the slaves really sought and this was economically unacceptable. Instead, working in no sense for themselves and with no hope of improvement in a system from which all those involved in it tried to escape, slaves rarely produced more than the minimum, not even caring that thereby they gained a reputation for incurable slug-gishness, laziness, and dishonesty.[47]

The pessimistic stereotyping of "Negro" traits by frustrated whites can itself be seen as a subtle victory for the blacks in resisting the system. It took percipient outsiders who noticed the energy, thrift, and honesty of blacks working their own lands to detect the irony. Plantation whites were also notoriously blind, or forced to turn the blind eye, to the degree to which their slaves were covertly insolent. Even Edward Long recognized that some work-songs satirized the "obishas" and other "buckras," though there were innumerable more subtle ways of "putting on ole Massa" which escaped his notice.[48]

Running away was a far more obvious form of resistance though equally difficult to cure. The overall number of runaways at any one time was probably no more than 1 percent of the island's slave popu-lation, but the Worthy Park records suggest a rather higher propor-tion of the slaves went absent without leave at some time in their lives, perhaps as many as 5 percent. An increasing number of them, however, were the semi-assimilated who "pulled foot" for the towns,

---

[46] It may have been even less. Between 1776 and 1796 the cane-cutters at Worthy Park (who included a majority of women) probably cut no more than ⅔ ton of cane each per day on the average, compared with 3.42 tons of cane per man performing essentially the same tasks in 1968; Craton and Walvin, A Jamaican Plantation, pp. 103-104.

[47] It produced, however, the damaging phenomenon of the "Quashee" or "Sambo" mentality. See, for example, Patterson, 174-181; Stanley Elkins, Slavery, Chicago, 1959, pp. 82-87, 130-133, 227-229.

[48] Long, Jamaica, II, 423.

almost inevitably to return or be recaptured. Those few Africans who ran away, and those who escaped into the impenetrable forests and hills, were far more damaging to the system, for by so doing they were totally rejecting slave society, urban as well as rural.

A similar distinction in the nature of rejection can be detected in a study of Jamaican rebellions—the most extreme of all forms of resistance. Compared with the American mainland colonies (and later U.S.A.), where Herbert Aptheker was able to detect over the entire slavery period no rebellion involving more than 70 slaves, and only some 250 mutiny-like outbreaks of 10 or more slaves, Jamaica suffered several prolonged revolts involving at least 1,000 slaves, resulting in immense property damage and horrific loss of life.[49] Orlando Patterson tends to equate all these outbreaks,[50] but they should perhaps be distinguished into three main types, dating from the periods 1655-1739, 1740-1775, and 1807-1834, with the period 1775-1807 being one of significant transition and comparative, though uneasy, quiescence.

From the earliest period to 1739, the Maroons carried on a tradition from the days of the Spaniards that runaway slaves could find a refuge in the hills and defend their freedom against encroachment. This phase, in which a nomadic enclave of almost totally unassimilated Africans with Amerindian allies steadily expanded with fresh recruits such as those who fled after the St. John's rebellion of 1690, came to an end with the treaties signed by Cudjoe and Quao at the end of the First Maroon War. By these treaties the Maroons nominally agreed to hunt down and return runaways, alive or dead, in return for an acknowledgement of continued independence.

Thereafter, the Maroons somehow maintained their separation but gradually lost their dynamism as well as their bond of empathy with the plantation slaves. In due course they suffered much the same fate as the indigenous minorities of the American mainland in the face of the inexorable advance of the Europeans. In 1796, after a second war provoked more by the whites' paranoid fear of a spread of the Haitian Revolution than by Maroon provocation, the Windward Maroons were extirpated and the remainder shut up firmly in the western cockpits. In this Jamaican equivalent to Wounded Knee, slaves and free blacks assisted the whites in their campaign, many slaves, indeed, being manumitted as a reward for their faithful services.[51]

Tacky's five-month rebellion in 1760, though not the first such out-

---

[49] *American Negro Slave Revolts,* New York, 1943.

[50] *Op. cit.,* pp. 260-283.

[51] A lively but mythopeic account of the Maroons is Carey Robinson, *The Fighting Maroons of Jamaica,* London, 1970.

break, was a different case entirely; a classic revolt led by the fiercest of the unassimilated Africans, the Coromantines. It was possible only in a comparatively early stage of plantation development. The forces of control were distracted by a mercantilist war, yet far more important were the facts that the population in the areas most affected was overwhelmingly African, the tribes comparatively unsplit, and the natural leaders, for the most part, as yet uncorrupted by the attractions of limited power and ease within the system.[52]

Despite the paranoia and military power which enabled the whites to persecute the Maroons in the Second Maroon War and deport half of the survivors to Nova Scotia, it was not the strength of the forces of control or even the tightening of the slave code immediately after 1760 which chiefly explain the remarkable lack of Jamaican slave rebellions over the period of the American, French, and Haitian Revolutions. A far more plausible explanation is that Jamaican plantations were now relatively stabilized, with Creole slaves approaching parity and complete monopoly of subordinate power and status, and the Africans relatively divided and repressed.

Unrest revived after the French wars ended, reaching a dramatic climax in the Christmas Revolt in western Jamaica in 1831. Yet this phase, while no less serious in its manifestations, was of an entirely different kind again. The 1831 rebellion was led not by the most repressed, the African laborers, but (like the Guyanese revolt of 1823) by the Creole élite of craftsmen and drivers, particularly those who were active in the Baptist chapels. It was a response to the frustration of the rising expectations of open-ended economic improvement and social mobility consequent upon the last-ditch efforts of the whites to retain their socioeconomic and racial superiority.[53]

Since the "Silver Age" of 1783-1793, both the social equilibrium and the relative prosperity of Jamaican sugar plantations had been upset. Creole slaves were now in the majority, but conditions were actually deteriorating for them as well as for their masters. The general decline in the sugar industry which had begun in earnest after 1805 meant greater exploitation and hardship for the slaves. Masters tried to maintain profits by greater production, while having less money to

---

[52] The 1760 rebellion awaits a comprehensive scholarly treatment (as indeed do all Jamaican rebellions).

[53] Mary Reckord, "The Christmas Rebellion, 1831," *Jamaica Journal* (1970); "Missions in Jamaica before Emancipation," *Caribbean Studies* (1968). The most perceptive study of the relationship of religious revivalism to the post-1807 revolts seems to me to be Robert Moore, "Slave Rebellions in Guyana," unpublished paper, Slavery Conference, University of Guyana, 1971.

provide services.[54] At the same time the fund of money in general circulation, which the slaves had come to rely on, gradually dried up.

Moreover, outside the plantations tensions mounted as the result of changes which had occurred since 1807 or 1787. Following the great increase in manumissions, the growth of towns and the decay of many of the weaker plantations, the number of dissidents in the non-plantation Negro population increased. The number of free Negroes had risen by 1830 to 45,000, outnumbering the whites by 3:2, and town slaves probably numbered 25,000 exclusive of runaways and the unrecorded masterless.[55] Yet what set the seal on the general unrest was the intransigence of the whites. Their siege mentality was exacerbated both by their actual military weakness since the wars ended in 1815, and by the feeling that their economic plight and the pretensions of the Negroes alike were the products of an inimical and erroneous liberalism emanating from Westminster and the headquarters of the Missionary Societies. Only by a counterattack by the forces of law, order, and the Established Church, they considered, could they retain what they had.[56]

In many ways the 1831 rebellion was more akin to the 1865 Morant Bay Rebellion of the nominally free than to the true slave rebellions of a century earlier. In 1865 as in 1831, the rebels made appeals to African identity, just as the white-dominated régime in 1865 regressed to the form of retributive brutality employed in 1831, 1760, and 1690. But in the rebels' case this was now as much an appeal from the head as from the heart, and in the régime's case as much a calculated policy as an automatic reflex conditioned by two centuries of uneasy mastery. With even less realism than ever before, the Jamaican whites were resisting the fact that they were as much a part of Creole society as the free Negroes or the slaves themselves.

In conclusion then, it can be maintained that the distinctive unit in Jamaican slave society was the relatively stable, almost closed sugar estate, and that this was generally attained by about 1790. Moreover, as the determinants of health and mortality/fertility were "accidents" of geography, epidemiology, and demography, the most important factors in the development of Jamaican society—slave and postslave— were not the imposition of the slave system as such or even the re-

---

[54] The same effect has been noted in the French Antilles in the years just prior to the French and Haitian Revolutions by the *doyen* Gabriel Debien in, for example, *Plantations et Esclaves à Saint-Domingue*, Dakar, 1962, chap. VI.

[55] Brathwaite, *Development*, p. 168; Higman, 22.

[56] This impression is overwhelmingly clear from the evidence before the Graham Commission in 1832; *British Sessional Papers*, Reports, 1831-1832, 721, xx.

sistance to it. Rather, it was those elements of syncretization and symbiosis which contributed toward the insensible creation of an integrated society: not European or African (or even plural) but *Creole*.

Yet Jamaican slave society was characterized also by certain dynamic tensions, consequent upon the location, topography, and size of Jamaica, racial imbalance and ambivalences, absenteeism, the premature decline of the sugar economy, the ending of the slave trade, and the way in which the amelioration and emancipist policies were enforced from England and polarized the social elements. These factors together determined that while Jamaican society would be neither the unmodernized Africa transplanted of Haiti or the stagnant little black England of Barbados, it would not be the sick plural society which the U.S.A. has inherited from the American South.

TABLE 1. THE GROWTH OF JAMAICA, 1670-1830, COMPARED WITH THE BRITISH WEST INDIES, 1630-1830.[a]

Period	1. Jamaica: Slaves (thousands)[b]	2. Whites	3. Colored	4. Free Negroes (Black and Colored)	5. Barbados: Slaves	6. Whites	7. Leewards: Slaves	8. Whites	9. British West Indies: Slaves	10. Whites	11. B.W.I.: Annual Slave Trade	12. Jamaica: Annual Slave Trade	13. B.W.I.: Annual Sugar Production (thousand tons)	14. Jamaica: Annual Sugar Production (thousand tons)	15. Jamaica: Sugar Estates[c]	16. Jamaica: % Sugar Products of Total Exports, by Value	17. Jamaica: Sugar Profits: % of Capital
1630	—	—	—	—	—	2	—	1	4	7	—	—	—	—	—		
1650	—	—	—	—	15	25	2	3	17		1.4	—	2	—	—		
1670	9	8	—	—	35	25	4	4	49	40	3.0	1.0	10	1	57	75.0	20.0
1690	34	7	—	—	45	17	13	5	93		6.5	2.0	18	4	70		
1710	49	7	1	—	42	13	27	7	120	32	7.8	2.5	25	5	150	85.0	17.5
1730	80	8	4	1	46	16	55	11	188		9.5	4.5	45	16	300		
1750	122	11	9	2	57	15	73	10	255	43	12.4	6.7	42	20	525	90.0	12.0
1770	185	17	23	6	63	16	86	10	389		15.8	8.0	90	40	650		
1790	250	25	32	10	64	16	83	9	483	71	16.1	8.0	100	50	900	75.0	7.5
1810	325	30	55	17	69	14	82	9	670		—	—	150	75	750		
1830	312	30	60	45	82	15	70	8	702	75	—	—	230	70	600	75.0	2.5

[a] See Michael Craton, *Sinews of Empire; A Short History of British Slavery*, London, 1974, chaps. II, III. Population figures in cols. 1-10 largely from Great Britain, Commons, *British Sessional Papers*, A/P, 1789, XXVI, 646a, pt. IV; 1830, XXI, 674; 1838, XLVIII, 215; 1845, XXI, 426; also F. W. Pitman, *The Development of the British West Indies, 1700-1763*, New Haven, 1917, App. I, 369-390; Brathwaite; Sheridan, p. 41. Slave totals and trade figures in cols. 11, 12, largely from Philip D. Curtin, *The Atlantic Slave Trade; A Census*, Madison, Wis., 1969. Sugar production in cols. 13, 14, from Noel Deerr, *The History of Sugar*, 2 vols., London, 1949-1950, I, 176, 193-204. Sugar estates in col. 15 from Edward Long, *History*, I, 301; Edwards, *History*, II, 466. Percentage monoculture in col. 16 largely from Long, *Jamaica*; Edwards, *History*; R. M. Martin, *Statistics of the British Empire*, London, 1839. Profitability in col. 17 from Craton, *Sinews of Empire*, chap. III.

[b] All figures of persons in cols. 1-12 given in thousands.

[c] These figures, unfortunately, must remain approximate since, as is discussed in the text, authorities obviously differ as to criteria, without explanation given. Where possible the criterion used here has been estates growing a substantial amount of sugar, with their own mills and factory.

TABLE 2. PART 1. THE POPULATION OF A TYPICAL LARGE JAMAICAN SUGAR ESTATE AROUND 1793 (WORTHY PARK, ST. JOHN'S: 1,200 ACRES, 400 ACRES CANES, 577 SLAVES)

	Ages	Color	African or Creole	Male or Female	Salary or Approx. Value (Jamaica Currency, £) [a]
A. WHITES (10-11)					
Owner (absent in England) [b]			English		2,000-4,000
Attorney (in Kingston) [b]			C		200
Overseer	42	White	C		—
Overseer's Wife	40	White	C		100
Head Book-keeper	38	White	C		50-80
3 Under Book-keepers	20-30	White	3 C		100-150
Head Boiler	40	White	C		50-100
Head Distiller	42	White	C		6/8 d.p.slave
Doctor	47	White	C		—
Settler & Wife "to save Deficiency"		White	2 C		
B. NEGRO ELITE (21)					
7 Drivers & Driveresses	40-60	Black	5 A 2 C	5 M 2 F	120-150
2 Head Housekeepers [c]	35, 40	Sam./Mul.	2 C	2 F	60-80
Head Cooper	35	Mulatto	C	M	140-300
Head Potter	40	Black	C	M	140-160
Second Boiler	40	Black	C	M	180-200
Head Mason	50	Black	C	M	170-180
Head Sawyer	45	Black	C	M	150
Head Carpenter	65	Black	A	M	140-300
Head Blacksmith	50	Mulatto	C	M	180
Head Cattleman	35	Black	A	M	120
Head Muleman	45	Black	C	M	120
Head Home Wainsman	40	Black	C	M	150-200
Head Road Wainsman	23	Black	C	M	150-200
Head Watchman	50	Mulatto	C	M	80

C. SPECIAL WORKERS or LOWER ELITE (95)

	Ages	Color	African or Creole	Male or Female	Salary or Approx. Value (Jamaica Currency, £) [a]
2 Waiting Boys	15, 16	Mulatto	2 C	2 M	60-80
Groom	35	Sambo	C	M	80
2 Seamstresses	15, 20	Black	2 C	2 F	50-60
2 Washerwomen	19, 41	Black/Mul.	1 A 1 C	2 F	50-60
Cook	35	Black	C	F	50-60
Midwife	60	Black	A	F	150-200
2 Hothouse Nurses	30, 35	Black	1 A 1 C	2 F	90-120
Black Doctor	49	Black	A	M	140
6 Coopers	25-50	5 B./1 Sam.	1 A 5 C	6 M	120-200
9 Carpenters	25-50	7 B./2 Mul.	3 A 6 C	9 M	140-250
3 Sawyers	20-32	Black	3 A	3 M	100-120
2 Masons	22-35	Black	2 C	2 M	120-200
Under Blacksmith	31	Black	C	M	120-200
9 Boilers	40-50	Black	9 C	9 M	140-250
4 Distillers	30-45	Black	4 C	4 M	140-300
2 Potters	40-50	Black	1 A 1 C	2 M	120-200
2 Sugar Guards	25-30	Black	2 C	2 M	50-70
6 Home Wainsmen	25-40	Black	2 A 4 C	6 M	90-120
7 Road Wainsmen	20-40	Black	7 C	7 M	90-120
14 Mulemen	20-35	Black	7 A 7 C	14 M	90-120
3 Hog Tenders	10-40	2 B./1 Mul.	1 A 2 C	3 M	80
2 Poultry Tenders	55-60	Black	1 A 1 C	2 F	50-60
3 New Negro Tenders	30-60	Black	3 C	1 M 2 F	50-80
8 Cattlemen & Boys	15-60	5 B./3 Sam.	3 A 5 C	8 M	80-120
2 Ratcatchers	19-21	2 Mulattos	2 C	2 M	80-100

TABLE 2 (*Continued*)

	Ages	Color	African or Creole	Male or Female	Salary or Approx. Value (Jamaica Currency, £)
D. GANGS (364)					
147 Great or First Gang	26-40	Black	70% African	60% Female	50-125
67 Second Gang	16-25	Black	75% African	64% Female	50-100
68 Third Gang	12-15	Black	51% Creole	54% Female	50-80
21 Grass or Weeding Gang	5-11	Black	66% Creole	69% Female	50-60
13 Vagabond Gang[d]	18-40	Black	60% Creole	60% Female	50-100
48 "Pen Negroes" (at Mickleton & Spring Garden Pens)[e]					
E. MARGINALLY PRODUCTIVE OR UNPRODUCTIVE (97)					
25 Watchmen	35-70	Black	20 A 5 C	25 M	30-70
7 Grass Gatherers	60-65	Black	5 A 2 C	4 M 3 F	60
3 Child Watchers	60-70	Black	2 A 1 C	3 F	50
2 Pad Menders	60-65	Black	2 A	1 M 1 F	80
3 Women with Six Children	30-55	Black	1 A 2 C	3 F	50-80
18 Hopeless Invalids	15-50	16 B./2 Mul.	10 A 8 C	9 M 9 F	5
2 Superannuated	75-85	Black	2 A	2 F	5-10
37 Infants	0-5	33 B./4 Mul.	37 C	18 M 19 F	10-60

[a] The valuations in the last column are approximate, being estimated from data in the Wedderburn Papers at the Institute of Jamaica. Prices of new African slaves ranged £50-70 for males, £50-60 for females. For seasoned slaves, the ranges were £80-125 and £70-110.

[b] The Attorney's high salary was based on the management of 5-6 estates. Some managed 15-20 and may have made £8-10,000 a year.

[c] When the owner, or his son, was in residence, the nominal Great House staff of two may have been raised as high as 25.

[d] The Vagabond Gang consisted of persistent runaways and other miscreants.

[e] Mickleton Pen was 12 miles distant, Spring Garden 20. They were used as resting places to and from Kingston and Old Harbour respectively; also for breeding cattle, growing provisions and seasoning new slaves.

TABLE 2. PART 2. CLOTHING ISSUED TO WORTHY PARK SLAVES

		Osnaburgh (yards)	Baize	Checks	Hats	Caps	Knives	Coats	Blankets
B.	NEGRO ELITE (21)								
7	Drivers & Driveresses	10-12	3	3	1	–	1	1 [a]	–
2	Head Housekeepers	10	3	–	1	–	–	–	–
	Head Cooper	10	3	3	1	–	1	–	–
	Head Potter	7	2½	3	1	–	1	–	–
	Second Boiler	7	2½	3	1	–	1	–	–
	Head Mason	10	3	3	1	–	1	–	–
	Head Sawyer	10	3	3	1	–	1	–	–
	Head Carpenter	10	3	3	1	–	1	–	–
	Head Blacksmith	10	3	3	1	–	1	1	–
	Head Cattleman	10	3	3	1	–	1	–	–
	Head Muleman	10	3	3	1	–	1	–	–
	Head Home Wainsman	7	2½	3	1	–	1	–	–
	Head Road Wainsman	10	3	3	1	–	1	–	–
	Head Watchman	10	3	3	1	–	1	–	–
C.	SPECIAL WORKERS or LOWER ELITE (95)								
2	Waiting Boys	7	2½	3	1	–	–	–	–
	Groom	7	3	3	1	1	1	–	–
2	Seamstresses	10	3	–	1	1	–	–	–
2	Washerwomen	10	3	–	1	1	–	–	–
	Cook	10	3	–	1	1	1	–	–
	Midwife	7	3	–	1	1	1	–	–
2	Hothouse Nurses	7	3	–	1	1	–	–	–
	Black Doctor	12	3	3	1	1	–	1	–
6	Coopers	10	3	3	1	1	1	–	–
9	Carpenters	7-10	3	3	1	1	1	–	–
3	Sawyers	10	3	3	1	1	1	–	–
2	Masons	10	3	3	1	1	1	–	–
	Under Blacksmith	7	3	3	1	1	1	–	–
9	Boilers	7	3	3	1	1	1	–	–
4	Distillers	7	3	3	1	1	1	–	–

TABLE 2 *(Continued)*

	Osnaburgh (yards)	Baize	Checks	Hats	Caps	Knives	Coats	Blankets
2 Potters	7	3	3	1	1	1	–	–
2 Sugar Guards	10	3	3	1	1	1	–	–
6 Home Wainsmen	7	2½	3	1	1	1	–	–
7 Road Wainsmen	10	3	3	1	1	1	–	–
14 Mulemen	7	2½	3	1	1	1	–	–
3 Hog Tenders	7	2½	3	1	1	1	–	–
2 Poultry Tenders	7	2½	3	1	1	1	–	–
3 New Negro Tenders	7	2½	3	1	1	1	–	–
8 Cattlemen & Boys	5-10	2-3	3	1	1	1	–	–
2 Ratcatchers	7	2½	3	1	1	1	–	–
D. GANGS (364)								
147 Great or First Gang	7	2½	–	1	1	1	–	–
67 Second Gang	7	2½	–	1	1	1	–	–
68 Third Gang	5-6	2	–	1	1	–	–	–
21 Grass or Weeding Gang	3-5	2	–	1	1	–	–	–
13 Vagabond Gang	5-7	2½	–	1	1	–	–	–
48 Pen Negroes	7	–	–	1	1	1	1 [b]	1
E. UNPRODUCTIVE (97)								
25 Watchmen	7	3	–	1	1	1	–	–
7 Grass Gatherers	7	2½	–	1	1	1	–	–
3 Child Watchers	5	2	–	1	1	1	–	–
2 Pad Menders	5	2	–	1	1	1	–	–
3 Women with 6 Children [c]	10	3	–	1	1	1	–	–
18 Hopeless Invalids	5-7	2½	–	–	1	1	1 [b]	1
2 Superannuated	2½	2	–	–	–	–	–	–
37 Infants	2-4	1-2½	–	–	.	–	–	–

[a] The members of the Elite receiving coats were all the Head Drivers, the Blacksmith and the Black Doctor.

[b] Members of the Pen or Mountain Gang received a coat if female, a "frock" if male. Each of the "Yaws Negroes" received a coat, a frock and a blanket.

[c] Mothers who had borne children within the year received 5 yds. "Daccas," 5 yds. Flannel, 2 extra yds. Osnaburgh, and a dollar. Those females who were pregnant at issue time each received 5 yds. Daccas.

TABLE 3. PART 1. MOBILITY WITHIN THE WORTHY PARK SLAVE POPULATION, 1783-1838

			Total Entries	Av. Age 1783-1838	Av. Age 1793	Av. Age 1821	Av. Age 1834	% Males	% Creoles	% Colored
B	1	**NEGRO ELITE:** Heads & Drivers	277	47.3	54.7	47.6	51.3	78.8	87.5	12.1
C		**LOWER ELITE:**								
	2	Domestics	364	33.6	35.5	41.0	35.6	32.0	96.9	48.5
	3	Hospital	101	56.7	*	74.1	48.0	13.6	57.5	5.8
	4	Factory Craftsmen	210	35.3	37.1	38.5	34.7	100.0	66.5	10.2
	5	Other Craftsmen	316	36.4	39.7	35.0	37.5	100.0	79.5	18.0
D		**LABORERS:**								
	6	Factory	22	34.3	*	*	*	100.0	0.0	0.0
	7	Stockmen	214	32.7	35.9	37.5	35.0	92.8	66.2	1.8
	8	Other Specialists	18	43.9	*	*	*	38.9	2.9	11.1
	9	Field Gang 1	1590	32.3	30.0	36.8	31.9	28.2	67.3	1.1
	10	Field Gang 2	866	22.1	31.0	17.0	22.6	35.9	90.0	2.8
	11	Field Gang 3	773	12.5	13.2	13.0	15.4	46.3	91.4	5.1
	12	Field Gang 4	510	22.0	5.8	*	23.8	33.0	82.4	4.8
	13	Unspecified Field	1099	28.7	39.0	24.1	35.3	41.7	61.6	1.1
E		**UNPRODUCTIVE:**								
	14	Watchmen	407	52.6	47.8	59.8	56.8	97.4	26.4	1.9
	15	Miscellaneous	553	18.8	10.0	8.8	8.5	32.4	86.0	1.5
	16	Aged	267	63.2	57.7	64.5	70.8	19.9	37.7	3.6
	17	Young (under 6)	607	3.3	2.1	4.9	3.0	44.2	99.5	14.4
	18	Six Children	72	47.3	*	49.3	45.2	0.0	72.8	0.0
	19	Runaways	176	36.7	*	38.0	*	77.3	44.9	0.8
	20	Manumitted	32	7.1	*	*	2.4	51.4	100.0	45.7
		All			26.7	28.1	30.2	47.0	74.1	7.0

TABLE 3. PART 2

RIGHT TRIANGLE = DOWNWARD MOBILITY
LEFT TRIANGLE = UPWARD MOBILITY
DIAGONAL = STATIONARY

GROUP	1	2	3	4	5	6	7	8	9	10	11	12	13	14	15	16	17	18	19	20
1	188	3	2	3	12	0	9	0	11	0	2	1	10	12	3	5	0	0	2	0
2	2	231	8	1	11	0	10	3	6	14	10	3	7	5	1	13	1	1	1	5
3	2	6	43	0	1	0	0	0	5	3	1	2	2	1	9	15	0	0	0	0
4	6	0	1	132	1	3	4	1	13	0	0	0	19	0	0	0	0	0	2	0
5	18	3	0	3	242	0	2	0	4	0	0	0	6	4	0	1	0	0	2	1
6	0	0	0	2	3	3	0	0	11	0	0	0	0	0	0	0	0	0	0	0
7	13	4	1	1	0	0	70	1	32	14	1	1	20	5	1	1	0	0	8	0
8	0	1	2	0	3	0	1	3	0	1	0	1	1	0	1	1	0	0	0	0
9	15	6	14	12	1	12	42	3	1013	50	0	0	96	18	1	3	0	9	22	0
10	1	6	4	3	4	0	5	1	119	932	2	27	20	10	1	13	0	2	11	0
11	4	10	0	5	3	0	6	1	5	111	496	17	28	0	1	4	0	0	6	0
12	3	19	4	1	4	0	0	0	12	12	74	273	33	0	16	6	1	0	3	1
13	10	29	5	26	5	4	37	0	266	71	69	42	384	15	3	11	2	1	15	0
14	4	1	0	1	0	0	2	1	2	0	0	0	4	307	8	11	0	0	5	0
15	1	4	6	1	0	0	0	0	0	1	39	55	2	0	275	8	45	0	0	17
16	2	5	4	0	1	0	1	2	1	1	0	5	10	2	15	176	0	1	0	0
17	2	10	0	0	1	0	3	0	0	0	18	58	82	0	13	4	365	0	2	5
18	0	0	1	0	0	0	0	0	0	0	0	2	1	0	3	3	1	59	0	0
19	3	3	1	2	4	0	3	0	27	9	0	1	25	9	2	3	0	0	105	0
20	0	3	1	0	0	0	0	0	0	0	0	0	0	0	0	0	0	0	0	0

NOTES:

1. This table is the result of an IBM computer program run at the University of Waterloo by William Ableson of the Department of Statistics from data collated by Garry Greenland from more than 30 Worthy Park slave lists, drawn from the period 1783-1838, but with gaps 1797-1812, 1817-20, 1825-29. This discontinuity should be borne in mind when evaluating the averages tabulated, as should the fact that job categories are not described with absolute consistency throughout the period when assessing the value of the mobility diagram.

2. The Fourth Field Gang was originally one of the very youngest working children, but later included a fair number of elderly "grass-cutters."

3. Listed Occupations in each Numbered Category:

1. NEGRO ELITE: Heads & Drivers—Head Carpenter, Head Blacksmith, Head Mason, Head Cooper, Head Wainman, Head Boiler, Head Muleman, Head Hogman, Head Cattleman, Head Wagonman, Stock Superintendent, Head Distiller, All Field Drivers, Driveresses & Superintendents, Assistant & Second Drivers & Driveresses, Head Watchman, Black Doctor.

2. LOWER ELITE: Domestics—All listed in Great House, Overseer's House, Bookkeepers' House, Attorney's House, Cooks, Washers, Housekeepers, Waiters, Grooms, Stablemen, Gardeners, Seamstresses, "Boatswain," as well as those listed simply as Domestics.

3. Hospital—Lay Doctor, Matron, Doctor's Assistant, Midwife; Hothouse, Yaws House or Children's Nurses; Field Nurse, Weaning Nurse, Hospital Attendant.

4. Factory Craftsmen—Cooper, Boiler, Potter, Distiller, with all Assistant & Apprentice Craftsmen.

5. Other Craftsmen—Carpenters, Joiners, Cabinetmakers, Blacksmiths, Masons, Sawyers, with those listed as "learning" and all listed as Tradesmen.

6. LABORERS: Factory—Stokers & Field Stokers.

7. Stockmen—Wainmen (Field & Road), Mulemen, Cattlemen, Stablemen, Hogmen, Wagoners, Stockmen, Fowlmen, as well as all boys listed with stock.

8. Other Specialists—Sugar Guards, Road Guards, Plowmen, Ratcatchers, Fence Trimmer, Bagwasher, Pad-mender, Seamstress (not domestic), "Candy," Negro House Mender, New Negro Attendant.

9. Field Gang 1—All in First, Big, or Great Gang and "First Class," after 1834.

10. Field Gang 2—All in Second Gang & Second Class.

11. Field Gang 3—All in Third or Small Gang & Third Class.

12. Field Gang 4—All in Fourth Gang & Fourth Class, Grass or Weeding Gang, "Field Girls," "Field Boys."

13. Unspecified Field—"Field," Field Cooks, "Pen Negroes," "Vagabond Gang" (of miscreants).

Categories 14-20, UNPRODUCTIVE are generally self-explanatory. The few listed as Invalids (5) and Hired Out (4) are placed under Miscellaneous. The Young include those corroborated as being under 6 though not specifically so listed. The women with six children exempted from Labor by the Jamaica Act of 1787, the Runaways, who by Law had to be reported, and the Manumitted are all corroborated from other sources.

TABLE 4. CALCULATED SLAVE POPULATION DATA, JAMAICA, 1702-1772

		(a) Slave Population First Year of Decade (000)	(b) Average Annual Increase (000)	(c) As a Percentage	(d) Average Annual Slave Imports (000)	(e) As a Percentage	(f) Average Annual Net Decrease (000)	(g) As a Percentage	(h) Average Annual Total Deaths (000)	(i) As a Percentage	(j) Males Present First Year of Decade (000)	(k) As a Percentage	(l) African-born First Year of Decade (000)	(m) As a Percentage
Figures extrapolated	1682-91	32	0.2	0.63	1.60	5.0	1.40	4.4	1.90	5.8	20.0	62.0	—	—
	1692-1701	34	0.6	1.77	2.20	6.5 }5.9	1.60	4.7 }4.4	2.20	6.0 }5.8	20.4	60.0	—	—
	1701-11	40	0.9	2.02	2.75	6.2	1.85	4.2	2.55	5.7	23.2	58.0	—	—
	1712-21	49	1.5	2.66	2.36	4.2	0.86	1.5	1.76	3.1	28.0	57.0	43.7	89.4
	1722-31	64	1.6	2.22	4.67	6.5 }5.2	3.07	4.3 }2.8	4.17	5.8 }4.4	36.9	57.6	48.7	76.3
	1732-41	80	2.0	2.22	4.44	4.9	2.44	2.7	3.74	4.2	45.7	57.4	65.1	81.5
	1742-51	100	2.2	2.00	5.22	4.7	3.02	2.7	4.72	4.3	57.2	57.2	76.4	76.4
	1752-61	122	2.8	2.06	6.67	5.0 }4.4	3.87	2.9 }2.4	5.87	4.3 }3.8	69.6	57.0	95.5	78.4
	1762-71	150	3.5	2.09	5.96	3.6	2.46	1.5	4.96	3.8	85.4	57.0	108.9	72.8
	1772-81	185	—	—	—	—	—	—	—	—	106.1	57.3	119.0	64.4

SOURCE: Taken from my "Jamaican Slave Mortality," *Journal of Caribbean History* 3 (November 1971).

XI

Mortality and the Medical Treatment of Slaves in the British West Indies

RICHARD B. SHERIDAN

SUCCESSIVE WAVES of peoples have occupied the Caribbean islands, beginning in pre-Columbian times with the Siboneys, Tainos, Arawaks, and Caribs. Only a handful of these indigenous peoples survived the coming of the Spaniard. The Spaniard's exclusive claim to the Antilles was successfully challenged by Dutchmen, Frenchmen, Englishmen, and Danes. For upwards of four centuries the inexorable demand for plantation labor was met by selling Africans into bondage. Following slave emancipation came contract and free laborers from India, China, and elsewhere. Dominating the population of the Caribbean today are the descendants of the African slaves who survived the health hazards of a complex tropical environment in an age of rudimentary medical science.

I

AT the outset it may be asked why Europeans transported Africans several thousand miles to the New World instead of establishing plantations in tropical Africa. This question can perhaps be answered briefly by reference to three environments—physical, technological, and social. Technologically superior Europeans found the coastal lowlands of West Africa both inaccessible and inhospitable. Treacherous surf, mangrove swamps, enervating climate, generally poor soils, and the difficulty of supporting animal husbandry in the face of the tsetse fly were some of the reasons for the failure to establish plantations in Africa. Caribbean islands, on the other hand, were capable of supporting livestock and plantation agriculture. They were in the path of the trade winds which determined sailing and trade routes, energized windmills, and made the climate less enervating. Slaves were less prone to run away or rebel when they were confined to small, densely populated islands and denied access to guns and sailing craft. Then it was possible for Europeans to replicate their old-world culture, albeit a culture corrupted by slavery, when they occupied sparsely populated or even depopulated West India islands.[1] Finally, as Philip Curtin has so ably demonstrated, Europeans suffered a lower mortality rate in the West Indies than they did in West Africa, while imported Africans worked better and lived longer than Indians and white indentured workers.[2]

Prior to 1816 only crude estimates of the slave population of the British West Indies are extant. In 1680, the colonies of Barbados, Jamaica, and the four Leeward Islands of Antigua, St. Kitts, Nevis, and Montserrat contained some 68,000 Negro slaves, of whom Barbados claimed about two-thirds. In 1700, there were some 116,000 slaves, of whom Barbados and Jamaica claimed 50,000 and 45,000, respectively. Jamaica moved ahead of Barbados in subsequent decades. Its slave population in 1750 was 125,000, while that of Barbados was 68,000, and the Leeward Islands, 64,000. The estimated total population in 1750 was 257,000. By the Treaty of Paris in 1763, Britain acquired the "Ceded Islands" of Dominica, St. Vincent, Grenada, and Tobago. Meanwhile, the several British Virgin Islands acquired enough slaves to be included in the estimates. By the eve of the American Revolution the eleven Caribbean islands contained some 416,000 slaves, as compared with 460,000 in the thirteen mainland colonies. Colonies acquired by conquest after 1775 included St. Lucia, Trinidad, Berbice, and Demerara. In 1800, fifteen British colonies contained about 674,000 slaves, nearly half of whom were in Jamaica. In 1834, at the time of slave emancipation, 651,912 slaves were enumerated in the British Caribbean.[3]

"The most striking demographic peculiarity of the South Atlantic System was its failure to produce a self-sustaining slave population in tropical America," writes Philip Curtin.[4] Whereas the slave population of the American South increased by natural means during and following the era of the slave trade, that of the West Indies depended on annual recruits from Africa merely to maintain the existing population. Only the island of Barbados had a slave population that increased by natural means, and this came after the African slave trade was prohibited by the British Parliament in 1807. Among the numerous causes of slave mortality in the West Indies were the high pro-

---

[1] Richard B. Sheridan, "The Development of the Plantations to 1750," in *Chapters in Caribbean History*, London, 1970, pp. 12-25.

[2] "Epidemiology and the Slave Trade," *Political Science Quarterly* 83 (June 1968), 190-216.

[3] Noel Deerr, *The History of Sugar*, London, 1949-1950, II, 278-279, 306.

[4] Curtin, p. 213.

portion of male to female slave imports, the difficulty of acclimating or "seasoning" newly imported slaves, unstable sexual unions which contributed to the low birth rate, high mortality among infants and young children, malnutrition, hard labor, cruel punishment, epidemic and other diseases, and accidents.[5]

Broadly speaking, slavery in the British Caribbean falls into three periods with respect to the mix of demographic and economic factors. Early slavery dates from about 1640 with the launching of the sugar industry in Barbados. It gradually gave way to near-monoculture slavery in that island during the 1680s, and to slave amelioration in the 1760s and 1770s. These stages came later in other Caribbean islands which lagged behind Barbados in developing slave-plantation economies.

The Caribbean colonies were initially colonies of settlement perhaps as much as colonies of exploitation. They attracted numerous smallholders who grew tobacco and other minor staples and foodstuffs with the assistance of indentured servants and a few black slaves. Compared with minor staples, sugar production required more land, labor, and fixed and working capital for efficient production. But for several decades sugar plantations were undercapitalized, depending on both white servants and black slaves to produce not only the sweetening substance but also the greater part of their food requirements. Planters conserved their human capital by assigning slaves to light tasks, feeding and clothing them well, and encouraging family life and reproduction. Contemporary accounts indicate that slave cargoes contained about as many females as males.[6]

Near-monoculture slavery followed in the course of decades the early slave economy. It was characterized by the consolidation of smallholdings into sugar plantations, rising land values, emigration of former smallholders and their servants, annual cropping of cane land, soil depletion and its correction by heavy application of fertilizer, dependence on imported foodstuffs and other supplies and equipment, and a slave population that failed to reproduce itself. Probably the chief cause of the excess of deaths over births was the low cost of imported slaves. Since it was generally cheaper to buy new workers than to bear the cost of breeding and raising a slave to working age in the colony, planters preferred to import more men than women.

---

[5] Richard B. Sheridan, "Africa and the Caribbean in the Atlantic Slave Trade," *American Historical Review* 77 (February 1972), 15-21.

[6] *Ibid.*, p. 20; Orlando Patterson, *The Sociology of Slavery: An Analysis of the Origins, Development and Structure of Negro Slave Society in Jamaica*, London, 1967, p. 105.

Not only did the birth rate decline, but the death rate increased because of hard labor, cruel punishment, malnutrition, epidemics, and accidents. Most of the deaths occurred during the seasoning, for the mortality among new slaves was greater than that among Creoles or island-born Negroes.[7]

Amelioration of the slave's condition seems to have been limited to estates of enlightened planters prior to the American Revolution. Trade interruption in conjunction with unusually severe hurricanes during the revolutionary struggle resulted in slave deaths, reputedly as many as 15,000 in Jamaica.[8] Planters not only grew more foodstuffs at a time of uncertain supplies from abroad but they were also concerned to increase the birthrate and longevity of their slaves. After 1790 the long and bitter slave rebellion in St. Domingue threatened to spread to the British colonies. Planters became fearful of large aggregations of African-born slaves and sought to substitute a more tractable and self-generating labor force of Creole blacks. The collapse of the sugar boom of the 1790s brought planter and politician demands to end the slave trade in an effort to deny laborers to foreign competitors and thus limit sugar production and raise prices to the comparative advantage of British planters. Meanwhile, amelioration had been encouraged by higher slave prices. Finally, the antislavery movement in England became a force which could not be ignored.[9]

II

THOUGH historians and demographers assign different weights to economic and noneconomic factors, they agree that mortality rates declined during the eighty to one hundred years prior to British slave emancipation. Crude annual rates of population decrease can be computed by relating net slave import figures to unofficial census returns. For Barbados the annual rate of decrease was 4.1 percent in the quarter century 1676-1700. It then rose to 4.9 percent in 1701-1725, after which it declined to 3.6 percent in 1726-1750, and 3.8 percent in 1751-1775. Import data are spotty for the years from 1776 to the end of the slave trade in 1807, but other evidence indicates that imports played a declining role in recruiting the slave population. Indeed, the Barbadian experience was unique, for the island's blacks increased from about 69,400 in 1809 to 83,150 in 1834.[10] (See also Appendix I.)

[7] Sheridan, "Africa and the Atlantic Slave Trade," pp. 20-27.

[8] William Beckford, A Descriptive Account of the Island of Jamaica, London, 1790, II, 311-312.

[9] George W. Roberts, The Population of Jamaica, Cambridge, England, 1957, pp. 234-235; Eric Williams, Capitalism and Slavery, Chapel Hill, 1944, pp. 145-153.

[10] Sheridan, "Africa and the Atlantic Slave Trade," pp. 27-30; Roberts, p. 36; Philip D. Curtin, The Atlantic Slave Trade: A Census, Madison, Wis., 1969,

The mortality experience of Jamaica and Barbados afford interesting points of comparison. My crude calculations for Jamaica give an annual rate of decrease of 3.1 percent in 1676-1700, 3.7 percent in 1701-1725, 3.5 percent in 1726-1750, and 2.5 percent in 1751-1775. Though the downward trend was reversed for a time in the 1790s, the annual rate declined to 2.0 in 1776-1800 and to 0.43 percent from 1817 to 1829.[11] (See also Appendix I.) While the computed rates of population of the two islands rose and fell, Jamaica's rate not only lagged behind but was consistently lower than that of Barbados. The lag can be explained by the later economic development of Jamaica, while the consistently lower rates were probably due to the more diversified economy of Jamaica. Barry Higman has demonstrated statistically that in Jamaica the slaves increased generally on coffee plantations and cattle ranches or pens, and decreased on sugar estates. He cites a contemporary observer who attributed the heavy mortality on sugar plantations to cane-hole digging, night work, and the use of the whip.[12]

Recent studies have recounted the mortality experience of individual sugar plantations. J. Harry Bennett, Jr. has told the tragic story of the slaves on the Codrington plantations in Barbados from 1712 to 1748. In an average year there was only one birth to every 100 of the population, one out of every two infants died before reaching 5 years of age, four or five of every hundred seasoned slaves died annually, and deaths during the seasoning claimed four or five in every ten of the Africans imported as replacements. Despite the purchase of an average of nine slaves a year, the Codrington community declined from 292 to 209.[13]

African recruitment and the hiring of seasoned slaves were abandoned by the managers of Codrington in 1761. There followed after some delay a new policy of amelioration to prolong the life of the slaves and encouraged them to breed. That the new policy was successful is evident from the increase of the labor force by one third from 1793 to 1823.[14]

---

pp. 52-72; George R. Mellor, *British Imperial Trusteeship 1783-1850*, London, 1951, pp. 433-442.

[11] Gisela Eisner, *Jamaica, 1830-1930: A Study in Economic Growth*, Manchester, 1961, pp. 131-132.

[12] Douglas G. Hall, *Free Jamaica, 1838-1865: An Economic History*, New Haven, 1959, pp. 17-18; Barry W. Higman, "Slave Population and Economy in Jamaica at the Time of Emancipation," unpublished Ph.D. dissertation, University of the West Indies, 1970, p. 92.

[13] *Bondsmen and Bishops, Slavery and Apprenticeship on the Codrington Plantations of Barbados, 1710-1838*, Berkeley and Los Angeles, 1958, p. 61.

[14] *Ibid.*, pp. 138-141.

Slavery on Worthy Park estate in Jamaica has been analyzed by Michael Craton and James Walvin. The work force increased from 318 in 1783 to 357 in 1791. Massive purchases of new slaves during the sugar boom of the 1790s increased the death rate from 3.0 percent to 5.7 percent, while the birth rate remained fairly stable at 2.3 percent. By the turn of the century the mortality rate had probably resumed its downward trend. Over the entire period 1811-1837, when a policy of amelioration was vigorously pursued, the annual average death rate was 2.60 percent, and the birth rate 2.33 percent. This gave a natural decrease of 0.27 percent, or approximately six slaves every five years out of a population of about 500.[15]

The slave mortality experience can now be summarized briefly. After an initial period of relatively mild slavery, sugar monoculture ushered in a more demanding labor regimen. Most of the slaves who survived the Middle Passage arrived in a debilitated condition. Substantial numbers died during the seasoning. Illnesses multiplied on the plantations after periods of drought, night work, and toil in wet weather. Overwork and malnutrition contributed to the decline of the blacks. From time to time epidemics of smallpox and measles took a heavy toll. When the cost of imported slaves was low in relation to the cost of breeding and rearing children to the age of labor, planters purchased many more males than females. From this followed unstable sexual unions which, in turn, contributed to the low birth rate and the high infant mortality. But far more women tended to survive than men, leading in time to an equalization of the sex ratio. Finally, natural increase depended upon the combination of sexual balance, a reasonably healthy birth rate, and a moderate death rate.

III

It may be argued from the foregoing discussion that demographic conditions improved because of natural forces operating on slave fertility and mortality rates, and that amelioration as a conscious policy of slaveholders was ineffectual. On the other hand, declining mortality might be explained as a consequence of such expedients as lightened discipline and labor tasks, and improved food, clothing, housing, and medical attention. A third hypothesis would attribute demographic improvement to a combination of natural and con-

[15] *A Jamaican Plantation: The History of Worthy Park 1670-1970*, Toronto, 1970, p. 130; Michael Craton, "Jamaican Slave Mortality: Fresh Light from Worthy Park, Longville and the Tharp Estates," *Journal of Caribbean History*, 3 (November 1971), 1-27.

trived elements. The remainder of this paper will marshal evidence in an effort to support the third hypothesis in its medical dimensions.

"As an economic measure," writes Harry Bennett, "amelioration can be defined with substantial accuracy as a system by which money that would otherwise have been spent on hiring and buying Negroes was used to improve the lot of the existing stock of slaves in order to induce them to breed their replacements." [16] From the standpoint of medical treatment of slaves, amelioration would depend on the number of medical practitioners in the islands, their professional qualifications, the number and quality of medical assistants and nurses, the provision of hospitals and other physical facilities to isolate and treat patients, sanitary measures, the state of medical science and especially tropical medicine, and, of course, the extent to which these resources were concentrated on the black people.

Modern medical progress dates from the sixteenth century when old wisdom was challenged by devastating epidemics stemming from interpenetration of disease environments which accompanied wars, urbanization, and intercontinental migration and trade. Exploration of new lands brought new diseases as well as new drugs with which to treat them. Knowledge of infectious diseases advanced. Physical and chemical discoveries reacted on physiology, medicine, and surgery. In an age when qualified physicians were far outnumbered by quacks and mountebanks, notable developments occurred in immunology, surgery, obstetrics, medicine, and especially medical education.

As the commercial revolution shifted north from Italy, so did the centers of medical education. Padua was the educational center of medicine in Renaissance Italy. In the seventeenth century the center shifted to Leyden, Holland. Here Hermann Boerhaave (1668-1738), the great teacher of clinical medicine, attracted students from many lands: from England, Scotland, and even from the West Indies and North America. Through his students Boerhaave was the founder of the Edinburgh Medical School, which succeeded Leyden as the center of European and American teaching and research.[17]

"The specialty of tropical medicine deals with all diseases prevalent in the tropics and with the complex of interrelationships between man and disease in the tropical environment," writes Dr. Thomas

---

[16] Bennett, p. 140.

[17] Douglas Guthrie, *A History of Medicine*, London, 1945, pp. 193-195, 220-231; Lester S. King, *The Medical World of the Eighteenth Century*, Chicago, 1958, pp. 1-29, 297-325.

291

Huckle Weller.[18] Since the navy was Britain's first line of defense and imperial defense extended into tropical latitudes, it is not surprising that a naval surgeon pioneered tropical medicine. Scurvy was the scourge of seamen, and it was James Lind, the Scottish naval physician, who, in 1754, published *A Treatise on Scurvy*, which recommended the use of lemon juice with highly successful results. He also wrote an *Essay on Diseases of Europeans in Hot Climates*, which is said to have opened the campaign for the conquest of the tropics for the white man.[19] Included among the Europeans who ventured into hot climates were numerous doctors. Several of these medical men became famous for their scientific achievements.

Foremost among the physicians who practiced in the West Indies was Sir Hans Sloane (1660-1753). He was born at Killileagh, Ireland, the son of a tax collector. In 1683 he graduated M.D. at the University of Leyden, having earlier studied medicine at Paris and Montpellier. Four years later he went to the West Indies as physician to the Duke of Albemarle, Governor of Jamaica. During his stay of fifteen months on the island, Sloane made many natural history observations and collections, returning to London with some 800 species of plants. His great work was published in 1702 under the title, *A Voyage to the Islands Madera, Barbados, Nieves, S. Christophers, and Jamaica, with the Natural History of the last of those Islands*. During his long life he received many honors, including his appointment as first physician to George II. Sloane is best known for his great collection of natural history specimens, manuscripts, and books which he bequeathed to the nation on condition that £ 20,000 should be paid to his family. Indeed, Sloane's bequest became the first collection of the British Museum.[20]

Although it is uncertain if Sloane ever treated slaves, no such doubt concerns two other medical men who combined practice with scientific pursuits in Jamaica. Testifying before a committee of the Privy Council in 1789 was John Quier (1738-1822), practitioner in physic and surgery. He said that he had studied surgery in London and physic at Leyden and served as assistant surgeon in military hospitals in the former war. For upwards of twenty-one years he had practiced in Jamaica, where he had from 4,000 to 5,000 slaves con-

---

[18] "Tropical Medicine," in *Encyclopedia Britannica*, Chicago, 1955, XXII, 495; H. Harold Scott, *A History of Tropical Medicine*, Baltimore, 1939, I, 1-96; II, 982-1010.
[19] Charles Singer, "History of Medicine," in *Encyclopedia Britannica*, XV, 203.
[20] *The Dictionary of National Biography*, ed. Sidney Lee, London, 1897, LII, 379-380.

stantly under his care. Quier reduced infant deaths from tetanus or lockjaw, was a pioneer in inoculation for smallpox, and anticipated European doctors by more than a century in the diagnosis of measles. He closed his testimony by saying that "within these last Twenty Years the Treatment of new Negroes in this Island has been greatly altered for the Better; that these People are now in general treated with great Humanity and Tenderness, both before and after they are become seasoned to the Country; and that he does not conceive the great Mortality amongst them commonly to arise from want of Food or severe Labour." [21]

The career of Dr. William Wright, F.R.S. (1735-1819), was similar in many respects to that of Dr. Quier. He was born in the village of Crieff, Perthshire, Scotland, where he attended the grammar school. At the age of seventeen he was apprenticed to a surgeon at Falkirk, and in 1756 entered the Edinburgh Medical School. Two years later he was licensed at Surgeons' Hall, London, after which he served as surgeon's mate on several men-of-war as well as in military hospitals in the West Indies. At the end of the Seven Years' War he returned to London and obtained the degree of doctor of medicine.[22]

Because of the scarcity of medical opportunities in England, Dr. Wright was induced to seek his fortune in Jamaica. There he met Dr. Thomas Steel, a young surgeon who had been his fellow student at Edinburgh. Forming a partnership, the young doctors took up residence on Hampden Estate in St. James Parish, the property of James Sterling, who was an absentee in Scotland. According to Dr. Wright's *Memoir*, "The Negroes under the medical charge of the two partners amounted to 1200, which, at 5 shillings each per annum, produced a considerable item of ascertained revenue." From the income of his medical practice and his plantation, Dr. Wright was able to retire to Edinburgh after 1776 and, with the exception of two military assignments in the West Indies, devoted his remaining years to scientific and literary pursuits. That many Scots doctors had followed him to Jamaica is suggested by the remittance of some £11,000 which he

---

[21] Great Britain, *Parliamentary Papers*, 1789, vol. xxvi, no. 646a, pt. iii, Jamaica Appendix, no. 8, "Report of the Lords of the Committee of Council for Trade and Plantations on the Slave Trade,;" Heinz Goerke, "The Life and Scientific Works of Dr. John Quier, Practitioner of Physic and Surgery, Jamaica: 1738-1822," *West Indian Medical Journal* 5 (1956), 23-26. Dr. Quier treated the slaves on Worthy Park estate. See Craton and Walvin.

[22] *Memoirs of the Late William Wright, M.D., Fellow of the Royal Societies of London and Edinburgh, etc., With Extracts from His Correspondence and a Selection of His Papers on Medical and Botanical Subjects*, Edinburgh, 1828, pp. 1-19.

solicited from his friends in Jamaica to rebuild the University of Edinburgh.[23]

Dr. Wright's medical practice was undertaken with the aim of advancing medical science. He was a close observer of nature and was said to have pried with a curious eye into her most secret recesses. His remedies, while few, were efficacious. Patients, including pregnant women, were kept in well-ventilated, airy, and sanitary quarters and black nurses and midwives were properly instructed. For the cure of fevers, and especially lockjaw, he administered cold baths. By these and other means few women died of puerperal fever and the proportion of children who died of lockjaw was small in comparison with the numbers of former times.[24]

Much of Dr. Wright's fame rested on his natural history collections and the scientific papers he wrote. For many years he collected plants in Jamaica, supplying specimens to the Royal Gardens at Kew and the botanical gardens in Liverpool and Glasgow. He was a voluminous correspondent, a bibliophile, and a member of numerous learned societies. The work which issued from his original mind "brought him to be favourably known in that select circle of science, where Banks, Solander and Fothergill, Smith, Lind and Pulteney, Black, Hope and Rutherford, Hutton, Home and the two Hunters, were the burning and the shining lights." [25]

James Grainger, M.D. (1721?-1766), had an extensive medical practice among the slaves and also wrote an essay on West India diseases and remedies. Born in Scotland, he attended medical classes at Edinburgh University for three years and was apprenticed to a surgeon of that city. After service as an army surgeon, he toured Europe and then returned to Edinburgh and graduated M.D. in 1753. During the next six years he lived in London. Failing to obtain patients, he depended chiefly on his pen for a livelihood. His poems, essays, and translations from the classics brought him to the attention of such luminaries as Samuel Johnson and Oliver Goldsmith.

Grainger came to the West Indies in 1759 as the companion and tutor of the heir to a sugar fortune. Soon after his arrival in St. Kitts he married the daughter of a leading planter. Grainger not only practiced medicine and managed a plantation which belonged to an in-law, but he also found time to indulge his favorite study of botany and to write poetry. During his rides to different parts of the island to treat patients he composed a poem which was published in 1764 under

---

[23] *Ibid.*, pp. 23, 86.
[24] *Ibid.*, pp. 90-92.
[25] *Ibid.*, p. 175.

the title, *The Sugar Cane, A Poem in Four Parts.* The same year saw the publication of his *An Essay on the More Common West-India Diseases.*[26]

The principal design of Grainger's *Essay* was "to enable those who are intrusted with the management of Negroes to treat them in a more scientific manner than has hitherto been generally prac-tised. . . ." He wrote of the choice of new slaves, their seasoning, the diseases to which they were most exposed, and their management with respect to diet, clothing, punishment, and medical treatment. Grainger was probably an innovator in prescribing medicines con-cocted from indigenous plants. "The islands contain innumerable medicines of high efficacy," he wrote "not known in Europe; and doubtless a much greater number still remain to be investigated by future inquiry." Dr. William Wright saw the second edition of Grainger's *Essay* through the press in 1802, to which he added an introduction, practical notes, and a "Linnean Index." Wright said that he knew of physicians and surgeons who had profited much by it, "both in the knowledge of the diseases of the Negroes, and of the indigeneous remedies; in which respects it is, in my opinion, an ex-cellent model for a more scientific and general treatise on tropical diseases, especially among the Blacks."[27]

Dr. John Coakley Lettsom, F.R.S. (1744-1815), was an eminent Quaker physician and philanthropist. He was born on the island of Little Jost Van Dykes in the British Virgin Islands, the son of Edward and Mary Lettsom, who were Quakers. His father owned about fifty slaves who worked his cotton plantation on Little Jost Van Dykes and his sugar plantation on the neighboring island of Tortola. Because of his frail health, Lettsom was sent to England to live with Quaker friends of the family. At the age of sixteen he was apprenticed to a surgeon and apothecary at Settle in Yorkshire. He continued his medi-cal education in London under the patronage of Dr. John Fothergill, leading Quaker practitioner and philanthropist. At Fothergill's home Lettsom met Benjamin Franklin and David Barclay, the great city merchant.[28]

---

[26] *The Dictionary of National Biography*, ed. Leslie Stephen and Sidney Lee New York, 1890, xxii, 368-369.

[27] James Grainger, M.D., *An Essay on the More Common West-India Diseases; and the Remedies which that Country Itself Produces: To which are added, Some Hints on the Management, &c., of Negroes. The Second Edition. With Practical Notes, and a Linnean Index, by William Wright, M.D. F.R.S.*, Edinburgh, 1802, pp. i-viii.

[28] James Johnston Abraham, *Lettsom: His Life, Times, Friends and Descendants*, London, 1933, pp. 1-47.

Lettsom's experience as a doctor to the slaves was short and dramatic. In 1767 he sailed to Tortola with a view to getting money to finish his medical education. He refused one source of money, for his Quaker antislavery scruples impelled him to free the ten slaves that he inherited from his father's estate. Lettsom then turned with great zeal to the practice of medicine on Tortola and neighboring islands. He wrote that he often saw from fifty to a hundred people before breakfast. Indeed in the short space of six months his practice yielded the surprising sum of nearly £2,000.[29]

Lettsom studied at the Edinburgh Medical School and the University of Leyden, where he took his M.D. degree in 1769. He succeeded to Fothergill's practice in London and at the height of his career earned £12,000 in a single year. He founded the Medical Society of London, the Royal Sea Bathing Hospital, and was active in the Royal Humane Society and prison reform. From Fothergill he acquired a keen interest in natural science. The botanical garden at his country villa at Camberwell included specimens from remote lands and climates. One of his numerous books was the *Naturalist's and Traveller's Companion* (1772). He also published *Reflections on the General Treatment and Cure of Fevers* (1772), which drew on his medical experience in the West Indies.[30] As a vigorous supporter of causes and no mean controversialist, Lettsom made enemies and did not escape the satirists, who wrote of him:

> I, John Lettsom,
> Blisters, bleeds and sweats 'em.
> If after that they please to die,
> I, John Lettsom.

Not all of the white doctors regarded with scorn and ridicule the medical treatment of slaves by slaves. One of these was James Thomson, M.D., a graduate of the Edinburgh Medical School and friend and protégé of Drs. William Wright and John Quier. As a doctor who treated slaves in Jamaica and as a scientist who diligently carried on the work begun by Wright and Quier, Thomson observed closely the relationship between medicinal plants and the slave doctors who collected, prepared, and prescribed them. He wrote that it was the serious duty of every planter to provide a proper black person to superintend the management of the sick. Thomson candidly acknowledged that the effects of his most labored prescriptions had

[29] *Ibid.*, pp. 48-60.
[30] *Ibid.*, pp. 61-127, 150, 208, 276, 295-298.

been often superseded by the persevering administration of the black doctors' most simple remedies. He wrote at length of his and other doctors' experiments with the medicinal plants of Jamaica, of which he recommended that as many as twenty-eight varieties be kept on every estate.[31]

IV

BIOGRAPHICAL sketches of leading doctors obviously need to be supplemented with descriptive and quantitative data. Though many gaps in our medical knowledge remain to be filled, the remainder of this essay will summarize the data I have collected from primary and secondary sources pertaining to Barbados, Jamaica, and Antigua.

Doctors may have been attached to Barbadian plantations as early as 1690. In that year Sir Dalby Thomas wrote that a sugar plantation of 100 acres would require fifty black slaves, seven white servants, an overseer, farrier, carter, and a doctor whose salary amounted to £20 per annum.[32] A century later Joshua Steele, a leading planter, submitted evidence on slavery to Governor Parry of Barbados. He testified that it was the general practice in plantations to give a standing salary as far as five shillings per slave "to some medical person, apothecary, or practitioner, to supply medicines and attendance annually." Some planters went further and not only gave a salary for daily attendance, but also imported at their own charge the necessary medicines.[33] Dr. George Pinckard, an army surgeon who was stationed in Barbados, wrote in 1796 that the island contained many members of the medical profession who were an honor to their profession and an ornament to society. There were others, however, who were "preeminent in ignorance . . . and the very *negro doctors* of the estates too justly vie with them in medical knowledge." [34]

Harry Bennett has calculated the cost of maintaining the Codrington slaves during the eighteenth century. During the first half of the century the average cost per slave was £2. 2s. 11 1/4d. a year. Of this amount, £1. 11s. was for food, 8s. 5 1/4d. for clothing, and 3s. 6d. for medical care. In the latter half of the century, the whole of the annual charge had risen to £3. 16s. 5 1/4d., with £3 for food,

---

[31] *A Treatise on the Diseases of Negroes, As they Occur in the Island of Jamaica with Observations on the Country Remedies,* Jamaica, 1820, pp. 1-2, 8-11, 112, 143-168.
[32] *An Historical Account of the Rise and Growth of the West-India Collonies,* London, 1690, p. 14.
[33] William Dickson, *Mitigation of Slavery. Part I. Letters and Papers of the late Hon. J. Steele,* London, 1814, pp. 150-153.
[34] *Notes on the West Indies,* London, 1806, i, 388-392.

8s. 5 1/4d. for clothing, and 8s. 0d. for medical care. Medical care increased from 8.1 percent to 10.5 percent of total maintenance charges. Bennett writes that amelioration proved to be the most effective method of insuring a continuing supply of labor. In fact, the slave population which earlier had suffered such a high mortality rose from 266 to 355 from 1793 to 1823.[35]

Jamaica seems to have been well supplied with doctors who differed widely in their professional qualifications. Charles Leslie, who lived on the island before 1740, said that the physicians there of any note generally made fine estates. He went on to say that the island was

> quite crowded with raw unexperienced Youths, who imagine this the properest Place for a Settlement; and when they come over, are generally set to prescribe to a parcel of Negroes in some Country-plantations. Their Numbers make but dull Business for most of them; and in the Towns there are generally one or two eminent Men who have the Employment, and soon get to be rich.[36]

The quality of practice had improved by the latter part of the eighteenth century according to Bryan Edwards, the planter-historian. Every plantation that he was acquainted with in Jamaica was under the daily or weekly inspection of a practitioner in physic and surgery who frequently resided on the estate. The planters had become intolerant of "illiterate pretenders in medicine" and sought for and encouraged "young men of skill and science." The usual payment to doctors for attendance and medicines was six shillings a head per annum for all the Negroes on the estate, whether sick or well. Extra payments were made for amputations, inoculation, and difficult cases of midwifery. On an estate having 500 slaves the doctor's compensation was about £150 sterling per year, plus such prerequisites as board, washing, and lodging. Edwards was of the opinion that few plantation doctors had less than 500 slaves under their care; while several, with their assistants, had upwards of 5,000.[37]

Early nineteenth century practices in Jamaica were described by Robert Renny. He maintained that the health of the slaves was very punctually attended to. Newly imported slaves were "generally inoculated with the small, or the cow pock, matter." Every large estate had

---

[35] Bennett, pp. 43, 139-141.

[36] *A New History of Jamaica from the Earliest Accounts to the Taking of Porto Bello by Vice-Admiral Vernon*, London, 1740, p. 50.

[37] *The History, Civil and Commercial, of the British Colonies in the West Indies*, Dublin, 1793, II, 127-128; for another favorable impression of the medical treatment of slaves, see Beckford, II, 304-306.

a doctor in residence or in the immediate neighborhood. The slaves were attended in the sick-room, or hospital, over which an aged Negress presided as nurse. The proprietor commonly furnished blankets, rice, sugar, oatmeal, and flour; while those of a more liberal disposition supplied beef and mutton, and even sometimes spices, sago, and wines. Renny said that "the Negroes are subject to the same diseases as the Europeans; though they are seldom affected, and more seldom carried off, by those fevers, which usually prove so destructive to the white settlers." [38]

The new policy of amelioration, according to the Jamaican demographer George Roberts, appears to have had some success. The wastage of human life which had been compatible with slavery when Africans could be easily and cheaply imported, would have led to depopulation after the prohibition of the slave trade in 1807 if measures had not been taken to increase fertility and decrease mortality. [39]

Since a College of Physicians and Surgeons was not established in Jamaica until 1832, and before this no proof of qualification or registration was required, it is difficult to ascertain the number of doctors or pass on their professional standing. Some idea of the number of doctors and their wealthholding can be gained, however, by searching the *Inventorys* series at the Island Record Office at Spanish Town. In the five-year period 1741-1745, the personal property inventories of twenty-four physicians and surgeons are recorded. Omitting shillings and pence, they range from £39 to £6,522, the average being £874 in Jamaica currency, or £624 sterling. Thirty years later, in 1771-1775, a total of twenty-six doctors' estates were inventoried. They range from £51 to £9,931, and average £2,237 currency, or £1,597 sterling. Whereas the doctors in the first period held most of their personal property in the form of accounts receivable, those in the latter period not only claimed debts outstanding but a sizable number also owned slaves which they either leased or worked on their own plantations and pens. [40]

Fifty-one doctors' inventories are recorded in the years from 1791 to 1795 in Jamaica. They range from £10 to £56,815, and average £4,481 currency, or £3,199 sterling. At least half of these doctors were Scotsmen or Irishmen, whose personal property inventories were generally on the high side compared with all doctors. Dr. Alex-

---

[38] *A History of Jamaica*, London, 1807, pp. 176-179.
[39] Roberts, pp. 238-245.
[40] Jamaica Public Record Office, Spanish Town, *Inventorys*, vols. XXI-XXV, LI-LVI.

ander McLenan of St. James parish was a man of substance; his personal property amounted to nearly £12,171 currency. Of this amount, nearly £5,520 consisted of household furnishings, 33 slaves, and livestock; the remaining £6,651 consisted of claims on individuals in the form of book debts and amounts owing from ten estates and pens presumably for the treatment of slaves.[41]

One of the paradoxes in the demographic history of Jamaica is that within a decade after full emancipation the black population began to grow, while the number of doctors practicing on the island declined sharply. Compared with the 200 doctors in 1830, the number had declined to 87 in 1861 and 84 in 1871. The island's population, on the other hand, increased from 377,400 in 1844 to 506,100 in 1871. Some of the reasons for the growth in population lie outside the practice of medicine and surgery. It seems reasonable to assume, for example, that the high rate of abortion and child neglect that was reported in slave times declined after emancipation when stable sexual unions became more common. Also, the growth of peasant agriculture probably lightened the labor tasks of the blacks by comparison with the slave-plantations, thus helping to reduce mortality.[42]

V

THE medical history of Antigua is better documented than that of other British Caribbean colonies. In part, this is owing to the monumental genealogical history of the island by Dr. Vere Langford Oliver, himself a descendant of a prominent Antiguan family and also a medical practitioner. Moreover, the letter books and account books of Dr. Walter Tullideph afford insights not only into his own career as a doctor, merchant, and planter, but also of his doctor friends and business associates who like himself were Scotsmen.[43]

Medical practitioners increased in number and professional attainment as Antigua moved into front rank as a slave-plantation colony. From an estimated five to ten doctors in the first decade of the eighteenth century, the number increased to twenty-two in 1731, when a roster was drawn up in connection with the assignment of doctors

[41] *Ibid.*, vols. LXXXIII-XC.
[42] Eisner, pp. 133-140, 165-166, 337-340.
[43] Vere Langford Oliver, *The History of the Island of Antigua*, London, 1894-1899; *Letters Books of Dr. Walter Tullideph of Antigua and Scotland*, 1734-1767, 3 vols., "Dr. Tullideph's General Ledger"; "Dr. Tullideph's Medical Ledger." I am indebted to the late Sir Herbert Ogilvy, Bart., for permission to quote extracts from these records.

to militia regiments. At least half of the doctors enumerated in 1731 would appear to have been Scotsmen. Beginning in 1732, new doctors had to be certified and licensed. From these records we learn that nineteen new doctors were licensed from 1732 to 1750, of whom twelve arrived on the island after 1742. Most of the entries include only the date and name of the licensee, but a few give more particulars. We learn, for example, that a Dr. Forgus presented his diploma from the faculty of physicians of Angiers in France, Dr. Adam Byrne presented his certificate from Dublin University, Dr. John Tod presented his certificate from a chirurgeon and apothecary at Edinburgh, and Drs. Patrick Malcolm and Ashton Warner presented diplomas from Surgeon's Hall.[44]

Antigua may have had more qualified doctors in the middle years of the eighteenth century than at any other time during slavery. Compared with the nineteen doctors who were certified and licensed from 1732 to 1750, only nine were added to the rolls in the third quarter of the century, and only six in the fourth quarter.[45] That these figures understate the number of practitioners is suggested by the changing structure of medical practice. Whereas the doctors practiced individually for some years, they later employed assistants who treated slaves under their supervision. John Luffman wrote in 1787 that sick slaves were attended by young doctors whose principals contracted with the owners of estates or their attorneys at the common price of three shillings and nine pence sterling per slave. It was the business of these assistants to make twice weekly visits to the estates that had been put under the care of their employers. Their pay was so meager that Luffman doubted if it covered their expenses.[46]

At midcentury Antigua had approximately thirty-two qualified doctors in a population that was predominantly black. At that time the island contained approximately 30,000 blacks and 3,500 whites. The ratio of one doctor to 1,047 inhabitants compares favorably with the Jamaican ratio of one to 1,855 in 1830, and even the Mississippi ratio of one to 1,448 in 1970.[47]

Of the thirty-two Antiguan doctors, nineteen have been identified as Scotsmen or educated in Scotland, seven were Antiguans, one an Irishman, and five not identified. Foremost among the Antiguans was

[44] Oliver, I, xcviii-cix.

[45] *Ibid.*, cxxiii-cxlvii.

[46] *Brief Account of the Island of Antigua, together with the customs and manners of its inhabitants, white as well as black; as also an accurate statement of the food, clothing, and labor,* London, 1789, reprinted in Oliver, I, cxxxiii.

[47] Eisner, p. 337; Jack Star, "Where Have Our Doctors Gone," *Look* 35 (29 June 1971), 15-17.

Dr. Ashton Warner (1721-1789), descendant of the founder of the colony and member of a prominent planter family. For a time he practiced in London as did his brother Joseph Warner, F.R.S. (1717-1801).[48] But whereas Joseph remained to become one of the city's leading surgeons, Ashton returned to Antigua in 1749. Besides his medical practice, he was President of the Council and owner of two sugar plantations.[49] Dr. George Crump was the son and heir of an Antiguan barrister and planter, and nephew of a lieutenant-colonel of militia who was made governor of Guadeloupe at the British conquest in 1759. That the Crumps were among the best educated families of Antigua is evident from the fact that the doctor as well as his father and uncle were graduates of Leyden University.[50] The first Jarvis in Antigua was a bookkeeper. His son, Dr. Francis Jarvis, married the widow of a leading planter. Dr. William Jarvis, who was licensed to practice in 1746, was first cousin to Dr. Francis Jarvis. Dr. Thomas Jarvis, another cousin, produced a diploma from the College of Physicians at Edinburgh and was licensed to practice medicine in Antigua in 1790. He inherited property on the island which he claimed to be worth £50,000.[51]

Numbered among the nineteen Scots doctors was Walter Tullideph (1703?-1772), who had a successful career in the West Indies. He was born at Dumbarney, the son of a Presbyterian minister. After attending the high school at Edinburgh, he was apprenticed to a chirurgeon of that city in 1718. About 1726 he went to Antigua where several friends and relatives were already established as doctors, merchants, and government officials.[52]

We first learn of Tullideph from his letters to Sir Hans Sloane. He wrote from Antigua on 5 July 1727:

> When I had the honour to wait upon you in London you were pleased to recommend to me the Study of our West India Vegetables, in obedience to which desire, I have made it my endeavour

---

[48] *The Dictionary of National Biography,* ed. Sidney Lee, London, 1899, LIX, 396-397.

[49] Oliver, III, 186-187.

[50] *Ibid.,* I, 184-186.

[51] *Ibid.,* II, 96-103.

[52] Charles B. Boog Watson, ed., *Register of Edinburgh Apprentices, 1701-1755,* Edinburgh, 1929, p. 88; Tullideph to Andrew Aiton in Scotland, dated Antigua, 16 May 1757, Tullideph Letter Book, vol. II; Oliver, I, 223-225; III, 128-133, 155-162; R. B. Sheridan, "The Rise of a Colonial Gentry: A Case Study of Antigua, 1730-1775," *Economic History Review,* 2d ser., 13 (1961), 342-357.

to examine several of them in their perfection and to put up a dryed specimen of each of them as often as I could conveniently.[53]

From time to time Tullideph shipped growing plants and dried specimens to Sloane, but his scientific interest soon became subordinated to his professional and business activities. Sloane was informed in a letter of 25 June 1734 that the laborious practice of physic and surgery engrossed most of Tullideph's time. The young doctor had left the country and settled in the town of St. John where he was endeavoring to get a modest fortune.[54]

That the move to town did not interfere with the treatment of plantation slaves seems evident from the entries in Tullideph's medical ledger. Though part of the ledger has decayed, enough remains to show that his practice was considerable. While his white patients were treated individually, his far more numerous black patients were treated mainly on a contract basis. For example, one entry in his account with Samuel Byam's plantation is as follows: "To ye care of 125 negroes fm. Janry. 25, 1734/5 to Do. 1735/6 is one year @ 6/ . . . [£] 37. 10. 0." In other words, Tullideph contracted to treat Byam's slaves on an annual basis at six shillings per head. Twenty-two such accounts are entered in the ledger from 1731 to 1735, some for periods of less than five years. In 1733 Tullideph had 14 accounts for the care of 1,198 slaves at a total charge of nearly £360. The next year he had seventeen accounts for 1,408 slaves at £422.[55]

Other Negro slaves, especially those owned by smallholders and artisans, were treated by Tullideph on an individual basis. For example, he charged £1. 8s. for dressing a wound, the same for visiting a Negro wench in labor, £2 for the "Cure of a Clap," £2. 16s. for maintaining two slaves at his hot house with nursing and lodging, and £5 for laying open a mortification in a slave's leg with dressing and care involving several visits.[56]

To augment his modest fortune the young doctor sold medicines and other goods at retail and wholesale. He sent to London for upwards of £160 worth of medicine in the early 1730s, most of it coming from Alexander Johnston, "Chymist and Druggist at the Golden Stead in Fan Church Street over against Magpie Alley." Small quantities were retailed to local inhabitants, the greater part

[53] Great Britain, British Museum, Sloane MSS, 4049, vol. xiv, fol. 3, "Original Letters to Mr. H. Sloane."

[54] Tullideph to Sir Hans Sloane, dated Antigua, 25 June 1734, *Tullideph Letter Book*, Vol. i.

[55] "Tullideph's Medical Ledger," fols. 1-247.

[56] *Ibid.*, fols. 52, 54, 62, 108, 135.

being dispensed at wholesale to doctors in Antigua and neighboring islands. Tullideph also acted as Johnston's attorney in collecting debts owed by doctors in the West Indies.[57]

Tullideph came to Antigua at the invitation of his cousin Dr. Walter Sydserfe, who became a planter, assemblyman, councilor and lieutenant-general in the militia. Having come out to join his cousin in the practice of medicine, Tullideph, in turn, found that he needed assistance. On 24 March 1735 he wrote to another cousin who was a sugar factor in London: "If you can agree with any Sober Young Surgeon who has been educated at Edinburgh (if possible) for three years, he to pay his own passage . . . I will give him ye first year £ 30, ye second 40, and the third £ 50. . . ."[58] The following year a Dr. William Mercer was licensed to practice in Antigua, and two years after this Tullideph ordered his London chemist to charge a small invoice of medicines to "Messrs. Walter Tullideph & Wm. Mercer in Compy."[59]

The transition from doctor to planter was accelerated in 1736 when Tullideph married a young widow and came into possession of a small plantation. To his brother David, a Scottish merchant trading to Antigua, he wrote in the fall of 1738: "I have resigned all business in favour of Dr. Mercer, it was too great fatigue & he allowed me in consideration £ 300 (which keep a secret), & I still hold all business that side of the creek next my self which may be £ 200 per Ann. gott with much ease. You may acquaint Brother Thomas of this."[60]

Meanwhile, Tullideph had written to Brother Thomas in Scotland about the prospects for combining medicine with planting in Antigua:

If any of our nephews will Study Physick and Settle as a Planter I can allow such a one £ 100 Sterlg. pr. Ann. to manadge my Estate and take care of my negroes when I resolve to come home, besides ye Care of adjoining plantations Tomie [Thomas] don't stand for a small matter in ye purchase of an Estate. . . .[61]

[57] Tullideph wrote to Alexander Johnston on 21 October 1734, 2 February 1735, 22 October 1736, 23 May 1736, 27 June 1737, and 10 August 1738—all in vol. I of the *Tullideph Letter Books.*

[58] Tullideph to William Dunbar, Merchant in London, dated Antigua, 24 March 1734, *ibid.*

[59] Tullideph to Mr. Alexander Johnston in London, dated Antigua, 17 April 1738, *ibid.*

[60] Tullideph to David Tullideph in England, dated Antigua, 3 November 1738, *ibid.*

[61] Tullideph to Thomas Tullideph in Scotland, dated Antigua, 28 April 1736, *ibid.*

Although none of his nephews followed his advice, Tullideph found several doctors who eagerly enlisted his support in climbing the ladder of plantership.

As doctor-planters with influential connections in Scotland, England, and Antigua, Tullideph and Sydserfe came in time to direct a Scots colonial community consisting of doctors, merchants, bookkeepers, overseers, plantation attorneys, and planters. Both of these cousins married into planter families, served in the legislature and militia, managed the estates of absentees, and acted as guardians, executors, and trustees. In these and other capacities they found opportunities to recommend their fellow countrymen. Fourteen of the nineteen doctors who are mentioned in the Tullideph correspondence from 1734 to 1758 were Scotsmen, of whom at least eight became members of the colonial gentry.

Population growth, enclosures, and a low level of material well-being coexisted in eighteenth century Scotland with a high level of primary and secondary education, the flowering of university life, and intellectual and cultural achievement. As Richard Pares has observed, theological Calvinism was losing its hold on the people, and the great mental and moral energies which it generated were transferred to secular studies and secular interests. Many Scotsmen sought a new life in the colonies. The Scottish family system helped to make the migration a continuous one, for one Scotsman was hardly established abroad before he sent for his brothers, cousins, nephews, and fellow townsmen. Politics aided the outward movement, for the Scottish M.P.'s at Westminster generally voted in a bloc and they traded their votes for posts in the colonies which they conferred on their relatives and friends. Another source of strength were the Scotsmen who fought in colonial wars.[62]

VI

IT might be concluded that Scots doctors and medical progress did much to improve the health and longevity of slaves in the West Indies. But it should be emphasized that the Scots' contribution was reinforced by other developments. These included the relative rise in the price of slaves, the threat of slave rebellion, competition from rival slave-plantation colonies, the growing proportion of Creole to African slaves, and the rise of the antislavery movement in England.

[62] "A Quarter of a Millennium of Anglo-Scottish Union," in *The Historian's Business and Other Essays,* ed. R. A. and Elisabeth Humphreys, Oxford, 1961, pp. 84-94.

Since mortality and medical care began on the Middle Passage, it is interesting to speculate about the relationship between the Parliamentary Act of 1788 which required qualified doctors on all slave vessels and the loss of fewer Africans in transit to the plantations during the later decades of the slave trade.[63] Economic and humanitarian forces combined to induce colonial legislatures to adopt ameliorative measures which included provisions regarding the medical care of slaves. The Leeward Islands Act of 1798, for example, required every plantation to provide a "commodious" hospital, employ a doctor who was obliged to call at the estate twice a week unless he was notified in writing that his presence was not required, give special attention to pregnant women and infants, and record vital statistics.[64]

Yet it may be argued that what was achieved by investment in medical care of slaves was partly negated by factors that were beyond the control of planters, their medical assistants, and reformers.[65] Orlando Patterson writes that "the most important factor in any consideration of reproduction during slavery is an analysis of the attitudes toward pregnancy and child-rearing on the part of both masters and slaves." [66] We have seen that most planters adopted a new policy toward reproduction in the later part of the eighteenth century. There is dramatic evidence that male slaves valued medical services, for only the white doctors were spared in the bloody slave revolts which occurred on the Danish island of St. John in 1733, and in French St. Domingue in 1791.[67]

Most important in negating the policy of reproduction was the attitude of female slaves themselves. Irregular sexual unions were fostered by the excess of black males over females, the large number of unmarried white males attached to plantations, planter opposition to slave family life and their own cavalier attitude toward concubinage.

[63] C. M. MacInnes, "The Slave Trade," in *The Trade Winds: A Study of British Overseas Trade during the French Wars 1793-1815*, ed. C. Northcote Parkinson, London 1948, pp. 254-255; Curtin, *Atlantic Slave Trade*, pp. 275-286.

[64] Elsa V. Goveia, *Slave Society in the British Leeward Islands at the End of the Eighteenth Century*, New Haven, 1965, pp. 191-198.

[65] Cultural barriers which impeded European doctors in treating patients in colonial countries are discussed perceptively by Frantz Fanon in chap. 4, "Medicine and Colonialism," of his book, *A Dying Colonialism*, New York, 1967, pp. 121-145.

[66] *Sociology of Slavery*, p. 105.

[67] *Ibid.*, p. 105; Waldemar Westergaard, *The Danish West Indies Under Company Rule*, New York, 1917, p. 169; C.L.R. James, *The Black Jacobins: Toussaint L'Ouverture and the San Domingo Revolution*, 2d edn., New York, 1963, p. 88.

In the absence of venereal disease, irregular relations need not have inhibited reproduction. But there is evidence that such diseases did inhibit the birth rate. Moreover, slave women disliked the idea of bringing more slaves into the world and often found ways to induce abortion. Finally, there is reason to believe that many infants died because of maternal neglect.[68]

Having ventured to analyze some of the mortality and medical variables of Caribbean slavery, I end this essay with a challenge to press forward with improved data and analytical tools, and especially to undertake comparative studies of mortality and the medical treatment of slaves in the Atlantic world.

[68] Patterson, pp. 106-112.

APPENDIX 1

COMPUTATION OF RATE OF DECLINE OF SLAVE POPULATION

THE data needed for computing a rough rate of population decline (see Appendix Table 1) are net slave imports, that is, total imports less reexports, and the slave population at selected intervals of time. Annual imports and reexports were recorded in Jamaica from 1702 to 1800, and imports in all but a few years from 1676 to 1701. Similarly, except for the decade 1736-1746, annual imports into Barbados were recorded during the century from 1676 to 1775. These two series have been adjusted where necessary to show both gross and net imports for quarter-century periods. Given the net slave imports and slave population at the beginning and end of each period, the problem is to compute the annual rate of population decline of both the Creole and imported slaves.

APPENDIX TABLE 1. ESTIMATED ANNUAL RATE OF POPULATION DECLINE, 1676-1800 (POPULATION AND IMPORTS IN THOUSANDS)

	1676	1701	1726	1751	1776	1800
	BARBADOS					
Estimated slave population	33.0	45.0	55.0	65.0	74.4	68.0
Total net slave imports for 25-year period	52.4	70.9	63.6	75.8	n.d.	
Estimated annual rate of population decline for 25-year period	4.1%	4.9%	3.6%	3.8%	n.d.	
	JAMAICA					
Estimated slave population	9.0	43.0	75.0	121.0	200.0	300.0
Total net slave imports for 25-year period	54.0	86.1	132.1	177.6	222.8	
Estimated annual rate of population decline for 25-year period	3.1%	3.7%	3.5%	2.5%	2.0%	

SOURCES: Slave import and population data have been compiled from numerous sources, of which the following are most comprehensive: Great Britain, Public Record Office, *Colonial Office* 1/43, no. 37; Great Britain. *Parliamentary Papers*, 1789, vol. 26, no. 646a, pt. 3, Jamaica Appendix, "Report of Lords' Committee on the Slave Trade," *ibid.*, 1790, vol. 29, no. 697; K. G. Davies, *The Royal African Company*, London, 1957, p. 143, 363; Noel Deerr, *The History of Sugar*, London, 1949-1950, II, 278-279; Frank W. Pitman, *The Development Of the British West Indies 1700-1763*, New Haven, 1917, pp. 71-90, 369-392.

The computation of the estimated annual rate of population decline for each twenty-five year period was computed by first calculating the estimated annual excess of deaths above births over the period, and then dividing that by the estimated population in the middle year of the period. The total excess of deaths over births was calculated as the difference between: (1) the sum of the population at the start of the period plus the total net imports during the period; less (2) the population at the end of the period. This difference was divided by twenty-five to obtain the annual excess. The estimated middle year population was the arithmetic mean of the population in the terminal years of each twenty-five year period.

XII

Religion and Magic in Mexican Slave Society, 1570-1650

COLIN A. PALMER

THE CONTENTION that slaves in the New World were unable to develop and maintain their social customs and institutions is now being questioned by some scholars. Indeed, it is becoming increasingly clear that slaves were able to create a way of life for themselves which was quite unlike that of their masters. Slavery, wherever it existed in the New World, may have been an institution of total control, but there were some crucial areas of the slaves' life that managed to resist complete obliteration. The experiences of the slaves in early colonial Mexico demonstrate the resilience of some of their customs and beliefs in spite of persecution and in the face of efforts to eradicate them.

The slave population in Mexico in the early years was essentially an immigrant population. Most of them had come from West and Central Africa and included such peoples as the Wolof, the Akan, the Benguela, and the Bakango.[1] According to the estimates that exist, the average working life of a slave rested somewhere between ten and twenty years.[2] The slaves who were imported tended to be predominantly male, outnumbering females by a margin of approximately three to one. In addition, it appears that the reproductive rate of these slaves, at least that of African with African, was not very high. The sexual imbalance of the slaves, their low reproductive rate, and their high mortality rate meant that masters had to rely on fresh importations from Africa to replenish their labor supply. These slaves brought with them to Mexico a large variety of beliefs ranging all the way from religion to medicine.

On arriving in Mexico, the slaves were, quite naturally, exposed to the cultural influences of the Indians and the Spaniards. In time, the Africans would acquire some of the cultural traits of these two

[1] There was an annual average of between 30,000 and 45,000 slaves in Mexico during the period 1570-1650.

[2] See, for example, Ward Barrett, *The Sugar Hacienda of the Marqueses del Valle*, Minneapolis, Minn., 1970, p. 84.

peoples and out of this intermixture a new culture would emerge for them.[3] The slaves manifested a great capacity to extract from their new environment those cultural ingredients that would be of some value to them. It would be a very rewarding study if it were possible to identify precisely those features of the slaves' folk culture that were African or Indian or Spanish in origin. Yet this appears to be impossible since none of the component parts apparently survived in a pure form. This difficulty notwithstanding, it is possible to get some understanding of the life style of the slaves by examining some of their religious beliefs and folk practices.

Those Africans who came to Mexico as slaves hailed from an intensely religious peoples. Indeed, religion has traditionally pervaded every facet of the African's existence. According to John S. Mbiti, "because traditional religions permeate all the departments of life, there is no formal distinction between the sacred and the secular, between the religious and the non-religious, between the spiritual and the material areas of life." [4] With this kind of religious heritage, it would, therefore, be no easy task for the Spaniards to eliminate the slaves' traditional beliefs and convert them to Catholicism. For conversion would mean not only a change in the nature of the African's religious beliefs but also in his life style and the way in which he perceived himself and the world around him. As Mbiti expressed it, "conversions to new religions like Christianity and Islam must embrace his [the African] language, thought patterns, fears, social relationships, attitudes and philosophical disposition, if that conversion is to make a lasting impact upon the individual and his community." [5]

However difficult the task might have been, the Spanish Crown from the outset insisted on the conversion of the African slaves to Catholicism. As early as 1501 when Ferdinand and Isabella gave their approval to the introduction of slavery into Hispaniola, they advised Nicolás de Ovando, the governor, to admit only "Negro slaves or other slaves who were born in the power of Christians, our subjects and natives." [6] In later years, when slaves were imported directly from

---

[3] For a study of the beliefs and practices of the Indians, see the famous work by Fray Bernardino Sahagún, *Historia General de las cosas de Nueva Espanã*, 5 vols., Mexico, 1938. For the Spaniards, see Gonzalo Aguirre Beltrán, *Medicina y Magia: El proceso de aculturación en la estructura colonial* (Mexico, 1963).

[4] John S. Mbiti, *African Religions and Philosophies*, New York, 1970, p. 2.

[5] *Ibid.*, p. 4.

[6] Antonio de Herrera y Tordesillas, *Historía general de los hechos de los Castellanos en las islas y Tierra Firme de la Mar Oceano*, Madrid, 1601, dec. 1, lib. 4, cap. 12.

Africa, the Crown required that they be baptized before they disembarked in the New World.

In accordance with the policy of both the church and the state, the slaves were not excluded from the sacraments of the church. Charles V actively supported measures for the Christianization of the Africans. In fact, the Emperor was convinced that "all Negroes are, by nature, capable of becoming Christians." [7] Consequently, in 1537 he ordered that all slaves be released from their duties at a certain hour each day in order that they might receive religious instruction.[8] Four years later, the Emperor prohibited slaves from working on holidays and feast days and decreed that they should attend mass on those days like the other Christians.[9]

There is no evidence that the church avoided its responsibilities to Christianize the slaves. In fact, the First Provincial Council of the church held in Mexico acknowledged that "we are obliged, as with new plants, to provide for their [the slaves] spiritual nourishment and sustenance as guardians of their souls." [10] On their part, the Jesuits, when they arrived in 1572, manifested an active interest in the spiritual life of the slaves. By initiating a program of religious instruction through the creation of special centers for this purpose, the Jesuits were able to report in 1583 that "in public we do not see such obvious sins as before we were accustomed to seeing." [11] To supplement the spiritual efforts of the church and the state, some of the larger sugar plantations and haciendas employed resident priests to minister to the needs of all the people, including the slaves.

In spite of the active interest of the church and the state in making good Catholics of the slaves, it would be erroneous to conclude that these slaves totally rejected their own traditional African religious beliefs and embraced the Spanish variant of Catholicism both in its form and in its substance. The evidence is impressive that it was the nonmaterial aspects of their culture, chiefly their religious beliefs that survived in Mexico. Thus, despite the determination of the church, the state, and the Holy Office of the Inquisition to ensure religious conformity, the slaves from time to time reverted to some of their traditional religious practices and beliefs, or combined them with their practice of Catholicism. This conclusion can be supported by

[7] Richard Konetzke, ed., *Colección de documentos para la historia de la formación social de Hispanoámerica, 1493-1810*, 3 vols., Madrid, 1953, I, 235.

[8] *Recopilación de leyes de las Indias*, 3 vols., Madrid, 1943, lib. 1, t. 1, ley 12.

[9] *Ibid.*, lib. 1, t. 1, ley 13.

[10] Francisco Antonio Lorenzana, ed., *Concilios Provinciales, primero segunda*, Mexico, 1769, p. 138.

[11] Felix Zubillaga, S.J., ed., *Monumenta Mexicana*, Rome, 1959, II, 147.

COLIN A. PALMER

data derived from an examination of cases involving slaves who appeared before the Inquisition in the seventeenth century.

Slaves were denounced before the Holy Office for committing two major religious offences. In the first place, slaves tended to blaspheme or to renounce God with great frequency and this generally earned them a denunciation before that institution. Secondly, the practice of some of their traditional beliefs, loosely defined by the Holy Office as witchcraft, sorcery, and divination provided the basis for a large number of *procesos*. These offences are important for understanding the nature of slave religion in Mexico.

In its efforts to foster religious orthodoxy, the Holy Office relentlessly pursued blasphemers among the slave population. A noted scholar of the Inquisition, Henry C. Lea, defines blasphemy as "an imprecation derogatory or insulting to the Divinity." [12] For punitive purposes, the Inquisitors made a distinction between blasphemy and heresy since "words uttered in anger, while emotionally distraught were generally considered to be blasphemy and not heresy." [13] In seventeenth century Mexico, the slaves who were denounced usually committed blasphemy during periods of stress. The records are full of such cases.

There were three channels by which such cases came to the attention of the Holy Office. On some occasions slaves voluntarily denounced themselves; on other occasions a master was the informant, but often it was just an ordinary citizen who reported this infraction of the religious law. Once a slave had been accused of blasphemy, if the evidence warranted it, the Holy Office would order the arrest of the slave in question. During the ensuing trial, the slave would not be told the names of his accusers nor the offense for which he was charged. The Inquisitors would ask the accused person whether he knew the reason for his trial. If the answer was in the affirmative, the slave would be asked to relate his side of the case. In the event of a slave's ignorance of the reason for the proceedings, the Inquisitors would ask such leading questions as would indicate to him the nature of the charges. After a generally lengthy trial, the judgment of the court would be handed down.

The members of the Inquisitorial tribunal usually undertook a thorough investigation of the charges leveled against the accused. In order to sustain a charge, it was first necessary to establish whether the slave had been baptized and confirmed. The judges also tended

[12] Henry C. Lea, *A History of the Inquisition of Spain*, New York, 1908, IV, 328.
[13] Richard E. Greenleaf, *Zumárraga and the Mexican Inquisition, 1536-43*, Washington, 1961, p. 100.

314

to ask whether the accused went to confession and received communion at the times appointed by the church. All those who gave evidence against the slave would be required to give their opinion of the accused as a Christian, to comment on his character, and also to mention what they thought of the slave as a person after he had blasphemed. In addition, such witnesses would be asked whether the slave was sober when he renounced God.

The Inquisition imposed stringent punishments on those found guilty of blasphemy. Such slaves would generally receive between one hundred and two hundred lashes, publicly administered. In addition, they would be exposed to public humiliation and their offense announced to the populace. A typical punishment would read: "We order that in the chapel of this Holy Office he hears mass, praying without a ribbon or hat, with a wax candle in his hands and a rope tied to his neck and a gag in his mouth . . . that he be taken through the public streets of this city upon a beast of burden naked to the waist, with the rope and the gag and with the voice of the crier making his offence known." [14] In certain instances, the Inquisition would order that the slave be kept in chains for up to a period of a year. For habitual blasphemers, the penalty was exile.

Most slaves uttered blasphemous words while they were being whipped by their masters. One slave blasphemed when his head had been cut in three places while being beaten.[15] Another slave renounced God while she was about to be branded.[16] A third slave renounced God when her master tied her while she was nude and then began to beat her cruelly and squeeze her flesh with a pair of pincers.[17] A male slave blasphemed after he had been tortured by his master for an entire night.[18] The chronicle of similar reasons for blasphemous acts is endless. Yet, the Inquisition seemed not to have been concerned at the violence which directly contributed to these religious offenses.

A closer examination of some of these cases will illustrate the circumstances that led the slaves to blaspheme. In 1603, for example, Jerónimo Ambrosio, a Mulatto slave of Luis de Dueñas of Mexico City, was denounced for blasphemy. It transpired that one night his master punished him by putting him in a pit in the *obraje* he owned. Finding this kind of torture unbearable, the slave renounced God,

---

[14] Mexico, *Archivo General de la Nación*, Ramo de Inquisición, hereafter referred to as *A. G. N. Inquisición*, vol. 288, fols. 224-246; vols. 145, 148, 275.
[15] *Ibid.*, vol. 256, no. 15.
[16] *Ibid.*, vol. 271, no. 6.
[17] *Ibid.*, vol. 148, no. 4.
[18] *Ibid.*, vol. 142, no. 7.

the Virgin Mary, and the saints. As a result, he was denounced to the Holy Office by his master and by several witnesses who had heard the renunciation. Brought up before the tribunal, the slave at first denied the offense, but later admitted that he had committed it.[19]

The witnesses who gave evidence against the slave all agreed that he was sober when he blasphemed. In his turn, Ambrosio said that he was a Christian, baptized, and confirmed, and that he received Holy Communion on those occasions ordered by the church. Under the observation of the tribunal, he made the sign of the cross, repeated the Pater Noster, Ave Maria, Credo, Salve Regina, and the Ten Commandments. According to the record of the proceedings, these were all "well said." [20]

For his offense, the slave received a severe punishment. The court ordered that he be given two hundred lashes in addition to a public humiliation and penance. His master was required to keep him in chains for a period of one year.[21]

Another case of blasphemy involved a slave, Juan, who renounced God after he had been beaten and locked in a room late at night by his master. His accusers declared that he was sober when he committed the offense. In addition, he was a "bad Negro who was a thief and drunkard." [22] They felt that he was "a bad Christian" for having renounced God.[23]

When he gave evidence, Juan declared that he was a Christian, baptized, and confirmed. He also recited correctly all the various prayers that the Inquisitors asked him to repeat. Pleading that the offense occurred while he was under the influence of alcohol, Juan begged the tribunal for mercy. The court considered the case, found him guilty, ordered that he be publicly humiliated and do penance for his acts. In addition, he should receive one hundred lashes and should be kept in chains by his master for a period of six months.[24]

In 1610, Juan, a slave of Luis de Villanueva Zapata of Mexico City, appeared as the defendant in a blasphemy case. It turned out that the slave had renounced God after he had received between thirty and forty lashes from his master. The slave in question was sixteen years old and had been born in New Spain.[25]

When Juan testified, he too, admitted that he was a Christian, bap-

---

[19] *Ibid.*, vol. 172, fols. 1-22.
[20] *Ibid.*
[21] *Ibid.*
[22] *Ibid.*, vol. 139, fols. 139-162.
[23] *Ibid.*
[24] *Ibid.*
[25] *Ibid.*, vol. 288, fols. 224-247.

tized, and confirmed. He repeated the usual prayers but said he was still in the process of learning the Ten Commandments. He stoutly denied, however, that he had ever blasphemed while he was being punished. After several audiences with the tribunal, the slave boy eventually broke down and confessed that he had blasphemed, but only because he thought this would free him from his master's punishment. He immediately repented his offense and threw himself upon the mercy of the court.[26]

After due deliberation, the Holy Office found him guilty and pronounced sentence. He was required to do penance and to undergo public humiliation in the usual way. Furthermore, he would be given one hundred lashes. According to the record, these punishments were duly administered.[27]

It would be tedious to enumerate any more of these cases. They all followed the familiar pattern of blasphemy, usually during a period of stress, denunciation, trial, and punishment. The Holy Office, despite its ardor, was never able to eradicate the high incidence of blasphemy among the slaves. For the act of blasphemy was but one manifestation not only of the nature of slave religion but also of the nature of slavery in Mexico.

There are three general conclusions which can be drawn from blasphemous acts by the slaves. In the first place, and on a superficial level, blasphemy appeared to be the instinctive reaction by a slave to a situation which he found unpalatable. In this sense, he was no different from the ordinary Spaniard who used blasphemous words as a matter of course. According to Henry C. Lea, the Spaniard employed a number of expressions "which seem to have been in the mouth of everyone, ineradicable by the most severe legislation, such as 'Mal grado aya Dios' ('May it spite God'), 'Pese a Dios' ('May God regret'), 'Reniego a Dios' ('I renounce God'), 'Descreo de Dios' ('I disbelieve in God'). . . ."[28] Since the slave in Mexico acquired his basic vocabulary from the Spaniard, he could hardly avoid learning the profane as well.

The blasphemous acts of the slaves also indicated the nature of the slave system in Mexico. Slaves blasphemed while they were being beaten and tortured, and the frequency with which blasphemy cases were tried reflected the fact that such punishments were a normal feature of the slaves' existence. The slave girl who cried "I renounce God and his saints, I only need a knife to kill myself," while she

[26] *Ibid.*
[27] *Ibid.*
[28] Lea, IV, 331.

was being beaten, was probably articulating the mood of her peers.[29] By severely punishing offenders, the Holy Office ignored the conditions which produced such expletives by the slaves. If the Inquisition had actively pursued those masters whose violence provoked the slaves to blaspheme, it might have rendered such slaves a humanitarian service.

In a deeper sense, the incidence of blasphemy probably reflected the existence of a type of folk Catholicism among the slave population. There is, for example, some resemblance between the blasphemy of the slaves and one form of the Ashanti oath. In this instance, according to Busia, "a man might swear an oath to prevent another from doing him bodily harm." [30] It is likely that the renunciation of God by the slave probably was intended to have a similar restraining effect on the person who was performing the whipping. If this was the intention, it invariably had the desired effect since the beating would cease and the slave would be denounced before the Holy Office. By blaspheming, the slave was probably appealing to the Inquisition to adjudicate the dispute between himself and his master as was the case with the Ashanti where "the oath was used to secure the backing of the central authority in the settlement of the issue involved." [31]

It is also conceivable that the slaves may have established with the Christian God the same dependent relationship which characterised his association with his master. The findings of Emanuel DeKadt for contemporary Brazil that "the key concepts of folk Catholicism [promise, protection, request, miracle and the showing of respect] are very nearly identical to the key concepts operating in the socio-political sphere" may have some applicability to the master-slave relationship and to slave religion in colonial Mexico.[32] In other words, the slave may have conferred on the Christian God the same qualities that he gave to his master. Thus, the God who failed to offer "protection" or to work "a miracle" when the situation demanded it was not playing the role ascribed to him and so could be renounced. It could have been this thinking which allowed one slave girl to lament while she was being whipped that "God is worth nothing to me; I

[29] A. G. N. Inquisición, vol. 291, no. 1.

[30] I am indebted to Professor Philip Curtin for suggesting a possible similarity between the two phenomena. See K. A. Busia, The Position of the Chief in the Modern Political System of Ashanti, Oxford, 1958, p. 78.

[31] Ibid.

[32] Emanuel De Kadt, "Religion, the Church, and Social Change in Brazil," in Claudio Veliz, ed., The Politics of Conformity in Latin America, Oxford, 1969, p. 196.

renounce God." [33] These conclusions, of course, are all speculative. It is quite tempting, however, to dismiss these blasphemous acts of the slaves as simply irrational behavior. Such may well have been the case but this does not appear to be a sufficiently adequate explanation for so widespread a phenomenon.

The slaves' practice of a number of folk beliefs also engaged the vigorous attention of the Holy Office. The Inquisition characterized such practices as either witchcraft, divination, or sorcery. It is obvious from an examination of the records, however, that the Holy Office misunderstood the nature of some of these beliefs and practices. In addition, some of the records also demonstrate the degree of religious syncretism in the slave population.

In attempting to understand these practices of the African slave, terminology is of utmost importance. There has always been some controversy over whether such practices should be classified as religion or magic. Modern scholars are becoming increasingly convinced that since magic possesses a spiritual character, no distinction can be made between the two phenomena. Geoffrey Parrinder concludes that "the efficacy of magical practices does not merely reside in things done or said, but in the employment of a supernatural agency, a psychic power." [34] Accordingly, some scholars question the continued usage of the term magic since there is no method of determining where magic stops and religion begins.

Perhaps, if any distinction can be made between magic and religion, that distinction should ultimately depend on the beliefs of the practitioner. If the individual believed that he benefited from some power inherent in the object he used, then that could be considered magic. On the other hand, if the practitioner believed that the object was devoid of any inherent power, but derived its efficacy from God, then that would constitute a religious belief. It is not possible for the historian who uses the records of the Holy Office of the Inquisition to determine the extent to which the slaves appreciated these distinctions. Yet, a study of the literature on African traditional religions would lead one to conclude that the belief in the mystical power of a God as manifested through certain objects was so generalized that one can characterize the slaves' beliefs as religious rather than magical.

The practice of "witchcraft" was one of the more frequent offenses of the slaves. To the Inquisition in Spain, a witch was a woman who "has abandoned Christianity, has renounced her baptism, has wor-

[33] A. G. N. Inquisición, vol. 274, no. 3.
[34] Geoffrey Parrinder, *African Traditional Religion*, London, 1962, p. 26.

shipped Satan as her God, has surrendered herself to him, body and soul, and exists only to be his instrument in working the evil to her fellow creatures, which he cannot accomplish without a human agent." [35] In view of the number of slaves who were accused of this practice in Mexico, and in view of the nature of their alleged spells, the preceding definition of witchcraft was obviously given a very broad interpretation in that colony.

The definition of witchcraft has, of course, changed over the years. A witch today is "one who is believed to harm others mystically and illegitimately by means of psychic emanations from an inherent physiological condition that is transmitted biologically." [36] Whatever definition is used, whether that of the Inquisition or that of the contemporary scholars, the documents consulted for this work make it clear that the slaves were not guilty of witchcraft, but rather, were involved in their own traditional practices or in practices learned from the Indians and the Spanish themselves. Slaves resorted to such practices in order to attract the opposite sex, to ameliorate their master's treatment of them, or to acquire some quality which they did not possess.

There is extensive documentary evidence regarding the use of folk practices by the slaves to further amorous desires. Where physical attraction proved insufficient to win the affections of a certain man or woman, the slave resorted to the supernatural to expedite the process. The belief was widespread that the carrying of certain specified articles on one's person would achieve this desired end. John Mbiti relates that among Africans, "charms, amulets, medicines drunk or rubbed into the body, articles on the roofs or in the fields . . . and many other visible and invisible, secret and open precautions" are used for a variety of purposes. [37] Aguirre Beltrán notes that Spaniards and Indians behaved in a similar fashion in Mexico. [38] Accordingly, among the slaves in Mexico, Agustín carried "an idol," [39] while Mateo carried "a stick." [40] One woman, Lucia, kept "a purse with hair," [41] while another had "a dead bird and red silk, some fragrant things and herbs." [42]

---

[35] Lea, IV, 206.

[36] See M. Fortes and G. Dieterlen, eds., *African Systems of Thought*, London, 1966, p. 22.

[37] Mbiti, *African Religions*, pp. 262-263.

[38] Aguirre Beltrán, pp. 163-179.

[39] A. G. N. *Inquisición*, vol. 372, no. 14.

[40] *Ibid.*, vol. 380, fols. 302-350.

[41] *Ibid.*, vol. 435, no. 51.

[42] *Ibid.*, vol. 513, no. 34.

Certain objects were more popular than others. Various kinds of herbs were thought to possess extraordinary qualities. If used by the supplicant, they could be expected to relieve his anxieties and help him achieve his objective. One woman named María possessed a herb "that is called *doradilla*." [43] Antonio Pardo received from a friend a certain kind of herb "to give to any woman to make her love him." [44] In order to be efficacious, certain functions would have to be performed by the supplicant. Absolute purity of body was essential. The individual would have to abstain from food for a specified period of time if he wanted a favorable answer. Thus, one woman was advised that if she wanted to win the favors of a certain man, she would have to fast for three Sundays. [45] A male slave was told to fast on the day he gave the magic herb to the woman of his choice. [46] Another slave fasted "one day without eating salt." [47]

A variety of methods could be used to take advantage of these mystical herbs. The victim would sometimes have the powerful charm thrown all over his or her body. If thrown on the victim's clothes, a similar effect would be created. A prospective victim who walked on such herbs would, of course, fall prey to its charms. If taken orally, the herb would be equally effective. One slave advised another that "she should take in her chocolate a little bark from a tree in order that a man may love her better." [48] María, a slave from Cuencamé, "knew a herb . . . which if it is chewed and spat out on the clothes of any man, or when he walks on the floor where it is, . . . although he may not want to see a woman, he would fall in love with her." [49]

There were other herbs which were effective if an unrequited admirer applied them to parts of her body or to the victim's clothes. Such herbs were usually ground to a fine powder. For example, Gabel, a slave, gave to "this informer some powder tied up in a purse and told her that they were effective for by carrying them and rubbing her hands with them, the men will love her." [50] Another slave received a similar powder which would be potent if she applied it to the collar of her husband's shirt. [51] A third slave had some herbs

[43] *Ibid.*, vol. 530, no. 17.
[44] *Ibid.*, vol. 380, fols. 302/354.
[45] *Ibid.*, vol. 685, no. 27.
[46] *Ibid.*, vol. 380, fols. 302/354.
[47] *Ibid.*, vol. 360, fol. 354.
[48] *Ibid.*, vol. 380, fols. 302/354.
[49] *Ibid.*, vol. 356 ii, fol. 352.
[50] *Ibid.*, vol. 363, no. 30.
[51] *Ibid.*, vol. 380, fol. 356.

concealed in her bosom so that "the men would love her well." [52]

There were other objects which were thought to possess super-natural powers. The bones of certain animals, the eyes, feathers, or heads of special birds, if held in one's possession would help one attain certain ends. María had a crow's head and feathers in a box which "was good for making people sleep." [53] Another woman used the eyes of a swallow for a similar purpose. [54] In order to induce sleep in others, a nail driven into a shoe would be efficacious. One slave woman testified that "in order that a person may go out at night, it is good to nail a shoe with a knife under her master's bed in order that they sleep." [55]

A special kind of earth also possessed revered qualities. Earth taken from graveyards and mountains seemed to have played a significant role in the practices of the slaves. It is quite possible that, in the case of earth from the cemetery, the practice was African in origin. For the Africans, in spite of their tribal variations, shared the custom of ancestor worship. Perhaps the efficacy of earth from the cemetery derived from its association with the dead ancestors. Martín, a slave, claimed that "earth from the cemeteries was good to make one sleep whoever had it under his bed." [56] Juana de la Cruz told another woman that "she should take a little stone from a sepulchre and place it under the pillow of her master's bed, for the purpose of going out at night without their knowing it." [57] This preoccupation by the slaves with efforts to induce sleep in their masters reflected their desire for liberty to do whatever they wanted, especially in the nights. On the other hand, it demonstrated the kind of isolated and cloistered existence that masters forced their slaves to lead. The slave attempted, through such practices, to defeat a system which had him totally confined. That he was willing to expose himself to the persecution from the Inquisition testified to the strength of his beliefs.

Earth from the mountains could also be used, especially to induce love in another person. For example, an Angolan slave, Francisco, "gave to this informer some earth which in the mountain he had dug at the foot of a little tree . . . and told this informer that they were good for attracting women." [58] The earth which contained the

[52] *Ibid.*, vol. 292, no. 28.
[53] *Ibid.*, vol. 498, no. 8.
[54] *Ibid.*, vol. 561, no. 1.
[55] *Ibid.*, vol. 360, no. 21.
[56] *Ibid.*
[57] *Ibid.*
[58] *Ibid.*, vol. 363, no. 18.

footprints of a prospective victim could be collected and used against that person. Thus, Antonio advised a woman that by "taking earth from that part of the soil where the man whom this witness desired placed his foot . . . [then] that man would love her and desire her although he may be at the other end of the world." [59] With this kind of claim for the efficacy of such charms, it is no wonder that the slaves experimented with them.

One of the constant preoccupations of the slave was how best to get his master to ameliorate his punishment. A resort to his folk practices was held to be an effective means to this end. Juan Sebastian received from a friend of his "a little rue, onion, and garlic and that taking a little blood from the arm he should mix these things together and he should do this two times in order that his master should treat him well." [60] Similarly, by chewing certain articles, a master could be coerced into selling a slave to a different owner. The slave, Francisco, became ill after he had chewed some roots he received from an elderly black man. Complaining that his master maltreated him, Francisco received from his benefactor "something which he should chew and that mixing it with saliva, he should apply it to his face and that would be enough to make his master hate him and sell him." [61] The result of this was not that the slave obtained his objective, but rather he became so violently ill that he "almost died" and a confessor had to be called. [62] In the end, he appeared before the Holy Office to answer for his crime.

In the event of illness, the slaves would also resort to the use of traditional means to effect a cure. Certain herbs were thought to possess healing qualities. These were generally taken orally. At other times the treatment could be administered externally in the form of an ointment applied to the skin. Often these rites would be accompanied by the recitation of certain charms. The following description of one such ceremony is instructive, for not only does it reveal the type of ritual involved, but it also indicates an interesting admixture of traditional beliefs and Christianity. The accused woman, Ana de Pinto, was denounced by the patient. In his testimony before the Holy Office, the patient declared that

she said to this witness, I will make you well in eight days, and saying this, she took a little bag in which she carried some powder

---

[59] *Ibid.*, vol. 480, fol. 359.
[60] *Ibid.*, vol. 380, fols. 302/337.
[61] *Ibid.*, vol. 376, fol. 87.
[62] *Ibid.*

and asked that they bring her a lighted stove and bowl with a little water to which she added the powder and then she applied it on my right side and on the stomach of this witness, and after having annointed it and bandaged it, she uttered some words naming the Most Holy Trinity, Our Lady and Saint Juana, but in detail I do not remember the words owing to the pain that afflicted me; only that on applying the ointment, she made the sign of the cross above the pain, on the chest, on the forehead and on the ears, and blowing in my mouth she said some words which I was not able to understand, and on the following day she asked whether I would take a certain beverage that she would prescribe, and, replying that there was nothing I would not take in order to regain my health, and the said Mulatto went outside and in the presence of María Palaez, my wife, she ground something in a cup of water and . . . having drunk the water I was intoxicated the entire day and had a severe pain in the stomach . . ., and the following day, Ana de Pinto came, asked for a needle and silk and with her hands sewed upon my shirt above the heart, a small bag she brought, and on it was a cross which appeared to be made of yellow silk, and afterwards she applied the same ointment about six or eight times, always making the sign of the cross, and blowing, and crossing herself, and saying the aforementioned words and, at this time, she sent me from her house a jar of water, saying I have to keep it in the sun and in the night air, and that I was to drink it with the left hand.[63]

Although the Holy Office unleashed its great might against the practitioners of what it considered to be religious deviance, it was fighting a losing battle. For the Inquisition had confused witchcraft with the practice of folk beliefs. The female slave who concealed a certain herb in her bosom in order to attract the attentions of a man was by no means a witch. Unlike witchcraft, which is malevolent, this practice was harmless. The slave was simply acting in the same way her ancestors had done. It is true that she acquired some new practices in Mexico and probably used different herbs, but her faith in the efficacy of these practices never wavered.

As in the case of the practitioners of "witchcraft," sorcerors engaged the attention of the Holy Office. Sorcery, usually defined as the practice of destructive or "black" magic, had been a feature of Spanish as well as of various African societies. The Inquisition undertook, in the

[63] *Ibid.*, vol. 318, fols. 468-471.

fifteenth century, to extirpate its practice in Spain.[64] Consequently, in the New World the Holy Office merely continued its fight against these individuals.

Sorcerors in Mexico, as was customary everywhere, were both hated and feared. They were thought to have made a pact with the devil, an act which gave them unusual power. In order to make themselves known and perhaps to add to their appeal, such individuals had various marks put on their bodies. Juan Andrés had an illustration of "the devil" painted on two parts of his body.[65] Pablo Gómez had "certain figures carved on his stomach and on his back in order to make him brave." [66] Some sorcerors were accused of having the ability to fly. A female slave, Leonora, was denounced for having the power of "flying wherever she wanted." [67]

Sorcerors in Mexico used various animals or articles in the practice of their craft. One slave woman, Francisca,

> had an ointment to smear the joints of the body . . . Then they assembled in a field where the devil appeared in the form of a goat, and while singing and dancing, they were kissing it under the tail . . . and afterwards they returned to wherever they wanted, and being sorcery, they had to give to the devil one finger from the left hand . . . and the devil was marking them with a very faint mark on one eye or on one cheek.[68]

To aid her in her practice, one woman had a snake under her bed.[69] A male slave who had made a pact with the devil with his blood and had promised him his soul had books with devils painted on them.[70]

While the Inquisition pursued such slaves with great ardor, there is no evidence that sorcery actually declined among the black population in New Spain. Slaves probably became only more careful in its practice. As long as the slaves believed that the sorcerors could avenge a wrong or harm an enemy, their services continued to be demanded.

Divination, "the art or practice of foreseeing future events or discovering hidden knowledge through supernatural means," [71] was also

---

[64] For a short discussion of the practice of sorcery in Spain, see Henry Kamen, *The Spanish Inquisition*, New York, 1965, pp. 201-204. For sorcery in Africa, see Parrinder, pp. 116-119.

[65] *A. G. N. Inquisicion*, vol. 636, no. 4.

[66] *Ibid.*

[67] *Ibid.*, vol. 316, fols. 514-521.

[68] *Ibid.*, vol. 342, no. 12.

[69] *Ibid.*, vol. 376, no. 44.

[70] *Ibid.*, vol. 366, no. 43.

[71] See William A. Lessa and Evon Z. Vogt, eds., *A Reader in Comparative Religion*, New York, 1965, p. 299, and Parrinder, pp. 119-122.

prevalent among the slaves. Those slaves who possessed this gift were the objects of respect among their peers. Some diviners claimed that their powers derived from association with saints. One mulatto said he knew about the future from "a saint who is so friendly that he is almost always at my side." [72] Another slave claimed that he was in constant communication with his ancestors "in order to know hidden things and what is going to happen." [73] Because of the dependence on the wisdom of the ancestors in this case, this practice appeared to be African in origin.

A fairly common practice in the art of divination was that of "speaking through the chest." In essence, this was a form of ventriloquism where the diviner carried on a conversation supposedly with a spirit. This also appears to have been an African practice.[74] In his attempt to cure a patient, Francisco Puntilla demonstrated this art. The patient related that

> being sick in the face, they told me to seek aid from a Negro belonging to Cristóbal Martínez called Francisco de Puntilla and the cure that he effected was to wash my face with water and said it was from certain herbs which he carried in two jars of clay, one red and the other dark; and there were some ugly figures of faces engraved in them, and when he washed my face, he was saying: "Wait for me; I will ask if you will get better," and he asked in Spanish and turned my face towards his armpit saying "You must get better, and one heard in that place a shriek like that of a rabbit that it appeared to answer the question, and he stopped and said that I would be cured.[75]

By the use of divination, the slaves and others attempted to discover the identity of wrongdoers, especially thieves. By this method, the location of lost items would also be discovered. The rites of divination were very interesting, both from the point of view of the tools that were used and from the Christian features that they involved. One witness before the Holy Office described the process by which a thief was identified in the following words,

> I saw that between Dona Ruez Gómez de Anzures and Diego Martín, Mulatto slave of Diego Sánchez de Coca, they chose a

---

[72] A. G. N. Inquisición, vol. 471, fol. 148.
[73] Ibid., vol. 828, no. 1.
[74] See Aguirre Beltrán, p. 188.
[75] A. G. N. Inquisición, vol. 278, fol. 243.

small statue of Christ and a sieve, placing it upon the finger of Dona Ruez de Anzures and some large scissors arranged in the form of a cross nailed upon the sieve, and a rosary hanging from the sieve, and the said mulatto questioned thus: "Sieve, tell me for God's sake, and by your faith do not move from side to side nor tell anybody else, but tell us the truth about who committed the crime, if it was Cota de Monzon," but the sieve did not move, and thus interrogating it by calling the names of all those who were in the house until it came to the name of Juan de Vera, and then the sieve shook.[76]

The method of divination could, of course, vary. Each diviner had his own ritual, but most of them possessed a statue of Christ or the Virgin Mary. Perhaps this gave a stamp of authenticity or legitimacy to their practices. On the other hand, it was a very clear manifestation of religious syncretism. Leonora de Sosa described the ritual performed by a slave in Guadalajara in order to discover the whereabouts of his mules in the following way:

I spoke with the said Negro, whose name I do not know, about the missing mules to which he said I need not worry, and the Negro placed two lighted candles in front of an image of Our Lady and a jar of water and with a wand stirring the water he said: "Now your mules have appeared; go to your home, send an Indian and in a clearing he will find them," and I sent the Indian and he found them tied.[77]

Whether contrived or not, the diviners administered to the needs of a grateful population. The diviner calmed their fears in times of stress by providing answers to their problems. In addition, he served a useful function by identifying, whether accurately or not, such wrongdoers as thieves who had incurred the wrath of the group. By isolating offenders, and perhaps making them available for social sanctions, the diviner played a role in the maintenance of social cohesion.

The slave's practice of a form of folk Catholicism as well as the continued vitality of his other folk beliefs and customs manifested his success in maintaining a way of life somewhat different from that of his master. In addition, the resort to his folk practices represented, in part, an attempt to cope with his life situation. Such slaves found solace and security in the observance of such beliefs especially in

---

[76] *Ibid.*, vol. 435, fol. 293.
[77] *Ibid.*, vol. 486, fol. 555.

times of stress and crises. The Holy Office wanted to enforce religious orthodoxy and attempted to eradicate all manifestations of religious deviance and syncretism. But the tribunal was doomed to fail. As long as the belief in the efficacy of such practices continued, the slaves would continue their observance, Inquisitorial persecution notwithstanding.

PART THREE:
THE SLAVE AND FREE PERSON
OF COLOR IN AN
URBAN ENVIRONMENT

XIII

The Free Person of Color in Mexico City
and Lima: Manumission and
Opportunity, 1580-1650

FREDERICK P. BOWSER

THIS STUDY concerns a little-known but important racial component of colonial Spanish America and employs historical evidence which has rarely been used in a systematic fashion. More specifically, this essay attempts to delineate, on the basis of notarial records, certain aspects of the lives of free persons of color in sixteenth and seventeenth century Lima and Mexico City.

First, a consideration of the evidence. Documents prepared by notaries public are the minutiae of history: bills of sale, wills, letters of manumission, apprenticeship and labor contracts, promissory notes, and the like. Taken singly, most such records tell us very little about the individuals involved or the society in which they moved. However, examined in quantity, notarial documents shed much light on the social and economic history of colonial Spanish America; each legal transaction then becomes a tiny fragment of the mosaic of historical reality.[1]

Notarial records are of particular value for the study of the free colored population. Although there is sufficient evidence to indicate that the free black was an important member of colonial society,[2] this racial group excited little interest among those agencies and individuals who generated the documents which have been preserved for our study. Therefore, the historian who attempts a detailed examination of this segment of the population on the basis of the standard range of documentation soon finds himself frustrated. In general, government correspondence mentions the free person of color only intermittently and then usually in the vaguest of terms. Often born

---

[1] See, for example, the brilliant employment of notarial records in James Lockhart, *Spanish Peru, 1532-1560: A Colonial Society*, Madison, Wis., 1968.

[2] My article, "Colonial South America," in David W. Cohen and Jack P. Greene, eds., *Neither Slave Nor Free*, Baltimore, 1972, pp. 19-58, attempts to pull together the evidence in print.

out of wedlock and of mixed blood, the presence of the free person of color was deplored by a home government which, at this date, greatly preferred a colonial society composed of three hierarchically arranged racial groups: whites, browns, and blacks. Illegitimate mixed bloods did not fit readily into this scheme, and it was believed, perhaps with some reason, that their presence encouraged disorder and insurrection among the slave population.[3] When the number of free coloreds became sufficiently large, a development which by chance corresponded more or less precisely with the growing financial needs of the Spanish crown, sporadic and often ineffectual attempts were made to compel the former to pay tribute, in common with the Indian. These efforts generated a certain amount of official correspondence, including financial records, but the imposition of tribute was bitterly resented and often successfully circumvented by flight, "passing," or influence. Therefore, these documents, too, shed little light on the free person of color and, even in a demographic sense, are of marginal utility. The records of the church are scarcely more useful: an occasional lament by a prominent clergyman concerning the manners and morals of the free person of color, the odd report to the home government detailing the organization and financial resources of the religious brotherhoods organized for this group, and the all too rare marriage license which records the vows made by the more respectable free persons of African descent. Beyond these two sources, there are only travelers' accounts. But the majority mention blacks only in passing, lump the free with the slave, and, in most instances, necessarily concentrate upon the surface of things: dress, customs, manners, and the like.[4]

---

[3] Concerning the problem of disorder and insurrection among the colored populations of Peru and Mexico during this period, see D. M. Davidson, "Negro Slave Control and Resistance in Colonial Mexico, 1519-1650," *Hispanic American Historical Review* 46 (1966), 235-253; Carlos Federico Guillot, *Negroes rebeldes y negros cimarrones: Perfil afro-americano en la historia del Nuevo Mundo durante el siglo XVI*, Buenos Aires, 1961; and my recent book, *The African Slave in Colonial Peru, 1524-1650*, Stanford, 1973.

[4] The present writer must acknowledge that these assertions are based upon a detailed examination of the evidence for Peru only. An astute and indefatigable student of the free person of color in Mexico may disprove my contentions, and my own research there has been limited to notarial records. For example, one possibly fruitful line of investigation concerning the Mexican of African descent would be the voluminous records of the Holy Office, still preserved almost intact in the Archivo General de la Nación. Daniel Lockwood, a graduate student of Latin American history at Stanford University, is at present researching this documentation for information concerning free coloreds under my direction. See also Gonzalo Aguirre Beltrán, *Medicina y magia: El proceso de aculturación en la estructura*

For a closer glimpse of the free person of color, the scholar must turn to notarial records. For example, to legally free a slave, letters of manumission or provisions in wills had to be prepared, and from these we may gain some idea of the conditions under which slaves gained their liberty, and of their age and sex. More than one historian has concluded that frequency of manumission has something to do with prevailing economic conditions and their impact on slave prices. Bills of sale found in notarial archives enable us to evaluate this interpretation.[5] In addition, apprenticeship and labor contracts, as well as promissory notes and wills, provide the historian with valuable evidence concerning the economic and social ascent, such as there was, of the free person of color.

Even notarial records, of course, can distort historical reality. For example, in certain contexts the standard legal formulae employed in these documents may well have imposed a spurious Spanish mentality on free coloreds. To consider but one instance, no one in Spanish America made a will without commending their souls to God, and all but the poorest (including free coloreds) specified a sum of money, however modest, to be used for masses for the salvation of their souls. That all were equally devoted to Catholicism is doubtful. Similarly, the wording employed in letters of manumission may cloud the true attitudes held by masters toward the slaves whom they freed; very nearly all such documents mention the "love and good will" which the former bore the latter, even though the conditions of liberation were harsh. Further, many of the poorest of free coloreds probably do not figure in notarial records at all; their business affairs were too modest, and they died intestate. Their lives are lost to us. Nevertheless, notarial records are perhaps more useful than all of the other historical evidence combined in tracing the growth and fortunes of the free

colonial, Mexico, 1963. For Peru, archival riches of this nature are no longer available. All that is left are the summaries of the cases and the decisions handed down by the Holy Office and sent to Spain, housed in the Archivo Histórico Nacional (Madrid) and consulted by the author in 1963-1964. With this exception, it is doubtful that colonial documentation for the two countries is very different in quality, at least as these records concern the free person of color. Extant parish records might also shed additional light on those of African descent, but here, as with tribute, the historian faces the problem of passing. As regards this point, see Magnus Mörner, *Race Mixture in the History of Latin America*, Boston, 1967, pp. 68-70. In addition, a letter of December 19, 1971, from Professor Colin A. Palmer informs me that materials concerning the free colored person are to be found in the *Bienes Nacionales* and *General de Parte* sections of the Mexican National Archive.

[5] For example, see Mörner, pp. 116-117.

333

colored population, and this essay has been written to demonstrate that fact.[6]

This essay rests upon one further assumption: that manumission, in an age when few questioned the morality of slavery, was largely an urban phenomenon.[7] In accordance with the well-known Iberian preference for urban life, in Spanish America rural argriculturalists rarely lived on their estates, did not know their slaves well, and seldom freed them. By and large, rural slaves were in no position to accumulate the money with which to buy their freedom, and, in their isolation and ignorance, most probably did not know that legal avenues to freedom existed. The situation was different in the cities and towns. Above all, urban slavery involved household service and skilled labor: the opportunity to ingratiate oneself with the master, to earn a little money, to gain awareness of the Spanish world and its ways. At least in the sixteenth and seventeenth centuries, when the foundations of the Spanish colonial order were laid, the free colored population found its origin and its base in the urban areas.

To compare the fate of the free person of color in Mexico City and Lima during this period seems logical since the two cities present an interesting combination of similarities and differences. Both were the glittering capitals of viceroyalties which divided Spanish America between them, and centers of commercial and social dominance as well, sustained by the silver from far-away mines. By modern standards, both cities were small in size, but, in a period of sharp native population decline, the demands of their inhabitants for labor and provisions placed a heavy strain on the regions around both capitals and spurred the importation of African slaves to compensate for the shrinking numbers of Indians.

---

[6] The chronological limits of this study were determined by the author's previous research in Peru and by the fact that very few notarial records for Mexico City prior to 1580 have been preserved. Concerning the latter point, see A. Millares Carlo and J. I. Mantecón, "El Archivo de Notarías del Departamento del Distrito Federal," *Revista de Historia de América*, no. 17 (1944), 69-118. In future references, the abbreviation "AGN" will designate this archive. My previous work concerning the free person of color (see above, nn. 2, 3) makes extensive use of Peruvian examples. Therefore, in this essay I use evidence from AGN where possible.

[7] This assumption is justified in greater detail in my essay cited in n. 2. Here I add merely that there were exceptions to this rule. To cite one for Mexico, in 1647 Doña Catalina de Villaseca, the widow of a Mexico City alderman, freed without conditions one Diego Rodríguez, a black of 70-odd years who was then acting as majordomo of a cattle ranch owned by the mistress. In the letter of manumission Doña Catalina praised the long and faithful service of Diego and mentioned that her husband had considered him more as a son than as a slave. AGN, register of Francisco Flores, 15 November, unnumbered fols.

Lima faced the problem of a dependable labor supply first. For reasons which are still unclear, the native population of the Peruvian coast dwindled at a far sharper rate than that of the highlands during the Conquest and the civil wars which followed. For a time, it was possible to commandeer labor from the *sierra* to serve the needs of the capital, but, by the last several decades of the sixteenth century, the steadily shrinking Indian population of the highlands could supply very little manpower for the coast. As a result, the importation of Africans increased, and slave prices remained steady from 1580 to 1650, indicating a continuing demand for blacks (see Figures 1 and 2). By 1636, the inhabitants of Lima numbered 27,394, of whom 14,481 were blacks and mulattoes, and reliance on forced Indian labor had shrunk to negligible proportions.[8]

The case of Mexico City is more complex.[9] The capital of the Mexican viceroyalty was surrounded by a relatively dense, if declining, Indian population, one which was made to serve the Spanish first through the forced labor (*repartimiento*) system and, beginning in the early decades of the seventeenth century, more and more through debt peonage and sheer economic necessity. But native labor was not enough. Available demographic data for Mexico City, crude but consistent, indicates a larger city than Lima, with more Spaniards served by still greater numbers of blacks and mulattoes. Further, the Mexican Venice faced a problem which rainless Lima did not: drainage. The Spaniards drastically modified the drainage system of the Aztecs without substituting an adequate one of their own, and this negligence, combined with a prodigal disregard of the erosion caused by the cutting of the surrounding forest, produced intermittent but disastrous flooding of the capital in the seventeenth century. The worst years were 1604, 1607, and 1629. These floods forced the initiation of a massive project, the *Desagüe General*, to cut a tunnel through the mountains at the northwestern corner of the Valley and thereby drain off the excess water at critical periods of high rainfall. Work on the project continued throughout the colonial period, absorbing large amounts of scarce native labor, and the effect, as Figures 1 and 2 demonstrate, was to keep the demand for African

[8] These trends are explored in greater detail in my book cited in n. 3. The 1636 population figures for Lima are to be found in a letter of April 29 to the crown from the archbishop in Archivo General de Indias (Seville), Lima 47. The name of this archive will hereafter be abbreviated as AGI.

[9] The discussion of Mexico City which follows is based on Charles Gibson, *The Aztecs Under Spanish Rule: A History of the Indians of the Valley of Mexico, 1519-1810*, Stanford, 1964, esp. pp. 220-256, 377-381.

335

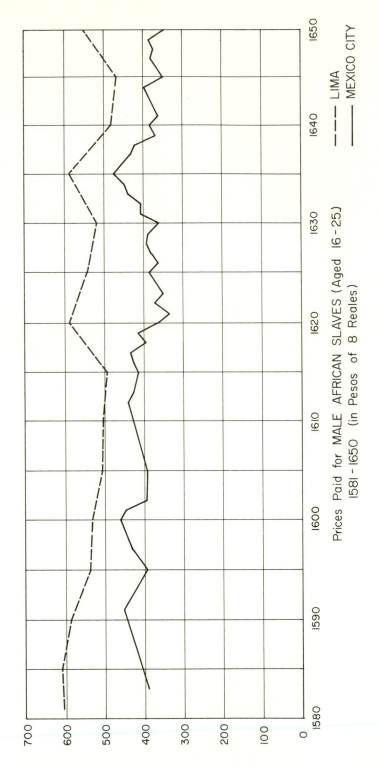

Prices Paid for MALE AFRICAN SLAVES (Aged 16-25)
1581-1650 (in Pesos of 8 Reales)

------ LIMA
—— MEXICO CITY

Figure 1

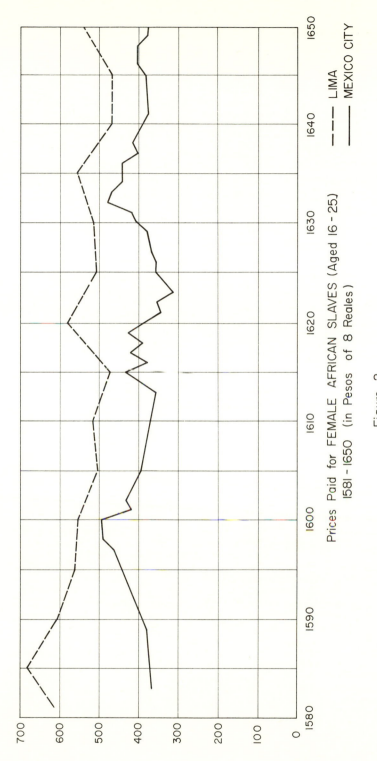

Prices Paid for FEMALE AFRICAN SLAVES (Aged 16 - 25)
1581 - 1650 (in Pesos of 8 Reales)

——— LIMA
——— MEXICO CITY

Figure 2

slaves at high levels, at least until 1650. To be sure, prices paid for slaves in Mexico City were consistently lower than those which prevailed in Lima at the same time, but higher transportation costs to Peru largely explain this difference. However rough the transit from Veracruz to Mexico City, it did not compare with the time and expense involved in freighting slaves from the Caribbean port of Cartagena down the Pacific coast to Lima.[10]

Within this context of tight labor supply, high slave prices, and (at least in Mexico) general economic distress,[11] slaves managed to obtain their freedom, and free persons of color slowly increased in numbers. Of course, free blacks and mulattoes were to be found in both capitals from the earliest days of the conquest. Some came from Spain as part of the entourage which surrounded all prominent conquistadores and high government officials. Others, who arrived as slaves, distinguished themselves through military prowess and profited by the free-and-easy atmosphere of the conquest period to gain their freedom. In addition, more than one conquistador freed his slaves for faithful service during the exertions of the conquest period.[12] The free person of color was considered a serious problem in Lima as early as 1538, and in 1560 the number of mulattoes in Mexico City, most presumably free, was set at 1,000.[13]

By 1580, however, the exuberance and liberality of the conquest period had given way to the hard task of building a society in America. Traditional attitudes and principles came to the fore, and the

[10] I discuss the operation of the Peruvian slave trade from Cartagena to Lima in my book cited in n. 3. For Mexico, see the following works by Gonzalo Aguirre Beltrán, *La población negra de México, 1519-1810*, Mexico, 1946, and "The Slave Trade in Mexico," *Hispanic American Historical Review* 24 (1944), 412-431. Two additional points must be mentioned. First, the graph of Mexico City slave prices before 1615 is based on fragmentary data and should be regarded as only the crudest indication of reality. Second, Oriental slaves obtained via trade with Manila were present in both cities, but notarial evidence indicates that their numbers were far greater in Mexico City, and this fact no doubt also served to depress prices paid for African slaves. Concerning this trade, see William Lytle Schurz, *The Manila Galleon*, New York, 1939.

[11] For Mexico, the classic statement of the economic consequences of native population decline is Woodrow Borah, *New Spain's Century of Depression*, Berkeley, 1951, which should now be supplemented by the appropriate sections of Gibson, *Aztecs*, and J. H. Parry, *The Spanish Seaborne Empire*, New York, 1966, pp. 213-228. For Peru, the present state of research does not permit generalizations concerning the extent to which demographic decline adversely affected the Spanish colonial economy.

[12] For additional details, see my essay cited in n. 2.

[13] Lockhart, p. 191; Gibson, p. 380. The figure for Mexico City becomes more impressive when it is realized that the number of Spanish males was estimated at only 8,000 for the same date.

processes of manumission were affected as a matter of course. But in this connection generalization is difficult. The Spanish empire in America was noted for the large body of law which regulated its operation, but this great mass of legislation, far from being a detailed statement of general principles, was, in the words of Magnus Mörner, "a series of administrative decisions arrived at in certain cases and with regard to local jurisdiction." [14] That is, the legal web which bound the lives of slave and free in Mexico City was not necessarily the same as that of Lima.

In general, however, the colonial authorities attempted to govern the American empire in accordance with both Spanish legal principles and legislation, modified when necessary by New World realities. As this effort concerned the colored population, both free and slave, the model was the famous legal codification known as *Las Siete Partidas*, drawn up in the thirteenth century by the order of Alfonso the Wise.[15] As David Brion Davis has observed, the *Partidas* is "a body of ideal law . . . (which) had little relation to the living law of Castille." [16] In other words, we deal with a statement of legal and moral principles and not with a compilation of specific legislation which could be taken from the *Partidas* and automatically be applied to America. Nevertheless, the principles embodied in this compilation, although sometimes mocked by colonial conditions, guided Spanish lawmakers in their task and therefore deserve consideration.

Those who compiled the *Partidas* viewed liberty as one of the greatest of human possessions and regarded slavery as a necessary evil, as a transitory condition which did not alter or diminish the nature of the person in bondage. Further, the compilation declared freedom to be a legitimate goal for the slave, and stated that society should do its part by sanctioning such means as manumission by the master, liberation by a third person, and self-purchase with gift money.[17] Specific legislation attempted to implement these precepts. In a 1540 decree addressed to the *audiencias* of Spanish America, the crown commanded that if black slaves "should publicly demand their liberty, they should be heard, and justice done to them, and care be taken that they should not on that account . . . be maltreated by

[14] Mörner, p. 35.
[15] *Las Siete Partidas del Rey Don Alfonso el Sabio cotejadas con varios códices antiguos por la Real Academia de la Historia*, 3 vols., Madrid, 1807.
[16] *The Problem of Slavery in Western Culture*, Ithaca, N.Y., 1966, p. 103.
[17] *Las Siete Partidas*, Partida III, título ii, ley 8; título v, ley 4; título xiv, ley 5; título xxxiii, regla 1; Partida IV, título v, prólogo; título xxi, ley 1; título xxii, ley 1; título xxii, ley 13.

their Masters." [18] It is doubtful if many slaves obtained their freedom in this fashion, although the immorality of the African slave trade outraged an occasional brave churchman. Moreover, there were many repressive features in the body of legislation which the crown and various agencies of local government slowly framed to govern and protect the slave. Nevertheless, the strictures of the *Partidas* were not only adhered to but even expanded to favor the achievement of free status. Specifically, as the institution of slavery evolved in Spanish America, the paths to freedom became three: manumission by the master, various forms of purchase, and (indirectly) the continuing process of racial mixture. We will examine each of these means in turn as they operated in Lima and Mexico City during the period under study.

Voluntary manumission by the master was a fixture of slavery until its abolition, and was usually granted as a reward for long and faithful service or perhaps out of simple love and charity. In its simplest form, the slave was freed in the master's last will and testament, or perhaps in a letter of manumission while the latter was still living. For example, in 1623 Francisca de San Gerónimo, a nun in the Mexico City convent of San Gerónimo, freed Ana Bañol (aged 60) in return for the long years during which Ana had served both Francisca and her parents.[19] Juan del Corral, a prominent builder in early seventeenth century Lima, liberated his slave Luisa Berbesi by testament in gratitude for the "fidelity and love" with which she had nursed him through various severe illnesses.[20] In another instance, Dominga Conga, aged forty-five, was freed by her mistress "for the service of God" (a phrase frequently employed in such documents), for her faithful service, and for the fact that she had successfully reared five children.[21] There were other variations: slave children, for example, might be liberated while the parents remained in bondage.[22]

---

[18] I use the translation of Sir Arthur Helps, *The Spanish Conquest in America and its Relation to the History of Slavery and to the Government of Colonies,* 2d ed., 4 vols., London & New York, 1900, iv, 250.

[19] AGN, register of Andrés Moreno, 13 November, fol. 403.

[20] The will, dated in 1611, is printed in Emilio Harth-terré and Alberto Márquez Abanto, "El puente de piedra de Lima," *Revista del Archivo Nacional del Perú* 24 (1960), 55-74.

[21] Archivo Nacional del Perú, Sección Notarial (hereafter ANP, SN), register of Cristóbal de Pineda (1620), 1 August, fols. 245-246.

[22] For example, in 1626 and 1630, Mariana de Montesdoca (a woman who suffered from both poor health and limited means) freed the mulatto children of her female slave Francisca de Santiago to express gratitude for the latter's services. Clearly, however, Francisca herself, the only support her mistress had, was too valuable to manumit. AGN, register of Pedro de Santillan (1635), statement of

Were a slave owned by both husband and wife, voluntary manumission was sometimes accomplished by stages. In 1599, for example, Doña Francisca de Esquivel freed Leonor Negra in her will, bequeathed her fifty *pesos*, and was careful to mention that her husband had relinquished half-interest in the slave on his death several years before.[23]

It must also be observed that manumission was not an act of generosity to aged and infirm blacks, perhaps no longer fit for service, but with no one but their owners to fall back on for support. Selfish masters, to avoid the cost of supporting such slaves, occasionally freed them, but such motives were rarely stated, and the frequency of such cases is therefore very hard to determine. Here we cite one reasonably clear-cut example: that of Diego de Aranda, a *mulato* in his forties when his master died in 1643. The executor of the estate, on behalf of the minor heirs, soon petitioned the authorities for permission to free Diego, claiming that the latter "for a long time" had been crippled and unable to move, rendering him unfit for service and a burden on the modest resources of his new masters. In addition, it was observed that Aranda's free *mulata* wife had offered fifty *pesos* toward his liberation. The request of the executor was granted.[24]

On the other hand, many masters freed slaves in their wills with selectivity, and this practive may indicate a realization that liberty was a cruel illusion for aged and helpless slaves. Indeed, some slaveholders were explicit concerning this point. For example, Doña Melchora de Guzmán provided in her 1614 will that Cristina Bran, a slave of advanced years who had reared her two sons, was to live with the latter as long as they maintained a joint residence and was not to be sold under any circumstances. In the event her two children ever decided to live apart, Cristina was to be free, no doubt

---

March 14 which confirmed the two manumissions, fols. 24v-25v. In a much more rare case of 1633, the mistress of Manuela Negra (aged 30) provided in her will that Manuela might be freed on her death, or the latter could choose to liberate instead one of her two slave children. AGN, register of Juan de Ovieda Valdivieso, 8 July, fols. 301v-304v.

[23] AGN, register of Juan de Porras, 20 November, fols. 55-59.

[24] AGN, register of Juan Santos de Rivera, letter of manumission of 13 November and related documents, fols. 284v-288v. In another example of this practice, in 1638 the executors of the estate of one Diego de Sousa declared that among the deceased's worldly possessions was Isabel Negra, described as "old, sick in her bed, and crippled." Sousa had left Isabel 100 *pesos* to aid her in the purchase of freedom, and, since no buyer could be found for the black, the executors accepted the money and signed a letter of manumission. The fate of Isabel is unknown. AGN, register of Gabriel López Haedo, 27 February, fols. 27-28.

with the hope that one of her former masters would take her in.[25] Other slaveholders near death were equally scrupulous concerning the welfare of infant slaves, who likewise would have found a simple declaration of freedom a hardship. In 1640, Martín de Ribadeneira, a free black citizen of Lima, provided that his slave Miguel (aged 10) serve his wife for an additional decade, after which he was to be free. To take an example for Mexico City, in 1615 Andrés de Villegas, a clothier, willed his slave Magdalena Mulata (then aged 7) to serve the poorest nunnery in the capital for twelve years; at the end of that period, the executors of his estate were instructed to grant her a letter of manumission.[26]

In other instances, voluntary manumission might be hedged about with conditions prompted by the master's piety, his desire to ensure his own spiritual salvation, or his wish to protect the economic welfare of relatives and friends. Adult slaves, for instance, might be willed to serve religious institutions for a period of years before liberation.[27] Or, to cite another example, in 1620 Leonor Jiménez freed Guiomar Negra (aged 60 or more) on condition that the latter turn over to her executors the sum of one-half *peso* a week, to be spent for a mass for Leonor's soul.[28] In a 1597 codicil to her will, Doña Isabel de Luján freed two of her six slaves unconditionally, but three others were to serve her sister for periods which ranged from three to twenty years before liberation, and yet another was willed to a nephew for two years of service prior to manumission.[29] Very rarely, slaves were liberated on condition that they advance the future of their own kind. María de Jesús, for example, was emancipated by her master in his will on condition that for the next four

[25] AGN, register of Juan Pérez de Rivera, 15 September, fols. 57-62. For another example, in 1646 the master of a black woman named Valentina de Morales (aged 40) freed her in his will and bequeathed the usage of a house in Mexico City until her death. AGN, register of Diego de los Ríos, 29 October, fols. 68r-73r.
[26] In the order of mention: ANP, SN, register of Antonio de Tamayo (1640), 10 November, fols. 915v-917v; AGN, register of Pedro de Santillán (1635), 24 December, fol. 259. In fact, Magdalena served the nunnery for sixteen years instead of twelve, and did not ask for legal proof of her liberty until the above date, when she planned to leave Mexico City for Zacatecas.
[27] See, for example, AGN, register of Juan de Oviedo Valdivieso (1636), 27 March, fols. 189r-196r.
[28] AGN, register of Andrés Moreno, will of 9 September, fols. 290v-292v.
[29] AGN, above notary, January 16, fols. 104r-109r. Occasionally, such testamentary provisions were waived by the heirs in exchange for money. For example, in 1613 Doña Maria de Castañeda willed Juana Negra to her daughter for nine years, after which the slave was to be free, but the executor of the estate liberated Juana instead in return for 300 *pesos*. For both the will and the letter of manumission, see AGN, register of Juan Pérez de Rivera (1614), fols. 16r-22r.

years she pay one *peso* a week to the executors of his estate. This sum was to provide a dowry for still another slave, Isabel de Jesús, at the time in the service of the convent of San Gerónimo in Mexico City, and freed in the same testament.[30]

In many cases, it must have been difficult for masters to strike a balance between sentiment and economic interest. In her will of 1643, for example, Doña María de Castilla Altamirano freed one Luis Mulatto in gratitude for the "many good works" performed by his ex-slave mother, Juana Negra. Doña María was at pains to mention that Juana "nursed me at her breasts along with the said Luis," but she nevertheless provided that the slave must serve her children for four years before manumission.[31] Other masters were less sentimental. Some slaves were freed, for example, on condition that they continue to work for their former owners for a certain period of time each day, or a black held by a partnership might become, say, one-third free upon manumission by one of the partners, thereafter dividing his time between his own occupations and continuing service to the partnership.[32] Further, intelligent and restless slaves might be placated by the promise of freedom contingent upon a continued period of service. In 1605, for example, María de Cevallos, a slave born in Lima, was freed by her master on condition that she serve him for an additional four years. In other instances, letters of manumission were granted to take effect on the master's death. Such were the intentions of Juan Fresco, resident in Mexico City and about to begin the long journey to New Mexico in 1625. In his letter of manumission, Fresco praised the fidelity of his female slave, expressed the hope that she would behave in the same fashion on the trip, and promised liberation as a reward once he should die.[33]

With regard to the purchase of freedom, Spanish American practice was more liberal than that envisioned by the *Partidas.* The latter compilation sanctioned the use of gift money to purchase liberty, but, unlike the Roman tradition, slaves were forbidden to own property

---

[30] AGN, register of Diego de Los Ríos (1643), 23 December, fols. 72r-77r.

[31] AGN, register of Juan de Barrientos, 30 April, fols. 216v-224r. Doña Maria also willed 100 *pesos* to one Francisco de Losa, a free mulatto, "in order that he clothe himself because he brought me up and he has served me during my illnesses and for the love and good will that I bear him."

[32] See Emilio Harth-terré and Alberto Márquez Abanto, "El artesano negro en la arquitectura virreinal limeña," *Revista del Archivo Nacional del Perú* 25 (1961), 27-31, for the details of these examples.

[33] In the order of mention: ANP, SN, register of Juan de Altamirano, 15 July, fols. 561v-563v; AGN, register of Andres Moreno, 3 July, fols. 136r-137r.

(*peculium*).³⁴ In America, however, the crown restored the slave's right to *peculium*, although it is not certain that the decision was a conscious one. In any event, in 1526 royal officials were asked if it would be feasible to establish a scale of prices, depending on the slave's age and condition, which, if raised and paid by the black to his master, would entitle him to freedom.³⁵ The crown may well have had nothing more than gift money in mind, and certainly such price scales were never established for the empire as a whole, but it was not long before the custom of liberation-by-purchase took hold.

During the period under study here, such arrangements were individualistic, informal, and dependent upon the generosity and good will of the master. Available evidence indicates that slaveholders were under no legal obligation to liberate their charges in exchange for payment, although, as reflected in the *Partidas*, there was considerable moral pressure to do so. Ordinarily, provisions for purchase of freedom were made in two ways. First, master and slave might agree on the latter's worth, perhaps with the aid of an appraisal by a disinterested third party, and the slaveholder then swore not only to free the black if this sum were paid but also to never sell the slave for more than this amount. All subsequent buyers of the black were then obliged to agree to these conditions.³⁶ Other masters chose to grant their slaves this privilege in their wills. For example, Isabel Álvarez provided in her will that Catalina Negra might purchase her freedom for the sum of 200 *pesos*, payable to the executor of her estate, and in the interval she was to serve a friend of the deceased.³⁷ Even more generous terms were granted on occasion. In 1619, for

³⁴ *Las Siete Partidas*, Partida III, título ii, ley 8; título xxix, ley 3; Partida IV, título xxi, ley 7; Partida V, título v, ley 45.
³⁵ Richard Konetzke, ed., *Colección de documentos para la historia de la formación social de Hispanoamérica, 1493-1810*, 3 vols. in 5, Madrid, 1953-1962, I, 88.
³⁶ For example, on 14 March 1616 the slave Mencia Mulata was purchased for 250 *pesos* with the proviso that she was to be liberated when this sum was paid to her new master. Mencia managed to raise the amount by 3 December of the same year (AGN, register of José de la Cruz, fols. 244r-245r). However, many slaves paid off their purchase price more slowly in small installments. In her will of 12 May 1645, for example, Catalina Ortíz de Arri mentioned that she had agreed earlier to free two of her female slaves for 350 and 400 *pesos* respectively. The first had paid all but some 53 *pesos* of this amount while the second (mother of the first) still owed 115. Catalina reminded the executors of her estate that letters of manumission were to be granted when these sums were paid, and it is known that the second slave completed payment some three years later. AGN, registers of Diego de los Rios (1645), fols. 38-40; (1648), fol. 5.
³⁷ AGN, register of José de la Cruz (1623), 2 June, fols. 93r-96r. The *mulata* daughter of Catalina (aged 18) was freed in the same will on condition that she pay for a mass per week for the soul of her dead mistress, and was consigned to the care of the same friend.

example, a *mulata* named Ursula de Vergara, whose age is not recorded, was sold in Lima for 270 *pesos* on condition that she was to be free if this sum were paid and with the further proviso that the amount was to be reduced by 25 *pesos* for each year of service. A year later, her free mulatto mother persuaded a Spaniard to loan her the requisite amount.[38]

The last example underlines an obvious fact. A slave's right to purchase freedom would have been meaningless without gift money, loans, or the willingness of the master to allow the black a certain amount of free time to accumulate the sum. Fortunately, a considerable amount of charity prevailed in both capitals. For one thing, free persons of color endured what must have been considerable sacrifices to liberate family and friends. For example, the free black woman Ana Hernández stated in her will of 1593 that she had freed her husband, Cristóbal Negro, with her earnings, although perhaps the frankness which often comes with approaching death also led her to declare, with some acidity, that her worldly possessions had suffered as a result of the marriage.[39] In 1618, María Andrada (African-born but free) left the entire proceeds from her modest estate to her godchild, a slave of the dean of the Mexico City Cathedral, in order that he might purchase his freedom.[40] Children were among the chief beneficiaries of all forms of liberation, as we shall have occasion to observe later in more detail, and in this process free persons of color played an important role. To choose but one example among many, Gerónima de Otalora, a free *mulata*, in 1615 paid some 150 *pesos* to liberate Isabel Mulata, one year of age and the slave of Cristóbal de Molina. The mother of Isabel was likewise a slave of Molina and remained in bondage; the relationship between the child and her benefactress was not recorded.[41]

Persons of color, whether free or slave, were often able to borrow the money necessary for liberation. In 1622, for example, María Bran, the widowed slave of an architect resident in Mexico City, borrowed "from various persons" the sum required to free Melchor Hernández, her son of fourteen years and slave of the same master. In 1637, Beatriz de Mayorga, a free black woman, obtained a loan from a

---

[38] ANP, SN, register of Francisco González Balcázar (1620), letter of manumission dated 21 January, fols. 88v-90v. The mother had approved and signed the sale contract of 1619.

[39] AGN, register of Andrés Moreno, 20 July, fols. 38-39. Ana, who owned two slaves in her own right, relinquished her interest in a third, and provided for his freedom if he would pay her husband half of his current value.

[40] AGN, register of Alonso de Santillán, 3 December, fols. 724-725.

[41] AGN, register of above notary, 15 July, fol. 350.

345

Spanish patron to free her muleteer husband.[42] Regrettably, such transactions do not reveal the motives of the patrons. That is, were these sums advanced out of nothing more than kindness and charity, or was the intention to ensnare the newly liberated, through debt, into a more subtle form of bondage? Lacking firm evidence, the historian can do no more than suggest that, as in most human affairs, good and evil were both present.

In other instances, slaves were allowed a certain amount of free time, or permitted to apply a portion of their wages toward the purchase of freedom. To take an example from seventeenth century Lima, Gaspar Mandinga, by the terms of his master's will, was required to work three days a week on the estate of the heirs, but the rest of his time was his own, and he eventually accumulated the 200 *pesos* necessary for liberation.[43] For Mexico City, we may cite the 1636 case of Domingo Criollo, permitted by the testament of his deceased masters to buy his freedom for the same amount. But Domingo's savings totaled only some 87 *pesos,* and therefore the executor of the estate agreed to hire him out for 4 *pesos* per month. Of this salary, Domingo was to keep half with which to clothe himself, the other half was to go to the executor and apply toward his estimated value, and the employer agreed to provide room, board, and medical care.[44]

Race mixture played an important role in the creation of the free black and mulatto populations of both cities. This development displeased the colonial authorities. As noted before, the intention of the Spanish crown was to populate the American colonies with three distinct racial estates: the European, the Indian, and the African. This policy was endorsed by the church, and reflected the widely held belief that racial mixture produced types who combined the worst defects and vices of both their parents, and, of course, prejudice tended to make this view a self-fulfilling prophecy. Crown and church opposed sexual unions between Africans and Indians with particular zeal. It was feared that the African would reinforce the Indian's attachment to paganism and perhaps even infect him with the infidelity of Islam. Further, the products of such unions, which usually

[42] In the order of mention: AGN, register of Joseph de la Cruz, 6 April, fols. 80r-81r (in addition to the money, Melchor was required to serve the master for an additional two years); register of Andrés Moreno, 4 July, fols. 143v-145r.

[43] ANP, SN, register of Cristóbal de Arauz (1635), 28 November, fols. 929-933.

[44] AGN, register of Juan Oviedo Valdivieso, 6 July, fols. 407-408. At least in Lima, this practice was fairly common among black artisans. For examples, see Harth-terré and Márquez Abanto, "El artesan negro," *passim.*

involved African men and Indian women, would be free since in law the child acquired the mother's status.[45]

However, all official efforts to prevent racial mixture were to no avail. Spaniard, Indian, and African interacted sexually over the years to produce a bewildering variety of racial mixtures (*castas*),[46] and this development inevitably strengthened the formation of a numerous class of free "blacks." The lot of the Afro-Indian, product as he was of the two most despised racial groups in Spanish America, was frequently unenviable; neither his father nor his mother was able to provide him with many advantages except freedom as he made his way in the larger, and frequently hostile, Spanish urban world.[47] The fate of the mulatto, and of the still lighter products of Afro-Spanish sexual unions, was in many instances somewhat more pleasant. Sexual contact between Spanish men and African women was widespread and persistent throughout the colonial period, and prompted much comment from travelers. Writing of early seventeenth century Peru, one observer noted maliciously that the Spanish males of the colony seemed to favor colored women over their own, and ascribed the tendency to the fact that most of them had been suckled by African wet nurses.[48] Things were no different in Mexico City, at least if we may place any credence at all in the often notoriously prejudiced testimony of Thomas Gage. Speaking of the "tawny young maids" of that viceroyalty's capital, Gage writes that: "The attire of this baser sort of people of blackamoors and mulattoes . . . is so light, and their carriage so enticing, that many Spaniards even of the better sort (who are too too prone to venery) disdain their wives for them." [49]

[45] For Mexico, a useful survey of this problem is provided by Edgar F. Love, "Legal Restrictions on Afro-Indian Relations in Colonial Mexico," *Journal of Negro History* 55 (1970), 131-139.

[46] See, for example, the lists of racial terminology in Mörner, pp. 58-59, and the minute racial and physical discriminations recorded in Gonzalo Aguirre Beltrán, "Races in 17th Century Mexico," *Phylon* 6 (1945), 212-218.

[47] Unfortunately, it is difficult to study the Afro-Indian of Mexico City during this period since such persons, in common with the products of Afro-Spanish sexual unions, were termed "mulattoes." Only in those instances where the racial ancestry is given can the Afro-Indian be singled out. In Lima, on the other hand, the Afro-Indian was labeled as a *zambaigo* in notarial records, a term later shortened to *zambo*.

[48] Very rarely did affairs between Spanish women and African men come to light. For example, see Juan Antonio Suardo, *Diario de Lima,* ed. Rubén Vargas Ugarte, 1936, II, 35-36. An additional example will be discussed below.

[49] In the order of mention: Boleslao Lewin, ed., *Descripción del virreinato del Perú: Crónica inédita de comienzos del siglo XVII*, Rosario, Argentina, 1958, p. 39; J. Eric S. Thompson, ed., *Thomas Gage's Travels in the New World*, Norman, Okla., 1958, p. 68.

Whatever the reason, colored women seem to have held an overpow-ering attraction for the Spanish, and the inevitable result was the creation of a numerous group of Afro-Spaniards.

Such offspring assumed their mother's status, and therefore more often than not were slaves. Indeed, in 1563 even the crown capitu-lated to social reality. In that year, it was decided that Spanish fathers were to be given preference in the sale of any children they had fathered in the wombs of slaves who belonged to another master, provided that the purchase was made for the purpose of liberating these offspring.[50] This decree, of course, did nothing more than sanc-tion a societal practice which dated from the earliest days of the conquest and which continued to the end of slavery in Spanish America. Throughout this period, compassionate Spanish fathers frequently freed their slave children and provided for them. In 1618 in Mexico City, for example, Pedro González (a Spanish swordmaker) purchased for a handsome sum the freedom of his two mulatto daughters, the products of his marriage to a female slave owned by the same master.[51] Other Spanish fathers, while less than candid about the question of parenthood, were not so callous as to evade its responsibilities. In 1600, for example, Melchior de Sintra, a resident of Lima, manumitted María Mulata (aged 5) "for reasons which move me," and still others preferred to remain anonymous.[52] Also frequent were cases which involved Spanish males who purchased infant slaves of no possible utility in the immediate future. In 1619, for example, one Juan Torrejano purchased Isabel Mulata, an infant barely twenty months old, from Pedro Cortés, Marqués del Valle.[53] In this not-un-common instance, the historian can only conclude that Torrejano was the father of the child (or acting as an agent for the male parent), and that possession was desired for liberation at a more discreet time. There were still other variations, when liberation was triggered by the obvious fact of race mixture. Slave mothers sometimes found kindly godfathers to liberate their mixed-blood offspring, or, if the child was startlingly white, even the master himself was occasionally moved to manumission by the fact.[54]

---

[50] *Recopilación de leyes de los reynos de las Indias: Edición facsimilar de la cuarta impresión hecha en Madrid el año 1791*, Madrid, 1943, Libro VII, título v, ley 6.

[51] AGN, register of Alonso de Santillán, 22 November, fol. 734.

[52] In the order of mention: ANP, SN, register of Rodrigo Gómez de Baeza, 15 December, fol. 991; *ibid.*, register of Bartolomé de Toro (1630), 8 August, fols. 653-654.

[53] AGN, register of Alonso de Santillán, 16 March, fols. 154v-155r.

[54] For examples in the order of mention: ANP, SN, register of Cristóbal de Aguilar Mendieta (1593), 7 February, fols. 182v-183r; *ibid.*, register of Cristóbal de Aldana (1653), 17 July, fol. 390. Clearly, in many instances it is very difficult

If frequently blessed with freedom, Afro-Spanish children were nevertheless burdened not merely by color prejudice but also by the stigma of illegitimacy. For example, in labor and apprenticeship contracts which involved minor children it was customary to record the names of the parents. In a sample of 78 such contracts for Mexico City, 40 of the free colored minors involved (or 51 percent) were listed as orphans. To be sure, a few of these cases must have been genuine, but 13 (or 32.5 percent) of these children were only *huérfanos de padre*, while the mother's name was recorded. In short, however powerful the sexual allure of the colored women, however strong the affection of the father for his mulatto child, few Spaniards cared to drastically lower their social status through marriage to a female of an inferior racial group. Cases such as that of the swordmaker González and his slave wife, mentioned above, were rare in both capitals. In general, concubinage characterized sexual unions between Spaniards and Africans, although such relationships might last for years, and the children continued to be illegitimate. At worst, these unfortunates might be abandoned by both parents. At best, they might obtain their freedom, and even share in their fathers' estates, but in either case the burden of illegitimacy had to be shouldered.[55]

It must also be mentioned that race mixture became an increasingly complex phenomenon as the numbers of free colored increased. Spaniards and free colored women produced offspring who were automatically free, if not advantaged, and these latter in turn mingled with the European and Indian elements, and with the other castes, to produce an ever-larger and more bewildering variety of offspring who, depending upon their pigmentation or luck, might or might not enter the ranks of the free "blacks." That is, the reproduction and growth of the free colored population, while never divorced from slavery, depended upon that institution less and less with each generation.

Before we take our leave of the subject of manumission, it is neces-

---

to establish the motives of those who liberated Afro-Spanish infants. In a letter of manumission of 1626, for example, the master of Juana Mulata declared that his slave was in the last stages of pregnancy and that "several persons" had urged him to free the as yet unborn child. The deciding factor seems to have been the 50 *pesos* offered by one Lázaro Sánchez, but the historian does not know why the latter was moved to part with this sum. AGN, register of Pedro de Santillán, 30 December, fol. 703.

[55] This issue is explored in more detail in my essay cited in n. 2. In addition, the fairly common practice of branding slaves burdened many who achieved freedom with a symbol of servitude as enduring as color and more so than illegitimacy. In the 1633 letter of manumission which freed the *mulata* Agustina de Castro, her mistress noted that she was branded on the face with an "s" and the representation of a nail (*clavo* in Spanish), i.e., esclavo. AGN, register of Juan de Oviedo Valdivieso, 17 March, fols. 118r-119r. Agustina was far from alone.

349

TABLE 1. MANUMISSIONS, PERU, 1580-1650

Age of Slave	Sex		Terms of Liberation				
	Males	Females	Uncondi-tional	Future Service	Other Obliga-tions	By Payment	For Future Payment
over 45	7	20	15	2	1	9	1
36-45	5	21	8	1	—	15	1
26-35	9	22	6	6	—	18	1
16-25	2	17	5	2	—	10	3
8-15	8	26	15	12	—	5	3
under 8	48	29	33	8	1	34	2
unknown	16	64	19	19	3	28	13
TOTALS	95	199	101	50	5	119	24

NOTE: Table 1 is a sample taken from 207 notarial registers for Lima.

sary to consider the frequency of the various types of liberation, the sex and age of the slaves involved, and the possible significance of any patterns which are revealed. Tables 1 and 2, which illustrate trends of manumission in Lima and Mexico City, have been prepared from extensive sampling of notarial registers for both capitals.

The similarities in the patterns of manumission for the two cities are striking. Of particular interest is the fact that in both Lima and Mexico City, freedom was a goal obtained for the most part by women and small children. In the case of the Peruvian capital, those

TABLE 2. MANUMISSIONS, MEXICO CITY, 1580-1650

Age of Slave	Sex		Terms of Liberation				
	Males	Females	Uncondi-tional	Future Service	Other Obliga-tions	By Payment	For Future Payment
over 45	3	5	6	—	1	1	—
36-45	4	2	3	—	—	3	—
26-35	6	4	4	1	1	5	—
16-25	2	4	1	—	1	4	—
8-15	2	6	3	3	—	3	—
under 8	11	16	12	5	—	8	3
unknown	12	27	13	13	1	10	2
TOTALS	40	65	42	22	4	34	5

NOTE: Table 2 is a sample taken from 91 notarial registers for Mexico City.

two groups compose 84 percent of the sample while adult males in the prime of life (ages 16-35) make up only 4 percent. In the case of Mexico City, the respective percentages are 72 and 8. The obvious conclusion, at least for these two very important centers of Spanish American civilization, is that during the early period of colonization the adult free colored population was heavily female and that a balance between the sexes must have been struck only slowly, as generation after generation of free male infants attained manhood. These figures also reveal that various forms of purchase and unconditional manumission by the slaveholder were the most important paths to liberty, with liberation contingent on future service ranking third. In addition, both tables support the assumption that the attitudes held by slaveholders toward liberation were influenced by economic conditions. In the case of both Lima and Mexico City during this period, labor was scarce, and few prime adult slaves of either sex were freed unconditionally; the percentage for Lima is 3.7 and that of Mexico stands at 5.

Clearly, these various types of manumission in combination with reproduction produced in both capitals a growing number of free coloreds, but population estimates constitute difficult and thankless tasks. Although the authorities deplored the presence of free individuals of African descent, attempts at official enumeration did not begin until the late sixteenth century, when the home government decided to impose a tribute obligation. Unfortunately, many free coloreds were able to evade the tax by various means, and the royal treasury officials, burdened with other duties, farmed out the tax on the basis of the roughest of estimates. However, it seems reasonable to assume that by 1650 ca. 10 percent of Lima's colored population was free, i.e., perhaps 2,000 in a total black population of 20,000.[56] The case of Mexico City is even more difficult since even estimates of the total free colored population are little more than impressions. We will take those of an observer whose unreliability can at least be calculated with some assurance: Antonio Vázquez de Espinosa, whose *Compendium and Description of the West Indies* was written sometime in the second decade of the seventeenth century.[57] Vázquez estimated the colored population of Lima at some 30,000, a figure which every official census indicates should be cut by at least fifty percent. Vázquez assigned to Mexico City a colored population of 50,000; if we assume that he was consistent in his exaggerations, this

---

[56] For a more detailed discussion, see chap. XI and Appendix I of my book cited in n. 3.

[57] Trans. Charles Upson Clark, Washington, 1942, p. 156.

number can be cut in half and arbitrarily multiplied by ten percent to yield a free colored population of some 2,500 at the end of the period under study. It is to be hoped that future archival research will find the data necessary to confirm or modify this pathetically crude estimate. It must also be observed that these numbers are impressive percentages of the relatively small populations of both capitals.

By whatever means liberation was achieved, persons of African descent soon discovered that freedom was far from absolute. The attitudes of crown, church, and society assured that this would be the case. In law, the condition of the free colored was significantly better than that of the slave, but inferior to the status of Spaniards, Indians, and mestizos. The policy of the home government reflected a combination of contempt, fear, and solicitude which, however, was not always enforced by colonial authorities. In the first place, Madrid reasoned that free blacks, mulattoes, and Afro-Indian mixtures, who had profited by the richness of Spanish America to free themselves and to accumulate modest fortunes, could reasonably be obligated to pay tribute each year in compensation for the peace, justice, and freedom which they enjoyed.[58] Further, since tribute was obligatory, freedom did not mean that free persons of color had the right to spend their days in sloth and debauchery. Rather, they must hire themselves out to, and live with, Spanish employers. In this fashion, their whereabouts would be known and the tax easily collected.[59]

The crown regarded the free person of color as a source of modest revenue, but his presence in Spanish America was also feared as the possible origin of unrest and insurrection. For this reason, Madrid and the colonial authorities sought to restrict the movements of free coloreds and to prohibit them from owning firearms.[60] At the same time, as foreign intrusion increased in Spanish America in the late sixteenth century and thereafter, the crown did not hesitate to rely more and more upon colored militia units, supplemented by similar white contingents, to ward off these attacks. The present writer does not know if this development occurred in Mexico City before 1650, and perhaps, since the capital was well inland and most of the threats were directed at the Pacific port of Acapulco, there was no

[58] Konetzke, I, 482-483, decree of 24 April, 1574. The wording of this legislation implies that the crown considered the purchase system a more important avenue to freedom than voluntary manumission by the master.

[59] *Ibid.*, 502-503, decree of 29 April, 1577.

[60] An empire-wide prohibition concerning the bearing of arms by free persons of color appeared in 1551 (*Recopilación*, Libro VII, título v, ley 15) but local ordinances against this practice may have been framed still earlier.

need. But coastal Lima was more exposed to attacks by foreign enemies, and viceroys stationed there assumed that free coloreds could be useful in case of emergency. In 1624, for example, when a Dutch fleet seriously threatened the Lima area, companies of mulatto militia were sent first to the nearby port of Surco to prepare fortifications and were then ordered to return to Callao where they were held in readiness for an attack that never came. Available evidence indicates that they were not armed during this emergency, although things might have been different had the Dutch assault materialized.[61]

From time to time, the government concerned itself with the manners and morals of the free colored population. Free persons of African descent, along with slaves, were subjected to the scrutiny of the Holy Office.[62] In addition, decrees came periodically from Spain which commanded that free blacks and mulattoes be properly indoctrinated in the principles of Christianity, in order that they might lead orderly and upright lives, and occasionally the crown also inquired about the medical care given to this segment of society.[63]

In general, however, as the free person of color lived his life he encountered more contempt and discrimination than solicitude. His illegitimacy was taken for granted, and this often-correct assumption was a serious legal impediment to socioeconomic advancement.[64] The shadow of illegitimacy, combined with the weight of color prejudice, was sufficient to bar blacks and mulattoes from most educational institutions, from public office,[65] from the possession of grants of Indian tribute and labor, and from the professions, including the priesthood. In a comment on the possibility of the free person of color entering the service of God in any institutionalized fashion, the crown expressed the fear that the public would be scandalized to see "such unworthy people so highly placed." [66] Spanish artisans clung to the medieval guild system during this period, and, fearful of competition and wishing to monopolize the profits to be made from colonial demand, were very nearly as discriminatory as the crown against the

---

[61] Petition to the crown by the free mulattoes involved, Lima, 18 March 1627, in AGI, Lima 158.

[62] Concerning this point, see n. 4.

[63] Konetzke, I, 435-436, 444-445, 496; II, 1, 135, 365. In 1623, an interesting decree provided that free, married colored women could not be forced to attend the public dances held on the various religious holidays. Ibid., II, 1, 278, July 21.

[64] Mörner, pp. 40, 68.

[65] At least in Lima, however, quadroons seem to have been able to purchase appointment as notaries public. See my essay cited in n. 2.

[66] Konetzke, I, 256, 607-608; II, 1, 65-67.

free person of color. Guild after guild excluded those of African descent although free coloreds were valued as journeymen.[67]

The church discriminated against those of African descent at ¡a lower level than the priesthood, although the doctrine that all men were equal in the eyes of God was never abandoned. In 1614, for example, the city fathers of Lima forbade the use of coffins among the African population as a grave affront to the superior status of the Spaniards.[68] In the same year, a synod presided over by the Archbishop of Lima decided that no blacks, mulattoes, or Indians were to be buried in the cathedral. Despite the strenuous objections of at least one member of the civil arm of the government, there is no evidence that this decision was reversed.[69] Perhaps even more irritating, although less insulting in spiritual terms, was the sumptuary legislation directed against colored women, no doubt in part because of the lure they held for Spanish men. Such regulations were promulgated with monotonous regularity, perhaps a sign of their ineffectiveness, and at times included a very wide range of items: silk, pearls, gold, slippers ornamented with silver bells, canopied beds, and rugs or cushions to sit on at church.[70]

Free coloreds found it relatively easy to circumvent or ignore much of this discriminatory legislation. For example, Thomas Gage describes in great detail the silks, laces, and fancy footwear worn by the *mulatas* of seventeenth century Mexico City, and adds: "Most of these are or have been slaves, though love have set them loose, at liberty to enslave souls to sin and Satan."[71] The frequency with which free coloreds were forbidden to carry weapons belies the effectiveness of this restriction as well. Even tribute was successfully evaded by most of the colored population. At least until 1650, this fiscal obligation was collected only irregularly in Lima, and the quadroons of the colony managed to obtain formal exemption from the crown.[72] During

[67] *Ibid., passim,* for numerous examples. See also my book cited in n. 3 and Manuel Carrera Stampa, *Los gremios mexicanos,* Mexico, 1954, pp. 223-243.

[68] *Libros de cabildos de Lima* (hereafter cited LCL), ed. Bertram T. Lee and Juan Bromley, continuing publication begun in Lima, 1935, xxvii, 506-507, 526.

[69] Letter to the crown from Cristóbal Cacho de Santillán, crown attorney before the *audiencia,* Lima, 16 April 1617, in AGI, Lima 96.

[70] Diego de Encinas, *Cedulario indiano: Reproducción facsimil de la edición única de 1596,* Madrid, 1945-46, iv, 387, decree of 4 August, 1574, which was addressed to the *audiencia* of Panama, but which had wider application; *LCL,* xix, 401, session of 26 September 1622; Suardo, i, 155, entry of 14 April 1631; Konetzke, ii, 1, 182-183; Josephe de Mugaburu and Francisco de Mugaburu (hijo), *Diario de Lima, 1640-1694: Crónica de la época colonial,* ed. Horacio H. Urteaga and Carlos A. Romero. 2 vols. Lima, 1917-18.

[71] *Op.cit.* p. 69.

[72] These issues are discussed at length for Lima in my book cited in n. 3.

certain periods, the Mexican situation may have been much the same. In 1594, for example, Viceroy Don Luis de Velasco informed the crown that free coloreds were fleeing fixed residences and wandering from place to place rather than pay the tax.[73]

However, there is evidence to indicate that the free coloreds of Lima enjoyed considerably more independence, and perhaps even more opportunities for advancement, than their Mexico City counterparts. The Spaniards of both capitals feared the blacks around them, and the more so since the latter grew in numbers as the danger of foreign intrusion increased in the seventeenth century, but the whites of Mexico City appear to have been more jittery than the *limeños*.[74] Free coloreds were always regarded as potential allies and leaders of the slave population. Gage, for example, vividly describes the Spanish fear of the former in Mexico City: "And there are so many of this kind, both men and women, grown to a height of pride and vanity, that many times the Spaniards have feared they would rise up and mutiny against them. The looseness of their lives and public scandals committed by them and the better sort of Spaniards were such that I have heard those who have professed more religion and fear of God say often they verily thought God would destroy that city, and give up the country into the power of some other nation."[75]

Evidence from notarial records indicates that the free coloreds of Mexico City, feared more than those of African descent in Lima, were also more tightly controlled by the authorities. During this period, it was not a question of additional restrictive legislation, but merely one of better enforcement. For example, as we have seen, the free coloreds of both capitals were commanded to hire themselves out to, and live with, Spanish employers. In Lima, employment contracts (*cartas de servicio*) demonstrate that the authorities from time to time rounded up free coloreds and held them in jail if necessary until they agreed to take employment with a Spaniard. However, the records also show that such vigilance was spotty, and, when relaxed, free coloreds promptly rented the houses and stores necessary to conduct their businesses and give them shelter. In Mexico City, the situation appears to have been different. The notarial registers examined by the present writer indicate that rentals by free persons of color were rare.[76]

[73] Konetzke, ii, 1, 18, letter of 29 May.
[74] Contrast Davidson, "Negro Slave Control," *passim*, with the appropriate chapters of my book cited in n. 3.
[75] Gage, pp. 69-70.
[76] The only two instances discovered thus far for Mexico City are as follows: AGN, register of Francisco Flores (1645), rental contract of 4 October, whereby

To be sure, the floods which endangered Mexico City in the first half of the seventeenth century may well have curtailed construction and thereby produced a shortage of housing. In turn, this development perhaps forced free persons of color to live in the homes of advantaged Spaniards whether they liked it or not, and no doubt serve those who housed them in return for the favor. However, additional evidence indicates that the free coloreds of Mexico City were more supervised by the authorities, and therefore more disadvantaged, than those of Lima. In the latter city, and well before the middle of the seventeenth century, free colored artisans were publicly acting as master craftsmen, signing contracts and conducting their businesses according to their own lights. This development seemingly did not occur in Mexico City. There were skilled blacks in plenty, but the notarial records indicate that few became certified masters, able to act as free agents. Rather, perhaps because of the power of the Spanish guilds, or the number of skilled Indians, or both, free coloreds who had mastered a craft continued as journeymen. The present writer has discovered very few contracts signed by skilled free persons of color in Mexico City. This is in sharp contrast to Lima, and the implications are obvious. However devastating the demographic decline in the Valley of Mexico, the pace was slow enough to permit Spaniards, Indians, and mestizos to dominate the arts and crafts, to exploit skilled persons of African descent, and to narrow their opportunities for advancement. In Lima, on the other hand, the shortage of skilled labor came too early, and the efforts of Spanish artisans to monopolize the status of master were frustrated.[77]

That is, Mexico City did not suffer from a shortage of skilled free persons of color: tailors, makers of saddles and hats, butchers, and the like. And some skilled coloreds did very well for themselves. In 1622, for example, the free mulatto Juan Bautista de Villar agreed to serve the man who had won the contract to supply Mexico City with beef for two years, arranging for the receipt and slaughter of these livestock, in return for the handsome salary of 700 *pesos* per year, a supply of maize, all the beef he could eat, and a quantity of clothing.[78]

---

a free *mulata* and her son rent a house for two years at the rate of 7.5 *pesos* per month; *ibid.*, register of Hernando de Arauz (1636), 15 March, fol. 270, whereby Francisco Camacho, a free mulatto rents a "store" for one year for 90 *pesos*.

[77] In addition to the sources cited in note 66, see Harth-terré and Márquez Abanto, "El artesano negro," *passim*.

[78] AGN, register of Joseph de la Cruz, 14 March, fols. 73v-75v. Free persons of color appear to have been very prominent as butchers in the operations of the slaughterhouse which supplied Mexico City with meat. See also AGN, register of Pedro de Santillán (1618), fols. 218-219, 222-225.

All too often, however, the skilled person of color in Mexico City found himself under the thumb of a Spanish master, working not merely for wages inferior to those which could have been obtained with a shop of his own, but also to pay off a debt. In 1601, for example, Francisco Morales, a free mulatto and skilled in the making of saddles, agreed to serve a Spanish artisan of the same specialty in return for board and "the usual wages" until a debt of forty *pesos* had been paid.[79] Seemingly, the free colored artisans of Lima rarely found themselves in such an unfortunate position.

It must be stressed that in both capitals skilled free persons of color were far from constituting a majority of their racial group. Yet many free blacks obviously appreciated the advantages to be had from apprenticeship in the arts, or at least their wiser parents did. In 1584, for example, the *mulata* Antonia Jiménez placed her son, aged eighteen, with a Spanish embroiderer for 2.5 years to learn the skill. To take another, in 1624 a mulatto of the same age, named Miguel Alvarado and a native of Puebla, apprenticed himself to a caps and headwear-maker (*gorrero*) for three years for the same reason.[80] Except in the case of the very young, the length of such apprenticeship contracts ranged between one and four years, and usually included room, board, medical care for all but the most serious illnesses, often a modest amount of clothing, and occasionally a token salary. Skilled adults usually preferred to hire themselves out for no more than a year's time (perhaps two), and the pay they received was subject to considerable individual variation. Nevertheless, it seems reasonable to state that the average colored artisan in Lima during this period earned ca. 37.5-62.5 *pesos* per month, depending upon his skill and journeyman or master status. His counterpart for Mexico City might have averaged no more than 45. In short, the colored artisans of the latter capital enjoyed neither the status nor the monetary rewards which were available to skilled blacks in Lima.[81]

In addition, a greater percentage of the free colored population of Lima seems to have gravitated toward the lucrative arts and crafts. For the period under study, a sample of some hundred labor contracts signed by free coloreds in Lima reveals that 35.5 percent were skilled, or apprenticed to craftsmen, while the percentage for Mexico City (in a sample of roughly equal size) is 28 percent.[82] Of itself, this

---

[79] AGN, register of Juan de Porras, 30 June, fol. 441.

[80] In the order of mention: AGN, register of Juan Pérez de Rivera, 1 September, unnumbered fols.; Joseph de la Cruz, 7 January, unnumbered fols.

[81] These assertions are based upon a mass of pinpoint data in AGN and ANP; for more detail concerning Peru, see my work cited in n. 3.

[82] As in n. 81, only a footnote of inordinate length can document these assertions.

deviation is not statistically significant, but still other evidence argues that free persons of color in Mexico City were economically disadvantaged in comparison to those of Lima.

If we take, for example, the wage scales which applied to unskilled free coloreds, in the Peruvian capital domestics in their teens might command some 5-6 *pesos* per month, adults as much as 8-12, and wet nurses as much as 13 to 15. In Mexico City, free blacks of the same status, if they were fortunate, might earn 5 *pesos* in thirty days, together with room, board, and medical care (along with their *limeño* comrades), but 87.5 percent of the former earned less than this amount.[83] In addition, unskilled free coloreds, were as liable as their skilled counterparts to subjection to what can only be called an urban form of debt peonage, and the examples for Mexico City greatly outnumber those for Lima. To give but one example, in 1584 the *mulata* Francisca Gutiérrez agreed to serve one Doña María de Castañeda in household work for the time necessary to pay a debt of 30 *pesos* at the rate of 1.5 *pesos* per month.[84] The present writer cannot generalize with certainty, but it is easy to visualize free coloreds such as these permanently trapped in a web of debt to Spanish creditors, equally as much as their Indian and mestizo counterparts in the rural areas. If the same held true for Lima, it is not reflected in the notarial records.

In both capitals, free colored women were placed in a particularly unfortunate position. Although they were such an important part of the world of free persons of African descent, participation in the arts and crafts was largely reserved for males. Some, to be sure, found other ways of attaining modest prosperity (perhaps as vendors of various commodities including themselves), but most found themselves condemned to the treadmill enjoyed by housekeepers and wet nurses. In 1583, for example, the mother of Mariana Mulata (aged 9) had no alternative but to hire her out to a Spanish employer for four years with the agreement that Mariana was to be taught to sew and become a laundress. All too often, agreements such as the above led to a pattern of life which could not be reversed. In 1623, for

---

[83] Clearly, these comparisons would be more meaningful if something were known concerning the cost of living in the two capitals. What is needed are monographs along the lines of Woodrow Borah and Sherburne F. Cook, *Price Trends of Some Basic Commodities in Colonial Mexico, 1531-1570*, Berkeley, 1958.

[84] AGN, register of Juan Pérez de Rivera, 14 April, unnumbered fols. Further, many blacks, skilled and unskilled, found themselves serving Spanish masters in Mexico City who had advanced them the money to pay the tribute owed the crown or to bail themselves out of other unspecified difficulties. See, for example, AGN, register of Hernando de Arauz (1621), fols. 11v-12r, 13v-14r.

example, the free *mulata* Melchora de Morones appeared before the judicial authorities, declared that she had served the same Spanish master for a decade without salary (although all her worldly necessities except ambition for advancement were met), and signed to serve another two years.[85]

Despite these many disadvantages, the free coloreds of Mexico City and Lima often managed to accumulate modest fortunes for themselves and to provide for their offspring. To consider here no more than the example of Mexico City, free persons of color traded in fabrics, livestock, and other merchandise, owned slaves of their own, operated inns, and at least the most fortunate acquired houses and house lots even if the majority were compelled to live with Spanish employers.[86] This economic advancement is all the more impressive if the historian bears in mind the low wages earned by most free persons of color and the weight of the prejudice directed against them.

We must not, however, permit these small and painfully achieved advantages to blind us to the fact that most free persons of color began and ended their days in poverty, under a cloud which all their efforts could not dissipate. For one thing, the opportunity to purchase liberation was a mixed blessing, tempting many free coloreds to buy the freedom of family members and friends with slender resources that might have otherwise have been more economically profitable. Further, the operation of Spanish inheritance laws, which favored nearly equal division among the heirs, caused generation after generation of free coloreds to fragment their meager estates. In addition, of course, bad luck or poor judgment often played a hand. Let us take the case of Marcos Pérez, a fruit vendor in the *plaza mayor* of Mexico City. Pérez' pigmentation was so light that he was permitted to describe himself as *"de color pardo"* in his will, rather than employ the customary *"mulato libre."* Pérez had used his fair skin to marry a Spanish woman, a very rare event at that time, and his wife had

[85] In the order of mention: AGN, register of Juan Pérez de Rivera, 27 July, unnumbered fols.; AGN, register of Andrés Moreno, 24 May, fols. 193r-194r.

[86] For both cities, these generalizations are based on masses of notarial documents whose bulk prohibits individual citation. It might be added that even slaves managed to accumulate property under exceptional circumstances. In 1634, for example, the Spaniard Diego Treviño threatened to sue one Juan Jolofo, a free black, for the value represented by a female slave and other goods possessed by María Jolofa on her death. María was Treviño's slave, but died in the house of Juan, who seems to have claimed her possessions, human and otherwise, for his own. Under threat of suit, however, Juan paid 350 *pesos* to Treviño in compensation, and legal action was dropped. AGN, register of Juan López de Rivera, 14 November, fols. 147-148.

359

brought him a modest dowry in jewelry. Two children had resulted from the marriage, and their status as whites was assured.[87] But Pérez' luck went bad. At the time of his death, all of his wife's jewels were pawned, he was behind in the payment of debts, and his financial situation was so uncertain that the arrangements for his burial and the number of masses to be said for his soul were left to the discretion of his executors. His wife and the children were assigned equal shares of anything that remained of his estate.[88]

The Pérez saga illustrates more than the frustrated ambitions of many free coloreds in both capitals. A point of equal or greater importance is the fact that the ambivalent racial attitudes of Spanish American society operated against solidarity based upon race among free persons of color, and this phenomenon goes far to explain the disappearance of those of African descent in present-day Lima and Mexico City.

To explain the assimilation of the free person of color, so prominent in colonial times, we must begin by observing that the policies of the Spanish crown, always an odd combination of inflexibility and pragmatism, changed at some point in the seventeenth century. Reality belied the original plan of three distinct racial groups in Spanish America, and if the free person of color existed, however mixed of blood and illegitimate of birth, Madrid reasoned that he might as well be organized to more usefully serve the government. The present writer has no evidence for Mexico City, but in Lima during the late 1620s an effort was made to organize free "mulattoes" into a guild, and to make the officers of that organization responsible for the collection of tribute, the recruitment of colored militia, and the collection of special contributions for various religious and civic festivities.[89] The experiment appears to have been less than successful. The

---

[87] In the notarial records of the period, the names of those presumed by all to be Spaniards were rarely qualified by racial descriptions. Pérez, it is clear, did not quite "pass." His wife had obviously lowered herself in the eyes of society by the marriage, and Peréz was therefore at pains to describe her as an *española*. The children, however, seem to have been accepted as whites, since no racial classification was attached to their names.

[88] AGN, register of Francisco Flores (1645), 17 May, fols. 171-172.

[89] It is unclear whether "mulattoes" was meant as a rubric for all free persons of color. My information comes from a lawsuit in AGI, Escribanía de Cámara 1023b, "Pedro Martín de Leguisamo, oficial de platero y vecino de la ciudad de Lima, con el Gremio de Mulatos de ella, sobre que se declarse no ser de este gremio, y sí de los españoles," 1632, *passim*. Leguisamo's mother was a *mulata*, but his father was a Basque *hidalgo*, and Leguisamo managed to avoid payment of tribute and service in the mulatto militia on the strength of his father's noble status.

officers of the guild flatly refused to collect tribute from their fellows, although in 1631 the organization participated on a lavish scale in the festivities which honored the birth of Baltasar Carlos, heir to the Spanish throne.[90]

The colonial authorities preferred to let the issue of racial classification rest at roughly this point: to distinguish the mulatto from the black, the Afro-Indian from the aborigine, and even to recognize the quadroon. But the Pandora's box of racial mixture, once opened unconsciously by thousands of individuals, could not be closed by government fiat. Together with the emergence of the mestizo, it was clear to all but the most stiff-necked bureaucrat, and well before the dawn of the seventeenth century, that Spanish America could not be divided into neat racial compartments, each capable of separate treatment. This is not to say that there was not a clearly recognizable colored community. Notarial records clearly indicate this trend, one reinforced by prejudice. In the main, free persons of color married or cohabited with those of African descent (whom they often helped to free), found their friends, and transacted their business with those of similar racial origins.

In both cities, however, a powerful counter-trend existed which made for the constant splintering and ultimate absorption of the free colored community into an emerging, but anonymous, mixed-blood population. This development did not reach fruition during the period under study, but the basic outlines were clear by 1650. Outwardly, Spanish society was violently opposed to racial mixture, but the process was a fact, and with it came an almost morbid fascination with racial classification, culminating in the elaborate nomenclature of the late colonial period. One curious consequence of all this, discernible by the seventeenth century, was that race mixture was despised, but the mulatto, for the white blood which coursed through his veins, was regarded as superior to the "pure" black. He was thought, perhaps, to be more arrogant, lazier, but nevertheless more acceptable.

Intelligent and ambitious free persons of color were quick to notice these distinctions, to see the advantages of "whitening" both for themselves and their children. They readily sacrificed racial solidarity to socioeconomic advancement. Clearly, the perception of an advantage does not equal its achievement: the case of the fruit vendor Pérez illustrates this point. His light color, his Spanish wife and her

---

[90] Suardo, I, 133-135, 137-142, describes the festivities, which include floats, theatricals, and bullfights.

FREDERICK P. BOWSER

dowry, gained him nothing, but *their* children, however poor, were accepted as white. Further, a Spanish male who fathered a child by an attractive *mulata* did not do so to further the racial assimilation of the American colonies; his thoughts were elsewhere.

Nevertheless, the pattern remained: generation by generation white society slowly mixed with the colored population beneath it, allowed its inferiors liberation in various ways, and then absorbed them. The process was largely unconscious, but there was a degree of calculation, particularly on the part of the Africans involved. In Lima, for example, the confraternity organized by the Jesuits for blacks in the sixteenth century made no distinctions in the beginning: blacks were blacks, free or slave. However, sometime between 1630 and 1650 the sodality fragmented into three groups. First, Peruvian-born persons of color, those who had mastered the Spanish language and customs, split with their slave counterparts fresh from Africa. The former group then divided yet once again: Creole mulattoes did not wish to honor the Faith in the company of "blacks" born in Peru.[91] However, self-interest should not be exaggerated. The identification of many free coloreds with Spanish culture appears to have been genuine, especially as regards the church, and had nothing to do with schemes for advancement. For example, more than a few free persons of color bequeathed what few worldly possessions they had to the various churches, convents, and hospitals which dotted both capitals.[92]

In any event, the assimilation of the free person of color was slow and uncertain, often costly in terms of human dignity and pride, and not very rewarding even in economic terms. The generalizations in this paper cannot be applied to all of the urban centers of colonial Spanish America, even for the sixteenth and seventeenth centuries, and much less thereafter; too many potential variables exist. However, at least for the two capitals under study, it seems clear that the majority of free persons of color remained at the bottom of the societal ladder, whatever their ambitions and beliefs, gradually "whitening" through the process of racial mixture and in isolated instances bettering their economic position.[93]

[91] Luis Martin, *The Intellectual Conquest of Peru: The Jesuit College of San Pablo, 1568-1767,* New York, 1968, pp. 133-134. Unfortunately, the proportion of free coloreds to slaves in these squabbles is unknown, but logic would argue that the number of the former was high.

[92] See, for example, my book cited in n. 3, esp. ch. XI.

[93] This process is exceedingly difficult for the historian to document. Even the crown agreed that African blood did not taint those who were quadroons or lighter, and it was to the advantage of those who could do so to "pass," not perhaps as whites but merely as members of the relatively dark-skinned masses.

362

Prejudice, of course, continued. The lot of those whose lives we have briefly sketched was unenviable, and the process by which the urban free person of color was assimilated can hardly be defended in terms of morality or social justice. It is also ironic, although perhaps fortunate for the societies involved, that the person of African descent, so prominent in Lima and Mexico City during the sixteenth and seventeenth centuries, has very nearly been denied living proof of his historical importance. An odd face or feature here and there strikes the visitor, but those who came from Africa are now most visible in historical documentation. This fact stands as a flawed monument to the flexibility of Iberian racial attitudes.

As we have seen, society developed a complex system of racial castes, but these classifications had no legal force, were therefore not used in notarial records, and, at least among the poor, probably had very little practical effect. Free persons of color who gained some economic advantage, as Pérez attempted, could often ignore the question of pigmentation, and at a later date purchase legal certificates of whiteness from the government. Concerning this last point, see my essay cited in n. 2.

APPENDIX

THIS essay is based on a limited number of printed sources cited in the footnotes and upon an occasional document from the Archivo General de Indias (Seville). In general, however, the information in this essay has been taken from notarial records for Lima and Mexico City, and these are listed below.

ARCHIVO GENERAL DE NOTARIAS DEL DISTRITO FEDERAL (MEXICO CITY):

Arauz, Hernando: 1619-1627, 1630-1650.
Arauz, José: 1604-1612.
Barrientos, Juan de: 1638-1643.
Bernal, Esteban: 1629.
Caballero, Jusepe: 1613.
Cobián, Torivio: 1648-1655.
Contreras, Miguel: 1622.
Cruz, José de la: 1615-1628.
Espinosa, Cristóbal de: 1631.
Flores, Francisco: 1633-1650.
Lópes de Rivera, Juan: 1630-1634, 1638-1643.
López, Haedo, Gabriel: 1630-1650.
Molina Guerra, Martín de: 1645-1650.
Moreno, Andrés: 1591-1598, 1600-1602, 1607, 1613, 1616, 1619-1620, 1623, 1625, 1629, 1630-1640.
Oviedo Valdivieso, Juan: 1633-1634, 1636-1641.
Pérez de Rivera, Juan: 1582-1585, 1588-1592, 1611-1615, 1619, 1623-1627, 1630-1631, 1633.
Porras, Juan de: 1599-1605, 1613-1615, 1617-1618.
Ríos, Diego de los: 1642-1650.
Santillán, Alonso de: 1615-1619.
Santillán, Pedro de: 1614-1650.
Santos de Rivera, Juan: 1624-1631, 1633-1635, 1642-1644.
Sariñana, Martin: 1637-1650.
Valdivieso, Francisco: 1631-1636, 1641.
Veedor, Jose: 1633-1639.
Vicente, Cristóbal: 1628-1645.

ARCHIVO DE NOTARÍAS, No. 1 (TOLUCA, MEXICO). The records listed below are those of notaries who divided their time between Toluca and Mexico City:

Amunares, Bernardino de: 1620-1623.
Cáceres, Andrés Luis de: 1604-1609.

ARCHIVO NACIONAL DEL PERU (LIMA), SECCION NOTARIAL:

Sixteenth century
Alejandro, Francisco: 1595
Arias Cortés, Pedro: 1582-1583, 1595.
Aguilar Mendieta, Cristóbal: 1595, 1600

The above with Diego de la Torre Sabá and Agustin Atencia: 1589-1592.

Bote, Ramiro Francisco: 1595.
Cueva, Alonso de la: 1580.
Franco de Esquivel, Marcos: 1581-1583.
Gómez de Garnica, Martín: 1595-1597.
Gómez de Baeza, Rodrigo de: 1585, 1590-1591, 1595.
Gutiérrez, Juan: 1585, 1595.
Herrero, Alonso: 1583.
Hernández, Blas: 1581-1583, 1590-1591, 1595, 1600.
Hernández, Alonso: 1585.
López, Esteban: 1591, 1595-1598.
Moscoso, Ambrosio de: 1580-1582, 1584-1587.
Manuel, Juan: 1585-1590.
Nuñez de la Vega, Sebastián: 1593-1595.
Pérez, Esteban, with Bartolomé Gascón: 1583-1585, 1589.
Rios, Pedro de los: 1589-1590.

Seventeenth century
Aguilar, Mendieta, Cristóbal: 1605, 1615, 1625, 1630.
Acuña, Francisco de: 1620, 1625, 1630, 1635, 1640, 1645, 1650.
Aldana, Cristóbal de: 1625, 1635, 1640, 1645.
Alférez, Miguel de: 1610, 1615, 1620, 1625.
Atencia, Agustin de: 1615, 1620, 1625.
Aguirre y Urbina, José de: 1645, 1650.
Arauz, Cristóbal de: 1605, 1610, 1620, 1630, 1635, 1640, 1645.
Aparicio de Urrutia, Juan: 1605, 1609, 1610.
Alcocer, Pedro Luis de: 1620.
Alvarez de Quiroz, Pedro: 1625, 1630, 1635.
Arroyo, Pedro de: 1601, 1602, 1605, 1610, 1635.

Altamirano, Juan: 1605.
Aguila Bullón, Juan: 1630.
Bustamante, Francisco de: 1615, 1640.
Barrientos, Cristóbal de: 1605, 1610, 1615.
Balcázar, Martín de: 1640, 1645.
Bello, Juan: 1600-1602.
Carrión, Alonso de: 1615, 1620.
Carbajal, Juan de: 1645, 1650.
Cívico, Bartolomé de: 1625, 1635.
Cámara, Bartoloméde la: 1615, 1620.
Florez, Cristóbal: 1605, 1610.
Fernández, Fabian: 1645.
Figueroa, Marcelo Antonio de: 1645.
Gómez, José Felipe: 1620, 1625.
Grados de Lícera, Miguel: 1600.
Gonzáles Pareja, Juan: 1615, 1620.
Gonzales de Soto, Alonso: 1630.
Gómez de Garnica, Martín: 1600-1601, 1605.
García de León, Diego: 1645.
Gómez de Baeza, Rodrigo: 1600, 1605.
Gonzáles Balcázar, Francisco: 1605, 1610, 1620.
Herrera, Juan Bautista: 1630, 1640, 1645, 1650.
Hernández, Francisco: 1620, 1625.
Ita Hervás, Baltasar de: 1635.
Jaramillo, Diego de: 1645.
Jácome Carlos, Juan: 1645.
López Salazar, Diego: 1610.
López Mallea, Pedro: 1615.
López Almagro, Pedro: 1610.
Luna, Miguel de: 1630.
López, Esteban: 1600, 1605.
López Chico, Gregorio: 1630.
López Lízar, Diego: 1620, 1630.
López de Mendoza, Juan: 1630.
Martínez, Francisco: 1610, 1615.
Mendieta, Juan de: 1600.
Medina, Melchior de: 1625, 1630.
Martínez Llorenta, Juan: 1635.
Mota, Antonio de la: 1650.
Nieto Maldonado, Diego de: 1610, 1615, 1620, 1625, 1630, 1635.
Ordoñez, Francisco: 1640, 1645.

Ochandiano, Martín de: 1645.
Pérez Gallegos, Diego: 1625, 1630, 1640.
Pineda, Cristóbal de: 1610, 1620.
Postigo, Luis del: 1611.
Quintero, Martín de: 1640, 1645, 1650.
Quesada, Cristóbal de: 1600.
Rosa, Luis de la: 1650.
Rodríguez, Cristóbal: 1610, 1640.
Rivera, Juan de: 1615, 1630.
Sánchez Vadillo, Diego: 1635.
Sobarzo, Juan de: 1650.
Samudio, Juan: 1610, 1640, 1645.
Santisteban, Marcos: 1645, 1650.
Toro, Bartomé de: 1630, 1640.
Tamayo, Antonio de: 1620, 1640.
Taboada, Francisco de: 1645, 1650.
Valenzuela, Juan de la: 1630.
Vargas, Cristóbal de: 1610.
The above with Clemente de Obregón: 1605.

XIV

From Porterage to Proprietorship: African Occupations in Rio de Janeiro, 1808-1850

MARY KARASCH

THE BEAUTY of the city of Rio de Janeiro, the capital of Brazil, served as a constant theme for many European travelers who visited Brazil during their nineteenth century voyages. In frequently inept and florid style, they tried to portray the visual impact of a red-tiled multicolored city on a blue bay edged by green mountains. As their ships passed other white-sailed ships in the bay, the sights and sounds of the harbor fascinated them. They even observed slavers bringing in their cargoes and watched the faces of the slaves as they too viewed the natural beauty of their future home. These harbor scenes prepared some travelers for what they would see when they eventually landed, but others were continually surprised at the nature of the population. From the time a visitor was rowed ashore until he was settled in a private home or in a hotel, he was surrounded by black slaves who rowed his boat, carried his luggage, or tried to sell him something. If he was observant, he noted the tattooed faces, filed teeth, and African styles of dress that would almost convince him he had landed in Africa instead of Brazil; for in the first half of the nineteenth century Rio was a city of slaves, but especially of African slaves.

The slaves who so attracted the attention of the travelers were employed in a large variety of occupations. Accordingly, this essay will undertake an examination of these occupations, as well as an analysis of the number of slaves who worked in Rio in the first half of the nineteenth century. A study of the various census figures should clarify the origins of Rio's slave population and the percentage of slaves in the total population. As early as 1808, for example, an official tabulation revealed that the city then held 54,255 individuals. On a less official basis, but also revealing, are the estimates of Luccock, who counted houses to arrive at a total population of 60,000.[1] He

[1] Luiz Gonçalves dos Santos, *Memórias para servir à história do reino do Brasil*, Rio de Janeiro, 1943, p. 55; "Memoria Estatistica do Imperio do Brazil," *Revista*

369

obtained this figure by taking an average of fifteen persons per dwelling times 4,000 dwellings. In order to explain the large number of people in each house, he noted that generally more than one family lived together with their slaves. In this total, however, he did not include foreigners—that is, 6,000 working on shore and 10,000 involved in shipping. Of particular interest are his figures on slaves (12,000) and "free Negroes" (1,000). Perhaps 20 percent of the total population was enslaved, while only 1 percent were "free Negroes," who may or may not have been freedmen.

By the time of the census of 1821 (Table 1), the number of households had increased to 10,151 and slaves to 36,182. Including the free persons, who numbered 43,139, the total population numbered 79,321; and the slaves had risen to 46 percent of the total population.[2] Given that the slave population was not fully enumerated, the number of slaves must have been greater.

Between 1821 and the next official census in 1838, one can only conjecture about the dimensions of population change. In 1823 Kotzebue guessed at the total population of 250,000 for the city of Rio, of whom two-thirds were "Negroes." His estimate, which is far

TABLE 1. TOTAL POPULATION OF THE CITY OF RIO DE JANEIRO, 1821

Parishes	Freemen	Slaves	Total	Households
Inside the City				
Sacramento	12,525	9,961	22,486	3,352
São José[a]	11,373	8,438	19,811	2,272
Candelaria	5,405	7,040	12,445	1,434
Santa Rita	6,949	6,795	13,744	1,742
Santa Anna	6,887	3,948	10,835	1,351
	43,139	36,182	79,321	10,151
Outside the City				
Engenho Velho	1,871	3,006	4,877	546
Lagoa	937	1,188	2,125	246
	2,808	4,194	7,002	792
TOTAL	45,947	40,376	86,323	10,943

SOURCE: AN, Cod. 808, vol. IV, Estatística, 1790-1865, fol. 17.
[a] Included Gloria.

Trimensal do Instituto Histórico e Geográphico Brasileiro (hereafter *Revista do IHGB*), tomo LVIII, parte 1, (1895), 93; and John Luccock, *Notes on Rio de Janeiro and the Southern Parts of Brazil* . . . London, 1820, pp. 41-42.
    [2] The 1821 census is held at the Arquivo Nacional (hereafter AN), Cod. 808, vol. IV, Estatística, 1790-1865, fol. 17.

370

too high, seems to be based on his impression that a "white face is seldom to be seen in the streets; but the blacks are so numerous, that one might fancy oneself in Africa." Two years later Schlichthorst estimated that the number of slaves then surpassed the number of free men and that the whites were outnumbered three to one.[3]

When Walsh visited the city in 1828 and 1829, he also tried to arrive at a population total by counting the houses as Luccock had done. At that time, he found that the number of inhabited houses had risen to 15,623 in contrast to the 10,151 households of the 1821 census. Instead of the fifteen persons per dwelling that Luccock used, he decided that the average was about six persons per dwelling, thus putting the total population at close to 100,000. In order to take into account the large number of slaves in many households, he raised the figure to 150,000 and, as Kotzebue had done, estimated that two-thirds of this figure were black. Perhaps Walsh's verbal description of the population in 1828 suggests a better picture of Rio than his figures provide. First he admitted that many slaves were sent to the country; but "a great proportion remains in the town, to supply the demands of the expanding white population, so that their increase has been beyond all ordinary calculation; my eye really was so familiarized to black visages, that the occurrence of a white face in the streets of some parts of the town, struck me as a novelty."[4]

Although Walsh's estimates appear to be too high because the 1838 census recorded less than 100,000 people, his figures are conservative in comparison with other travelers. At the same time, Stewart claimed that the city had 200,000 people and that the number of slaves was "fearfully great."[5] Whatever the true figures, the reports of travelers on the whole confirm that significant population growth, both free and slave, took place between 1821 and 1838.

On the other hand, the questionable 1838 census (Table 2) suggests that there was no great increase in population; in fact, some parishes showed a decline. Nevertheless, despite the fact that its data are suspect, the census is useful because it does illustrate that growth occurred in the suburbs. By the time of the 1838 census, three parishes had been added to the city proper, but even with these parishes, the 1838 census is still too low. Furthermore, it shows an unusually low total for the slave population. The figures clearly do

---

[3] Otto von Kotzebue, A New Voyage Round the World, in the Years 1823, 24, 25, and 26, London, 1830, I, 44; C. Schlichthorst O Rio de Janeiro como é, 1824-1826, trans. Emmy Dodt and Gustavo Barroso, Rio de Janeiro, 1943, p. 48.

[4] R. Walsh, Notices of Brazil in 1828 and 1829, London, 1830, I, 463-465, 467.

[5] C. S. Stewart, A Visit to the South Seas . . ., London, 1832, pp. 82-83.

371

TABLE 2. TOTAL POPULATION OF THE CITY OF RIO DE JANEIRO, 1838

Parishes	Freemen	Slaves	Total	Male	Female	Total	House-holds
Sacramento	15,922	8,334	24,256	12,478	11,778	24,256	3,322
São José	9,326	5,084	14,410	7,874	6,536	14,410	1,648
Candelaria	5,816	4,297	10,113	7,162	2,951	10,113	1,153
Santa Rita	8,850	5,707	14,557	8,599	5,958	14,557	2,095
Santa Anna	10,282	5,491	15,773	8,188	7,585	15,773	2,499
Engenho Velho	3,876	4,290	8,166	5,071	3,095	8,166	1,212
Gloria	3,950	2,618	6,568	3,551	3,017	6,568	982
Lagoa	2,003	1,316	3,319	1,688	1,631	3,319	512
TOTAL	60,025	37,137	97,162	54,611	42,551	97,162	13,423

SOURCE: AN, Caixa 761, pacote 2, Mapas de População de Províncias, 1809-1889.

not agree with the large numbers of slaves imported or with travelers' reports. In general, travelers estimated that the slave population equaled one-half to two-thirds of the total population, but the 1838 census recorded that slaves made up little more than a third of the population (38 percent).[6]

As a result, one must seriously question the accuracy of this census, not only for slaves but also for freemen. Shortly after the count was done, a passage in the *Resumo Corographico da Provincia do Rio de Janeiro* of 1841 reported on the difficulties of taking an accurate census. It cited the practice of substituting dead slaves for those brought in by means of the contraband slave trade. In addition, it claimed that many masters hid their slaves to evade taxes, while others allowed their slaves to live and work in a place other than their home. As for freemen, it noted that they were not adequately counted because they hid themselves to avoid being forcibly recruited into the army; and it concluded that many foreigners who made up much of the population escaped the census takers.[7]

Finally, what most makes the 1838 census suspect is that the more accurate 1849 census reveals that the population doubled in little more than ten years from about 100,000 to over 200,000, which suggests that the 1838 figures were far too low. On the other hand,

[6] AN, Caixa 761, pacote 2, Mapas de População de Províncias, 1809-1889; Francis Castelnau, *Expedition dans les parties centrales de l'Amerique du Sud, de Rio de Janeiro à Lima . . .*, Paris, 1850, i, 138; and Melchior Yvan, *Voyages et Récits*, Brussels, 1853, i, 63.
[7] *Resumo corographico da provincia do Rio de Janeiro e do Municipio da Corte*, Rio de Janeiro, 1841, p. 43; William Hadfield, *Brazil, the River Plate, and the Falkland Islands*, London, 1854, p. 144.

this sharp rise does point to increased white immigration, as well as to an extraordinary expansion of the slave trade. Thus, both white and black "immigrants" flooded the city in the 1840s. Although they did not all remain in the city but went on to the coffee plantations in the Paraíba Valley, enough stayed to alter the nature of the population. The enumerated slave population more than doubled, but the free white population also rose. It is in this period that cheap, white, immigrant labor "whitened" the city and moved into occupations formerly left to slaves. By 1850 the abolition of the slave trade confirmed the whitening process because urban slaves were then moved to the plantation areas, where the demand for slave labor was intensive, while the poor white immigrants filled their places.[8]

The 1849 census, taken on the eve of these important changes, reveals many facets of the city's population (Table 3). It is the most accurate of any Rio census of the first half of the nineteenth century, since it was carefully taken and cross-checked with tax records. Of the 21,694 households listed in the tax records, the census takers succeeded in compiling lists on 21,336 of them, or all but 358. When the results were finally compiled, there was considerable surprise at the increase in population in comparison to the 1838 census. Dr. Haddock Lobo, who was in charge of the census, attributed this to deficiencies in the 1838 census and to the influence of the slaves,

TABLE 3. TOTAL POPULATION OF THE EIGHT PARISHES OF
RIO DE JANEIRO, 1849, BY CIVIL STATUS

Parishes	Freemen	Freedmen	Slaves	Total	Households
Sacramento	25,435	2,206	14,215	41,856	5,054
São José	15,412	1,638	10,357	27,407	2,671
Candelaria	9,949	194	8,540	18,683	1,825
Santa Rita	18,095	1,413	12,304	31,812	2,964
Santa Anna	23,190	2,687	12,840	38,717	4,352
Engenho Velho	9,758	1,367	9,759	20,884	2,386
Gloria	8,168	723	6,779	15,670	1,461
Lagoa	6,312	504	4,061	10,877	981
TOTAL	116,319	10,732	78,855	205,906	21,694

[8] Schlichthorst, p. 48. By 1860 the drain of slaves was so great that Soares wrote that one only had to look at the streets to see the difference. Sebastião Ferreira Soares, *Notas Estatísticas sobre a Producção Agrícola e Carestia dos Géneros Alimentícios no Imperio do Brazil*, Rio de Janeiro, 1860, p. 136.

who contributed to an unusual population density of nine inhabitants for each house.[9]

The census clearly reveals that households, slaves, and the population as a whole had at least doubled between 1821 and 1849. Although the slave population had almost doubled to 78,855, it had lost ground in relation to the total population. In 1849 about 40 percent were enslaved, while the freedmen ran to about 5 percent of the total population. The explanation for this percentage decline was the increase in foreign immigration from Portugal, the African islands, England, France, Germany, Spain, and Italy. What is surprising, however, is the magnitude of this "immigration," which shows that almost half of the city's population was foreign born, including African-born slaves and freedmen, as well as Europeans. It is probable that the true population is even higher because the government had difficulty in accounting for all of the foreigners in the city. Without its African slaves and foreign freedmen and freemen, the city's population would have been closer to 100,000 than the more than 200,000 indicated in the census. By this time Rio was truly an international city: native-born Brazilians held a bare majority.

Since the immigrants were generally men or boys, whether African

---

[9] Thus far, the original of the 1849 census has not been located. About the turn of the century it was held by the Biblioteca Nacional when Noronha Santos did a biographical study of Haddock Lobo. Francisco A. Noronha Santos, "Haddock Lobo," *Revista do IHGB*, tomo 76, parte 1 (1913), 278-279. Unfortunately, the manuscript section of the Biblioteca Nacional could not find the census. Investigations at the other major archives and libraries did not uncover it. In order to reconstruct the census, therefore, it is necessary to rely on less complete printed materials. This is indeed unfortunate, since information was collected on each parish, with the inhabitants categorized by sex, nationality, age, marital status, profession, and civil status. Not all of these categories appear in the printed sources.

One of the most complete printed versions appears in a travel account, Hermann Burmeister, *Viagem ao Brasil através das províncias do Rio de Janeiro e Minas Gerais*, trans. Manoel Salvaterra and Hubert Schoenfeldt, São Paulo, 1952, p. 325. The final census totals that appear in the tables are the result of careful comparisons of this version with the following printed materials that give more abbreviated versions of the census: Joaquim Norberto de Souza Silva, *Investigações sobre os recenseamentos de população geral do Imperio e de cada provincia de per si tentados desde os tempos coloniaes até hoje feitas em virtude do aviso de 15 de Março de 1870*, Rio de Janeiro, 1870; *Almanak* (Laemmert) *Administrativo Mercantil e Industrial do Rio de Janeiro para o anno bissexto de 1851*, pp. 236-240; AN, *Relatorio do Ministerio do Imperio*, 1851, pp. 22-23.

One final point should be made about the census. Because 358 household lists out of a total of 21,694 were not received, the census takers raised the totals by 5% to account for the missing lists. Thus, the final totals include this estimated 5%. Serviço Nacional de Recenseamento, *Resumo Histórico dos Inquéritos Censitários Realizados no Brasil*, Rio de Janeiro, 1951, p. 22.

or European, the city also had an unbalanced ratio of men to women in certain categories of the population. In every parish of the city, males outnumbered females. While Brazilian-born men and women were relatively equal in number in the categories of freemen and slaves, freedwomen of *crioulo* origin outnumbered Brazilian freedmen. In the foreign group, however, only in the freedman category did females outnumber males. For every foreign free woman, there were four foreign free men; but there were two African slave men for every African slave woman. Therefore, because of this unbalanced situation in which foreign men were not accompanied by their women, it was natural for them to draw on Brazilian free women as wives and on freedwomen and slaves as sexual partners or common-law wives. The uneven sex ratio certainly encouraged miscegenation, and it was more likely the dearth of women that accounted for racial mixture in Rio than any special Portuguese "genius" or color blindness toward other races.

These population characteristics revealed by the census had an influence on the evolution of Cariocan society, endowing it with a nature different from other Brazilian cities and from cities of the American South. For example, although there are many points of similarity between slavery in the southern cities and in Rio, there are significant differences that begin with the population. First, female slaves outnumbered male slaves in the cities of the South in 1850 (except Richmond), while the 1849 Rio census reveals the exact opposite. As Wade explains, the majority of urban slaves in the South were used as domestics; but, as will be shown later, this was not true of Rio. The functions of slaves in Rio were far more diverse than in the American urban South. Second, the urban southern slave population never approached the numerical size it did in Rio. While the 1849 census illustrates that close to 80,000 slaves lived in Rio, at the most no more than 20,000 resided in even the largest southern city in 1850. Third, no southern city had such a significant percentage of African-born slaves as did Rio. In fact, the total number of slaves in New Orleans did not even equal Rio's more than 50,000 slaves of African birth in 1849.[10]

Comparison with the American urban South suggests that geography and demography were most crtitcal in determining the nature of slave life in Rio. While the beauty of the mountains and the tropical scenery drew praise from comfortable travelers, the mountains also

---

[10] Richard C. Wade, *Slavery in the Cities: The South 1820-1860*, New York, 1964, pp. 325-330, 30, 24.

confined and restricted the city and created conditions of over-crowding that particularly affected slaves. The congestion even led one Brazilian to protest the number of urban slaves and to request that they be sent to the country.[11] Such a large number of slaves in the city, of whom 60 percent were of African birth by 1849, had to leave its imprint.

The figures raise a question: Why did the city require so many slaves? The majority of slaves were used for manual labor, but what is unique to Rio in the first half of the nineteenth century is the variety of semiskilled and skilled manual occupations that were open to slaves. Ewbank was typical of many observers when he noted that Brazilians had a "horror" of manual employments and believed that they alone were born to command. According to his informant, Doctor C., young white men would rather starve than become mechanics. When the doctor had once advised a widow to have her sons learn a trade, she was so insulted that she never spoke to him again.[12] As long as these attitudes toward manual labor prevailed, and as long as the masters associated it with slavery, the slaves of the city enjoyed a wide choice of occupations. When increasing numbers of white immigrants began to demand more ways to earn a living, slaves began to lose those opportunities. They were more and more confined to the unskilled and semiskilled occupations. In fact, they even began to lose control over their specialties, such as street selling. This happened especially after 1850, but in the period under consideration slaves worked at a remarkable variety of occupations, whose diversity can only be suggested in this brief discussion.[13]

Unskilled manual occupations occupied the majority of the slave population. Unless selected for special training, the average imported slave found himself assigned to an unskilled job. Whether he then improved his position or occupation frequently depended on the will of his master or on his own initiative. As he mastered new skills, he often changed occupations. The number of advertisements for slaves with multiple occupations illustrate that a slave was expected to be versatile in and adept at as many occupations as profited his

[11] Frederico Leopoldo C. Burlamaqui, *Memória Analytica acerca do commercio d'escravos e acerca da escravidão domestica*, Rio de Janeiro, 1837, p. 88.

[12] Thomas Ewbank, *Life in Brazil* . . . New York, 1856, p. 184.

[13] Many conclusions regarding the occupations slaves held are based on the reading of slave advertisements in the newspapers of the period. In particular, *O Diario do Rio de Janeiro* is an excellent source for the variety of occupations slaves performed. Newspapers, however, do not provide information on total numbers of slaves involved in each type of occupation or the progression of slaves from one occupation to another. Thus far, such information is lacking.

master. If the labor market demanded a man to pave roads or carry coffee or row a boat, the slave had to be able to perform all of those tasks. In some cases the movement from one occupation to another meant increased status or higher wages that might enable a man to buy his freedom.

In dealing with unskilled manual occupations, what one must remember is that, although the jobs might be among the lowest in status, even slaves who merely toted water received wages for their labor. Of course, the master obtained his share of the wage, but the slave could often keep and save or spend what he earned over and above what his master required. Many masters did not even stipulate what occupation the slave had to pursue—unless he was already specially trained—but left it up to the slave to choose the work he preferred, as long as he returned with the specified sum of money on a daily or weekly basis. In fact, something like employment agencies existed for the placement of slaves sent by their masters to find the work of their choice.[14]

Within the unskilled occupations slaves who labored as porters, stevedores on the docks, and boatmen most frequently worked for wages and so earned the designation *negro de ganho*. Because they had access to money, *negros de ganho* were the ones among the unskilled slave workers who were most likely to accumulate enough funds to buy their freedom. In fact, Rugendas estimated that an industrious *negro de ganho* could save his purchase price within nine to ten years.[15] Thus, an African slave could buy his freedom even if he worked at an unskilled occupation.

There was a definite hierarchy within the category of unskilled manual occupations; that is, many of them were considered better than others, and the preferred ones gave status to slaves. To move into a more prestigious job often meant a greater degree of satis-faction for an ambitious slave—or vice versa. When merchants began to use horses and carts in preference to slave porters in the early 1850s, the slaves protested the change, since it meant the loss of

[14] Luccock, p. 108; and Vivaldo Coaracy, *Memórias da Cidade do Rio de Janeiro,* Rio de Janeiro, 1965, p. 364.

[15] *Negros de ganho* were slaves who worked for wages or sold goods in the streets and returned a specified sum of money to their masters on a daily or weekly basis. Whatever they earned above the amount due their masters they could keep for themselves. A slave who went *ao ganho* thus had to earn money for his master. While this system often gave slaves freedom of movement or choice of occupa-tion, they were punished for failure to meet the masters' requirements. João Maurício Rugendas, *Viagem Pitoresca através do Brasil,* trans. Sérgio Milliet, São Paulo, 1941, p. 187.

their favored positions as *negros de ganho*. It was also likely that because of the change they would be sent to rural plantations.[16] Although their work as porters may have involved heavier physical labor than that of a field slave, they still viewed agricultural labor as less desirable. Being sold or rented to a plantation meant that they would have little or no opportunity to buy their freedom once they moved out of the urban environment; furthermore, they would be deprived of the sort of freedom of movement they enjoyed within the city.

Even within the city, or at least in its environs, there were slaves who performed agricultural labor or who worked as gardeners on the small farms and country homes that surrounded the city. On the *chacaras* of rich men, slaves cultivated fruits, vegetables, flowers, and coffee trees. Occupations related to agricultural work but allowing more freedom were hunting and gathering activities around the environs of Rio. The artist Debret pictured the return to the city of the slave hunters, who, in return for supplying their masters with food from the forests, were allowed to live a relatively free life. Besides hunting, they often accompanied convoys of mule teams into the interior, hunted escaped slaves, or served as naturalists for foreign collectors. Evidently, slave naturalists were considered trustworthy, since they were allowed to roam the forests at will, sometimes staying away for months before returning to Rio with their specimens for natural history collections. If they served a foreign naturalist, they were given their freedom at the end of their services, and continued in the occupation as freedmen.[17]

Other slaves who enjoyed freedom to travel between the city and the interior were those who accompanied mule trains. The head of the train was generally a freeman or freedman, but the individual mule drivers were slaves. Many slaves, besides those who worked the long-distance routes, acted as mule drivers, bringing in provisions from the immediate countryside. Others worked as herdsmen of cattle and pigs. Still others accompanied bullock carts or carried in foodstuffs on their heads.[18] In general, slaves were the most useful in

[16] John Candler and Wilson Burgess, *Narrative of a Recent Visit to Brazil . . .*, London, 1853, p. 40.

[17] Jean B. Debret, *Voyage Pittoresque et Historique au Brésil*, 1834, rpt. Rio de Janeiro, 1965, II, 67-68, pl. 19; and William S. W. Ruschenberger, *Three Years in the Pacific . . .*, Philadelphia, 1834, pp. 40-41.

[18] J. B. von Spix and C.F.P. von Martius, *Travels in Brazil, in the Years 1817-1820*, London, 1824, I, 233; Auguste de Saint-Hilaire, *Voyage à Rio-Grande do Sul (Brésil)*, Orléans, 1887, pp. 493-494; Walsh, II, 3-4; Debret, II, 62, pl. 16; and Gilbert F. Mathison, *Narrative of a Visit to Brazil, Chile, Peru and the Sandwich Islands . . .*, London, 1825, p. 22.

collecting and transporting food and goods to and from the rural areas.

As the preceding section has suggested, one of the major activities of slaves in Rio was porterage—carrying everything from chickens to pianos. Since unwritten custom decreed that masters never carried anything, slaves moved everything in the city, including the master's person. When travelers landed in the city, they quickly learned they had to hire a slave to carry a package of letters or an umbrella. When Luccock left the ship with a gun in his hand, a Brazilian advised him to hand it to a slave because it was wrong to deprive slaves of their hire. Moreover, Luccock ran the risk of angering one of them, who would take revenge for depriving him of his rightful work.[19] Whatever they carried, the slaves who worked as porters clearly served as the city's "beasts of burden."

Related in function to the porters, but operating in Guanabara Bay and on the ships that sailed to Africa were slave boatmen and sailors, who also earned their living by transportation. Goods and people had to be moved between ship and shore not only in Rio's harbor but also between Rio and various points along the bay, particularly São Cristovão, where the royal family had its residence, and the city of Praia Grande (Niterói). For this service there were many small boats and canoes, generally manned by from two to eight slaves. Besides small sailing vessels, one of the most common styles was a *falua* with two masts, each with a large sail, four to eight slave oarsmen, and a covered stern to protect customers from the sun. The Portuguese owner generally acted as steersman in the larger passenger boats, but frequently slaves alone navigated the smaller boats that carried cargo or one or two passengers.[20] The slaves who served as oarsmen on most of the boats were generally Africans, and many of them worked for wages as *negros de ganho*. Others were rented to captains as oarsmen or sailors on larger vessels. In fact, it was common to rent slaves to serve on ocean-going vessels. While many were used in the coastal trade between various states in Brazil, owners also rented their slaves to captains of slave ships as cooks, cabin boys, common seamen, or barber-surgeons.[21]

---

[19] Luccock, p. 110.

[20] George Gardner, *Travels in the Interior of Brazil*, London, 1846, p. 38; Ewbank, p. 112. One of the travelers who did detailed pictures of the slave-operated small boats in the harbor was Paul Harro-Harring, whose work has been published as *Tropical Sketches from Brazil, 1840*, Rio de Janeiro, 1965.

[21] *Diario do Rio*, II, no. 2 (3 November 1821), 10, advertised the sale of an African slave who was a sailor and a cook and who had made "many voyages" to Africa. Arquivo Histórico do Itamaratí, III, Coleções Especiais, 33, Comissões Mistas (Tráfico de Negros), Lata 4, Maço 3, *Embarcação Brilhante*, 1831-1838.

In addition to serving as boatmen and sailors, unskilled slaves were also used in factories in this period. Although the factories were generally small in terms of the number of workers employed, an unknown number of Rio's slaves worked in factories, making everything from gunpowder to chocolate. Industrial slavery was a part of slave life in Rio, although it never reached the proportions it did in the southern United States. In Rio one simply did not find large industries employing many slaves.

In 1843 a listing was made of the factories in Rio, revealing that they were largely food- or raw material-processing plants.[22] Such shops as foundries, firecracker-makers, and a window-glass factory were exceptions. In contrast to the privately owned small-scale factories, the government owned and managed an ironworks and a gunpowder factory, both of which employed sizable labor forces. On the whole, there were probably only two factories that approached the size of those in the United States, while some 228 small shops employed the majority of slave factory laborers. The largest number of factories made candles, cigars, hats, tobacco, and metal products. On an average, each factory appears to have employed ten to twenty slaves in the manufacture of its product.[23]

Of these industries, cigar factories—of which there were sixty-two in 1843—employed the most slave labor. By 1860 some 2,000 workers were engaged in the production of cigars. How many slaves worked in each shop can only be estimated, but the factory of the Frenchman J. Bouis employed eleven. When he sold these slaves and the shop, he had more than 250,000 cigars in stock. In 1831 and in 1852 there were complaints about the bad treatment of the slaves in these fac-

---

This ship included Joze Bruno, a freedman, and at least three rented slave sailors: Joaquim Benguela, Lourenço, and Joze, *preto de Nação*. When the British captors held these men, the owners of the first two slaves requested that they be returned to them, while Joze had to petition for his release from the Casa de Correção, where he had been held a year. As the petition said, it was not his fault that he had been engaged in the slave trade; his master had forced him to sail on the slave ship.

[22] Divisão do Patrimonio Histórico e Artístico do Estado da Guanabara (hereafter PHAEG), 43-1-43, Estatistica de casas de commercio, numero de rezes, embarcações, vehiculos terrestres e notas sobre licenças para obras, alvarás de negocio e receita e despeza, 1843.

[23] In any advertisements for the sale of a factory and its slaves, generally ten to twenty slaves were listed. For example, the sale notice of a bakery noted that it employed and owned fourteen slaves. *Diario do Rio*, i, no. 12 (14 July 1821), 90. One exception to this was the paper factor of Zeferino Ferrez that employed 80 to 90 persons. However, it is unclear whether the workers were slaves. Gilberto Ferrez, "Os Irmãos Ferrez da Missão Artística Francesa," *Revista do IHGB*, 275 (April-June 1967), 28.

tories, the unusual illnesses they suffered and died from, and their terrible working conditions. As one young doctor wrote, there was no illness proper to the profession of cigar-making; rather, the workers suffered from illness brought on by forced labor in overcrowded, poorly ventilated rooms.[24]

A final group of unskilled workers was that employed by the city government on public works projects. These jobs often involved hard labor in the company of chained criminals. Because of the difficulty of recruiting slaves, the government tended to fill its quota with *Africanos livres*.[25] Thus the so-called "free Africans" performed many of the most onerous or unpleasant jobs in the city. In general, rented slaves and *Africanos livres* built roads, paved and cleaned the streets, cared for the whale-oil lamps that illuminated the city, fought fires, or served as dogcatchers.

Semiskilled Manual Occupations

Whatever the occupation, there was constant movement between jobs and levels of skill. A slave who could be rented to pave roads one month could be ordered to sell produce or cook food the next. It was usually slaves of poor masters who had to perform a variety of jobs, while those of rich owners were often trained in a specialty. The general impression is that specialization was the exception. During their lifetime, most slaves worked at a variety of unskilled and semiskilled occupations. This lack of specialization is particularly true of the two major types of occupations under consideration in the semiskilled category; that is, sales and domestic service.

Selling things door-to-door through the streets of Rio was a major activity for slaves. Those who worked at other occupations frequently took advantage of free time on Sundays or in late evenings to sell food or handmade (or stolen) articles to obtain extra money. If they had their own gardens in the suburbs, their masters often allowed them to sell their fruits and vegetables in the city. It is probable that some of the slaves who made their living full-time from

---

[24] Adolfo Morales de los Rios Filho, *O Rio de Janeiro Imperial*, Rio de Janeiro, 1946, p. 242; PHAEG, 58-2-1, Cemiterios dos "negros novos," proximo ao morro da Saude, no Vallongo . . ., 1829-1839, fol. 5; Antônio do Nascimento Silva, "Que molestias predominão sobre os que se empregão nas fabricas de tabaco, e charutos estabelecidos na cidade do Rio de Janeiro? . . .," Tese apresentada à Faculdade de Medicina do Rio de Janeiro, Rio de Janeiro, 1852, pp. 14-15; and Soares, p. 73.

[25] IHGB, Lata 364, no. 4, Collecção Senador Nabuco, Importação de africanos livres . . ., 1855; and PHAEG, 39-1-28, Africanos livres empregados em trabalhos e obras publicas da Municipalidade, 1852, fol. 1.

street selling began on a part-time basis; finding they could do it successfully, they received permission from their masters to go *ao ganho*. The only limitation on street sales was the size of the merchandise: whatever could be carried or led from door to door was offered for sale. Balancing goods in baskets, on boards, or in cases carried on the head, slaves of both sexes hawked everything from articles of clothing, novels and books, skillets, water pots, kitchen utensils, baskets and mats, and candles to love potions, herbs and flowers, birds and animals, and jewelry.

Besides door-to-door selling, slaves and freedmen also sold goods in the various city markets. In fact, African freedwomen appear to have owned many of the market stalls. Obtaining a stall in a market evidently conferred status on its possessor, since it often meant that the individual not only had bought his freedom but had also risen above door-to-door selling. Moreover, he was a person of property. For many slaves, it was the most one could hope to achieve: to be a freedman and to own some property.

One final and notable aspect of life in the city was slave prostitution. As with most other occupations, it was pursued on a part- or full-time basis. Schlichthorst, for example, described the pretty black women on the streets, who sold pastries, cakes—and their own charms. Although they labored during the day to return a specific sum to their masters, at night they frequently obtained extra money on their own. Thus, many prostitutes were frequently pictured as freedwomen. If they were still slaves, it was not uncommon for their masters to solicit business for them or to send them into the streets on an *ao ganho* basis. As Dr. Lassance Cunha observed in 1845, prostitution was more common in Rio than was generally believed because most of it was clandestine and exercised almost exclusively by slave women.[26]

---

[26] Schlichthorst, p. 101, Morales de los Rios Filho, p. 51; F. Dabadie, *A travers l'Amérique du Sud*, Paris, 1859, p. 57. Masters also used the newspapers to solicit business for their slave women. One provocative advertisement appears in the *Diario do Rio*, ii, no. 24 (29 September 1821), 188. Harro-Harring, pl. 23, depicts a woman selecting for prostitution a young slave woman at the slave market. Herculano Augusto Lassance Cunha, "Dissertação sôbre a prostituição, em particular no cidade do Rio de Janeiro," Tese apresentada à Faculdade de Medicina do Rio de Janeiro, Rio de Janeiro, 1845, pp. 17-23, 32, 60; Miguel Antônio Heredia de Sá, "Algumas reflexões sobre a cópula, onanismo e prostituição do Rio de Janeiro," Tese apresentada à Faculdade de Medicina do Rio de Janeiro, Rio de Janeiro, 1845, pp. 31-32; and Theodor von Leithold and L. von Rango, *O Rio de Janeiro visto por dois prussianos em 1819*, trans. Joaquim de Sousa Leão Filho, São Paulo, 1966, p. 32.

Domestic Service

UNDOUBTEDLY, much of the clandestine prostitution involved domestic slave women and their masters. Like most other services slaves performed, there was likewise a profusion of duties for domestic slaves. Young mulatto slave women whom masters advertised in the newspapers for household work in a single gentleman's home also served as sexual partners. Besides caring for the house and cooking the food, the woman might also be sent into the streets to sell prepared food or to obtain outside employment. Domestic slaves in Rio —especially those belonging to low- or middle-income families— performed all the household duties and often outside occupations as well. Except in the case of wet nurses and stablemen, both sexes did the household work. Because of the shortage of female slaves, young boys were trained as domestic servants; they provided all the services of a slave woman, including the sexual, except that of wet nurse.[27] In fact, they seem to have been preferred as domestic help, since they could also work at other occupations that brought in higher wages than those of female slaves.

In large households there was more labor specialization. The elite among the slave women were the richly dressed ladies-in-waiting who served wealthy women and who were known as *mucamas* (or *mocambas*).[28] Not infrequently of mulatto ancestry, a *mucama* was often the half-sister, child, or mistress of her master, or was related in some other way to the family. In a middle-income family, particularly if the master was unmarried, she served as housekeeper or as supervisor in charge of the other slaves. In that case, she frequently owed her position to the fact that she was her owner's mistress. In some cases, the *mucama* was also the nurse for the master's children, in many households not only nursing the children but rearing them as well. If the master had no wet nurse among his own slaves at the time his child was born, he rented one through an advertisement in a

---

[27] Given the shortage of women in the later period when so many boys entered domestic service, one suspects that homosexual practices were not uncommon. Heredia de Sá, pp. 15-16, discreetly commented on "that atmosphere of depravation which envelopes our youth, impregnating in them vices so much more perilous. . . . It is for that reason that bodies from ten to twelve years enclose souls already aged."

[28] Raymond S. Sayres, *The Negro in Brazilian Literature*, New York, 1956, p. 152; Debret, II, 47, pl. 10; and *Diario do Rio*, II, no. 9 (10 October 1821), 64, gives but one example of an advertisement for a mulatto freedwoman as a housekeeper.

newspaper or through a rental agency. As Schlichthorst observed, every young slave woman had milk for two children, her own and a white child.[29]

After *mucamas*, housekeepers, and nurses, the next in status in a large household were slave children of the master. They were commonly brought up in the house with the master's legitimate offspring, and served as playmates or babysitters. As they grew up, girls were trained in skilled household tasks as *mucamas* and boys as pages or valets.

Male slaves of the household served as coachmen, livried footmen, and *cadeirinha* (hammock) carriers; either men or women worked as cooks, buyers, and launderers. Many women slaves also specialized in sewing, lace-making, starching and ironing clothes, or spinning cotton.[30] Slaves who lacked skills—quite often the newly imported, the children, or the aged—were assigned menial tasks, such as cleaning, carrying water, kitchen work, or emptying refuse containers. Yet, whatever their position in the household, domestic slaves were privileged in terms of material comfort. In general, they possessed better clothing than other slaves because a master's prestige was enhanced by the sartorial elegance of his slaves, and they tended to receive better food. If a master had many slaves, the individual work load was considerably lightened, since each performed only his particular specialty. Since a master's status was often determined by the number of his slaves, many domestic slaves were more for display than for labor. Burlamaqui complained that wealthy masters frequently spent more on clothes for slaves than the slaves could earn in wages. On the other hand, domestic slaves, especially women, often suffered from the confinement and seclusion imposed on Brazilian women. While they may have enjoyed better living conditions than other slaves, they nevertheless suffered severe restrictions in personal freedom.[31]

---

[29] The *Diario do Rio,* as well as other newspapers, had many advertisements regarding the buying and selling of wet nurses. A typical one followed the form of one in the *Diario do Rio,* I, no. 20 (24 July 1821), 157: "For sale a black wet nurse with a baby of a month and a half from her first pregnancy Nation Rebola." The advertisement went on to list her age as eighteen and to enumerate her many household skills. See also Schlichthorst, p. 93.

[30] This specialization is made clear in advertisements offering for sale slaves who were starchers, ironers, or laundrymen. See also Leithold, p. 30; and Debret, II, 147, pl. 48.

[31] Advertisements for female domestic slaves often mentioned that the woman had never left the house except to attend Mass. See, for example, *Diario do Rio,* II, no. 14 (18 September 1821), 108.

THE CRAFTS AND RETAILING

DOMESTIC service, sales, and unskilled manual occupations were
not the only opportunities for slaves. After the arrival of the Portuguese court in 1808, and before immigrants again flooded the city
in the 1840s, slaves were apprenticed to and worked at the majority
of skilled crafts in the city. Although usually supervised by a white
master craftsman, skilled slaves built the cabinets, made the jewelry,
or printed the books. Because of the shortage of whites willing to
work with their hands, slaves and freedmen had access to the arts
and crafts and skilled occupations throughout this period. According
to Spix and von Martius, slaves in Rio actually had more opportunities to enter the skilled crafts than European workers, who were excluded because of craft restrictions.[32]

In contrast to domestic service, where women were more important,
the skilled occupations were almost entirely in the hands of male
slaves, who thereby gained the chance to earn money on an *ao ganho*
basis, to buy freedom, and to support themselves as freedmen. Since
the arts and crafts demanded a high order of training, the critical
factor for a slave was his master's decision to apprentice him, to send
him to a school for slaves, or to put him into a situation where he
could learn by working. A common practice was to buy young slaves
just off the slave ships and teach them a trade or apprentice them to
a master craftsman. By having his slaves taught a trade, a master
could double or triple their value and obtain a good return on his
investment. Since skilled slaves also worked for wages on an *ao ganho*
basis, masters often lived off their wages. According to Ewbank,
the Carmelite monks of the Lapa Church in Rio raised slaves for
this purpose on their estate in the province of Rio. At the time Ewbank
described the situation, the Carmelites had six men and fifty women
slaves. When the boys reached a certain age, the monks apprenticed
them in the city instead of putting them to work in the fields. According to Ewbank's estimate, the monks realized twice the profit
they would have made had the slaves been kept on the estate.[33]

Although a slave might have had no choice in the craft to which
he was apprenticed, the degree of his skill was often his responsibility,
as well as whether he used his skills to earn the price of his freedom.
Newspaper advertisements reveal how skilled many slaves became.
Slaves were generally designated by such terms as *aprendiz* (apprentice), *meio-official* (semiskilled worker), *official* (skilled worker),

---

[32] Spix and von Martius, I, 124.
[33] Schlichthorst, p. 275; Ewbank, p. 370.

and *mestre* (master);[34] the most common were *official, bom official, aprendiz,* or some other indication that the slave was still learning his trade. Also common was the practice of training slaves in one or more occupations: a slave was often described as trained in one occupation but learning another, such as a skilled painter who was a beginning tailor. Another possibility was for a new slave to be trained in two occupations at once, such as the African boy who was learning cooking while training simultaneously as a bricklayer's apprentice.

In such manner, a slave learned his trade and improved his skills, and if he were sold, the newspapers would describe him as *bom official* or *muito bom official* (very good skilled worker). To indicate that he was particularly proficient, the master printed the top wages that he could earn while working at his trade. Finally, the designation *mestre* was rare, but it did appear. A Calabar slave of thirty years of age was advertised as a master candlemaker and soapmaker. On the whole, one suspects that many slaves had the skills of master craftsmen but were seldom accorded the position or the status of a free white master craftsman.

One of the more common skilled occupations for slaves and freedmen was that of carpentry, or more generally any of those skills required in the construction crafts, including masonry. As Horner observed, most of the builders were blacks, either free or enslaved.[35] They did everything: splitting logs and sawing wood, laying bricks and tiles, and making the furniture and carriages required for a completed household.

All the metal crafts also employed slaves, who worked in iron, tin, copper, gold, and silver. Skilled slave blacksmiths frequently commanded some of the highest prices and earned good wages. Of less stature were the tinsmiths, who made lanterns, bugles, trumpets, military ornaments, and the *funils* widely used during Carnival. Coppersmiths were invaluable in the manufacture of the kettles and other objects used in the homes and the sugar mills. When Ewbank visited two copper shops, he observed one establishment where all fourteen workers were slaves who were supervised by a slave foreman and

---

[34] The discussion in the following two paragraphs is based on advertisements in the *Diario do Rio.* Specific references are from ii, no. 22 (27 November 1821), 171; i, no. 7 (7 June 1821), 31; i, no. 9 (9 June 1821), 46; ii, no. 14 (18 September 1821), 108; and ii, no. 7 (9 November 1821), 51.

[35] Debret, ii, 65, pl. 18; ii, 109, pl. 34; Ewbank, pp. 187, 195; and Gustavus R. B. Horner, *Medical Topography of Brazil and Uruguay,* Philadelphia, 1845, p. 56.

the Portuguese owner. In the other, twenty blacks did all the work themselves; only the clerks, who sold the copper objects, were white.[36]

Slaves also handled valuable silver and gold, turning out admirable jewelry and dinner services. Even the highly critical traveler, Ida Pfeiffer, admired their gold and silver work. In addition, they cut and shaped the precious stones that filled the gold and silver settings.

One of the more uncommon types of metal work produced by slaves was the manufacture of shackles, iron collars, chains, iron masks, and other instruments of control and punishment. Debret and Ewbank both described a shop where the slaves performed this labor. In fact, Ewbank was waited on by a black man who tried to sell him some chains.[37]

Slaves were also important in the skills connected with clothing, making every item from hats to shoes, including simple sun hats woven of natural fibers, wooden platform shoes called *tamancos*, leather belts and shoes, gloves, and suits. Because of the clothing demands of a growing city, slave tailors were particularly common, and good ones could succeed in buying their freedom. One example of opportunities for tailors is that of an African freedman who had been imported as a slave about 1820. Thirty years later he was a tailor who had purchased his freedom "with wages earned for work in extra hours." In 1851 he applied to the British consulate for protection to transport himself and a "large number of his countrymen to Ambriz [Angola], declaring that there were upwards of 500 similarly situated free Africans desirous to return to Africa."[38]

In the early period, however, when European tailors had monopolized the craft, many master tailors used slaves merely to carry their equipment when they visited their clients. Increasingly, they had slaves do the expert work involved in making suits. When Robertson visited the street of the tailors, he observed the black and mulatto slaves who sat on benches in front of "every" door working with the needle.[39] Another craft that slaves took over in this period was

[36] For the discussion of metal workers, see: Ewbank, pp. 72, 100, 193, 195; Ida Pfeiffer, *A Lady's Voyage Round the World*, London, 1852, p. 7; PHAEG, 44-1-24, Funileiros e Latoeiros, 1815, fol. 16. Two workers, one in gold and the other in precious stones, appeared for sale in the *Diario do Rio*, II, no. 16 (20 November 1821), 122; and no. 27 (31 October 1821), 210.

[37] Debret, II, 132; and Ewbank, pp. 437-438.

[38] Great Britain, Foreign Office, *British and Foreign State Papers*, 1851-1852, XLI, "Correspondence of Great Britain, relative to the Slave Trade, 1851, 1852," 378.

[39] John Parish Robertson and William Parish Robertson, *Letters on Paraguay . . .*, London, 1838, I, 146; Gilberto Freyre, *O escravo nos anúncios de jornais brasileiros*

that of shoemaking. Prior to 1813 many poor white families had earned their living by fashioning and selling shoes, but in that year 101 members of the brotherhood and guild of shoemakers protested the increasing use of slave labor in the manufacture and sale of shoes. By 1821 this practice had become so prejudicial to poor whites that they again protested; their protests were ignored, and the slaves continued to make and sell shoes. In the 1830s, Debret observed that the slaves of German and French shoemakers were as skilled as their masters.[40]

Another skilled profession in which slaves were important and which produced a number of freedmen who owned their own businesses was that of barber-surgeon. According to Debret, the man who cut beards and styled hair was "nearly always" a black or mulatto. The barbershop Debret frequented belonged to two "energetic" freedmen who had bought their freedom by saving their wages when they had worked for artisans.[41]

To be a barber, however, required a number of skills besides those of cutting and trimming beards; that is, barbers also worked as surgeons, bloodletters, dentists, and musicians. In 1820 the slave Vicente applied to be licensed as bloodletter and dentist. At first there was some reluctance to give a slave a license; but the officials decided to admit him and other slaves to the profession because there was a shortage of free men trained in the occupation, and the public good required that skilled men, even if they were slaves, fill this office.[42]

Since barbers were also bloodletters, they were also expected to treat illnesses and even perform minor surgery.[43] Because of the shortage of doctors, barbers were often the only source of medical care for the poor and the slaves. During the days of the slave trade, the "surgeons" who made the crossings to and from Africa were

---

do século XIX, Recife, 1963, p. 162; Diario do Rio, I, no. 23 (25 June 1821), 161; and no. 25 (27 June 1821), 177.

[40] PHAEG, 50-1-12, Sapateiros, 1813-1827, fols. 2-3, 17-18, 22; Debret, II, 91-92, pl. 29.

[41] Debret, II, 50-51, pl. 12.

[42] Ibid.; A. de La Salle, Voyage autour du Monde Exécuté pendant les années 1836 et 1837 . . ., Paris, 1851, I, 144; Ewbank, pp. 195-196; and PHAEG, 6-1-23, Documentos sobre a Escravidão e Mercadores de Escravos, 1777-1831, fols. 92-93.

[43] Bloodletting was also a practice in Angola. Leeches were used in both Africa and Brazil; in fact, they were imported into Rio from Angola. Joachim J. Monteiro, Angola and the River Congo, London, 1875, II, 263, 266.

barber-surgeons. Masters commonly rented or sold their slave barber-surgeons to captains of slavers.[44]

Other slaves and freedmen were also medical specialists. Often of African origin, they frequently mixed African cures and Portuguese medical practice in their treatments. Prominent among such specialties was midwifery. Except for the Frenchwomen who became the midwives of the rich in that period, black women were most important as midwives. Frequently employing African customs, which Doctor Imbert severely criticized, they were the major source of medical care for women in childbirth. For many an African slave woman, being a skilled nurse or midwife was an important and prestigious occupation which gave her "the respect and consideration of all."[45]

The above are but a few of the crafts and skilled occupations that slaves pursued. They were also important in the arts as musicians, painters, sculptors, and actors. Like so many of the professions, the arts were often practiced only on a part-time basis; rare were the slaves who painted, carved, or played music to the exclusion of other pursuits. In general, the pattern was for the slave to work primarily at the occupation decreed by the master while using his artistic talents to earn extra money. Maria Graham knew one slave, probably typical of many, whose proper job was to sell fruit for his master, but who, after he had sold his wares, earned additional money by dancing, singing, and telling stories in the streets. Debret pictured such slaves, playing African instruments for crowds of slaves gathered around the public fountains.[46]

Slaves also played European instruments. The largest employer of slave musicians was the royal family, and, in 1816 at least, fifty-seven slaves performed on special occasions. According to Spix and von Martius, who heard them, they performed vocal and instrumental music with skill for a white audience. They also contributed their talents to the African-style celebrations in honor of the black patroness, Nossa Senhora do Rosario, at which the slaves and freedmen danced to their music.[47]

---

[44] An example appears in *O Correio Mercantil*, I, no. 18 (10 September 1830), 72.

[45] Ewbank, p. 247; *Diario do Rio*, II, no. 7 (9 November 1821), 52; PHAEG, 47-1-47, 47-1-48, Parteiras, 1820-1878; João B. A. Imbert, *Manual do Fazendeiro ou Tratado Domestico sobre as Enfermidades dos negros*, Rio de Janeiro, 1839, II, 252; and Morales de los Rios Filho, p. 114.

[46] Maria Graham, *Journal of a Voyage to Brazil and Residence There, During Part of the Years 1821, 1822, 1823*, London, 1824, p. 166; and Debret, II, 129, pl. 41.

[47] Spix and von Martius, I, 112.

Slaves who painted or sculpted were largely employed in the decoration of churches or homes. According to Ewbank, both slaves and free blacks did sculptures in stone and saints' images in wood. He knew one old African, once an "excellent" sculptor, who had degenerated into a beggar and an habitual drunk. In the Church of Lampadosa, Ewbank saw a sculpture of a dead Christ that had been carved in the eighteenth century by a slave named Fulah.[48] Besides these more lasting examples of slave creativity, the common employment of slave painters and sculptors was in fashioning images of saints, ornaments, decorations, stage scenery, and whatever else was needed in the many and elaborate processions with which Cariocans celebrated the religious holidays. Slaves also arranged and set off the elaborate fireworks that accompanied major celebrations.

Ambitious and trained slaves who labored in the construction, metal, and clothing crafts or who learned a skill like barbering or painting earned among the highest slave wages in the city. It was possible for them to save sufficient funds from their earnings not only to buy their freedom but also to become property owners. Thus, not even business management or property ownership were closed to slaves and freedmen.

Slaves could own other slaves. Although there was always the danger of the master claiming the slave as his own, if the master were cooperative, a slave could buy another slave out of his savings, much as a master allowed him to buy clothing, food, or jewelry. One example was the woman slave who bought herself by exchanging her own slave plus a sum of money for her freedom.[49] One suspects, however, that this practice was uncommon and that ownership of slaves was largely restricted to freedmen rather than to slaves.

As far as the records indicate, there were certain groups of freedmen who owned slaves. The most common examples, which come from the manumission records, were those of freedwomen who evidently had been married to freedmen, who had given them slaves. Since many of them were widows, they had inherited the slaves from their husbands.[50] Another group of women owning slaves were freedwomen who were prostitutes. Street sellers and laundrywomen also bought slaves to assist them in their work. On the whole, it seems that freedwomen had more opportunities to own slaves than freed-

---

[48] Ewbank, pp. 195, 400; José Vieira Fazenda, "Antiqualhas e Memórias do Rio de Janeiro," *Revista do IHGB*, tomo 88, 142 (1920), 391-392.

[49] Ubaldo Soares, *A Escravatura na Misericórdia*, Rio de Janeiro, 1958, p. 123.

[50] AN, Secção Legislativa e Judiciaria, Livro do 1° Oficio de Notas, no. 218, fol. 24, records one of many cases in which a freedwoman manumitted her slave.

men; yet clearly some *negros de ganho* bought and trained slaves to follow their trade, and barbers and artisans did likewise. One other factor that appears to have encouraged freedmen to own slaves is that, while the slave trade continued, they had the opportunity to buy members of their own people. This pattern clearly emerges from the *negros de ganho* records where Yoruba freedmen owned Yoruba slaves.[51]

While the number of slaves and freedmen who owned slaves was limited, every slave woman and freedwoman made an attempt to own jewelry. The more gold and silver jewelry she possessed, the greater her status and wealth. One suspects that many slaves and freedmen who could not invest in other forms of property accumulated jewelry. The poorest managed with beaded necklaces and copper bracelets, anklets, and earrings; the more prosperous black women collected gold and silver ornaments. A British merchant, who warned his superior not to send poorly made African goods to Brazil, reported on the wealth of the Brazilian blacks: "The domestic negroes of the Brasils wear none but solid gold trinkets, consisting of collars, bracelets, and chains; and plates for the forehead, breast and shoulders, and crucifixes and molten images to suspend from these various articles. And the field negroes, and mertchoes wear none but trinkets of pure materials."[52]

Thus, slaves could accumulate items of value for their personal use, but freedmen could also own businesses. In 1843 a count was made of the owners of businesses and properties in the city of Rio and its surrounding rural parishes.[53] The figures established that there were 166 African-born individuals who owned businesses or property in the city but not one in the rural areas. Since the accounting was by nationality, it also revealed that only the Brazilians, Portuguese, and French surpassed the Africans in number of proprietors, while the English or any other nationality counted fewer owners than the Africans.

The figures suggest that Africans as a group were more successful than most other foreigners, but the proportions must be put in perspective. In the first place, African-born individuals outnumbered other foreigners in the city. Given their numerical advantage, they

---

[51] PHAEG, 6-1-46, Escravos ao ganho, 1845-1863, fol. 47.

[52] Thomas Ashe, *A Commercial View, and Geographical Sketch, of the Brasils* . . ., London, 1812, p. 17.

[53] PHAEG, 43-1-43, Estatistica de casas de commercio, numero de rezes, embarcações, vehiculos terrestres e notas sobre licenças para obras, alvarás de negocio e receita e despeza, 1843.

should have done better than the French, who were a definite minority. Second, specific data from one of the urban parishes, Santa Rita,[54] strongly suggest that African ownership was almost entirely limited to two types of businesses, barbershops and *quitandas* (grocery stores), both of which were generally small-scale operations. In fact, it is possible that these *quitandas* were no more than one- or two-room stalls, not much more than a market stall. Moreover, the Santa Rita figures reveal that Africans had a definite majority in those businesses in that parish. (See Table 4.)

As this brief discussion has suggested, it was possible for a slave to begin as a newly imported African and work his way up to ownership of business property as a freedman. What is important to remember, however, is that the incidence of such individuals was small in proportion to their total numbers in the population. Only a limited number of Africans succeeded in entering businesses which, being low in prestige, were avoided by whites.

The traveler Rugendas ably summed up the chances for occupational mobility for Rio's slaves. To paraphrase, the most slaves could achieve as freedmen was to join the ranks of the "inferior classes," for the number of those who succeeded in elevating themselves to the level of the bourgeoisie as businessmen or proprietors was small; on the other hand, it was easy for freedmen to earn a living because of the good wages for manual laborers.[55]

Because of the growing demand for workers to fill manual occupations between 1808 and 1850, slaves and freedmen had significant opportunities open to them, as long as the work involved labor that whites disdained. Moreover, as long as European immigration did not exceed certain limits and the slave trade kept prices relatively low and made slaves easily available, slaves and freedmen in Rio

TABLE 4. BARBERS AND SHOPOWNERS IN SANTA RITA, 1841

	Barbers (Male)	Shopowners (Male)	(Female)	Total
African	5	10	16	31
Crioulo	2	4	4	10
TOTAL	7	14	20	41

[54] PHAEG, 43-1-42, Estatistica da Freguezia de Santa Rita: Rellação nominal das cazas de Negocios da Freguezia de Santa Rita pertencente a anno de 1841, 1841.

[55] Rugendas, p. 192.

moved into occupations that had once been the special preserve of the whites, such as shoemaking. While slaves could aspire to buy their freedom and to work at the skilled crafts, this is not to suggest that slaves rose easily within Cariocan society or that their masters treated them benevolently. In many cases, what they achieved was due to their own hard labor in the face of difficult living conditions and a hostile disease environment. This, then, is part of the record of slave achievements in an urban environment in spite of the conditions of servitude.

But these conditions did not last. When European immigrants and a rising demand for labor on the interior coffee plantations combined to produce an exodus of slaves from the city, the result was a sharp reduction in the slave population and a restriction of African occupational mobility. The diversity of occupations open to African slaves and freedmen in Rio was unique to this particular period, but records of the episode indicate the diversity of skills and talent acquired and exercised by slaves when given the opportunity by economic necessity and their masters.

XV

Free-Born and Slave-Born Blacks
in Antebellum Philadelphia

THEODORE HERSHBERG

CENTRAL TO THE study of the Afro-American experience is the assessment of the impact that slavery had on the slaves.[1] A direct

[1] This essay is part of a larger study known informally as the Philadelphia Social History Project. The research deals with comparative social mobility in 19th-century Philadelphia focusing on the patterns of three distinct groups: blacks, Irish, and Germans. The research, originally funded in April, 1969, was recently expanded to include native-white-Americans in order to study, in the most comprehensive comparative perspective, the relationships between social mobility and social stratification, industrialization, family structure, neighborhood, and transportation. The author wishes to express his appreciation to the Center for Studies of Metropolitan Problems, NIMH (Grant no. MH 16621), whose financial support has made this research possible.

The data are derived from five distinct sources. First, the Population Manuscript Schedules of the U.S. Census for Philadelphia County, 1850-1880. From these census records enumerated decennially by the federal government, information was taken describing each of approximately 500,000 black, Irish, German, and native-white American inhabitants—that is, a large sample of native-white American and all Irish and German males above the age of seventeen, a large sample of Irish, German, and native-white American households including all members of each sample household, and all black men, women, and children. The major variables listed in these census schedules include name, age, sex, color, occupation, property, and place of birth.

The second data source is the Manufacturing Manuscript Schedules of the U.S. Census for Philadelphia County, 1850-1880. All places of business in the county with an annual product of $500 or more were included in the census. In all, data describing over 27,000 individual firms, ranging from 4,700 in 1850 to 8,500 in 1880, have been recorded. Although the information included in the census varied slightly from year to year, each firm was described in terms of the following variables: company name, name of business or product, amount of capital, number of employees (males, females, youths), wages, source of power, machines, materials, and product (the latter two in kinds, quantities, and value), the number of months per year in operation, etc.

The third data source consists of three unusually detailed household censuses of the entire free-black population of antebellum Philadelphia taken in 1838 and 1856 by the Pennsylvania Abolition Society and in 1847 by the Society of Friends. These censuses describe 11,600 households and include, in addition to those variables listed in the U.S. Census of Population, membership in specific church, beneficial and temperance societies, income, education, school attendance, house, ground and water rent, slave birth, how freedom was acquired, the amount of

comparison of free-born and slave-born blacks should consider two dimensions of historical experience: socioeconomic condition and social status. Demographic characteristics, distribution of the work force, property accumulation, and the vital institutions of the black community such as family, church and beneficial society, constitute important socioeconomic measures. These should be complemented by information describing the role of status-at-birth in the emerging black social structure. It is critical to our understanding and interpretation of the 19th century black experience that we know whether and to what extent blacks themselves may have preferred the free-born over the slave-born. The place of the slave-born in the social stratification of the black community will be discussed at another time.[2] In this essay I shall discuss some of the methodological problems involved in constructing a research design to compare free-

---

property brought to Pennsylvania, and marital status. The data used in this essay are drawn entirely from this source.

The fourth data source consists of the City of Philadelphia's business directories for the entire period, 1850-1880. Similar to today's "Yellow Pages," the directories listed all the "business" firms in the city under each business "type," e.g., "Butchers: George J. Amos, 1526 N. 5th Street, William Buehler, 1545 Germantown Ave." Approximately 140,000 entries are included in the directories in the four census years 1850, 1860, 1870, and 1880. Each entry is being put into machine-readable form and will be sorted by address to allow for the study of business development by type and neighborhood, the impact of transportation, etc.

The fifth data source consists of a reconstruction of all means of transportation available to nineteenth-century Philadelphians. All omnibus, trolley, and tram car routes and railroad lines in the County of Philadelphia are being plotted in order to observe the relationships between transportation, urbanization, and industrialization.

The five data sources described above are being coded in spatial units slightly larger than a square block so that the relationships between the spatial dimensions and all other aspects of the research can be studied.

Finally, the data describing each individual, household, manufacturing and business firm, and the transportation network are being put into machine-readable form. When all the data are verified, a sophisticated record linkage program will instruct the computer in tracing specific individuals, households, and firms from census to census and within each census. When identifications are made it will be possible to proceed with analysis of the dynamic aspects of the research: an intra- and inter-generational approach to a study of change over time.

[2] Also, and perhaps of more importance, the role of color: black and mulatto. The draft of this essay originally submitted to the Conference on Comparative Systems of Slavery included a considerable amount of data describing the distribution of the slave-born and free-born, and of the black and mulatto as members and leaders of Philadelphia's Negro elite organization. In all, the membership patterns by status-at-birth and color of twenty elite organizations were presented. This information has been removed from the present essay and is included instead in "Mulattoes and Blacks: Intra-Group Color Differences and Social Stratification in Nineteenth-Century Philadelphia" (presented at the 67th Annual Meeting of the Organization of American Historians, April 1974).

born and slave-born blacks and describe the preliminary empirical findings resulting from a socioeconomic comparison of these two groups in antebellum Philadelphia.[3]

THE RESEARCH DESIGN

IT is important to recognize that we are dealing with three, not two, groups within the black population: (1) free-born, (2) slave-born freed *before* the Civil War, and (3) slave-born freed *after* the Civil War. In determining "when" one should study the question, scholars would agree that a point in time after 1865 would be appropriate; to do otherwise would mean comparing the free-born with the slave-born freed before the Civil War. Such a comparison would be inappropriate, for the latter group, it would be argued, is probably not representative of the far larger slave-born population freed after the Civil War. In determining "where" one should study the question, one must consider the characteristics of the local black population and hope to find: *first*, free-born blacks as distinct from those who were slave-born and freed before the Civil War, and *second*, slave-born blacks freed after the Civil War.

On both counts, however, the historian is faced with formidable obstacles. If one turns to a southern location where the second condition is easily satisfied, the first condition is not met. Most available data, especially that in the U.S. Census, distinguish only between blacks who were slave or free at a point in time, and not between slave and free *birth*. Moreover, even if data were found which did distinguish status-at-birth, it is highly likely that most locations in the South would be ruled out because there were not enough free-born blacks in the population to allow for comparative study. Such free-born blacks as there were in the South, however, were only the exception in their local environments.[4] In a northern location such

[3] I want to make it clear at the outset that the research design is constructed to measure only the effects of *direct* contact with slavery. In so doing I do not want it to appear as though I am underestimating the negative effects on blacks of *indirect* contact with slavery. Whether prejudice toward blacks preceded the establishment of the institution of slavery in the seventeenth century, or vice versa, or whether they evolved simultaneously, is not very important in this context; what is, is that by the nineteenth century the central perception held by whites of blacks in America was that of inferiority. Proslavery propaganda reinforced this perception, and it pervaded the values and institutions of the entire society. Free-born blacks were indeed affected indirectly by the institution of slavery; it remains significant, nevertheless, to determine the consequences of *direct* contact with slavery.

[4] I may be wrong in these observations. Perhaps the number of free-born is larger than I anticipate. Perhaps the data which distinguish status-at-birth is available. I just think it unlikely.

as Philadelphia, for example, where status-at-birth data are available *before* the Civil War, free-born blacks were the rule: they comprised 90 percent of the black population, all of which was free.

A city like Philadelphia satisfied the first condition, but not the second. Status-at-birth data are *not* available to describe the black population *after* 1865. To obtain the second condition—numbers of slave-born blacks freed after the Civil War (freedmen)—we might assume that because 94 percent of the blacks in the South were slaves in 1860, a very large percentage of the blacks who migrated to Philadelphia after the Civil War must have been freedmen, too. But even discounting the fact that migrants from Maryland, Delaware, or the District of Columbia [5] were more likely to have been free than slave before the Civil War (55 percent of all blacks in these areas were in fact free in 1860), one is left with the problem of representativeness.

To put it another way, even if we had data which distinguished the freedmen who migrated to Philadelphia (or to any other northern city) after the Civil War from the free-born blacks already living in the city, we would still be left with a *migrant* and not a typical ex-slave. Migration is a highly selective process and it is unlikely that the post-Civil War migration was an exception. The observations of Carter G. Woodson, made over fifty years ago in his *Century of Negro Migration,* remain unchallenged. If Woodson is correct, the migrants who came to the North before the Great Migration were not typical of those who stayed behind, but representatives of the "Talented Tenth."

The migrants who came *after* 1910, and especially after 1915, although still not "typical" of the millions of southern blacks who did not migrate, were, according to Woodson, far more representative of the southern black masses than those who migrated before them. They came to the North for different reasons than did those who had left the South earlier. The "push and pull" factors (floods, drought, and the boll weevil, and the demand for industrial labor, created in part by the war and heightened by the end of European immigration) which led to the Great Migration simply were not operative in the earlier period. Those who came *before* 1900 were probably motivated for different reasons; the problems they faced in the South and the opportunities they saw in the North, if not different in kind, were certainly different in degree. Whatever the motivation of the

[5] Most migrants to Philadelphia, in fact, came from these areas. According to the U.S. Census of 1860 only two of ten migrants came from other slave states and most of these came from Virginia, which in 1860 had a free-black population of 58,042.

earlier migrants, however, the numbers alone of those who came after 1910 make this latter group far more representative.

The thrust of this argument is to study a northern city during the years of the Great Migration which had a large free-born black population and which experienced a substantial in-migration of southern blacks, thus coming closest to satisfying the two conditions described above. The problem with this approach is twofold: first, and familiar by now, the data necessary to distinguish between these two groups are not available; second, with a new twist, even if the data were available one would no longer be dealing with "typical" freedmen as migrants, but with their children, and that would destroy the original intent of the research design—to study the effects of *direct* contact with slavery.

In summary, then, the construction of a research design to study blacks in either a southern or northern location who were representative of those free-born and slave-born freed after the Civil War proves highly problematic, even when allowing for the discovery of data which would distinguish between these two groups.

The comparison of free-born and slave-born blacks is too important to abandon, however, simply because the ideal conditions for their comparative study are difficult to obtain. In its place I offer a comparison of free-born and slave-born blacks freed *before* the Civil War. To date, so little is known about ex-slaves in antebellum America that the group might just as well not have existed. The data presented below, although limited in this essay to comparisons of socioeconomic characteristics, make possible the difficult but potentially significant task of understanding the contribution made by ex-slaves in shaping the values and institutions of free-black communities. With the interaction between free blacks and freedmen after the Civil War just beginning to be studied, the insight into the ex-slave subgroup of free blacks might prove of considerable value.

Socioeconomic Condition: 1838, 1847, 1856

The data presented below are derived from manuscript household censuses. A household census differs from an individual enumeration such as that taken by the U.S. Bureau of the Census (beginning in 1850) in several important respects. The only name given is that of the household head and the only information provided describes the members of the household in aggregated form. Although the groups which took the censuses cooperated with each other, the data contained in one survey differ in various ways from those collected in the others. Few variables, for example, were common to all three years. The 1838 census was the most specific of the three in its description of the different types of ex-slave households, while the 1847 census contained much richer detail describing all households. Finally, the 1856 census was the least valuable because it confined itself to questions of education and skilled occupations.

Cutting across the three censuses was the dimension of the sex of the household head. Where data on wealth were available, as was the case in 1838 and 1847, a strong and direct relationship was found between household size, wealth, and male sex, so that the largest households had the most wealth and the greatest likelihood of being headed by a male. When significant differences emerged between ex-slave and free-born households, they almost invariably occurred between male-headed households. Ex-slave households headed by females resembled their free-born counterparts much more closely and consistently than did the males. Tables 1 to 6, therefore, do not explicitly describe female-headed households of either birth.

1838

DEMOGRAPHIC VARIABLES

Among the approximately 3,300 households and 12,000 persons included in the 1838 census, about one household in four contained at least one person who, although free in 1838, had been born a slave (see Tables 1 and 2). Living in these 806 households were some 1,141 ex-slaves (or 9 percent of the entire population). In 1838, ex-slaves differed from their free-born neighbors in a variety of significant social indicators.[6]

The family size of all ex-slave households was 10 percent larger than households all of whose members were free-born: 4.27 persons as compared to 3.88. Families of ex-slave households headed by free-born males and those families headed by males who bought their own freedom were 20 percent larger: 4.70.

Two-parent households were generally larger for the ex-slaves. Taken together, two-parent households were found 80 percent of the time among ex-slaves, while the figure for the free-born was 77 percent. A significant difference, however, was found in the case of ex-slave household heads who bought their own freedom. In this group 90 percent were two-parent households. Small groups of

---

[6] The discussion of the differences in socioeconomic condition between the ex-slaves and the free-born in 1838 draws heavily on my article, "Free Blacks in Antebellum Philadelphia: A Study of Ex-Slaves, Free-Born and Socioeconomic Decline," *Journal of Social History* 5 (Winter 1971-1972), 183-209.

TABLE 1. ANALYSIS OF 1838 CENSUS TAKEN BY PENNSYLVANIA ABOLITION SOCIETY, ALL HOUSEHOLDS [a]

	Households			
	With Free-Born (1)	With Ex-Slaves (2)	Headed by Ex-Slaves (3)	Headed by Ex-Slaves Who Bought Themselves (4)
DEMOGRAPHIC				
Number of households	2,489	806	314	96
Number of persons	8,867	3,217	1,013	358
Percentage two-parent households	77.0	79.8	79.3	90.5
Average size of households (with two or more persons)	3.88	4.27	3.84	4.12
SOCIAL				
Church affiliation (percentages): [b]				
Non-churchgoers	17.8	9.3	5.4	3.2
White churches	5.5	5.1	5.7	7.5
Baptist	8.7	10.3	11.4	12.9
Methodist	70.7	76.5	74.1	76.3
Episcopalian	7.0	4.8	4.7	2.2
Catholic	4.1	1.1	1.3	1.1
Presbyterian	7.6	5.3	6.7	5.4
Miscellaneous	1.9	2.0	1.7	2.2
Beneficial society membership:				
Percentage of households with members	56.4	56.1	60.8	64.6
Percentage of persons who were members	27.1	27.0	35.1	32.4
School attendance:				
Percentage of households with children attending	27.6	29.2	29.0	35.4
Percentage of households with children not attending	22.5	25.4	15.9	22.9
Percentage of children attending	55.0	67.1	71.7	71.2

TABLE 1 (*Continued*)

		Households		
	With Free-Born (1)	With Ex-Slaves (2)	Headed by Ex-Slaves (3)	Headed by Ex-Slaves Who Bought Themselves (4)
ECONOMIC				
Wealth:				
Average total wealth ($)	$252	$268	$295	$388
Wealth distribution (percentages)				
$ 0-$ 20	23.9	19.6	17.5	10.4
$21-$ 40	21.1	19.6	19.7	11.5
$41-$ 90	17.8	15.1	14.6	11.5
$91-$240	18.6	21.1	18.8	25.0
Above $241	18.6	24.6	29.3	41.7
Property holdings:				
Average personal property ($)[c]	$176	$175	$191	$223
Average real property ($)	$ 76	$ 93	$105	$164
Average real property, owners only ($)	$987	$730	$567	$527
Percentage real property owners	7.7	12.8	18.5	31.2
Occupations (percentages):				
White-collar	4.0	5.4	8.2	4.9
Skilled	17.6	16.6	18.8	20.7
Unskilled	78.4	78.1	73.1	74.4

[a] All households for which the census was taken were classified into households with all free-born and households with ex-slaves. The latter category includes households headed by ex-slaves, and households headed by ex-slaves who bought themselves are a composite of that group.

[b] Some households held more than one church affiliation.

[c] There is little observable difference between the average personal property for all households and average personal property for owners only. Over 95% of all households owned personal property.

TABLE 2. ANALYSIS OF 1838 CENSUS TAKEN BY PENNSYLVANIA ABOLITION SOCIETY, MALE-HEADED HOUSEHOLDS [a]

	Households		Households with Ex-Slaves		Households with Ex-Slave Head of Household	
	With All Free-Born (1)	With Ex-Slaves (2)	Free-Born Head of Household (3)	Ex-Slave Head of Household (4)	Manumitted (5)	Bought Self (6)
DEMOGRAPHIC						
Number of households	1,760	601	394	207	85	81
Number of persons	6,966	2,643	1,852	791	312	327
Percentage two-parent households	99% of all male-headed household with 2 or more persons were two-parent households.					
Average size of households (with two or more persons)	4.06	4.40	4.70	3.99	3.80	4.72
SOCIAL						
Church affiliation (percentages): [b]						
Non-churchgoers	18.5	10.5	13.5	4.8	7.1	3.7
White churches	5.2	4.3	4.1	4.6	3.8	5.1
Baptist	8.1	11.0	10.0	12.7	13.9	12.8
Methodist	71.1	75.1	77.7	70.6	70.9	75.6
Episcopalian	8.1	4.6	0.4	5.1	3.8	2.6
Catholic	2.6	1.3	0.9	2.0	2.5	1.3
Presbyterian	7.8	5.8	4.7	7.6	7.6	5.1
Miscellaneous	2.3	2.2	2.4	2.0	1.3	2.6
Beneficial society membership:						
Percentage of households with members	52.0	57.7	53.8	65.2	62.3	69.1
Percentage of persons who were members	25.5	26.2	22.6	34.5	34.6	33.0
School attendance:						
Percentage of households with children attending	29.7	35.9	35.3	37.2	36.5	38.3
Percentage of households with children not attending	25.2	28.3	32.2	20.1	17.6	24.7
Percentage of children attending	54.9	61.4	55.7	72.7	75.0	70.8

TABLE 2 (Continued)

	Households		Households with Ex-Slaves		Households with Ex-Slave Head of Household	
	With All Free-Born (1)	With Ex-Slaves (2)	Free-Born Head of Household (3)	Ex-Slave Head of Household (4)	Manumitted (5)	Bought Self (6)
ECONOMIC						
Wealth:						
Average total wealth ($)	$257	$317	$284	$380	$388	$409
Wealth distribution (percentages)						
$ 0-$ 20	21.8	16.3	19.0	11.1	16.5	6.2
$21-$ 40	18.6	18.1	19.5	15.5	16.5	8.6
$41-$ 90	16.7	14.0	14.7	12.6	12.9	11.1
$91-$240	20.9	23.0	22.6	23.7	24.7	28.4
Above $241	22.1	28.6	24.1	37.2	29.4	45.7
Property Holdings:						
Average personal property ($)[c]	$181	$204	$180	$249	$269	$252
Average real property ($)	$ 69	$113	$103	$131	$119	$157
Average real property, owners only ($)	$768	$770	$1,017	$564	$776	$472
Percentage real property owners	9.0	14.6	10.1	23.2	15.3	33.3
Occupations (percentages):						
White-collar	4.2	5.4	4.4	7.0	7.3	5.1
Skilled	17.5	15.6	14.2	18.4	17.1	20.3
Unskilled	78.3	79.0	81.4	74.5	75.6	74.7

[a] All male-headed households were divided into those with all free-born and those with ex-slaves. These households were then classified by characteristic of the head of household. Those headed by ex-slaves were broken down in accord with the response to a question about the termination of bondage, the two groups shown being the most frequent answers.
[b] Some households held more than one church affiliation.
[c] There is little observable difference between the average personal property for all households and average personal property for owners only. Over 95% of all households owned personal property.

ex-slaves clustered disproportionately in the outlying districts of Kensington, Northern Liberties, and Spring Garden. Twenty-five percent of the entire black population of Philadelphia, they comprised about 35 percent of the black population in these areas. Most ex-slaves, however, lived in the same proportions and in the same blocks as did the free-born population.

More interesting than the pattern of their distribution throughout the city, however, was the level of population density in which they lived, i.e., the number of black neighbors who lived close by. To calculate the number of black households in a grid of approximately one and one-quarter blocks square, three density levels were used: 1-20, 21-100, and in excess of 100 households per grid.[7]

The less dense areas were characterized by larger families, greater presence of two-parent households, less imbalance between the sexes, and fewer families whose members were all not native to Pennsylvania. In these areas lived a disproportionately greater number of wealthy families, and among them, a correspondingly overrepresented number of real property owners. Here white-collar and skilled workers lived in greater percentages than elsewhere in the city, and unskilled workers were decidedly few in both percentage and absolute number. The major exceptions to the distribution of wealth and skill came as the result of the necessity for shopkeepers and craftsmen to locate their homes and their businesses in the city's more densely populated sections.

Ex-slave households were more likely than free-born households to be found in the least dense areas (one in four as compared with one in five). Conversely, ex-slave households were less likely to be found in those areas with the greatest density of black population.

SOCIAL VARIABLES

For two basic reasons the all-black church has long been recognized as the key institution of the community: first, an oppressed and downtrodden people used religion for spiritual sustenance and for its promise of a better life in the next world; second, with the ability to participate in the political, social, and economic spheres of the larger white society in which they lived sharply curtailed, blacks turned to the church for fulfillment of their secular needs.

---

[7] Admittedly crude at this stage of research, the population density technique of analysis nevertheless yields interesting and important information; and with refinement promises to be an invaluable tool for the study of neighborhood, and its relation to social mobility, class ecology, and community structure.

405

Important in the twentieth century, the church was vital to blacks in the nineteenth. Philadelphia blacks were so closed off from the benefits of white society that church affiliation became a fundamental prerequisite to a decent and, indeed, bearable existence.[8] For this reason, non-church affiliation, rather than poverty, was the distinguishing characteristic of the most disadvantaged group in the community. Non-churchgoers must have enjoyed few of the benefits and services which accrued to those who were affiliated with a church in some manner. The socioeconomic profile of non-churchgoers is depressing. They fared considerably less well than their churchgoing neighbors in all significant social indicators; they had smaller families, fewer two-parent households, high residential density levels, and they were disproportionately poor; their ratios for membership in beneficial societies and for the number of school-age children in school was one-fourth and one-half, respectively, that of the larger community; occupationally, they were decidedly overrepresented among the unskilled sectors of the work force.

In this sense, then, the percentage of households with no members attending church is a more valuable index of general social condition than any other. Eighteen percent of the free-born households had no members attending church; for all ex-slave households the figure was *half* as great. Ex-slave households were one in four in the community-at-large; they were less than one in ten among households with no members attending church. The ratios were even lower (one in twenty) for ex-slave-headed households and lowest (one in thirty) for ex-slaves who bought themselves.

About 150 households, or 5 percent of the churchgoing population of the entire community, attended twenty-three predominately white churches. These churches had only "token" integration, allowing a few blacks to worship in pews set apart from the rest of the congregation. Ex-slaves of all groups attended white churches in approximately the same ratio as did the free-born: one household in twenty.

The churchgoing population of the entire community consisted of 2,776 households distributed among five religious denominations: Methodists (73 percent), Baptists (9 percent), Presbyterians (seven percent), Episcopalians (seven percent), and Catholics (three percent). Methodists worshipped in eight and Baptists in four all-Negro

---

[8] The data describing church affiliation are derived from the Abolitionist and Quaker census categories "name of religious meeting you attend" and "number attend religious meeting." These terms and the very high percentage of positive respondents make it clear that we are not dealing here with formal, dues-paying, church membership, but rather with a loose affiliation with a church.

congregations scattered throughout the city and districts. Together they accounted for more than eight of every ten churchgoers. The various ex-slave groups were found an average of 11 percent more frequently among Methodists, and 30 percent more frequently among Baptists.

In any case, Methodists and Baptists differed little from each other and to describe them is to characterize the entire community: poor and unskilled. Within each denomination, however, a single church— Union Methodist and Union Baptist—served as the social base for their respective elites. And while ex-slaves attended all of the community's all-black churches, it was in these two churches where the ex-slaves were most frequently found. The ex-slave members of these two churches shared the socioeconomic and cultural characteristics of the community's elite denominations, the Episcopalians and the Presbyterians, and it should not be surprising, therefore, to find ex-slaves of all groups underrepresented in each of these last two denominations.

Next to the church in value to the community were the all-black beneficial societies. These important institutions functioned as rudimentary insurance groups which provided their members with relief in sickness, aid during extreme poverty, and burial expenses at death.

There were over one hundred distinct societies in antebellum Philadelphia. They grew out of obvious need and were early manifestations of the philosophy of "self-help" which was so popular in the nineteenth century. Almost always they were affiliated directly with one of the all-black churches. The first beneficial society, known as the "Free African Society," was founded in 1787. A dozen societies existed by 1815, 50 by 1830, and 106 by 1847.

Slightly more than 50 percent of free-born households were members of the various societies. Making good the philosophy of "self-help" half a century before Booker T. Washington, the societies found ex-slaves more eager to join their ranks than the free-born. Each group of ex-slaves had a higher percentage of members, especially ex-slave–headed households (61 percent), ex-slaves who purchased their own freedom (65 percent), and the males among the latter group (70 percent).

Membership in beneficial societies varied significantly by wealth and status. Ranking the entire household population in 30 distinct wealth categories revealed that, beginning with the poorest, the percentage of membership rose with increasing wealth until the wealthiest six categories. For this top 11 percent of the population, however, membership in beneficial societies declined from 92 percent to 81 percent. Among the wealthiest, and this applied equally to ex-slaves, there was less need for membership in beneficial societies.

One household in four among the free-born population sent children to school. For ex-slave households the corresponding figure was more than one in three. Ex-slave households had slightly fewer children, but sent a considerably greater percentage of their children to school. For free-born households the percentage was 55 percent; for all ex-slave households, 67 percent; and for ex-slave-headed households, the figure rose to 72 percent. To the extent that education was valuable to blacks the ex-slaves were better off.

ECONOMIC VARIABLES

The antebellum black community was extremely poor. The total wealth—that is, the combined value of real and personal property holdings—for three out of every five households amounted to only $60 or less. Poverty, nevertheless, did not touch all groups equally. The average total wealth for the ex-slave–headed households was 20 percent greater than that for the free-born households; for ex-slave males, 53 percent greater; and for ex-slave males who freed themselves, 63 percent greater.

The most significant differences in wealth by far occurred in real property holding. One household in thirteen among the free-born, or slightly less than 8 percent, owned real property. For all ex-slave households the corresponding ratio was one in eight; for ex-slave-headed households, one in five; for males who were in this group, one in four; and most dramatically, for males who purchased their own freedom, one in three owned real property. To these ex-slaves, owning their own home or a piece of land must have provided something, perhaps a stake in society, of peculiarly personal significance. Distribution of wealth, to view the matter from a different perspective, was less unequal for ex-slave households, particularly ex-slave household heads. The poorest half of the free-born and ex-slave-headed households owned 5 and 7 percent, respectively, of the total wealth; for the wealthiest quarter of each group the corresponding figure was 86 and 73 percent; for the wealthiest tenth, 67 and 56 percent; and for the wealthiest one-hundredth, 30 and 21 percent. Overall wealth distribution, in other words, while still skewed toward pronounced inequality, was more equally distributed for ex-slave household heads in the middle and upper wealth categories.

The final area of comparison between the ex-slaves and the free-born is occupation.[9] Analysis of the data, using the same classification schema for blacks as for white ethnic groups, confirms an earlier suspicion that, although such schema are necessary in order to compare the black to white ethnic groups, they are entirely unsatisfactory tools of analysis when social stratification in the black community is the concern. Despite the fact that the blacks who comprised the labor force of antebellum Philadelphia described themselves as engaged in 400 different occupations, a stark fact emerges from the analysis: there was almost no occupational differentiation!

Five occupations accounted for 70 percent of the entire male work force: laborers (38 percent), porters (11.5 percent), waiters (11.5 percent), seamen (5 percent), and carters (4 percent); another 10 percent were employed in miscellaneous laboring capacities. Taken together, eight out of every ten working men were unskilled laborers. Another 16 percent worked as skilled artisans, but fully one-half of this fortunate group were barbers and shoemakers; the other skilled craftsmen were scattered among the building construction (3.2 percent), home-furnishing (1.3 percent), leather goods (1.2 percent), and metal work (1.2 percent) trades. Less than one-half of 1 percent of blacks, as pointed out in another context, found employment in the developing factory system. The remaining 4 percent of the labor force were engaged in white-collar professions. They were largely proprietors who sold food or second-hand clothing from vending carts, and should not be considered as "storeowners."

The occupational structure for females was even less differentiated than for males. More than eight out of every ten women were employed in day work capacities (as opposed to those who lived and worked in white households) as domestic servants: "washers" (52 percent), "day-workers" (22 percent), and miscellaneous domestics (6 percent). Fourteen percent worked as seamstresses, and they accounted for all the skilled workers among the female labor force. Finally, about 5 percent were engaged in white-collar work, which,

---

[9] The construction of meaningful occupational categories had thus far proven to be the most difficult part of the research. While constructing such categories for the Irish, German, and native-white American work force (currently underway) is certainly complex, one at least has the benefit of considerable occupational differentiation which provides vertical distance, a prerequisite for the study of social mobility and social stratification. Some 13 vertical categories including white collar/skilled/unskilled, nonmanual/manual, proprietary/nonproprietary, and combinations of these schema, and 102 horizontal categories including building construction, food, clothing, and domestic services were constructed for the study of the Negro occupational structure.

as with the males, meant vending capacities in clothing and food selling categories.

It should come, then, as no surprise that there are few distinctions of significance to make between the occupational structure of the ex-slaves and free-born work forces. The differences in vertical occupational categories find male ex-slave household heads more likely to be in white-collar positions (7 percent as opposed to 4 percent for the free-born), equally distributed in the skilled trades, and slightly less represented in the unskilled occupations (75 percent as opposed to 78 percent). Within the horizontal categories there were few important differences. Male ex-slave household heads were more likely than the free-born to be employed as porters, carpenters, blacksmiths, preachers, and clothes dealers.

In summary, then, we find the ex-slaves with larger families, with greater likelihood of two-parent households, with higher affiliation rates in church and beneficial society, sending more of their children to school, living more frequently in the least dense areas of the country, and generally wealthier, owning considerably more real property and being slightly more fortunate in occupational differentiation. By almost every socioeconomic measure the ex-slave fared better than his free-born brother.

1847

DEMOGRAPHIC VARIABLES

The population in the 1847 census—4,300 households and 16,000 persons—was an increase of about one-third over 1838. (See Tables 3 and 4). The number of ex-slave households (810) and individual ex-slaves in the population (1,083) remained about the same, but the percentage of each declined: from 25 to 20 percent of all households and from 10 to 7 percent of all ex-slaves. Importantly, eight of ten ex-slave households in 1847 did not appear in the 1838 census.

Ex-slaves had larger households than the free-born, but they had a slightly smaller percentage of two-parent households. Ex-slave households whose members bought their own freedom were more likely than the free-born to have both parents present, but only by a narrow margin. Both the ex-slaves and the free-born had seriously imbalanced sex-ratios: for every 1,000 males the former had 1,397 females and the latter 1,311. The imbalance existed even in households headed by males, although it was considerably lower: 1,154 and 1,081, respectively. This helps to explain the fact that, among both the ex-slaves and the free-born, roughly three households

TABLE 3. ANALYSIS OF 1847 CENSUS TAKEN BY SOCIETY OF FRIENDS, ALL HOUSEHOLDS [a]

		Households			
	With all Free-Born	With Ex-Slaves	With Ex-Slaves Who Bought Freedom	With Ex-Slaves Who Were Manumitted		
				All Causes	Self-Manumitted	Manumitted by Master
	(1)	(2)	(3)	(4)	(5)	(6)
DEMOGRAPHIC						
Number of households	3,488	810	229	616	201	403
Number of persons	12,877	3,161	918	2,410	714	1,643
Percentage of males in households	43.3	41.7	42.5	41.6	40.6	42.1
Percentage of households headed by male	70.2	66.7	71.2	66.7	57.2	70.5
Average size of Households (with two or more persons)	4.07	4.24	4.22	4.26	4.04	4.36
Marital status (percentages):						
Married	65.0	63.5	66.8	64.1	52.2	69.0
Single	6.6	4.9	2.2	5.5	8.5	4.2
Widow	22.4	27.5	25.8	26.9	33.3	24.6
Widower	2.6	1.6	2.2	1.3	2.0	1.0
Wife forsaken	2.8	2.2	2.6	1.9	3.5	1.2
Husband forsaken	0.6	0.2	0.4	0.2	0.5	0
Percentages of various age groups:						
0-4	15.3	12.6	9.8	12.9	10.8	13.8
5-14	19.0	18.9	20.0	18.8	18.0	19.2
15-49	57.9	50.2	49.1	50.3	50.8	50.1
over 50	7.7	18.3	21.1	18.0	20.4	17.0
Percentage of households in high density (ghetto) areas	48.7	46.3	45.0	46.9	56.2	42.9

TABLE 3 (Continued)

	With all Free-Born	With Ex-Slaves	Households With Ex-Slaves Who Bought Freedom	With Ex-Slaves Who Were Manumitted		
				All Causes	Self-Manumitted	Manu-mitted by Master
	(1)	(2)	(3)	(4)	(5)	(6)
SOCIAL						
Church attendance:						
Percentage of households with at least one person attending	83.7	91.0	93.9	91.2	95.5	88.8
Percentage of persons attending	60.8	73.8	86.9	84.7	81.6	70.0
Beneficial society membership:						
Percentage of households with at least one member	62.2	68.0	74.2	67.0	66.7	67.5
Percentage of persons (age 15 and over) who were members	45.9	49.9	55.9	49.0	49.5	49.2
Temperance society membership:						
Percentage of households with at least one member	13.2	16.5	18.3	16.6	13.4	18.1
Percentage of persons (age 15 and over) who were "intemperate"	3.0	2.1	1.4	2.2	3.3	1.8
School attendance:						
Percentage of households with children in school	26.1	29.5	34.9	28.7	24.4	30.8
Percentage of children (age 5 to 14) in school	63.4	63.5	59.8	53.5	59.7	61.6
Literacy:						
Percentage of households with at least one person who could read	68.1	73.9	81.2	73.7	76.1	72.7

	With all Free-Born (1)	With Ex-Slaves (2)	With Ex-Slaves Who Bought Freedom (3)	Households Ex-Slaves Who Were Manumitted All Causes (4)	Self-Manumitted (5)	Manumitted by Master (6)
Percentage of persons (age 5 and over) who could read	48.6	52.1	58.6	50.3	54.3	48.6
Percentage of households with at last one person who could write	33.7	42.2	48.5	41.7	48.3	38.5
Percentage of persons (ages 5 and over) who could write	22.5	24.4	27.7	23.1	27.9	21.6
Percentage of households receiving public aid	8.6	17.3	15.7	18.3	23.4	16.4
ECONOMIC Wealth:						
Average Total Wealth ($)	$248	$263	$348	$239	$232	$217
Average Personal Property ($)	$160	$162	$197	$155	$149	$158
Average real property ($)	$86	$101	$150	$84	$83	$59
Percentage of households with real property	6.14	8.15	12.2	6.98	6.47	6.95
Average real property of households with real property ($)	$1,404	$1,236	$1,232	$1,203	$1,277	$845
Occupations (percentages): White-collar Skilled Unskilled	None	None		None		

ª All households for which the census was taken were classified into households with all free-born and households with ex-slaves. Households with ex-slaves were divided in accordance with the answer to the question of how freedom was obtained. Since some households contained more than one ex-slave, and these might have obtained freedom in different ways, the number of households in cols. (3) and (4) is slightly in excess of the number in col (2). Several households included slaves manumitted for other reasons, so the number of households in cols. (5) and (6) are slightly less than those in col. (4).

TABLE 4. ANALYSIS OF 1847 CENSUS TAKEN BY SOCIETY OF FRIENDS, MALE-HEADED HOUSEHOLDS[a]

| | Households | | Households With Ex-Slaves Who Bought Freedom | Households With Ex-Slaves Who Were Manumitted | | |
| | With All Free-Born | With Ex-Slaves | | All Causes | Self-Manumitted | Manumitted by Master |
	(1)	(2)	(3)	(4)	(5)	(6)
DEMOGRAPHIC						
Number of households	2,447	540	163	411	115	284
Number of persons	9,954	2,419	729	1,839	477	1,309
Percentage of males in households	48.0	46.4	45.7	46.3	46.1	46.5
Percentage of households headed by male						
Average size of households (with two or more persons)	4.20	4.53	4.49	4.33	4.32	4.62
Marital status (percentages):						
Married	92.3	94.8	93.9	95.6	90.4	97.5
Single	2.3	1.1	0.6	1.2	3.5	0.4
Widow						
Widower	3.7	2.4	3.1	1.9	3.5	1.4
Wife foresaken						
Husband forsaken	0.9	0.4	0.6	0.2	0.9	0
Percentages of various age groups:						
0-4	16.8	14.0	11.2	14.1	12.6	14.6
5-14	18.9	19.8	20.8	19.7	18.6	20.1
15-49	58.0	50.7	49.0	51.0	51.2	50.9
over 50	6.2	15.6	19.2	15.3	17.6	14.4
Percentage of households in high density (ghetto) areas	46.3	43.0	43.0	42.8	56.5	38.0

	Households		Households With Ex-Slaves Who Bought Freedom	Households With Ex-Slaves Who Were Manumitted		
	With All Free-Born	With Ex-Slaves		All Causes	Self-Manumitted	Manumitted by Master
	(1)	(2)	(3)	(4)	(5)	(6)
SOCIAL						
Church attendance:						
Percentage of households with at least one person attending	82.9	91.7	96.3	91.5	94.8	89.8
Percentage of persons attending	70.8	84.0	88.2	84.0	89.4	81.3
Beneficial society membership:						
Percentage of households with at least one member	64.8	70.7	76.7	69.6	72.2	69.0
Percentage of persons (age 15 and over) who were members	35.5	38.4	42.8	37.8	40.8	37.3
Temperance society membership:						
Percentage of households with at least one member	15.2	17.8	19.6	18.5	14.8	20.1
Percentage of persons (age 15 and over) who were "intemperate"	3.3	2.2	1.4	2.5	4.0	1.8
School attendance:						
Percentage of households with children in school	29.0	35.9	40.5	34.5	31.3	36.3
Percentage of children (age 5 to 14) in school	58.6	55.8	58.6	55.2	56.2	55.1
Literacy:						
Percentage of households with at least one person who could read	68.8	80.0	85.9	80.0	80.9	80.3

TABLE 4 (Continued)

	Households		Households With Ex-Slaves Who Bought Freedom	Households With Ex-Slaves Who Were Manumitted		
	With All Free-Born	With Ex-Slaves		All Causes	Self-Manumitted	Manumitted by Master
	(1)	(2)	(3)	(4)	(5)	(6)
Percentage of persons (age 5 and over) who could read	47.8	54.4	61.4	52.6	54.4	52.1
Percentage of households with at least one person who could write	35.7	46.8	54.0	45.0	52.2	43.7
Percentage of persons (age 5 and over) who could write	22.6	25.8	29.8	24.4	28.5	23.6
Percentage of households receiving public aid	4.8	7.8	8.0	8.3	7.8	8.8
ECONOMIC						
Wealth:						
Average total wealth ($)	$295	$319	$394	$294	$258	$275
Average personal property ($)	$192	$200	$241	$190	$159	$204
Average real property ($)	$101	$119	$153	$105	$99	$71
Percentage of households with real property	7.15	9.81	14.11	8.27	6.96	8.45
Average real property of households with real property ($)	$1,418	$1,217	$1,085	$1,265	$1,422	$840
Occupations (percentages):						
White-collar	9.6	9.8	13.5	8.2	10.0	7.4
Skilled	18.3	13.7	17.9	11.0	9.1	11.9
Unskilled	72.1	76.4	68.6	80.9	80.9	80.7

ᵃ All households for which the census was taken were classified into households with all free-born and households with ex-slaves. Households with ex-slaves were divided in accordance with the answer to the question of how freedom was obtained. Since some households contained more than one ex-slave, and these might have obtained freedom in different ways, the number of households in cols. (3) and (4) is slightly in excess of the number in col. (2). Several households included slaves manumitted for other reasons, so the number of households in cols. (5) and (6) are slightly less than those in col. (4).

in ten were headed by a female. The imbalance in the sex ratios explains, too, why the male household heads of both groups were married between 90 percent and 97 percent of the time. To a considerable degree female household heads of both groups claimed to be widows and the only significant difference in marital status appears when female ex-slaves, especially those manumitted by "self," report being widowed: 33 percent against 22 percent for the free-born. The age structure of the households varied slightly where children under fifteen and adults 15 to 49 were concerned, but the percentage of adults 50 and above was two to three times higher among the ex-slaves than among the free-born.[10]

The final demographic variable for comparison deals with the density and location of the two groups. The increase in residential segregation over the past decade brought both the ex-slaves and the free-born to high levels of density with no significant variation between them. Their location, characterized by almost identical distribution patterns in 1838, however, underwent considerable change. The ex-slaves began to cluster disproportionately in a few grid squares in the "old city."

SOCIAL VARIABLES

Church attendance among both households and persons remained higher for the ex-slaves than for the free-born. Ninety-six percent of the households headed by males who bought their freedom had at least one person in attendance. Congregational or denominational data were not included in the 1847 survey, but no evidence suggests any change in such distributions from 1838. Membership in the other major institution in the community, the beneficial society, showed no appreciable difference between the groups, except for a higher percentage of members among those ex-slaves who bought their own freedom. Data on membership in temperance societies were reported only in the 1847 census. Intemperance itself was not much of a problem, at least according to the census: only about 3 percent of adults in both groups "confessed" to this condition. In any event,

---

[10] This statistic is somewhat puzzling because migrants are characteristically young males, not persons over 50. Too few Pennsylvania-born ex-slaves would have been alive in 1838 to account for this because the state's gradual emancipation act was passed in 1780. The probable explanation is that many ex-slave in-migrants brought their relatives with them. Leaving the slave South certainly provided sufficient motivation, even for the elderly. This interpretation is supported by the fact that the highest percentages of persons over 50 (21%) were found among ex-slaves who bought their own freedom.

15 percent of the community's households were members of the
societies and ex-slaves had a slightly higher membership rate than
the free-born. Membership will probably prove a good indicator of
the desire to be socially mobile and contemporary sources note that
abstinence was strictly practiced at parties given by the city's leading
black families.[11]

School attendance statistics show the ex-slaves with a greater
percentage of children in school; once again, the largest margin
separating ex-slaves from the free-born was found among the ex-slave
households whose male heads bought their own freedom, 40.5 percent to 29 percent, respectively. The same margin of difference in
favor of the same group of ex-slaves appears in the information describing the percentage of households with at least one member who
could read—86 to 69 percent—and who could write—54 to 36 percent.

The only social variable in which the ex-slaves were worse off than
the free-born was the number "receiving public aid" (usually a cord
or two of wood). All ex-slave groups of both sexes received this assistance more often than did the free-born, but the greatest margin
by far involved the households headed by female ex-slaves.

ECONOMIC VARIABLES

The ex-slaves were better off in all wealth categories. The most
important differences, familiar to us by now, were among the ex-slaves
who bought their freedom. Their total wealth was one-third greater
than the free-born ($394 to $295) and they owned real property twice
as often (14 percent to 7 percent).

Occupational distinctions were few and insignificant for both sexes,
in both groups, and in all occupational categories. Porters, waiters,
and laborers, were the most numerous male occupations, as were day
work and washers for females; domestic service trades, building
construction, clothing, and food dominated the horizontal categories;
and seven or eight out of every ten workers were unskilled in the
vertical categories. Once again, however, male ex-slaves who bought
their own freedom had the fewest unskilled occupations (69 percent
as opposed to 72 percent for the free-born and 80 percent for the
manumitted) and the most white-collar occupations (14 percent
as opposed to 10 percent for the free-born and 8 percent for the
manumitted).

Although the margin which separated the ex-slaves from the free-

[11] Joseph Willson, *Sketches of the Higher Classes of Colored Society in Philadelphia*, Philadelphia, 1841, pp. 62-63.

born narrowed considerably in certain variables between 1838 and 1847, the ex-slaves remained better off in all social indicators but the receipt of public aid. As in 1838, the most well-off group of ex-slaves were males who bought their own freedom.

1856

DEMOGRAPHIC VARIABLES

The population in the 1856 census—3,861 households and 14,700 persons—was a decrease of about 10 percent from 1847, but the number of ex-slave households (910) increased 12 percent and the number of ex-slave individuals in the population (1,234) increased 14 percent over 1847 (see Tables 5 and 6). The 1856 census purported to include black households in the "new" City of Philadelphia, which in 1854 consolidated with the County of Philadelphia, a far larger and more populated area, but when comparing the count to that of the U.S. Census for Philadelphia County in 1850 and 1860, the black household population appears to be understated by at least one-fourth. The volatility of the population remained high: only one household in four in the 1856 census was found in the 1847 census.

According to those who took the 1856 census, its purpose was to survey "Education and Higher Occupations." As a result, little of the rich detail found in the earlier manuscripts is available. The size of ex-slave households remained larger, for instance, but because no wealth data were contained in the census of 1856, it is not possible to determine whether the strong, direct relationship between household size and wealth which existed in 1838 and 1847 held in 1856. The percentage of male-headed households was identical (73 percent) although a new census category, those "free-born in slave state," was highest (78 percent). Density remained high for all groups and the distinctive residential clustering pattern of the ex-slaves which emerged for the first time in the 1847 census appeared again a decade later.

SOCIAL VARIABLES

For the first time in 1856, the education profile of the ex-slaves was *worse* than that of the free-born. Ex-slave households had a higher percentage of "children over 8 not in school," and the same percentage of children in school. In a series of education categories, ex-slaves had more households in which persons "cannot read" (83 to 64 percent), slightly more in which persons could "read only" (38 to 35 percent), and less in which persons could "read and write"

419

TABLE 5. ANALYSIS OF 1856 CENSUS TAKEN BY PENNSYLVANIA ABOLITION SOCIETY, ALL HOUSEHOLDS [a]

	Households		Households With at Least One Member Free-Born in a Slave State
	With All Free-Born (1)	With Ex-Slaves (2)	(3)
DEMOGRAPHIC			
Number of households	2,952	909	2,197
Number of persons	10,876	3,803	8,603
Percentage of households headed by male	73.2	73.5	77.9
Average size of households (with two or more persons)	3.93	4.35	4.09
Percentage of households in high-density (ghetto) areas	45.6	41.2	46.3
SOCIAL			
School attendance:			
Percentage of households with children (age 8 and over) not in school	26.6	31.9	27.3
Percentage of households with children (age 5 and over) in school	26.7	32.6	29.4
Literacy:			
Percentage of persons (age 8 and over) who cannot read	28.6	39.1	33.8
Percentage of persons (age 8 and over) who can read	12.8	12.6	12.8
Percentage of persons (age 8 and over) who can read and write	12.4	8.4	10.6
Percentage of persons (age 8 and over) who can read, write, and cipher	14.6	7.0	11.5
Total Percentage of persons (age 8 and over) who can read	39.8	28.0	34.9
Total Percentage of persons (age 8 and over) who can write	27.0	15.5	22.2
ECONOMIC			
Percentage of households with persons "having trades"	32.5	26.8	33.3
Percentage of persons "having trades"	14.7	10.1	13.8
Percentage of persons "having trades," working at them	64.5	62.2	61.5
Percentage of persons, clerks and higher	0.2	1.5	0.1
Percentage of persons, teachers	0.2	1.8	0.1
Percentage of persons, artists	0.1	0	0.1
Occupations (percentages):			
Barber	16.4	10.2	13.1
Blacksmith	1.5	6.4	2.2
Bootmaker	5.5	4.5	4.9
Brickmaker	4.9	3.2	3.8
Cabinetmaker	1.2	3.2	1.5
Carpenter	3.3	9.6	5.3
Dressmaker	26.7	19.1	27.9

TABLE 5 *(Continued)*

	Households		Households With at Least One Member Free-Born in a Slave State
	With All Free-Born (1)	With Ex-Slaves (2)	(3)
Shoemaker	4.8	6.4	4.6
Tanner	2.3	2.5	2.7
Shirtmaker	2.5	3.2	2.6
Industrial groups (percentages):			
Bldg. constr.	12.1	18.5	14.2
Clothing	48.5	42.7	49.0
Food	3.3	1.9	2.7
Home furn.	3.7	4.5	3.5
Leather	3.2	3.8	4.2
Metal work	3.2	9.6	4.6
Service trades	17.4	10.2	14.0

[a] All households for which the census was taken were classified into households with all free-born and households with ex-slaves. Those households with a member free-born in the slave states are shown in col. (3).

(25 to 33 percent), or "read, write, and cipher" (18 to 32 percent). Only 28 percent of ex-slave persons could read, against 40 percent for the free-born, and only 16 percent who could write, against 27 percent for the free-born.[12]

ECONOMIC VARIABLES

No wealth data were included in the 1856 census, leaving for discussion only information about "higher occupations." Again for the first time in 1856, the ex-slaves were worse off than the free-born. Only 10 percent of the ex-slaves, as opposed to 15 percent of the free-born, "had trades." Slightly less than two-thirds in both groups "worked at trades." The numbers of "clerks and higher," "teachers," and "artists" were so few that percentage comparisons are not meaningful.

[12] The decline in basic educational skills possessed by ex-slaves might be explicable in terms of the southern white reaction to the Nat Turner revolt and the publication of the *Liberator*. After 1831 it might have become increasingly difficult for slaves and even free blacks to acquire these rudimentary skills. An analysis of the age structure might explain why the ex-slaves in the 1847 census appear better equipped than the ex-slaves in 1856.

421

TABLE 6. ANALYSIS OF 1856 CENSUS TAKEN BY PENNSYLVANIA ABOLITION SOCIETY,
MALE-HEADED HOUSEHOLDS [a]

	Households		Households With at Least One Member Free-Born in a Slave State
	With All Free-Born (1)	With Ex-Slaves (2)	(3)
DEMOGRAPHIC			
Number of households	2,154	666	1,708
Number of persons	8,350	2,918	6,973
Percentage of households headed by male			
Average size of households (with two or more persons)	3.98	4.48	4.16
Percentage of households in high-density (ghetto) areas	42.7	41.7	43.9
SOCIAL			
School attendance:			
Percentage of households with children (age 8 and over) not in school	24.4	30.0	25.9
Percentage of households with children (age 5 and over) in school	28.9	35.9	31.3
Literacy:			
Percentage of persons (age 8 and over) who cannot read	27.9	38.3	33.0
Percentage of persons (age 8 and over) who can read	12.3	12.9	12.6
Percentage of persons (age 8 and over) who can read and write	12.9	8.8	10.9
Percentage of persons (age 8 and over) who can read, write, and cipher	16.1	7.6	12.6
Total Percentage of persons (age 8 and over) who can read	41.3	29.3	36.1
Total Percentage of persons (age 8 and over) who can write	29.0	16.4	23.5
ECONOMIC			
Percentage of household with persons "having trades"	36.2	28.7	35.8
Percentage of persons "having trades"	15.6	10.4	14.4
Percentage of persons "having trades," working at them	64.6	62.0	62.2
Percentage of persons "clerks and higher"	1.7	1.6	0.1
Percentage of persons "teachers"	0.2	0.2	0.2
Percentage of persons "artists"	0.1	0	0.1
Occupations (percentages):			
Barber	18.3	11.6	14.6
Blacksmith	1.7	7.2	2.5
Bootmaker	6.3	5.1	5.6
Brickmaker	5.6	3.6	4.3
Cabinetmaker	1.4	3.6	1.6
Carpenter	3.8	10.9	6.0
Dressmaker	22.0	16.7	24.3

TABLE 6 (*Continued*)

	Households		Households With at Least One Member Free-Born in a Slave State
	With All Free-Born (1)	With Ex-Slaves (2)	(3)
Shoemaker	5.5	6.5	5.1
Tanner	2.4	2.9	2.9
Shirtmaker	2.0	1.4	1.9
Industrial groups (percentages):			
Bldg. constr.	13.9	20.3	16.0
Clothing	43.4	36.2	44.9
Food	2.9	2.2	2.5
Home furn.	4.1	5.1	3.7
Leather	3.5	4.3	4.5
Metal work	3.7	10.9	5.1
Service trades	19.5	11.6	15.6

[a] All households for which the census was taken were classified into households with all free-born and households with ex-slaves. Those households with a member free-born in the slave states are shown in col. (3).

Selected occupations show ex-slaves to be blacksmiths, carpenters, and cabinetmakers more often than the free-born, and less often as barbers and brickmakers. In selected horizontal categories, ex-slaves were more often in building construction (the wood sector as opposed to brick and stone) and metal work, and appeared less often than the free-born in clothing and the personal service trades. Both these distributions square with our understanding of what skills the ex-slaves would have developed while in slavery.

CONCLUSIONS

A general conclusion emerges from the socioeconomic data presented describing the ex-slaves and the free-born: the margin of difference which favored the ex-slaves in every instance in 1838 narrowed in 1847, and reversed itself in several variables in 1856, leaving the ex-slaves in these cases worse off than the free-born.

There are two general explanations for the narrowing of the margin between the ex-slaves and the free-born. The first deals with the city as a destructive environment. In the decades before the Civil War "all social indicators—race riots, population decrease, disfranchisement, residential segregation, per capita wealth, ownership of real property, family structure, and occupational opportunities," I have documented elsewhere, "pointed toward socioeconomic deterioration within Philadelphia's black community." [13] The city, with its racist structures and institutions, offered blacks few opportunities for socio-economic mobility. When waves of Irish and German immigrants poured into Philadelphia in the fifteen years preceding the Civil War, an already unenviable situation deteriorated rapidly. After living in the city for a decade or more, the socioeconomic condition of the ex-slave in-migrant eroded. While this erosion was not unique to the ex-slave, it reduced the initial advantages he enjoyed at a rate faster than the decline in the socioeconomic condition of free-born blacks, bringing the ex-slave to the level (and in some instances slightly below that) of the free-born black native to the city.

The second explanation lies in the socioeconomic characteristics of those blacks, especially ex-slaves, who migrated to Philadelphia. There appear to have been very high rates of population turnover for ex-slaves. Only one household in five among the ex-slave popula-tion in 1838 was found in the city a decade later; although the rate of turnover slowed somewhat in the next ten years, only one house-hold in four in 1847 was found in 1856 and only one household in seven survived from 1838 to 1856. The changing characteristics of the ex-slave population suggests that the typical ex-slave in-migrant, appearing in Philadelphia for the first time in 1847 and especially in 1856, was not as well-endowed with the occupational skills or education as was his counterpart who migrated to Phila-delphia before 1838. This interpretation is further supported by data describing the households receiving public aid in 1847. Although ex-slaves received public assistance disproportionately, the 1838 census did not include such information; therefore, we do not know if this constituted a decline. But we do know that only one ex-slave household in eight which received public aid in 1847 had been in Philadelphia in 1838.

The second explanation is the more persuasive, but it should be kept in mind that the two explanations are in no sense mutually ex-clusive. It is highly probable that an increasingly hostile urban en-vironment awaited a somewhat less well-off ex-slave in-migrant.

Despite the narrowing over time of the margin which favored the ex-slaves over the free-born, two features of the socioeconomic profile of the ex-slaves stand out. It is very striking that the condition of the great majority of the ex-slaves was not *markedly* inferior to that of the free-born. In this matter we are dealing with large numbers of

[13] Hershberg, p. 192.

ex-slave households, comprising between one-fourth and one-fifth of the entire black household population. This knowledge should serve as an important corrective to the notion that "slavery" was in all instances a totally destructive experience. Second, the consistently superior position of the ex-slave males who "bought their own freedom and often that of their nearest relations," confirms the belief that the adverse conditions could be molded by some to their advantage.

The question that remains, however, is whether those in the process of "freeing themselves from bondage" and perhaps in internalizing the ethic of deferred gratification which "made them useful and respectable citizens," [14] were a unique group, or whether they were in some way representative of other blacks who experienced American slavery? The question is a good deal more complex than might be expected. Of whom were the ex-slaves in Philadelphia representative: of other ex-slaves in nearby states who did not migrate? of slaves in those states who would not be freed until after the Civil War? of ex-slaves and slaves throughout the South? It is probably impossible to answer these questions with any certainty, but if ex-slaves in Philadelphia were representative of the slave experience, "our insight would necessarily be limited to the effect of the mildest slavery system as it was practiced in Maryland, Delaware and Virginia," [15] for, in fact, this is from where the ex-slaves in Philadelphia had come.

Although the consideration that not all ex-slaves in Philadelphia were alike complicates these questions yet further, it does offer an intriguing hypothesis. The peculiarly high achievement levels of those who bought their own freedom makes it important to differentiate among ex-slaves according to the manner in which they gained their freedom. While it remains speculation at this point, it is likely that ex-slaves throughout the South who bought their own freedom also achieved a disproportionately high measure of success. Eugene Genovese has pointed to the little understood role of the black slave driver during slavery and suggested that such individuals might have assumed positions of leadership in black communities after the Civil War. It is quite possible that ex-slaves who bought their own freedom may have played a similarly valuable role in the emerging black social structure. Such a hypothesis, however, should be sensitive to the role of ex-slaves in different settings. Ex-slaves would probably

[14] Society of Friends, *Statistical Inquiry into the Condition of the People of Colour of the City and Districts of Philadelphia*, Philadelphia, 1849, p. 31.
[15] Hershberg, p. 201; for the statistics on where the migrants came from, see above, n. 5.

play a far less prominent role in older and established communities such as Philadelphia, whose population was largely free-born, whose institutions had developed long before Emancipation, and whose social structure would not be affected by the Civil War, than they would in newly forming southern communities whose populations were composed overwhelmingly of freedmen, whose institutions would in most instances first have to be built, and whose social structures would undergo severe shocks as a result of Emancipation. In any case, it is clear that the research necessary to answer these questions remains to be done.

XVI

A Model to Explain the Relative
Decline of Urban Slavery:
Empirical Results

CLAUDIA DALE GOLDIN

I. Definition of the Problem

THE economics of American Negro slavery has generated much interest and many articles during the past ten years by both historians and economists.[1] Out of these years of debate has evolved a set of positive statements concerning the profitability, and viability of rural slavery. Works by Conrad and Meyer, Evans, and others have shown that rural slaveowners made competitive profit rates on their slaves.[2] Yasuba's contribution to this continuing series of papers demonstrated that slavery was not only profitable, but was indeed a viable industry, that is, it was profitable to raise new slaves and perpetuate the system.[3]

During this decade of debate the historical fact that the South did not industrialize and urbanize under slavery has entered the discussions in only a limited way.[4] If slavery was both profitable and viable in the production of agricultural staples, why did it not flourish in the production of urban services and industrial goods? After all,

[1] This essay is a portion of my doctoral dissertation, and the reader is referred to that work (University of Chicago, 1972) for clarifying comments. I wish to acknowledge the encouragement and help of my thesis committee, Robert W. Fogel, H. Gregg Lewis, and Donald McCloskey. Stanley Engerman provided very useful comments on this draft. NSF Grant #s 27262 and 2782 supported the collection of data on slave price and hire rates used in this research.

[2] A. H. Conrad and J. R. Meyer, "The Economics of Slavery in the Antebellum South," *Journal of Political Economy* (April 1958), 95-130, reprinted in *The Economics of Slavery and Other Studies in Econometric History,* Chicago, 1964, pp. 43-92; R. Evans, Jr., "The Economics of American Negro Slavery," unpublished Ph.D. dissertation, University of Chicago, 1959, portions reprinted in *Aspects of Labor Economics,* ed. H. Gregg Lewis, Princeton, N.J., 1962, pp. 185-243.

[3] Y. Yasuba, "The Profitability and Viability of Plantation Slavery in the United States," *The Economic Studies Quarterly* 12 (September 1961), 60-67.

[4] See Eugene D. Genovese, *The Political Economy of Slavery,* New York, 1967, chap. 8.

slavery enabled a control of labor which should have encouraged certain investments in human capital not otherwise profitable.

Slavery did exist in industry in the South [5] and in its urban centers.[6] But, whereas the plantation slave population grew steadily from its inception until its forced demise with the close of the Civil War, its urban, and perhaps industrial, counterparts reached a peak in their growth sometime between 1830 and 1850 and declined during their last decade.[7] Some cities showed a weakening in their slave populations earlier, and a few declined throughout the forty year period, 1820 to 1860.

Many historians and students of the antebellum period have tried to discover the cause of this decline, and their answers have been quite varied. Some, it appears, were correct, but many were in fact without warrant.

It appeared to some that slavery was incompatible with urban life, and that this was the reason for slavery's apparent difficulties in the cities. Frederick Douglass, who as a slave spent much of his life in southern cities, expressed this rather tersely. "Slavery dislikes a dense population" was Douglass' explanation for what appeared to have been a decline in urban slavery.[8]

John Elliott Cairnes more carefully isolated the problems with slavery inherent in the city environment. He noted "[t]he conduct of manufacturing industry on a great scale always brings with it the congregation in towns of large masses of workmen. The danger incident to this, where the workmen are slaves, is . . . obvious. Manufacturing industry, where slavery exists, could only be carried on at the constant risk of insurrection. . . ."[9] Cairnes, then, believed that the problems of slavery specific to urban areas were those of control. Charles Wesley agreed with this reasoning and stated that slavery did not flourish in urban areas, not "because the slaves being Negroes were incapable of attaining the necessary skill," but, like Cairnes's reasoning above, because "[the] incompatibility between slavery and industrialism [was] inherent in the entire antebellum economic system. . . ."[10] It was inherent because Wesley believed there was

---

[5] See R. S. Starobin, *Industrial Slavery in the Old South*, New York, 1970.

[6] See R. C. Wade, *Slavery in the Cities*, New York, 1964.

[7] This essay will deal only with urban slavery, and therefore will include certain industry, e.g., iron, but will omit manufacturing industry in rural areas, e.g., milling.

[8] Frederick Douglass, *My Bondage and My Freedom*, New York, 1855, pp. 143-148.

[9] J. E. Cairnes, *The Slave Power*, London, 1862, rptd. New York, 1969, pp. 70-71.

[10] C. H. Wesley, *Negro Labor in the U.S. 1850 to 1925*, New York, 1927, p. 24.

a greater probability of insurrection the larger the percentage of skilled slaves.

In a similar vein, Richard C. Wade in *Slavery in the Cities* concluded that "wherever it touched urban conditions [slavery] was in deep trouble." [11] "The cause of slavery's difficulty in the city was the nature of urban society itself,"[12] for the distinction between master and slave broke down and with it the institution itself. Wade believed that the master-slave relationship was destroyed in the cities because the slave was allowed more freedom in work and social life. Many slaves lived apart from their masters, hired out their own time, married other slaves and raised families; in general they were, in Wade's words, "beyond the master's eye." It was not just this lack of control which, to Wade, destroyed slavery in the cities, but the change in the entire institution to merely a worker-employer relationship. The roots of this deeply entrenched institution were eroded by urban life. Urbanization and slavery were basically incompatible because urban life demanded certain freedoms for slaves and these freedoms in turn relegated bondsmen almost as free as the white urbanites.

Any thesis which attempts to explain changes in, for instance, the location of labor must involve factors which affect either the demand or the supply functions for labor services. The main problem with arguments which rest on the incompatibility of slavery with urbanization is that they fail to reveal the mechanism which results in transferring labor services from city to countryside. Without specifying such a mechanism it is difficult to explain why slavery declined in some cities but not in others, and in some decades but not in others.

One possible line of causation suggested in the writing of Wade, is that the costs of keeping slaves in the cities compared to those for the rural areas, rose over time. Translated into the language of the economist, Wade has suggested that the demand function for urban slaves was either declining over time or moving less rapidly to the right than otherwise would have been the case. Wade asserted that as the urban population became denser the costs of maintaining control of slaves rose at a disproportionate rate. More importantly, policing, jailing, and adjudicating costs were shifted from the community at large to owners of slaves through the imposition of specific taxes and license fees on slaves.

Cairnes and Wesley suggest insurrections, runaways, or the entire

[11] Wade, p. 3.
[12] *Ibid.*, p. 246.

problem of control as the reason for rising costs in the cities. The cities were areas which harbored many free blacks, and it was possible that escape by slaves was simple because they could easily blend into the existing life. As escapes became more numerous the expected value of an urban slave decreased, and the demand for the services of such bondsmen would move correspondingly to the left. In addition, the problem of mass rebellions or insurrections was, to these writers, enough to scare potential urban owners of slaves not to purchase them and to convince present owners to sell. Again, these explanations imply a lowering in the expected value of the slave's services, a decline in the demand for urban slaves.

There are other reasons to doubt the incompatibility argument, even as expressed in its most sophisticated form in terms of declining demand for urban slaves. As an empirical fact, license fees, taxes, and jailings were very small during the period from 1820 to 1860, and in many of the cities they did not increase during 1850 to 1860, the decade of large decreases in urban slave populations. The white citizenry might have been fearful of slave rebellions but they did not, to any substantial degree, internalize these anxieties.

The Wesley and Cairnes statements concerning the greater probability for insurrections in the cities is not entirely consistent with the facts. Other than the Vesey Conspiracy in Charleston in 1822 most major slave insurrections after 1820 occurred in rural areas. This, of course, can be due to extreme police protection in the cities, but to the extent that these costs were not internalized the demand function for urban slaves should have remained unaffected.

Other writers of this period saw slavery, not as an institution which was incompatible with cities, but one which was more highly desired in the countryside. Some versions of this argument are couched in racist tones; others are more plausible and will be translated into economics.

John Elliott Cairnes in *The Slave Power* was one of the first to pose the problem of slavery in an urban and industrial setting as a function of education and control. He asserted that, "slave labor is unskillful . . . having no interest in his work [he] has no inducement to exert his higher faculties. . . . He is therefore unsuited for all branches of industry which require the slightest care. . . . He cannot be made to cooperate with machinery . . . ; he is incapable of all but the rudest forms of labor."[13] Ulrich B. Phillips concurred with Cairnes in that slave labor could be profitable only if "the work required was simple"

[13] Cairnes, pp. 45-46.

for then "the shortcoming of negro slave labor were partially offset by the ease with which it could be organized."[14]

Lewis Cecil Gray, with racist overtones similar to those of Phillips and Cairnes, believed that the Negro was "primitive" and difficult to control. Thus, the plantation system was adopted because it afforded "more powerful stimuli than the rewards of industry. . . ."[15]

Certain students of the antebellum era saw slavery as being more compatible with rural areas than cities because of the nature of plantation work. One writer who implied this was Robert Russel. In his words, "[s]laves were better adapted to the routine of the plantation than they were to the more varied tasks of general farming with considerable household manufacturing."[16] This same view concerning the relative compatibility of slaves in agricultural and urban pursuits is implied in the natural limits thesis. In its original form expressed by Charles W. Ramsdell, the natural limits thesis stated that slavery would end after all available lands had been brought into cultivation, and if the price of cotton fell substantially.[17] Slavery, to Ramsdell, could be profitable only in staple agriculture. He may have been implying that the use of slaves in producing staples enabled certain economies of scale and methods of control to be utilized. Most importantly, Ramsdell did not believe that slavery could survive in an environment other than one which was agricultural.

The explanation for the decline of urban slavery which has been most accepted by the profession, if we are to use textbook content as our standard, is that of Richard C. Wade in *Slavery in the Cities*.[18] In much of this book, Wade expresses the view, noted before, that slavery was *per se* incompatible with urban life. But, if we were to read a causal relationship into this work, we would conclude that slavery declined in the cities because of declining demand for slaves in those areas.

Wade confuses two issues. His main assertion is that the demand for urban slaves declined over time. But he also implies that the number

[14] U. B. Phillips, "The Economic Cost of Slaveholding in the Cotton Belt," *Political Science Quarterly* 20 (June 1905).

[15] Lewis Cecil Gray, *History of Agriculture in the Southern U.S. to 1860*, Washington, D.C., 1958, I, 470.

[16] Robert Russel, "The General Effects of Slavery upon Southern Economic Progress," *Journal of Southern History* 4 (February 1938), 45.

[17] Charles W. Ramsdell, "The Natural Limits of Slavery Expansion," *Mississippi Valley Historical Review* 16 (September 1929), 151-171.

[18] For example, see John White and Ralph Willet, *Slavery in the American South: Seminar Studies in History*, Great Britain, 1970, p. 38; also R. Farley, "The Urbanization of Negroes in the U.S.," *Journal of Social History* 1 (Spring 1968), rptd. in the Bobbs-Merrill reprint series.

of slaves in the cities during the entire forty-year period studied was lower than would have been if purely profit motivations were considered. This is a more difficult point to refute. If the South had an enormous comparative advantage in agriculture, then for a large range of factor prices, the region would not have urbanized. We could then conclude that the South became a slave labor area because of its natural advantages in the production of staple crops, and not that it produced agricultural goods because of slavery. But if slavery in some way changed this comparative advantage which the South had in agriculture, then it is possible that the South did not urbanize, in part, because of slavery. This essay begins with the year 1820 and asks questions concerning the changes in urban slavery from that point. It does not, in any direct way, attempt to answer the second point; that is, whether the level of urbanization was stifled because of slavery.

The general difficulty with all the explanations outlined above is that they are too broad and sweeping; they do not explain the considerable variation in the course of urban slavery. They do not help the investigator to explain why slavery declined in some cities while increasing in others, or why slavery declined in certain decades while increasing in others. What is required then, is an explanation broad and flexible enough to cope with all of the experiences in the cities during 1820 to 1860.

In establishing such a broad and general explanation it will be useful to regroup the above quotations into those which suggested that slaves were pulled out of cities and those which implied that slaves were pushed out. Those writers who stated or implied that slavery declined in the cities because of a declining demand for the services of these chattel, were stating that slaves were pushed out of the cities. Wade, Cairnes, Douglass, and Wesley all implied that costs of keeping slaves in the cities increased over time, relative to those in rural areas. Writers such as Ramsdell and Russel, who stressed slavery's greater compatibility with agriculture, were suggesting that if slavery declined in the cities it was due to the pull of slaves from cities into staple crop production. This may have been owing to a variety of causes and each of the writers invoked slightly different ones. If this pull explanation is correct we should then observe the rural demand function for slaves increasing at a rate more rapid than the urban schedule. But, if the urban function was increasing at all, then push factors were not important.

Push or pull factors each would imply certain concommitant changes. If push factors were most important we would expect an

432

absolute decline in city slave prices. Much of the city slave labor force had skills specific to urban areas, but the selling price to plantations of these slaves would be equal to that paid for any other prime field hand. If the city demand were declining, city slave prices should fall absolutely from their previous levels. In addition, transfer costs, within limits, would put a wedge between the price of a slave in a growing area and that in a declining city. The puzzling feature about an explanation which relies solely on a declining demand for city slaves is that urban slave prices and hire rates continued to rise during the periods 1830-1840 and 1850-1860, when the quantity of slaves in these areas fell dramatically.

If slaves were pulled out from the cities we should observe that those slaves with training specific to the cities remained there, while the less skilled slaves were sold to the countryside. If push factors, especially those outlined by Cairnes and Wesley, were operative we should expect those slaves who were most inimical to urbanization, the skilled and the males, to be sold. Much of this depends upon how social pressures, if they existed, became internalized. The push and pull theories predict very different changes in the skilled slave populations in the cities, as well as different patterns of slave price changes.

A more general explanation must be consistent with all the facts of the period, and in particular must be able to predict the variations from city to city and from decade to decade. It must come to grips with the fact that the rates of change for the slave population in the various cities fluctuated in magnitude and even in sign over the four decades. While some urban areas had large decreases, others had large increases, in their slave populations. Neither simple push nor pull theories enable us to predict these differences. In fact, the push theory is inconsistent with the finding that the heavily industrial city, Richmond, showed increases in its slave population throughout the forty-year period 1820-1860. According to a declining demand theory based on control problems, Richmond should have lost slaves as time wore on, since it contained an unusually high proportion of skilled slave labor. This concentration should have created more severe problems for Richmond than for other cities.

Moreover, the exodus of slaves from cities seems to have been greater among the unskilled than the skilled. As 1860 approached, the cities were left with a more skilled male slave labor force than they had in earlier periods. Unskilled male slaves were sold to the plantations, but the skilled, especially those with skills specific to urban areas, remained in the cities. This, again, is inconsistent with a push theory for the decline in urban slaves. That is, if demand for all types

433

of urban slaves were declining we would not expect any change in the skill composition of those remaining. Furthermore, if Wade's thesis that urban masters sold their chattel because they no longer felt they had control over them is correct, again we would not expect a change in the male skill mix of the type indicated. Presumably the educated and skilled slaves were more inimical to slavery, and hence constituted a greater threat than the uneducated slave.

Not only were the cities left with a more skilled male slave population, but they had more females, especially old ones, and fewer children by the eve of the Civil War than previously. Thus, if the cities pushed their slaves out, they did so with much discrimination. While one might be inclined to rationalize the greater exodus of unskilled males and children on the grounds that they constituted a more acute threat to safety than skilled males and women, no evidence to support such a view has yet been marshaled.

These facts make one doubt that the simple versions of the pull and push theories can describe accurately all factors during this period. They contradict the push hypothesis to a greater extent, and it will be shown that the pull explanation contains some elements of truth. A portion of this paper will explore two complementary alternative hypotheses. The first is the pull thesis: that is, slaves were pulled out of the cities because the rural demand for their services was increasing at a more rapid rate than that of the cities. This need not be a necessary condition to explain the observation that slavery declined in cities during specific decades. The more important hypothesis predicts that urban slaves could have been sold from the cities, especially during 1850 to 1860, even, if the demand for their services was increasing at a rate greater than that in rural areas. It will be shown that this hypothesis seems correct for most cities, while a combination of this and the pull thesis can explain the data for other urban areas.

I shall argue that the urban demand for slaves was probably increasing over time, accounting for the evidence we have on city slave prices. In general, rural demand was also increasing, probably at an accelerating rate. Nevertheless, there is evidence to suggest that many city demand functions were increasing at a rate even greater than the increase in overall supply. It may seem contradictory to argue that the urban slave population was declining even though the demand for urban slaves increased more rapidly than the aggregate slave population. The contradiction is only apparent. It can be resolved by considering the difference between the elasticities of demand in rural and urban areas. Differences in these elasticities may

434

also explain changes in the *rate* of change in the quantity of urban slaves. The alternative hypothesis is consistent with the facts observed previously: that unskilled male slaves were sold to the plantations from the cities during periods when the price of slaves was very high, and that male and female slaves with skills more specific to the cities were retained there.

Although the remainder of this essay will demonstrate that slaves were, in part, pulled out from southern cities, certain urban areas may have suffered declines in demand, during specific decades. In addition, even if demand was increasing in the cities it may have been dampened by factors which served to increase costs specific to cities. It is possible, then, that the costs for holding slaves in cities, versus rural areas, increased over time as per Wade, Cairnes, and Wesley. But, in very few cities, and in only a small number of decades, did this ever result in a declining demand for slaves. That is, these increased costs may have resulted in a more sluggish acceleration in demand for slave services, but rarely dampened this to zero or negative growth.

It will also be shown that during some decades and again for some cities the rural demand for slaves was growing more rapidly than that for urban areas. But in many cases this was not true, and for most cases the demand for urban slaves was increasing quite rapidly. In fact, for almost the entire period, 1820 to 1860, the growth in demand for urban slaves was greater than that of supply. That is, urban areas contributed to the increases of slave prices in general.

The model which will be developed will build on the suggestions of authors such as Ramsdell, Cairnes, Russel, Wesley, Douglass, and Wade. Most of the theories expounded by these writers appear to be wrong only in omission. Each could explain only a portion of the labor movements which occurred during these four decades. The crucial departure which my analysis makes from theirs is the stress placed on the changes of demand and supply over time, and not just their levels at a point in time. In addition, my model appears to be more general. It explains not only the overall patterns of urban versus rural slave labor movements but also why certain cities suffered losses and others gains and when these occurred.

II. An Empirical Estimation of a Model to Explain the Relative Decline of Urban Slavery

This section will present data on the rate of change of the slave labor force and population for ten southern cities and for the United

435

States, and price data for certain regions. A simple model will be developed and econometrically estimated with these data. Conclusions will then be drawn from the regression coefficients and constant terms.

A. THE DATA

Table 1 shows the average annual rates of change of the slave population and labor force for the major southern cities during 1820 to 1860 and for the United States. Focusing first on the United States totals, note that the slave population and labor force oscillated somewhat. They increased at a rate close to 3 percent per year during the 1820s; at a rate of 2 percent per year between 1830 and 1840. The rate returned to 3 percent in the 1840s and then fell again to 2 percent during slavery's last decade. That is, the rate of increase for slaves was not constant, but had small cycles, with greater rates of increase for the first and third than for the second and fourth decades. These cycles have been attributed to the "echo effects" of the increased importation of mature Negroes prior to the embargo placed on slave importations.[19]

The cities show the same variations, but with a much more marked pattern. Every city, with the sole exceptions of Mobile and New Orleans, shows a cyclical pattern in the percentage rate of change of slaves over the four decades. The percentage increase in slaves for the ten year period 1820 to 1830 and 1840 to 1850 is greater (or equivalently, the decrease, as in the case of Baltimore, is smaller), than for the other two decennial periods. In addition, the swings of these cycles are very large. Many cities experienced large increases in their slave populations during the first and third decades and decreases during the other two decades. Other cities, such as Richmond, experienced increases in their slave populations throughout this forty-year period, but despite this, the rates of increase had a cyclical pattern. Therefore, it seems clear that an explanation for why slavery declined in the cities during its last decade must be consistent with these large cycles in slave population and labor force change.

The slave price and hire rate data presented in Tables 2 and 3 also show cycles. In those periods for which the cities were losing slaves, the prices of these laborers were increasing rapidly; in the other decades, those for which the cities were gaining slaves or losing them less rapidly, prices were rising at a slower pace or even declining. The model must also be consistent with these price variations.

---

[19] See Conrad and Meyer, p. 69. In addition, cholera epidemics in the 1830s and 1850s served to lessen the rate of increase of slaves during those decades.

TABLE 1. AVERAGE ANNUAL RATES OF CHANGE OF SLAVE POPULATIONS AND LABOR FORCES FOR TEN CITIES, THREE REGIONS, AND THE UNITED STATES [a]

	Total Population				Labor Force [c]			
	1820-30	1830-40	1840-50	1850-60	1820-30	1830-40	1840-50	1850-60
Baltimore	−.006	−.025	−.008	−.028	+.004	−.023	−.006	−.031
Charleston	+.019	−.005	+.029	−.034	+.018	.000	+.036	−.035
Louisville	+.085	+.035	+.046	−.010	+.098	+.031	+.054	−.018
Mobile	+.034	+.119	+.056	+.011	+.037	+.122	+.062	−.001
New Orleans	+.025	+.091	−.032	−.024	+.015	+.097	−.028	−.028
Norfolk	+.014	−.001	+.015	−.027	+.014	.000	+.016	−.017
Richmond	+.037	+.017	+.028	+.016	+.044	+.025	+.031	+.020
St. Louis	+.043	−.060	+.055	−.054	+.045	−.052	+.055	−.060
Savannah	+.026	+.016	+.028	+.021	+.028	+.017	+.033	+.016
Washington, D.C.	+.018	−.031	+.021	−.017	+.026	−.028	+.021	−.029
Total U.S.	+.027	+.021	+.025	+.021	+.025	+.023	+.029	+.021
New South Cities [b]	+.026	+.095	−.014	−.013	+.017	+.100	−.009	−.019
Old South Cities [c]	+.030	−.003	+.027	−.009	+.024	+.009	+.032	−.008
Border State Cities [d]	+.024	−.017	+.029	−.023	+.032	−.014	+.032	−.030

SOURCE: *Census of the United States*, 1820, 1830, 1840, 1850, and 1860.

[a] Although certain cities underwent boundary changes during these decades, most of these extensions do not affect the conclusions about the cycles of slave population change. In fact, a few cities grew by annexing nearby towns during those decades when the aggregate slave population declined or grew slower than previously.

[b] Mobile, New Orleans.

[c] Richmond, Savannah, Charleston, Norfolk.

[d] Louisville, Baltimore, Washington, D.C., St. Louis.

[e] Defined as the population between 10 and 55.

TABLE 2. AVERAGE ANNUAL RATES OF CHANGE OF SLAVE PRICES

Period	Richmond (1)	Charleston (2)	Mid-Georgia (3)	New Orleans (4)	Virginia Cities [a] (5)
			1. Undeflated		
1820-30	−.050	−.047	−.031	−.032	−.015
1830-40	+.057	+.044	+.025	+.022	+.044
1840-50	−.007	+.003	+.011	+.010	+.003
1850-60	+.054	+.043	+.059	+.049	+.053
			2. Deflated		
1820-30	−.035	−.032	−.016	−.017	.000
1830-40	+.053	+.040	+.021	+.018	+.040
1840-50	+.002	+.012	+.020	+.019	+.012
1850-60	+.043	+.032	+.048	+.038	+.042

SOURCES: Undeflated Slave Prices:
  Col. (1)-(4), U. B. Phillips, *American Negro Slavery*, p. 370.
  Col. (5), collected from Probate Records, Slave Sales and Inventories, Genealogical Society, Salt Lake City.
  The price deflator (Warren-Pearson Wholesale Price Indexes), from *Historical Statistics of the U.S. Colonial Times to 1957*, Washington, 1960, p. 115.
[a] Richmond, Fredericksburg and Lynchburg. These data are for slaves living and working in these cities.

TABLE 3. AVERAGE ANNUAL RATES OF CHANGE OF SLAVE HIRE RATES

	North Carolina		Virginia Cities male and female combined
	male	female	
		1. Undeflated	
1820-30	n.a.	n.a.	−.004
1830-40	+.051	+.059	+.016
1840-50	−.010	+.003	−.010
1850-60	+.054	+.054	+.079
		2. Deflated	
1820-30	n.a.	n.a.	+.011
1830-40	+.047	+.055	+.012
1840-50	.000	+.013	.000
1850-60	+.043	+.043	+.068

SOURCES: Undeflated hire rates collected from Probate Records, Slave Sales and Inventories, Genealogical Society, Salt Lake City.
  The price deflator (Warren-Pearson Wholesale Price Indexes), from *Historical Statistics of the U.S. Colonial Times to 1957*, Washington, 1960, p. 115.

It is possible to construct an economic model which can rationalize the relative change in urban and rural slave populations and labor forces and be consistent with the price data presented. This model will be presented first and then will be empirically estimated with the data from Tables 1, 2, and 3. Assume that there is a demand function for rural (plantation) slaves which takes the following form:

$$(1) \quad Q_r = D_r P^{-e_r}.$$

Similarly, the cities have a demand schedule for slaves,

$$(2) \quad Q_c = D_c P^{-e_c},$$

where e_r and e_c are the (constant) price elasticities of demand for rural and urban slaves respectively, D_r and D_c are the shift parameters, P is the price of a homogeneous slave input, and Q_r and Q_c are the quantities of rural and urban slaves. There is reason to assume that e_c is greater than e_r.[20] This assumption is vindicated in the empirical analysis, to follow shortly.

If we differentiate the logarithmic transforms of (1) and (2) totally, we get:

$$(3) \quad \overset{*}{Q}_r = \overset{*}{D}_r - e_r \overset{*}{P}, \text{ and}$$

$$(4) \quad \overset{*}{Q}_c = \overset{*}{D}_c - e_c \overset{*}{P},$$

where an asterisk ($*$) over any variable or parameter indicates the rate of change of that variable over time.

In order to derive the aggregate demand function for slaves, we define the total number of slaves,

$$(5) \quad Q = Q_r + Q_c.$$

Substituting from (1) and (2), we get

$$(6) \quad Q = D_r P^{-e_r} + D_c P^{-e_c}.$$

For convenience let $R = P^{-e_r}$ and $C = P^{-e_c}$, and by substitution from (6),

---

[20] There are two justifications for this. In the first place the substitution possibilities for urban slaves were much greater than those for rural slaves. That is, there were more and closer substitutes for industrial and domestic urban slaves than for agricultural bondsmen. Secondly, the elasticity of demand for the final goods and services produced in urban areas was probably greater than that for agricultural commodities.

$$(7) \quad Q = D_r R + D_c C.$$

Taking the total differential of (6), gives us,

$$(8) \quad dQ = D_r dR + R dD_r + D_c dC + C dD_c.$$

Dividing (8) through by Q and rearranging terms to get the expression in terms of rates of change gives us,

$$(9) \quad \overset{*}{Q} = \frac{Q_r}{Q} (\overset{*}{D}_r + \overset{*}{R}) + \frac{Q_c}{Q} (\overset{*}{D}_c + \overset{*}{C}),$$

and now letting $\alpha = \dfrac{Q_r}{Q}$ and substituting back from before for R and C,

$$(10) \quad \overset{*}{Q} = \alpha(\overset{*}{D}_r - e_r \overset{*}{P}) + (1 - \alpha)(\overset{*}{D}_c - e_c \overset{*}{P}).$$

Rearranging (10) to get the expression in a more convenient form yields,

$$(11) \quad \overset{*}{Q} = (\alpha \overset{*}{D}_r + (1 - \alpha) \overset{*}{D}_c) - (\alpha e_r + (1 - \alpha) e_c) \overset{*}{P}.$$

Thus, from (11) we see that we have an expression of the form,

$$(12) \quad \overset{*}{Q} = \overset{*}{D} - e \overset{*}{P},$$

where $\overset{*}{Q}$ is the rate of change in the total slaves demanded, $\overset{*}{D}$ is a convex combination of the shift terms, in rate of change form, from the two demand functions, and e is a convex combination of the price elasticities of demand for rural and city slaves.

If we define the supply schedule in a manner similar to the above,

$$(13) \quad Q = SP^\gamma,$$

where S is the shift parameter and γ is the (constant) elasticity of supply, we can express it in rate of change form as,

$$(14) \quad \overset{*}{Q} = \overset{*}{S} + \gamma \overset{*}{P}.$$

We will assume that for each ten year period $\gamma = 0$.[21] This assump-

---

[21] Conrad and Meyer point out that all slave labor of working age was employed during the working season; therefore, no changes in the equilibrium price or rental rate could elicit an increase in the working time of those already in the labor force, and no price changes could increase the percentage of slaves in the labor force. In addition, on the production side, it appears as if changes in the fertility rates were independent of demand considerations. Even if planters attempted

tion enables us to fit the model by estimation of the demand functions alone, since the change in the quantity of slaves supplied is equal to the exogenous shift in the total number of slaves, or more accurately just those in the labor force. The equilibrium value of $\dot{Q}$ is, therefore, determined solely by the aggregate rate of change supply function, given values for e, $\dot{S}$, $\dot{D}$, and that $\gamma = 0$.[22] The intersection of the rate of change aggregate demand and supply function determines the rate of change in the price of slaves $\dot{P}$. Given $\dot{P}$ we can then substitute into equations (3) and (4) to get values of $\dot{Q}_c$ and $\dot{Q}_r$, specifying either e_c, e_r, $\dot{D}_c$, and $\dot{D}_r$, or the share of rural slaves in the total and the parameters of only one of the demand functions.

The assumptions that $e_c > e_r$ and $\gamma = 0$ enable certain conclusions to stem from the model, even in this simple form. If the rate of growth of supply is low ($\dot{S}_2$ on Figure 1), that is if it intersects the rate of change demand schedules to the left of their intersection (point O on Figure 1), then $\dot{Q}_c$ will be less than $\dot{Q}_r$, ($\dot{Q}_{c_2} < \dot{Q}_{r_2}$). If the supply schedule is increasing at a faster rate ($\dot{S}_1$), and intersects the rate of change demand schedules to the right of point O, the opposite will result, ($\dot{Q}_{c_1} > \dot{Q}_{r_1}$). Therefore, we should expect the following to have occurred if the model is properly specified. (1) The cities should have had larger relative changes in their slave populations than the rural areas. (2) Those decades for which the aggregate rate of change in supply was low, the cities should have been losing more slaves, or gaining fewer than those decades for which the rate of change in supply was great. (3) Prices for slaves should have oscillated, increasing at a low rate, or decreasing, during those decades for which the rate of change in supply was large, and vice versa for the other

---

to alter the birth rate such efforts would have had no effect on the labor force supply for at least ten years. See M. Zelnick, "Fertility of the American Negro in 1830 and 1850," *Population Studies* 20 (July 1966), 77-83. Most of the change in the equilibrium quantity of slaves in the United States, therefore, seems to have come about through random elements, such as cholera epidemics, and the embargo of 1807.

[22] When "rate of change" precedes either "supply" or "demand" it refers to the type of function given by equations (3, 4, 12, 14) to differentiate them from what we normally consider as being demand or supply functions, as given by equations (1, 2, 5, 13). The difference between the two is that the former are in rate of change form, and, in essence, are the latter increasing at some constant or changing rate.

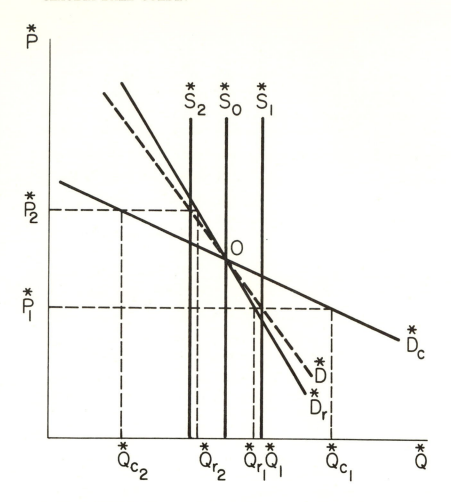

A GENERAL GRAPHICAL REPRESENTATION
OF THE MODEL

periods. All of these conclusions are apparent in the tables presented above.

C. AN EMPIRICAL FIT OF THE MODEL

Estimating a model which has only four data points is, at best, difficult to manage; but to the extent the model is correctly specified, even four observations can yield interesting results. This appears to be the case for the model presented above. For most cities and for the aggregate, the assumption that $\overset{*}{D}_c$ and $\overset{*}{D}_r$ are constant, i.e., $d\overset{*}{D}_c = d\overset{*}{D}_r = 0$, seems to be valid. That is, either the variables determining $\overset{*}{D}_c$ and $\overset{*}{D}_r$ were growing at constant rates, or else their rates changed differently thus canceling out. For two cities, Mobile and New Orleans, this was not the case; the growth in their free populations for the period 1830 to 1840 was so enormous that the exclusion of this variable yielded insignificant results. The inclusion of this one additional variable aided the fit dramatically. If more observations were available, the addition of all the variables determining the $\overset{*}{D}$'s probably would have afforded even better results for all equations in the model. But, this section will demonstrate that the most simple model goes very far in explaining the shifts in urban slave populations.[23]

Table 4 gives the results of regressions performed on equations,

$$(4) \quad \overset{*}{Q}_c = \overset{*}{D}_c - e_c \overset{*}{P} \text{ and}$$

$$(12) \quad \overset{*}{P} = \frac{\overset{*}{D}}{e} - \frac{\overset{*}{Q}}{e}$$

Equation (12) is a simplified expression for

[23] The following tabulation of the "t" distribution for 1 and 2 degrees of freedom for various levels of significance is helpful in interpreting the coefficients and constant terms. Because of the very limited number of observations the usual 5% level of significance will not be used. Even where the coefficients are extremely insignificant they are still the maximum likelihood estimates. The homogeneity of the results reinforces the use of coefficients which otherwise would be rejected at even the 20% level.

THE "t" DISTRIBUTION FOR 1 AND 2 DEGREES OF FREEDOM

Degrees of Freedom	.5	.2	.1	.05	.02	.01
2	.816	1.886	2.920	4.303	6.965	9.925
1	1.000	3.078	6.314	12.706	31.821	63.657

TABLE 4. PART 1. ESTIMATION OF THE MODEL [a]

	$\overset{*}{D}$	$-e$	R^2 [b]
United States [c]	.025	−.075	.978 (.967)
	(9.41)	(−9.83)	
[d]	.026	−.159	.687 (.530)
	(2.28)	(−2.09)	
Baltimore [e]	−.004	−.537	.968 (.953)
	(−2.03)	(−7.83)	
Charleston [f]	.009	−.534	.377 (.065)
	(.061)	(−1.10)	
Louisville [e]	.078	−1.64	.765 (.648)
	(4.07)	(−2.55)	
Mobile [d]	.056	−.091	.002 (.000)
	(1.60)	(−.064)	
New Orleans [d]	.026	−.746	.091 (.000)
	(.63)	(−.449)	
Norfolk [e]	.019	−.783	.693 (.539)
	(1.71)	(−2.12)	
Richmond [e]	.036	−.473	.980 (.971)
	(25.39)	(−9.99)	
St. Louis [e]	.062	−2.80	.897 (.845)
	(3.10)	(−4.17)	
Savannah [f]	.024	−.118	.498 (.247)
	(9.44)	(−1.41)	
Washington, D.C. [e]	.025	−1.15	.857 (.786)
	(2.52)	(−3.47)	
Old South [e]	.033	−.948	.963 (.944)
	(8.58)	(−7.18)	
New South [d]	.031	−.542	.059 (.000)
	(.833)	(−.354)	
Border States [e]	.032	−1.23	.903 (.854)
	(3.80)	(−4.31)	

NOTE: Part 1: $\overset{*}{Q}$=average annual rate of change in slave population. Regressions run in the form: $\overset{*}{Q_c}=\overset{*}{D_c}-e_c\overset{*}{P}$, for cities and city aggregates, $\overset{*}{P}=\overset{*}{D}/e-\overset{*}{Q}/e$ for U.S. See text for rationale.

$$(11) \quad \overset{*}{P}=\frac{(\alpha \overset{*}{D_r}+(1-\alpha)\overset{*}{D_c})}{(\alpha e_r+(1-\alpha)e_c)}-\frac{\overset{*}{Q}}{(\alpha e_r+(1-\alpha)e_c)}.$$

If α, or the share of the total slaves which are rural, is very high then estimation of (11) for all slaves is approximately equivalent to that for slaves in agriculture.

The econometric rationale for the regressions is as follows. The cities are assumed to be price takers; therefore, $\overset{*}{P}$ is given and $\overset{*}{Q_c}$ is determined by (4). The rural equation assumes $\overset{*}{Q}$ to be given, since

444

TABLE 4. PART 2.

	$\overset{*}{D}$	$-e$	$R^{2\,\text{b}}$
United States [c]	.030	−.166	.332 (.000)
	(1.08)	(−.98)	
[d]	.032	−.435	.125 (.000)
	(.663)	(−.534)	
Baltimore [e]	.004	−.753	.971 (.957)
	(1.37)	(−8.24)	
Charleston [f]	.011	−.485	.266 (.000)
	(.630)	(−.851)	
Louisville [e]	.091	−2.11	.829 (.744)
	(4.53)	(−3.12)	
Mobile [d]	.059	−.306	.019 (.000)
	(1.53)	(−.194)	
New Orleans [d]	.022	−.581	.051 (.000)
	(.515)	(−.328)	
Norfolk [e]	.018	−.637	.754 (.632)
	(2.39)	(−2.48)	
Richmond [e]	.0410	−.468	.884 (.826)
	(11.54)	(−3.90)	
St. Louis [e]	.063	−2.82	.910 (.865)
	(3.41)	(−4.50)	
Savannah [f]	.026	−.170	.431 (.147)
	(6.05)	(−1.23)	
Washington, D.C. [e]	.031	−1.42	.971 (.956)
	(5.98)	(−8.15)	
Old South [e]	.0311	−.717	.716 (.574)
	(3.29)	(−2.25)	
New South [d]	.0284	−.426	.033 (.000)
	(.706)	(−.260)	
Border States [e]	.039	−1.47	.919 (.878)
	(4.32)	(−4.76)	

NOTE: Part 2: $\overset{*}{Q}$ = average annual rate of change in slave labor force.

[a] Figures in parentheses for all tables are "t" values. The "t" statistics for all the aggregate equation coefficients are for $\dfrac{\overset{*}{D}}{e}$ and $\dfrac{1}{e}$.

[a] Figures in parentheses for all tables are "t" values.
[b] Figures in parentheses are R^2 adjusted for degrees of freedom in all tables.
[c] Phillips' Richmond prices
[d] Phillips' New Orleans prices
[e] "Va. City" prices
[f] Phillips' Charleston prices

All prices deflated by the Warren-Pearson Wholesale Price indexes.

$\overset{*}{Q} = \overset{*}{S}$, and the price is determined by (11). Table 5, Part 1 was computed on the assumption that $d\overset{*}{D}_c$ might not have been equal to 0. The only proxy I have at the present time for growth in value added for industrial and domestic urban production is the rate at which the

TABLE 5. PART 1. ESTIMATION OF EXTENDED MODELS [a]

		$\overset{*}{D}{}'$	b	$-e$	R^2
	$\overset{*}{Q}$=slave:				
Baltimore:	pop.	−.010	.159	−.493	.996 (.989)
		(−4.18)	(2.73)	(−13.3)	
	labor force	.005	−.025	−.760	.972 (.915)
		(.492)	(−.112)	(−5.33)	
Charleston:	pop.	−.006	.675	−.361	.591 (.000)
		(−.237)	(.0725)	(−.596)	
	labor force	−.007	.794	−.281	.520 (.000)
		(−.231)	(.728)	(−.397)	
Louisville:	pop.	−.054	1.42	−6.73	.999 (.999)
		(−8.91)	(22.26)	(−11.28)	
	labor force	−.047	1.50	−1.09	.999 (.996)
		(−3.97)	(11.88)	(−9.30)	
Mobile:	pop.	.0175	.806	−.847	.918 (.753)
		(.949)	(3.33)	(−1.36)	
	labor force	.018	.861	−1.11	.864 (.592)
		(.683)	(2.49)	(−1.25)	
New Orleans:	pop.	−.011	.991	−1.71	.979 (.938)
		(−1.08)	(6.55)	(−4.46)	
	labor force	−.017	1.07	−1.62	.997 (.991)
		(−4.26)	(17.94)	(−10.74)	
Norfolk:	pop.	.001	.736	−.653	.798 (.394)
		(.053)	(.723)	(−1.42)	
	labor force	.004	.614	−.529	.875 (.626)
		(.234)	(.984)	(−1.88)	
Richmond:	pop.	.039	−.118	−.451	.985 (.960)
		(6.81)	(−.581)	(−6.52)	
	labor force	.054	−.503	−.374	.966 (.898)
		(6.04)	(−1.56)	(−3.24)	
St. Louis:	pop.	.014	.444	−.376	.799 (.388)
		(1.73)	(1.21)	(−1.6)	
	labor force	.020	.256	−.319	.472 (.000)
		(.96)	(.279)	(−.564)	
Savannah:	pop.	.033	.324	−2.63	.998 (.997)
		(6.31)	(7.52)	(−20.6)	
	labor force	.039	.277	−2.67	.985 (.954)
		(2.51)	(2.20)	(−7.17)	
Washington, D.C.:	pop.	.010	.253	−5.99	.893 (.679)
		(.380)	(.578)	(−.581)	
	labor force	.017	.242	−.901	.995 (.984)
		(2.42)	(2.11)	(−3.35)	

NOTE: Part 1: $\overset{*}{Q}=\overset{*}{D}{}'+b\overset{*}{Q}_{fp}-e\overset{*}{P}$; $\overset{*}{Q}_{fp}$=average annual rate of change in the free population.

446

TABLE 5. PART 2.

	$\overset{*}{D}{}'$	b	$-e$	R^2
Richmond Prices:				
U.S. Slave Population	.026	.019	−.08	.994 (.982)
	(13.26)	(1.62)	(−12.57)	
U.S. Slave Labor force	.019	.127	−.04	.910 (.731)
	(3.29)	(2.54)	(−3.13)	
New Orleans Prices:				
U.S. Slave Population	.023	.055	−.14	.812 (.437)
	(2.09)	(.818)	(−2.07)	
U.S. Slave Labor force	.019	.015	−.07	.953 (.857)
	(4.55)	(4.19)	(−4.48)	

NOTE: Part 2: $\overset{*}{P} = \frac{1}{e}\overset{*}{D}{}' + \frac{b}{e}\overset{*}{C} - \frac{1}{e}\overset{*}{Q}$, where $\overset{*}{C}$=average annual rate of change of the value of cotton production.[b]

[a] Slave prices used are the same for Table 4. $\overset{*}{D}{}'$ is interpreted as the rate of change in demand neglecting that change due to $\overset{*}{Q}_{fp}$ in Part 1 and $\overset{*}{C}$ in Part 2.

[b] Cotton prices are deflated by the Warren-Pearson Wholesale Price indexes.

free population was growing. The addition of this variable aided the fit for the New South cities. Part 2 of Table 5 adds the growth rate of the deflated value of cotton production to the aggregate equation, improving the explanation of the changes in the price of slaves.

The results of the regression runs are impressive. For most cities the fit is good for both labor force and for population. Since the labor force was estimated by sampling the census manuscripts there is error in its measurement, and this is the reason for estimating the functions using both the labor force and the population figures. This econometric fit of the simple model shows that the assumption made previously concerning the relative magnitudes of e_c and e_r is probably correct. In all cases e_r is less than e_c. The estimates of both elasticities are probably biased downward because the rate of change of the wage rate for free labor was excluded. If slave and free labor were substitutes then a combination of the own and the cross elasticities is actually being estimated. The cross elasticity would be positive, therefore the true own elasticity is greater than the estimated elasticity.

The elasticity of demand for urban slaves varies among cities. We would expect that the elasticity of demand would be greater in those cities which had greater influxes of immigrants and in those cities where slaves performed in less skilled occupations. These appear to

447

be the case. The Border State cities, Louisville, St. Louis, and Washington, D.C., all have elasticities of demand which exceed one, based on fitting the model using the rate of change in slave population as the dependent variable.[24] The elasticities for the Border State cities are also greater than those for the Old South cities, when the $\overset{*}{Q}_{fp}$ term is added, although the elasticities are now lower. That is, these Border cities did experience larger changes in free population and this explains, to some extent, the large changes in slave populations, although enough variance is felt so that the elasticity remains fairly large. The New South cities have greater elasticities of demand than those of the Old South. This is probably due to the greater availability of substitutes. The Old South cities have the lowest elasticities of demand, and it was in these regions that slaves were used the most intensively for manufacturing purposes. The census manuscript slave schedules show that a large percentage of Richmond's slaves were employed by the tobacco and iron factories. In fact, over 50 percent of Richmond's slaves were hired out in 1860.[25]

The rate of growth in demand for urban slaves appears to have been very rapid. The simple model shows that the rate of growth in urban demand for the three regions was greater than that for the aggregate United States, although the constant term for the New South is rather insignificant. The only city which shows a negative rate of growth in demand is Baltimore, but this is positive when the slave labor force is used as the dependent variable. For all cities, the addition of the rate of change in the free population reduces the $\overset{*}{D}'$ term, which is construed as the agglomeration of all shift factors other than $\overset{*}{Q}_{fp}$. That is, if the free population had not been increasing, demand would have increased less rapidly or decreased at a faster rate. Three cities would have had demand schedules for slaves which moved to the left if their free population had not grown. The others would have grown from between 1 to 5 percent per year. The $\overset{*}{D}$ term for the aggregate would have grown at about 2 percent per year if the rate to change or the value of cotton production was zero, but was actually growing at slightly under 3 percent per year.

---

[24] These Border State cities attracted far more immigrants than their more southern counterparts. See *Reports of the Immigration Commission: Statistical Review of Immigration, 1819-1910*, Washington, 1911; rptd. New York, 1970.

[25] See the manuscript census schedules for 1860, Richmond, Virginia, National Archives, microfilm.

448

III. Concluding Remarks

It has been shown that the demand for slaves in the urban South from 1820 to 1860 was not declining. In fact, most of the estimates presented in that part indicate that $\overset{*}{D_c}$ was greater than $\overset{*}{Q}$ for most cities and urban aggregates. The decline of urban slavery in its last decade, 1850 to 1860, was almost entirely due to rapid increases in the price of slaves in general, which led urban owners to cash in on their capital gains. Even if urban and rural demands were increasing at the same rate, large price increases would have caused the equilibrium changes in the two areas to have been different because of the greater elasticity of demand for slaves in the cities. In fact, even if $\overset{*}{D_c}$ was greater than $\overset{*}{D_r}$ the equilibrium rates of change during the last decade could still be generated solely because of differences in elasticities. $\overset{*}{D_c}$ might have been lower than $\overset{*}{D_r}$; therefore part of the relative loss of slaves by the cities could have been due to "pull" factors. It has been demonstrated that there is no necessary reason to assume that the relative loss of slaves by the cities during 1850 to 1860 was due to decreases in the urban demand function. In fact, the urban demand function was probably not decreasing at all, and in some cities was increasing at a rather rapid rate.

Slavery in the cities was not, therefore, dying because of any factors inherent in the urban milieu itself. This may be less true of some Border State cities, but, rural Border State regions should also have been experiencing the same problem with runaways, the underground railway, and abolitionists. It may, therefore, be interesting to hypothesize about what the equilibrium growth of urban slaves would have been had emancipation not occurred. I assume that the regression lines, computed in Table 4, Part 1, apply to the period following the war. That is, the shift terms, $\overset{*}{D_c}$, are assumed the same and the elasticities are held constant. Table 6 gives estimates of $\overset{*}{Q_c}$ for the three urban regions, and the $\overset{*}{Q}$ in the total U.S., for the period 1860 to 1890. The rate of change in prices, $\overset{*}{P}$, has been calculated to have been .0129 or 1.29 percent per year for the period 1860 to 1890, had slavery continued.[26]

---

[26] This has been computed by R. W. Fogel and S. L. Engerman in chap. 24 of their book, *The Reinterpretation of American Economic History*, New York, 1971, pp. 330-331.

449

TABLE 6. HYPOTHESIZED AVERAGE ANNUAL RATES OF GROWTH OF URBAN SLAVES, 1860 TO 1890, FOR THREE URBAN REGIONS AND THE U.S.

Regions	e_c or e	$\overset{*}{D_c}$ or $\overset{*}{D}$	$\overset{*}{Q_c}$ or $\overset{*}{Q}$
(1) Old South	−.95	+.033	.0207
(2) Border States	−1.2	+.031	.0154
(3) New South	−.54	+.032	.0250
(4) U.S. Total	−.2	+.026	.0234

NOTE: e_c, e, $\overset{*}{D_c}$, and $\overset{*}{D}$ are the regressions results from Table 4, Part 1.

The results are very interesting. The average annual growth in the aggregated slave population of 2.34 percent is very close to the rate of growth of the southern black population. In addition, all the urban $\overset{*}{Q}$'s are positive and are close to the $\overset{*}{Q}$ for the aggregate. Therefore, a 1.29 percent per year change in prices is approximately that $\overset{*}{P}$ at which the rural and urban functions cross. The decline of slavery in 1850 to 1860 would have been temporary; if the growth in prices had slowed down, the cities would have begun to gain slaves again. In addition, these estimates are probably much too low. Industrial slavery had just begun to spread over the South by the 1850s, and the increase of industrialization after 1860 would have strengthened the shift terms.

XVII

Comment

HAROLD D. WOODMAN

USING THE methods of the so-called new economic historians Professor Goldin attempts to explain the relative decline of urban slavery in the American South. More precisely, she uses regression analysis to develop supply and demand schedules for urban and rural slaves during the years 1820-1860 in order "to formulate a rationale for the relative decline of urban slavery which is consistent with the facts of the period." The key facts, according to Professor Goldin, are: (1) "the rates of change for the slave population and labor force in the various cities fluctuated in magnitude and even in sign, over the four decades"; (2) urban slave prices rose even during the periods of relative decline in urban slavery; (3) the relative decline in urban slaves during the 1850s was mainly among the unskilled males and children, with skilled males and females remaining in the cities in larger numbers. She argues that these facts are not consistent with the argument that the decline in urban slavery is attributable to a decline in urban demand, a position which she says is "most accepted by the profession" and comes mainly from Richard C. Wade's *Slavery in the Cities.*

Professor Goldin's analysis shows that in fact urban demand for slaves was *not* decreasing during the 1850s, but was, on the contrary, increasing. Nevertheless, the cities lost slaves because prices for slaves in the countryside were rising rapidly enough to pull slaves out of the cities. In her words: "The decline of urban slavery in its last decade, 1850 to 1860, was almost entirely due to rapid increases in the price of slaves in general, which led urban owners to cash in on their capital gains." She concludes that had the Civil War not intervened and had slave price increases slowed, the urban areas would have once again gained slaves, this serving as additional proof that the urban environment was not responsible for the changing numbers of slaves in the southern cities.

Although I must leave a detailed critique of Professor Goldin's regression analysis to someone trained in the area, I would raise one question concerning the way in which she uses her data. When she calculates the rate of change in the numbers of slaves in southern cities over the years 1820 to 1860, Professor Goldin discovers a "cyclical pattern in the percentage rate of change of slaves over the four decades" which implies that the notion of a steady decline in urban slavery is not consistent with the facts. I would argue, however, that a better measure of the relative decline of slavery in the cities would be a calculation of the number of slaves relative to the whole population in the urban areas. When such calculations are made (see Table 1 below) the cyclical patterns tend to disappear. Southern cities, with a couple of minor exceptions, show a steady decline in the proportion of slaves to the total urban population. By this measurement, then, Wade's generalization that urban slavery was on the decline gains impressive support.

At the same time, however, my figures do not invalidate Professor Goldin's central point that the absolute numbers of slaves in the urban South tended to fluctuate. But this fluctuation occurred in the midst of a general decline. Therefore, Professor Goldin's conclusions do not contradict what I consider the most important point in Wade's analysis, i.e., that the urban environment was detrimental to and corrosive of the institution of slavery. What Professor Goldin has done is to offer convincing evidence to explain the minor fluctuations in the numbers of urban slaves during the antebellum period. Within the context of the market for slaves, some owners would buy and sell in

TABLE 1. SLAVES AS PERCENTAGE OF TOTAL POPULATION, SOUTHERN CITIES AND ENTIRE SOUTH

	1820	1830	1840	1850	1860
Baltimore	6.94	5.11	3.13	1.74	1.04
Charleston	51.06	50.69	50.15	45.44	34.32
Louisville	25.70	23.27	16.17	12.58	7.21
Mobile	31.29	36.79	30.53	33.16	25.93
New Orleans	27.06	31.60	22.94	14.62	7.94
Norfolk	38.46	38.27	33.97	29.98	22.46
Richmond	36.36	39.51	37.26	36.01	30.86
St. Louis	18.01	19.79	9.30	3.41	.96
Savannah	40.87		41.86	40.69	34.60
Washington, D.C.	14.68	12.38	7.33	5.28	2.90
New South Cities [a]	27.44	32.10	23.78	17.40	10.60
Old South Cities [b]	44.23		42.75	39.91	31.73
Border State Cities [c]	10.15	9.40	6.04	3.98	2.08
South	34.14	34.70	34.93	34.70	34.48

[a] Mobile, New Orleans.
[b] Richmond, Savannah, Charleston, Norfolk.
[c] Louisville, Baltimore, Washington, D.C., St. Louis.

response to profit incentives. Moreover, Professor Goldin is undoubtedly correct when she notes that the availability of substitutes for slave labor in the cities made sales of urban slaves profitable in times of rising prices. In all cities the white population increased steadily and in every city except Charleston, New Orleans, and Norfolk the free black population also increased steadily. Presumably, at a certain point in a rising market for slaves, the urban slaveowner would find it economically advantageous to sell his slave and hire a free worker; conversely, in a falling market, an urban dweller might find it profitable to buy a slave rather than to hire free labor.

Yet the fact remains that these short term decisions dictated by the exigencies of the market took place in the midst of a general decline in urban slavery. Therefore, Professor Goldin's evidence, when viewed in the context of Wade's argument that urban life undermined the peculiar institution offers evidence that slavery was detrimental to the development of urban economic endeavors—industry, trade, commerce—and hence to southern economic development. Of course, she would not agree with this conclusion because she explicitly avoids treating the larger issue by construing Wade's argument in narrow economic terms.

There is ample evidence that slaves could be trained for city work as artisans or other skilled workers and, indeed, they were. But training requires more than the mastery of a manual (or mental) skill if we view the process in group or class rather than in individual terms. Training requires also the absorption of certain attitudes and discipline. The incentives of free workers are much different from those of slave laborers and these incentives (wages, leisure, promotion, fear of being fired, opportunities for social mobility, etc.) are denied the slaves, or, if given, tend to undermine the entire nature of slavery. Moreover, in an industrializing, urban society, worker skills are learned in the context of a particular social milieu in which general discipline, requisite education, and a general ideological commitment to the system are instilled. The question, then, is not whether a master can teach a slave—or even a group of slaves—to run a machine or keep accounts, but rather whether a society that has need for these services can use slave labor to perform them without altering the nature (even the existence) of slavery and the nature of the political and economic power relations in the slave society.

For the planter, the weakening of the bonds of servitude carried the danger of the destruction of the system upon which his political, social, and economic well-being depended and we could expect to hear his voice raised to express concern over the menacing features of

453

urban slavery. Urban slaveowners and hirers might be less concerned with this problem and might be willing to accept the corrosive changes in slavery that urbanism brought had not an alternative—and a profitable one at that—been available to them. As Professor Goldin ably shows, when slave prices did not so dictate, the urban owners kept their slaves. Yet in the long run, the South's urban labor needs were increasingly met by free labor. Wade noted that, as time went on, more and more urban jobs were closed to slaves and became monopolized by whites. These developments cannot be explained by Professor Goldin's economic model.

If Professor Goldin's excellent paper has not destroyed Wade's argument, it has added another dimension to it and for this reason her paper is an important contribution to our understanding. It should also be noted that her analysis suggests an additional line of inquiry. She has shown that the South's urban labor needs were met by a declining slave population and a growing free population, but it is important to remember that the southern cities were growing more slowly than those in the North. In other words, the South's urban labor needs were met by a relatively small population. It would be interesting to speculate what might have happened had the urban demand been greater. We would expect (following Professor Goldin) to find an influx of slaves into the cities and this (following Wade) would have tended to undermine the slave system. I raise this question not to propose a counter-factual research plan but to suggest that the dominant planter class might be aware of such potential dangers and therefore be motivated to oppose those economic changes that could result in the urbanization of the South. In the absence of such changes, the influence that urbanism could exert on the institution of slavery was limited. The existence of plantation agriculture in the countryside and the resulting demand for slave labor, the very limited urban development (due in large part to the limited industrial development) which made the substitution of free for slave labor relatively easy, and the slight political and social influence of the urban areas—all these factors made it impossible for the urban areas to exert a significant influence on the institution of slavery which always remained a rural phenomenon.

It is to Professor Goldin's credit that her paper has deepened our understanding of southern history and suggested profitable avenues for further research.

XVIII

The Reconstruction of Plantation Labor after Emancipation: The Case of British Guiana

ALAN H. ADAMSON

THE CONFIGURATION of post-emancipation Guyanese society has been shaped by one major theme: the survival and modernization of a plantation agriculture exporting sugar to metropolitan markets. Elsewhere,[1] I have attempted a general description and analysis of this development and wish in the present essay to isolate what is perhaps its critical aspect: the story of how the colony's planting interest built for itself a non-slave labor force between 1838 and 1900. Inevitably, one hopes that what follows will fit at least partially into the broad pattern of British West Indian, and even Caribbean, society, but there are limits beyond which it is dangerous to generalize from the experience of a single region. A host of special circumstances, including a low ratio of population to agricultural land, a vast and empty frontier, and a rich alluvial soil incapable of effective exploitation without large-scale capital investment in sea defense and drainage, have combined to make Guyana the extreme case in West Indian history. Nevertheless, she is not unique and there is a case for arguing that the extremity of her condition is of particular value to comparative historians precisely because it illuminates more clearly, if also more harshly, certain problems which in other parts of the West Indies tend to be obscured. Among these the problem of plantation labor merits special attention.

Difficulties related to the supply and control of labor were, of course, nothing new to the planting community. They were inherent features of slavery in the Western Hemisphere. But in the high period of the old plantation system the purely economic aspect of the labor question was modified to the benefit of the slaveowner by political

[1] *Sugar Without Slaves: The Political Economy of British Guiana 1838-1904*, New Haven, 1972.

considerations. Until the last decades of the eighteenth century, he could rely on the backing and support of the ruling sectors of British metropolitan society. Thereafter, this support diminished. The planting sector of the imperial system, based on slavery and high-cost production for protected markets, found itself in growing conflict with those industrial and commercial interests who now thought in terms of engrossing global markets through free trade. A temporary, but not the less intriguing, split occurred inside the ruling elements of British society. The ending of the slave trade, abolition, and emancipation were all products of this division and its curious side effect, the identification of one section of British capital with the slaves and their aspirations for freedom.[2]

However, this alignment of interests was temporary. When abolition became an accomplished fact, the fundamentally common interest of metropolitan and colonial capital reasserted itself through the generally received assumption that a viable and "civilized" West Indian society could only exist on the basis of a plantation economy. An important corollary was that such a society must have access to a large and dependent, though legally free, body of labor. Alexander Geddes, a Jamaican proprietor, expressed the position of the planting community. If estates were generally abandoned, he warned the West Indian Committee of 1842, the concentration of taxation on remaining plantations would become intolerable, roads would decay, the availability of cheap land would scatter labor over the face of the country, thus limiting access to churches and schools and destroying all chance of carrying on the best estates. "The cultivation of exchangeable commodities thus ceasing (for the black population cultivate nothing for export) commerce, the handmaid of civilisation, would cease also, and with it the consumption of British and British colonial manufacturers and products. . . . The vast capital sunk in land, buildings, cultivation and live stock would be lost, and the charge of maintaining the colony would fall on the mother country. . . . Foreigners in slave countries would be confirmed in their view that emancipation was a failure."[3] George Carrington, an absentee with two estates in Barbados, put the matter in more openly racist terms. "The black man is totally unable to conduct his affairs with any success whatever, supposing the whites were annihilated"; the experience of San Domingo had demonstrated that "in proportion as

[2] It is obvious, I trust, that this radically simplified account omits consideration of a host of other forces that played a part in this complex movement.

[3] Great Britain, *Parliamentary Papers* (henceforth *P.P.*), vol. 13 (1842), no. 479, p. 474.

you reduce the whites, you lessen the chance of prosperity and moral improvement on the part of the blacks." [4]

Metropolitan statesmen now accepted these doctrines, sometimes formulating them in terms that even planters found indiscreet. Thus Lord Howick, one of the architects of abolition in the 1830s, directing himself to a witness before the 1842 West Indian Committee: "Do you not conceive that some means might be adopted to check that tendency of labourers to withdraw and to establish themselves on land of their own?. . . Do you conceive there would be any injustice in taking measures that would render land more expensive and make a greater amount of labour necessary before the labourer could establish himself on the land?. . . Do you not conceive that it is greatly to the advantage of the negro population . . . that a state of civilised society should be maintained, which can only be maintained by a system of combined labour? . . . Do you not think . . . that the nature of taxation ought to be so altered as to make it fall more on the labourer and less on the proprietor?" [5] And Sir John Pakington in the same vein: "Do you not think it is most desirable, for the fair protection of the planter, that some means should be devised of making the labourers work fairly every day of the week . . . and work more hours in the day than they do?" [6] Howick, later Earl Grey, and Pakington were both future colonial secretaries. Their questions reflect the weakening of the humanitarian impulse after emancipation and the growth of a conviction that the transition from slavery to freedom ought not take place outside the plantation context and that the personal dependence of slavery ought to be replaced by the economic dependence of the wage laborer, Marx's "other man . . . compelled to sell himself of his own free-will."

The unity of metropolitan and colonial capital is thus a cardinal political factor in post-emancipation British Caribbean history. Planters and colonial administrators might continue to bicker over marginal issues, but they were agreed that the plantation system must be preserved. If the "natural" superiority of sugar production was insufficient to ensure its survival in competition with less "civilized" sectors of the economy, then some degree of compulsion, short of slavery, would have to be employed. Thus the key to victory in the struggle which ensued lay in the control of labor.

In the decisive years, between 1838 and 1900, the planters resorted

[4] *Ibid.*, p. 140.
[5] *Ibid.*, pp. 406-407.
[6] *Ibid.*, p. 314.

ALAN H. ADAMSON

to a variety of devices and policies to secure this control. Some were pursued persistently, others were designed to meet and solve temporary problems, but all were related to the grand strategy of plantation survival. The most important were: (1) the regulation of undiluted creole labor; (2) the circumscription of peasant economy; (3) immigration; (4) indenture and reindenture; (5) income redistribution through control of fiscal policy; and (6) the monopoly of political authority.

REGULATION OF CREOLE LABOR

WELL before emancipation, the old slave plantation system had run into labor supply problems. It is one of the grimmer comments on the peculiar institution that after the abolition of the slave trade the slave population of British Guiana fell from 100,000 in 1812 to some 82,800 in 1838. The planters' reaction to this problem demonstrated that they were not prepared to solve it by liberalizing the master-slave relationship. Instead, they stiffened manumission conditions and accepted Canning's famous resolutions of 1823, aimed at ameliorating slave conditions, with an ill-will and ineptitude that caused a slave uprising in 1823. The experience of 1823 was bitter enough for the slaves. Subsequent events were to confirm their apprehension that plantation laborers would never be truly free, whatever their legal status. Shortly after the apprenticeship period began, the widespread destruction of fruit trees along the front lands of estates signified that the planters were ready to drive their bondsmen into the cane fields if need be under the threat of starvation.

Then, in the summer of 1838, on the eve of emancipation, the planter-controlled legislature passed a series of laws to regulate affairs when the slaves achieved full freedom. A vagrancy ordinance provided that "persons wandering abroad, . . . able to maintain themselves wholly or in part, wilfully refusing or neglecting to work, were punishable on the view of a single magistrate with thirty days' confinement and hard labour." [7] It also abolished the stipendiary magistracy, established in 1834 to remove from the jurisdiction of local justices of the peace questions relating to masters and servants. A poor-law ordinance declared that servants might be punished for any misdemeanor with imprisonment and hard labor for one month, or a fine of five pounds, while masters were punishable only by voidance of contract or a maximum £5 fine. Finally, a militia ordinance made ex-apprentices ineligible to serve in the militia.[8]

[7] *Ibid.*, p. 209.
[8] *Ibid.*, p. 300.

460

These statutes were disallowed in London, but their intent was clear enough and merely confirmed the creole population in its revulsion from plantation labor, a revulsion expressed with deep feeling in the way the apprentices treated "Stanleys," those children under 6 who had been freed unconditionally on 1 August 1834. Throughout the West Indies, the parents of these children would not permit them to work on the estates, declaring that they were born free and that they would rather work "their own fingers to the bone before they would [make] their children do the slightest work." "They have a notion," observed Henry Barkly, a future governor of the colony, "that exemption from the cultivation of sugar cane is the real secret of what freedom is." [9]

Against this background, the shrinkage of the plantation labor force immediately after emancipation was virtually guaranteed. Children, old men, and many women stopped working within a few weeks. The formation of quasi-peasant villages (see below) affected the regular supply of what labor was left, so that the number of "effective" workers was estimated to have declined from 63,000 at the end of apprenticeship to 25,000 in 1841.[10] Even if it is granted that these figures were exaggerated to present the plight of the planters in the most desperate terms, there can be no question that the magnitude of the decline was staggering and contributed more than any other factor to an average annual reduction of sugar production in British Guiana of some 38 percent between 1838 and 1846.[11]

The diminishing size of the labor force was not the only facet of the problem. The planters had also lost effective control over those they continued to employ. Ex-slaves soon found that they were operating in a seller's market. As long as that market remained free and the supply short, planters inevitably drove up wages by bidding against each other. The basic wage at the outset of emancipation was a uniform 32 cents per task.[12] By 1847 it was quoted at 40 cents, while heavier types of work paid up to 48 cents.[13] Nevertheless, the most perceptive planters agreed that their major problem was not high wage rates, but the loss of absolute command that an army of slaves,

---

[9] *Ibid.*, pp. 122, 193.

[10] *Ibid.*, p. 173.

[11] Based on Noel Deerr, *The History of Sugar*, London, 1951, I, 303ff.

[12] At the beginning of the apprenticeship period, when planters first faced the question of how much to pay for what quantity of work, a governor's committee broke down the work involved in sugar growing into twenty basic types of "tasks." To each task was assigned the amount of work an able-bodied laborer could perform in a seven-and-a-half hour work day.

[13] Great Britain, *Colonial Office* (hereafter *C.O.*) 111/379, pp. 276ff; *P.P.*, vol. 23 (1847-1848), pt. 2, no. 184, p. 59.

whatever its other shortcomings, had always assured them. "The dis-advantages," said Henry Barkly, "under which most of the British colonies labour . . . do not arise . . . from the dearness of Free Labour. [They] are attributable almost entirely to the great difficulty of commanding continuous labour, which always constituted a crying evil in countries where there exists a great deal of waste land and a very small population. A planter has a capital of so many thousand pounds invested in his estate, which, provided he could keep his machinery going so many days in the year would yield him a fair return, but he cannot make sugar this week because half the labourers choose to go fishing—and he cannot attend to such a cane-piece till the weeds have choked the cane-sprouts, because they are taking advantage of the weather to plants their own yams." [14]

In the years immediately following emancipation, these three de-fects in the labor force—its diminished size, its augmented cost, and its discontinuous availability—threatened the plantation system with extinction. The need to cut production costs through technological renovation was also recognized if free sugar was to compete with the slave-made product of Cuba and Brazil, but planters argued that the capital required for this transformation would not be risked in a colony where the labor supply was an uncertain as it was in British Guiana. The survival of sugar therefore resolved itself into the ques-tion of how an adequate body of plantation workers was to be re-constituted from the chaotic aftermath of slavery.

Barring a sufficient supply of alternate (immigrant) labor, the planters' initial solution consisted of a unilateral effort to reimpose some of the disciplines of slavery. At the end of 1841 they issued a series of "Rules and Regulations for the Employment of Labourers on Plantations." These were to be effective on 1 January 1842. Among other things, they stated that every field laborer was to turn out at 7 a.m., and if not at work by 8 a.m. should forfeit any claim to wages, irrespective of the work performed; that a resident laborer absent without "sufficient cause" should be fined 16 cents for each absent day; that laborers would "not have any provision grounds allowed to them; if they choose to plant provisions, it is on sufferance and at their own risk"; that the price of labor was to be standardized (in effect, reduced) to 32 cents per task; that no person could hunt, shoot, fish, cut grass, or pick fruit without permission of the manager; and that any person not willing to accept this dispensation was to leave the estate by 1 January 1842. [15]

[14] *C.O.* 111/269, Barkly to Grey, no. 30, 30 October 1849.
[15] *P.P.*, vol. 13 (1842), no. 479, pp. 643-644.

Governor Henry Light pointed out immediately that some of these regulations, by depriving laborers of "their right to claim the value of their labour," contravened the order in council of 7 September 1838—the so-called Stephen code—which governed relations between masters and emancipated servants.[16] The workers responded by striking generally along the coast. On 4 and 5 January, delegations from various estates visited the governor "to see whether these rules and regulations had the sanction of Her Majesty or the Government." [17] Their understanding of the situation can be seen in a letter which the laborers of Plantation Walton Hall sent to their local stipendiary magistrate:

> We free labourers . . . are already to work our liberty hours in putting hands and heart, providing in we getting what is right. As to say for taking one guilder [32 cents] per day, we cannot take it at all. Sir, you will be pleased to understand us to what we say (those few years since we got free), and so soon brought on a reducing price, which is now offered to we labourers. We certainly think it to be very hard.
>
> If you take it in consideration when calling on us. We shall be proud to know from, if such laws come from the Queen, or Governor, or any of Her Majesties Justice of Peace.
>
> During our slavery we was clothed, ration, and seported in all manner of respets. Now we are free mens (free indeed), we are to work for nothing. Then we might actually say, we becomes slaves again. We will be glad to know from the proprietors of the estates, if they are to take from us our rights altogether.[18]

The strike lasted for approximately one month. Although some planters appear to have succeeded in reducing wage rates, work was generally resumed only when it became apparent that the rules and regulations would not be enforced. Labor had won a battle, but the war had only begun. At the end of 1847, following a drastic fall in sugar prices, the planters launched a second combined assault on the wage level. This time there was no attempt to introduce the hated rules and regulations and Governor Light, who had cautiously opposed planter "imprudence" in 1842, now sent a private circular to the stipendiary magistrates, instructing them to "exert themselves among the labourers" to accept a 25 percent wage cut.[19] Once again, a gen-

[16] *Ibid.*, p. 646.
[17] *Ibid.*, p. 642.
[18] *Ibid.*, pp. 656-657.
[19] *C.O.* 111/246, Light to Grey, no. 224, 31 December 1847.

eral strike occurred, but the outcome was more ambiguous than in 1842. Although there was no regular labor in January and early February 1848, immigrant workers failed to maintain solidarity with the creoles and thereby helped to drive the main body of strikers back into the fields at reduced rates.[20] However, the planters' success may have been counterproductive. The number of people living in villages rose from 29,000 in June 1847 to 44,000 in December 1848, a direct result, argues Allan Young, of the 1847-1848 strike. "It brought home to the great mass of the labourers still living on the estates their utter insecurity of tenure. . . . [They] were mere tenants-at-will." [21]

CONTROL OF THE PEASANTRY

THE spread of creole villages brought home to the planters their own insecurity as employers of labor. As long as a man could buy land on abandoned estates he could make himself at least partially independent of the plantation system. The planters had been powerless to stop this process in the 1840s. They could, and did, impede its further development as the base of an independent peasant economy. Elsewhere I have dealt with this in some detail and will merely summarize here the more important methods used to block the "natural" growth of village life.[22] In what follows, however, I do not wish to imply that the villages would have provided a sturdy, yeoman alternative to plantation life if they had been left to their own devices, but merely that their frustration, induced in part by policies outside their own control, precluded *any* kind of development.

The assault on peasant independence began with the passage of legislation in 1852 and 1856, which was directed against the further spread of those villages which had been purchased communally in the 1840s. These laws prohibited the acquisition of land by more than twenty persons, and required that if more than nineteen people bought an estate, the land would have to be partitioned among the individual shareholders. The end of communalism, it was hoped, would divert ex-slaves from large-scale land buying and to this extent make them more amenable to plantation labor. In 1861 the legislative encirclement of the peasant was completed by an ordinance which raised the upset price of crown land from $5 to $10 an acre and set the minimum parcel at 100 acres. At a time when "abandoned estates

---

[20] *P.P.*, vol. 23 (1847-1848, pt. 1, no. 167, p. 331; pt. 2, no. 206, pp. 9, 135.
[21] Allan Young, *The Approaches to Local Self-Government in British Guiana*, London, 1958, p. 16.
[22] "Monoculture and Village Decay in British Guiana: 1854-1872," *Journal of Social History* 3 (Summer 1970), 386-405.

on the coast could be purchased for one-fifth that amount and river estates at an even lower rate," [23] this effectively contained the bulk of the peasantry along the coastal strip.

The subsequent story of village life in British Guiana is one of stagnancy and decay. While total village population more than doubled between 1851 and 1891, the number of native-born Negro villagers grew by only 46 percent, and in the 1850s and 1880s appears in fact to have declined. While many of the disabilities under which the villagers labored—microculture, capital starvation, high land cost, poor education, limited markets, usurious rates of interest, and defective transport—are generic to most forms of peasant production, the villagers of British Guiana had as well to face difficulties associated with the high cost of drainage and sea defense. The plantation, system was not responsible for these problems: indeed, it had to wrestle with some of them itself. Nevertheless, in addition to the restrictive legislation described above, the planting interest was able to weaken the villages and strengthen itself through its control of fiscal policy, to which we shall return later. The point to be observed here is that even as early as the 1850s many villagers were finding it difficult to subsist. Only one outlet presented itself: a return to labor on the plantations. Necessity gradually reversed the contraction of creole estate labor which had occurred in the forties. The number of nonresident laborers at hire, estimated at 17,252 in 1852, rose slightly to 18,469 in 1861 and to 22,000 in 1868. By then it was admitted that "hundreds, perhaps thousands, who would now work on estates cannot find employment." [24]

Thus, while the planter was gradually recovering command over that large body of continuous labor which he had lost after emancipation, the ex-slave population seemed to have failed to establish an existence independent of the estates. The villages did not disappear. They merely survived in a state of suspended animation, always compelled to offer part of their labor to sugar and to do so, as the century wore on, in an increasingly weaker bargaining position.

IMMIGRATION

EVEN before emancipation the planting community had anticipated that the slaves would reject estate labor when they became free and that it would have to look to immigration to replace them. After a

[23] W. T. Veness, *El Dorado: or British Guiana as a Field for Colonization,* London, 1867, p. 7.

[24] *C.O.* 116/222, Blue Book 1853; *Royal Gazette,* 14 September 1864, 12 and 14 May 1868.

number of abortive experiments in the 1830s and 1840s, the flow of labor from abroad became a permanent feature of the Guyanese economy until the end of World War I. Between 1855 and 1904 almost a quarter of a million immigrants were registered in the colony, a figure roughly equal to the entire population in 1880. Indeed, if they had not come population would have declined as it had after 1807. British Guiana, it would appear, devoured free men as voraciously as slaves.

Most of these immigrants were of East Indian origin. In the second half of the nineteenth century, four out of five arrivals were from Calcutta or Madras. Ultimately, the sheer weight of their numbers was far more significant than the containment of the Negro village economy in shifting the balance of power from labor back to capital under post-emancipation conditions. By the end of the century the resident estate population per acre was almost three times what it was in 1852. No wonder Trollope's Demerara planter could boast: "Give me my heart's desire in Coolies, and I will make you a million of hogsheads of sugar without stirring from the colony!" [25]

CONTROL THROUGH INDENTURE

THE planters, however, were not satisfied that simple quantitative expansion would give them the degree of control over the labor force they considered essential for efficient sugar production. Only continuous labor would assure optimum conditions; barring outright slavery, this could only be obtained from men compelled to place themselves under contracts or indentures of service lasting several years. In confirmation of this argument they pointed to the failure of free immigration to supply the plantations with the amount of labor they wanted. Between 1834 and 1848 British Guiana had received 46,514 immigrants, most of them under short contracts (12 months) or none at all. At the end of that period only 12,872 remained as predial laborers on the estates, and only 19,122 in the colony. Apart from a few who had returned home, the rest were dead. The cost to the public treasury since 1841 had been 360,000 pounds.[26]

The position of the Colonial Office was crucial in determining the issue of indenture. While the new orthodoxy assumed that white capital employing black or colored labor must form the basis of post-emancipation colonial societies, it also assumed that resource markets,

[25] Anthony Trollope, *The West Indies and the Spanish Main*, London, 1859, p. 164.
[26] James Rodway, *History of British Guiana, Georgetown*, 1891-1894, III, 106.

including labor, should operate freely and without controls. At least that was the theory. In some places, however, and British Guiana was one of them, theory collided with the force of special circumstance. Thus Lord Grey, the key figure in the indenture controversy, could argue like a good liberal: "All experience tends to prove that no legal regulations, . . . if they stop short of the extreme compulsion which is characteristic of slavery, can succeed in enforcing really efficient labour . . . from men who have no interest in being efficient. . . . Whenever the rate of wages is not left to be settled by free bargaining between the parties . . . disturbances are sure to occur." But he was aware also that in parts of the West Indies "the facility of obtaining land effectually prevents the prosecution by voluntary labour of any enterprise requiring the co-operation of many hands." [27] From here it was a short step to the view of Herman Merivale that the free laborer ought to be "by a law of nature dependent on capitalists"; and that, where this dependence did not exist, as in British Guiana immediately after emancipation, it "must be created by artificial means." [28] Once Grey agreed, as he did for Mauritius in 1847, that immigrants introduced at public expense must sign one-year labor contracts or pay a fine, the principle of compulsory labor received official sanction. Indenture became the chief means of creating dependence.

In British Guiana the immigration ordinance of 1854 provided the framework which, with some later amendments, regulated indentured labor for the rest of the century. It empowered the immigration agent-general to assign to various plantations all immigrants who did not choose one specifically. After allotment each immigrant was compelled to sign a three-year contract, following which he had the option of reindenturing for one or two years, or of commuting the remaining two years of his "industrial residence" at the rate of $12.00 per annum. After five years he was free, but to earn a free return passage to India ten years of industrial residence was required. An immigrant who accepted a $50.00 bounty on the completion of his first period of industrial residence was reindentured for another five-year period. An immigrant under contract could be apprehended without a warrant if found more than two miles from his estate without a ticket of leave signed by his employer. When apprehended anywhere without a contract, the onus of proof was always on the immigrant. Lack of documents thus constituted *prima facie* evidence of guilt. For every day away from work the immigrant not only forfeited his wages, but

[27] *C.O.* 111/266, minute attached to Barkly to Grey, no. 72, 4 May 1849.
[28] Quoted in K. Marx, *Capital*, New York, i, 770.

was also required to pay his employer 24 cents. Six dollars per annum for lodging and $3.00 for medical expenses were deducted from his wages. Finally, an immigrant who refused to sign a contract on arrival in the colony was required to pay a monthly fine of $1.50, and for every fine unpaid could be sentenced to fourteen days at hard labor.[29]

These regulations represent a genuine counterrevolution. They provided the planter with a workable substitute for slave labor, and for several generations provided the conditions for the growth of an enclave subculture which was in, but not yet of, the creole community. Guyana has been called an island almost entirely surrounded by land. The indentured immigrants might quite properly be defined as a subculture almost entirely surrounded by legislation. Slavery had gone, but what Eric Williams has called the nineteenth century counterpart of the *encomienda* had taken its place.

While this initial legislation was rigorous enough, the controls governing work, wages and freedom of movement were reinforced further in the years between 1855 and 1870. One of the few liberties left to the indentured immigrant after 1854 was his right to commute at the end of his third or fourth year of industrial residence. He took this right seriously as the threefold increase in commutation payments between 1859 and 1862 indicates. In these years it was not uncommon for a planter to offer a bonus to a seasoned immigrant if he would commute and transfer to his estate. If continued, this practice would have injected an element of bargaining and competition into the labor market and to that extent would have eased the rigidities inherent in the new system. But that was precisely what the planting community feared. In 1862, therefore, the right to commute was abolished and in the following year reindenture for five years certain was established. Even the option of changing employers at the point of reindenture was removed. As this last escape hatch to freedom closed, the Colonial Office, which continued to regard itself as the trustee of the unenfranchised, let the matter slip by unnoticed. The 1870 Commission of Enquiry, however, called it "the most important change that has been effected by the legislation of the last ten years. . . . The effect . . . has been to keep the immigrant population as a whole out of the labour market."[30]

An additional means of discipline and control was secured through the work quota, which required an immigrant to complete five tasks

---

[29] Enclosed in *C.O.* 111/300, Wodehouse to Newcastle, no. 21, 7 June 1854.
[30] *P.P.*, vol. 20 (1871), no. 393-1, p. 721; *C.O.* 111/339, Hincks to Newcastle, no. 19, 19 January 1863; *C.O.* 114/22, Sessional Papers, Court of Policy and Combined Court, *C.O.* 111/379, p. 744.

per week or 260 per annum. These tasks had been defined by a committee of planters at the time of emancipation. Their high output level, derived from slave conditions, prevented the mass of the indentured East Indian labor force from fulfilling its legal minimum. In 1870, for instance, 56 percent appear to have fallen below the norm required by law. In effect, this gave the employer a legal weapon over more than half his indentured laborers. He could obtain a conviction against them whenever he wished. He could also convict for badly done or unfinished work, for neglecting or refusing to perform work, for drunkenness at work, abusive language, carelessness with employer's property, inciting to strike, or desertion.[31]

There was thus every facility for estate managers to procure convictions against immigrants they might wish to punish. And they did use the courts extensively, sometimes as a means of labor discipline, sometimes directly as punishment, and often as a threat to secure docility in the future. In the five years between 1866 and 1870, 31,900 cases involving breaches of immigration ordinances were brought before stipendiary magistrates. Each year, in other words, warrants were served on something over 18 percent of the indentured population. While over half these cases resulted in convictions, many were withdrawn or dismissed on the promise of the defendant to behave better and pay the cost of the summons. Indeed, the withdrawal of cases under circumstances which were virtually the equivalent of coercion seems to have been used by employers almost as widely as prosecution. In 1872, a not untypical year, 47 percent of the cases ended in conviction and 40 percent were withdrawn. Only 12 percent were acquitted. "To be prosecuted," concluded the 1870 Commission of Enquiry, "is . . . almost the same thing as to be convicted and sentenced."[32]

Employers could use this apparatus with considerable flexibility and without too nice a regard for the actual nature of the offense. Normally they favored one of three charges: (1) failure to perform five tasks per week; (2) neglect of, or refusal to, work; and (3) absence from work without leave. When a decision of chief justice Beaumont in 1867 made it difficult to convict for not performing five tasks per week, the planters simply altered the nature of the charge, usually to one of absence without leave, so that while the number charged with not performing a sufficient number of tasks decreased, total convic-

---

[31] *P.P.*, vol. 20 (1859 Sess. 2), no. 31, p. 93; *P.P.*, vol. 20 (1871), no. 398-1, p. 115.

[32] *C.O.* 111/379, pp. 1160, 1182, 1186; *C.O.* 111/398, Rushworth to Kimberley, no. 10. 108, 5 July 1873.

tions under the labor laws actually rose. When the task-work clause was reinstated in 1868 convictions under it again became "popular." The planters, in other words, pretty well orchestrated the law without regard to actual offenses and primarily for the purpose of labor discipline.[33]

A paradoxical, but illuminating, consequence of this reestablished control over labor, may be seen in the planter's changing attitude to reindenture. In the 1850s and 1860s he regarded this as an integral feature of his economy, almost as vital as indenture itself, and as late as September 1873 was defending it vigorously with the argument that steady wages and a chance to use the reindenture bounty gave the immigrant a degree of security he could never hope to achieve as a free man. Yet three months later reindenture had "silently expired without one word of regret from its former most strenuous supporters."[34] The immediate occasion for this sudden change was an alteration in the method of financing immigration which raised the cost to the planter and left him proportionately less to pay out in reindenture bounties. But the surprising indifference of most planters suggests a more important change. By the 1870s steady immigration had expanded the labor force to the point where the planter could control it with less resort to ultraeconomic devices. For the first time since emancipation more or less chronic unemployment and its complement, a sizable reserve pool of labor, became permanent features of the economy. And although creole villagers suffered most painfully from this development, resident immigrants also felt its effects as is suggested by the growing number of returnees to India after 1876 and the beginnings of an East Indian village movement.[35] Immigration continued at a respectable level right up to the major collapse of sugar prices in 1894-1895, but the relative importance of the indentured laborer dropped from 74 percent of the labor force resident on estates in 1873 to 24 percent in 1884. At the same time, the number of resident laborers per acre of cane rose from .67 in 1871 to .83 in 1884.[36] By 1881 some large estates—notably those owned by James Ewing and Company—were running almost exclusively on free labor.[37] It

[33] C.O. 111/379, pp. 744, 819, 1192-1211.

[34] C.O. 111/400, Rushworth to Kimberley, no. 201, 24 December 1873.

[35] Stipendiary Magistrates' reports enclosed in C.O. 384/123, Young to Hicks Beach, no. 203, 20 August 1879; Dwarka Nath, *A History of Indians in British Guiana*, Georgetown, 1950, p. 187; *Royal Gazette*, 24 February 1880; C.O. 384/118, Kortright to Carnarvon, no. 1, 2 January 1878.

[36] Based on data from the Blue Books for the period and reports of the immigration agent general.

[37] C.O. 384/139, Young to Kimberley, no. 53, 1 March 1882; C.O. 114/29, Minutes of Court of Policy, 1st quarter, p. 15.

was becoming difficult to defend indenture except as a means of keeping labor cheap. In the longer perspective, it now appears as the principal, though temporary, device by which the plantation system delayed and modified the transition from slavery to full freedom until conditions had been established that would ensure that full freedom and dependence on the estates were interchangeable terms.

CONTROL THROUGH FISCAL POLICY

THE cost of immigration was not low, nor was it ever borne entirely by the sugar estates on whose exclusive behalf it was carried on. In the nineteenth century a variable fraction of the expense was always financed out of the public revenue, "a bonus," as one governor described it, "paid by the community for the production of sugar." [38] From 1847 to 1873 this bonus, including public debt charges attributable to immigration, absorbed between 22 and 34 percent of total public expenditure. Thereafter, these costs began to decline, particularly after the world sugar crisis of 1884, but even at the beginning of the twentieth century, immigration and public debt charges accounted for 13 percent of public outlay. [39]

At the same time, the fiscal system devised after emancipation shifted the main burden of taxation from the planters to the emergent peasantry and—as their numbers grew—the immigrant labor force. This was done by converting from the essentially direct system of taxation, characteristic of slavery, to indirect taxation. Before 1838, the chief sources of revenue had been a poll tax on slaves, an income tax, and a produce tax on exports. After emancipation these all disappeared and the colonial treasury was principally replenished through import duties, retail spirit licenses, and an excise tax on rum. Between 1850 and 1904 these three sources accounted for never less than 50 percent and often as high as 72 percent of total public revenue. In 1850, flour, rice, dried fish, and salt pork alone contributed more than half the total value of import duties. That this pattern was deliberately arranged so as to strike the immigrants and peasantry, while avoiding the planters, is obvious when one examines the list of articles exempt from duty in the same, not untypical, year. This included diamonds, ice, fresh fish, meat, fruit and vegetables, manures, and machinery. [40]

The connection between this fiscal pattern and public assistance to immigration is equally transparent. Lord Stanley, then colonial secretary, made it in 1842 when he accepted the principle that the colonial

---

[38] *Colonist*, 2 March 1855.
[39] Based on Blue Book returns of public expenditure in *C.O.* 116/224-273.
[40] *Ibid.*, and *P.P.*, vol. 39 (1851), no. 624, p. 310.

ALAN H. ADAMSON

share of immigration expenses should be defrayed through raising import duties on articles of mass consumption. These duties were thus a kind of punitive levy against the peasantry for refusing to orient its labor exclusively toward the plantations. Certainly Stanley was quite explicit about the matter when he related their introduction to the difficulties the planters were experiencing as a result of the "high price and scarcity of labour." [41] But whatever the motivation, fiscal policy reinforced other forms of labor control to the extent that it diminished the peasants' capacity for independent action and helped to hold the immigrants—indentured or free—within the orbit of the plantation system.

THE MONOPOLY OF POLITICAL POWER

THE coping stone of this complex edifice of control, and the ultimate weapon in the hands of the planting community, was the virtual monopoly over policy formation which it enjoyed under the constitution of British Guiana. When Anthony Trollope saw this curious mechanism at work in 1859, he characterized it as a mild despotism tempered by sugar. The truth is that it was never mild, and sugar, if anything, hardened its despotic nature. Clementi described it as "neither Crown Colony Government nor Representative Government, but a travesty of both." [42] Henry Taylor, watching matters from the Colonial Office, gave perhaps the most accurate description when he called it "a merchants' and planters' oligarchy not much tempered . . . by any apprehension that the Crown will really exert the latent power it claims of supreme and absolute legislation." In theory, this latent power resided in the Crown's power of veto and the ability to impose policy through orders in council. In practice, it was rarely exerted because, as Taylor perceived, "where taxation and the purses of the planters are in question, the West India Committee and the House of Commons make a formidable appearance in the background." [43] Hence the residuary legatees of power in British Guiana were the elective members of its Court of Policy and Combined Court. Because of high property qualifications and a narrow franchise these were the spokesmen of the planting community.

The situation was not without its ironic aspect. Westminster, having destroyed slavery in the name of humanity and free trade, now

[41] C.O. 111/379, p. 381.
[42] Trollope, p. 162; Sir Cecil Clementi, A Constitutional History of British Guiana, London, 1937, p. 377.
[43] Minutes by Taylor attached to C.O. 111/387, Scott to Kimberley, no. 160, 7 November 1871, and C.O. 111/383, Scott to Kimberley, no. 25, 23 January 1871.

472

seemed indifferent to the reconstruction of some of the worst features of the pre-emancipation agrarian system. Naturally, the mode by which the planting establishment secured its ends changed radically with the disappearance of slavery. Mediated and indirect restraint replaced the naked force characteristic of the old system, but the substance of control remained the same.

I suggested at the beginning of this essay that the critical factor in the survival of sugar after 1838 was the creation of a nonslave plantation labor force. It was this above all which made it feasible to renovate and modernize the technical base of the Guyanese sugar industry between 1850 and 1895, and to make it—despite falling prices and uncertain markets—one of the most competitive in the cane-producing world. The methods employed were varied and complex and their effectiveness cannot be understood exclusively in simple economic terms. Ultimately, the efficient production of sugar without slaves must be traced to the operation of political factors, both local and metropolitan, which enabled the planters to concentrate the lion's share of labor, capital and well-drained land within the polders of their own estates. While this assured the relative efficiency of their own sector of the economy, it virtually guaranteed the underdevelopment of the rest of the colony. "The shadow of the sugar cane," as one observer wrote in 1873, "kills all other vegetation and kills all other industries." [44]

[44] R. H. Whitfield, *Hints on Villages*, Demerara, 1873.

PART FIVE:
SUMMARY REMARKS

XIX

History and Anthropology: A Brief Reprise

SIDNEY W. MINTZ

WERE ONE to dip into the long-accumulated literature on the relationship between history and anthropology, one would discover that the problems arising from the convergence of these disciplines are neither new nor now resolved.[1] I do not propose an essay on the intellectual history of such a convergence, but it may be useful to note in very broad outline some background features for this discussion. Anthropology, described by one of its distinguished contemporary practitioners as "the most scientific of the humanities, the most humanistic of the sciences," has for very long stood at the frontier between these large and often poorly-bounded bodies of intellectual endeavor.[2] Much of what can justifiably be called early anthropology was concerned with the history of peoples, particularly (though not exclusively) non-literate peoples. But at least two quite different emphases marked these anthropological trespasses upon historical terrain. First of all, there was the greater inclination of anthropologists to abstract from the stream of events a pattern or series of supposed regularities, on the basis of which some sequence of stages or levels could be postulated. As Sturtevant points out, anthropologists were usually readier than historians to perceive "the events with which they deal as instances of more general types."[3] Secondly, there was the readiness to interpret oral tradition, myth, and folklore as a mode of access to history, in the case of societies for which—from the historical perspective, strictly conceived—no *history* really existed.

Both of these emphases opened historical anthropology to lively criticism, both from within and from without. Two of the most

---

[1] I am grateful to Jacqueline W. Mintz and to Professor Richard S. Price for reading and criticizing earlier drafts of this essay, and to Professors Stanley Engerman and Eugene Genovese for encouraging me to write it. Professor Robert Fogel has made a particularly telling defense of the methods used by him and by Professor Engerman in their forthcoming book, which I criticize only in passing in this essay. I hope that the points I make have some substance, nonetheless. Needless to add, any errors that remain are my own.

[2] Eric R. Wolf, *Anthropology*, Englewood Cliffs, N.J., 1964, p. 88.

[3] William C. Sturtevant, "Anthropology, History, and Ethnohistory," in James Clifton, ed., *Introduction to Cultural Anthropology*, Boston, 1968, p. 452.

important field ethnographers of this century, Bronislaw Malinowski and A. R. Radcliffe-Brown, were eloquent in their denunciations of history as practiced by anthropologists, though they denied that they shared any common theoretical ground otherwise. They called for the serious *field study* of non-literate peoples, and for an end to armchair theorizing (the latter admonition, however, being one that both were guilty of honoring mainly in the breach). A society had to be understood in terms of its present character; the present could not be "explained," other than speciously, in terms of the past. The relationships among coexisting institutions gave to a society its characteristic quality, explaining in a way that references to "the past" could not. In a modern version, ahistoricism or antihistoricism of this kind is exemplified in the early work of one of the best of contemporary ethnographers of the Caribbean region, Raymond T. Smith:

> . . . it is imperative to explore fully the interrelations between the co-existing parts of the social system before trying to "explain" certain social facts in terms of their antecedent states over a long time span. Such "explanations" are not invalid or without value, but they are not sociological explanations, and they may sidestep the crucial issues of sociological analysis.[4]

Malinowski's and Radcliffe-Brown's criticisms were more sweeping, and have withstood less well the arguments of historically minded anthropologists. We need to remember, however, that anthropologists were given to speculative reconstructions in lieu of history in its more familiar senses, and that tradition was at times invoked as "explanation" in the absence of serious sociological analysis. The antihistorical, so-called "functionalist" position developed as a reaction to what was often naive historiography and the substitution of speculation for fieldwork. As anthropologists moved toward the study of peoples whose history was documented at least in part through written records—frequently not their own, but those of their conquerors—the anthropological interest in history reasserted itself. In this regard, a major value of the ahistorical or antihistorical bias may have been the recognition that even written history must be approached with the genuine skepticism of those who realize that things not only aren't what they used to be, but also that they probably never were.

Nonetheless, the historical perspective has long been part of the intellectual habits of mind of anthropology's practitioners, past and

---

[4] Raymond T. Smith, *The Negro Family in British Guiana*, London, 1956, pp. 259-260.

present. While functionalist theory strode the stage, many serious historically minded anthropologists sought to reconcile the advantages of synchronic analysis of social relationships to the perspective provided by interpretations of past events. One of the clearest and most eloquent of these, Alexander Lesser, specialized in the study of nonliterate peoples, but saw no reason therein for downgrading the analytic value of an understanding of the past:

> We see such and such events going on. Many things are always happening at the same time, however. How are we to determine whether or not those things which happen at the same time are related to one another? For it is obvious that they may be contemporary events, or even serial events, not because they are related to one another but because their determinants, unknown and unobserved, have caused them to happen at the same or subsequent times. In short, contemporary or associated events may be mere coexistences. Culture, at any one time, is first and foremost a mass of coexistent events. If we are to attempt to define relationships between such events it is impossible in view of the known historicity of things to assume that the relationships lie on the contemporary surface of events. Whatever occurs is determined more by events which happened prior to the occasion in question than by what can be observed contemporaneously with it. As soon as we turn to prior events for an understanding of events observed, we are turning to history. History is no more than that. It is a utilization of the conditioning fact of historicity for the elucidation of seen events.[5]

Since Lesser wrote this passage, the antihistorical movement in anthropology appears to have peaked. Scholars such as Gonzalo Aguirre Beltrán, Pedro Carrasco, Bernard Cohn, Jerome Handler, John V. Murra, Richard Price, William C. Sturtevant, Jan Vansina, William Willis, and many others have pioneered a new rapprochement between history and anthropology. We need not accept the assertion that anthropology would ultimately be history or else it would be nothing at all, in order to discover that the usefulness of history for anthropology, and of anthropology for history, is genuine and important, at least in much of what both historians and anthropologists do.[6] Still,

[5] Alexander Lesser, "Functionalism in Social Anthropology," *American Anthropologist* 37 (July-September 1935), 392.

[6] For a thoroughly charming commentary on the differences between anthropologists and historians, see Bernard S. Cohn, "An Anthropologist Among the Historians: A Field Study," *The South Atlantic Quarterly* 61 (Winter 1962), 13-28.

the interpenetration of these fields has in no way been fully mapped out, and most of us who plunge today into problems that appear to require the skills of both disciplines for their solution continue to feel with justice rather like the blind men charged with describing the elephant.

If I seem to do an injustice to my own discipline in the preceding paragraphs, I believe that it is not so much by documenting certain excesses on the part of illustrious predecessors, as by compressing a rich and complex intellectual tradition into a few (and hence, unavoidably misleading) paragraphs. Recent work on the study of the pasts of non-literate peoples [7] and the use of documentary materials for the study of peoples in contact whose pasts were largely unrecorded [8] demonstrate not only the value of history for anthropology but also, I believe, the value of anthropology for history. The historical study of non-literate peoples *within the ambit of literate societies* reveals that what anthropologists do, their characteristic turns of mind, and their definition of the problems that interest them, may turn out to be at least as valuable for historians as the corresponding characteristics of history's practitioners are for anthropologists. The recognition that different societies (including those without writing) have different self-perceived histories; [9] the repeated confrontation with the idea

[7] See, for instance, J. Vansina, R. Mauny, and L. V. Thomas, eds., *The Historian in Tropical Africa*, London, 1964; I. M. Lewis, Introduction to I. M. Lewis, ed., *History and Social Anthropology*, London, 1968, pp. ix-xxviii; Sturtevant, *op. cit.;* Jan Vansina, "The Use of Ethnographic Data as Sources for History," in T. O. Ranger, ed., *Emerging Themes of African History*, Dar es Salaam, 1968, pp. 97-124.

[8] See, for instance, Jerome Handler, "Aspects of Amerindian Ethnography in Seventeenth Century Barbados," *Caribbean Studies* 9 (January 1970) 50-72; John V. Murra, "Rite and Crop in the Inca State," in S. Diamond, ed., *Culture in History*, New York, 1960, pp. 393-407; Murra, "Current Research and Prospects in Andean Ethnohistory," *Latin American Research Review* 5 (Spring 1970), 3-36; Richard S. Price, "Caribbean Fishing and Fishermen: An Historical Sketch," *American Anthropologist* 68 (December 1966), 1363-1383; William C. Sturtevant, "Taino Agriculture," in Johannes Wilbert, ed., *The Evolution of Horticultural Systems in Native South America: Causes and Consequences*, Caracas, 1961.

[9] One of the most thoughtful of contemporary anthropologists working at the borderline between anthropology and history has been William C. Sturtevant. Examples of his historical scholarship include "The Significance of Ethnological Similarities Between Southeastern North America and the Antilles," in Sidney W. Mintz, ed., *Papers in Caribbean Anthropology*, New Haven, 1960, pp. 3-58; and "Taino Agriculture." He has given special attention to that subdiscipline called ethnohistory, a term whose definition appears invariably to escape consensus. In a paper that is a model of clarity ("Anthropology"), Sturtevant writes:

Three dimensions are thus most important for characterizing ethnohistory, even though they are not sufficient to delimit the field: concentration on the past or the present; the use of written or nonwritten 'documents'; and a diachronic or synchronic emphasis. Among additional dimensions are: concern with history as we understand it, or with the characterization of other, 'folk' views of history;

that social reality is not what *is*, but what people *believe to be so;* the development of cultural ecology, as an analytic tool for relating the adaptations of particular societies to the environmental and technical conditions in which they find themselves; the holistic conception of culture; the conceptual distinctions between the cultural and the social; the persistent emphasis on the linked relationships, often hidden, among phenomena; these, and many other anthropological perspectives for the study of the way societies encounter each other, grow and change, may eventually inform history with a point of view the full promise of which is not yet fully grasped.

Since the essays which this commentary accompanies are concerned in large measure with slavery in the New World, they partake of a particular historical epoch and of particular conditions which, for very long, failed to catch the eye of anthropologists. The study of New World slavery—I restrict myself here to the historical questions concerned with enslaved Africans and their descendants in this hemisphere from the dawn of the sixteenth century to the dusk of the nineteenth—received little attention from anthropologists before the pioneering work of Melville J. Herskovits.[10] Since that time, however, Herskovits' students and many others have endowed this field of inquiry with considerable new meaning.[11] Several general points deserve to be mentioned in this connection.[12] First of all, anthropology

---

whether the society studied is a Western or Oriental civilization or a more exotic one; the value placed on typologizing cultural or social phenomena and their changes, that is, on generalizing or abstracting principles or theories from concrete data as opposed to emphasis on the uniqueness of events, on the study of a specific period or sequence for its own sake rather than as an example of general processes.

Readers interested in the relationship between anthropology and history, or between history and ethnohistory, cannot do better than to begin with Sturtevant's contribution.

[10] Melville J. Herskovits, "The Negro in the New World: The Statement of a New Problem," *American Anthropologist* 32 (January-March 1930), 145-155; Herskovits, *The Myth of the Negro Past,* New York, 1941; Sidney W. Mintz, "Melville J. Herskovits and Caribbean Studies: A Retrospective Tribute," *Caribbean Studies* 4 (July 1964), 42-51.

[11] Richard A. Waterman, "African Patterns in Trinidad Negro Music," Ph.D. dissertation, Northwestern University, 1943; Alan P. Merriam, "Songs of the Afro-Bahian Cults, a Musicological Analysis," Ph.D. dissertation, Northwestern University, 1951; William Bascom, "Acculturation Among the Gullah Negroes," *American Anthropologist* 43 (January-March 1941), 43-50.

[12] I have dealt with some of these issues at greater length in earlier papers. See my "Melville J. Herskovits and Caribbean Studies"; "Foreword" to Norman E. Whitten, Jr. and John F. Szwed, eds., *Afro-American Anthropology,* New York, 1970, pp. 1-16; "Creating Culture in the Americas," *Columbia University Forum* 13 (Spring 1970), 4-11; and "Toward an Afro-American History," *Cahiers d'Histoire Mondiale* 13 (1972), 317-332.

as a discipline was reluctant to recognize the study of "non-primitive" peoples as part of its justifiable concerns—and this reluctance was not limited to the doubtful acceptability of Afro-America. Just as the hill peoples of Southeast Asia traditionally received more anthropological attention than their lowland neighbors, so the Huichol and Tarahumara of Mexico were considered more proper anthropological subjects than the settled peasant cultivators of that country. Similarly, Afro-Americans throughout the hemisphere were not viewed as fit anthropological subjects of study, even though anthropology constantly vaunted its interest in man in all his variety. Secondly, Afro-Americanist studies by anthropologists generally tended to concentrate on some aspects of culture, to the exclusion of others. Folklore, music, dance, and religion were considered most fitting; family and domestic organization came next and, for very long, dominated anthropological interest in Afro-America; [13] other aspects of culture came last, if they were of interest at all.[14] Thirdly, there existed for long a gap or cleavage between the efforts of anthropologists and historians of Afro-America, even when dealing with the same problems: historians concentrated on documentary materials, anthropologists on field studies of living people, a genuine interest in the past notwithstanding. Finally—and it is to this last point that I shall wish to devote most of my commentary—practitioners of the two disciplines viewed and weighed differently the nature of their evidence.

I think that we are entitled to ask ourselves whether the combined historical and anthropological study of some problem-area—such as slavery in the New World—is marked by any unique or distinctive features, when compared to the study of other problems in the same geographical region, or to the study of other problems for which our methods might be combined elsewhere. It can be argued that there are distinctive, if not unique, attributes pertaining to studies of this kind, I believe. These attributes inhere in the nature of slave societies, as these developed in the western world—and here I am particularly concerned with the New World—in the course of the last five centuries. It would be banal to repeat what is already well known, other than in a phrase or two; but consider the following. In the course of five centuries, a whole New World, discovered and conquered, was populated from afar. Its discoverers and conquerors brought with them what they could of their own cultural heri-

---

[13] See Mintz, "The Caribbean as a Socio-Cultural Area," *Cahiers d'Histoire Mondiale* 9 (1966), 933-935.

[14] A good case in point, perhaps, is Haiti. For each anthropological paper on peasant economy, for instance, there must be at least a hundred on *vodoun*, folklore, music, and dance.

tages, but these transmissions were always imperfect and incomplete, and had to be readapted in every way to the conditions of life posed by new situations. Labor was a central problem for the pioneers, and slavery became a major solution to the problem of more land than could be adequately policed, if settled by men who were free.[15] Africa thus became a *fons gentium* for the European conquerors, and a conservatively estimated nine and one-half million enslaved Africans were introduced into what were essentially pioneer societies, all ostensibly erected,[16] more or less, upon a European cultural and social base. The African victims of this saga were those least able to transfer any coherent body of belief and behaviors, articulated with viable institutional frames, from the Old World to the New.[17] It was they, together with the conquered masses of American Indians, who provided the vital labor power of these new societies; it is their descendants who survive *en masse* in that vast area stretching from Brazil to the United States South. We may ignore here the moral and ideological problems slavery brought in its wake. The point I wish to stress is that slavery, as an organized system, defined in large measure the context within which transferred European traditions would grow and change. From the first European outposts, created at the start of the sixteenth century, until the abolition of slavery in Brazil in 1888, the forced labor of Africans and their descendants was not so much a mere aspect of New World history in this region, as its essential nature.[18]

[15] Herman J. Nieboer, *Slavery as an Industrial System,* The Hague, 1900; Mintz, "Review of *Slavery* by Stanley Elkins," *American Anthropologist* 62 (June 1961), 579-587; Stanley L. Engerman, "Some Considerations Relating to Property Rights in Man," *The Journal of Economic History* 32 (March 1973), 43-65.
[16] Philip D. Curtin, *The Atlantic Slave Trade: A Census,* Madison, Wis., 1969, p. 268.
[17] There is a good deal of polemical argument still current in regard to this assertion. On the one hand, the difficulties inherent in the perpetuation of ancestral cultures under conditions of oppression should be obvious. On the other, the concept of Africans and their Afro-American descendants as cultureless and physically destroyed has repeatedly been pressed into the service of racist philosophies and policies. The problem cannot be solved if one assumes that culture is a closed system, passed on as some kind of omneity of behavior and belief. Moreover, as I seek to make clear at a later point in this paper, it is essential to distinguish conceptually between institutions, as expressed in organized groups, or personnels (courts, guilds, priesthoods, lineages), and the beliefs, values, and attitudes through which culture is commonly manifested and "given life." Institutions, in turn, are not all of the same order; the personnel required to maintain a monarchical order differs in many ways from that required to maintain a folkloric tradition or a religious cult.
[18] Surely it need not be pointed out that European institutions and life-styles were as much affected by the presence of slavery and the slaves as were the institutions and life-styles of enslaved Africans. One way to discover what happened to African culinary, folkloric, and musical traditions in the American South is by

SIDNEY W. MINTZ

The speciality of the subject matter anthropologists confront in their attempts to study New World slavery, then, has to do both with the ways in which enslaved Africans entered into new societies, and the continuing patterns of segregation, oppression and control wielded upon their descendants. The history of the masses has always posed problems for the historian; the masses, characteristically, do not write about themselves—if, indeed, they are able to write at all—and those who observe them as contemporaries necessarily do so from a perspective that is bound to conceal many of the realities of social life. In the case of enslaved masses, living in the midst of the free and more powerful, the problem is quite possibly compounded. The difficulties posed by an ethnocentric perspective are obvious; nor should it be thought that anthropologists are liberated from them, simply because they may acknowledge their existence. For example, the languages associated with slavery in the New World—the Papiamentu of the Dutch Antilles, the Taki-Taki and Bush Negro languages of Surinam, the lexically French-derived Creole of Haiti, etc. —were for long viewed as imperfect or deformed versions of Indo-European languages, if the question came up at all. Again, the marital unions of lower-class people in these societies were commonly thought to be little more than incomplete or distorted renderings of European marriage patterns. The whole approach to these societies was, even on the part of anthropologists, Europe-centered, even when a relativistic view was touted and proclaimed. That the histories of these peoples should have been evaluated in comparable terms is, then, not surprising.

But what has consistently added to the distortion of our interpretations was the realization that enslaved Africans were unable to transfer in any intact fashion the institutional frameworks within which their cultural heritage could be perpetuated or reorganized. To clarify the problem, I wish to draw—here, only in the most superficial terms—the distinction between the social and the cultural, as these terms are often used. I shall stress the view that these terms serve best to describe different perspectives from which to interpret Afro-America, rather than mutually exclusive kinds of analysis. By "cultural" I refer here to the historically derived values, behavior patterns, and practices that made up the repertory of socially learned and inculcated resources of the enslaved: religious rituals, expressive media, social norms for mating and socializing, craft skills and value-

---

examining so-called southern (white) culture. How "African" *all* Americans are is conventionally hidden by the assumption that, under conditions of oppression, acculturation is a one-way street.

484

systems—the pool, if you will, of patterns for and of behavior that could be transferred into new settings and new conditions of life. By "social," however, I refer to the actual acting-out of this cultural content in daily life—the dynamic expression of the culture in every-day behavior.

It needs repeated emphasis that no emigrant people, including the European conquerors and masters, was able to bring to the New World more than a fraction of their traditional culture so that the enslaved Africans shared much with others in the American setting.[19] But the Europeans were able to attach their incompletely transferred cultural heritage to newly created institutional frameworks, because freedom made easier the reconstruction of these frameworks, whether in politics, religion, or domestic life. In analogous (and emphatically not homologous) fashion, American English is to the English of the mother country what Creole languages were to the African languages of the speech communities from which enslaved Africans were drawn. But the analogy may not be pushed very far; language, while a part of culture, is not the same as the rest of culture; I make the comparison merely to illustrate a general point.

Let us examine the case more concretely. Representatives of many different African cultures were enslaved and transported; accordingly, many different African religions, kinship systems, political orders, etc., were represented among the slaves. But the bodies of knowledge involved in the perpetuation of any such institutional repertory were carried in individual minds, and the opportunities for aggregating any common tradition were restricted by slavery itself. This re-ordering of the past was acute because it was so rarely possible to reconstitute some single tradition through a specific body of per-sonnel. Slavery itself severely limited the slaves' ". . . capacity to transfer cultural materials that depended upon some kind of social organization—not simply a religion, but its priesthood; not simply iron-working, but a guild of smiths; not only a regal tradition, but a royal lineage."[20]

At the same time, two very important qualifications upon this assertion must be introduced. First, we need take note of the fact that institutional continuities are not all dependent on the same kind or scale of social aggregate. While it may require the personnel of a court, and much else, to maintain the tradition of a monarchical order, it takes fewer people, and much less formal organization, to

[19] Mintz, "Foreword" and "Creating Culture in the Americas."
[20] Mintz, "Creating Culture in the Americas," p. 6.

maintain a folkloric tradition, or even a mode of domestic organization. Hence it would be inaccurate to argue that all of the cultural content transferred from Africa to the New World was subject to the same kinds of disorganizing pressures. Second, it must be stressed —as Herskovits, above all, constantly repeated—that we need to take account of any commonalities of African tradition that may have underlain the highly differentiated West African region from which most of the New World's slaves originally came. I have been inclined to deemphasize just such commonality, for two reasons. On the one hand, those who have employed this idea as a basis for explaining Afro-American culture have often ended up with rather vacuous generalities, so that an institution such as the "nine-night" wake in Jamaica can be equally well traced to an African tradition, a European tradition or, least helpful of all, to a common Euro-African substratum—leaving the student of origins somewhat further back than when he started.[21] On the other hand, an emphasis on common African traditions inevitably oversimplifies to some extent the unusual complexity of pre-slavery West African societies and cultures, and cannot but produce a synthetic, somewhat unconvincing vision of Africa itself.[22] Nonetheless, if the concept of levels of sociocultural integration[23] is applied to the problem of continuities in African materials, then it is possible to leave room for a residual substratum of common culture that may, indeed, have been African in origin, and which did not require an elaborate institutional replication for its perpetuation.

I do not mean here to explore this problem in any serious way. But purely for purposes of argument, I would suggest that many motor habits, the emphasis on the folktale as a pedagogical device, ceremonial use of the drum, the trickster motif, and certain features of verse-singer and chorus refrain might be parts of a West African cultural substratum; possession by specific gods with specific characterological attributes would be attributable—at least in some measure —to culture-specific African traditions; some social-organizational features having to do with descent are conceivably traceable to lineage organizations; and—though very doubtfully—aspects of mother-child relationships may have been perpetuated in a "matri-

[21] Michael G. Smith, *A Framework for Caribbean Studies,* Mona, Jamaica, 1955; Mintz, "Melville J. Herskovits and Caribbean Studies."

[22] Janheinz Jahn, *Muntu,* New York, 1961.

[23] Julian H. Steward, *Theory of Culture Change,* Urbana, Ill., 1955.

central cell" unit in plantation life.[24] The principal point I wish to make, however, is that we cannot view the phenomenon "culture" as homogeneous and undifferentiated, whether we are seeking to trace the origins of particular values or practices, or to understand what happens when a culture changes and reintegrates.

I make these points with particular regard to the common efforts of anthropologists and historians who seek to untangle the past of Afro-American peoples. Whereas anthropologists may attempt to "reason backward" from what they know or observe in contemporary Afro-American cultures, historians expectably begin their study of the past with the past, insofar as it appears to be documented. This difference, together with the historian's greater sensitivity and experience in dealing with the written record, and no doubt because of other differences as well, means that anthropologists and historians will reckon somewhat differently the reliability of what is supposed to be known. The historian recognizes that such materials as planters' diaries, censuses, the reports of government commissions and boards of inquiry, records of baptisms and marriages are all subject to error. But in the absence of contrary evidence, he quite defensibly proceeds on the assumption that he must use what he has, while allowing for the widest variety of error.

Confronted with the same evidence, the anthropologist probably can do no better, and I would suppose that he is usually far less prepared to do as well. He commonly marches, however, to the beat of a different drummer; and that is because his ear is attuned to the persisting gap between behavior and its documented depiction. Let me begin to explore this question with a case drawn from the recent book by R. W. Fogel and S. L. Engerman, since it falls so close to our common concerns. The authors argue that United States slavery did not, in fact, *significantly* break up slave families, though they readily admit that some such families were broken up by the separate sale of parents and children. The New Orleans slave records upon which they base this assertion "cover thousands of transactions during

---

[24] See Meyer Fortes, Introduction to Jack Goody, ed., *The Developmental Cycle in Domestic Groups*, Cambridge Papers in Social Anthropology, no. 1, Cambridge, England, 1958, pp. 1-14; Mintz, "A Final Note," *Social and Economic Studies* 10 (December 1962), 528-535. Fortes distinguishes conceptually among the household, the family, and the matricentral cell, this latter consisting of the unit of the mother and her child or children. Though I cannot dwell on all of the implications of these distinctions here, they appear to me to have advanced significantly our understanding of the extremely variable and complex relationship between procreation and family—by no means solely with reference to the nature of kinship under conditions of slavery.

the years from 1804-1860, [and] indicate that 80 percent of all sales over the age of 14 involved unmarried individuals."[25] The authors are careful to base their characterization of the sexual habits of slaves on demographic data (age of mothers at first birth, age of mother at last birth, seasonal variations in birth patterns of first and subsequent children, number of months elapsed between births, etc.) and not on the claims of either slaveowners or their critics. Their conclusions as to the proportion of slave families broken up by the interregional slave trade are based on inferences drawn from the demographic data contained in the New Orleans sales records, data which are a by-product of commercial transactions.[26]

But even granting the admirable objectivity of the research, the New Orleans sales records can only tell us when *slave wives* were sold with or without their children or husbands; they cannot tell us when *slave husbands* were sold with or without their children or wives. Hence the thousands of transactions during the years 1804-1860 upon which the data are based do not, in fact, indicate that 80 percent of all sales over the age of 14 involved unmarried *individuals*, unless by "individuals" one means only *female* individuals. The assertion, though impressive, is wrong. It could only be right for the slave population passing through the New Orleans slave marts during the specified period if the inferences about slave males were as reliable statistically as are those about slave females. The facts of the case are such that it is difficult to see how such inferences about slave males could be made at all.

Treatment of the data of a very different kind—both data and treatment—is provided in a recent work by Carl and Roberta Bridenbaugh, dealing with the English in the Caribbean region in the seventeenth century.[27] Their book is a treasure-trove of information on British West Indian colonial society; but it is also loaded with some of the most remarkable non sequiturs—many of them dealing with the issues of marriage and the family—to be found in any recent work by recognized historians. I shall not discuss here some of the more egregious assertions concerning the African's predispositions to steal: the "pugnacity and contentiousness *bred in the bones of the blacks*";[28] the quite gratuitous assumption that black migrants were a more select body than the white migrants to the islands; and many

[25] Robert William Fogel and Stanley L. Engerman, *Time on the Cross: The Economics of American Negro Slavery*, Boston, 1974.

[26] Robert W. Fogel, letter of 15 November 1972.

[27] Carl and Roberta Bridenbaugh, *No Peace Beyond the Line*, New York, 1972.

[28] *Ibid.*, p. 359 (italics added.).

other nineteenth century assertions that betray the authors' rather touching attempts to be part of the modern historiographical scene. But their comments on marriage and family do deserve our notice. "The most attractive positive trait of the blacks of both sexes [they tell us], which stemmed in part from their great sexual desire, was their devotion to family life. . . . Indeed, the Africans valued the conjugal tie, given its difference from the European, quite as much as did the white men." [29] Without reflecting as to why white men could value equally the conjugal tie, though being less sexy, we discover that this depiction of Africa becomes the basis for similarly undocumented assertions about West Indian slave domestic life. One such assertion precedes the citation: "The greatest single advantage the black had was his family. If it had been broken up in Africa by war or by native black slave traders [and take note who broke it up!], the planters wisely and actively sought spouses for men who had lost their wives or who were unmarried. . . . The result was that every plantation with adult slaves also had black women and children." [30] Indeed they did; but the presence of women and children is not *in itself* evidence of anything concerning marriage or family life; and the proportions of men and women, the demographic evidence, and the stability of plantation populations—precisely the sort of evidence that Fogel and Engerman, and many others, would insist on—is conspicuous by its absence. The Bridenbaughs' claim is limited here to seventeenth century Barbados; but it later is expanded by them to form part of the general picture for the British West Indies.

It may certainly be contended that West Indian slave society presented whites and blacks with different situations and different opportunities, and hence resulted in differences in modes of social assortment, mating and domestic organization. But the authors in question seem unable to relate their data to their basic postulates, which are unproved: Africans prized family life (as much as Europeans, no less); enslaved Africans were selectively superior to free white colonists; the planters provided male slaves with spouses; black family life was stable in the West Indies, while whites were simply an inferior group. If this be social history, we have no need of libraries, let alone of anthropologists.

But it would be wholly unreasonable to confine my criticisms to historians, or to cite these problems without any constructive commentary at all. Fogel and Engerman's general thesis requires modifica-

---

[29] *Ibid.,* p. 234.
[30] *Ibid.,* p. 118.

tion. Their assertion is statistically unconvincing, because the sale of unaccompanied male slaves says nothing about the breakup of slave families, one way or the other. Bridenbaugh and Bridenbaugh are in much deeper trouble. Assertions about the sexuality of different groups, the relationship of sexuality to domestic grouping, the "superiority" or "inferiority" of one or another stock, and the like, bear so little relationship either to their data or to what is known (and not known) about mankind as to leave their work at the level of a document in intellectual history. In one of these cases, it seems to me that a generalization must be reduced in scope, lest the consolation of hard statistics conceal from us the fact that most human beings have two parents, not one. In the other case, one is more tempted to suggest an entirely fresh start.

My general position in this connection is that we remain more in the dark than we like to think, when dealing with so intimate a sphere as domestic life—and of oppressed groups, at that—while our interpretations of these phenomena cannot proceed from a wholly western or ethnocentric perspective. Such reservations in no way invalidate or even limit the unusual and impressive scholarship of Fogel and Engerman. But it would be interesting to know—and I am sure that they can tell us—what percentage of the slaves over 14 were males, what percentage females, in the New Orleans data, since it may be that many more men than women were sold. Separating a slave woman from her children was no doubt considered unethical even by many slave owners; was separating a slave father from his wife and children regarded as equally unethical? And is it not likely that many more slave fathers passed through the marts than slave mothers? And is the tie between slave mothers and their children considered somehow more sacred than the tie between slave fathers and their children? And would not such an assumption prove to be, in fact, consistent with the western view?

On a much more general level, we can probably assume that the behavioral norms of slaves, be it in the United States or in the West Indies, were at some expectable variance from the norms of the society in which they were compelled to live, and I cannot tell how significant this normative difference may have been. Allow me to clarify this assumption with another case, this one coming from an anthropologist, one of the foremost students of Caribbean domestic organization, Michael G. Smith. In an important historical paper dealing with St. Vincent and Jamaica around 1820, he writes:

> As property, slaves were prohibited from forming legal relationships of marriage which would interfere with and restrict their

490

owner's property rights . . . slaves lacked any generally accepted mode of establishing permanent mating relationships outside of legally recognized marriage, among themselves. . . .

As a consequence . . . mating of slaves was typically unstable. But their offspring were not regarded as either legitimate or illegitimate; the children of a slave woman were the lawful property of her owner, who could alienate them at will. The legitimacy-illegitimacy dichotomy only applied to persons born free, and was never applied to slaves, as it was meaningless in that context. If, therefore, after Emancipation for various reasons the majority of the slaves and their descendants continued to mate in unstable associations lacking legal recognition, the "illegitimate" status of the children had no significance among them. [Here] . . . another contemporary West Indian problem is elucidated by reference to historical conditions of social structure.[31]

This case certainly differs from that for North America; it could surely be argued that the slave segments of St. Vincent and Jamaican societies lacked marriage altogether. Note, for instance, Kathleen Gough's definition of marriage, intended to be cross-culturally valid: "Marriage is a relationship between a woman and one or more persons, which provides that a child born to a woman under circumstances not prohibited by the rules of the relationship, is accorded full birth-status rights common to normal members of his society or social stratum."[32]

Gough continues: "There may yet turn out to be whole societies— or more probably whole social strata—in which children acquire no birth-status rights except through their mother, by the simple fact of birth. It is possible for example that some slave populations do not have marriage in this sense of the term."[33]

But are we in a position to assume that the absence of *legal* marriage for slaves in Jamaica and St. Vincent, or even of marriage as Gough has defined it, means that there were present none of the features commonly associated with marriage elsewhere, or in other segments of the same society? Michael G. Smith writes, "Absence of any formal procedure for establishing unions, *except for the house-building and feast on a girl's first mating*, was paralleled by the in-

[31] Michael G. Smith, "Social Structure in the British Caribbean about 1820," *Social and Economic Studies* 1 (August 1953), 71-72.

[32] Kathleen Gough, "The Nayars and the Definition of Marriage," *Journal of the Royal Anthropological Institute* 89 (January-December 1959), 32.

[33] *Ibid.*, p. 33.

formality with which these unions were dissolved." [34] Smith is a highly competent anthropologist. But if we put his exception into the context of contemporary middle-class practice—in the United States, say—I must doubt whether the building of a house and a feast among Jamaican slaves could have meant less than what comparable contemporary ritual means to us today. As for the implication that even such ritualization declined after the first union, it seems fair to argue that contemporary North Americans, too, are likely to be less ceremonious about their second and third marriages—and not really because they fail to take marriage seriously.

All I have really intended to convey here is that anthropologists may puzzle inordinately over the meaning of some word—such as "marriage"—that others are prone to suppose confidently to be semantically exact. It may be thought that what is meant by this is that we are oftentimes trapped by a middle-class bias. While that may indeed be the case, it is not solely what I mean. In part, certainly, the problem may be one of simple ethnocentrism. Just as "superstition" turns out to be the other man's religion, so, too, the behavioral patterns by which we court, copulate, reproduce and socialize, marry, divorce, commit adultery and are homosexual, turn out to be the other man's "promiscuity." But the difficulty is more basic even than this, it seems to me. It inheres in the expectation that everyday terms such as "marriage," "household," and the like are self-explanatory, simply because they are made prosaic by use, and because each of us thinks himself, by virtue of being human, to be an unwitting expert on what they supposedly mean. This is a more serious danger, precisely because we perceive *with* it; we confuse our objective with the stage, to borrow a bad image from microscopy.

It may be worth my stressing that this is not, after all, merely a terminological or semantic difficulty, but several other difficulties instead. There is, firstly, the gap (if any) between official usage and conventional behavior, as in the difference between legal or sacramental marriage and the actual ways by which individuals accord what Gough calls "birth status-rights" to their children, own or adopted. There is, secondly, the question of the other kinds of rights and duties—sexual access, coresidence, socialization, economic obligations, etc.—that marriage, whether defined jurally or in terms of

[34] Michael G. Smith, "Social Structure in the British Caribbean," p. 72; italics added.

local norms, is intended to signalize.[35] Thirdly, there is the matter of patterning: to what extent we may speak of a subcultural or group norm to which individuals adhere, and in what ways, and to what degree. Finally, there is the question of the relationship or interdependence between such norms and those that may prevail for the society as a whole, or for other groups in it. To speak of marriage norms for a slave population without trying to get at the linkages between those norms and others, observed by different groups in the same society, is rather like describing middle-class monogamy without taking account of premarital sexuality, long-term affairs, adultery or prostitution in contemporary North America.

It is clear—depressingly so, I suppose—that these sociological cautions upon the interpretations we may make, employing documentary materials as our raw materials, provide no alternative solution. For most purposes we must use what we have, or do no interpreting at all. But it is certainly not my intention to hamper such research, so much as to inform it with an additional perspective; and unfortunately anthropology provides no panacea to the hard-pressed historian. Yet we are entitled to assume, at least for purposes of argument, that the gaps between actual behavior, the informant's description of such behavior, and the historical records themselves, are as serious in studying the past as they are in studying the present. We cannot postulate that a household occupied by what is called a "family" necessarily includes a coresiding sociological "father" (*pater*)

---

[35] In an important paper, "Polyandry, Inheritance and the Definitions of Marriage," *Man* 55 (December 1955), 182-186, Leach has sought to exhaust logically the "functions" of marriage and provides the following list of purposes:

a. To establish the legal father of a woman's children.
b. To establish the legal mother of a man's children.
c. To give the husband a monopoly in the wife's sexuality.
d. To give the wife a monopoly in the husband's sexuality.
e. To give the husband partial or monopolistic rights to the wife's domestic and other labor services.
f. To give the wife partial or monopolistic rights to the husband's labor services.
g. To give the husband partial or total rights over property belonging or potentially accruing to the wife.
h. To give the wife partial or total rights over property belonging or potentially accruing to the husband.
i. To establish a joint fund of property for the benefit of the children of the marriage.
j. To establish a socially significant relationship of affinity between the husband and his wife's brothers.

It is doubtless of interest that Gough's definition of marriage, which she intends to be cross-culturally valid, finds its meaning outside this logical list, while leaving room for the possibility that marriage, as she defines it, may not occur in some societies.

493

or *genitor*. We cannot equate household with family. We cannot equate "marriage" with a sacramental or civil marriage service. We cannot assume as given that the treatment of adoptive and "own" children will be the same, or that adoptive and "own" children will inherit equally. We cannot suppose that serial unions are the equivalent of "promiscuity," or that the *irrelevance* of societal norms means the *absence* of subsocietal norms. In short, terms like "family" and "marriage" raise the same problem as do "monarchy" and "theocracy," even though for many purposes we are inclined to suppose that such terminology has a genuine cross-cultural validity. This is not, it seems to me, a matter of semantic quibbling, but much more serious. If some historians find such reservations disturbing, then perhaps I will have achieved my purpose, which is not to impede the important research that historians of slavery are engaged in, but to multiply the questions they are able to put to the data.

The end of such research is, among other things, the documentation of a past not only obscure, but obscured. It must always have been thus with the oppressed; forgotten, ignored, despised, and ridiculed, they made their own history in the shadow of "great events." Without them, of course, the great events would not have been great; but that, too, is a part of hidden history. We may never be able to light up the chasm that separated the masters' perceptions from the slaves' reality, even though we know that the masters, as well as the slaves, were aware of it. But a serious attempt to decompose the social functions of single institutions, such as marriage or the family, is in the service of such illumination. I hope that I will be excused if I seem to insist too much on our obligations to pursue it.

XX

Comments on the Study of Race and Slavery

STANLEY L. ENGERMAN

ONE OF THE advantages of editing a volume such as this has been the ability to defer the writing of my comments.[1] In the year or so after the authors had submitted the final versions of their papers, I had the opportunity to read and reflect upon them several times, as well as to sample the continued outpouring of work on New World slavery. All of this indicates how data long available are now being systematically used to answer long-standing questions about slavery and slave societies, and to help to frame new questions.

While it is difficult to segregate the many themes covered in these papers into a limited set of categories, I have found it useful to discuss five issues in the study of slavery to which they make contributions. First, the nature and magnitude of the African slave trade; second, the issue of material treatment, raised most forcibly in the discussion of comparative demography; third, the evaluation of the racial attitudes toward slaves and freedmen, during and after slavery; fourth, themes dealing with the economics of the slave systems, and the possibilities of flexibility in economic adjustments to changing conditions; and fifth, the problem of the adjustments made to the ending of slavery, and the effects of the new legal arrangements upon economy and society.

I. THE AFRICAN SLAVE TRADE

ON the quantitative magnitude of the slave trade and the issue of African origins little can be added to the revisions Curtin has made to his earlier work, in the light of the contributions of Anstey and Postma. The importance of these estimates to specialists in African history is obvious, as is the story they tell about European

[1] These comments draw extensively upon the discussion at the conference, and I wish to acknowledge my debt to the participants in the shaping of my thoughts. The frequency of footnote citations to our joint work is indicative of the influence of my collaboration with Robert Fogel. In addition I should also like to thank Robert Fogel, Eugene D. Genovese, and Herbert S. Klein, as well as several participants, for comments on an earlier draft. Calculations were financed under National Science Foundation Grant GS-27262.

and colonial trade patterns. One is struck in these series by the magnitude of the shifts in the trade and the great flexibility suggested in the responses of both African and European traders. The shifts in the relative importance of different European carriers, the changing sources of African supply, and the temporal variations in the magnitude of the trade all suggest that the trade represented an interaction among dynamic societies on several continents. As is clear from the essays in this volume, and is shown dramatically in Curtin's forthcoming study of Senegambian trade, the image of a static African society, or more accurately, societies, out-bargained and out-maneuvered by European traders is not accurate, and is clearly in the process of revision.

This revision will also affect the interpretations of the role of slavery and the slave trade for European economic development. Anstey's essay discusses the issue of what was the magnitude of the contribution of the profits of the slave trade to the English Industrial Revolution—a position put forward most forcibly by Eric Williams. Having myself written on the subject, I am quite aware of the nature of the assumptions and technical issues involved in this type of analysis, but I am doubtful that further research will alter Anstey's conclusions in regard to the specific question asked.[2] LeVeen's essay includes some discussion of the reason that slave trade profits would not be excessively large, and the same conclusions are suggested by the ease of entry into this trade—both by traders of different nations under national monopoly charters and by unlicensed small carriers of these nations—which limited the value of monopoly grants. The bankruptcies of the British and Dutch monopolies, and the need for the French to subsidize the trade, point in the same direction.[3] The slave trade was risky, so that the existence of occasional very high profits, which attracted the attention of writers of those and subsequent times, need not imply any long-term abnormal profits. Occasional high payoffs were necessary to offset the losses on other voy-

[2] Stanley L. Engerman, "The Slave Trade and British Capital Formation in the Eighteenth Century: A Comment on the Williams Thesis," *Business History Review* 44 (Winter 1972), 430-443.

[3] The bankruptcies of the monopoly companies may have been due to the entry of smaller traders, taking advantage of the expenditures of the monopolies on forts and factories, and in establishing trading connections. This would not affect the basic conclusion.

In terms of any necessary connection between the slave trade and industrialization, we were reminded by Curtin that Portugal, the principal carrier in the earlier years of the slave trade, did not undertake industrialization. Genovese further noted the rather mixed pattern of economic growth among the French slave-trading ports.

ages. LeVeen shows the relationship between risk and high payoffs for the period of the illegal slave trade, and the same feature was no doubt true earlier. Thus it is relatively easy to dismiss the slave trade itself as a source of much new capital, even if the period examined were the earlier one asked for by Shepperson. Yet one could follow Shepperson and others in the claim that what Williams was discussing was the overall slave economy, thus including the profits made from the use of slave labor.

The nature of the African response and the African trading relations are vital to an analysis of this problem. For the magnitude of any abnormal profits made by Europeans from the slave economy depends quite crucially on the conditions of African supply. Curtin has distinguished between two models of African supply—the political model in which the number of slaves was a by-product of African political warfare, and the economic model in which the supply was based upon some profit-maximizing calculus of the African suppliers. These different models have important implications for the study of African history and the issues of African political formations and state-building. They also have implications for the question of the ultimate beneficiaries of the Atlantic slave trade. There is little debate that there was a clear loser—the African who was forced to move to the New World to meet a labor shortage, and was not, in the parlance of economists, adequately compensated for this move. The question of who gained is more complex: Was it the African suppliers, the European planters in the New World, or the consumers of slave-grown products? Several recent papers have tried to analyze this question.[4] The issue of African supply conditions is crucial, since the profits of the planters would be quite different depending upon whether the response to an increasing demand for slaves could not be met by any increase in the number of slaves forthcoming, necessitating a higher price paid to acquire slaves, or at the other extreme, if the supply had come forward relatively responsively with no price change. Now these are polar cases, and, as LeVeen suggests, there was probably some increase in the quantity of slaves supplied but with a higher price paid to the African suppliers. Thus some of the increased demand meant increased incomes to African providers of slaves. This probability is suggested in the discussions of the mech-

---

[4] Richard Nelson Bean and Robert Paul Thomas, "The Fishers of Men—The Profits of the Slave Trade" (forthcoming); Henry A. Gemery and Jan S. Hogdendorn, "The Atlantic Slave Trade: A Tentative Economic Model," *Journal of African History* (forthcoming); Robert William Fogel and Stanley L. Engerman, *Time on the Cross,* Boston, 1974, ii, 123-124 and Engerman, "The Slave Trade."

STANLEY L. ENGERMAN

anism of the trade, provided by Davies and by Postma, in which we
are reminded that the Europeans remained on the coast and were
left dependent upon inland sources of supply controlled by Africans.
The existence of many potential African suppliers no doubt reduced
the magnitude of African profits due to increased European demand,
but the many European purchasers meant also that higher prices
were paid and that abnormal profits to middlemen were limited.

The evaluation of the profits of the planters using slaves on New
World plantations has long been the subject of debate, and many
views on overall profitability as well as its time pattern have been
presented. Craton presents some estimates of the rate of return to
planters in the West Indies, showing a marked decline over the
course of the eighteenth century from the initially high profit levels
of the late seventeenth century.[5] Even Sheridan's estimates do not
show very large profits for the planters, since they indicate that most
of the gain from the West Indies went to British factors and merchants, not planters.[6] The relatively low planter profits may not be
too surprising when we remember that not only were many colonists
bidding for slaves, there were also many suppliers of slave-produced
commodities in the European market. The study by Bean and Thomas
concludes that the benefits of the lower price sugar and tobacco
made possible by slave labor went to the European consumer.[7]
Other studies, however, argue that, once we allow for all the costs
of colonial production paid for by the British consumers of colonial
products, the rate of return to the British population from ownership
of the West Indies was probably quite low.[8] To establish which of

[5] There is an important distinction to be made between planter profits and
benefits to Britain. The major costs of the West Indies were paid in Britain, and
not by the planters. These were the costs of defense and the higher sugar prices
due to differential tariffs. Therefore it would be possible for planters to have made
large profits, but the colonies to have been, overall, a drain on British resources.
Rather than increasing British incomes, there may have been a redistribution resulting from the differential distribution of benefits and costs.

[6] Richard Sheridan, *The Development of the Plantations to 1750; An Era of
West Indian Prosperity, 1750-1775*, Barbados, 1970, pp. 98-110.

[7] Sidney Mintz, in his Lewis Henry Morgan Lectures at the University of
Rochester, has gone one step further to provide a new justification for the
Williams conclusion, suggesting that the lower priced sugar and other tropical
crops permitted British capitalists to provide adequate energy input to their
workers at reduced costs, thus increasing their profits. There was little basic trend
in the real price of sugar during the eighteenth century, but there were sharp
drops from 1720 to 1740 and 1800 to 1810. In both periods there was a sharp rise
in per capita sugar consumption in Britain. See Nöel Deerr, *The History of Sugar*,
London, 1950, II, 530-532.

[8] Robert Paul Thomas, "The Sugar Colonies of the Old Empire: Profit or Loss
for Great Britain?" *Economic History Review* 2d ser., 21 (April 1968), 30-45; and

498

these possibilities holds most weight, we need to know more about the patterns of land distribution in these colonies, as well as the differential burden of the taxes and expenditures within the several colonial empires.[9]

While the question of beneficiaries thus remains open, the new information presented permits some estimation of the price-quantity responses in both segments of the trans-Atlantic slave trade. Of course, more needs to be known and, given that the trade persisted over several centuries, what may initially appear as inconsistencies might easily be explained as temporal shifts. For example, both Davies and LeVeen point to the high mortality of European sailors and traders in Africa, but disagree as to whether these risks led to higher compensation for them. Davies argues that there was little apparent wage differential for African service, claiming the whites as further victims of the slave trade, whereas LeVeen argues that higher wages were paid to compensate for the increased risk of death. This is perhaps a small issue in the overall evaluation of the economics of the slave trade, but it is suggestive of how much more data need be processed before we can fully come to grips with these issues.

Much of the data generated in these essays relating to the slave trade has wider implications. The question of the African origins is important in the evaluation of the sources of slave culture and the persistence of various mores, as discussed in Palmer's article. The imbalanced age and sex ratios in the African trade provide a demographic echo in the New World, an issue which will be discussed below.[10] The data on slave trade mortality presented by Anstey and

---

Philip R. P. Coelho, "The Profitability of Imperialism: The British Experience in the West Indies 1768-1772," *Explorations in Economic History* 10 (Spring 1973), 253-280. In both analyses, the cost to British sugar consumers is based on payment of a higher price for British West Indian sugar than would need have been paid for slave-produced French West Indian sugar. The causes of the lower supply curve in the latter case are not discussed, however.

[9] See Fogel and Engerman, *Time on the Cross*, II, 123-124.

[10] The causes of the imbalance in sex ratios are not certain. The prevalence of males is usually regarded as the choice of planters, indicative of their lack of desire to raise slaves in the New World. It has been argued, however, that the African demand was higher for females, so that the imbalance was supply-created. To analyze this issue it is necessary to disentangle the choices which would have been made by planters at, say, equal prices for the sexes, from the actual choices made given the equilibrium price differentials which existed. The price data may seem to indicate that planters had a "preference" for males, but until more work can disentangle productivity differentials from the value of offspring and yield better estimates of the magnitude of the longer survival of females, the question remains open. Apparently males and females were equally valued when used in gang work, the major difference being that training as skilled artisans was apparently reserved for males only. The prices shown by Bowser, for the early

by LeVeen indicate that concentration on exceptional cases had led to overstatement of the losses in transit. Lower-mortality rates are perhaps not surprising once we remember the economic incentives to complete the voyage with minimum deaths. In his thesis LeVeen, following Curtin, has shown the variation of mortality with the point of origin in Africa, demonstrating the importance' of length of voyage in accounting for some of the observed differences in mortality rates at a given time as well as changes over time.[11]

II. Material Treatment and Demographic Performance

In an insightful piece Genovese has presented the three alternative definitions of treatment which have confused the evaluation of the so-called Tannenbaum-Elkins thesis on comparative slave treatment.[12] He pointed to the crucial distinctions to be drawn among the slaves' material living conditions, their social conditions of life, and their access to freedom and citizenship. Based upon these distinctions it will be useful in the following sections to discuss the slave's material treatment and living conditions in contrast with the attitudes taken by white society toward the "humanity" of the slave and of the freedman both under the slave regime and afterward. This distinction had been noted by Tannenbaum, but has become obscured in subsequent debate. Obviously treatment in these two senses may go in opposite directions. As Denslow noted in a paper presented at the conference, economic rationality could indeed suggest a positive correlation between "favorable" treatment in the latter sense, reflected (at one extreme) in manumissions, and "unfavorable" treatment in the former sense, as seen in poor demographic performance. This, of course, is consistent with the behavior pattern evident in the British colonies and in the northern U.S., where attempts at gradual emancipation via apprenticeship or similar schemes within a fixed time span led to an increased work effort in attempts by owner to capture profits. And, in the debate about reproduction, we should note that the higher

---

years of the slave trade do, however, show higher female than male prices. This might reflect a peculiar pattern of urban demand, since the use of the native population for agriculture was still possible.

[11] For a further analysis of this point, suggesting the importance of the excess above expected "normal" sailing time from the different ports, see Herbert S. Klein and Stanley L. Engerman, "Shipping Patterns and Mortality in the African Slave Trade to Rio de Janeiro, 1825-1830" (forthcoming).

[12] Eugene D. Genovese, "The Treatment of Slaves in Different Countries: Problems in the Applications of the Comparative Method," in Laura Foner and Eugene D. Genovese, eds., *Slavery in the New World*, Englewood Cliffs, N.J., 1969, pp. 202-210.

500

apparent U.S. birth rate is used as evidence of more favorable material treatment, while, as indicated in the "breeding" argument put forward by Sutch, it might be taken to reflect the ultimate in a dehumanizing approach to slaves.[13] Clearly we need to distinguish these concepts of treatment in approaching any comparative discussion.

In the past the discussion of the demographic issue and its significance has tended to be quite loose and many speculations have been made on the basis of rather limited evidence. The importance of the contents of this volume has been not to resolve any of these issues, but to set forth more rigorously than had previously been the case the issues needing to be resolved and the evidence to be gathered for this purpose. In describing the contributions made, there is a feeling that much of what has been previously asserted is in need of reexamination, and that we have just begun our probings by this better framing of the issues.

Much of the previous discussion of the demographic issue has attempted to demonstrate that the observed patterns of natural increase and decrease were the result of conscious decisions of the planter class. It is frequently charged, for example, that West Indian planters took measures to reduce the fertility of females, and actively discouraged slave reproduction. While the planters may have had some control over aspects of demographic performance, limited attention has been given to the systematic separation of the relative importance of those variables over which such control could be exercised and the extent to which the ability to control was limited by objective circumstances. The differences in demographic performance in different areas of the New World could reflect differences in objective circumstances (climate and epidemiological factors) to a greater extent than they did variables which the planters might try to control. And, of course, if planters attempted to impose various behavior patterns, their ability to do so might be limited.

In pursuing the implications of such distinctions, it is useful in the discussion of slave material treatment and demographic performance to consider these as endogenous variables subject to control of the

---

[13] For a discussion of some of the implications of the differences in demographic performance in the slave colonies, see C. Vann Woodward, "Southern Slaves in the World of Thomas Malthus," in his *American Counterpoint: Slavery and Racism in the North-South Dialogue*, Boston, 1971, pp. 78-106. Although demographic variables may not always be easily correlated with economic conditions, such arguments have frequently been applied in studies of standards of material comfort of both slave and free societies, and such a treatment provides a useful framework for the subsequent analysis, as well as containing some plausibility for the specific cases under study.

masters, but within the context of certain fixed constraints, set by nature and by basic political and social factors. While such a formulation might be regarded by some as a typical game to be played only by economists, clearly the basic idea has been widely used by others as seen in the many places in which phrases suggesting such behavioral responses by planters appear in this book and elsewhere. The model is a rather complex one, since humans cannot be regarded the same as machines, and it is necessary to consider not only the social and psychological aspects of the slave response, but also the limitations placed upon the owners when dealing with other humans, no matter how lowly they might regard them. A suggestive paper presented at the conference by Denslow used the economic models of optimum machine depreciation and obsolescence to discuss issues of material treatment, but this meant an ignoring of the human, emotional responses of slave and master. There is some range over which people can be manipulated without adverse effects, while the fact that planters were dealing with humans and not machines might have limited their ability to pursue with rigor the optimum policies appropriate to the handling of machines. Even if the individual planter might wish to disregard the distinction, the social and political milieu generally precluded this, and the external reactions could impose limits on his behavior.

The sketching of a consistent model of planter treatment of slaves represents an attempt to isolate those variables which would affect the social and material conditions of slave life. The advantage of such formal treatment is clarificatory—a guide to organizing thought —while the absence of a satisfactory resolution at this time indicates the very complexity of the issue. The economic model of the planter decision is based upon the fact that slaves produce an output sold for a price in the world market (as well as other consumption and capital goods). The revenue obtained from sales depends upon the productivity of the slave and the price at which the commodities can be sold in the market. There are costs of acquiring slaves—either the purchase price paid for imports or the costs of raising infants to productive ages. There are annual subsistence costs from birth to death, including not only food, clothing, and shelter, but also medical care. To complicate the analysis, it is clear that the quantity of consumer goods, particularly food and medical care, will affect not only the slave's annual output but also the expected lifetime. There is a cost of funds to the planter, reflecting the interest rate at which future incomes and expenditures are discounted. Given information on the relationship between the costs of care and annual productivity, it is possible to predict the effects of some of the above-mentioned variables on material treatment. For example, the higher the cost of consumption goods, the less will be provided the slaves. An expected permanent rise in slave productivity (due either to technical improvements or a more favorable world demand for crops) could lead to better treatment (as well as higher infant prices) than a rise which was thought to be only temporary which would lead to harder working in the short-run, and not affect infant prices; indeed it might lead to the desire to have slave fertility deferred. A higher interest rate would make for a shorter optimum slave life, and a lower price of infants. Thus, clearly, much depends on the expectations and evaluations of the future held by planters.

There are several "givens" in this model, providing the framework in which planters make their decisions. One, discussed formally by LeVeen and underlying several discussions of the "breeding" issue, is whether the slave trade was open and a continued source of African imports was available (or else, as LeVeen asks, what are the terms on which illegal imports are available). Creole slaves and imported slaves are not perfect substitutes who would sell at the same price. Losses in "seasoning" alone would guarantee the existence of a price differential, as would the differences in the process of socialization pointed to by Craton. But given that the prices would not be the same, some equilibrium price differential should be established. Closing the slave trade, even when the illegal trade persists will, as LeVeen demonstrates, raise the equilibrium differential and increase the price of infants. Some data, including Craton's for 1793, show a positive valuation for infants even before the trade closed, but closing the trade should have raised this price.[14] Thus the availability of

[14] The one explicit comparison of the price of raising slaves and of importing them is provided by LeVeen. The calculation should be regarded as suggestive, for the mortality assumed is too low, both for Creoles and for imports. This may not, however, affect the conclusions since the higher infant mortality would mean death before any substantial costs had been imposed on those raising slaves.

Most previous work on West Indian slavery seems to have accepted the traditional argument that the planters there actively discouraged slave reproduction, but enough puzzles are suggested by the available evidence to make this issue worth more systematic study. In addition to the positive prices at young ages shown by Craton for Jamaica in 1793, he notes elsewhere the payment of a bonus to childbearing females at this time (see Michael Craton and James Walvin, *A Jamaican Plantation*, Toronto, 1970, pp. 140-141). Similarly Bennett points out that on the Codrington plantations on Barbados, "every newborn boy or girl of the 1770s was listed on the inventory as worth £5" (J. Harry Bennett, Jr., *Bondsmen and Bishops*, Berkeley, 1958, p. 14). While the Jamaica observations come after the introduction of amelioration, and that for Barbados after a period of improved demographic performance, detailed examination of the earlier years is needed. In particular

African slaves was a crucial variable in determining the treatment of slaves in the New World.

Another variable, perhaps so obvious that it is sometimes not given sufficient emphasis, is the basic climate and epidemiological environment. This would affect both blacks and whites, though, as Curtin pointed out, with differential incidence due to epidemiological factors.[15] There is some suggestion, however, of a positive correlation between white and black death rates in the same area, even if related to different factors. A response by white planters to climatic conditions seems to be present. The healthier areas apparently attracted more whites relative to blacks, leaving the relatively unhealthier areas with almost completely black populations.[16] Of course, as so often, we cannot yet disentangle the intercorrelations among settlement patterns, climate, and sugar production. The white settlement pattern might have been more a response to the massive use of slave labor in sugar production in those areas where it was profitable, than a response based on presumed health differentials. Sheridan shows the important provision of health care to slaves in areas such as the British West Indies, with expenditures of roughly similar magnitude to those in the U.S. Nevertheless, given the limited knowledge of the causes of diseases and factors in their control, such treatment may have been of quite limited usefulness, if not, owing to erroneous concepts, actually counterproductive.

The use of a model to discuss slave material and social treatment is not intended as a way to avoid the basic moral issues of slavery. Until we are better able to distinguish between objective constraints and planter control variables, it is doubtful whether there is much

---

more attention needs be paid to what methods the planters could have and did use to discourage reproduction. It seems curious that much of the evidence presented on planter actions concludes that rather than discourage or restrict intercourse, they rather promoted promiscuity. Is it that they did this as a long-run measure to lower fertility, or perhaps was it an inappropriate measure to encourage a higher rate of fertility? Given that the key variable subject to planter control was the age of the mother at the birth of the first child, and that the material seems to suggest that West Indian practices would provide for a lower age than in the U.S., the problem posed by Eblen from nineteenth-century Cuban data is quite applicable to the West Indies of the previous century.

[15] Philip D. Curtin, "Epidemiology and the Slave Trade," *Political Science Quarterly* 83 (June 1968), 190-216.

[16] Another aspect of this adjustment by whites to climatic differences should be noted. Is it coincidence that areas in which slavery was considered most paternalistic were areas in which white planters resided upon the plantations with their slaves and did not choose to become absentee owners? Cf. Eugene D. Genovese, *The World the Slaveholders Made*, New York, 1969, pt. 1, for a discussion of paternalism.

to be gained by linking the question of the morality of different slaveowners, or the lack of same, to issues of material treatment and demographic performance. To determine whether a particular response by planters represented paternalistic concern for slaves or a profit-maximizing action with only limited concern is not easy, if it is at all possible. The existing literature suggests many combinations of motive and treatment; some resting on different motivation, others on different objective conditions with the attribution of similar motives.[17] Thus to show "favorable" treatment need reflect no moral grandeur—greed can provide some benefits. And, to argue that planters in unhealthy climates took good care of their slaves and that there was no evidence of overt maltreatment is not to reduce the moral indictment of slaveowners—the basic point remains that in the absence of enslavement no doubt fewer workers would have been in these areas. The moral issue of maltreatment and care is not so much how slaves were treated once they were there—it is the fact of their involuntary presence in unhealthy areas of the New World.

The issues generally discussed in regard to treatment refer not only to the care of slaves, but also to death and birth rates. More generally the model would also include the choice of imports (their age-sex structure) when the international trade was still open. A basic issue to be examined is the validity of making the comparative demographic experience of the U.S. and other parts of the New World serve as an index of comparative material and social treatment. The problem, long known but raised most forcibly by Curtin's recent book, concerns the relatively high rates of natural increase in the U.S. contrasted with what have been called rates of natural decrease elsewhere.[18] As is seen in comparing the data presented by

[17] The profit motive could suggest either favorable material and social treatment or very harsh treatment, depending upon the conditions of production, climate, world market conditions, etc. Thus, to use Elkins' example, "unopposed capitalism" could lead either to favorable or harsh treatment, and without more knowledge of the constraints the issue remains open.

This argument is not meant to suggest that, at times, certain patterns of behavior might be formed which linger past the operation of the constraints which led to them, or that all planters were "rational." It is meant merely to suggest that different responses to different conditions tell us little about motives, and that in the discussion of the relative morality of different national slaveries, the customary description of material treatment might not be central.

[18] The latter is generally measured by the excess of imports over population change during a given time span. It does not necessarily reflect the change in population of those resident at the start of the period. Because of the heavy toll of "seasoning," many imports did not survive to the closing date; as an offset there were children born to imported slaves. Unless these births equal deaths among the imports, the measure is not strictly the rate of natural decrease.

Wood with that given in Craton and Sheridan, this differential rate of increase was true both of the period when the slave trade was open and when it was closed. Since the data indicate little difference in the sex ratio of imports into the U.S., the West Indies, Brazil, and elsewhere the differential in population change cannot be traced directly to the age and sex composition of the original African imports. This raises the question whether too much attention has been paid to this variable in discussions of comparative demography, since the important differences no doubt came after arrival in the New World, and these should become the focus of study.

The comparison of population growth by imports versus that by natural increase raises issues beyond that simply of material treatment. As Craton, Palmer, and others point out, it is an important question for analyzing the cultural dimensions of the slave experience. For in the U.S., with a high rate of reproduction and limited imports, a large proportion of the population was native-born; in the Caribbean areas, as Craton shows, there was generally a larger, but relatively declining, African-born population. Thus a greater carry-over of African styles, such as the religious attitudes Palmer points to in Mexico, and of a particular pattern of resistance to enslavement led by the unassimilated as argued by Craton, would not be expected in the U.S. where the greater relative number of Creoles would limit the direct impact of largely unaltered African patterns.[19]

In explaining the different patterns of demographic change of the slave populations, the discussion naturally concerns both birth and death rates. It is, perhaps, clear that planter attitudes toward birth and death rates cannot easily be predicted. These attitudes represented responses to different conditions, and both their desire and their ability to have had an effect upon slave fertility and mortality depended upon such factors as epidemiological environment, family life of slaves, and the dictates of the economic means of production. In the discussion it is essential to distinguish between those variables the planters could control and those which, owing to economic and other factors, they could not.

Often vital statistics must be inferred from the fragmentary evidence on population change, since at present we have little or no direct information. Craton has summarized his calculations of birth and death rates for Jamaica, and these provide a useful starting point.

Generally this won't effect the interpretation of the broad changes in population, but it will influence the treatment of specific issues, as seen in Eblen's discussion.

[19] For an attempt to apply similar arguments to the U.S., see Gerald W. Mullin, *Flight and Rebellion*, New York, 1972.

They indicate a higher death rate for the Jamaican slave population than among the whites in England, but not higher than those in London and other urban areas. This suggests some possible correlation at this time between population density and death rates. The importance of epidemics is shown, also, in that the high average death rates seem to result not from a continuously high annual mortality, but rather from large variation in annual death rates, with periodic pronounced peaks. Death rates were particularly high during "seasoning," but apparently those who survived that process would have a reasonably long life span by the standards of those, and our, times.[20]

While the issues related to the death rate seem somewhat straightforward, they apparently do not explain the major discrepancies in rates of population growth. More attention, therefore, has been paid to the issue of comparative birth rates and their implications. This issue is a rather complex one, and has implications not only for the analysis of treatment under slavery, but also in the discussion of the impact of slavery upon black family structure. This dual role has sometimes led to interesting comparisons among countries.[21] The West Indies are often pointed to as being a case where the imbalanced sex ratios and presumably resulting instability led to low birth rates;

[20] There is some material suggesting that mortality rates were affected by the level and nature of economic output, although it is still too soon to determine the specific relationships. Sheridan points to the increase in rates of natural decrease in the West Indies following the introduction of sugar, Wood to the shift to a natural decrease in South Carolina after the introduction of rice, and Eblen notes a shift to lower rates of natural increase with the mid-nineteenth century sugar boom in Cuba. For more details on the impact of the expansion of sugar on slave demography in the British West Indies, see Richard S. Dunn, *Sugar and Slaves*, Chapel Hill, 1972.
In a detailed study of Jamaica in 1832 Higman finds mortality highest on sugar plantations, and also that mortality was positively correlated with output per worker (Barry W. Higman, "Slave Population and Economy in Jamaica at the Time of Emancipation," unpublished Ph.D. dissertation, University of the West Indies, 1970). While some might assume this evidence of "working slaves to death," this could be a spurious correlation of the type which so frequently confounds analysis of these issues. His findings also point to the relationship between size of units and mortality. Given economies of scale in production, as was true of the slave-produced crops, larger units were more productive. Thus, the higher densities might explain the relationship between size and mortality without an implication of "working slaves to death" as a deliberate decision.
[21] It should be noted that there is some asymmetry in the discussion of family instability in the U.S. and in the West Indies. In the U.S. the instability has been attributed to interregional mobility and sales leading to family breakup; in the case of Jamaica and West Indies the incidence of mobility and sales was much less, so instability is attributed to the patterns of behavior within the plantation and not to any desire to obtain marketable offspring. In the U.S. family instability has been traced (inappropriately) to the desire to encourage reproduction; in the West Indies to an attempt to discourage reproduction.

Sutch, on the other hand, is telling us that in the U.S. imbalanced sex ratios (though of the opposite type) and family instability were the mechanism to generate high birth rates.[22] Often explicit discussion of planter "breeding" controls leaves it unclear whether harsh treatment meant encouraging or discouraging reproduction. Thus it might again be useful to separate issues of morality from those of planter attitudes toward, and actions concerning, reproduction.

The attribution of "breeding" to U.S. planters, and the charge that reproduction was discouraged elsewhere, is given some plausibility by the observed differentials in rates of natural increase. While the earliest direct observation of a fertility rate for Jamaica presented by Roberts for the post-slavery period was high by European, but not New World, standards, it is larger than the birth rates estimated by Craton for the period of slavery.[23] Given the apparent great differential between the Jamaican and the U.S. fertility rates for the same period, two central hypotheses have been generated. The first, presented in Sutch's paper, places responsibility for this upon a "breeding" mentality of U.S. planters. The second, presented by Sheridan and Craton, argues that the presumed lower reproduction rates in the West Indies are indicative of the severe social, psychological, and epidemiological impact of the slave experience as seen in promiscuity, venereal disease, and family instability. In neither case is there a systematic examination of the behavior of those variables concerning fertility over which the planters might have exercised control. Richard Steckel, in his study of U.S. slave fertility (see n. 24), explains differences in the fertility performance based upon differences in the ages at which the first and last child were born and the spacing of children in the intervening period. In a time in which breast-feeding was prevalent, there were distinct limitations upon the extent to which spacing could be effected, while, given the generally high age at last birth, it is doubtful that any prolongation of the reproductive span was possible in that way. Thus the major control variables must have been the age at first child and, to some

---

[22] It should be noted that most studies of free populations show higher birth rates with some increased ratios of males to females, the frontier pattern seen in the U.S.

[23] George W. Roberts, *The Population of Jamaica*, Cambridge, 1957, p. 269. The average birth rate estimated for the 1844-61 period was 40. For the period 1811-17, Craton and Walvin in *A Jamaican Plantation*, p. 196 estimate a birth rate of almost 40, much higher than Craton estimates for the earlier period, as well as above those shown by Higman for the early nineteenth century. The size of the differential, however, raises questions about the reliability of the birth and infant mortality data for earlier years which require further study.

extent, child spacing, and it is to direct evidence on these points useful research can be directed. By analyzing differences in these variables we might better be able to determine the extent to which these planters could have, and did, influence fertility, and to what extent interpretations based on observed differences in natural increase misread the planter intentions in situations where basic conditions were outside their control.

The long historical tradition on the presumed fertility differentials between the U.S. and the Caribbean is the focus of Eblen's analysis, and in his study of Cuba he raises the question of whether fertility rates were really lower, and by how much, in the Caribbean than in the U.S. By standardizing the data in manners familiar to demographers, Eblen adjusts the raw population statistics to allow for the effects of imports, with their rather peculiar sex and age composition, and their children. He then estimates the most plausible fertility and mortality rates which would characterize a closed population, with a stable age distribution. These adjustments, while not in any sense denying the actual mortality experience discussed in the treatment context, highlight a feature of the demographic experience which might otherwise go unnoticed. Eblen's data suggest that when the age-sex structure of the population is allowed for, and the mortality rates of infants and female adults considered, the number of children born per female surviving child-bearing age could have been about the same in Cuba as in the U.S.[24] This is not to deny the toll of the higher infant and adult mortality in Cuba, but to point out that these, based in part upon climate and other conditions outside the control of planters, tend to obscure the measurement of the basic fertility experience. To the extent that the issues discussed are based upon the implications drawn from the presumptions of fewer chil-

[24] The relationships between infant mortality and the number of children born are complex. Given child-spacing patterns prevalent in noncontraceptive societies, higher infant mortality should mean more children born during the child-bearing span. It would also mean, however, a higher cost of obtaining children, presumably discouraging "breeding."
There is also an arithmetic relationship which makes comparisons of fertility rates difficult. Most comparisons for this period are based upon census data which show the number of surviving children. In adjusting for infant mortality, therefore, the fertility rate calculated depends upon the presumed infant mortality rate, and the higher the infant mortality used the higher the calculated fertility rate. The effects of different adjustments for infant mortality on U.S. slave fertility comparisons can be seen by comparing the birth rates shown in Jack E. Eblen, "Growth of the Black Population in *ante bellum* America, 1820-1860," *Population Studies*, 26 (July 1972), 273-289, with those of Richard H. Steckel, "The Economics of U.S. Slave and Southern Free White Fertility," unpublished paper, June 1973.

dren per female and lower reproduction rates, Eblen's adjustments are valuable and his inferences very important for subsequent studies.[25]

The long persistence of the apparent higher birth rate in the U.S., going far back into the era when slave imports were possible, means that whatever demographic differences might be explained by the closing of the slave trade, these cannot provide a full answer to the problem. The sex ratios of imports shown by Wood, for South Carolina, and by others, indicate a similarity for slave imports throughout the New World. Wood's work focuses further attention on the demographic problem, because of his description of variations in rates of natural increase, as well as by his demonstration of the imbalance of sex ratios on South Carolina plantations early in the eighteenth century, an imbalance about as great as those seen in the West Indies.

Wood's data show varying rates of natural increase, high at first but then falling with the shift to the production of rice.[26] While the isolated census statistics suggesting fertility rates indicate that this pattern over time may hold elsewhere in the U.S. as well, we must be careful, as Wood notes, before we can accept the implications of the currently available data on imports and population. In the specific case of South Carolina we must remember that Charleston was an

---

[25] At this point we might note other of Eblen's findings. Eblen points to a decline in fertility with the sugar boom in the 1840s. While suggestive, such a movement over the course of the nineteenth century was characteristic of white and black populations in the U.S. and elsewhere. Eblen also argues for the probability of equal birth rates for slaves and for free persons of color in Cuba, a pattern different from that seen in Brazil (where free exceeds slave) as well as that of the U.S., as indicated by the census data and suggested by Hershberg's summary tables (where slave exceeds free). On Brazil see Peter L. Eisenberg, "Abolishing Slavery: The Process on Pernambuco's Sugar Plantations," *Hispanic American Historical Review* 52 (November 1972), 580-597, and Herbert S. Klein, "Nineteenth Century Brazil," in David W. Cohen and Jack P. Greene, eds., *Neither Slave Nor Free*, Baltimore, 1972, pp. 309-334. For another discussion of the Cuban case, arguing for higher free than slave birth rates, on the basis of raw data, see Franklin W. Knight, "Cuba," in Cohen and Greene, pp. 278-308. These two issues—the time pattern of changes in fertility rates and the comparison of free and slave birth rates—clearly warrant more study, being of importance not only in themselves, but also in providing a null hypothesis for the "breeding" argument presented by Sutch. The frequently commented upon differential fertility experience of African-born and creole slave females, shown also in Eblen's estimates, might be explained in some measure by the age at which slaves were imported. It is probable that many females were imported after their child-bearing period had begun, and thus had fewer child-bearing years in the New World.

[26] The basic shift from high natural increase to natural decrease is dated by Wood at about 1720. His trade data indicate a sharp shift to imports direct from Africa in about 1724, with a corresponding reduction in slaves from the West Indies. If the latter had been "seasoned" prior to shipment to Charleston, this might help explain part of the increased mortality in South Carolina.

importing center for several colonies, being large enough to import directly from Africa. This is important since to ignore the possibility of intercolonial trade would imply exceptionally high rates of increase elsewhere in the colonies at the time of measured decrease in South Carolina. The absence of much direct evidence on intercolonial trade, pointed out by Wood, combined with the discussions of apparent low fertility in northern colonies suggested by McManus and by Nash, raise the possibility that the currently available import statistics might be too low.[27] These statistics, broadly consistent with most qualitative evidence, are generally based upon Henry Carey's estimates, with their assumed rate of natural increase.[28] While it is doubtful that any revisions would affect the basic demographic comparison, the sex ratios among U.S. slave adults throughout the pre-Revolutionary period suggest the continued importance of imports. In one sense the high U.S. fertility may seem surprising, given the very little we know about slave cultural mores and marriage patterns. In the U.S. the size of plantation units was smaller than in the islands, particularly in the North, and it might be thought that this would restrict marriages and, for those marriages across plantations, the frequency of intercourse. Studies for the later period (1860) in the U.S. do show some decline in fertility with plantation size, though there is some positive relationship at the smallest sizes, with fertility in the U.S. highest on plantations of 10-30 slaves. For Jamaica Higman finds the pattern to be ambiguous, but any increase of the birth rate with plantation size was quite small. Further studies of fertility by plantation size and by crop promise very useful information on these issues, which hopefully could be extrapolated backwards.[29]

It is most difficult, as was made clear during the conference, to come up with a consistent and useful definition of "breeding." Given the natural tendencies of men and women, it is no doubt more difficult to stop reproduction than the reverse. Three logical possibilities among many may be noted: (1) sexual separation to prevent intercourse; (2) a policy of laissez-faire in these matters, with, perhaps,

[27] See Edgar J. McManus, *Black Bondage in the North*, Syracuse, 1973; and Gary B. Nash, "Slaves and Slaveowners in Colonial Philadelphia," *William and Mary Quarterly* 3d ser., 30 (April 1973), 223-256.

[28] For a fuller discussion and revision of Carey's estimates, see Fogel and Engerman, *Time on the Cross*, ii, 30-32. Carey's procedure worked back from an assumed decadal rate of natural increase of 25%, based upon the U.S. experience in the early nineteenth century. He therefore applied to the period in which the slave trade was open, a rate of increase based upon the adjustment to the closed slave trade, in addition to implicitly assuming that births to and deaths of slave imports were equal between the terminal years of his comparisons.

[29] See Higman, "Slave Population," for a study of Jamaica in 1832, and Richard Steckel, "Economics," for an analysis of the U.S. South in 1860.

the expectation that high rates of reproduction will follow without anything more than reasonable care; (3) a policy of deliberate use of studs and incentives to forced reproduction. The last case is perhaps best described by Frederick Douglass' case of two slaves locked into a room by a master.[30] However, that there may be no conflict between high reproduction and family life can be seen in the discussions of slaveowners. Hammond's instruction to his overseers claimed that stable family life encouraged offspring, and was thus the desired condition for slaves. A similar argument has been made by Roberts and Craton in explaining low Jamaican fertility. Both argue that there was a positive correlation between number of children and family stability. And the issue of incentives is itself most ambiguous, not only because some incentives existed in the West Indies, but also because it is possible to interpret proper child care and concern for the health of mothers both as an incentive to reproduction and as concern for the welfare of slaves. In addition, the current explicit and implicit incentives for childbearing in our tax and welfare laws may suggest some caution in attributing motives to past behavior.

In examining Sutch's clearly presented argument on "breeding" I find it necessary to exercise some restraint both because of the inherent interest in the question, and also because Fogel and I have written on this elsewhere.[31] Sutch has raised an often-made argument to a more sophisticated plane, and has presented some demographic patterns which suggest atypicality. Yet I find his principal argument unconvincing for what he wishes to prove, and, in fact, it appears that he himself concludes without pushing the breeding argument that hard. What he has shown are two things which have been noted by observers of the American slave scene. First, a high rate of reproduction of the slave population; high not only by the standard of other slave societies but of white societies of this time as well. Second, a high rate of interregional mobility, which was clearly nonrandom as to age and sex categories. Yet these points are not what he wants to show, which is deliberate interference with rates of sexual intercourse to produce more slaves in the eastern states to be sold in the western states to obtain profits in the east.[32]

[30] Frederick Douglass, *My Bondage and My Freedom*, New York, 1969, pp. 218-219.

[31] Fogel and Engerman, *Time on the Cross*, I, 78-86.

[32] Given the great attention given to Virginia as a "breeding state" it is of interest that that state had a particularly low ratio of females to males. The exporting state

512

The attempt to deny or disprove deliberate breeding is extremely hard to argue against because of its great plausibility. For we know that children had value, and what would seem more rational economic behavior than for slaveowners to deliberately "breed" slaves for market sale.[33] And, of course, plausibility is strengthened by observing the pattern of interregional movement. Altogether, the theoretical plausibility has always made "breeding" a difficult proposition to argue against. Yet there are some reservations, also based on plausibility. The basic argument ignores the point that the morale and other influences on slave productivity might encourage sexual noninterference and family stability as profit-maximizing actions. And, as indicated by Hammond, such a policy of noninterference and encouragement of family stability was seen as the way to increase the birth rate, acknowledged to be a desirable result. It is therefore possible that no conflict existed between the desire to have high birth rates and family and sexual stability.

To suggest reservations about drawing Sutch's conclusion from the existence of high birth rates and selective immigration, let me point to some demographic patterns of the white population in the South at that time. It is doubtful that, even with the reasonable adjustments for differential infant mortality, slave fertility was much above that of the white southerners in 1850 and 1860. If not equal, the maximum differential suggested is on the order of only 10 percent. The level of slave fertility was, therefore, not unique for the geographic area. Similarly, the selective pattern of migration among the white population was such that the differential between males and females in the areas of white inmigration exceeded that in areas of outmigration by considerably more than among slaves.

---

with most females relative to males was South Carolina. That this wasn't due to breeding alone is suggested by the fact that this ratio prevailed on rice plantations, and, as Swan's data show, characterized even relatively large plantations. Dale E. Swan, "The Structure and Profitability of the Antebellum Rice Industry: 1859," unpublished Ph.D. dissertation, University of North Carolina, 1972. Why this should occur—the peculiar dominance of females in the production of rice—is not yet clear. (Puzzling also for this region is the rather low death rate shown in the census data for 1850, surprising given the frequently commented upon health problems of that geographic area.)

[33] Sutch's n. 11 on the Conrad and Meyer assumption as to the number of children born per female slave seems to represent a misreading of their intent. They simply seemed to have assumed too many children, without meaning to argue, as Sutch implies, that these were the number of children needed to yield profitability of female slaves. The important point is that the more plausible figures yield profitability, and their conclusions are not dependent upon the high number of surviving children assumed. For details, see Fogel and Engerman, *Time on the Cross*, II, 54-85.

Thus, selective migration had less effect on the sex ratios for slaves than for whites.[34] For both groups migration rates were high in the late teens and 20s, ages at which marriages have not yet occurred. And the similarity in white and slave demography pertains also to the temporal pattern of changes in the birth rate, both falling over time. Given the pronounced rise in slave prices in this period, a falling birth rate is hard to reconcile with the full breeding argument.[35]

The conclusion which is most consistent with the present analysis is that Sutch's work, for all its ingenuity and data handling, has not really established the presence of "breeding." [36] Yet the demographic issue we began with remains—the U.S. slave population had a higher rate of population growth than slave populations elsewhere, and this was owing in part to the birth of more children, with more of them surviving, per female. The similarities of white and black fertility and mortality experience in different parts of the New World raise again the central importance of climate and epidemiological environment. This not only directly affected death rates, but, for reasons noted by Eblen, obscured the comparison of the fertility experience. In analyzing material treatment, therefore, it might seem easier to regard planters in different areas responding to economic incentives in roughly similar manners, with different observed behavior based upon differences in the physical and economic constraints they faced, than to argue as if these constraints were the same all over and planter motivations differed.

III. Racial Attitudes and the Free Black

The discussion of varying attitudes toward freedmen necessarily raises the problem of the initial racial attitudes held by Europeans. Without going into detailed analysis, let it suffice to note that there was some initial distinction drawn by Europeans between blacks and whites, as seen in the very fact that only the former were, and re-

[34] For slaves the 1860 sex ratio (male to female, aged 15-50) was 3% higher for importing divided by exporting states. For the white population, using the same geographic breakdown, the ratio was 15% higher in the importing states.

[35] For some more specific reservations to Sutch's argument, see the Appendix, below.

[36] There are two further points. First, there is no evidence to support Sutch's claim about the incidence of venereal disease in the slave population. Second, the sales figure provides estimated revenues before deducting costs of raising slaves. The latter deduction, which yields a profit estimate, is the appropriate one if the planter was making a decision as to the encouragement of fertility. See Fogel and Engerman, *Time on the Cross*, I, 83-85, for an estimate of the magnitude of such profits, which indicates they were much too trival to bear the weight placed upon them by proponents of the "breeding" hypothesis.

mained, enslaved. This attitude is reflected in the attitudes toward females, where there seemed no reluctance to use black females in gang labor. Whatever may have been the reinforcement to racial attitudes due to enslavement, it seems clear that Europeans held to some initial distinctions and prejudices.

The two essays dealing with free blacks in slave societies show that their life was not easy either under Iberian or American control. Bowser shows quite clearly that in Peru and Mexico, even early in the slave era, the life of the free person of color was not easy. Legislation of a quite restrictive variety was imposed upon their economic and social life, and these people had little occupational mobility. Even more, in legislation which suggests the post-emancipation response, laws to force labor were introduced so that the ability to restrict labor input was limited. And these were times in which the free person of color was generally mulatto, and resident in urban areas.[37] The description presented by Bowser provides little evidence of a more favorable racial attitude among slaveowners in Lima and Mexico City than in the British colonies.

While manumissions can be explained by many factors, Bowser shows that there was a clear economic dimension.[38] Few prime-aged males were manumitted and when prime-aged females were freed it was generally via self-purchase. The relative frequency with which children and females were freed suggests the owners' motivation, but it is to be noted how infrequent such an action was, and how little it led to opportunities for subsequent economic and social advancement.

Hershberg's extensive work, only part of which is presented here, indicates that the free Negro in the northern United States also was low in economic and social status. It has become clear that antebellum racism was strong in the northern states, leading to restrictive legislation and limitations on the social and economic mobility of those free Negroes residing there. To be antislavery at that time did

[37] In most slave societies there has been an urban concentration of free blacks, reflecting the limited ability to acquire land for farming and the lack of desire to work on gangs. The relative frequency of freeing mulattoes and their urban concentration helps explain the frequent exaggeration of the extent of miscegenation seen in reports by travelers.

[38] A study dealing with Brazilian manumissions points to the relatively greater frequency with which mulattoes, creoles, and females were freed (Herbert S. Klein, "Nineteenth Century Brazil"). Klein (p. 317) suggests that in the early part of that century relatively more female than male infant slaves were freed at birth, a point suggestive of the relative costs of importing vs. raising slaves. In Lima, the relatively greater frequency with which male infants were freed is consistent with the relatively higher female price for that period.

not necessarily imply an absence of strong antiblack feeling. Data from the 1850 census can be used to show that in terms of wealth and the ability to practice skilled occupations, the free black was better off in the South than in the North.[39]

Hershberg's major interest here is the comparison between those born as slaves and those born in freedom. He generally concludes that the former were at least as well-off as the latter, although little in the way of a clear-cut pattern emerges. For example, more ex-slave households tended to hold wealth, but these owners had less on average than did free-born owners. As Hershberg notes, most of the ex-slaves were probably from Virginia, Maryland, and Delaware, so that it still is not possible to ascertain the effects on the blacks of life and labor on the larger-scale units of the Deep South. Recent studies of slaves prior to and immediately after emancipation would, however, suggest that in many respects the ex-slaves did not suffer in social and economic development relative to the free blacks of the antebellum era.

Because of the limitations in the data collected by the various organizations, we cannot satisfactorily make some comparisons suggested by Hershberg's presentation. Most particularly, it is not always possible to distinguish between households with members who were ex-slaves and those in which the heads were ex-slaves. Similarly it is not possible for two of the censuses to segregate out those free-born in the North from those free-born in slave states, groups whose probable differences in motivation and ability have been pointed to by Carter Woodson. A further problem arises because the black population, as the white population of this time, saw a large percentage of disappearances between census intervals. Thus it is difficult to examine the status of the same individuals over a period of years. In the case of blacks this disappearance leads to some puzzles and worries about census undercounts, since the free black population throughout the North had low rates of growth similar to those of Philadelphia.

In the years studied by Hershberg the Negro population of Philadelphia was small, being less than 5 percent of the city's population. This group was not too small to go unnoticed, as seen in the restrictive legislation imposed upon them by the state. This black population had a sex ratio similar to that in other northern, and southern, cities, with a quite high percentage of females relative to males. Thus while most males resided in two-parent households, the surplus of females

[39] U.S. Bureau of the Census, Seventh (1850), *Statistical View of the United States*, Washington, 1854.

would leave some impact in a larger number of female-headed households. Yet overall the percentage of two-parent households is high, at least relative to expectations based upon earlier "descriptions" of the slave experience, while the small size of family is suggestive of low birth rates for this group.

The clearest pattern seen in the Philadelphia data is of a low social and economic status group. Hershberg shows a developing pattern of residential segregation in this period. Forced into unskilled occupations free blacks had little opportunity to acquire wealth or move upward. Consideration of the status of the northern free black indicates the great extent of racism in the North, more than a half-century after the legal termination of slavery there, making understandable some of the southern critique of the North. It also demonstrates the flaw in those arguments which attributed southern controls over their free black population solely to their role as potential troublemakers. Racism cut quite deeply throughout the nation.

Some controversy has recently developed about the factors in differential rates of manumission in slave societies, and differences in the attitudes toward the economic and social status of the freedmen. These have been attributed to differences in the extent of racial feelings and perception among European settlers, to differences in the age-sex composition of black and white populations, to economic expectations about the future prospects of slave labor, and to various combinations of these and more factors. The complexities in defining many of the differences to be explained, as well as in setting forth the relationships to the independent variables, defy easy analysis.[40] About the only point which seems clear is that no matter how large or small the percentage of freedmen, living conditions were poor and the economic and social status was low. Differences in occupational and social mobility generally seem quite trivial relative to the limitations faced by most nonwhites, even those legally free, in slave societies. Based on the two cases described in this book, despite the major differences in European origins of the population, in the ratio of blacks to whites, and in the nature of economic organization, one is hard pressed to see sufficient major differences between mid-nineteenth century Philadelphia and Lima and Mexico City two to three centuries earlier to argue that the status of a free black was preferable in one or the other of these places.

---

[40] For case studies of the freedmen in several different countries of the New World, see Cohen and Greene, *Neither Slave nor Free.*

IV. Economic Flexibility and Urban Slavery

A theme cutting through several papers, and leading to the only direct confrontation contained in this volume, concerns the economic flexibility and potential of the slave regime. This theme really combines several different questions, some of which can be answered with available data, others in which there remain problems in appropriate formulation. Yet the discussion of economic issues has moved forward in the past decade. Methodologically, the advance has been in the awareness that to use the tools of economics as an explanatory device does not indicate that the resolution must rest on "economic" as opposed to other influences, or that there must be an inherent conflict between the answers of economists and those of historians. The tools of supply and demand can be made to include all determinants of behavior—there is no necessary conflict between a historical analysis using these tools and an argument that noneconomic (or perhaps, more technically, nonfinancial profit-maximizing) behavior was important. The economic model can encompass these "noneconomic" elements, as seen in LeVeen's careful analysis of the impact of legislation affecting the slave trade, and in Goldin's discussion of the effects of internalizing the costs of slave control in urban areas upon the extent of urban slavery. Substantively, the debate now very clearly distinguishes between what is regarded as economic rationality in planter adjustments within a given set of socially determined constraints, and what might be the cost of those constraints which preclude certain types of seemingly profitable economic activity.

Although begrudgingly in some cases, it is apparently becoming accepted that within the context of a predominantly agricultural economy the slave system had a great deal of economic flexibility. The movements among crops and regions in response to changing world demand and supply conditions, the adjustments made in the prices of slaves at these times, and the basic patterns of international and intranational slave movements all suggest flexibility of response to economic incentives. It seems clear that slave prices and quantities adjusted, so that slavery was generally a profitable investment to planters. Indeed, that specific issue, which was instrumental in getting economists into the field is now regarded as somewhat unimportant and not really useful for answering any of the interesting questions. It has also been shown that slave societies have been quite capable of rapid expansion and aggregate economic growth, under certain conditions (which were the conditions existing in the eighteenth and nineteenth centuries) and for, at least, limited periods. And it has

518

become recognized that the populations and total incomes were higher as a result of slave imports than would have been the case if dependence had been placed on free labor, and that slaves worked on efficient plantations of a scale not achievable with free wage labor.

Moreover, as we learn more about plantation operations and look at the planters' manuals and instructions to overseers from a different perspective we see a well thought out agricultural operation, with a very extensive use of incentives utilized within the plantation, in daily operation. And, as suggested by the age patterns of skilled labor, there was an apparent use of lifetime incentive schemes. The mass of data collected and processed by Craton here and elsewhere shows these incentive systems in operation, while Craton further notes, in regard to incentives and treatment, that the whip could be "counterproductive." [41] Yet, Craton then makes the argument that the productivity of slaves was low because of slave resistance and because the system lacked effective incentives.[42] As he suggests, this could be due either to the failure to employ incentives or else to their lack of effectiveness as an inducement to slave productivity. But the existence of these incentives to slave's labor in the form of cash payments, occupational mobility, and enhanced consumption does point to the planter awareness of positive, and not just negative, incentives. To show that under slavery there were limited cash incentives relative to the free labor system is clearly not the same as showing that there was an absence of incentives to slave productivity, although the issue of the extent to which such incentives could be employed without undermining the system remains. Differences in institutional arrangements meant a different variety of incentive schemes, not their absence. In terms of labor control and incentive, and the detailed planning of operations by planters, the slave plantation resembled more the capitalist, industrial future than the feudal, agrarian past.

While these aspects of planter rationality within agriculture are generally accepted, some choose to regard them as rather secondary manifestations which take attention from what is regarded as the more important problem of the long-run inflexibilities of the slave system

[41] This argument applies more strongly to areas where slave sales were more frequent, since whipping left marks that provided warning to potential purchasers and therefore probably reduced the selling prices of slaves.

[42] The evidence for this contention may seem strange—a comparison of levels of productivity of labor 150 years apart. Such comparisons would probably indicate "resistance" by just about all workers at that, and other, times. However Craton's comparison is for cane-cutters, a task in which there was apparently little major change in technique over the interval. Nevertheless the cumulative impact of seemingly minor changes in tools and in crops merits further study.

which limit its growth potential. These questions remain more difficult to evaluate, and, stated briefly, a distinction exists between those who would argue that slavery made for a comparative advantage in agriculture worth pursuing at the time, and those arguing that the agricultural base was retained only by socially and politically caused restrictions upon urbanization and industrialization. It is not always clear whether the contention is that these types of adjustments would have been beneficial in the U.S. before 1860, or, rather, that such adjustments would have been required after 1860 but that the slave system would have been incapable of adjustment at that time.

One variant of this argument about the inflexibility of the slave economy in the U.S. was recently presented by Richard Wade, in a book which is the focus of an attack by Goldin and defended in Woodman's comment.[43] In this book Wade was making two arguments about urban slavery, run together in his presentation, but which are quite distinct. One issue concerns the level of urban slavery, the other the particular proof intended by Wade in pointing to a decline in urban slavery in the 1850s. This latter point is, however, easily dismissed. A similar decline had occurred in the 1830s, and was reversed in the 1840s. In both periods of urban decline there was a marked expansion in the price and output of cotton, suggesting a rather flexible response in the extent of urban slavery dependent upon the alternative uses of slave labor in agricultural production. Thus the decline of the 1850s does not indicate the imminent decline of urban slavery, a point well documented by Goldin.

The first of Wade's points would clearly seem to be the more important for discussion of the nature of the slave regime. Were there influences which reduced the extent of urban slavery below what it would have been if decisions had been made by southerners purely on the basis of financial profits? There are two interconnected arguments on this point, which do point to different mechanisms at work. Wade has emphasized the loss of control over the slaves generated by urban life, suggesting a possible cost to the individual slaveowner as well as a threat to the entire social fabric. Elsewhere the emphasis is on the threat to the social fabric posed by alternative urban and industrial uses of slaves, suggesting controls introduced by the planter class in opposition to urban-industrial interests. Both point to the same conclusion, but their interpretations of white and of slave behavior differ rather considerably.

Wade's contentions about the distinctions between urban and rural

---

[43] Richard C. Wade, *Slavery in the Cities*, New York, 1964.

520

slavery, and the potential loss of control faced by urban slaveholders, lead him to the conclusion that whatever may have been the extent of urban slavery, and however flexible the movement in and out of cities in response to changing economic conditions, the level was always below what it would have been in the absence of the problems of urbanization. Goldin does confront this issue in part, noting the estimates presented in her thesis of the component of the costs of police control which was passed on to the slaveowners or hirers in the form of taxes. These raised the relative costs of urban slavery. She concludes that these internalized costs were too small to account for a substantial reduction in the extent of urban slavery. Woodman contends, however, these internalized costs did not reflect all the possible costs of urbanization, and the extent of these possible omitted costs does remain an open question.

The econometric analysis presented by Goldin, though based upon a limited number of observations, provides a rather convincing demonstration of a clear response in the number of urban slaves to changing demand conditions in agriculture. Her results showing the relative elasticity of demand for rural and for urban slaves have important implications concerning the substitutability of free and slave labor in agricultural and other uses. They suggest that free and slave labor were poor substitutes in agricultural uses, as indicated by the restriction of gang labor to plantations of slaves. In urban uses there was more substitution possible between free and slave labor, as is suggested by the frequent attempts of urban workers to restrict slave employment. Even without this intriguing finding on elasticities the movements of slaves could be explained by the movements in cotton prices, shifting the demand curve for agricultural uses of slave labor. Goldin's conclusion, however, demonstrates the further possibility that there could have been an increase in the demand for urban slaves which exceeded that in the agricultural uses. Further, the different substitution possibilities in urban and rural areas, and the specific configuration of cotton demand and U.S. immigration, can explain the results presented by Woodman, showing a decline in percentage of the southern urban population which was slave in the years before 1860.

Woodman's attack on Goldin's findings accepts the point that within the observed range of urbanization, flexible adjustments of the type she points to were possible. He argues, however, both that economic considerations called for a larger urban sector, and that the system was incapable of meeting the threats which such an enlarged sector would have generated. While his data indicate that cities were becom-

521

ing predominantly white, which was true of northern cities as well, this is not the crucial variable for Wade's argument. Wade's contention is based upon the presumed inability of the slave to work in cities, and is tested by the relative portion of the slave population resident in urban areas. While this ratio fell slightly in this period, this can be explained within the framework presented by Goldin. We are still missing the detailed data which can indicate how costly the failure to use slaves in urban and industrial uses was in the antebellum situation, although elsewhere she has argued that the relatively small differential between the wage rates of free laborers and those of slaves indicates that the costs were probably minor.

Several suggestive comparisons with the U.S. case might be made on the basis of Karasch's paper dealing with slavery in Rio in the same time period.[44] There are some similarities: a higher skill mix in urban areas and an attempt by laboring whites to restrict the use of black labor which was apparently denied by the political power of slaveowners. Most important, however, is the decline in Rio's slave population with the coffee boom of the 1850s. This was also the period in which slave imports stopped. This made the labor supply more inelastic, causing the agricultural pull to reduce the urban slave population. The high skill mix of Rio's slaves may seem surprising, given the high percentage of Africans in the population, but since the slave trade was open perhaps the African presence reflects only the persistence of imports in transit to the agricultural sector.

There were important differences between slavery in Rio and in the U.S. South: Rio had relatively more males compared to females than did U.S. cities, although some part of the imbalance may have been due to the slave trade and the greater presence of Africans. Karasch's descriptions of living conditions suggest more "freedom" for the urban slaves in Rio than we have been led to believe existed in the U.S., but that latter point is clearly in need of more study. Perhaps the most interesting difference is that Rio's population was generally 40 percent slave, a figure in excess of that in any American city, though comparable with the early data for Lima and Mexico City presented by Bowser. Rio's slaves represented between 10 and 20 percent of the Brazilian slave population, and there was clearly an ability to permit a large proportion of the urban population to be enslaved without an apparent threat to the system. Urban slavery in

---

[44] For another discussion of slavery in Rio, consistent in all regards with that by Karasch, see Herbert S. Klein, "The Internal Slave Trade in Nineteenth-Century Brazil: A Study of Slave Importations into Rio de Janeiro in 1852," *Hispanic American Historical Review* 51 (November 1971), 567-585.

Brazil was expanding until the growing agricultural demand and the closing of the slave trade generated a labor shortage and pulled the slaves out into the countryside.

This similarity of response does lend some credence to the explanation of the pattern of urban slavery in the U.S. presented by Goldin, but it is doubtful that those favoring the position put forward by Woodman would be satisfied with that as an answer to the questions with which they are concerned. Those questions remain, but it does seem that some of the "unnecessary" and "irrelevant" side issues have now been examined and we can now proceed to the major sources of disagreement.

V. The Post-Emancipation Response

The economic rationale for slavery, as has been pointed out by Nieboer, and numerous others before and since, was the existence of a land-labor ratio sufficient to permit the product of labor to exceed subsistence under appropriate production arrangements, and the desire of owners to limit the payment to labor to "subsistence" (however defined).[45] A positive slave price measured the discounted value of the excess of the slave's marginal productivity above the costs of subsistence, and indicated that the ownership of slave labor was profitable. This loss of the excess of productivity above "subsistence" was not the sum of exploitation faced by the worker, however, since an important aspect of plantation slavery was the ability to force workers into a type of labor which they did not like in a climate which frequently would not have been voluntarily selected. Slavery forced a higher participation rate for slave women and children, and, also, led to a form of labor utilization, in large-scale gangs, which few white laborers were willing to voluntarily select at wages which planters were willing, or could afford, to pay. Goldin's regressions show a pattern of differential demand elasticities, consistent with a limited ability to get free workers to substitute for slaves in large-scale agriculture. Without the use of force, the supply of labor to plantations would have been considerably reduced, and there would be expected to be cries of "labor scarcity" after emancipation. In these cases, as Kloosterboer pointed out in her study of the post-emancipation responses in many countries, there would be a drive by the planters to enforce an increased labor participation among those freed,

---

[45] For a recent discussion of this point, see Stanley Engerman, "Some Considerations Relating to Property Rights in Man," *Journal of Economic History* 33 (March 1973), 43-65.

and an attempt to restrict their opportunities so that they need work on large plantations similar to those in the slave era.[46] We see that such restrictions could characterize not only the emancipation of entire slave populations, but as Bowser shows, even the limited number of freedmen in urban Lima.

What Kloosterboer called "premature emancipation" from an economic point of view was characteristic of most slave societies in the Western Hemisphere. In most such cases there was an initial fall-off in the output of the export crop, with the substitution of leisure and work on smaller units for plantation labor. We have ample evidence on the initial fall-off in export production with emancipation in Jamaica, British Guiana, the American South, and, indeed, just about all former slave societies to understand the problems and concerns of the planter class.[47] The paper by Adamson, based upon his book dealing with this subject, provides a detailed examination of the wide range of responses undertaken by the planters to obtain a labor supply and to maintain their land values. The responses cited by Adamson are familiar, and those American historians concerned with southern Reconstruction may note the similarity of the response of southern planters to those of planters elsewhere facing the same problem. There is an attempt to stop workers from increasing their leisure, with the use of vagrancy laws and similar restrictions to force labor. There is an attempt to force workers onto large plantations by preventing them from acquiring small plots of land on which to work themselves. This may be done as in British Guiana by simply raising the price of Crown land, or it may take more the form seen in the American South with various legal and nonlegal enforcement mechanisms. Not all societies will adjust in the same way, and the success of the planter class will vary depending upon a host of conditions, not the least being the land-labor ratio and the need for a larger labor pool.

The high land-labor ratio in Guiana was instrumental in explaining one important difference between the adjustment pattern there and that in the American South, as well as pointing to the cause of differences in the response among the British Caribbean islands. The

[46] See W. Kloosterboer, *Involuntary Labour Since the Abolition of Slavery,* Leiden, 1960. For a discussion of the issues relating to comparative responses to emancipation, see C. Vann Woodward, "Emancipations and Reconstructions: A Comparative Study," unpublished paper presented to the XIII International Congress of Historical Sciences, 1970.

[47] On British Guiana see also Michael Moohr, "The Economic Impact of Slave Emancipation in British Guiana, 1832-1852," *Economic History Review* 2d ser., 25 (November 1972), 588-607. On the American South, see Roger L. Ransom and Richard C. Sutch, *What Was Freedom Worth?* (forthcoming).

Guyanese planters moved to acquire immigrants under indenture from overseas to provide for their plantation labor force, a policy dictated by the relative failure of the earlier restrictive policies. And, in a manner which leads to some grudging admiration for their resourcefulness, much of the immigration was supported by a state subsidy financed by a scheme of regressive taxation. Thus the ability to maintain political control and to impose basic legislation dealing with land and labor policy permitted the planters to maintain a profitable system of large-scale agriculture, and, no doubt, reduced the benefits of freedom to the former slaves. Studies of the American South, such as those of Ransom and Sutch, indicate that the American planters were not as successful as the Guyanese. The southern planters were forced to accept the smaller-scale producing units implied by the rise of sharecropping. The specific mechanisms of that transition are under study, but the intricate web of legal, quasi-legal, and nonlegal controls over a labor force emancipated from enslavement provides some reflection to those drawing extremely clear-cut distinctions between slave labor and free labor markets.[48]

The essay by Adamson raises quite explicitly the question of what differences, really, does the distinction between slave and free labor imply, and how important are political controls over definitionally free labor in restricting living standards and social and economic opportunity. Differences there are, but, as Adamson points out, a resourceful political oligarchy can easily limit them. And, as indicated in several papers, racism among the dominant population also limits the gains from freedom, and, indeed, the best description of the status of the freedman in a slave regime is still "quasi-freedom." To point out these limitations on freedom, and the absence of razor-sharp distinctions is not to argue that slavery is not distasteful, but rather to raise the questions both of the meaning of political controls and of the enduring costs of racism. It is in answering these questions that studies, such as Adamson's, dealing with the post-emancipation response, become so intriguing.

VI. Concluding Remarks

A final comment, of a most general nature, concerns the new life in the scholarship on slavery, which recently seemed such a worked

[48] Peter Eisenberg, in discussing the process of abolition in Pernambuco, concludes "not only that most free workers in the sugar zone lived no better than slaves, but also that the transition from slavery to freedom benefited the planters far more than the group freed" (Eisenberg, p. 592). The Brazilian adjustment also included subsidized immigration, but mainly from southern Europe rather than India or China.

STANLEY L. ENGERMAN

over subject. Perhaps it is inevitable that new questions be asked about old subjects, that comparative studies increase considerably the variety of issues raised, and that fresh insights open up new aspects of analysis, but these developments are aided by new techniques and the availability of new bodies of data for systematic exploitation. What the essays in this conference volume indicate is that important as are social science techniques, such as the tools of economic analysis and the relatively complex means of statistical analysis, even the simplest methods systematically applied to useful bodies of data can generate much that is of historical importance. The massive amounts of data in notarial archives, in probate records, in tax lists, in plantation record books, and other diverse sources have only recently become systematically exploited on a large scale. The problems in using these sources have frequently been not so much a paucity of data, but rather that their great extent made systematic study difficult. With advances in sampling methods, with an increased ability to handle and process large amounts of data, and, perhaps most important, a willingness to spend large amounts of time going through and collecting these primary materials, we are now in a better position to obtain a fuller picture of slave societies and also to describe and understand the slaves themselves.

While some complain that quantitative analysis, whether formal or that implied in systematic surveys of archival records, may lose sight of the individual, in a curious way the rather impersonal public records often provide the best means to study the social and cultural life of the slaves, and of other lower classes. We have seen the use of court records, notarial records, censuses, and other such documents used to present information otherwise unobtainable about these groups, and, as seen in the demographic studies, to obtain information about the most personal of individual actions. None of these sources or methods are new—the novelty is more in the number of scholars than in what is being done. But the cumulative impact of such studies is bound to change our impressions and interpretations of the historical past, not only regarding slave societies, but over a wide range of other issues.

526

APPENDIX

A Critique of Sutch on "The Breeding of Slaves"

This appendix contains a more detailed evaluation of Sutch's "breeding" argument than presented in the main text. For those interested in continuity, the appendix can be read as a continuation of the remarks made prior to n. 35.

There were several differences in the regional pattern of white and slave fertility rates in 1850 and 1860 which raise significant issues. In the older areas of the South slave fertility apparently exceeded white. In the newer areas, where in the typical frontier pattern there were more males than females, the white southern birth rate exceeded that of whites in the older areas as well as that of blacks in the newer areas.[1] Thus the puzzle is that whereas white fertility at this time increased with the movement westward, that for slaves fell. But, and this is the issue, it meant that there was an overall approximate parity in the all-South average fertility rates for slaves and for whites.[2] Thus, it might seem as likely that there was deliberate restraint in the west as there was deliberate "breeding" in the east. This, of course, is based on a null hypothesis equating white and black fertility, but even if that is not accepted the geographic pattern of differentials is worth more study.

By restricting data to the decade of the 1850s, Sutch has tended to overstate the average magnitude of migration. The period of the 1850s was one of high mobility, as were earlier boom periods, and mobility rates exceeded those of the 1820s and 1840s, though not the 1830s. Thus Sutch's migration rates exceed the average which would be shown for both phases of the cycle. And by basing the discussion of Tables 6 and 7 on the 0-1 age category, some distortion in the change in the fertility ratio over the decade is introduced. While comparisons based on age groups 0-5 or 0-10, as is more customary for analysis in this period, would not affect the regional patterns for the decade, they

---

[1] This discussion is based upon the ratio of children 0-5 (and 0-10) to prime-aged females. Sutch's Table 7, using the ratio of children 0-1, indicates that white fertility was higher in both parts of the South, but that the relative differences between slave and white fertility were higher in the buying states of the Lower South.

[2] The 1850 census data on mortality shows a higher slave infant mortality rate, as well as a greater differential above whites, in the eastern, presumably "breeding" areas, than in the west, a perhaps unexpected pattern.

527

would reverse the increased fertility rate between 1850 and 1860 shown in the 0-1 category. Whether this reversal is due to some feature of census taking or to the implicit averaging over time is unclear, and the limited mortality data preclude any examination of that factor.

There is some overstatement of the interregional differentials in Sutch's data which can be explained by selective age-sex migration, albeit not of a sort argued for.[3] Let us assume, as makes sense in view of the economic costs and risks of shipment, that women who are pregnant do not move nor do women with young infants. It would take only an amount equal to about 30 percent of the migration of females ages 15-40 shown by Sutch for the decade to equalize regional birth rates, consistent with a situation in which those women pregnant and with infants moved at a differentially lower rate than females without children. Sutch's use of the word "barren" is misleading. It should not imply infertility, as he argues, but rather need pertain only to the condition in the year of movement and the preceding year.

A basic concern with "breeding" as part of the critique of slavery is the effect of such behavior upon the slave family and the legacy for the current black family. The weak link of the southern defense, and a most attractive part of the abolitionist attack in a Victorian era, had been the claim that there was frequent actual or threatened breakup of families and that this relationship was not only legally, but also de facto, denied to slaves.[4] Recognizing the important issue of voluntary choice in the separation of families, and its direct denial to slaves, we should note that the ages at which most slaves moved west were in the mid-teens and 20s, ages at which white migration was high, and which generally preceded marriage. Even though slaves had children about two or three years before whites, suggesting

---

[3] A pattern of age differentials in migration, quite similar to that in the U.S., is presented in Herbert S. Klein, "The Internal Slave Trade in Nineteenth-Century Brazil."

[4] It is important to separate out the issue of the pattern of slave migration from the recent discussion of the black family. The basic inconsistency in the link is that the effects on the family rest upon an ideal or concept of the family; the actual age at separation being somewhat irrelevant for discussing the ideal. As is clear in Hershberg, and has been shown elsewhere by Gutman, Pleck, and others, there was a high percentage of two-parent households for the nineteenth-century blacks. While the percentage may have been lower than among the whites, it was sufficiently high that what are small differences in the relative ratio of two-parent households will show up as a large difference when comparing the ratio of female-headed households. A big measured change in black family structure, as measured by two-parent households, occurred in the 1950s, not during the years of slavery and its immediate aftermath.

similar differentials in ages of marriage, the data are still suggestive of heavy migration prior to marriage and childbearing.[5] Elsewhere Fogel and I have estimated that about 9 percent of all slave marriages were broken by interregional and intraregional sales.[6] The usual overstatements of the impact of the westward movement on the slave family result from a failure to distinguish that part of the westward movement involving sales and that involving moving plantations, in whole or in part, generally by the owners or their heirs. Sales were not the most frequent means of the westward movement; and while the movement was selective by age and by parental status, this reflected a decision on which groups were cheaper to move, not "breeding." If "breeding" were a widespread intent, the higher migration rates for females than for males in the age groups 15-19, and 15-30, would be difficult to explain. One can, however, explain it on cost grounds, since it was easier to ship females before children are born. If children were valuable in the west the lowest cost solution to the transport problem was clearly to ship the female before children were born, rather than to ship the children one at a time after they reach age 15.

One of the more ingenious parts of Sutch's paper concerns the search for so-called "breeding" farms. Since about 80 percent of a female's value was based upon field productivity rather than breeding potential, the image of a farm devoted solely to raising offspring and not crops clearly cannot hold. Even "breeding" farms must have extensive market production of crops to be economically profitable, making the search for them extremely difficult. Sutch has presented a list of farms, taken from the Parker-Gallman tape, which had atypical sex ratios, and a high ratio of children to *males*, and he then suggests that these were "breeding" farms.[7] While these farms do have sex ratios which are atypical, the curious point to note is that these are not efficient breeders—having a below-average ratio of children per *female*. Ignored in the entire discussion by Sutch is the discussion of

[5] See Fogel and Engerman, *Time on the Cross*, I, 137-139, as well as Steckel, "Economics." This small differential involving deferred childbirth, which a rational "breeder" presumably would have chosen to avoid, does provide a basis for the observation of relatively more teen-age mothers among slaves than in the white population. That a difference in white and slave ages at first births existed is clear; however, the differential is too small to support most of the charges concerning slave sexual behavior.

[6] Fogel and Engerman, *Time on the Cross*, II, 114-116.

[7] He does not indicate what percentage of farms would have had these sex ratios based upon the probable mortality experience of males and females, so that the number of such farms expected is not really specified.

the well-known practice of marriage across plantations. This is an important point, given that the relatively small size and the relative absence of new purchases on most American farms would limit potential unions. The prevalence of those farms which Sutch suggests as "breeders" in the Old South, further, may merely reflect the greater density and contiguity of units in those areas, reducing the cost to owners of cross-plantation marriages compared to those in the western areas.

As a test of one hypothesis in Sutch's argument, plantations were arranged by the ratio of males to females in childbearing ages. On cotton, rice, and sugar plantations the general result was that, for most of the range of observations, the fertility per female was positively related to the sex ratio. This occurred in cotton areas, with an overall equality in the sex ratio; in rice areas, where there were more females; and in sugar areas, where males predominated.[8]

These results are generally consistent with those presented by Sutch in his Table 12, but whereas he interprets them as a "limitation" upon the success of slave breeding they might more plausibly be explained by the absence of such a pattern of deliberate interference. This relationship between sex ratios and female fertility is not only suggestive in evaluating Sutch's arguments but also raises the question of why it seems expected that the similar sex ratios in the West Indies (more males than females) generated lower rather than higher birth rates.

---

[8] Sugar plantations had a lower birth rate than those producing other crops, but these did not differ significantly from the birth rates of the rest of Louisiana. The generally low measured birth rates for slaves in rural Louisiana is an issue requiring further study. The low fertility rate for whites in Louisiana is explained by the low rate in New Orleans; the fertility rate for whites in the rest of the state is comparable with that in the other states of the region.

In making the comparisons among crops I have used the samples of the 1860 manuscript censuses kindly made available by William Parker and Robert Gallman (cotton), Dale Swan (rice), and Robert Gallman and Mark Schmitz (sugar).

XXI

Concluding Remarks

EUGENE D. GENOVESE

WHEN PROFESSOR Fogel first asked me to assist Professor Engerman in preparing this conference, I was, to say the least, skeptical about its prospects. I foresaw nothing but misery resulting from a meeting of economists, historians, and social scientists who, for all their common interest in slavery, represented the widest possible spectrum of methods, from the most elaborate econometric to the most steadfastly traditional. Most of us have attended one or more of those fiascoes in which the warring faiths have lectured the heathens about their own particular revealed truths in a conversion process that has not always stopped short of hurling brutal insults at the recalcitrants. The proponents of the most technically advanced quantitative work have been known to meet resistance even among their fellow economic historians; they have evoked positive outrage among historians and anthropologists dedicated to understanding the subtleties of social and cultural sensibilities, who have been heard to wonder aloud why they or anyone else need a "new history." Despite the professed commitment to indisciplinary work on all sides, these meetings have more often than not resembled a Hobbesian state of nature rather than a community in peaceful coexistence and equilibrium. As the preparations for the meeting advanced, I increasingly feared that the life of the conference would be nasty and brutish without the saving grace of being short, although I never doubted that the papers, discretely considered, would come up to a high standard.

As is apparent from this volume, the papers did not disappoint expectations; but their separate excellence can hardly portray the spirit of the conference. For the first time in my experience—and apparently in the experience of most other participants—econometricians and cultural historians, together with other social scientists, talked not past each other but to each other and, from all indications, learned a great deal from each other. Whatever else the conference may have accomplished, it convinced its participants that they could communicate across disciplinary and methodological lines and that, indeed, they could no longer easily live without each other if

531

they wished to raise their specific scholarship to higher levels of general significance.

The conference included formal criticism of the separate papers as well as a methodological critique by Stanley Engerman. Those of the formal commentaries we have been able to include here testify to the general lines of the discussion and point to the tasks ahead. Accordingly, I shall curb my impulse to add to the specific discussion, especially of the economic and methodological questions. Professor Engerman's qualifications far exceed my own; I shall leave that field to him and address these concluding remarks to the yet more general question of the relationships among the several disciplines and points of view.

Those economists and historians who have participated in the reconstruction of the economic history of the Old South since the appearance of the ground-breaking study by Conrad and Meyer of the profitability question in 1958, have sometimes vitiated their own efforts by parochialism. In the more extreme forms econometricians proclaimed that all previous work was useless, that the new methods in effect implied a wholly new and decisively more significant content, and that traditional historians and their accumulated body of learning could and indeed should be ignored; simultaneously, historians, quick to see the confusion of method and content inherent in such claims and quicker to see how readily economists would plunge into the interpretation of historical data without first immersing themselves in the social context, blithely dismissed the whole school as trivial or even foolish. Those who could not hope to master the high-powered techniques of econometric analysis and mathematical model-building frequently interpreted the growing pains of a new discipline as proof of a fundamental disorder; accordingly, they hoped that it would soon go away.

The more serious men and women in each group avoided these extremes and tried to put matters in perspective. For example, even as rather brash young men, Conrad and Meyer introduced certain qualifications into their analysis of the profitability question and admitted, however grudgingly, that their method and results left unresolved the deeper questions of the social character of the slave regime. But despite their admission, they came dangerously close to doing what they had too much sense to want to do—virtually identify social process with its economic manifestation. Whatever one's criticism of Conrad's paper on econometric methods and southern history[1] it

---

[1] Alfred H. Conrad, "Econometrics and Southern History," *Explorations in Entrepreneurial History*, 2d ser., 6 (Fall 1968), 34-53.

displayed a heightened sensitivity to the limits of the work of the new school and an admirable willingness to reconsider the relationship of econometric history to historical process as a whole. The same development can be traced in the work of Professors Fogel and Engerman. What it comes to, I think, is that the finest products of the new school have transformed themselves from economists who work on data from the past into economic historians in the full sense—into historians who are primarily concerned with economic processes within larger social processes and who therefore struggle to define the extent to which economic processes are autonomous and the ways in which they are contingent. The better traditional historians, analogously, did not deny a degree of autonomy to the economic sector and did not reject the new methods; they tried to take full account of the new work while reevaluating the relationship between economic behavior and social behavior as a whole. (The work of Stuart Bruchey, Harry Scheiber, and Harold D. Woodman may serve as examples.)

Still, if most of us, economists and historians alike, avoided extreme reactions, none has been entirely free from parochial stupidities. Too often we have settled for lip service to opposing points of view or used our sensitivity to the historical and methodological complexities merely to allow us to avoid the big questions in a more sophisticated and professionally acceptable way. Having criticized the Conrad-Meyer paper for gliding, however elegantly, over the implicit questions of historical process—much as Professor Woodman has rightly criticized Professor Goldin's provocative paper—I must readily admit that the same charge could be leveled at my own early book, *The Political Economy of Slavery*.[2] On the one hand, I doubted that the Conrad-Meyer estimates of profitability would stand up, and despite my admiration for the current work of Professors Fogel and Engerman, I retain some skepticism. On the other hand, I did not confuse skepticism with proof and chose to leave the question open. Thus, I tried to show that my own interpretation which argued for the existence of a general, i.e., essentially secular, political crisis, could absorb their results, if further work sustained them. Although this procedure was sound so far as it went, it nonetheless obscured a central question, which Professors Conrad, Fogel, and Engerman had no intention of allowing to remain obscure, even if their own work had contributed some equivalent obscurities. It is, after all, one thing to assert that an interpretation of southern society as essentially non-capitalist is compatible with evidence of an economic performance

[2] New York, 1965.

that meets the test of marketplace rationality, and it is quite another to pretend that the question may be left there. If, for example, the cotton sector behaved as if it were embedded in a capitalist economy, then of what significance is the attribution of noncapitalism to the society? There are answers to this question, as Professor Woodman's excellent remarks suggest. But Marxists, like other critics of the new economic history, have only themselves to blame if scholars of different viewpoints continue to define capitalism and other social systems in strictly economic terms, for Marxists have been among the greatest culprits when it has suited their polemical purposes. Even if we correct this error and distinguish sharply between the society as a whole and the economy in particular, as I have tried to do in a more recent book,[3] we thereby do not more than point toward a possible solution. The hard problems remain, for it would be meaningless to argue that a noncapitalist society absorbs a capitalist economy without significantly altering the behavior of the economy and its agents. And it if does, then we must know precisely how and why and must be able to trace the consequences specifically within the economic sphere as well as generally within the wider society. The current work of Professors Fogel and Engerman, notably their recent book, *Time on the Cross*,[4] challenges us to do so, and nothing will be gained outside the realm of polemical point-scoring if we satisfy ourselves with saying that they ought to practice more consistently what they preach.

The great majority of us agree that these difficulties have roots in the ambiguous reality of the Old South's social system, and of the New World slave systems in general, however perverse or dogmatic any or all of us may be in our interpretations. Stanley Elkins describes the Old South as a capitalist society flawed by racial slavery. Professors Fogel and Engerman describe it as a capitalist society modified by paternalism. Some older writers described it as a feudal (or seigneurial) society modified by capitalism. I have described it as neither feudal nor capitalist but as a slave system (to be understood as a category in itself) embedded within and profoundly modified by capitalism. Clearly, we are quarreling over the balance of a variety of elements to each of which we would all accord an important role. Since our efforts at definition seek to provide tools of analysis, rather than dogmas, the efficacy of one or another viewpoint depends primarily on the nature of the specific problem addressed. If, for example,

---

[3] Eugene D. Genovese, *The World the Slaveholders Made*, New York, 1969.
[4] Boston, 1974.

Professor Goldin's analysis withstands criticism and the economics of urban slavery are shown to be fully comprehensible on the assumption of that degree of economic rationality we associate with capitalist society, then the burden of proof will fall upon those who deny that the Old South can best be understood in such terms; they will then, at the least, have to demonstrate at a higher level of specificity than has previously been achieved that such evidence of capitalist rationality can be accounted for in an alternative model, which in turn can help solve problems that cannot be solved on the basis of the social assumptions inherent in Professor Goldin's model.

Without entering into a discussion of the specific theses and results of the papers here under consideration, we may consider their more general significance as contributions to the debate over the nature and dynamics of social process. Taken together, they demonstrate that we have moved beyond the trivial apologetics according to which historians and social scientists, economists and anthropologists, quantifiers and traditionalists "have something to offer each other" and "can learn something from each other." Everyone in this world has something to offer everyone else, if only a useful negative example, and only fools refuse to learn from fools. With such strained pleas, no wonder most of us paid little attention and restricted ourselves to ritualistic pronouncements and esoteric speculations.

What is now clear is that each discipline and each section of each discipline—e.g., the history of United States or Jamaican slavery discretely considered apart from the history of American slave societies in general—faces stagnation if it proceeds along familiar paths. Economic historians who safely restrict themselves to "purely economic" phenomena not only risk misinterpreting their results—this danger has always existed and caused them some concern—they risk trivializing their own painstaking efforts. The strictures of Professors Shepperson, Woodman, and Mintz must be understood in this light. It would be easy to read their demand for attention to the culture and sensibilities of the people who stand behind our statistics—for example, the black victims of the slave trade and the plantation system—as no more than a plea for some evidence of humane concern to accompany tough-minded analyses of objective data that can stand by themselves in historical interpretation. We are fortunate that these strictures come from men whose high intellectual seriousness and professional achievement virtually force us to look deeper, for they are saying something much more important. They are saying that the most apparently technical questions cannot be answered outside a social and cultural context; that the results of purely formal analysis will

535

always mislead us; and that the purpose of all intellectual work, including the most technical, is to enrich our knowledge of a world the complexity of which forbids the isolation of "factors" except as a momentary and dangerous device in a treacherous procedure that requires constant criticism and revision.

Thus, far from an attempt to romanticize or "soften" economic history, these criticisms rest on a respect for the dignity of that discipline and an appreciation of its indispensable contribution to history in general. When, for example, Professors Shepperson and Richard Ralston criticized the papers on the slave trade for ignoring its black victims, they suggested that economic historians and demographers cannot be excused from bringing their insights as well as their methods to bear on the fate of the people, white and black, whose story ultimately constitutes the only subject matter of importance that we have. Were this not the case, econometric historians would be mere technicians who accumulated and evaluated data in order to answer other people's questions; they would deprive themselves of that equality of stature attendant on their being critics whose special work helps us understand the limits of even the best theories and of the probable efficacy of policy-making.

Conversely, the criticism directed by econometricians against historians is only superficially a demand for greater rigor, precision, and care in specifically economic history, and it has nothing intrinsically to do with the neopositivist viewpoint according to which all historical process must either be measured or discarded so that we can make history "scientific." Rather, as a number of these papers show, it constitutes an attempt to understand the meaning, limits, and significance of partially autonomous processes within the totality of a general historical process.

To illustrate: The common African origin of New World slaves guaranteed certain cultural similarities to all Afro-American peoples, but many other forces intervened to generate dissimilarities. Among those forces have been the economic. Some peoples found themselves slaves and free Negroes in plantation societies based on slave labor, others in societies based on seigneurial or bourgeois labor systems in which slavery operated as supplementary. Yet as Professor Karasch shows and as Professor Bowser also shows both here and in his more general paper on the free Negroes in Spanish America,[5] the specific economic condition of the blacks did not arise simply from particular

[5] Frederick P. Bowser, "Colonial South America," in David W. Cohen and Jack P. Greene, eds., *Neither Slave Nor Free*, Baltimore, 1972, pp. 19-58.

economic conditions. Rather, those particular economic conditions, with their attendant opportunities for and obstacles to black advance, would be incomprehensible apart from a social context shaped by discrete Old World cultures and New World patterns of racial and class structures that reflected both the Old World legacy and the need to respond to different colonial conditions. The access of black freedmen or even skilled slaves to economic advancement varied not only according to supply and demand conditions in the labor market but to a wide range of noneconomic conditions. In the United States racism has taken extreme forms and has blocked the advance of qualified blacks even under favorable conditions of economic demand. The social position of the slaves and free Negroes in all New World societies was, therefore, "overdetermined," to use the language of Louis Althusser. It arose from a conjuncture of interacting but discrete social processes only some of which were economic. The rupture of this conjuncture, however, required much more than a major change in one of its components. For example, the increase in slave hiring, even under the most favorable circumstance known as "hiring your own time," did not undermine slavery itself in the United States by providing for a transition to freedom but actually strengthened the slave system by introducing considerable economic and social flexibility. In much of Spanish America, on the other hand, such economic tendencies, as Professor Bowser shows, produced different results because they appeared within a radically different pattern of race and class relations.

From this point of view, the more precise the analysis of the productive structure, the more able we ought to be to come to terms with the problem. To the extent that new and more sophisticated methods of economic analysis contribute to that end, the case for them cannot be questioned. It would be sheer madness to believe that an economic analysis of the productive structure would proceed very far— could serve as more than a first approximation—if it were abstracted from a consideration of the ways in which the other structures impinge upon it; but it would be no less madness to try to evaluate the extent to which the productive structure impinges upon the others if we eschew that vital first approximation. It is no longer a question, if it ever was, of historians and economists "helping each other." Rather, it is a question of not being able to attack fundamental problems without the methods and findings of the other.

We have seen, in a general way, how the attempt to answer the most specific and technical economic questions inevitably falls within the fundamental problem of the evaluation of American slave societies,

537

and the papers before us should help to clarify this relationship. But nothing that has been said should be understood as suggesting the existence of some imminent tendency in intellectual work toward the establishment of a unified interpretation. The significance of the growing cooperation lies not in the merger of viewpoints but, on the contrary, in the sharpening of ideological debate. When, for example, Professor Anstey employs his rigorous methods to undermine the particular Marxian interpretation of Eric Williams, he hardly refutes Marxism thereby. No general historical interpretation is likely to be so frail as to collapse under one such blow, and some Marxist historians, myself included, did not agree with Mr. Williams in the first place. The value of an effort such as Professor Anstey's—or that of Professors Sutch, Eblen, or Denslow—consists first and obviously in its contribution to the solution of a particular problem but second and in some ways more important, to the clarification of the philosophical questions that underlie contending interpretations of history. To the extent that subsidiary and derivative issues are resolved, the fundamental issues appear in heightened form. The quarrels, in the end, are not between historians and economists, or between sociologists and political scientist, or between social and cultural anthropologists, however much bloodletting occurs within those antagonisms. The quarrels arise from the different schools of thought underlying each discipline; they reflect philosophical differences. I have alluded to these in connection with the work of Professors Fogel and Engerman, but it would be inappropriate to pursue the subject here. It is enough to note that all contending schools of thought profit from the integration of different methods and disciplines, although it remains to be seen whether or not they will be able to profit equally.

Our immediate concern is the relationship between what we may loosely call econometric and cultural history. The paper least concerned with quantitative analysis is that of Professor Palmer, and we can only hope that no one arises to demand that he quantify Mexican Afro-Catholicism. Yet criticism of Professor Palmer's paper runs into the intrinsic difficulties with which he has had to grapple. He could, for example, push his ideas on religious synchretism only so far without slipping into sheer speculation, unless he first got substantial help from scholars in tangential lines of work. He would no doubt be able to develop his line of thought and provide a much richer analysis of the black contribution to Mexican culture if he had better data on the particular types of West African peoples with whom he is concerned. For religion and for culture in general we can homogenize the slaves as "West Africans" only so far, for the Ashanti were not Fon or

Yoruba. More precise knowledge of the origins and more direct demographic work, such as Professor Bowser's, will be needed if the kind of cultural analysis Professor Palmer has so suggestively offered is to go much beyond its present limits. Conversely, his paper demonstrates just how widely the most "technical" econometric and quantitative work can be employed, and it thereby suggests the path along which economic and cultural historians can enrich each other's work—or rather, can blend their work to attack the big historical questions. If, as I believe, these papers and the conference as a whole, have contributed toward showing the indispensability of collective work, then we shall have gotten from them everything we could have hoped for.

May I close with a personal word? Several participants shared with me the honor of having studied with Frank Tannenbaum or having had him as a colleague. He was a man of deep conservative disposition in more ways than one, and I am not sure that he would have approved of everything that is now going on in the study of slavery. But by his persevering effort in comparative history, by his disdain for pedantic lines between disciplines, and by his untiring insistence that all scholarship, whatever its methods, must tell us about the quality of human life, he had a profound and salutary influence on the course of our intellectual work. Whatever reservations he might have had about the specifics, I think he would have seen the conference as a long step down the road he so boldly charted. For myself, I am saddened that he did not live to see the fruit that his labors have brought forth, but am gratified that the work being done, in effect, constitutes a memorial to him. Given his intellectual seriousness, not to mention his modesty, it constitutes, I do believe, the kind of memorial that would most have pleased him.

List of Participants

ALAN H. ADAMSON, History, Sir George Williams University.

ROGER ANSTEY, Eliot College, University of Kent, Canterbury.

ANTHONY ATMORE, School of International and Area Studies, University of London.

FREDERICK P. BOWSER, History, Stanford University.

MICHAEL CRATON, History, University of Waterloo.

PHILIP D. CURTIN, History, University of Wisconsin.

K. G. DAVIES, Bristol, England.

DAVID BRION DAVIS, History, Yale University.

DAVID DENSLOW, JR., Economics, University of Florida.

JACK ERICSON EBLEN, Research Associate, Population Research Center, and Associate Professor of Sociology, University of Chicago, and Visiting Associate Professor of Demography, University of the Philippines Population Institute.

STANLEY L. ENGERMAN, Economics and History, University of Rochester.

ROBERT W. FOGEL, Economics and History, University of Chicago and University of Rochester.

EUGENE D. GENOVESE, History, University of Rochester.

CLAUDIA DALE GOLDIN, Economics, Princeton University

THEODORE HERSHBERG, History, University of Pennsylvania.

MARY KARASCH, History, Oakland University.

HERBERT KLEIN, Columbia University.

E. PHILLIP LEVEEN, Agricultural Economics, University of California, Berkeley.

KENNETH MAXWELL, Institute for Historical Studies, Princeton.

SIDNEY W. MINTZ, Anthropology, Johns Hopkins University

COLIN A. PALMER, History, Oakland University.

JOHANNES POSTMA, History, Mankato State College.

JOHN M. PRICE, History, Northwestern State University (Louisiana).

RICHARD RALSTON, History, University of Rochester.

MARY RECKORD, History, Dalhousie University.

STUART SCHWARTZ, History, University of Minnesota.

GEORGE SHEPPERSON, University of Edinburgh.

RICHARD B. SHERIDAN, Economics, University of Kansas.

ARNOLD SIO, Anthropology and Sociology, Colgate University.

RICHARD SUTCH, Economics, University of California, Berkeley.

Index

Abolition Society census (Philadelphia), 420-21, 422-23
absenteeism, 262-63
Accra, 40, 88; as source for Dutch slave trade, 44-47, 48
Adamson, Alan H., 524-25
Africa: domestic slavery in, 79n; slave stations in, *see* slave station employees
African middlemen, 39, 497
Africanos livres, 381
African response to slave trade, 497
African traditions, 486-87
Afro-Americans, 481; cultural heritage, 482-83, 484-87
Afro-Indians, 347
Afro-Spaniards, 347-49
age-specific death rates, 218, 236
agriculture, U.S.: slavery in, 431-32
Akan (tribe), 35-56, 311
Alabama
children of slaves, 206; ratio of, to couples on slave farms, 193; ratio of, to women on slave farms, 190
exportation and importation of slaves, 178, 180, 208, 210
fertility of slaves, 185
growth rates of slave and free populations, 177
infant-woman ratio, 183
sex ratio of slaves, 192
slaveholdings and slaves (number of), 187
slaveowners, 177
amelioration, 267, 288, 289, 291, 299
Anglican church, 265-66. *See also* Christianization; church affiliation; conversion
Angola, 13, 25 n. 3, 34 (map), 37; British slave trade from, 111; desirability of slaves from, 36; Dutch slave trade from, 37, 39, 40, 42, 48, 49; slaves exported to South Carolina from, 149, 150, 151, 152, 153, 167-71
Anstey, Roger, 101-2, 495-96, 499
anthropology and history, relation of, 477-94

Antigua, 286; medical care of slaves on, 300-305; shipments of slaves to South Carolina, 167-71
apprenticeship of slaves, 385
Arkansas
children of slaves, 206; ratio of, to couples on slave farms, 193; ratio of, to women on slave farms, 190
fertility of slaves, 185
growth rates of slave and free populations, 177
importation of slaves, 178, 180, 208, 210
infant-woman ratio, 183
sex ratio of slaves, 192
slaveholdings and slaves (number of), 187
slaveowners, 177
Arriaga mortality schedule: described, 219-20; in estimation of population increase, 232, 234; and intrinsic birth rate, 237, 238
Ashanti (or Asante), 123
Ashanti oath, 318
assimilation of slaves, 264-65
Atlantic economy: relation to slave trade, 101-2

Baltimore: slave population, 437, 452; slavery in, 444-46
Barbados, 286, 287; cost of maintaining slaves on, 297-98; decline of slave population, 309-10; doctors on, 297; growth of, 275; mortality of slaves on, 268 n. 45, 289; population decrease on, 288; shipments of slaves to South Carolina, 167-71
Beaufort, S.C., 146-47
beneficial societies, *see* Philadelphia, black population of
Benin, 13, 126; slaves exported from, 111, 112, 123, 124; slaves from considered undesirable, 36
Berbice, 286
Biafra, 13, 126; slaves exported from, 111, 112, 125, 126, 152; slaves from considered undesirable, 36
Birmingham (England), 104
birth rate: calculation of, 213. *See also* vital rates

543

city, the: as destructive environment, 423-24
Clarkson, Thomas, 16, 19
clearance lists, 4-6
clothing, 279-80, 384, 387
Coale-Demeny models, 246
coastal distribution of British slave trade, 12-13
coastal factoring, costs of, 57-58
Cocos Islands, 188, 189
Codrington plantations (Barbados), 289, 297-98
coloreds, *see* free persons of color
Congo, 13
Conrad, Alfred H., 532-33
continuous rate of increase: calculation of, 213
conversion (of slaves), 312. *See also* Anglican church; Catholicism; Christianization
Coromantines (or Coromantees; tribe), 152 n. 64, 265, 272
costs, *see* shipping costs; slaves: costs of
cotton farms, U.S., 187
cotton industry, 23-24
cotton planters, 186
Craton, Michael, 498, 503, 506, 508, 512, 519
Creoles, 503; in British Guiana, 460-64; on Jamaica, 264, 265, 269, 272, 273, 274, 288
Cuba, 510 n. 25
  black population of
    Arriaga mortality schedule applicable to, 240
    children in, 230, 232
    distribution of, by age and sex, 217, 218
    fertility of foreign-born women in, 242
    fertility (relative) of free blacks and slaves, 242-44
    foreign-born survivors at each census, 219-23
    foreign-born women in, 234, 238, 239, 240, 242, 243-44
    growth rate (crude) curve, 215-18, 226, 227
    intrinsic rates of change, 221, 244, 245
    mortality rates, 244
    native-born in, 223-27, 227-33, 234, 235

native-born women in: birth rates of, 239, 240; reproductive behavior of, 243-44
natural increase rate, 242, 243
reproductive behavior of native- and foreign-born women, 243-44
slave and free black populations compared, 221
slaves imported to, 216
and U.S. black population, compared, 245-46
vital rates for, 238-44, 244-45
women (native, and foreign-born) in, 227-29, 234, 239, 240, 243-44
demand for slaves in, 72- 81
manumission in, 77
prices of slaves in, 52-54, 64, 69
rate of return data for, 65
slave/population ratio, 76-77
slave ships captured by British navy, 68
slaves imported to, 53, 72, 73-74; shipping costs of, 59
slave supply cost data, 56
slave trade illegal in, 71
Curtin, Philip D., 77, 78 n. 44, 219
customs fee (for slaves imported to South Carolina), 145, 148-49

Dahomey, 38
Davies, K. G., 498, 499
death rates, 236, 504, 505, 507, 513 n. 32; for British West Indies, 288; calculation of, 213; for Jamaica, 268. *See also* mortality, slave; vital rates
death rates, age-specific, 218
Deficiency Laws, 255
Delaware: children of slaves, 206; exportation and importation of slaves, 178, 179, 207, 209; fertility of slaves, 185; growth rates of slave and free populations, 177; infant-woman ratio, 183; sex ratio of slaves, 192; slaveowners, 177
demand for slaves, *see* slaves: demand for
Demerara, 286
Denmark, slave trade of, 109
Denslow, David Jr., 500, 502
disasters: effect on population estimates, 232, 233
discipline, 462-63, 468-70. *See also* slaves: treatment of
distribution and selling costs of slaves, 70-71. *See also* shipping costs; slaves: costs of

Library of Congress Cataloging in Publication Data

Main entry under title:

Race and slavery in the Western Hemisphere: Quantitative Studies

(Quantitative studies in history)
Papers presented at a conference held at the University of Rochester,
Mar. 9-11, 1972, sponsored by the History Advisory Committee of the
Mathematical Social Science Board.

1. Slavery in America—Congresses. 2. Slave-trade—Congresses.
3. America—Race question—Congresses. I. Engerman, Stanley L., ed.
II. Genovese, Eugene D., 1930-   ed. III. Mathematical Social
Science Board. History Advisory Committee. IV. Series.
HT1048.R33   301.44'93'091812   74-2965

ISBN 0-691-04625-5
ISBN 0-691-10024-1 (pbk.)